Pretty Guardian Sailor Moon 1

Naoko Takeuchi

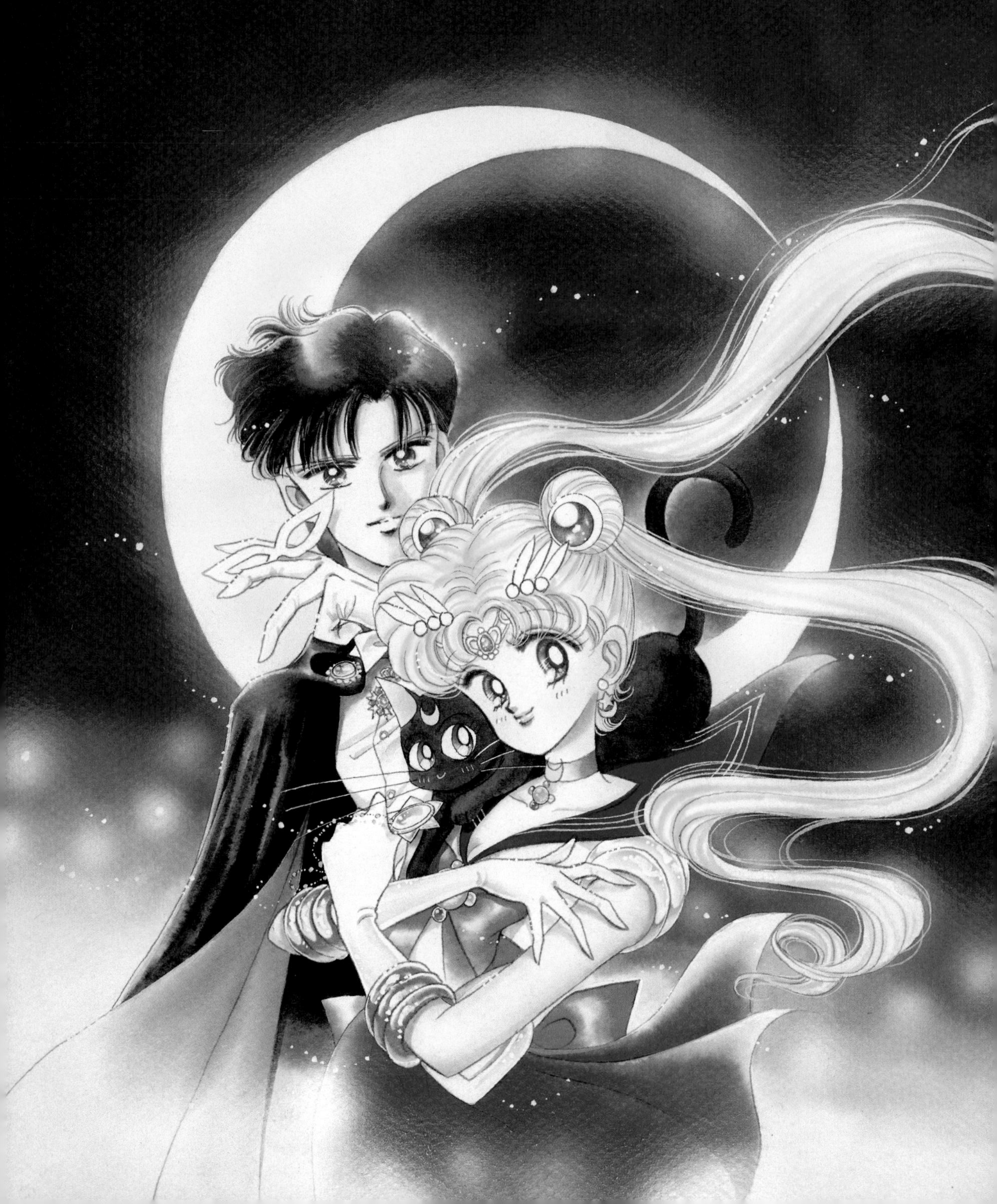

CONTENTS

Pretty Guardian
Sailor Moon

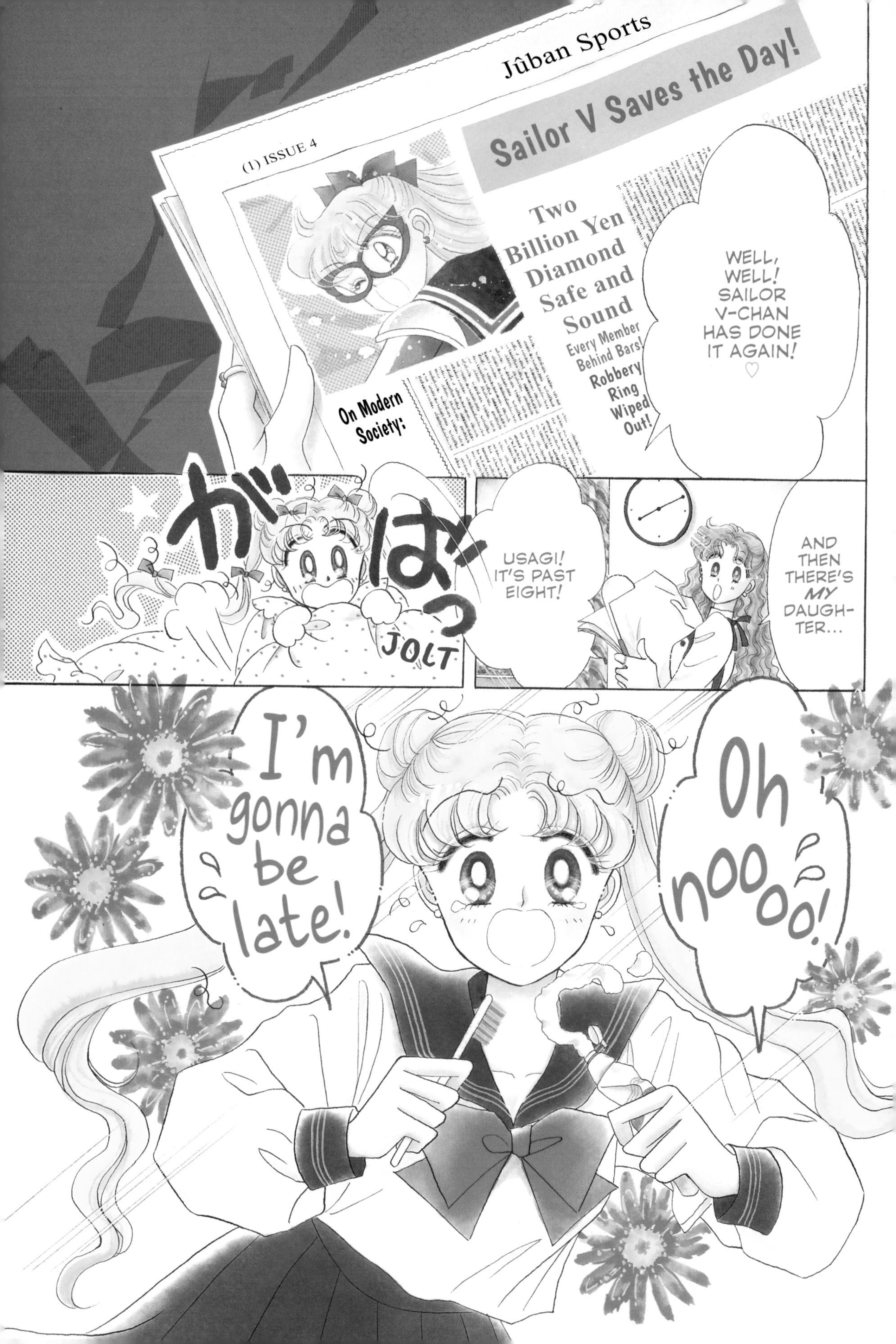

Jûban Sports
Sailor V Saves the Day!
(1) ISSUE 4
Two Billion Yen Diamond Safe and Sound
Every Member Behind Bars! Robbery Ring Wiped Out!
On Modern Society:
WELL, WELL! SAILOR V-CHAN HAS DONE IT AGAIN! ♡
AND THEN THERE'S *MY* DAUGHTER...
USAGI! IT'S PAST EIGHT!
がばっ
JOLT
Oh noooo!
I'm gonna be late!

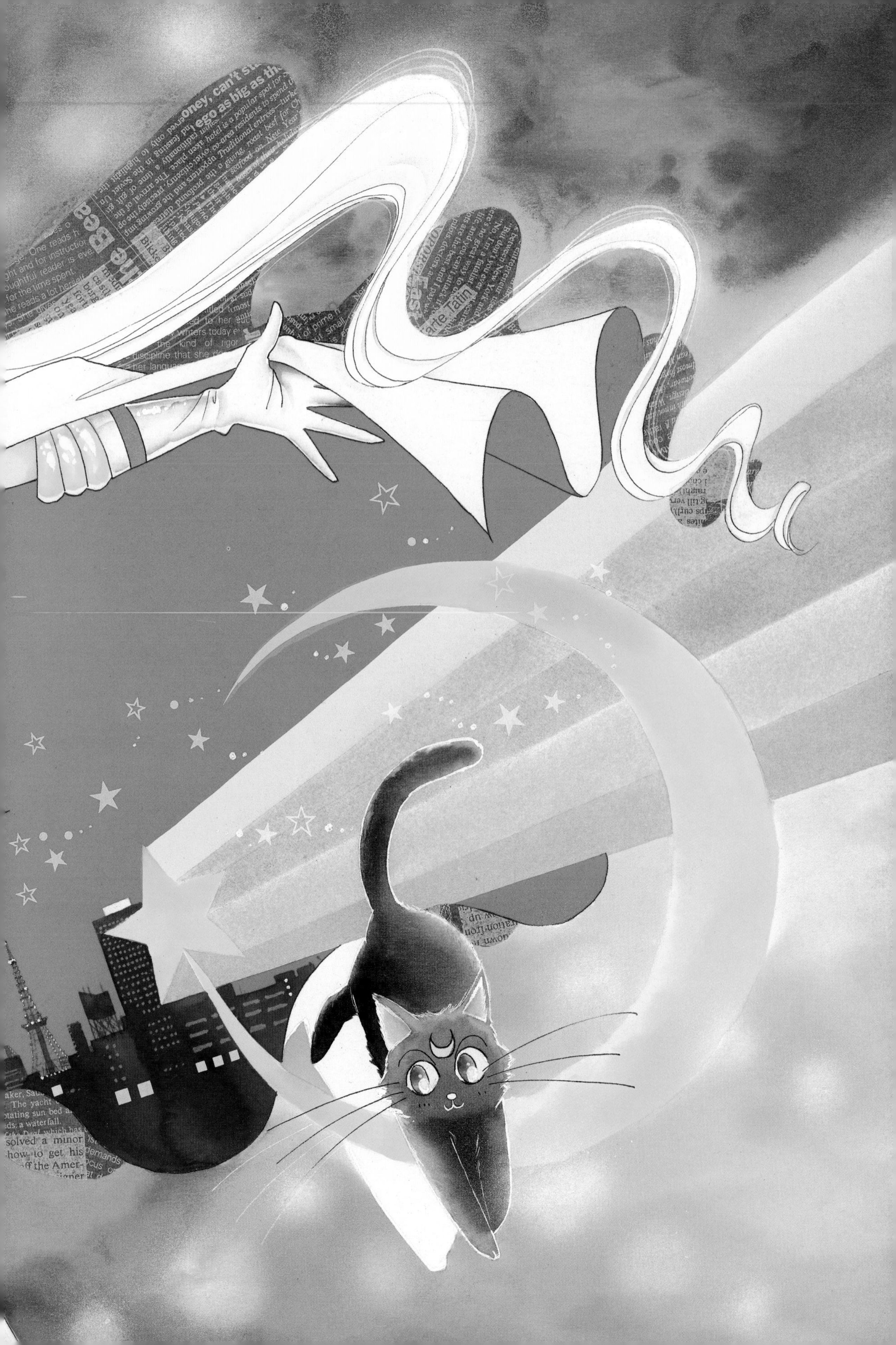

Act.1 Usagi: Sailor Moon

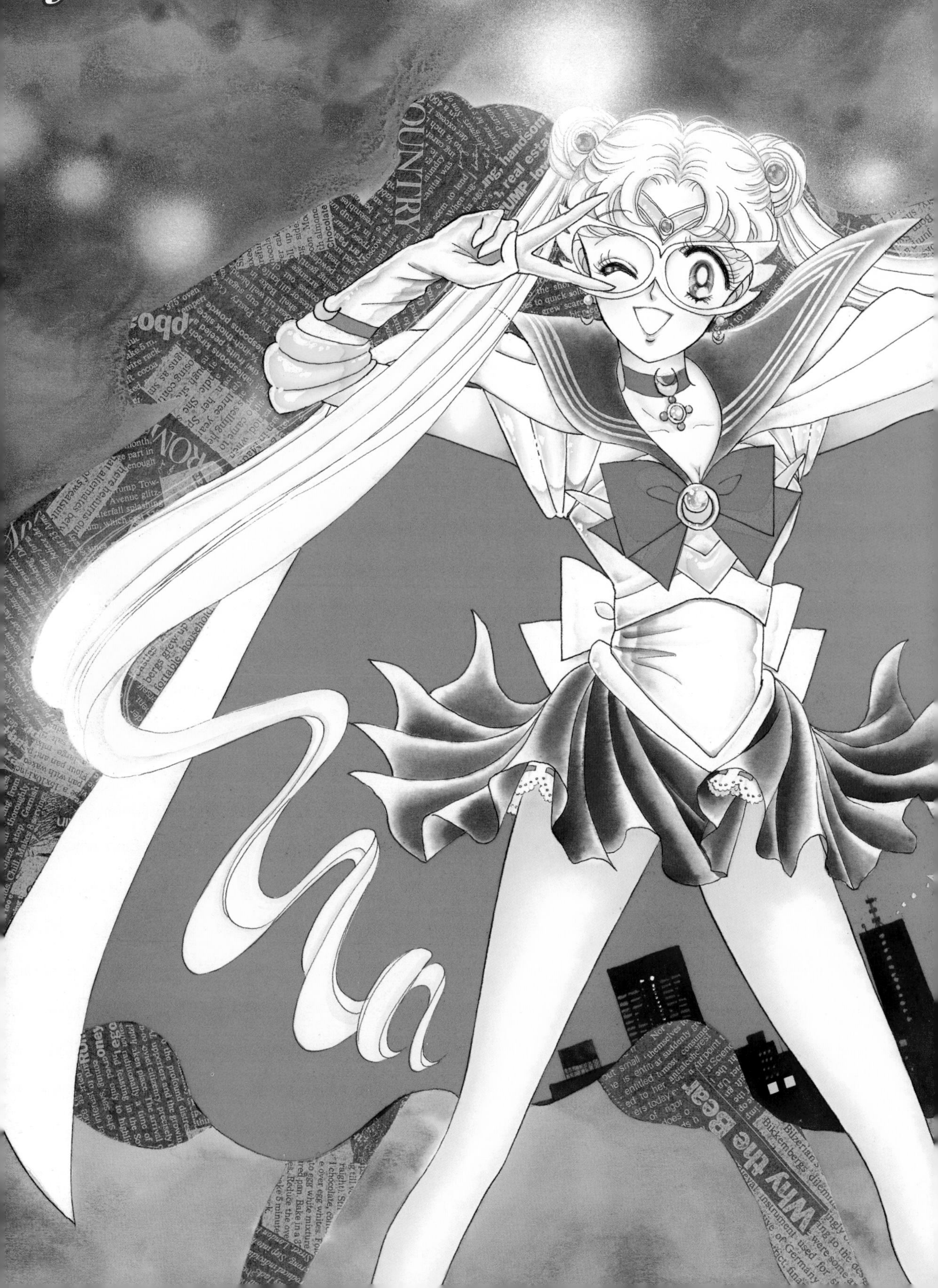

Pretty Guardian

Sailor Moon

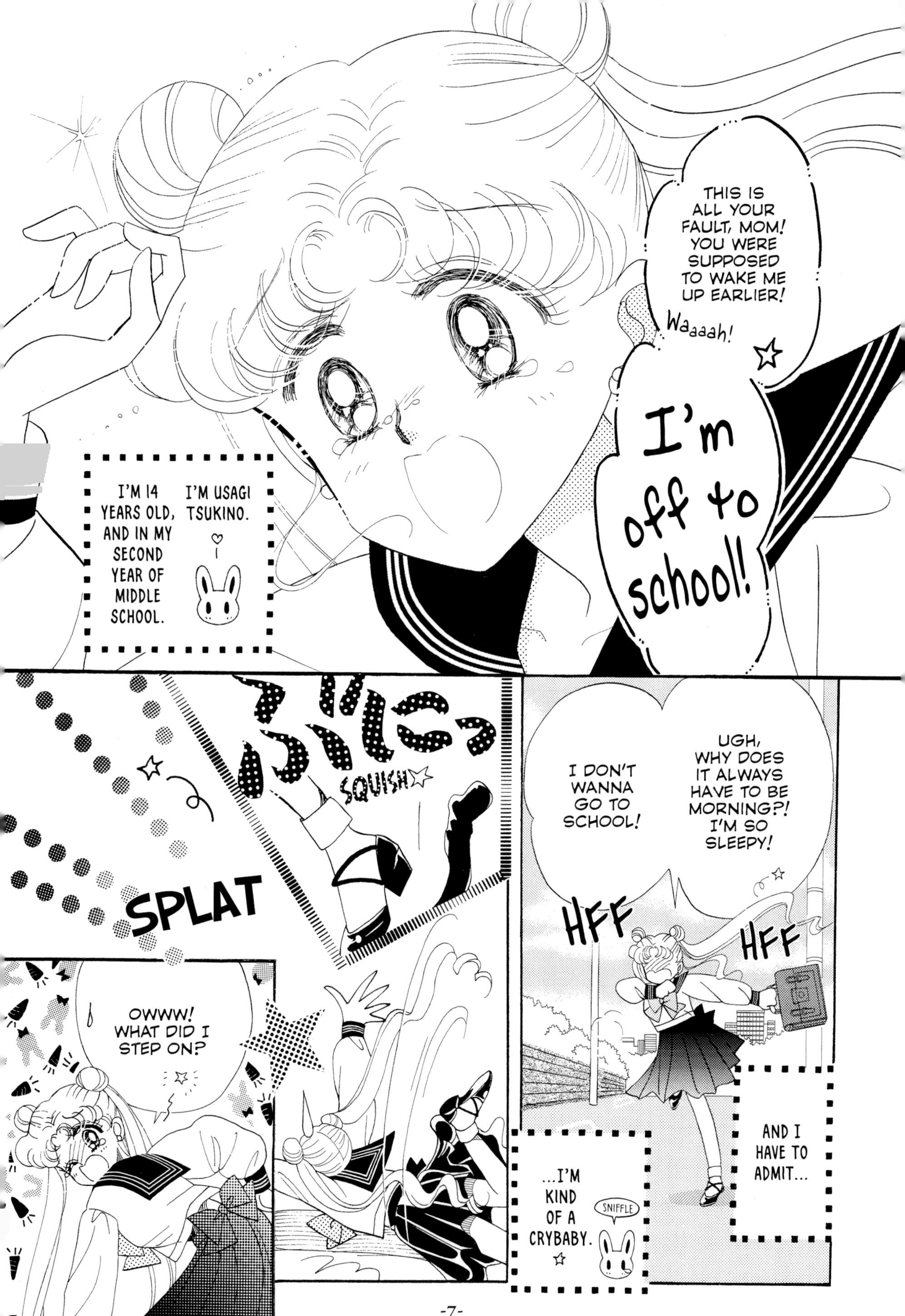
THIS IS ALL YOUR FAULT, MOM! YOU WERE SUPPOSED TO WAKE ME UP EARLIER!
Waaaah!
I'm off to school!
I'M USAGI TSUKINO.
I'M 14 YEARS OLD, AND IN MY SECOND YEAR OF MIDDLE SCHOOL.
UGH, WHY DOES IT ALWAYS HAVE TO BE MORNING?! I'M SO SLEEPY!
I DON'T WANNA GO TO SCHOOL!
HFF
HFF
AND I HAVE TO ADMIT...
...I'M KIND OF A CRYBABY.
SNIFFLE
ぶにっ
SQUISH
SPLAT
OWWW! WHAT DID I STEP ON?

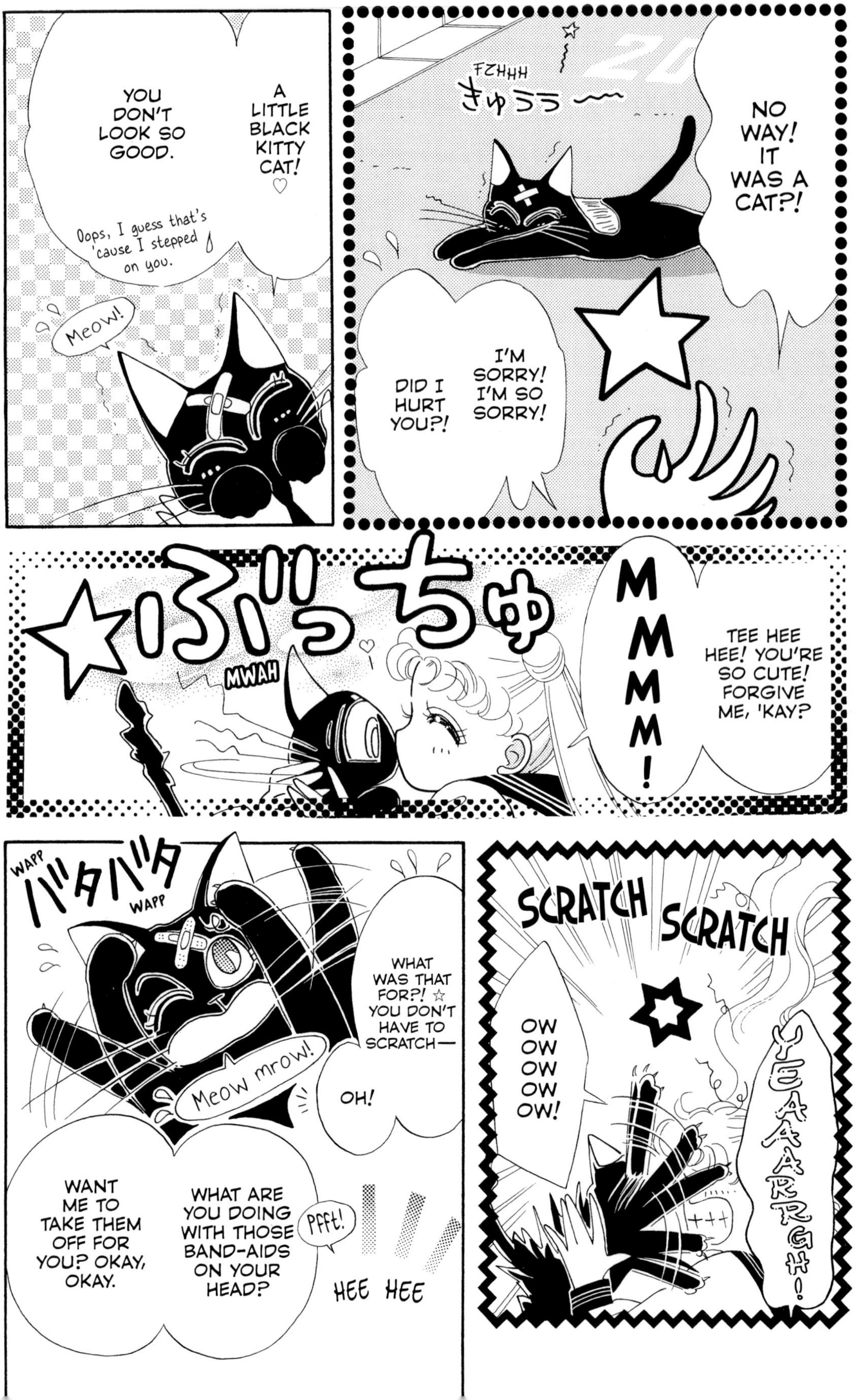

FZHHH
きゅうう〜
NO WAY! IT WAS A CAT?!
I'M SORRY! I'M SO SORRY!
DID I HURT YOU?!
A LITTLE BLACK KITTY CAT! ♡
YOU DON'T LOOK SO GOOD.
Oops, I guess that's 'cause I stepped on you.
Meow!
MMMM!
TEE HEE HEE! YOU'RE SO CUTE! FORGIVE ME, 'KAY?
ぶっちゅ
MWAH
SCRATCH SCRATCH
YEAARRGH!
OW OW OW OW OW!
バタバタ
WAPP WAPP
WHAT WAS THAT FOR?! ☆ YOU DON'T HAVE TO SCRATCH—
OH!
Meow mrow!
WHAT ARE YOU DOING WITH THOSE BAND-AIDS ON YOUR HEAD?
Pfft!
WANT ME TO TAKE THEM OFF FOR YOU? OKAY, OKAY.
HEE HEE

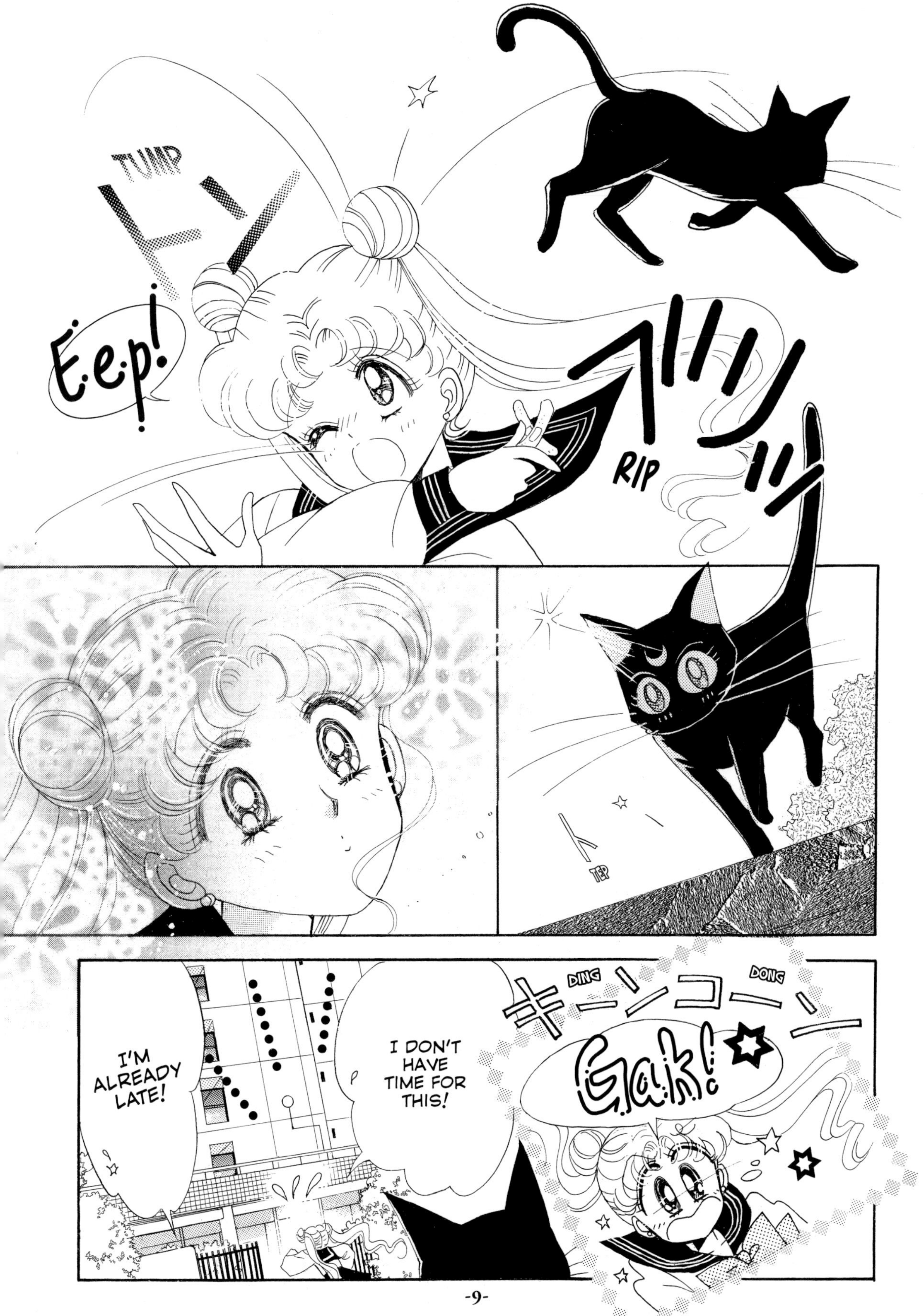

TUMP
Eep!
RIP
TEP
DING
DONG
Gak!
I DON'T HAVE TIME FOR THIS!
I'M ALREADY LATE!

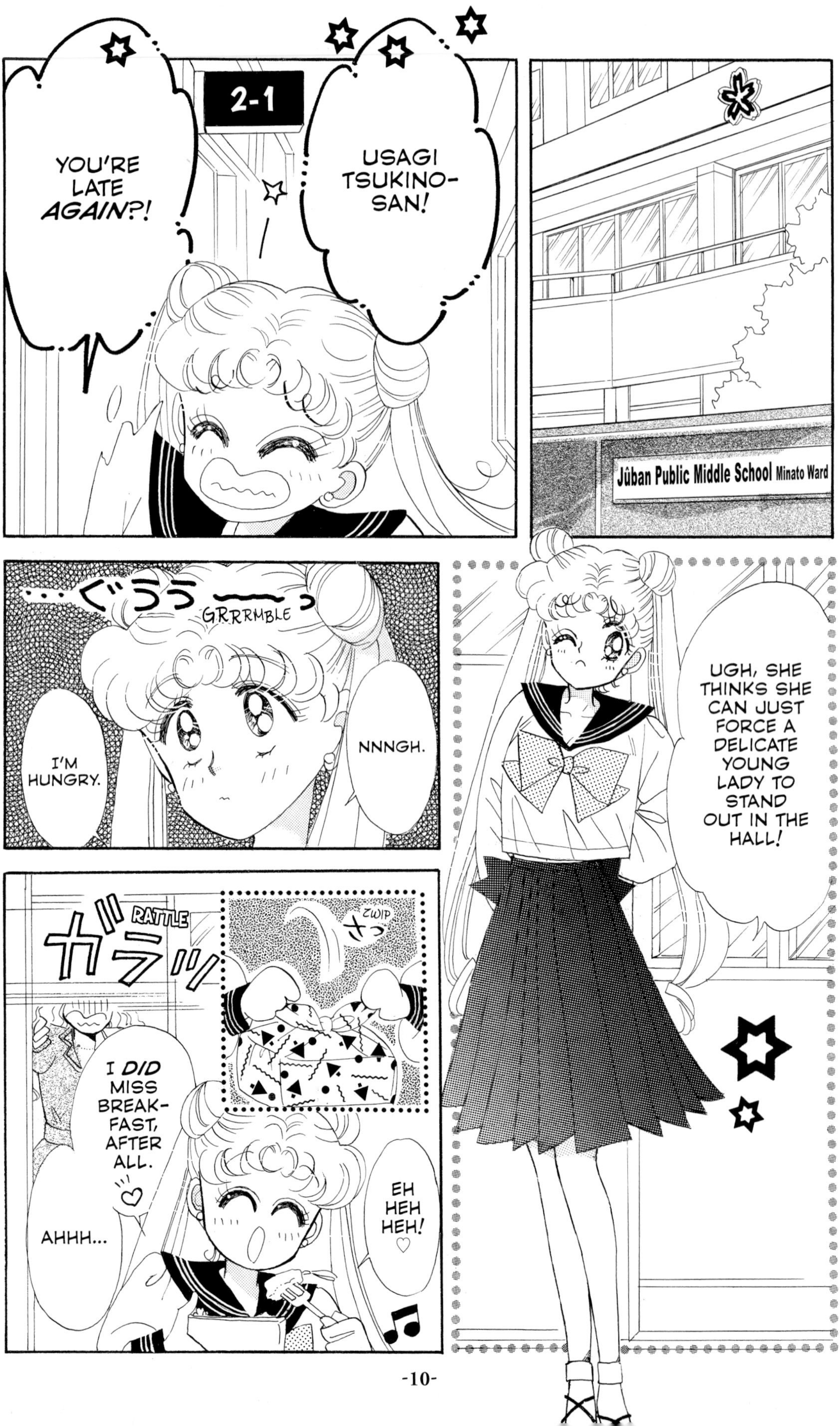
Jûban Public Middle School Minato Ward
2-1
USAGI TSUKINO-SAN!
YOU'RE LATE AGAIN?!
UGH, SHE THINKS SHE CAN JUST FORCE A DELICATE YOUNG LADY TO STAND OUT IN THE HALL!
…ぐううーっ
GRRRMBLE
NNNGH.
I'M HUNGRY.
さっ
ZWIP
ガラッ
RATTLE
EH HEH HEH! ♡
I DID MISS BREAKFAST, AFTER ALL.
AHHH…

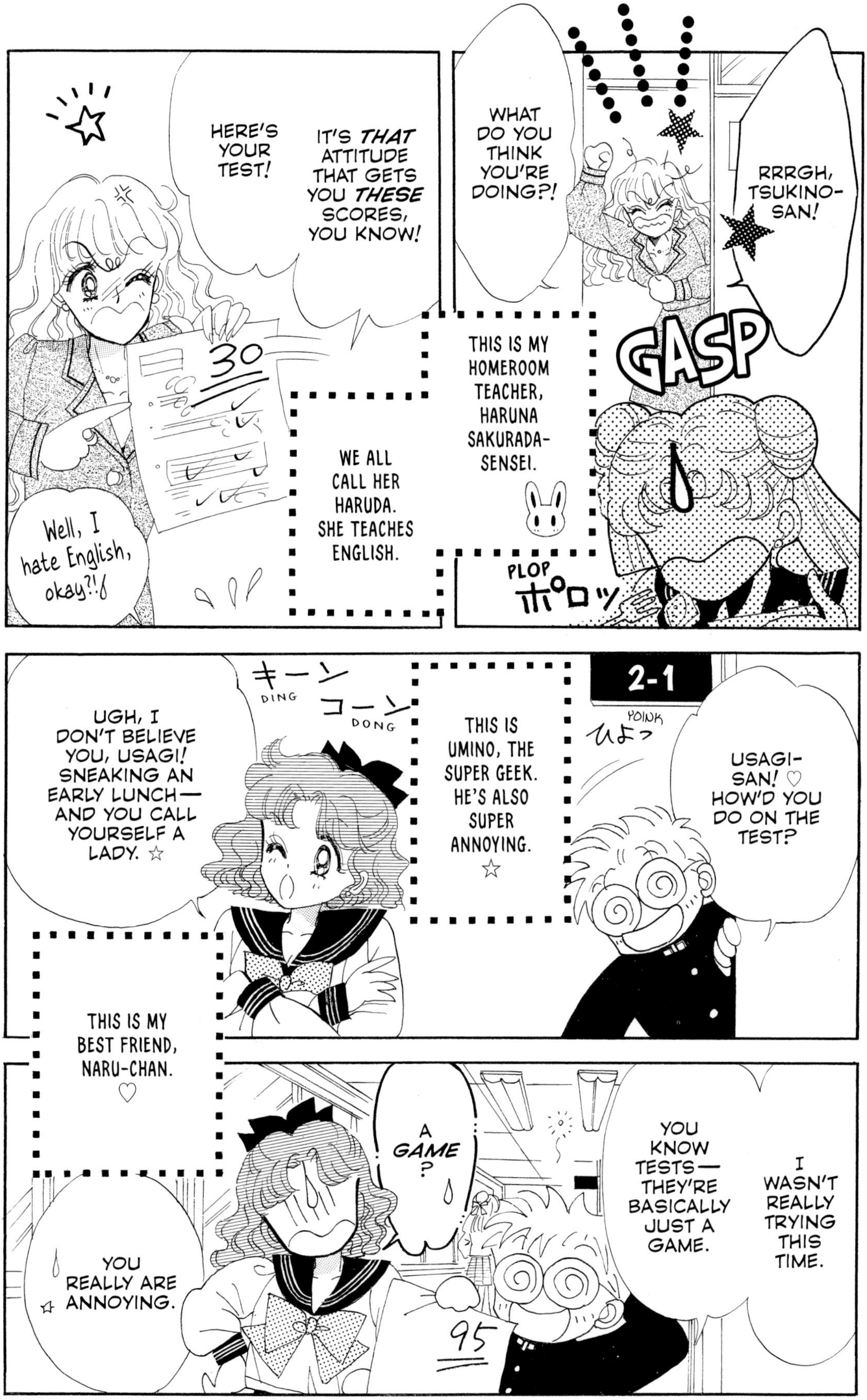
RRRGH, TSUKINO-SAN!
WHAT DO YOU THINK YOU'RE DOING?!
GASP
THIS IS MY HOMEROOM TEACHER, HARUNA SAKURADA-SENSEI.
PLOP ポロッ
IT'S *THAT* ATTITUDE THAT GETS YOU *THESE* SCORES, YOU KNOW!
HERE'S YOUR TEST!
30
WE ALL CALL HER HARUDA. SHE TEACHES ENGLISH.
Well, I hate English, okay?!
2-1
USAGI-SAN! ♡ HOW'D YOU DO ON THE TEST?
YOINK ひよっ
THIS IS UMINO, THE SUPER GEEK. HE'S ALSO SUPER ANNOYING. ☆
キーン DING コーン DONG
UGH, I DON'T BELIEVE YOU, USAGI! SNEAKING AN EARLY LUNCH—AND YOU CALL YOURSELF A LADY. ☆
THIS IS MY BEST FRIEND, NARU-CHAN. ♡
I WASN'T REALLY TRYING THIS TIME.
YOU KNOW TESTS—THEY'RE BASICALLY JUST A GAME.
A *GAME*?
95
YOU REALLY ARE ANNOYING.

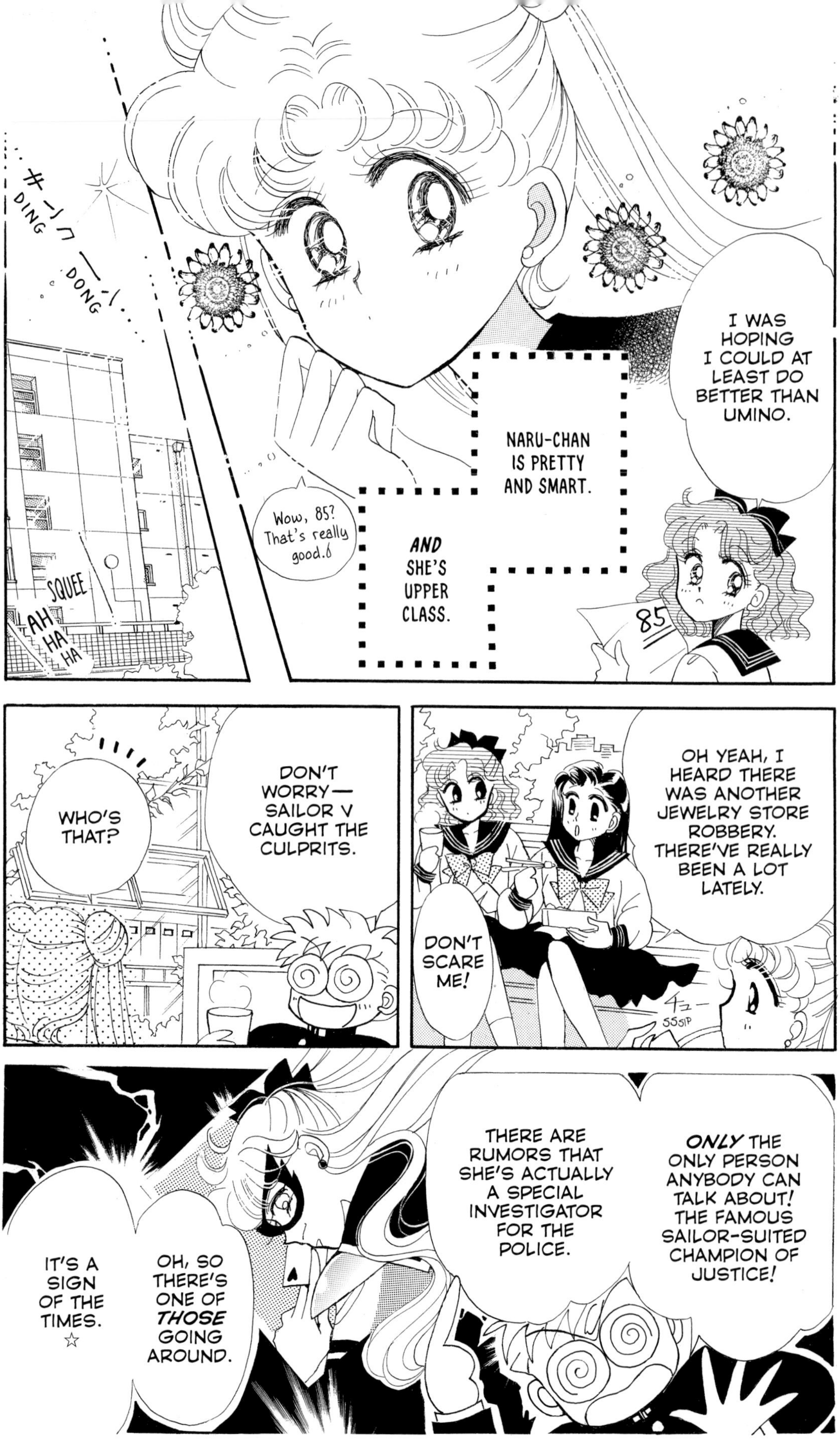
I WAS HOPING I COULD AT LEAST DO BETTER THAN UMINO.
NARU-CHAN IS PRETTY AND SMART.
AND SHE'S UPPER CLASS.
85
Wow, 85? That's really good.
DING DONG
SQUEE
AH HA HA
OH YEAH, I HEARD THERE WAS ANOTHER JEWELRY STORE ROBBERY. THERE'VE REALLY BEEN A LOT LATELY.
SSSIP
DON'T SCARE ME!
DON'T WORRY— SAILOR V CAUGHT THE CULPRITS.
WHO'S THAT?
ONLY THE ONLY PERSON ANYBODY CAN TALK ABOUT! THE FAMOUS SAILOR-SUITED CHAMPION OF JUSTICE!
THERE ARE RUMORS THAT SHE'S ACTUALLY A SPECIAL INVESTIGATOR FOR THE POLICE.
OH, SO THERE'S ONE OF *THOSE* GOING AROUND.
IT'S A SIGN OF THE TIMES. ☆

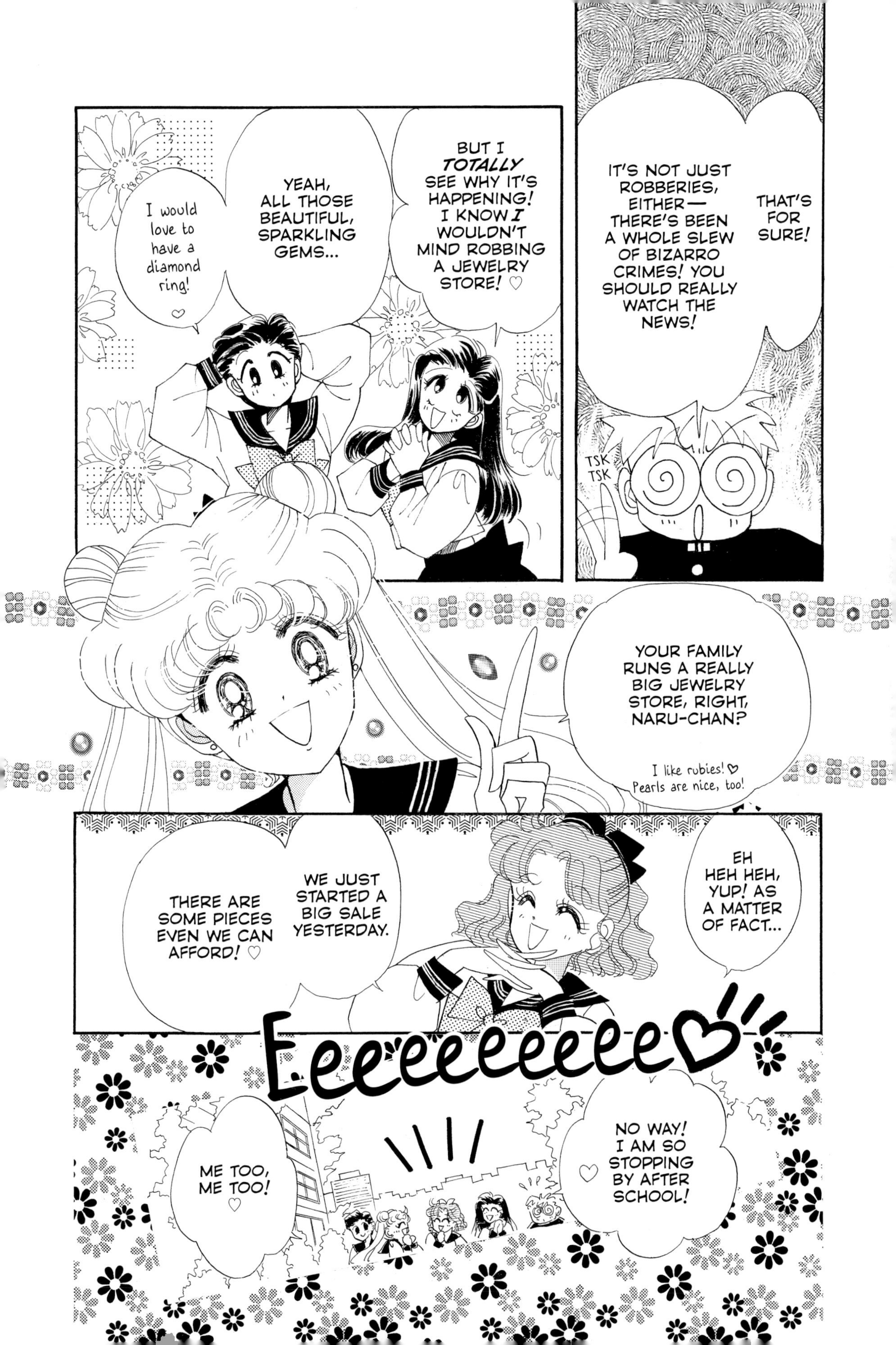
THAT'S FOR SURE!
IT'S NOT JUST ROBBERIES, EITHER— THERE'S BEEN A WHOLE SLEW OF BIZARRO CRIMES! YOU SHOULD REALLY WATCH THE NEWS!
TSK TSK
BUT I *TOTALLY* SEE WHY IT'S HAPPENING! I KNOW *I* WOULDN'T MIND ROBBING A JEWELRY STORE! ♡
YEAH, ALL THOSE BEAUTIFUL, SPARKLING GEMS...
I would love to have a diamond ring! ♡
YOUR FAMILY RUNS A REALLY BIG JEWELRY STORE, RIGHT, NARU-CHAN?
I like rubies! ♡ Pearls are nice, too!
EH HEH HEH, YUP! AS A MATTER OF FACT...
WE JUST STARTED A BIG SALE YESTERDAY.
THERE ARE SOME PIECES EVEN WE CAN AFFORD! ♡
Eeeeeeeee♡
NO WAY! I AM SO STOPPING BY AFTER SCHOOL! ♡
ME TOO, ME TOO! ♡

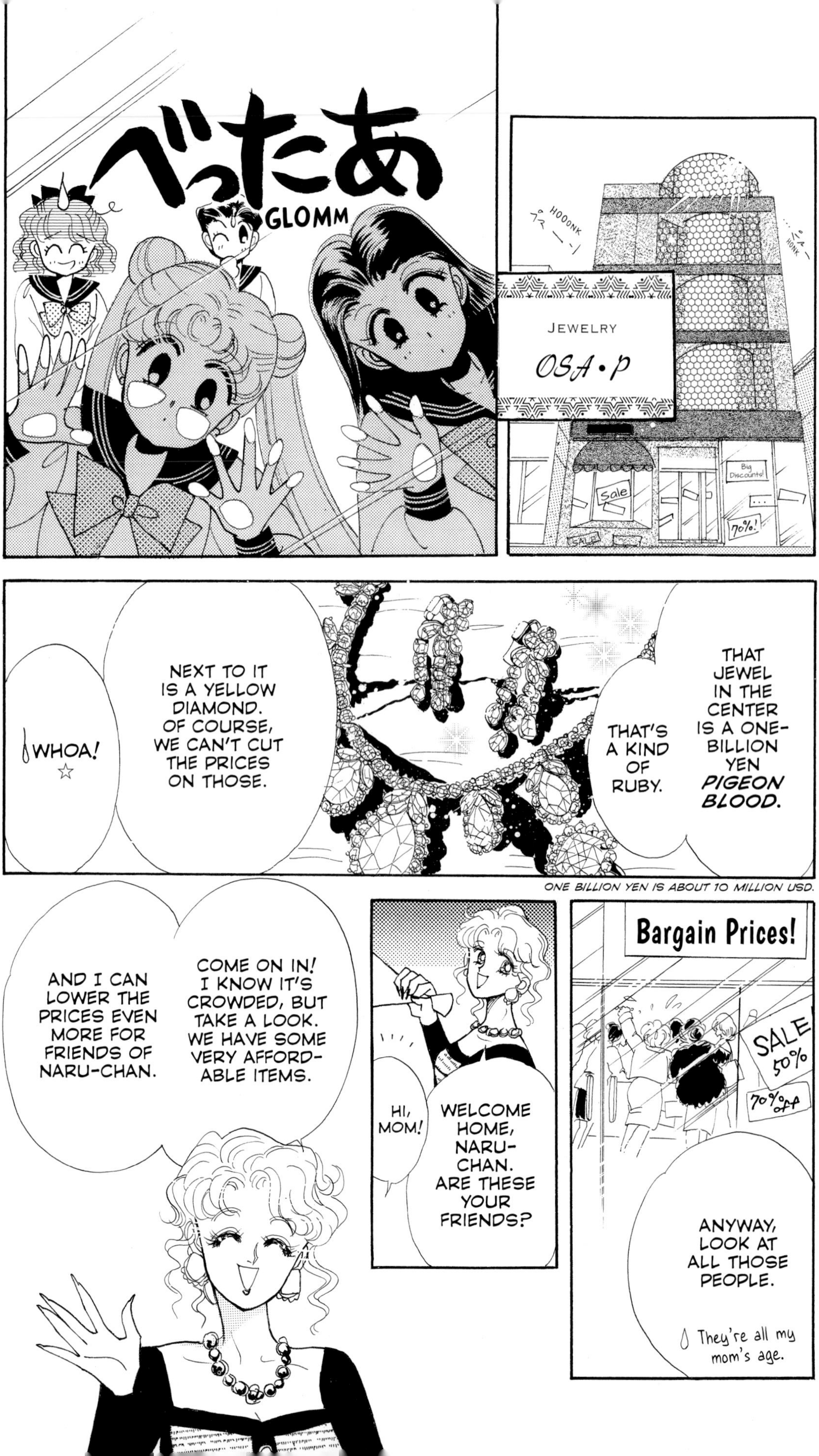
HOOONK
JEWELRY
OSA・P
Big Discounts!
Sale
70%!
べったあ
GLOMM
THAT JEWEL IN THE CENTER IS A ONE-BILLION YEN *PIGEON BLOOD.*
THAT'S A KIND OF RUBY.
NEXT TO IT IS A YELLOW DIAMOND. OF COURSE, WE CAN'T CUT THE PRICES ON THOSE.
WHOA! ☆
Bargain Prices!
SALE 50%
70% off
ANYWAY, LOOK AT ALL THOSE PEOPLE.
They're all my mom's age.
WELCOME HOME, NARU-CHAN. ARE THESE YOUR FRIENDS?
HI, MOM!
COME ON IN! I KNOW IT'S CROWDED, BUT TAKE A LOOK. WE HAVE SOME VERY AFFORDABLE ITEMS.
AND I CAN LOWER THE PRICES EVEN MORE FOR FRIENDS OF NARU-CHAN.

ONE BILLION YEN IS ABOUT 10 MILLION USD.

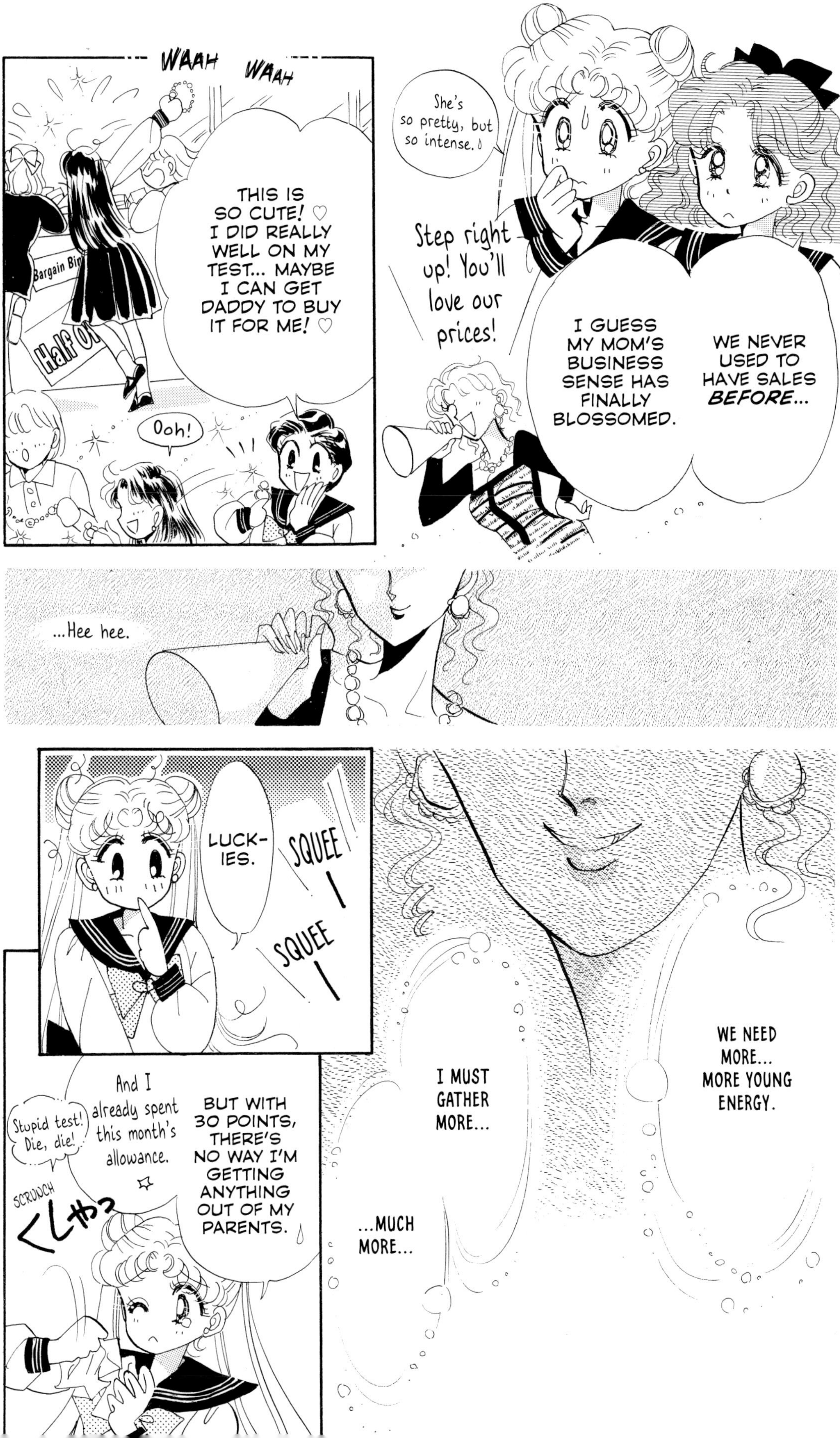
She's so pretty, but so intense.
WE NEVER USED TO HAVE SALES *BEFORE*...
I GUESS MY MOM'S BUSINESS SENSE HAS FINALLY BLOSSOMED.
Step right up! You'll love our prices!
WAAH
WAAH
THIS IS SO CUTE! ♡ I DID REALLY WELL ON MY TEST... MAYBE I CAN GET DADDY TO BUY IT FOR ME! ♡
Ooh!
Bargain Bin
Half Off
...Hee hee.
WE NEED MORE... MORE YOUNG ENERGY.
I MUST GATHER MORE...
...MUCH MORE...
LUCK-IES.
SQUEE
SQUEE
BUT WITH 30 POINTS, THERE'S NO WAY I'M GETTING ANYTHING OUT OF MY PARENTS.
And I already spent this month's allowance.
Stupid test! Die, die!
SCRUNCH
くしゃっ

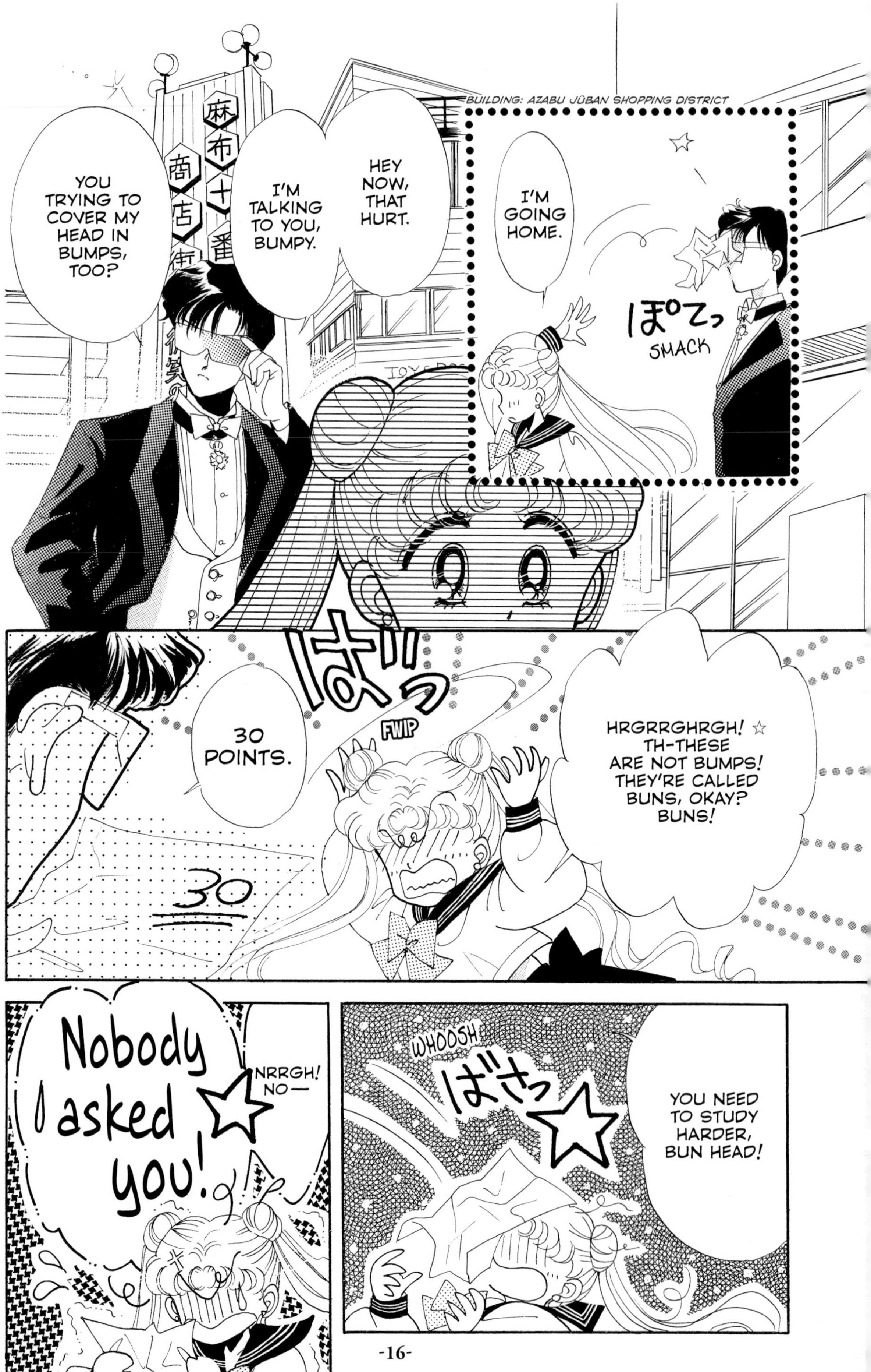
BUILDING: AZABU JŪBAN SHOPPING DISTRICT
I'M GOING HOME.
ぽてっ
SMACK
HEY NOW, THAT HURT.
I'M TALKING TO YOU, BUMPY.
YOU TRYING TO COVER MY HEAD IN BUMPS, TOO?
麻布十番商店街
HRGRRGHRGH! ☆ TH-THESE ARE NOT BUMPS! THEY'RE CALLED BUNS, OKAY? BUNS!
ばっ
FWIP
30 POINTS.
30
ばさっ
WHOOSH
YOU NEED TO STUDY HARDER, BUN HEAD!
NRRGH! NO—
Nobody asked you!

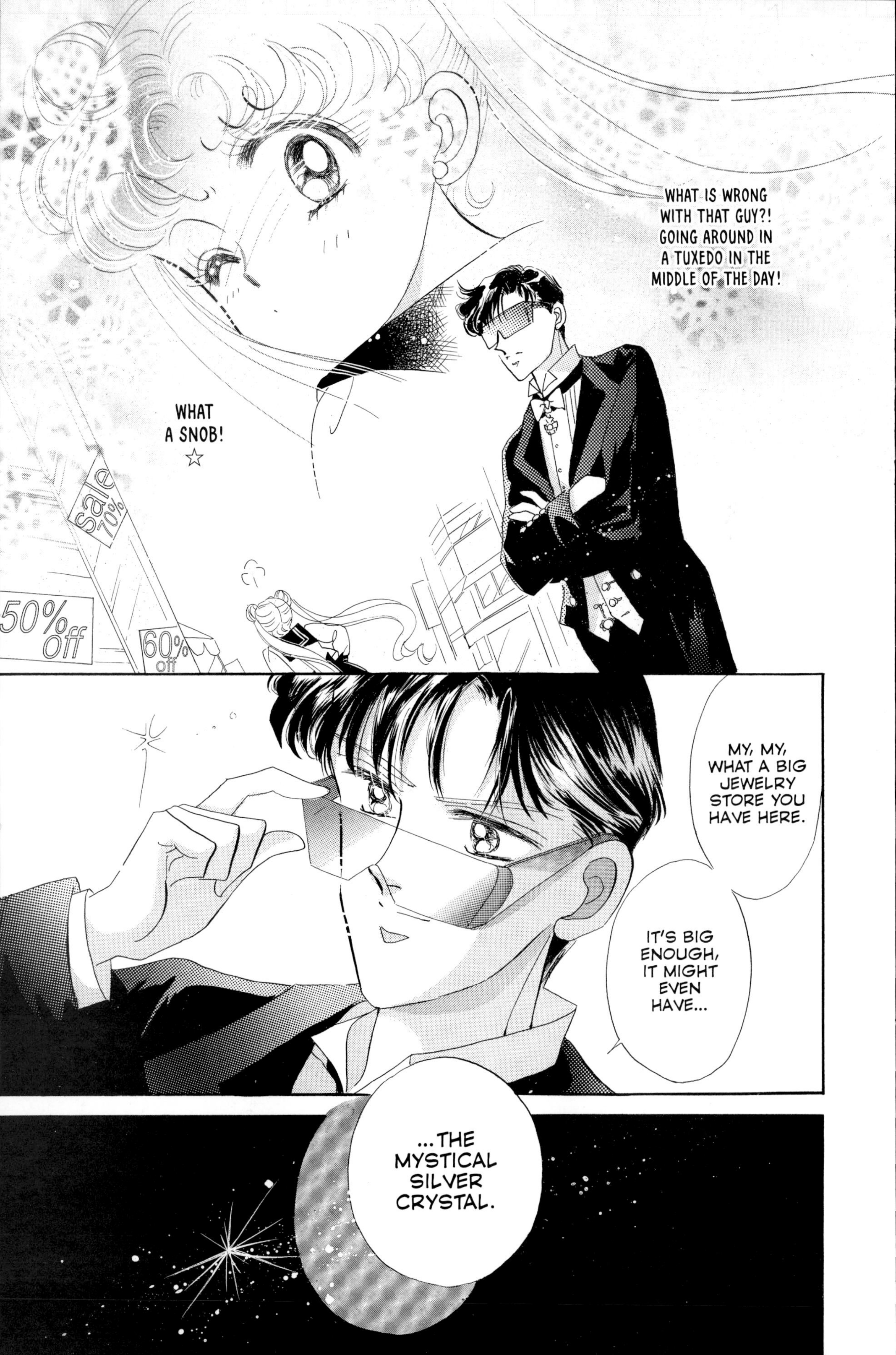
WHAT IS WRONG WITH THAT GUY?! GOING AROUND IN A TUXEDO IN THE MIDDLE OF THE DAY!
WHAT A SNOB! ☆
sale 70%
50% off
60% off
MY, MY, WHAT A BIG JEWELRY STORE YOU HAVE HERE.
IT'S BIG ENOUGH, IT MIGHT EVEN HAVE...
...THE MYSTICAL SILVER CRYSTAL.

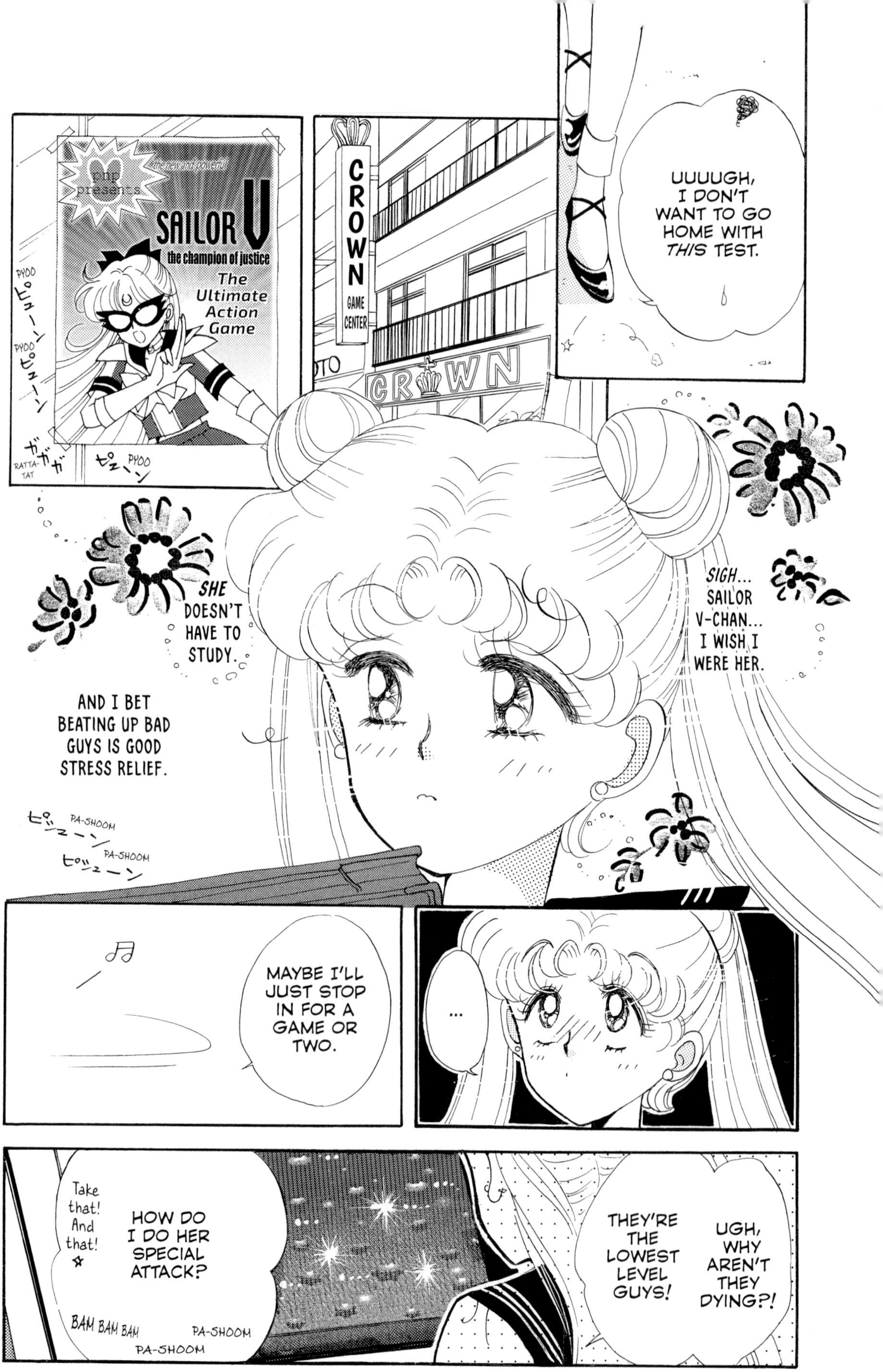
UUUUGH, I DON'T WANT TO GO HOME WITH *THIS* TEST.
CROWN GAME CENTER
CROWN
pnp presents
the new and powerful
SAILOR V
the champion of justice
The Ultimate Action Game
PYOO
PYOO
PYOO
RATTA-TAT
SIGH... SAILOR V-CHAN... I WISH I WERE HER.
SHE DOESN'T HAVE TO STUDY.
AND I BET BEATING UP BAD GUYS IS GOOD STRESS RELIEF.
PA-SHOOM
PA-SHOOM
...
MAYBE I'LL JUST STOP IN FOR A GAME OR TWO.
UGH, WHY AREN'T THEY DYING?!
THEY'RE THE LOWEST LEVEL GUYS!
HOW DO I DO HER SPECIAL ATTACK?
Take that! And that! ☆
BAM BAM BAM
PA-SHOOM
PA-SHOOM

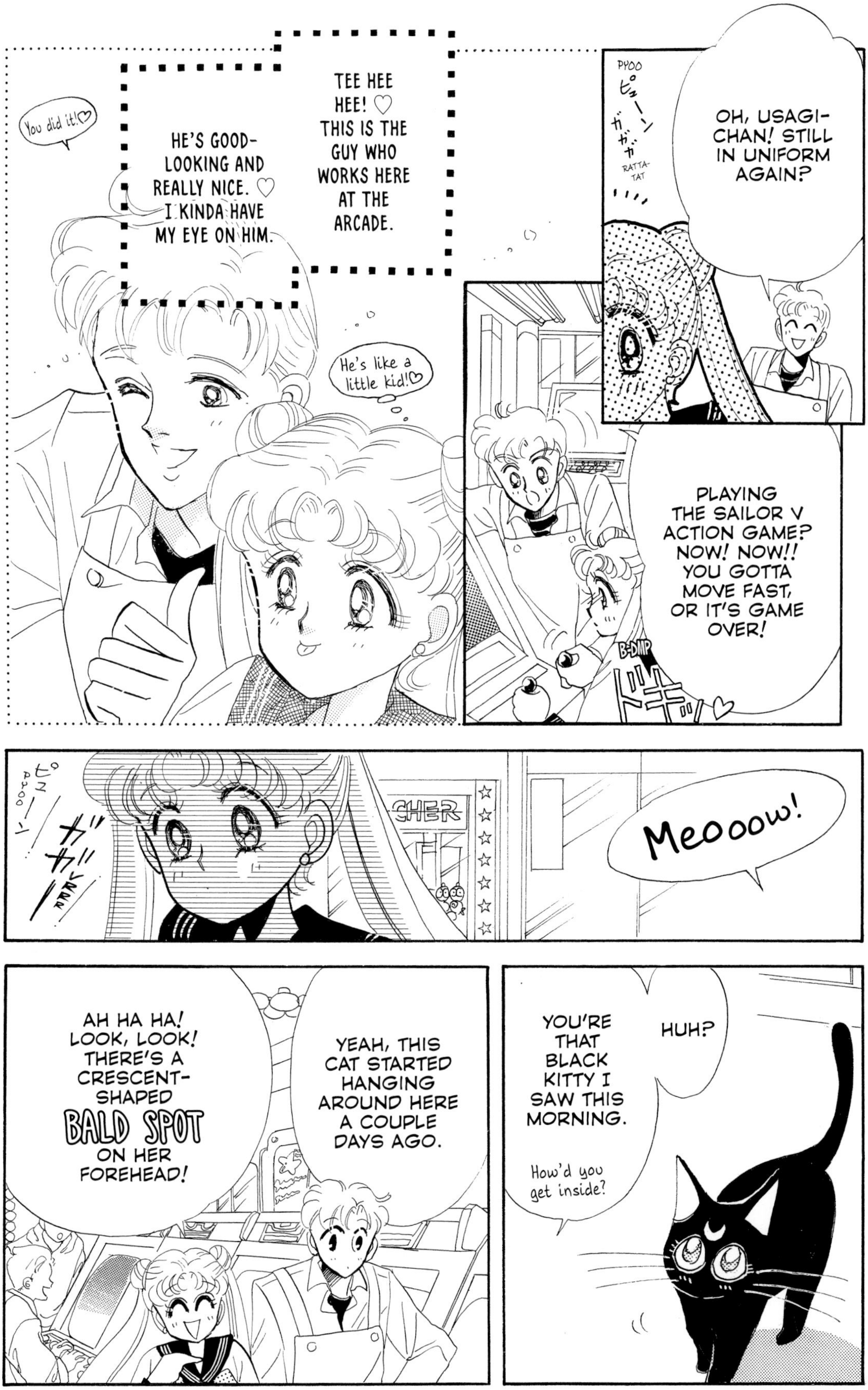
PYOO
RATTA-TAT
OH, USAGI-CHAN! STILL IN UNIFORM AGAIN?
PLAYING THE SAILOR V ACTION GAME? NOW! NOW!! YOU GOTTA MOVE FAST, OR IT'S GAME OVER!
B-DMP
TEE HEE HEE! ♡ THIS IS THE GUY WHO WORKS HERE AT THE ARCADE.
HE'S GOOD-LOOKING AND REALLY NICE. ♡ I KINDA HAVE MY EYE ON HIM.
You did it!♡
He's like a little kid!♡
Meooow!
PYOO
HUH?
YOU'RE THAT BLACK KITTY I SAW THIS MORNING.
How'd you get inside?
YEAH, THIS CAT STARTED HANGING AROUND HERE A COUPLE DAYS AGO.
AH HA HA! LOOK, LOOK! THERE'S A CRESCENT-SHAPED BALD SPOT ON HER FOREHEAD!

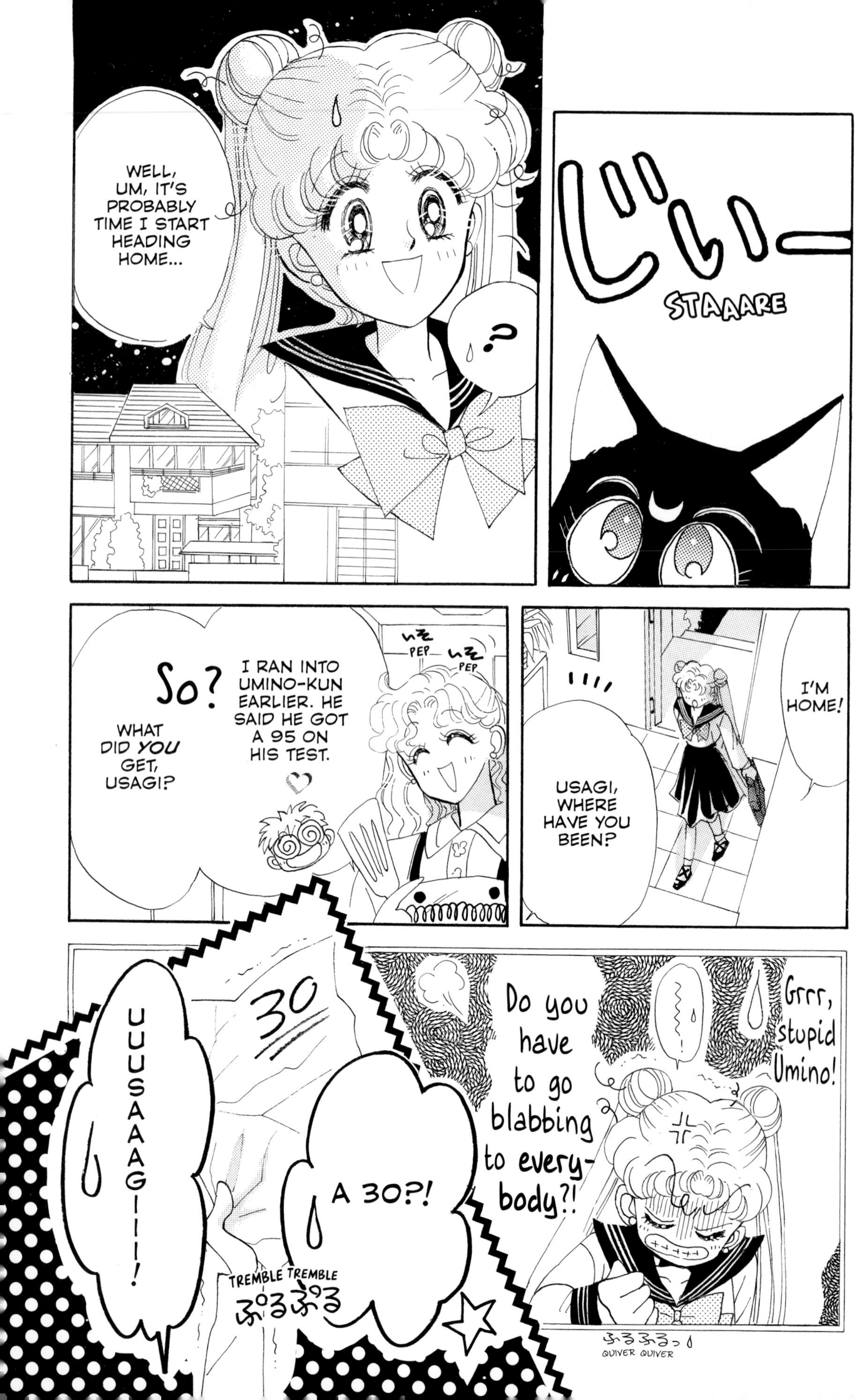

じぃー
STAAARE
WELL, UM, IT'S PROBABLY TIME I START HEADING HOME...
?
I'M HOME!
''''
USAGI, WHERE HAVE YOU BEEN?
いそ PEP いそ PEP
I RAN INTO UMINO-KUN EARLIER. HE SAID HE GOT A 95 ON HIS TEST.
So?
WHAT DID *YOU* GET, USAGI?
Grrr, stupid Umino!
Do you have to go blabbing to everybody?!
ふるふるっ
QUIVER QUIVER
30
A 30?!
UUUSAAAAG!!!!
TREMBLE TREMBLE
ぷるぷる

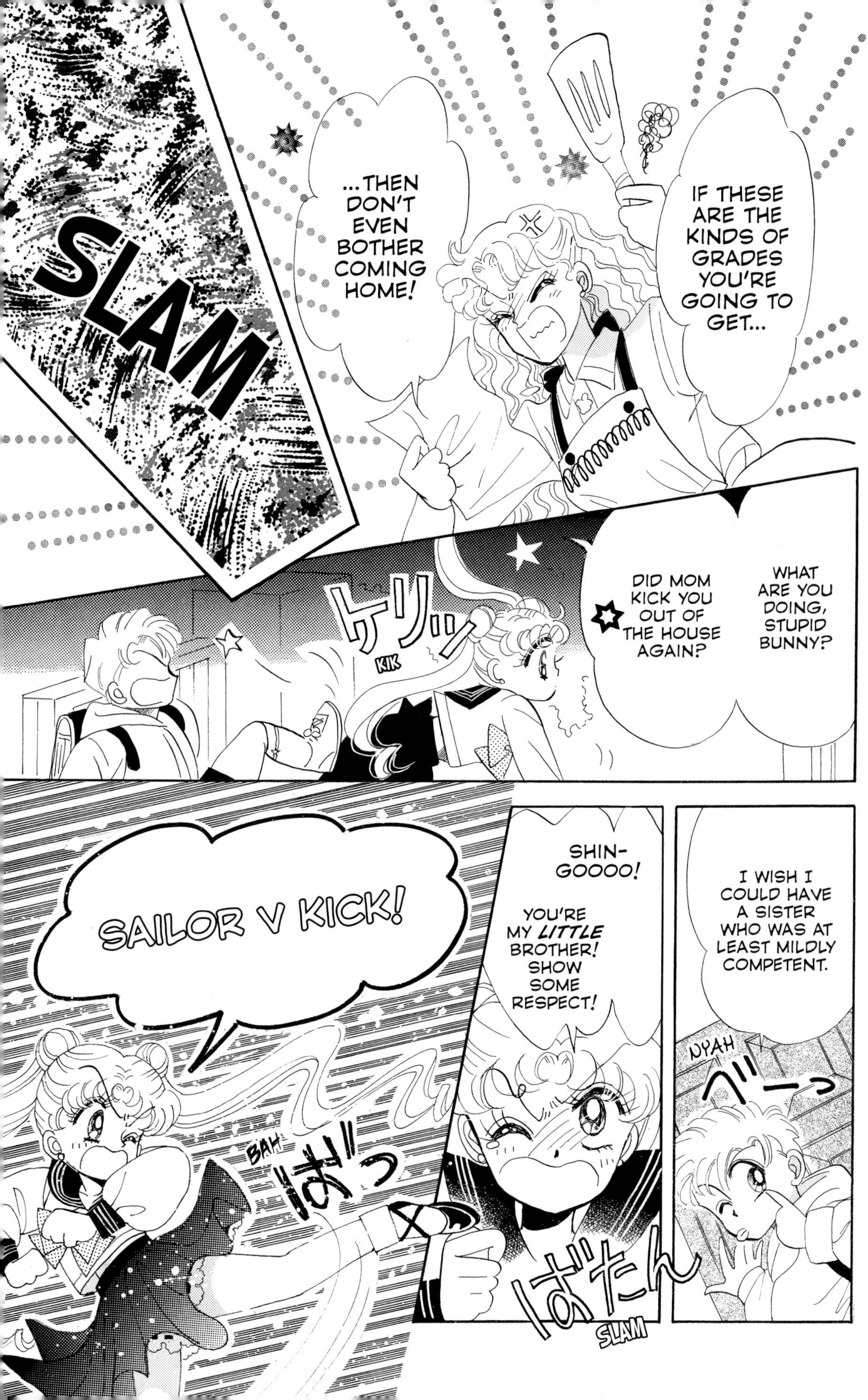
IF THESE ARE THE KINDS OF GRADES YOU'RE GOING TO GET...
...THEN DON'T EVEN BOTHER COMING HOME!
SLAM
WHAT ARE YOU DOING, STUPID BUNNY?
DID MOM KICK YOU OUT OF THE HOUSE AGAIN?
ケリッ
KIK
I WISH I COULD HAVE A SISTER WHO WAS AT LEAST MILDLY COMPETENT.
NYAH
べーっ
SHIN-GOOOO!
YOU'RE MY *LITTLE* BROTHER! SHOW SOME RESPECT!
ばたん
SLAM
SAILOR V KICK!
BAH
ばっ

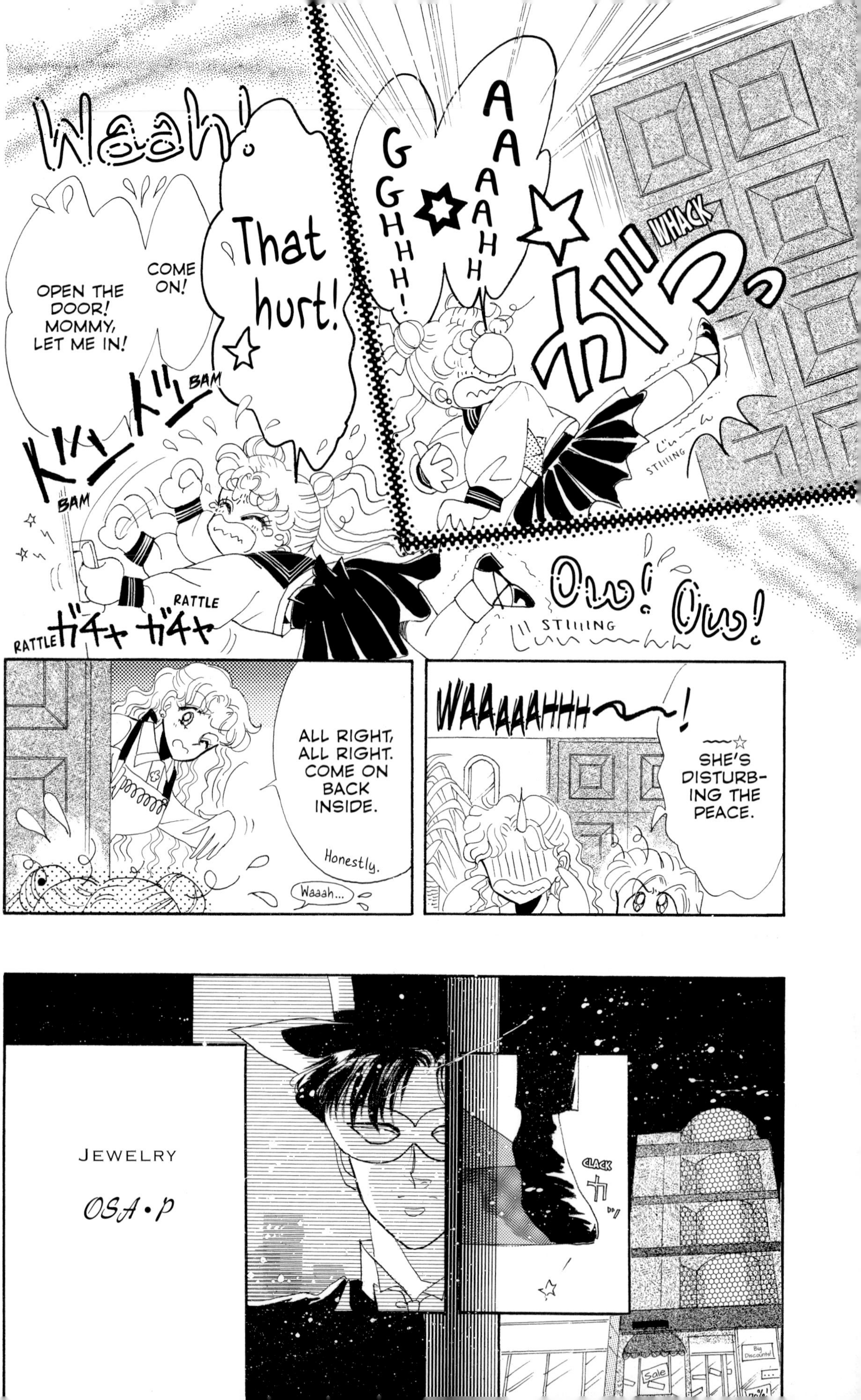
AAAAHH
GGHHHH!
WHACK
カドっ
STIIIING
Waah!
That hurt!
COME ON!
OPEN THE DOOR! MOMMY, LET ME IN!
BAM
ドンドン
BAM
RATTLE
ガチャガチャ
RATTLE
Ow! Ow!
STIIIING
WAAAAAHHH~!
SHE'S DISTURBING THE PEACE.
ALL RIGHT, ALL RIGHT. COME ON BACK INSIDE.
Honestly.
Waaah...
JEWELRY
OSA•P
CLACK
カ
Big Discounts!
Sale

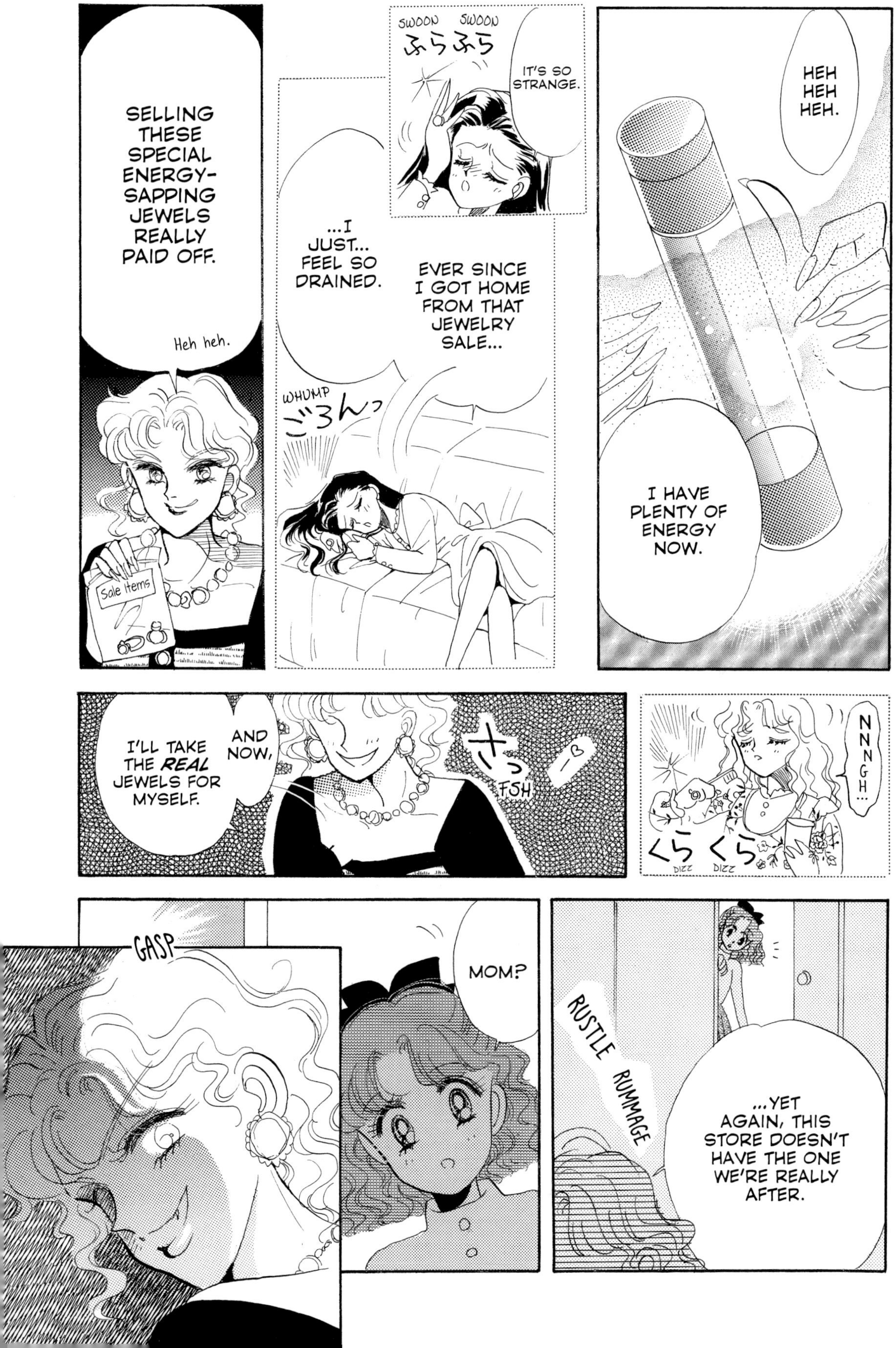
HEH HEH HEH.
I HAVE PLENTY OF ENERGY NOW.
SWOON SWOON
ふらふら
IT'S SO STRANGE.
EVER SINCE I GOT HOME FROM THAT JEWELRY SALE...
...I JUST... FEEL SO DRAINED.
WHUMP
ごろんっ
SELLING THESE SPECIAL ENERGY-SAPPING JEWELS REALLY PAID OFF.
Heh heh.
Sale Items
NNNGH...
くら くら
DIZZ DIZZ
AND NOW,
I'LL TAKE THE *REAL* JEWELS FOR MYSELF.
さっ
FSH
RUSTLE RUMMAGE
...YET AGAIN, THIS STORE DOESN'T HAVE THE ONE WE'RE REALLY AFTER.
MOM?
GASP

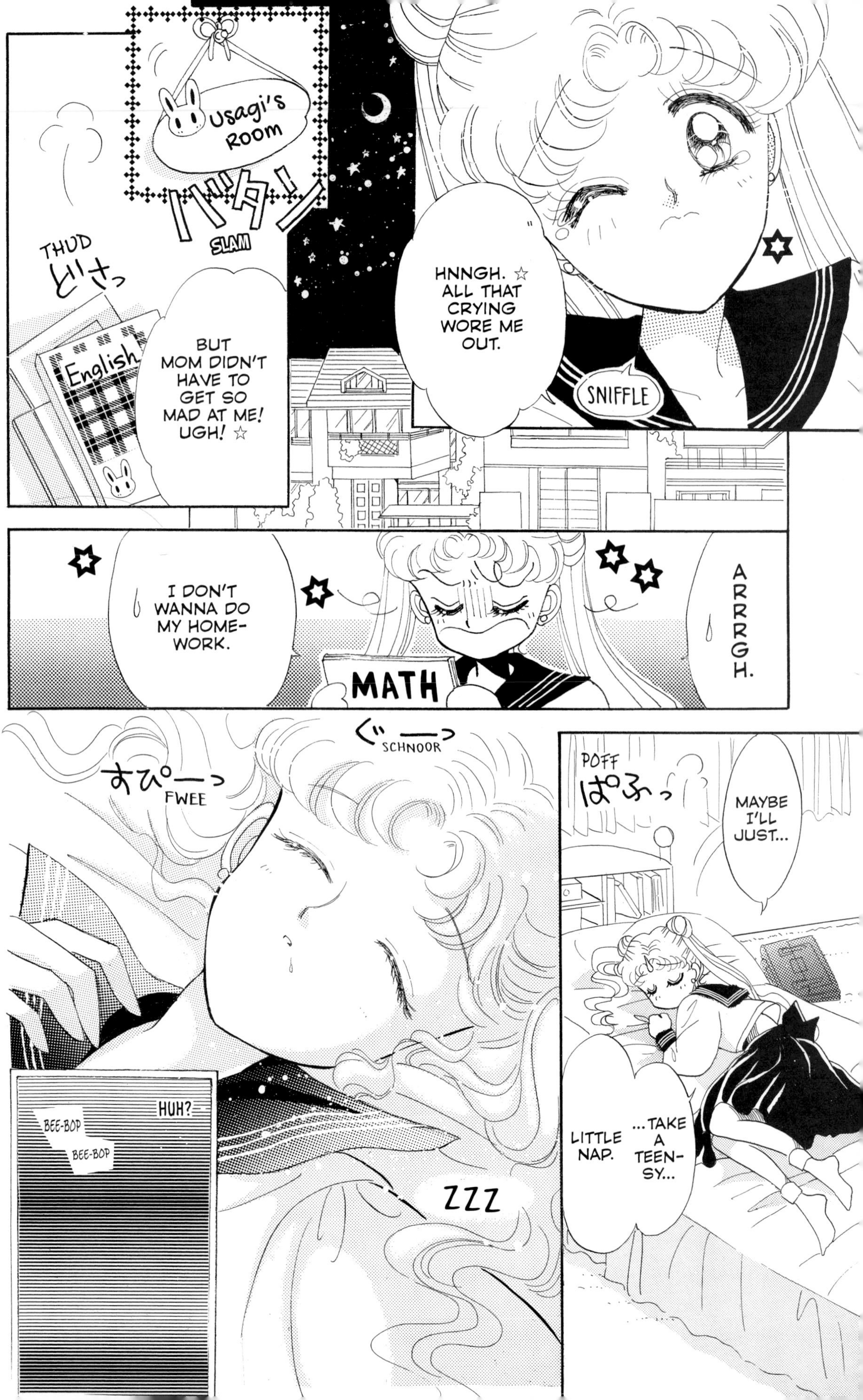
HNNGH. ☆ ALL THAT CRYING WORE ME OUT.
SNIFFLE
Usagi's Room
バタン
SLAM
THUD
どさっ
English
BUT MOM DIDN'T HAVE TO GET SO MAD AT ME! UGH! ☆
ARRRGH.
I DON'T WANNA DO MY HOME-WORK.
MATH
POFF
ぱふっ
MAYBE I'LL JUST...
...TAKE A TEENSY...
LITTLE NAP.
ぐーっ
SCHNOOR
すぴーっ
FWEE
ZZZ
HUH?
BEE-BOP
BEE-BOP

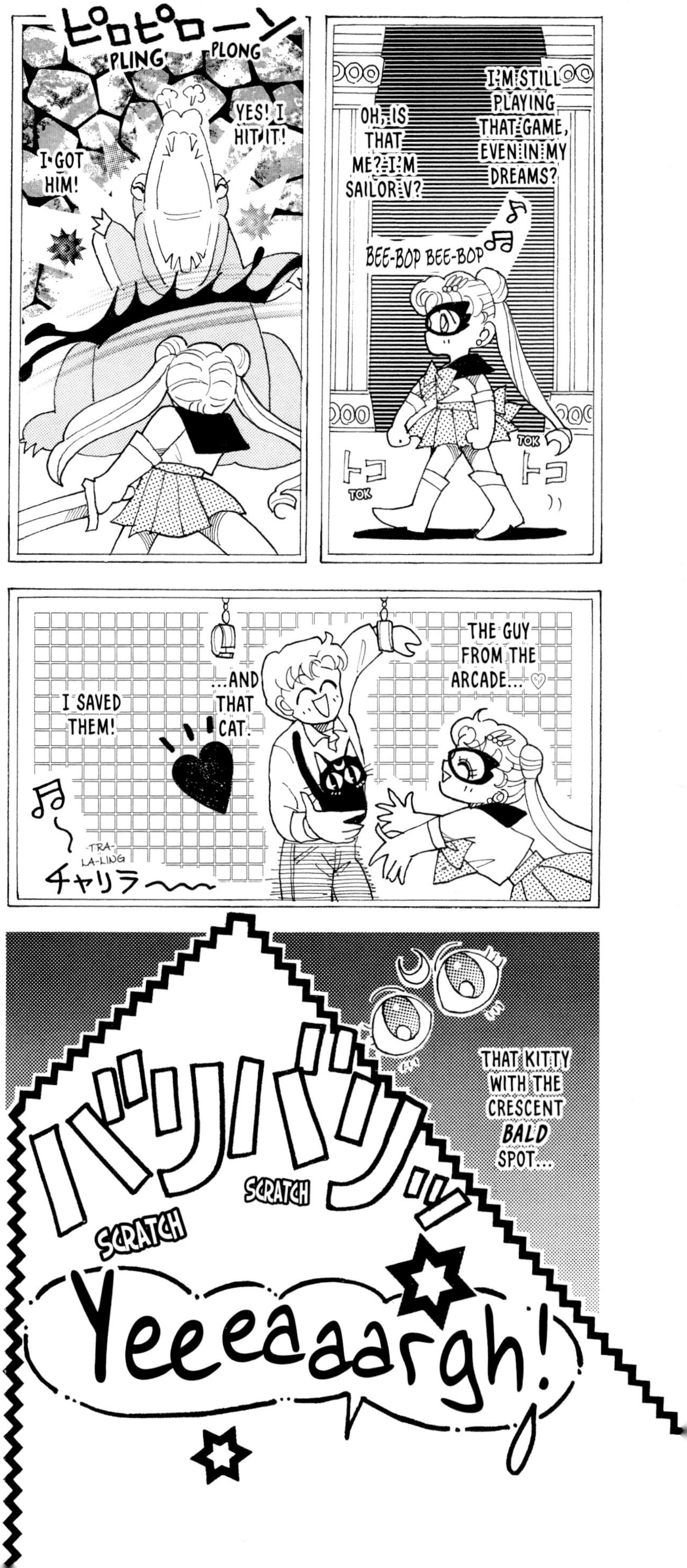
I'M STILL PLAYING THAT GAME, EVEN IN MY DREAMS?
OH, IS THAT ME? I'M SAILOR V?
BEE-BOP BEE-BOP
トコ
TOK
トコ
TOK
ピロピローン
PLING PLONG
YES! I HIT IT!
I GOT HIM!
THE GUY FROM THE ARCADE...
...AND THAT CAT.
I SAVED THEM!
チャリラ〜
TRA-LA-LING
THAT KITTY WITH THE CRESCENT BALD SPOT...
バリバリッ
SCRATCH SCRATCH
Yeeeaaargh!

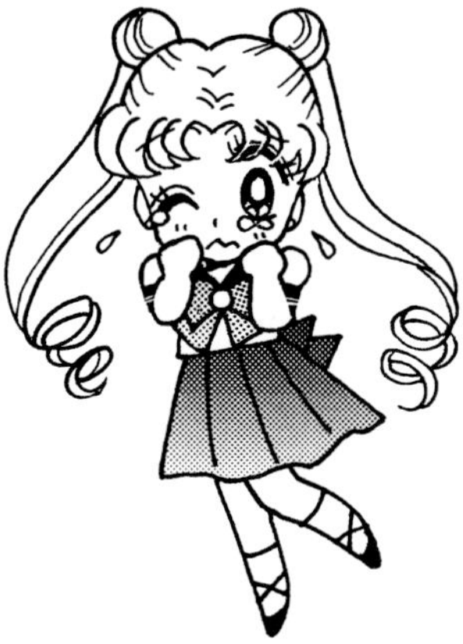

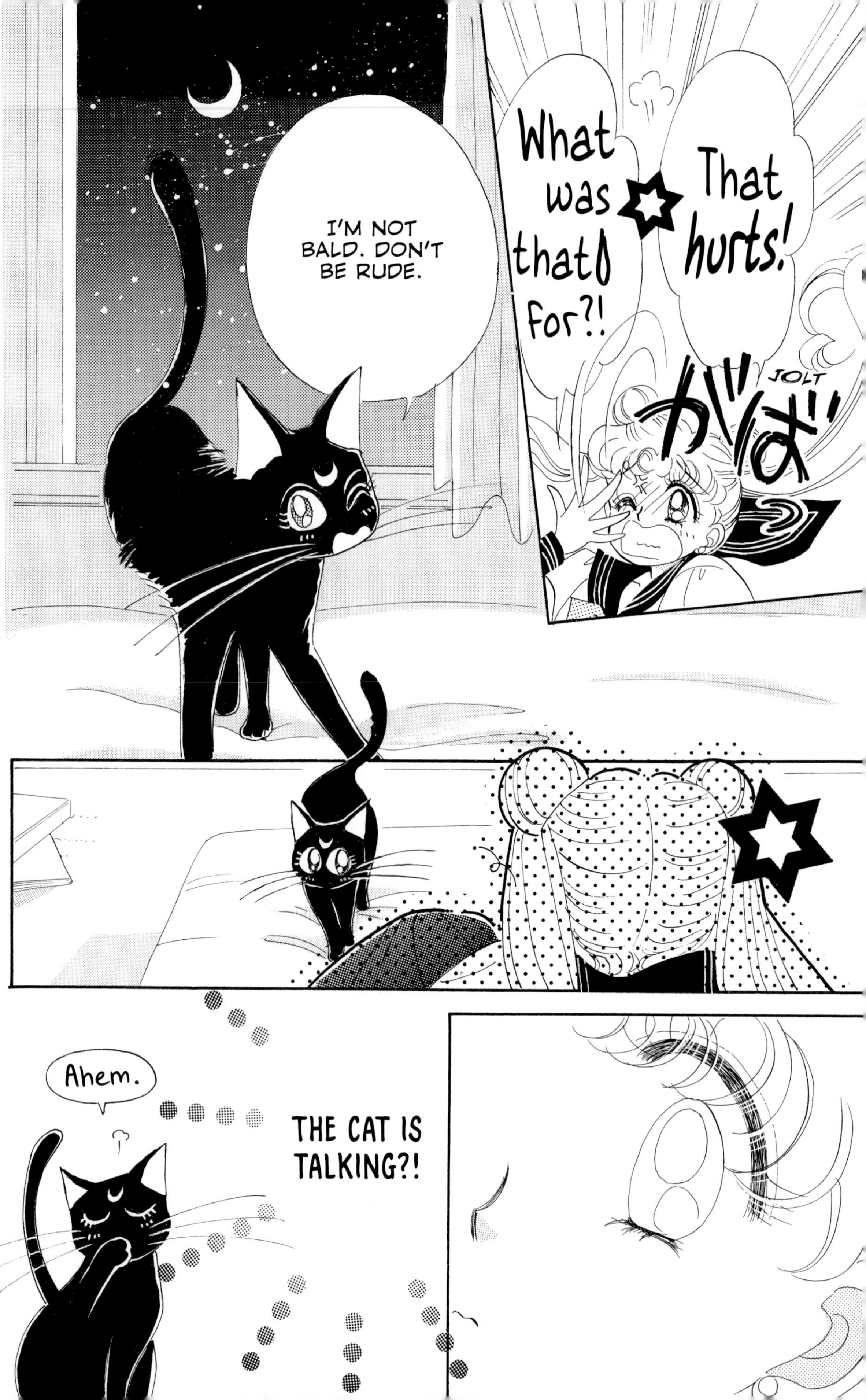

That hurts!
What was that for?!
JOLT
I'M NOT BALD. DON'T BE RUDE.
Ahem.
THE CAT IS TALKING?!

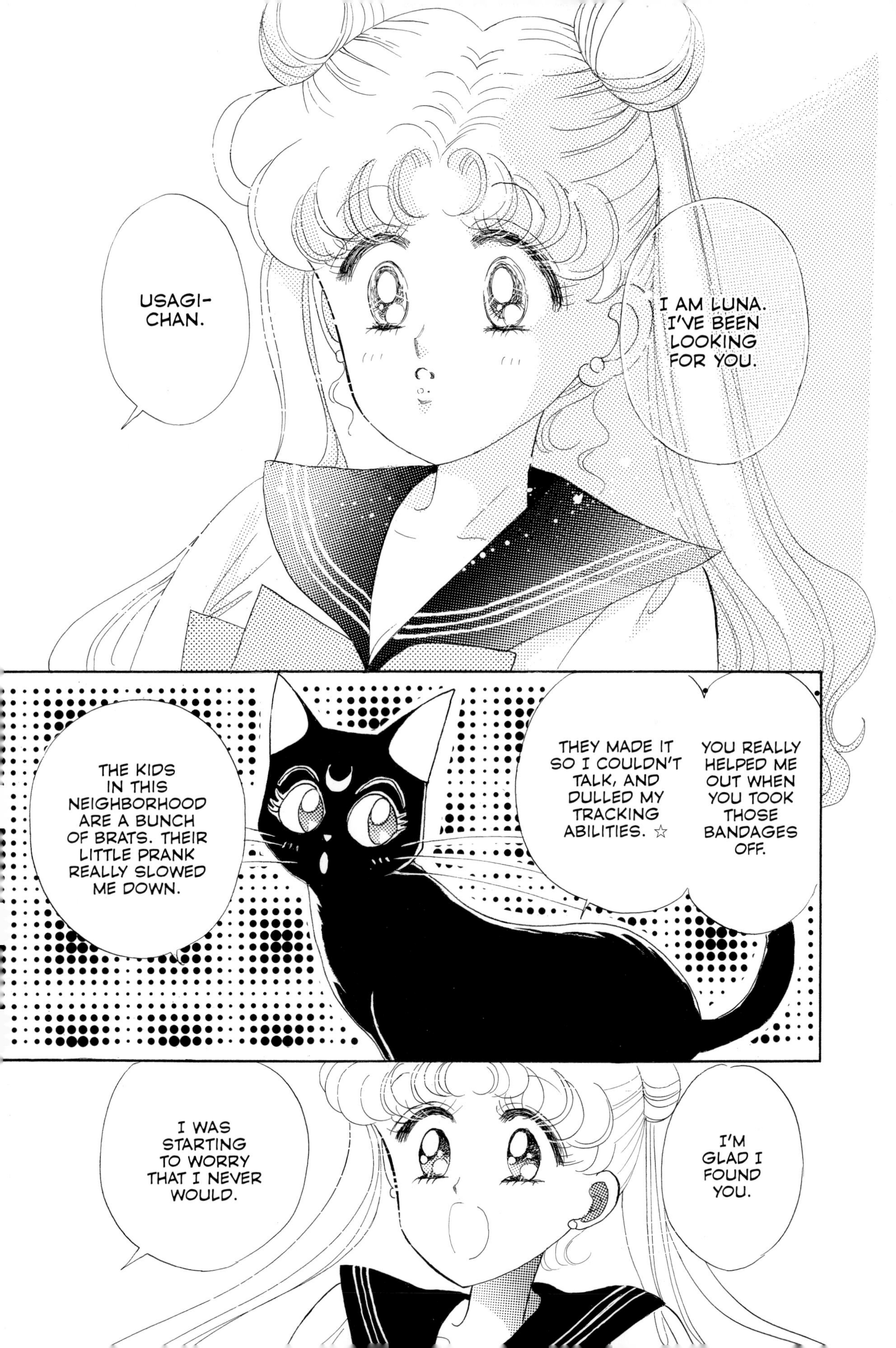
I AM LUNA. I'VE BEEN LOOKING FOR YOU.
USAGI-CHAN.
YOU REALLY HELPED ME OUT WHEN YOU TOOK THOSE BANDAGES OFF.
THEY MADE IT SO I COULDN'T TALK, AND DULLED MY TRACKING ABILITIES. ☆
THE KIDS IN THIS NEIGHBORHOOD ARE A BUNCH OF BRATS. THEIR LITTLE PRANK REALLY SLOWED ME DOWN.
I'M GLAD I FOUND YOU.
I WAS STARTING TO WORRY THAT I NEVER WOULD.

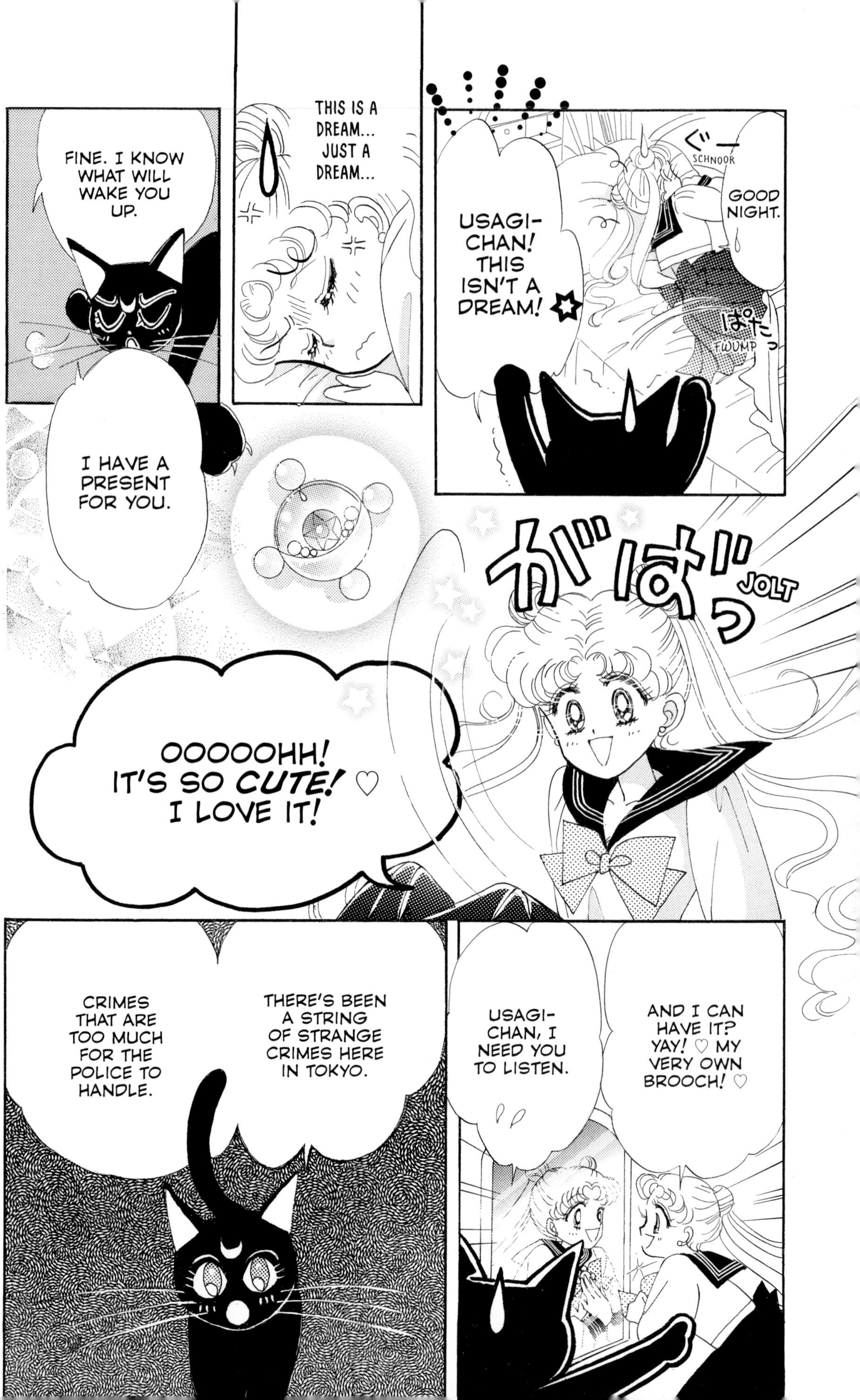
ぐー
SCHNOOR
GOOD NIGHT.
USAGI-CHAN! THIS ISN'T A DREAM!
ぱたっ
FWUMP
THIS IS A DREAM... JUST A DREAM...
FINE. I KNOW WHAT WILL WAKE YOU UP.
I HAVE A PRESENT FOR YOU.
がばっ
JOLT
OOOOOHH! IT'S SO CUTE! ♡ I LOVE IT!
AND I CAN HAVE IT? YAY! ♡ MY VERY OWN BROOCH! ♡
USAGI-CHAN, I NEED YOU TO LISTEN.
THERE'S BEEN A STRING OF STRANGE CRIMES HERE IN TOKYO.
CRIMES THAT ARE TOO MUCH FOR THE POLICE TO HANDLE.

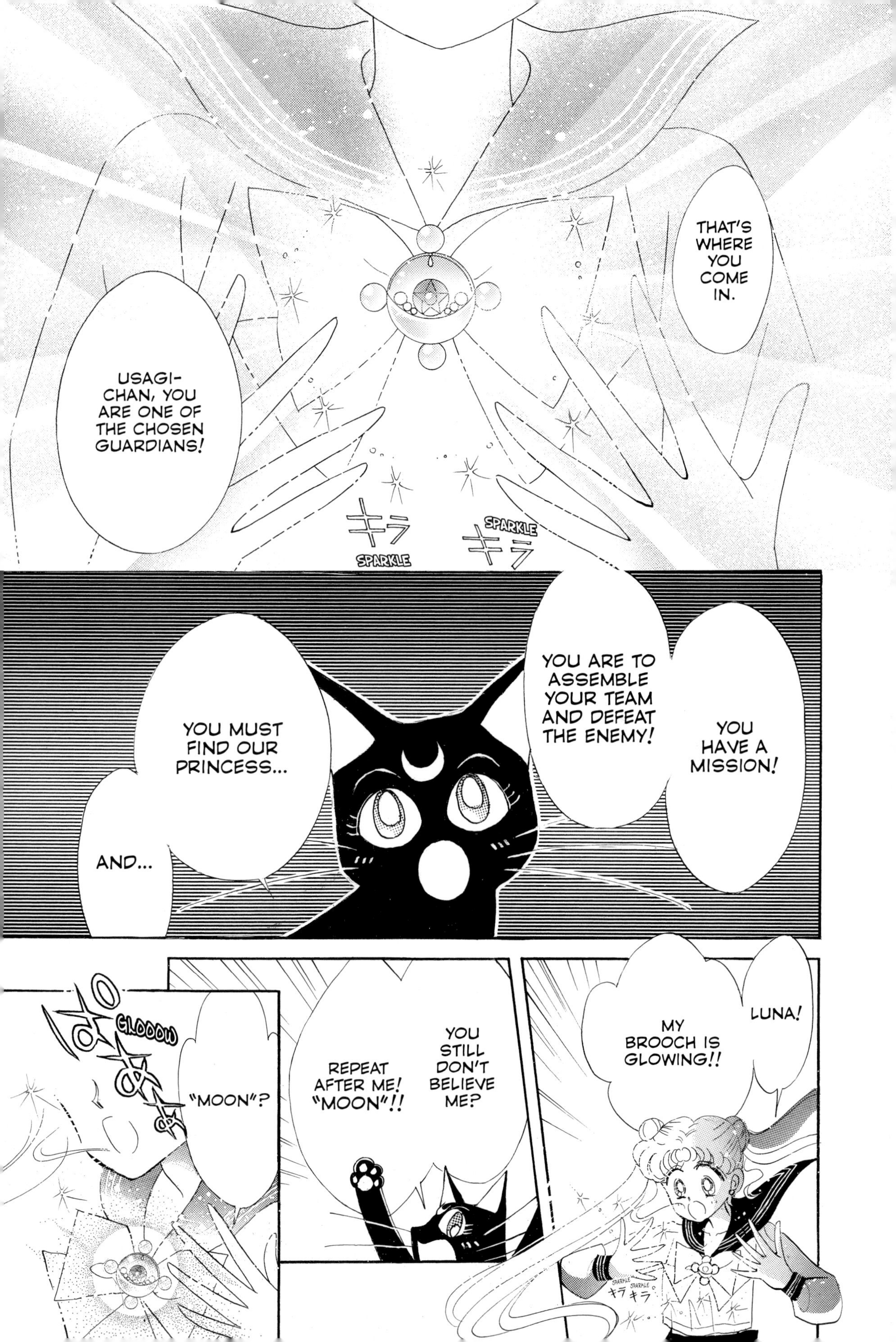
THAT'S WHERE YOU COME IN.
USAGI-CHAN, YOU ARE ONE OF THE CHOSEN GUARDIANS!
SPARKLE キラ
キラ SPARKLE
YOU HAVE A MISSION!
YOU ARE TO ASSEMBLE YOUR TEAM AND DEFEAT THE ENEMY!
YOU MUST FIND OUR PRINCESS...
AND...
LUNA!
MY BROOCH IS GLOWING!!
SPARKLE SPARKLE キラキラ
YOU STILL DON'T BELIEVE ME?
REPEAT AFTER ME! "MOON"!!
"MOON"?
GLOOOW

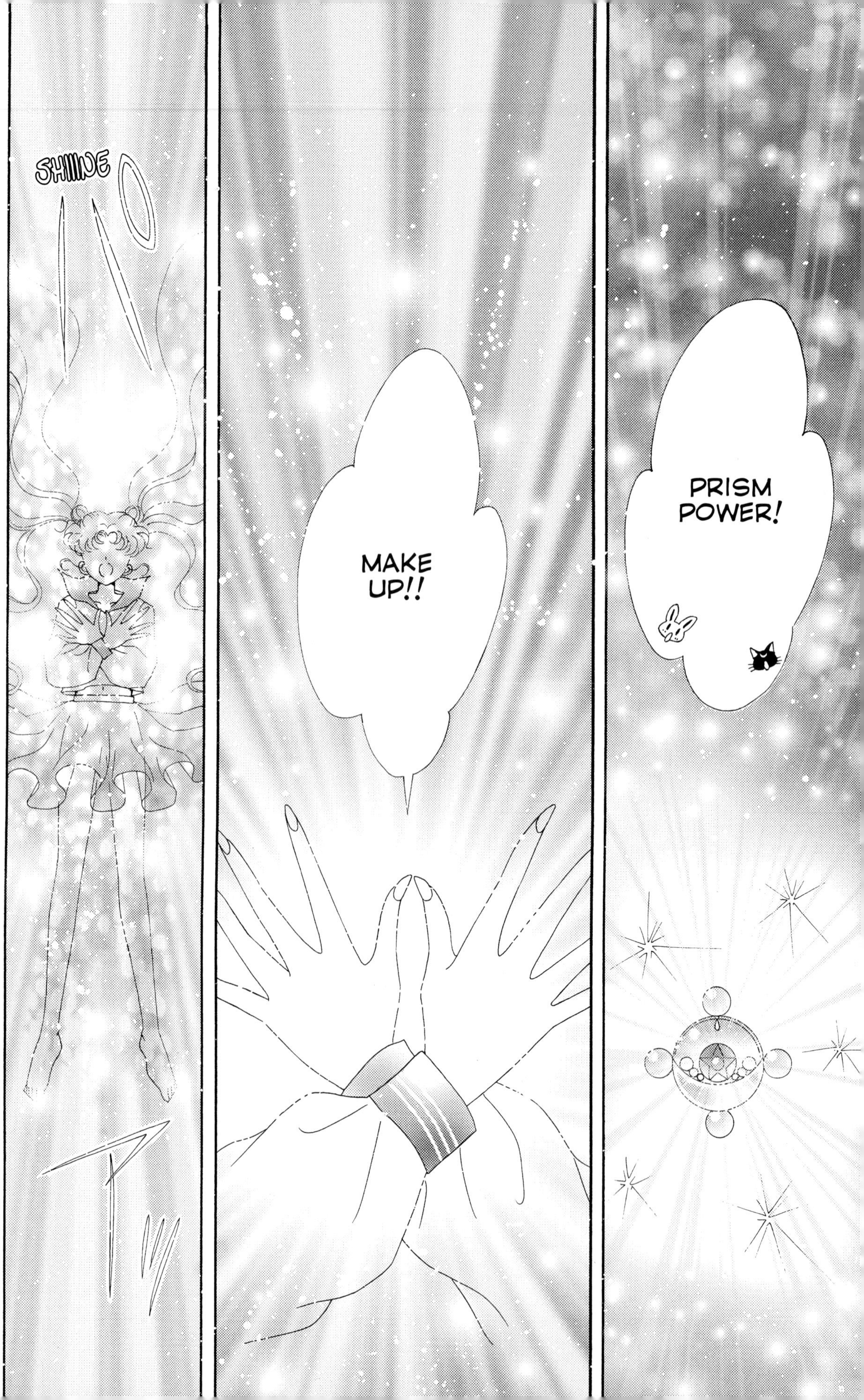
PRISM POWER!
MAKE UP!!
SHIIINE

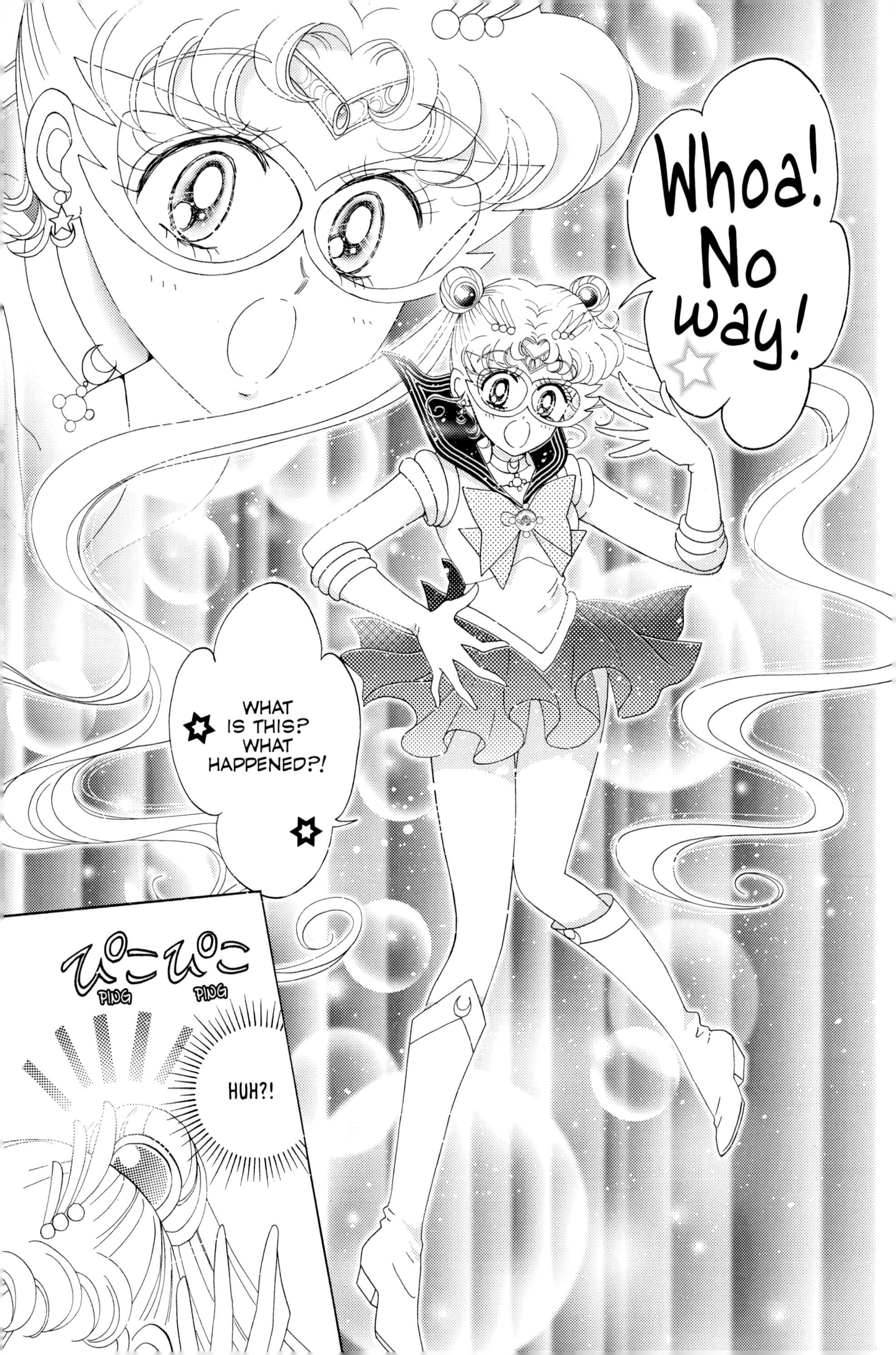
Whoa! No way!
WHAT IS THIS? WHAT HAPPENED?!
ぴこぴこ
PING PING
HUH?!

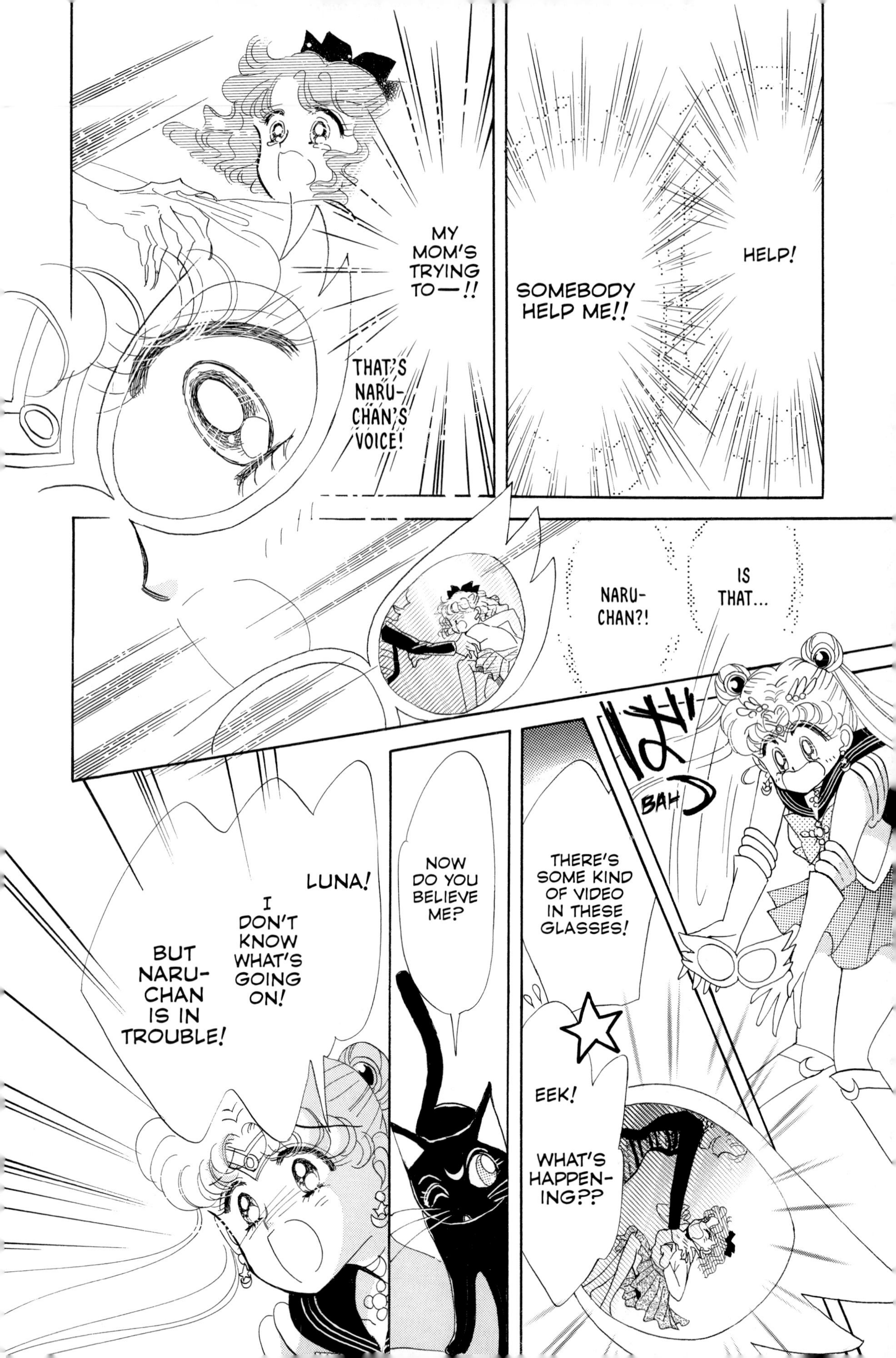
HELP!
SOMEBODY HELP ME!!
MY MOM'S TRYING TO—!!
THAT'S NARU-CHAN'S VOICE!
IS THAT...
NARU-CHAN?!
BAH
THERE'S SOME KIND OF VIDEO IN THESE GLASSES!
EEK!
WHAT'S HAPPENING??
NOW DO YOU BELIEVE ME?
LUNA!
I DON'T KNOW WHAT'S GOING ON!
BUT NARU-CHAN IS IN TROUBLE!

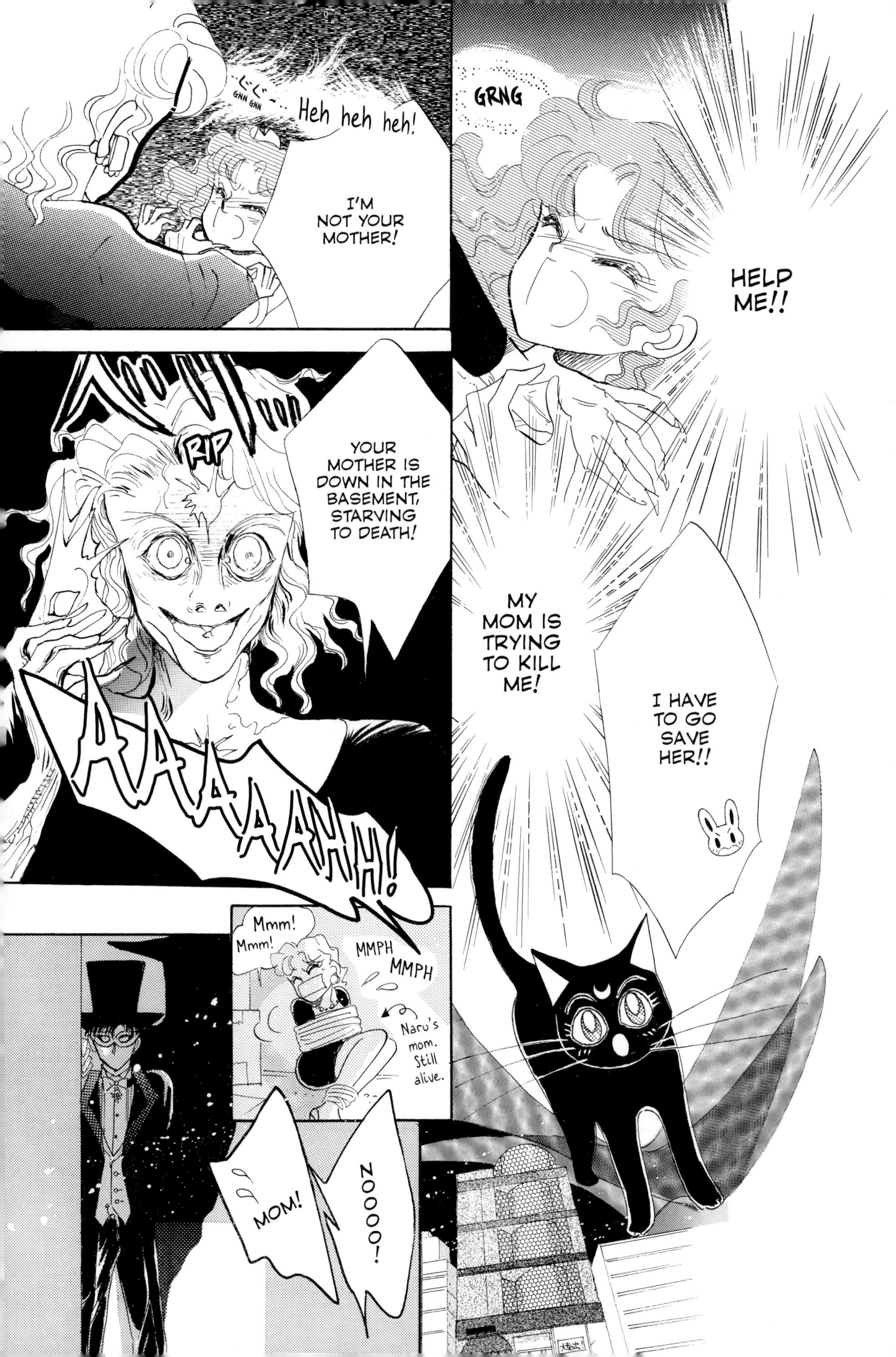
GRNG
HELP ME!!
MY MOM IS TRYING TO KILL ME!
I HAVE TO GO SAVE HER!!
GNN GNN
Heh heh heh!
I'M NOT YOUR MOTHER!
YOUR MOTHER IS DOWN IN THE BASEMENT, STARVING TO DEATH!
RIP
AAAAAHH!
Mmm! Mmm!
MMPH MMPH
Naru's mom. Still alive.
NOOOO!
MOM!

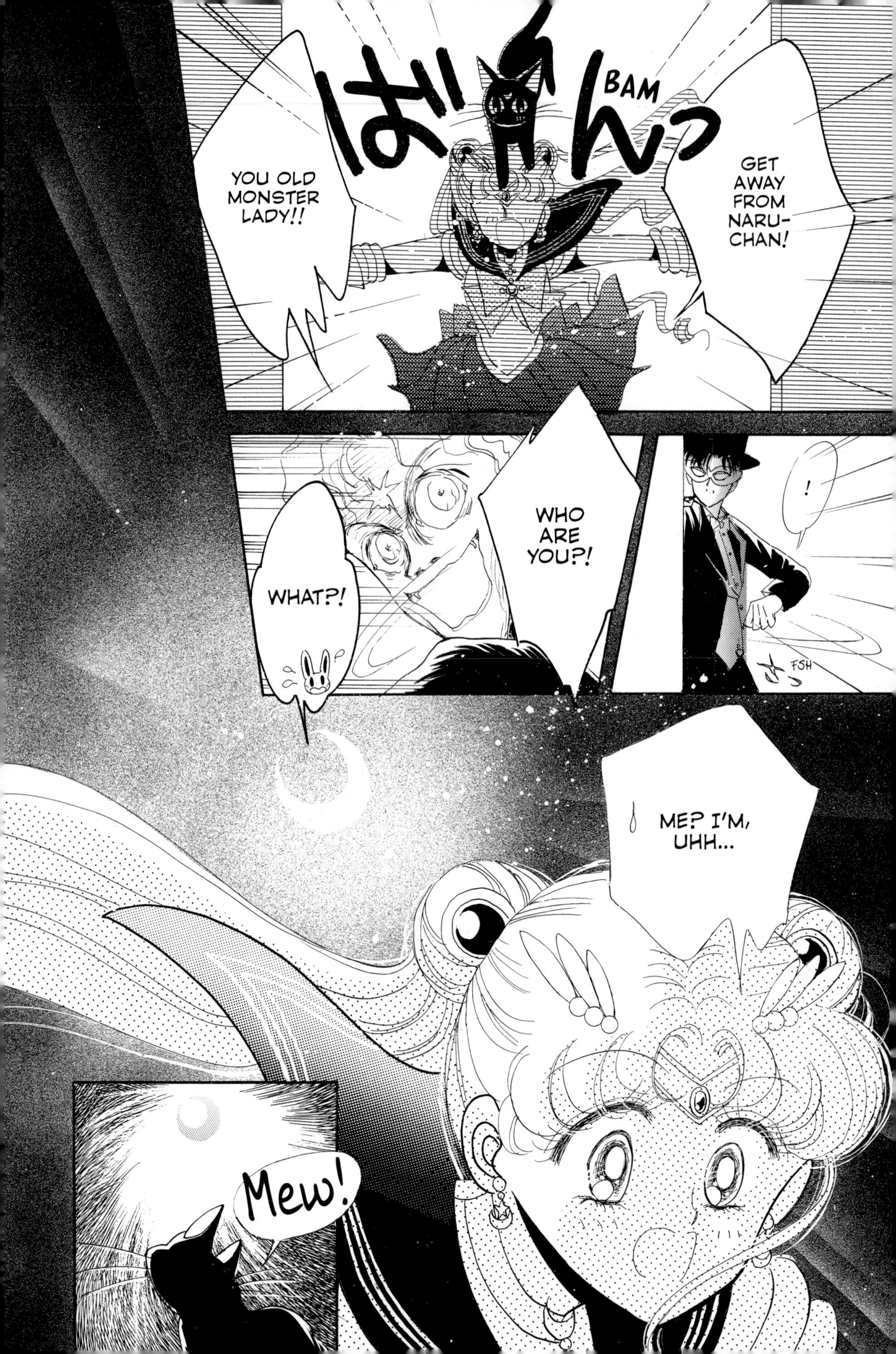
ばんっ
BAM
GET AWAY FROM NARU-CHAN!
YOU OLD MONSTER LADY!!
!
FSH
WHO ARE YOU?!
WHAT?!
ME? I'M, UHH...
Mew!

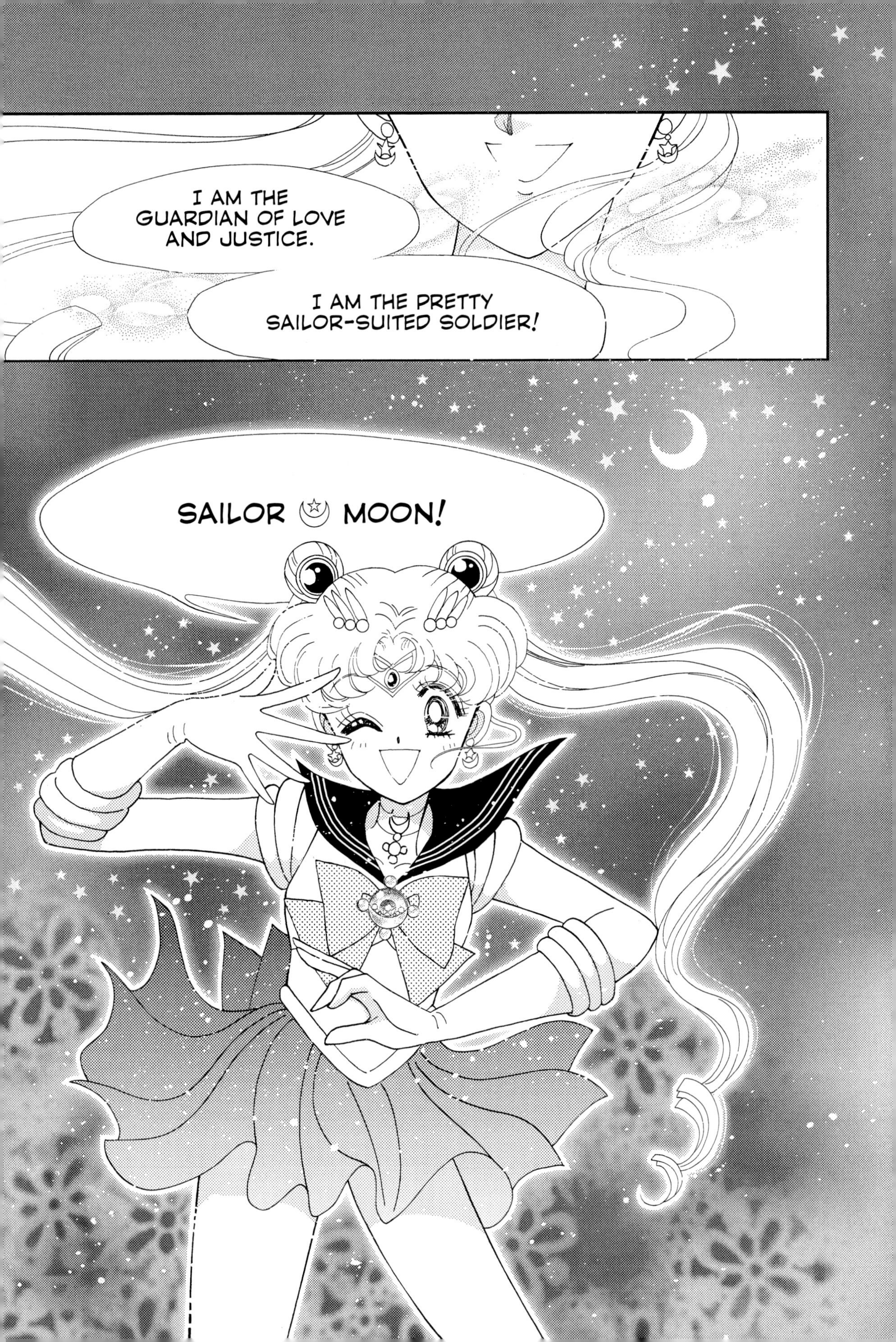
I AM THE GUARDIAN OF LOVE AND JUSTICE.
I AM THE PRETTY SAILOR-SUITED SOLDIER!
SAILOR MOON!

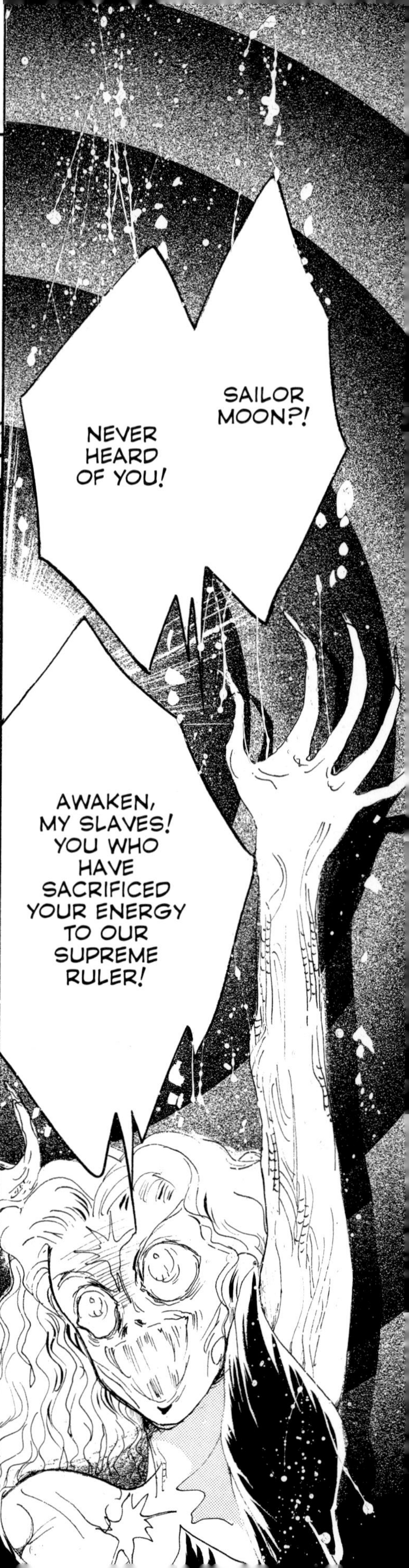
SAILOR MOON?!
NEVER HEARD OF YOU!
AWAKEN, MY SLAVES! YOU WHO HAVE SACRIFICED YOUR ENERGY TO OUR SUPREME RULER!

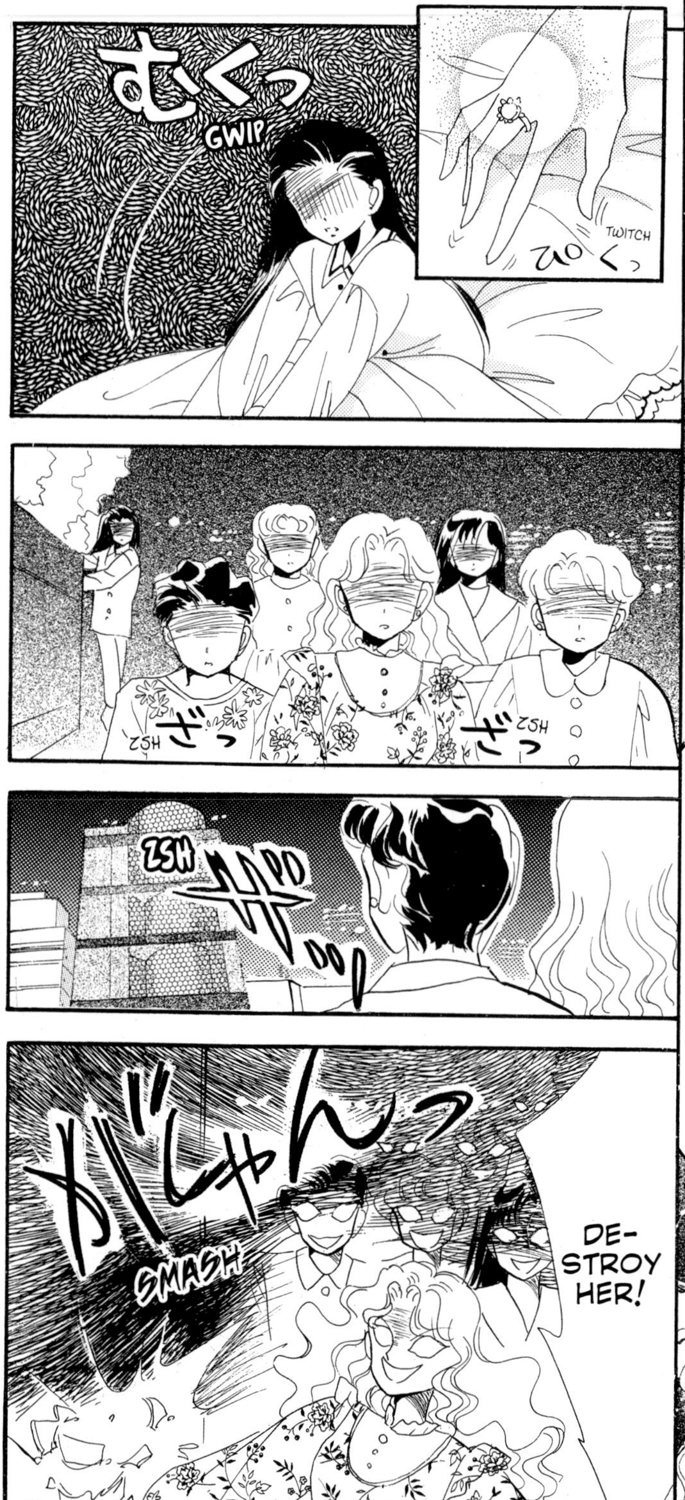
ぴくっ
TWITCH
むくっ
GWIP
ざっ
ZSH
ざっ
ZSH
ザッ
ZSH
がしゃんっ
SMASH
DE-STROY HER!

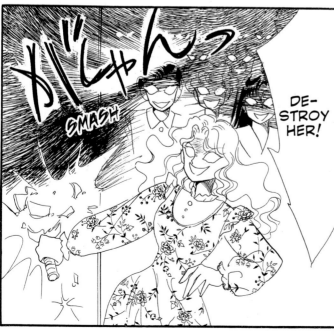

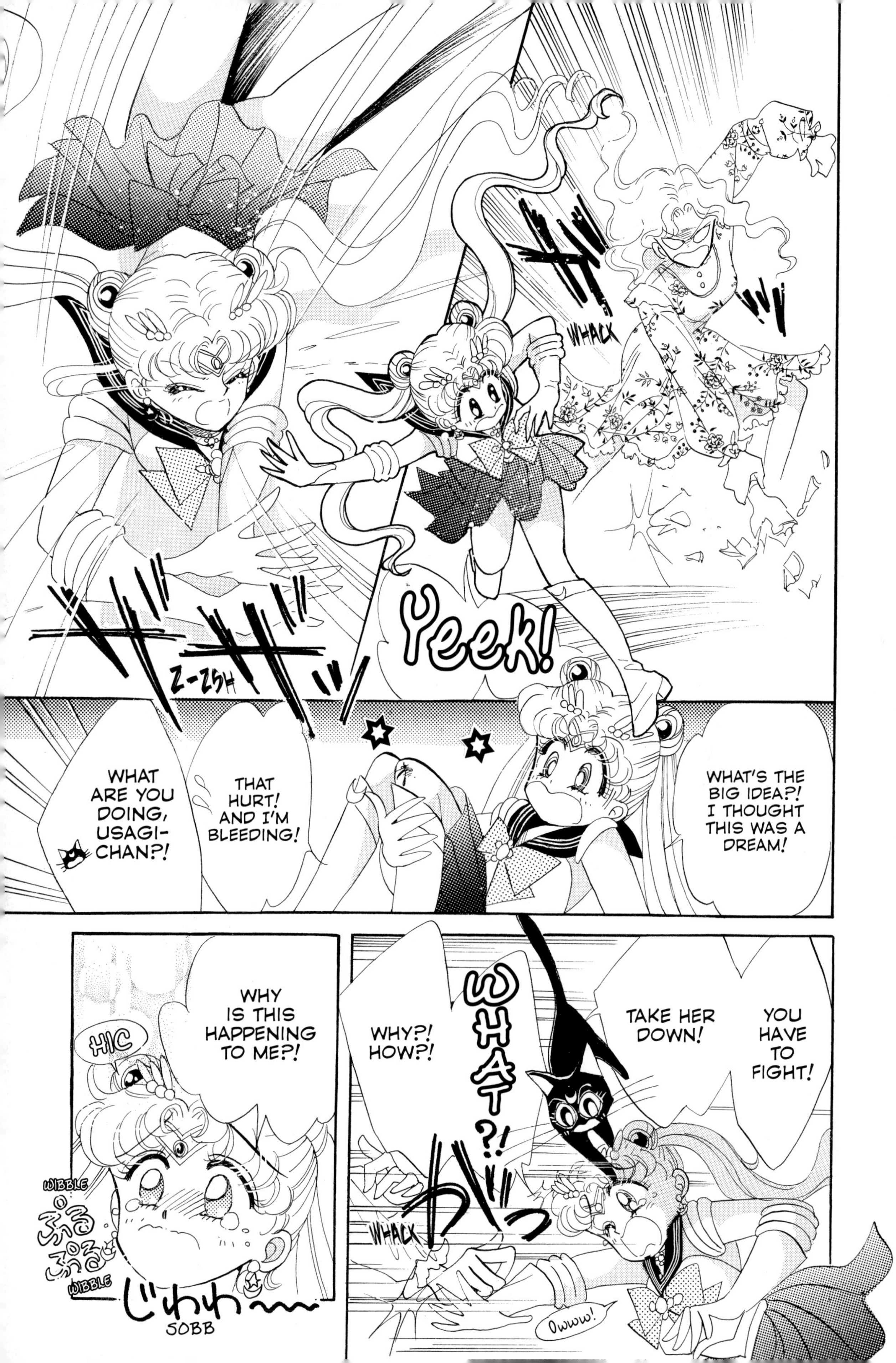
WHACK
Yeek!
Z-ZSH
WHAT'S THE BIG IDEA?! I THOUGHT THIS WAS A DREAM!
THAT HURT! AND I'M BLEEDING!
WHAT ARE YOU DOING, USAGI-CHAN?!
YOU HAVE TO FIGHT!
TAKE HER DOWN!
WHAT?!
WHY?! HOW?!
WHACK
Owww!
WHY IS THIS HAPPENING TO ME?!
HIC
WIBBLE
ぷるぷる
WIBBLE
じわわ～～
SOBB

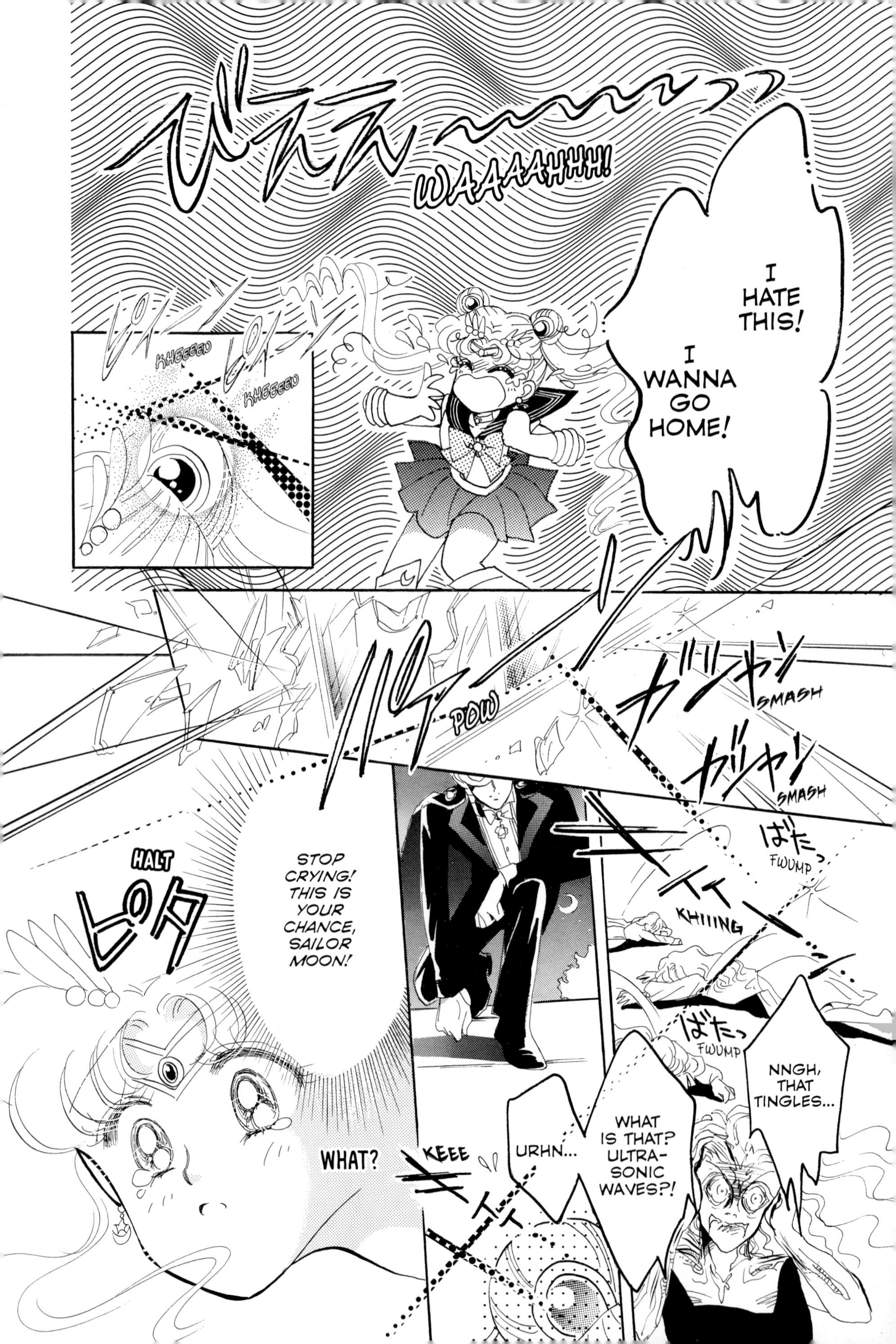
WAAAAHHH!
I HATE THIS!
I WANNA GO HOME!
KHEEEEN
KHEEEEN
POW
SMASH
SMASH
FWUMP
KHIIING
FWUMP
NNGH, THAT TINGLES...
WHAT IS THAT? ULTRA-SONIC WAVES?!
URHN...
STOP CRYING! THIS IS YOUR CHANCE, SAILOR MOON!
HALT
WHAT?
KEEE

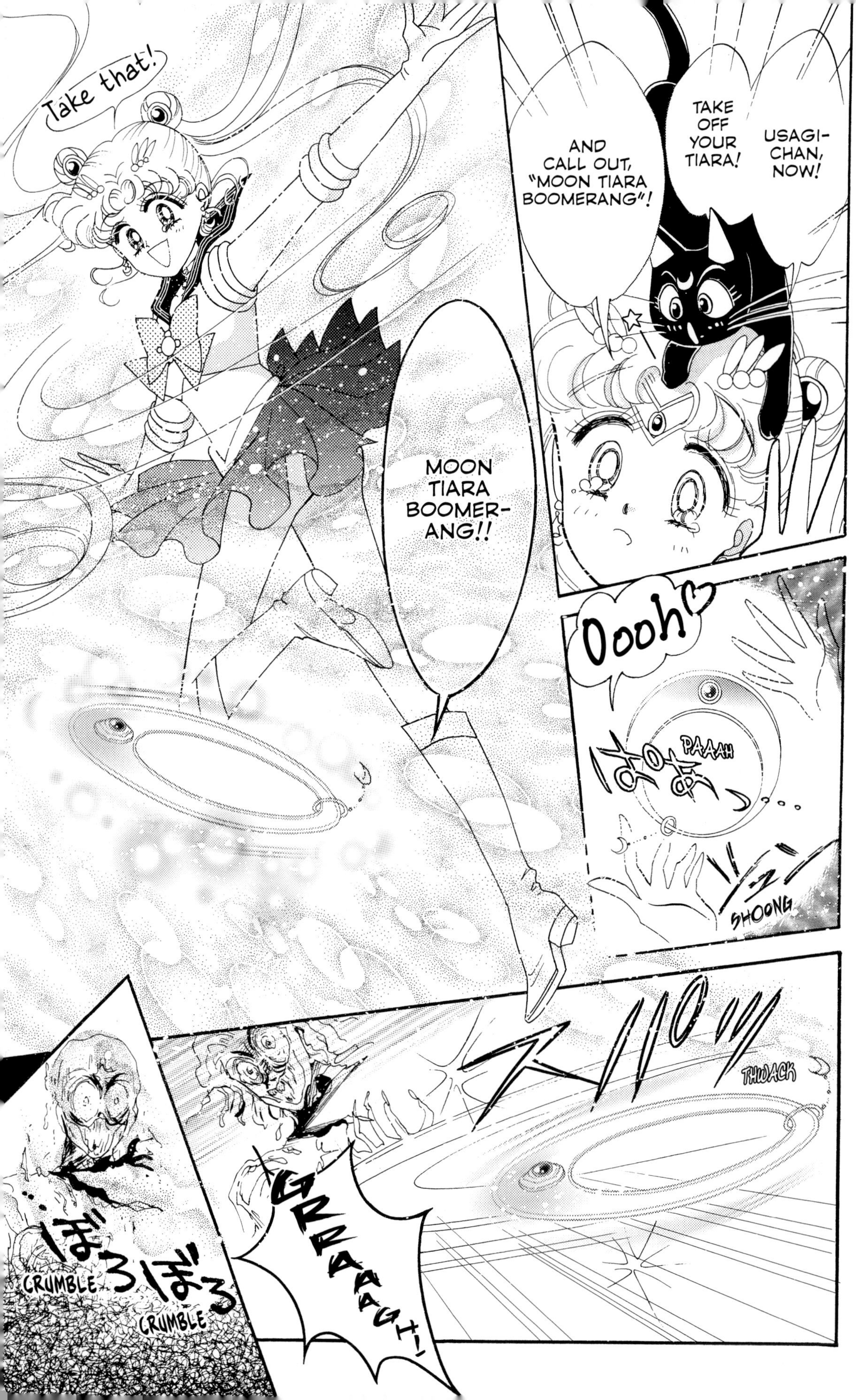
USAGI-CHAN, NOW!
TAKE OFF YOUR TIARA!
AND CALL OUT, "MOON TIARA BOOMERANG"!
Oooh♡
PAAAH
SHOONG
Take that!
MOON TIARA BOOMER-ANG!!
THWACK
GRRAAAGH!
ぼろぼろ
CRUMBLE
CRUMBLE

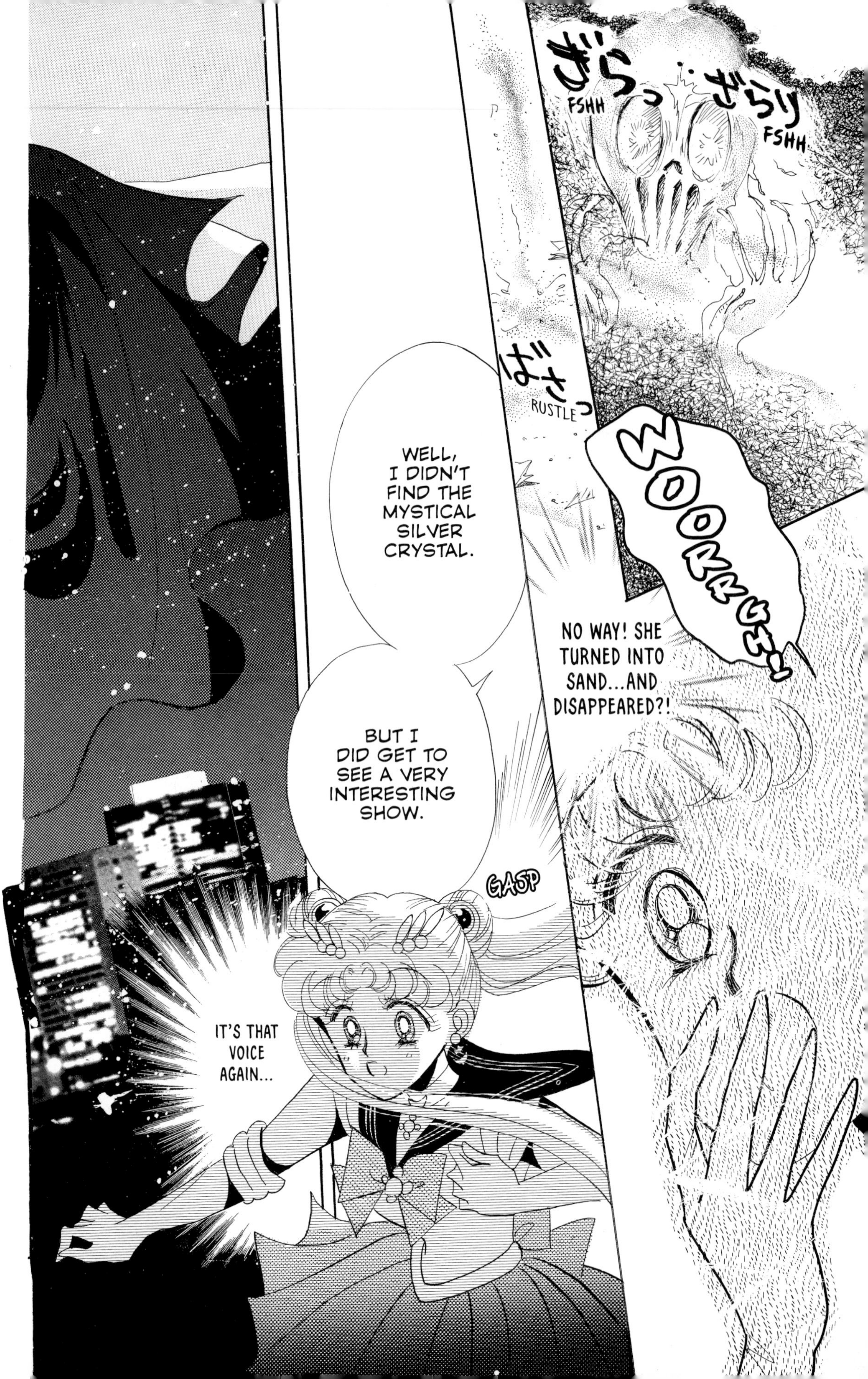

ざらっ
FSHH
ざらり
FSHH
ばさっ
RUSTLE
WOORRUH!
NO WAY! SHE TURNED INTO SAND...AND DISAPPEARED?!
WELL, I DIDN'T FIND THE MYSTICAL SILVER CRYSTAL.
BUT I DID GET TO SEE A VERY INTERESTING SHOW.
GASP
IT'S THAT VOICE AGAIN...

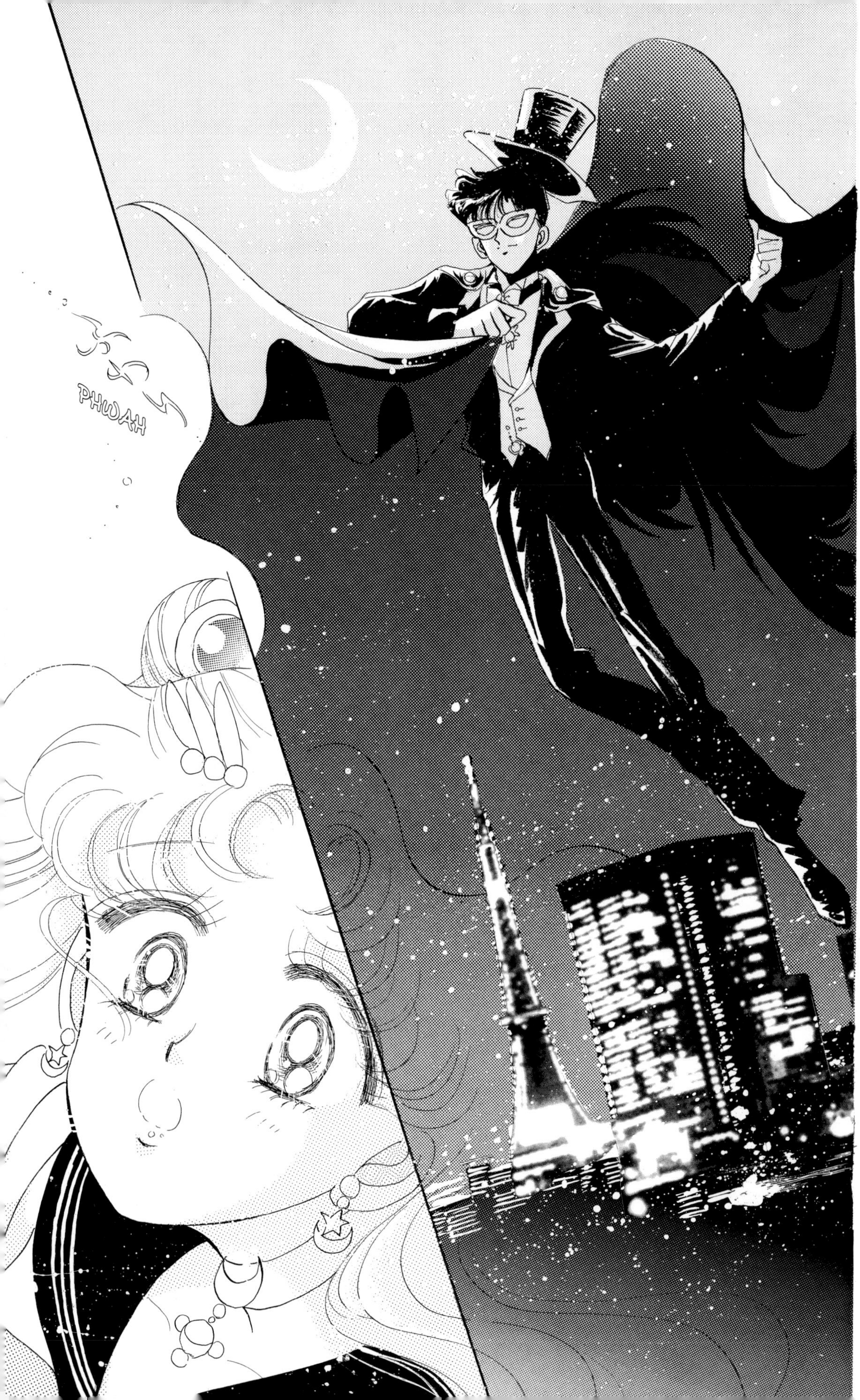
PHWAH

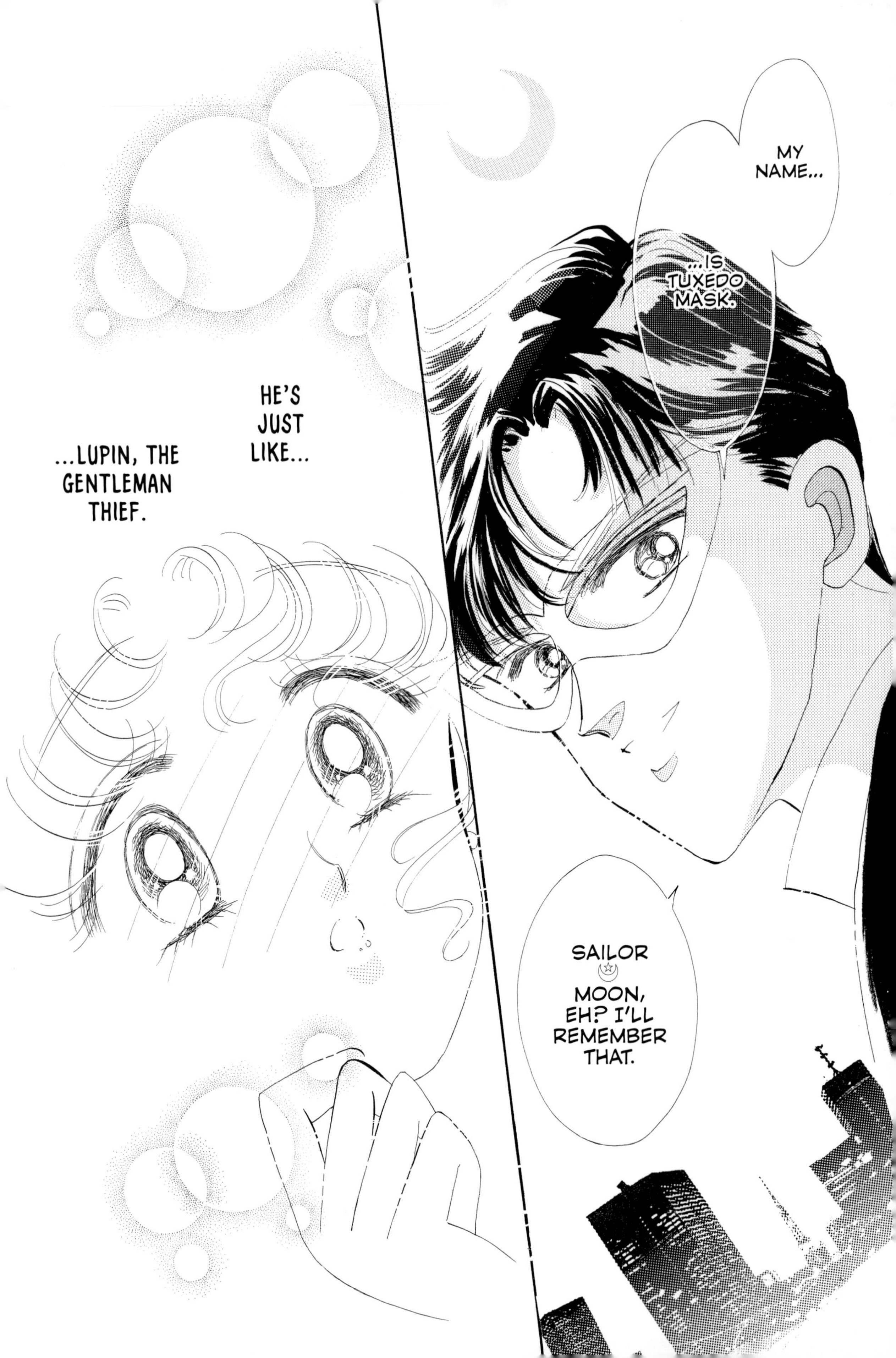
MY NAME...
...IS TUXEDO MASK.
SAILOR MOON, EH? I'LL REMEMBER THAT.
HE'S JUST LIKE...
...LUPIN, THE GENTLEMAN THIEF.

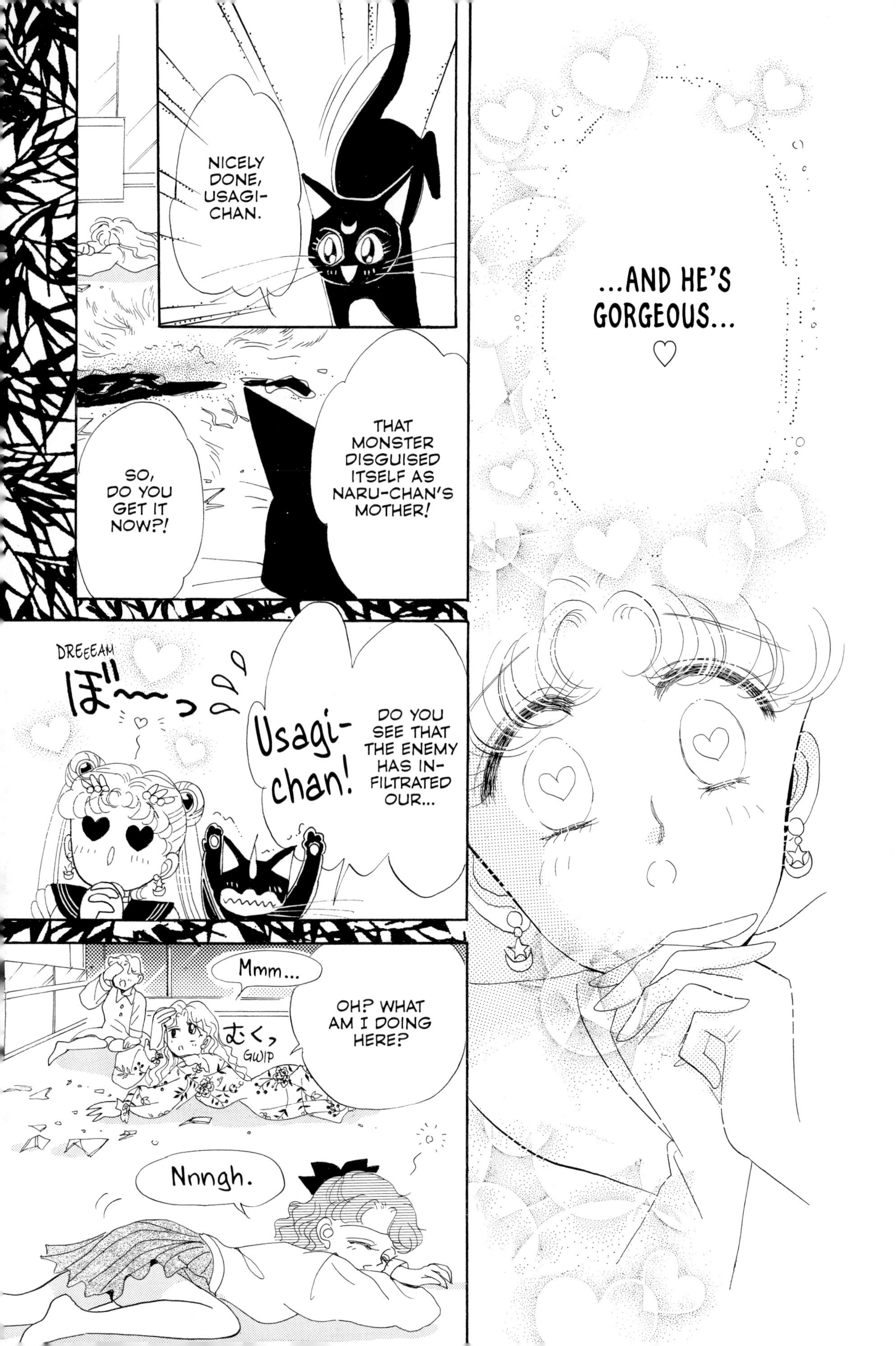
...AND HE'S GORGEOUS... ♡
NICELY DONE, USAGI-CHAN.
THAT MONSTER DISGUISED ITSELF AS NARU-CHAN'S MOTHER!
SO, DO YOU GET IT NOW?!
Usagi-chan!
DO YOU SEE THAT THE ENEMY HAS IN-FILTRATED OUR...
ぼ~~っ
DREEEAM
OH? WHAT AM I DOING HERE?
Mmm...
むくっ
GWIP
Nnngh.

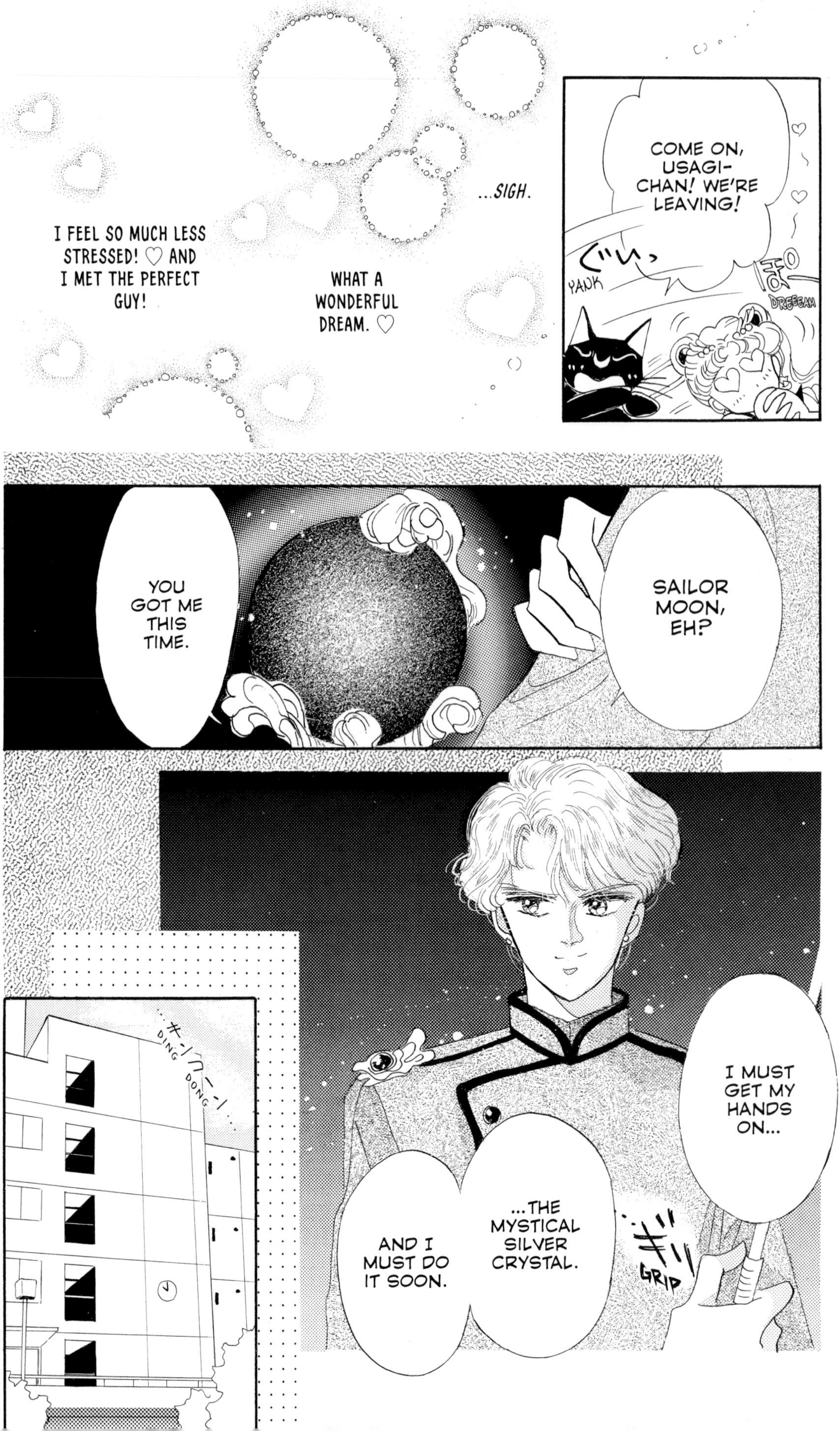
COME ON, USAGI-CHAN! WE'RE LEAVING!
ぐいっ
YANK
ぽー
DREEEAM
...SIGH.
WHAT A WONDERFUL DREAM. ♡
I FEEL SO MUCH LESS STRESSED! ♡ AND I MET THE PERFECT GUY!
SAILOR MOON, EH?
YOU GOT ME THIS TIME.
I MUST GET MY HANDS ON...
...THE MYSTICAL SILVER CRYSTAL.
AND I MUST DO IT SOON.
ギリ
GRIP
キーンコーン
DING DONG

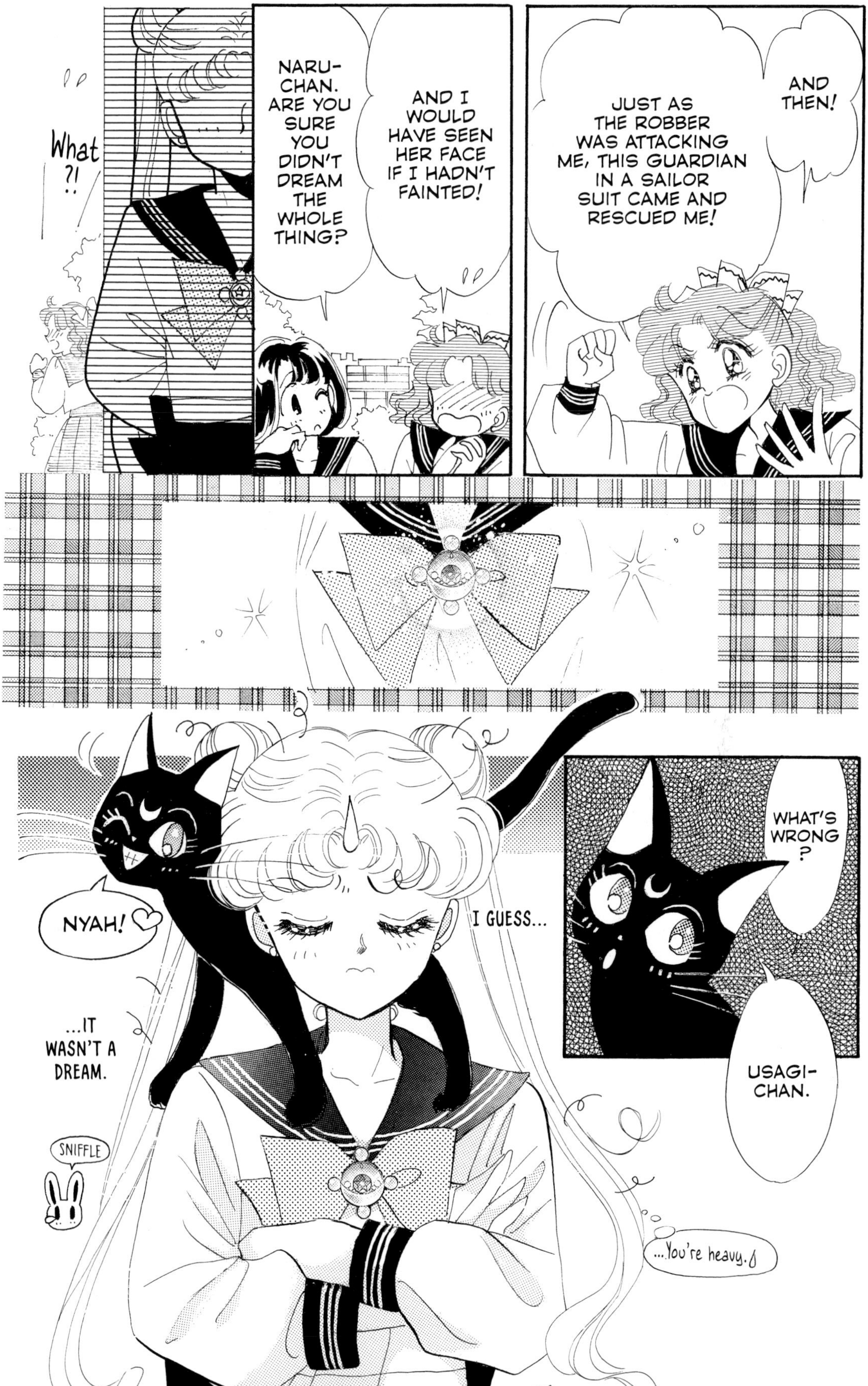
AND THEN!
JUST AS THE ROBBER WAS ATTACKING ME, THIS GUARDIAN IN A SAILOR SUIT CAME AND RESCUED ME!
AND I WOULD HAVE SEEN HER FACE IF I HADN'T FAINTED!
NARU-CHAN. ARE YOU SURE YOU DIDN'T DREAM THE WHOLE THING?
What?!
WHAT'S WRONG?
USAGI-CHAN.
I GUESS...
NYAH!
...IT WASN'T A DREAM.
SNIFFLE
...You're heavy.

Pretty Guardian

Sailor Moon

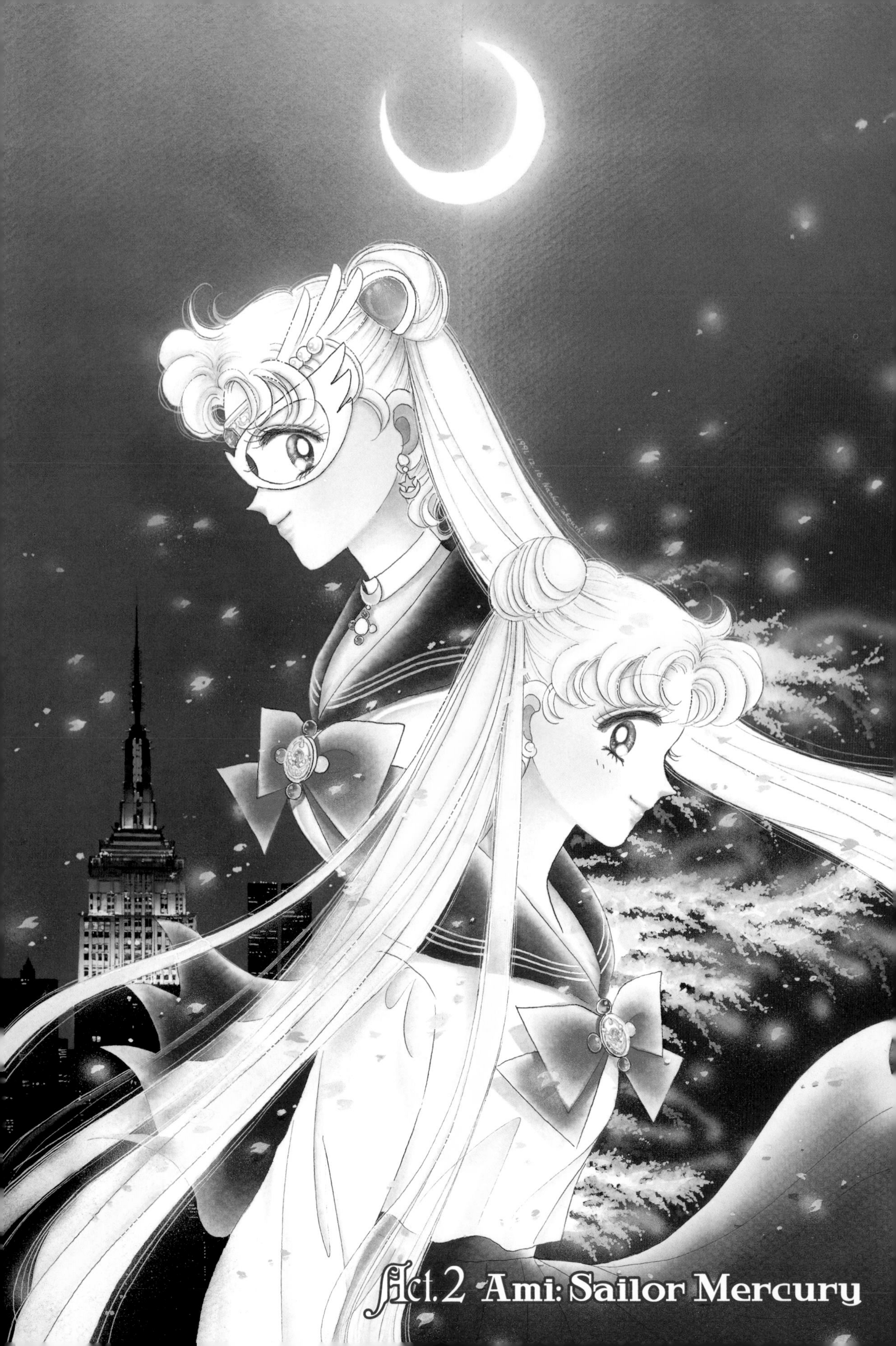

Act.2 Ami: Sailor Mercury

Pretty Guardian

Sailor Moon

WHOOSH

BWOH

HAVEN'T YOU FOUND THE MYSTICAL SILVER CRYSTAL YET?

WELL?

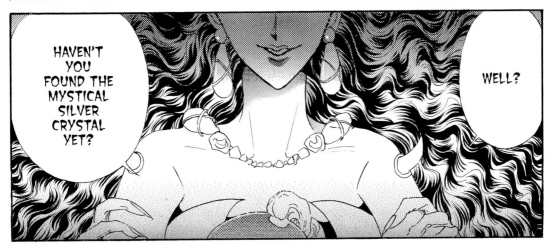

YOU HAVE MY HUMBLEST APOLOGIES.

NO, MY QUEEN.

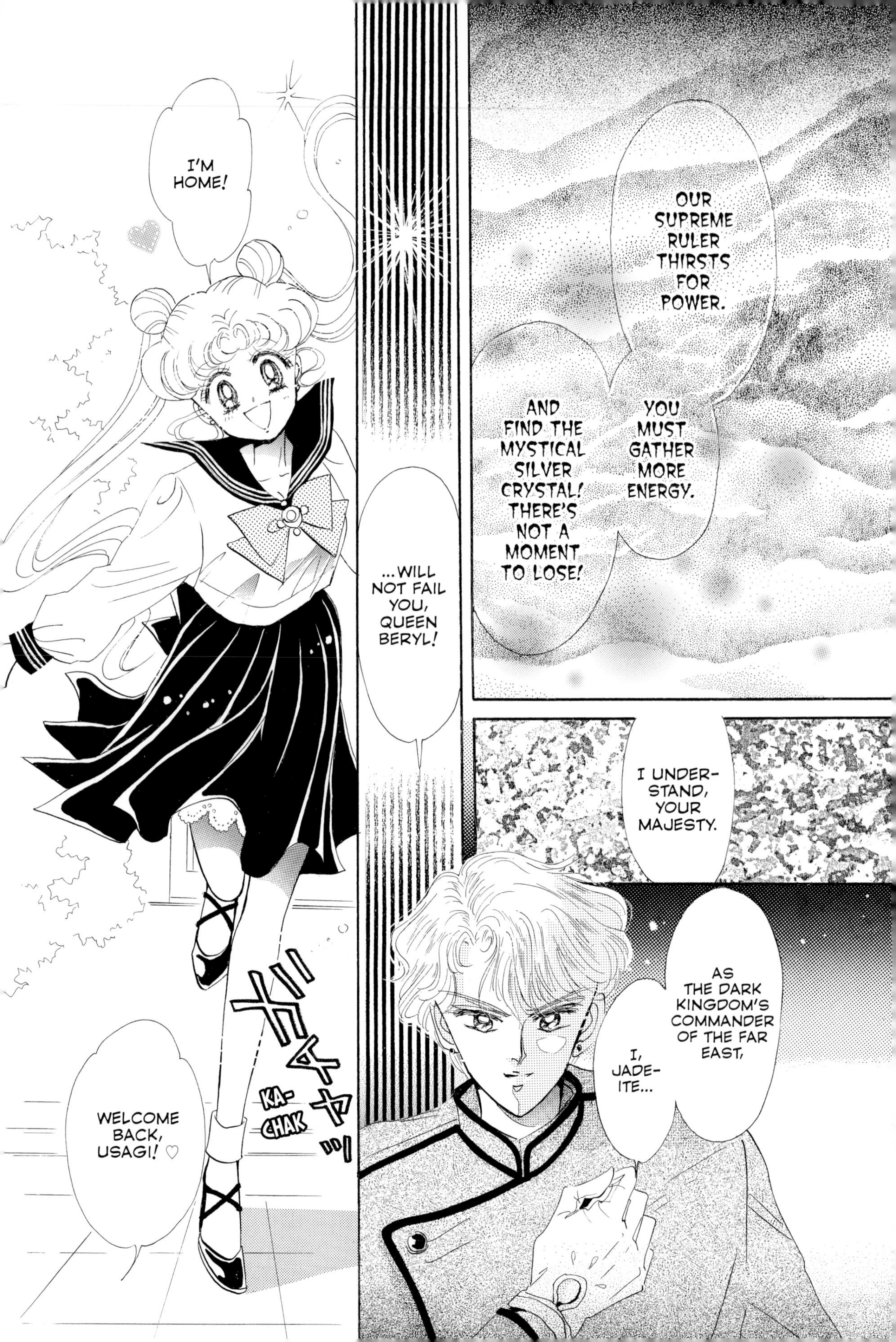
OUR SUPREME RULER THIRSTS FOR POWER.
YOU MUST GATHER MORE ENERGY.
AND FIND THE MYSTICAL SILVER CRYSTAL! THERE'S NOT A MOMENT TO LOSE!
I UNDER-STAND, YOUR MAJESTY.
AS THE DARK KINGDOM'S COMMANDER OF THE FAR EAST,
I, JADE-ITE...
...WILL NOT FAIL YOU, QUEEN BERYL!
I'M HOME!
KA-CHAK
WELCOME BACK, USAGI! ♡

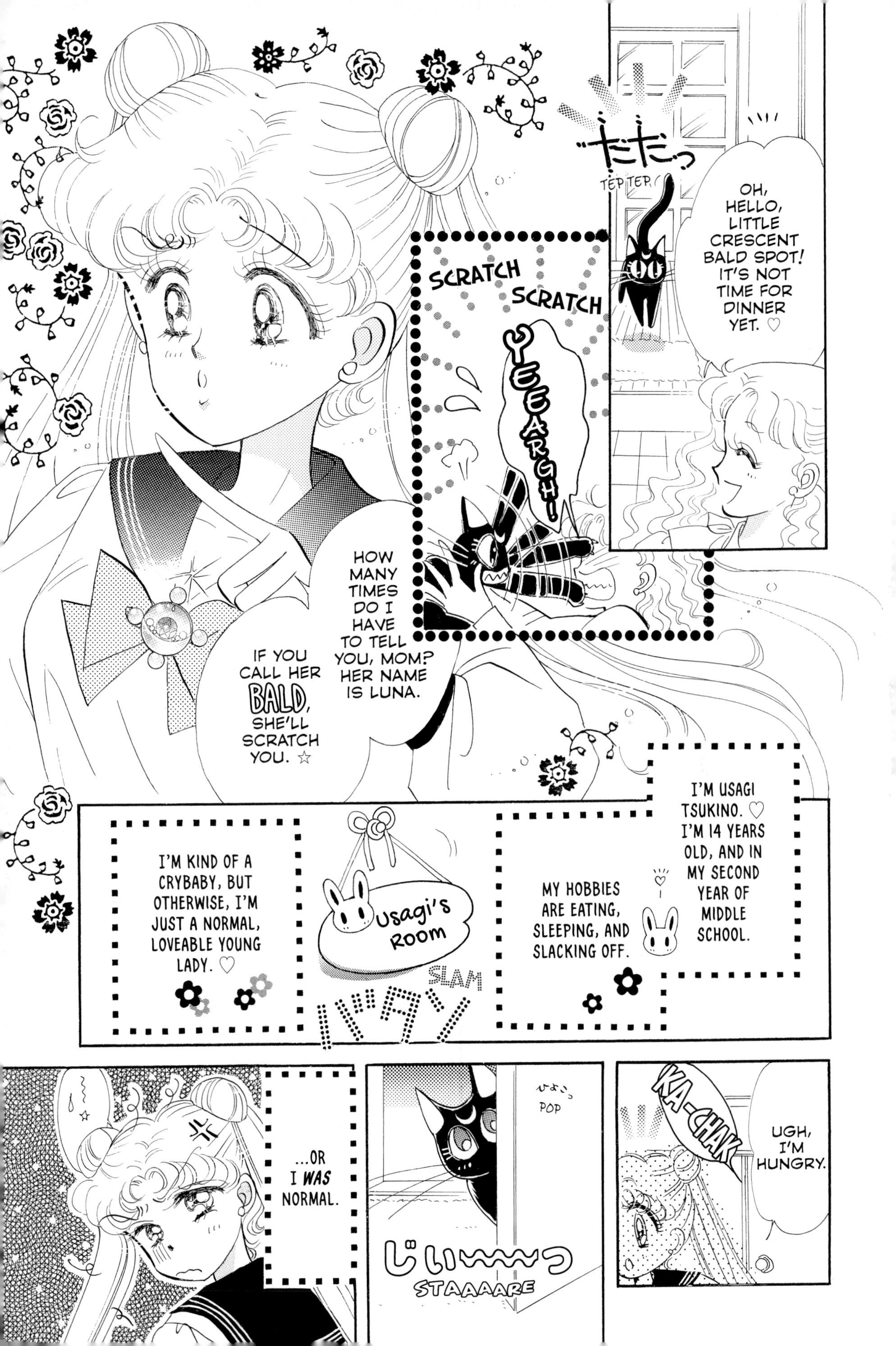

TEP TEP
OH, HELLO, LITTLE CRESCENT BALD SPOT! IT'S NOT TIME FOR DINNER YET. ♡
SCRATCH SCRATCH
YEEARGH!
HOW MANY TIMES DO I HAVE TO TELL YOU, MOM? HER NAME IS LUNA.
IF YOU CALL HER BALD, SHE'LL SCRATCH YOU. ☆
I'M USAGI TSUKINO. ♡ I'M 14 YEARS OLD, AND IN MY SECOND YEAR OF MIDDLE SCHOOL.
MY HOBBIES ARE EATING, SLEEPING, AND SLACKING OFF.
Usagi's Room
SLAM
I'M KIND OF A CRYBABY, BUT OTHERWISE, I'M JUST A NORMAL, LOVEABLE YOUNG LADY. ♡
KA-CHAK
UGH, I'M HUNGRY.
POP
STAAAARE
...OR I WAS NORMAL.

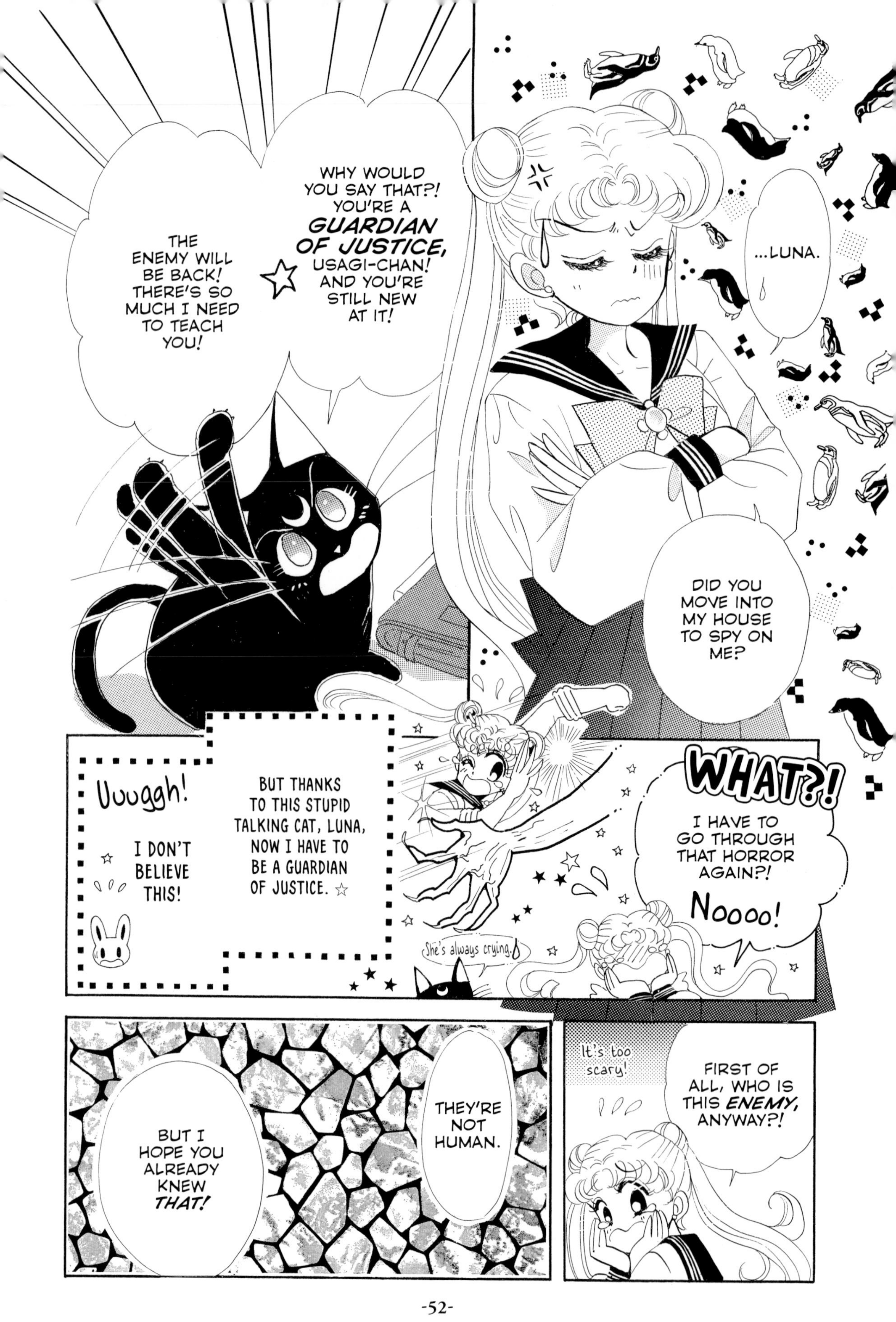
...LUNA.
DID YOU MOVE INTO MY HOUSE TO SPY ON ME?
WHY WOULD YOU SAY THAT?! YOU'RE A *GUARDIAN OF JUSTICE,* USAGI-CHAN! AND YOU'RE STILL NEW AT IT!
THE ENEMY WILL BE BACK! THERE'S SO MUCH I NEED TO TEACH YOU!
WHAT?!
I HAVE TO GO THROUGH THAT HORROR AGAIN?!
Noooo!
She's always crying.
BUT THANKS TO THIS STUPID TALKING CAT, LUNA, NOW I HAVE TO BE A GUARDIAN OF JUSTICE.
Uuuggh!
I DON'T BELIEVE THIS!
FIRST OF ALL, WHO IS THIS *ENEMY,* ANYWAY?!
It's too scary!
THEY'RE NOT HUMAN.
BUT I HOPE YOU ALREADY KNEW *THAT!*

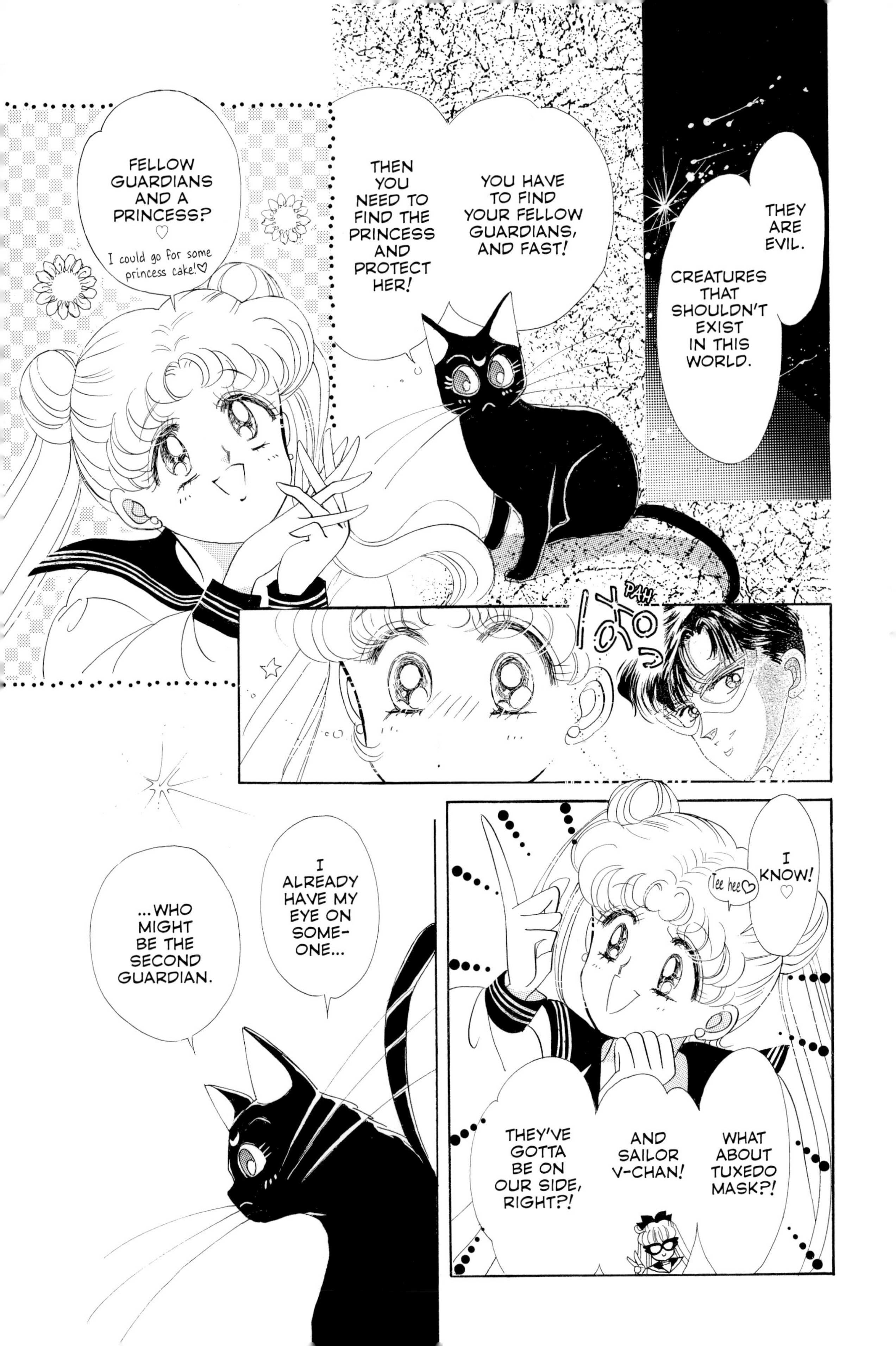
THEY ARE EVIL.
CREATURES THAT SHOULDN'T EXIST IN THIS WORLD.
YOU HAVE TO FIND YOUR FELLOW GUARDIANS, AND FAST!
THEN YOU NEED TO FIND THE PRINCESS AND PROTECT HER!
FELLOW GUARDIANS AND A PRINCESS? ♡
I could go for some princess cake!♡
PAH
I KNOW! ♡
Tee hee♡
WHAT ABOUT TUXEDO MASK?!
AND SAILOR V-CHAN!
THEY'VE GOTTA BE ON OUR SIDE, RIGHT?!
I ALREADY HAVE MY EYE ON SOMEONE...
...WHO MIGHT BE THE SECOND GUARDIAN.

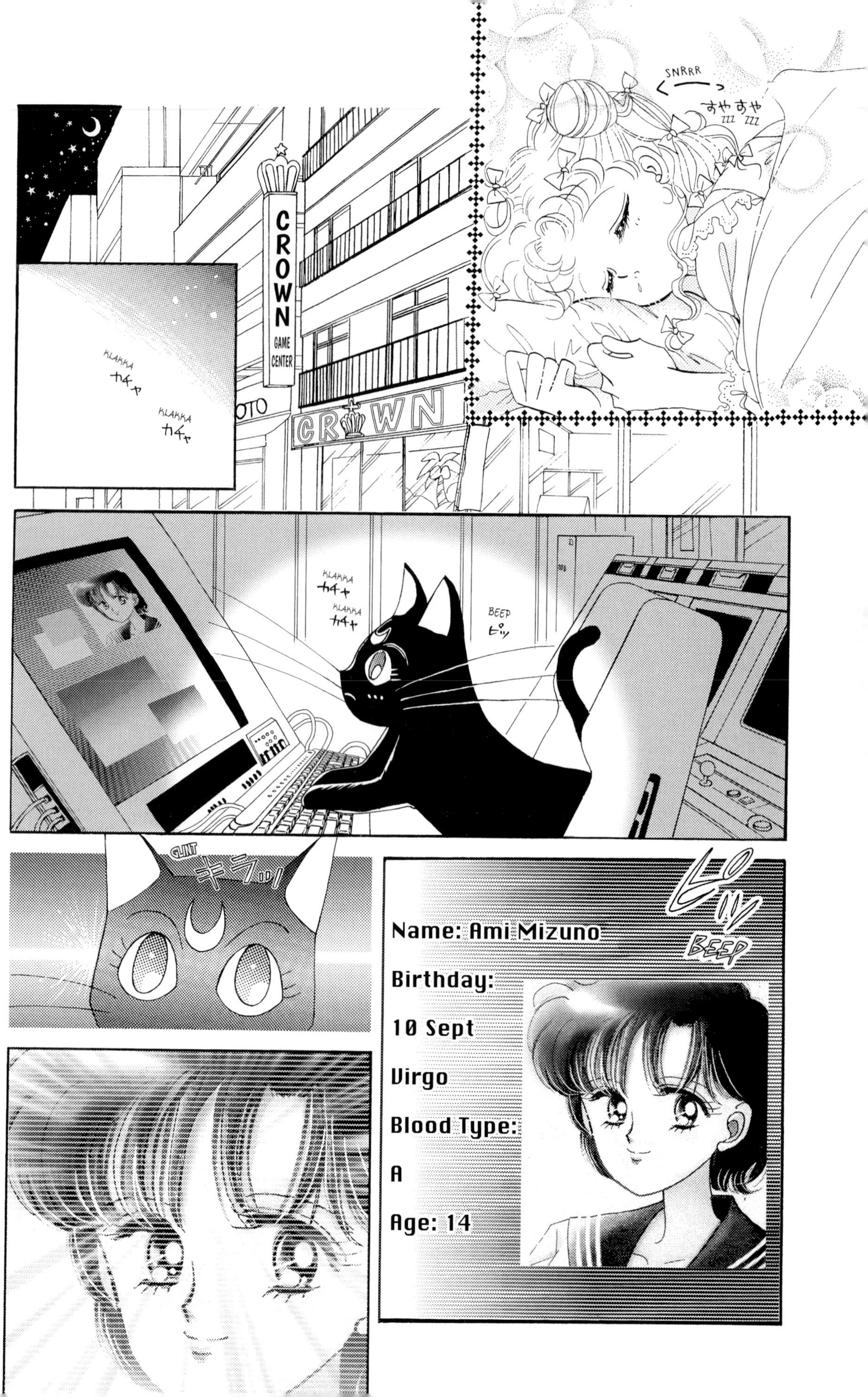
SNRRR
くーっ
すやすや
zzz zzz
KLAKKA
カチャ
KLAKKA
カチャ
KLAKKA
カチャ
KLAKKA
カチャ
BEEP
ピッ
ピッ
BEEP
Name: Ami Mizuno
Birthday:
10 Sept
Virgo
Blood Type:
A
Age: 14
GLINT
キラッ

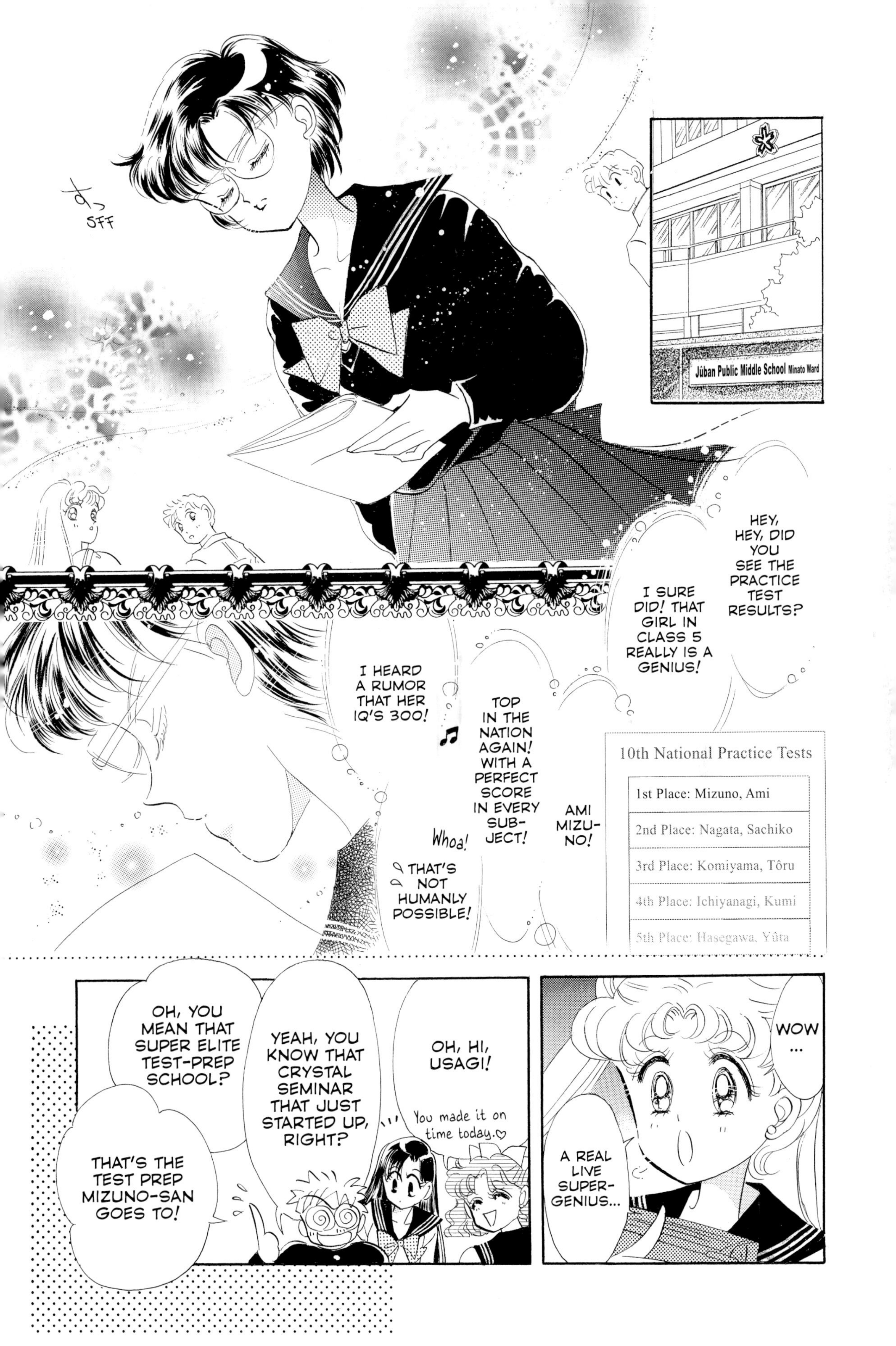
Jūban Public Middle School Minato Ward
すっ
SFF
HEY, HEY, DID YOU SEE THE PRACTICE TEST RESULTS?
I SURE DID! THAT GIRL IN CLASS 5 REALLY IS A GENIUS!
10th National Practice Tests
1st Place: Mizuno, Ami
2nd Place: Nagata, Sachiko
3rd Place: Komiyama, Tôru
4th Place: Ichiyanagi, Kumi
5th Place: Hasegawa, Yûta
AMI MIZUNO!
TOP IN THE NATION AGAIN! WITH A PERFECT SCORE IN EVERY SUBJECT!
I HEARD A RUMOR THAT HER IQ'S 300!
Whoa!
THAT'S NOT HUMANLY POSSIBLE!
WOW ...
A REAL LIVE SUPER-GENIUS...
OH, HI, USAGI!
You made it on time today.♡
YEAH, YOU KNOW THAT CRYSTAL SEMINAR THAT JUST STARTED UP, RIGHT?
OH, YOU MEAN THAT SUPER ELITE TEST-PREP SCHOOL?
THAT'S THE TEST PREP MIZUNO-SAN GOES TO!

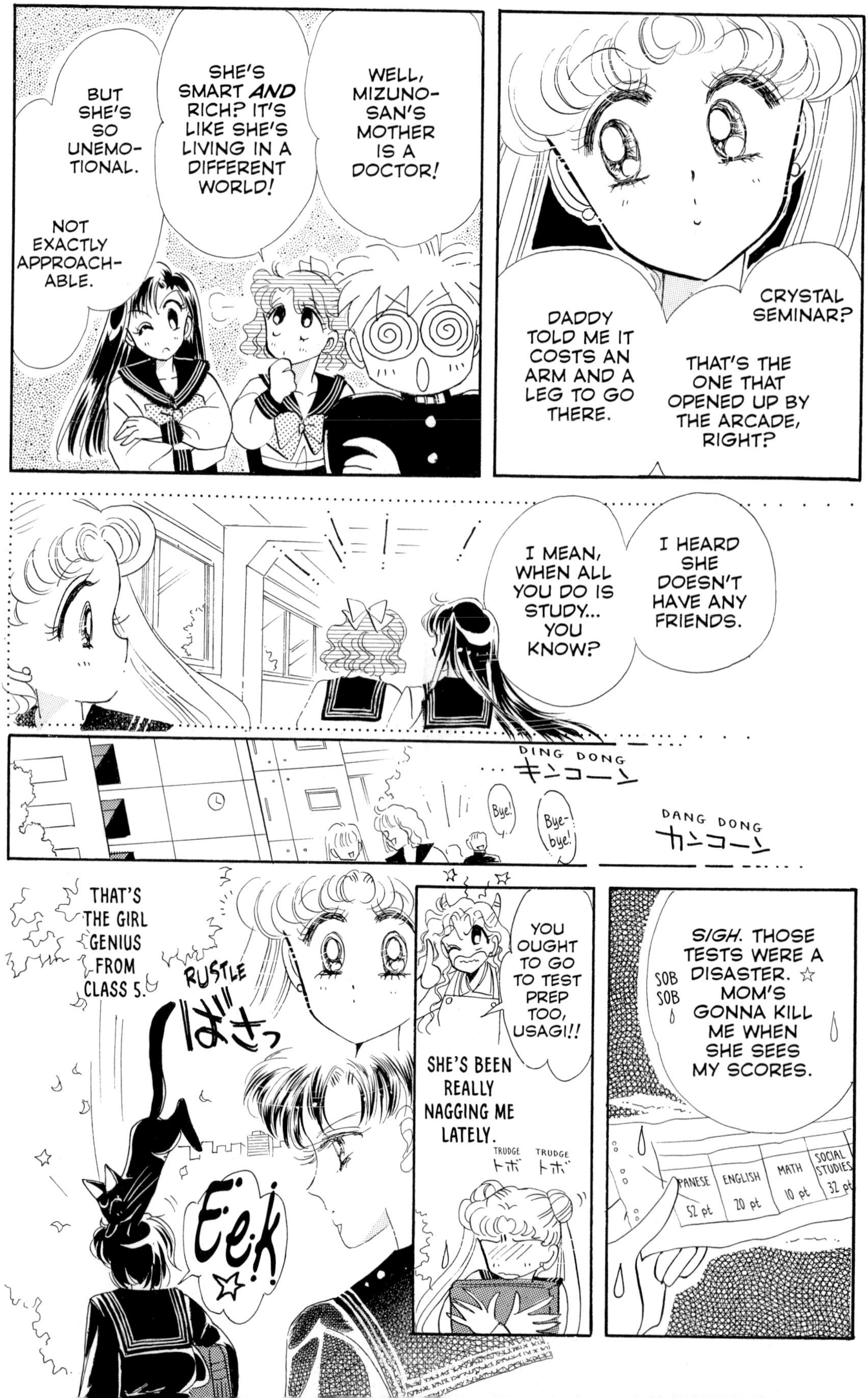
CRYSTAL SEMINAR?
THAT'S THE ONE THAT OPENED UP BY THE ARCADE, RIGHT?
DADDY TOLD ME IT COSTS AN ARM AND A LEG TO GO THERE.
WELL, MIZUNO-SAN'S MOTHER IS A DOCTOR!
SHE'S SMART *AND* RICH? IT'S LIKE SHE'S LIVING IN A DIFFERENT WORLD!
BUT SHE'S SO UNEMOTIONAL.
NOT EXACTLY APPROACHABLE.
I HEARD SHE DOESN'T HAVE ANY FRIENDS.
I MEAN, WHEN ALL YOU DO IS STUDY... YOU KNOW?
DING DONG キンコーン
DANG DONG カンコーン
Bye-bye!
Bye!
SIGH. THOSE TESTS WERE A DISASTER. ☆ MOM'S GONNA KILL ME WHEN SHE SEES MY SCORES.
SOB SOB
PANESE 52 pt
ENGLISH 20 pt
MATH 10 pt
SOCIAL STUDIES 32 pt
YOU OUGHT TO GO TO TEST PREP TOO, USAGI!!
SHE'S BEEN REALLY NAGGING ME LATELY.
TRUDGE TRUDGE トボトボ
THAT'S THE GIRL GENIUS FROM CLASS 5.
RUSTLE ばきっ
Eek!? ☆

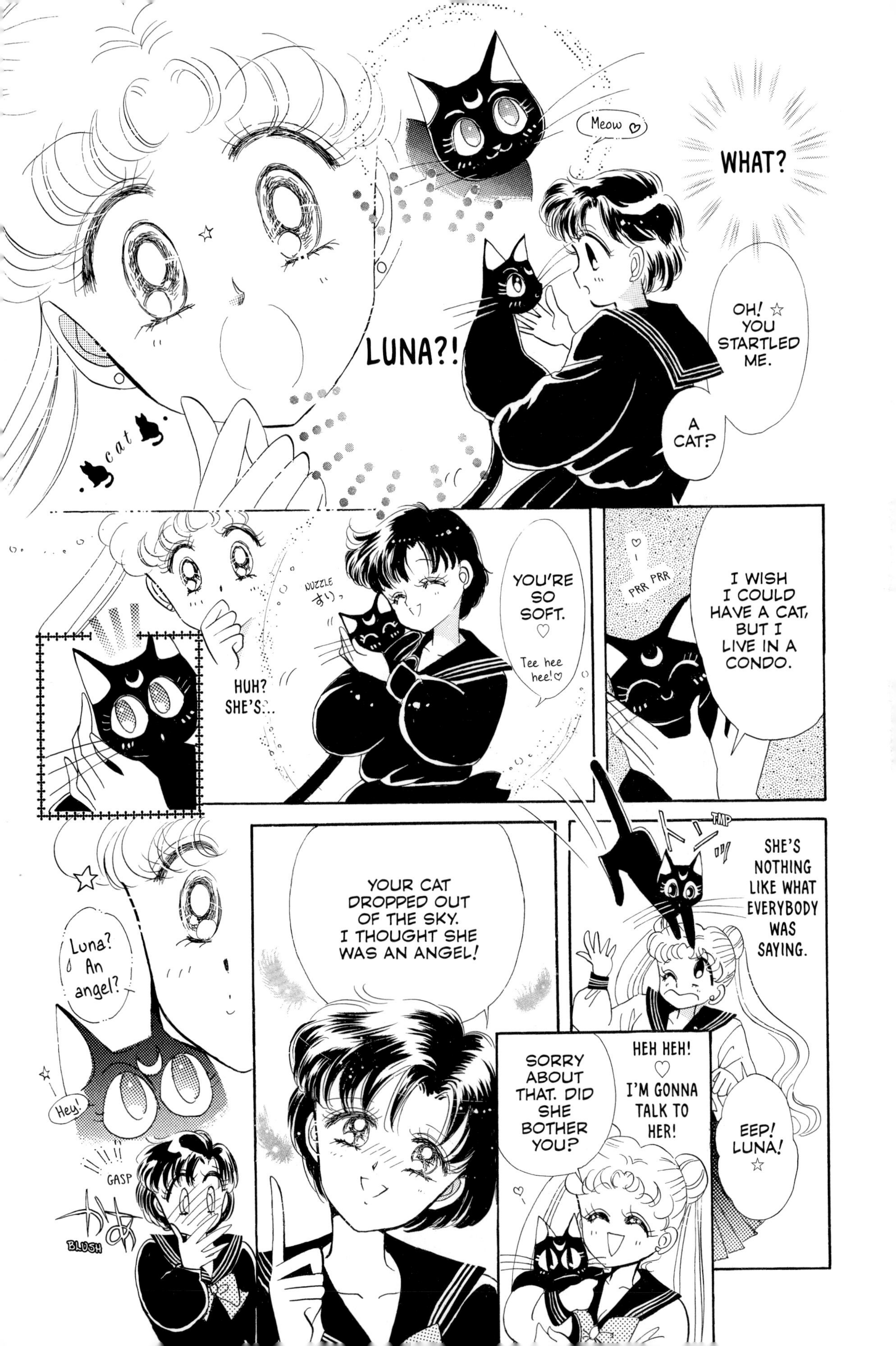
WHAT?
Meow ♡
OH! ☆ YOU STARTLED ME.
A CAT?
LUNA?!
cat
♡ PRR PRR
I WISH I COULD HAVE A CAT, BUT I LIVE IN A CONDO.
YOU'RE SO SOFT. ♡
Tee hee hee!♡
NUZZLE すり
HUH? SHE'S...
TMP
SHE'S NOTHING LIKE WHAT EVERYBODY WAS SAYING.
EEP! LUNA! ☆
HEH HEH! ♡ I'M GONNA TALK TO HER!
SORRY ABOUT THAT. DID SHE BOTHER YOU?
YOUR CAT DROPPED OUT OF THE SKY. I THOUGHT SHE WAS AN ANGEL!
Luna? An angel?
Hey!
GASP
BLUSH

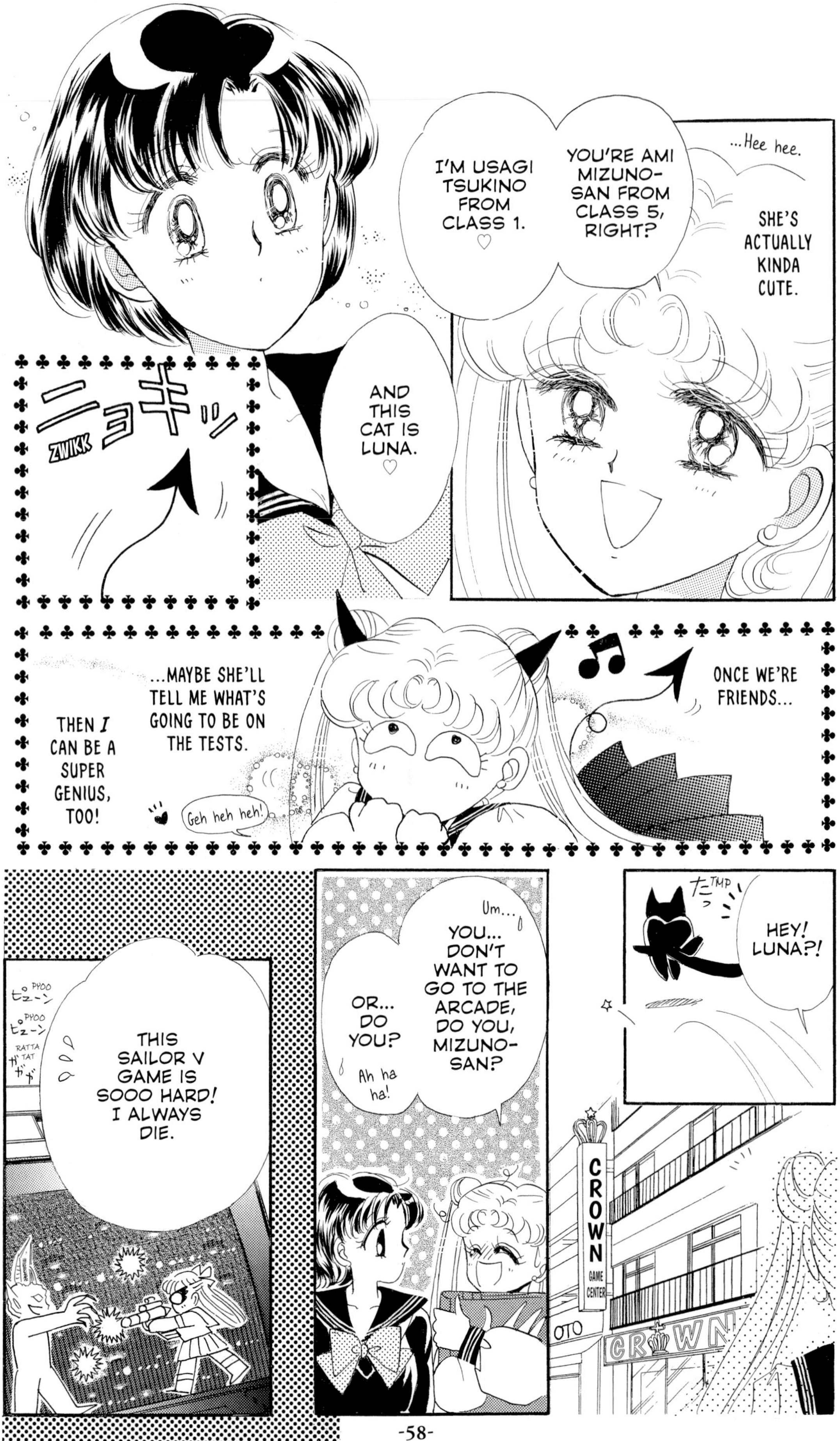

...Hee hee.
YOU'RE AMI MIZUNO-SAN FROM CLASS 5, RIGHT?
I'M USAGI TSUKINO FROM CLASS 1. ♡
SHE'S ACTUALLY KINDA CUTE.
AND THIS CAT IS LUNA. ♡
ニョキッ
ZWIKK
ONCE WE'RE FRIENDS...
...MAYBE SHE'LL TELL ME WHAT'S GOING TO BE ON THE TESTS.
THEN *I* CAN BE A SUPER GENIUS, TOO!
Geh heh heh!
た TMP
HEY! LUNA?!
CROWN
GAME CENTER
OTO
CROWN
Um...
YOU... DON'T WANT TO GO TO THE ARCADE, DO YOU, MIZUNO-SAN?
OR... DO YOU?
Ah ha ha!
ピューン PYOO
ピューン PYOO
ガガ RATTA TAT
THIS SAILOR V GAME IS SOOO HARD! I ALWAYS DIE.

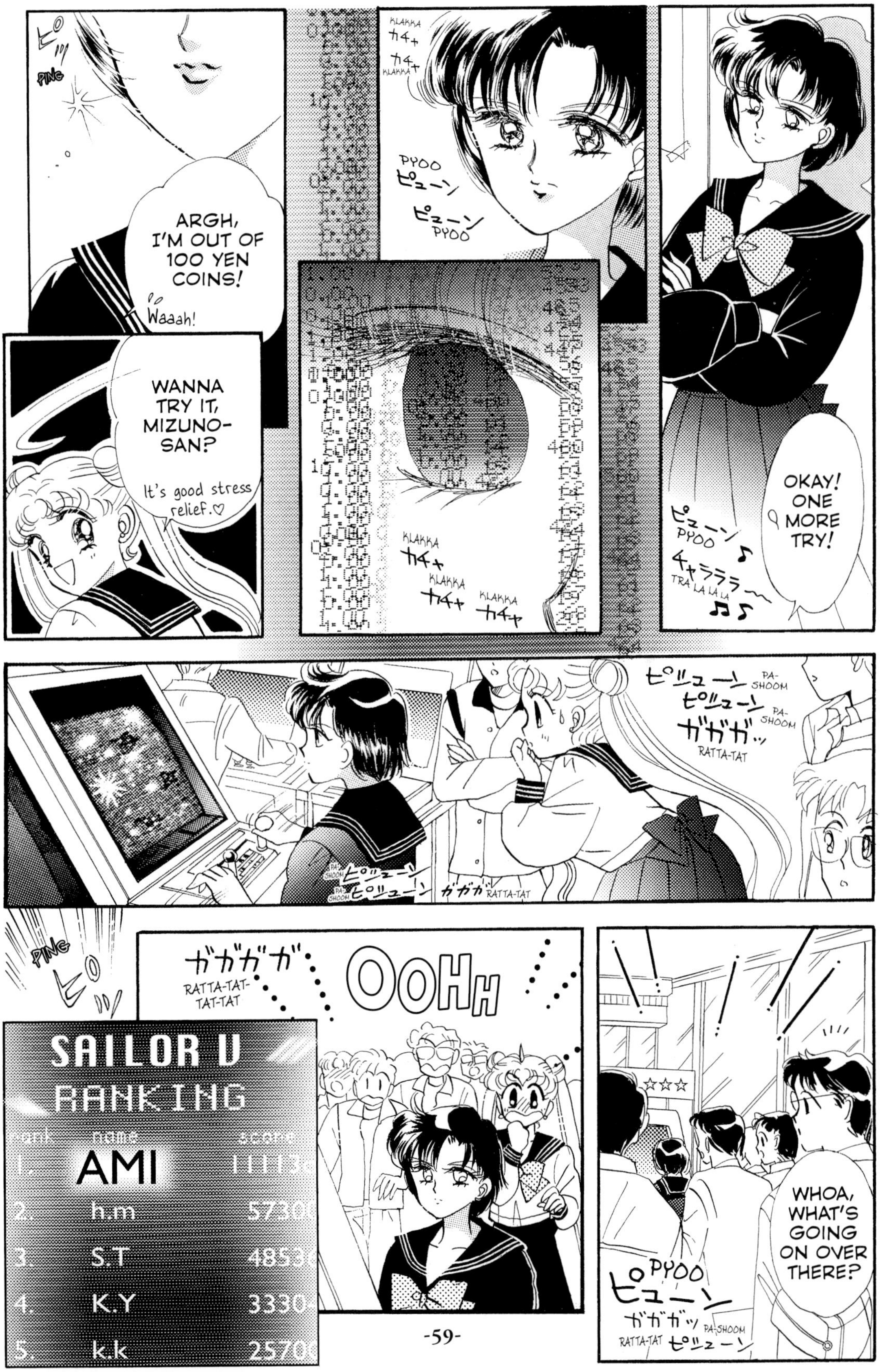

ピューン
PYOO
チャラララ〜
TRA LA LA LA
OKAY! ONE MORE TRY!
KLAKKA
カチャ
KLAKKA
PYOO
ピューン
ピューン
PYOO
KLAKKA
カチャ
KLAKKA
カチャ
KLAKKA
カチャ
ピ
PING
ARGH, I'M OUT OF 100 YEN COINS!
Waaah!
WANNA TRY IT, MIZUNO-SAN?
It's good stress relief.♡
PA-SHOOM
PA-SHOOM
RATTA-TAT
PA-SHOOM
PA-SHOOM
RATTA-TAT
WHOA, WHAT'S GOING ON OVER THERE?
PYOO
ピューン
RATTA-TAT
PA-SHOOM
ガガガガ
RATTA-TAT-TAT-TAT
OOHH
PING
ピ
SAILOR V
RANKING
rank name score
1. AMI
2. h.m
3. S.T
4. K.Y
5. k.k

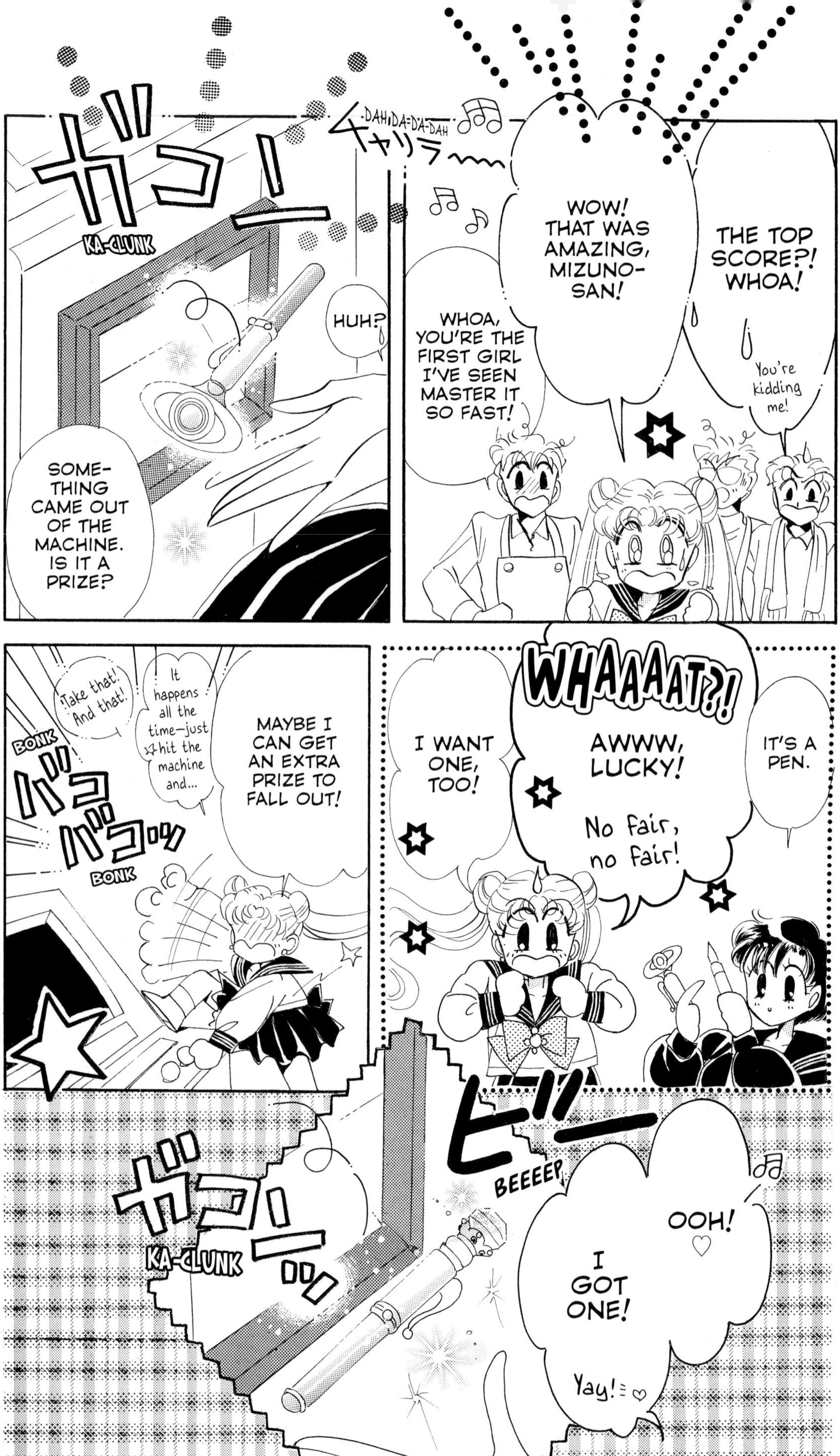

DAH-DA-DA-DAH
THE TOP SCORE?! WHOA!
You're kidding me!
WOW! THAT WAS AMAZING, MIZUNO-SAN!
WHOA, YOU'RE THE FIRST GIRL I'VE SEEN MASTER IT SO FAST!
KA-CLUNK
HUH?
SOME-THING CAME OUT OF THE MACHINE. IS IT A PRIZE?
WHAAAAT?!
IT'S A PEN.
AWWW, LUCKY!
No fair, no fair!
I WANT ONE, TOO!
MAYBE I CAN GET AN EXTRA PRIZE TO FALL OUT!
It happens all the time—just hit the machine and...
Take that! And that!
BONK
BONK
BEEEEP
OOH!
I GOT ONE!
Yay!
KA-CLUNK

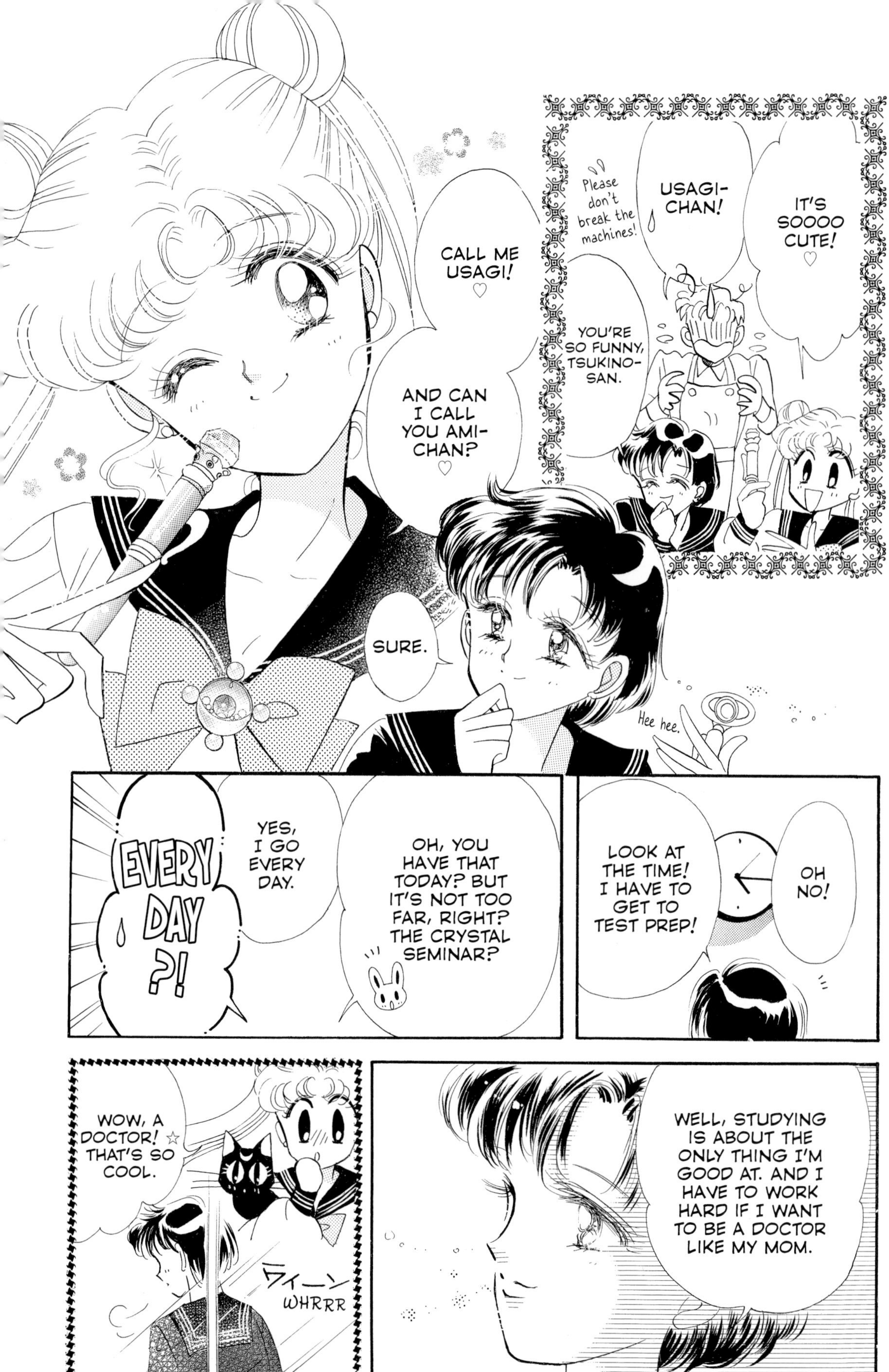
IT'S SOOOO CUTE! ♡
USAGI-CHAN!
Please don't break the machines!
YOU'RE SO FUNNY, TSUKINO-SAN.
CALL ME USAGI! ♡
AND CAN I CALL YOU AMI-CHAN? ♡
SURE.
Hee hee.
OH NO!
LOOK AT THE TIME! I HAVE TO GET TO TEST PREP!
OH, YOU HAVE THAT TODAY? BUT IT'S NOT TOO FAR, RIGHT? THE CRYSTAL SEMINAR?
YES, I GO EVERY DAY.
EVERY DAY ?!
WELL, STUDYING IS ABOUT THE ONLY THING I'M GOOD AT. AND I HAVE TO WORK HARD IF I WANT TO BE A DOCTOR LIKE MY MOM.
WOW, A DOCTOR! ☆ THAT'S SO COOL.
ワイーン
WHRRR

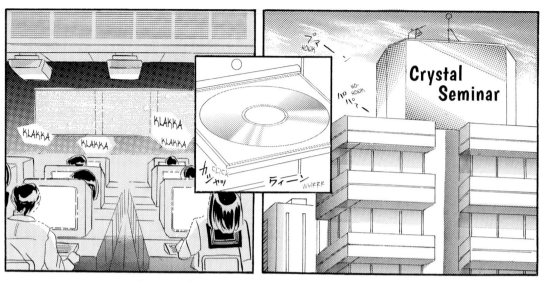

HONK
HO-HOOK
Crystal Seminar
CLICK
WHRRR
KLAKKA
KLAKKA
KLAKKA
KLAKKA
GASP
I HAVE HIGH HOPES FOR YOU, MIZUNO-SAN.
SUPERIOR HUMANS LIKE YOU CARRY THE WORLD'S FUTURE ON THEIR SHOULDERS, YOU KNOW.
YOU ARE WHAT EVERYONE ASPIRES TO BE. SO KEEP STUDYING, AND KEEP RAISING THAT BAR.
...YES, MA'AM.
DING DONG
キンコーン
DANG DONG
カンコーン
SQUEE
SQUEE
Girls Locker Room
HEY, WANNA GO TO THE FAUCHON SHOP ON THE CORNER FOR SOME ICE CREAM?
WHAT?! YOU KNOW I DO! ♡
ME TOO! ♡

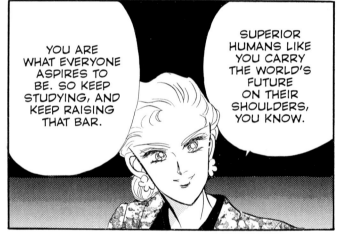

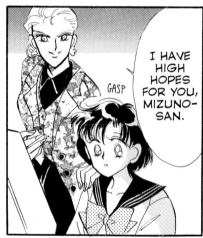

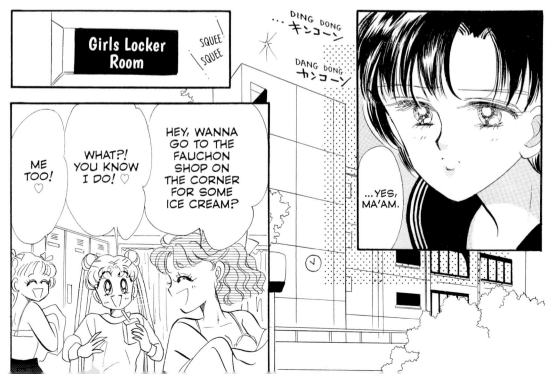

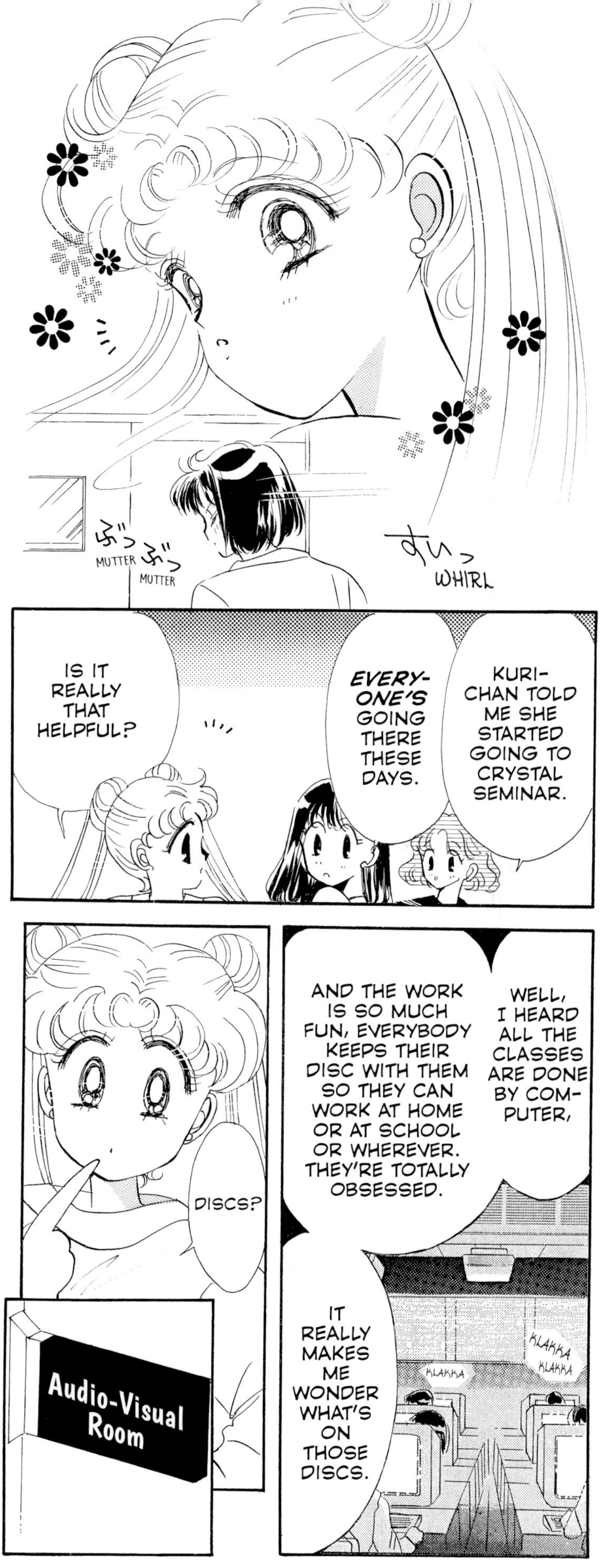
すいっ
WHIRL
ぶつっ
MUTTER
ぶつっ
MUTTER
KURI-CHAN TOLD ME SHE STARTED GOING TO CRYSTAL SEMINAR.
EVERYONE'S GOING THERE THESE DAYS.
...
IS IT REALLY THAT HELPFUL?
WELL, I HEARD ALL THE CLASSES ARE DONE BY COMPUTER,
AND THE WORK IS SO MUCH FUN, EVERYBODY KEEPS THEIR DISC WITH THEM SO THEY CAN WORK AT HOME OR AT SCHOOL OR WHEREVER. THEY'RE TOTALLY OBSESSED.
IT REALLY MAKES ME WONDER WHAT'S ON THOSE DISCS.
KLAKKA KLAKKA
KLAKKA
DISCS?
Audio-Visual Room
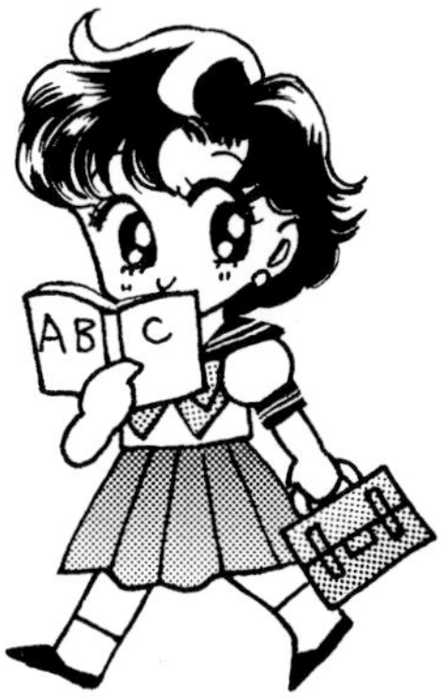
AB
C

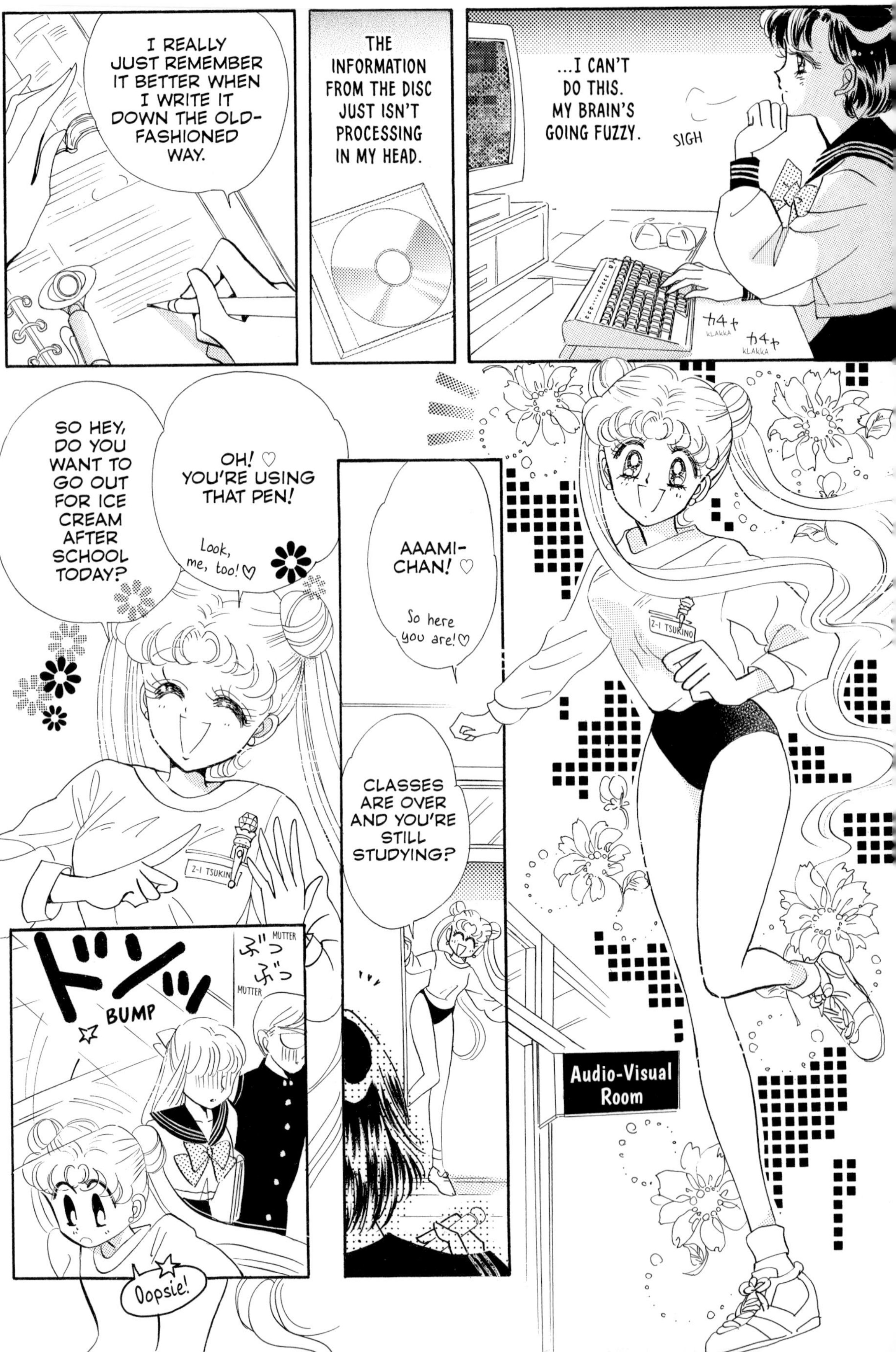

...I CAN'T DO THIS. MY BRAIN'S GOING FUZZY.
SIGH
カチャ KLAKKA
カチャ KLAKKA
THE INFORMATION FROM THE DISC JUST ISN'T PROCESSING IN MY HEAD.
I REALLY JUST REMEMBER IT BETTER WHEN I WRITE IT DOWN THE OLD-FASHIONED WAY.
AAAMI-CHAN! ♡
So here you are!♡
CLASSES ARE OVER AND YOU'RE STILL STUDYING?
Audio-Visual Room
2-1 TSUKINO
OH! ♡ YOU'RE USING THAT PEN!
Look, me, too!♡
SO HEY, DO YOU WANT TO GO OUT FOR ICE CREAM AFTER SCHOOL TODAY?
2-1 TSUKIN
ぶつ MUTTER
ぶつ MUTTER
ドン BUMP
Oopsie!

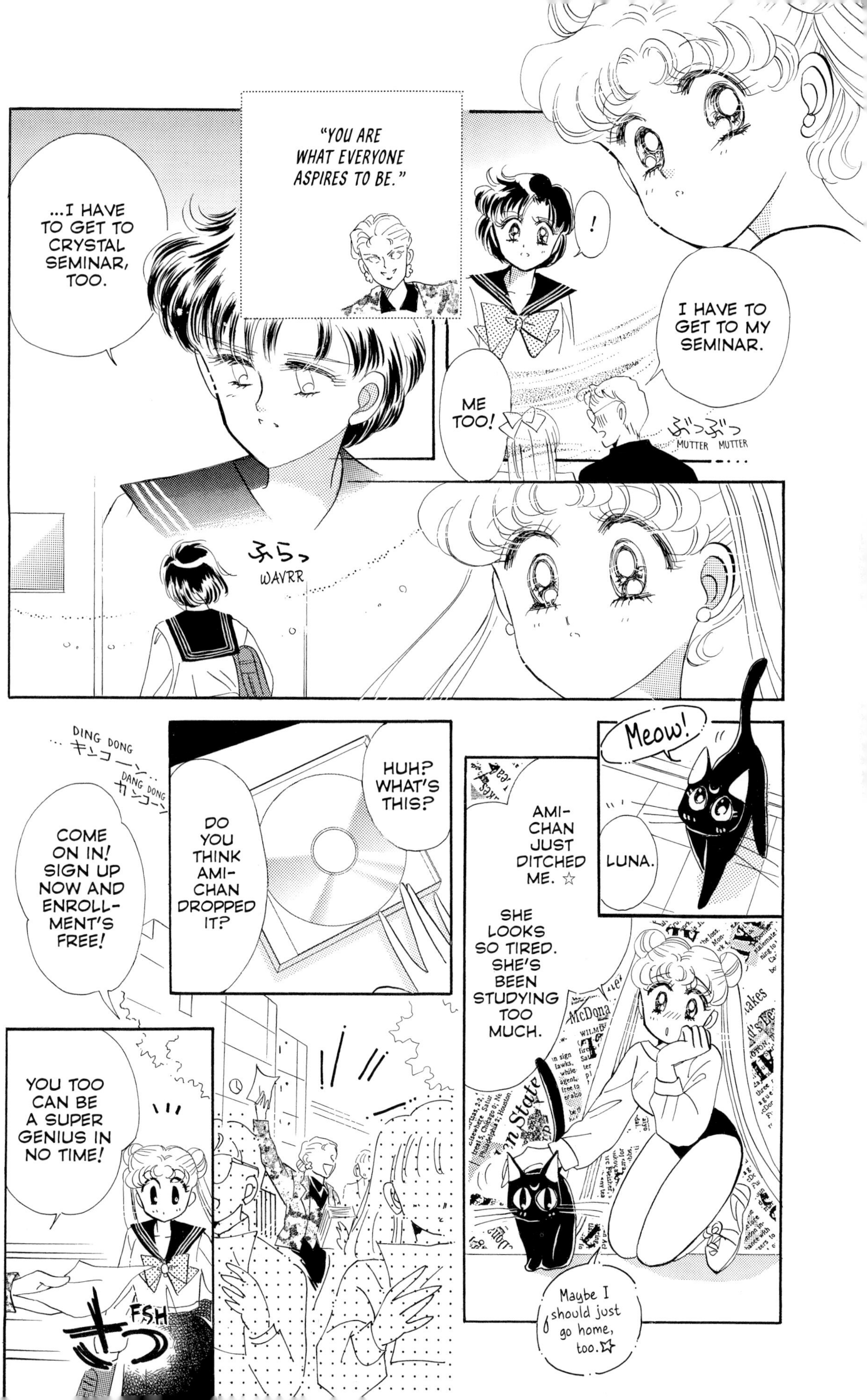
I HAVE TO GET TO MY SEMINAR.
ぶつぶつ
MUTTER MUTTER
!
ME TOO!
"YOU ARE WHAT EVERYONE ASPIRES TO BE."
...I HAVE TO GET TO CRYSTAL SEMINAR, TOO.
ふらっ
WAVRR
Meow!
LUNA.
AMI-CHAN JUST DITCHED ME. ☆
SHE LOOKS SO TIRED. SHE'S BEEN STUDYING TOO MUCH.
Maybe I should just go home, too.☆
HUH? WHAT'S THIS?
DO YOU THINK AMI-CHAN DROPPED IT?
キンコーン
DING DONG
カンコーン
DANG DONG
COME ON IN! SIGN UP NOW AND ENROLL-MENT'S FREE!
!/ //
YOU TOO CAN BE A SUPER GENIUS IN NO TIME!
さっ
FSH

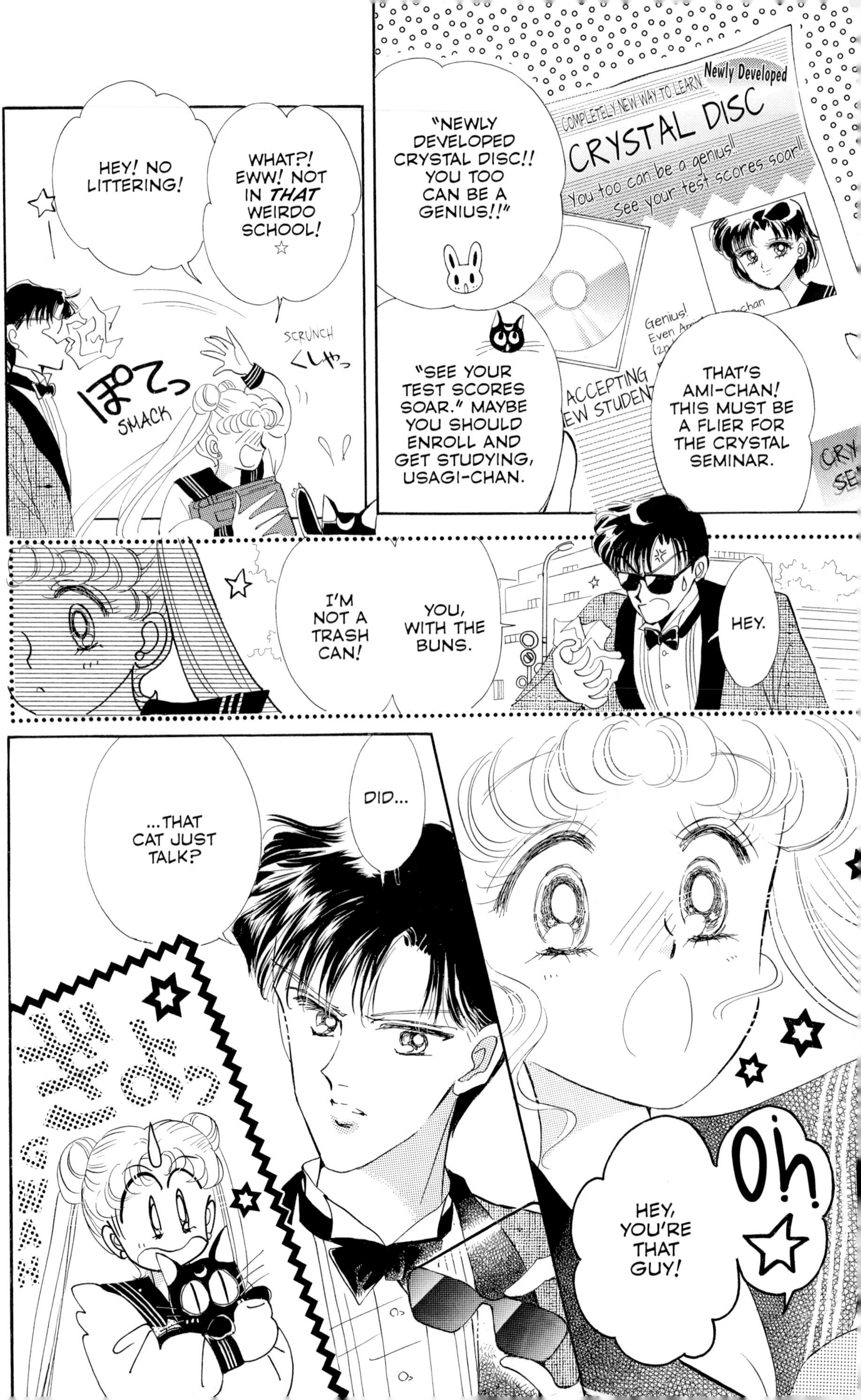
Newly Developed
COMPLETELY NEW WAY TO LEARN
CRYSTAL DISC
You too can be a genius!!
See your test scores soar!!
Genius!
ACCEPTING
THAT'S AMI-CHAN! THIS MUST BE A FLIER FOR THE CRYSTAL SEMINAR.
"NEWLY DEVELOPED CRYSTAL DISC!! YOU TOO CAN BE A GENIUS!!"
"SEE YOUR TEST SCORES SOAR." MAYBE YOU SHOULD ENROLL AND GET STUDYING, USAGI-CHAN.
WHAT?! EWW! NOT IN *THAT* WEIRDO SCHOOL!
SCRUNCH
くしゃっ
HEY! NO LITTERING!
ぽてっ
SMACK
HEY.
YOU, WITH THE BUNS.
I'M NOT A TRASH CAN!
Oh!
HEY, YOU'RE THAT GUY!
DID...
...THAT CAT JUST TALK?

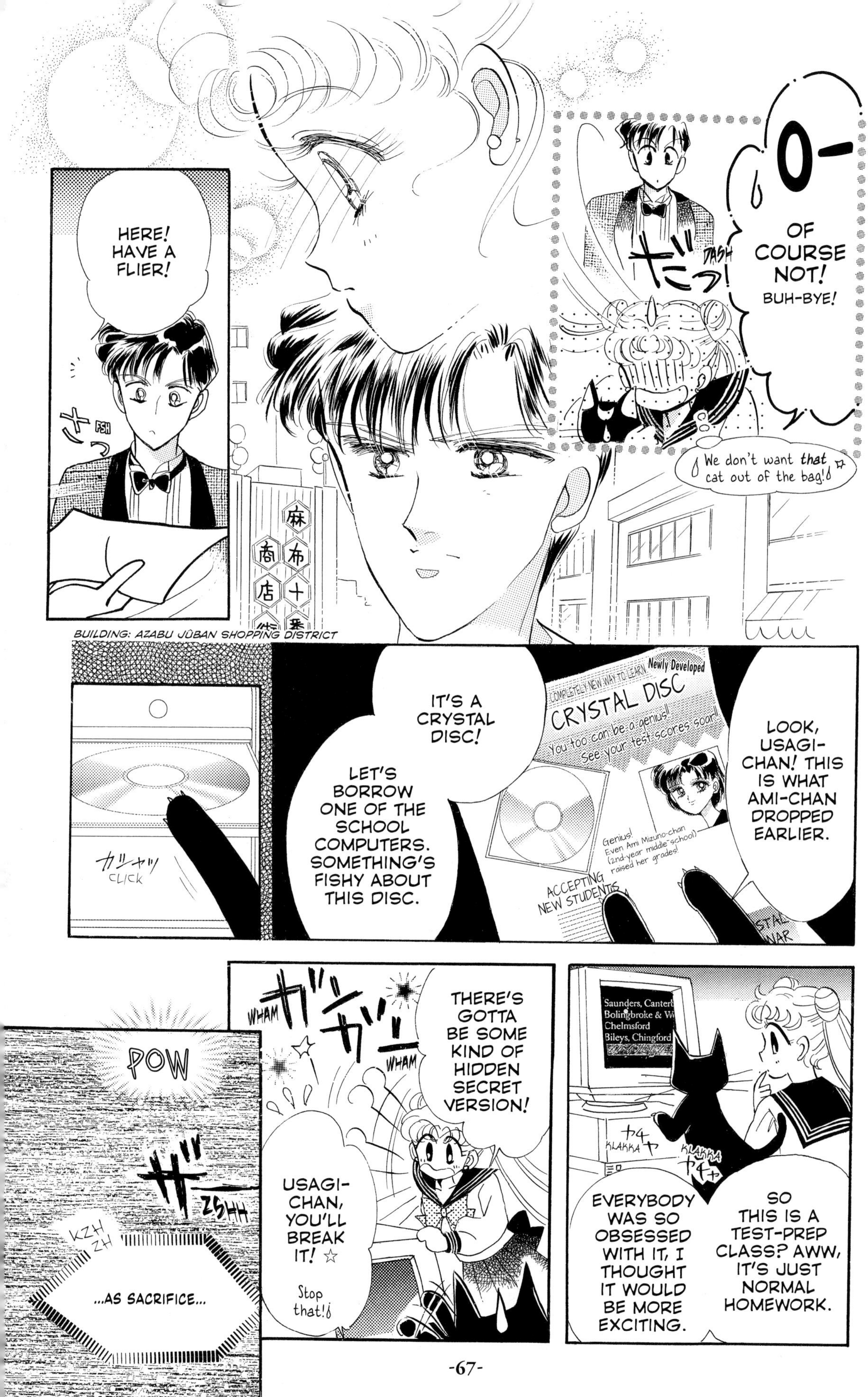
O-
DASH
OF COURSE NOT! BUH-BYE!
We don't want *that* cat out of the bag!
HERE! HAVE A FLIER!
FSH
BUILDING: AZABU JÛBAN SHOPPING DISTRICT
LOOK, USAGI-CHAN! THIS IS WHAT AMI-CHAN DROPPED EARLIER.
Newly Developed
COMPLETELY NEW WAY TO LEARN
CRYSTAL DISC
You too can be a genius!! See your test scores soar!!
Genius! Even Ami Mizuno-chan (2nd-year middle school) raised her grades!
ACCEPTING NEW STUDENTS
IT'S A CRYSTAL DISC!
LET'S BORROW ONE OF THE SCHOOL COMPUTERS. SOMETHING'S FISHY ABOUT THIS DISC.
CLICK
Saunders, Canterb
Bolingbroke & W
Chelmsford
Bileys, Chingford
KLAKKA
KLAKKA
SO THIS IS A TEST-PREP CLASS? AWW, IT'S JUST NORMAL HOMEWORK.
EVERYBODY WAS SO OBSESSED WITH IT, I THOUGHT IT WOULD BE MORE EXCITING.
WHAM
WHAM
THERE'S GOTTA BE SOME KIND OF HIDDEN SECRET VERSION!
USAGI-CHAN, YOU'LL BREAK IT! ☆
Stop that!
POW
ZSHH
KZH ZH
...AS SACRIFICE...

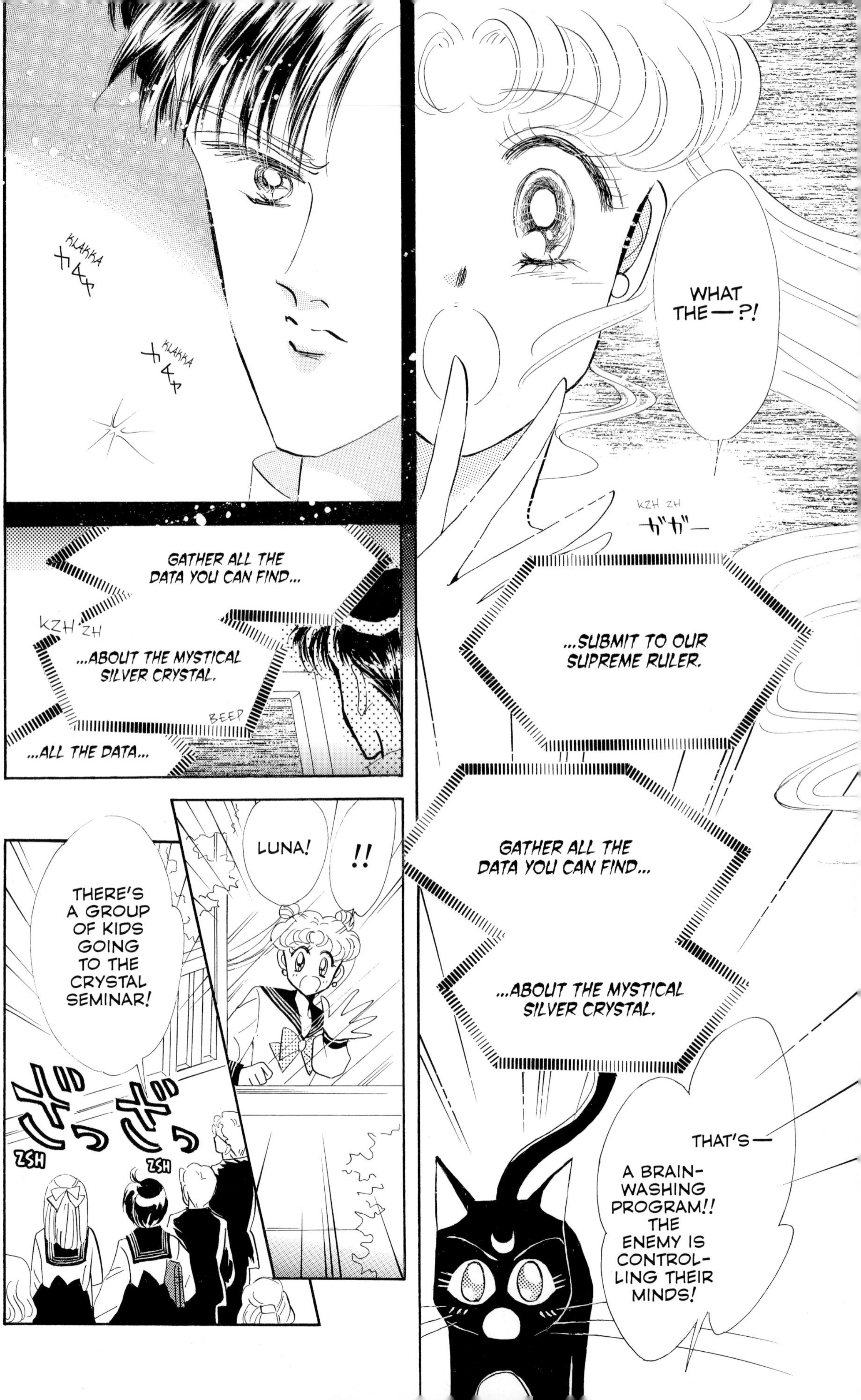
WHAT THE—?!
KZH ZH
...SUBMIT TO OUR SUPREME RULER.
GATHER ALL THE DATA YOU CAN FIND...
...ABOUT THE MYSTICAL SILVER CRYSTAL.
THAT'S—
A BRAIN-WASHING PROGRAM!! THE ENEMY IS CONTROLLING THEIR MINDS!
KLAKKA
KLAKKA
GATHER ALL THE DATA YOU CAN FIND...
KZH ZH
...ABOUT THE MYSTICAL SILVER CRYSTAL.
BEEP
...ALL THE DATA...
!!
LUNA!
THERE'S A GROUP OF KIDS GOING TO THE CRYSTAL SEMINAR!
ZSH
ZSH

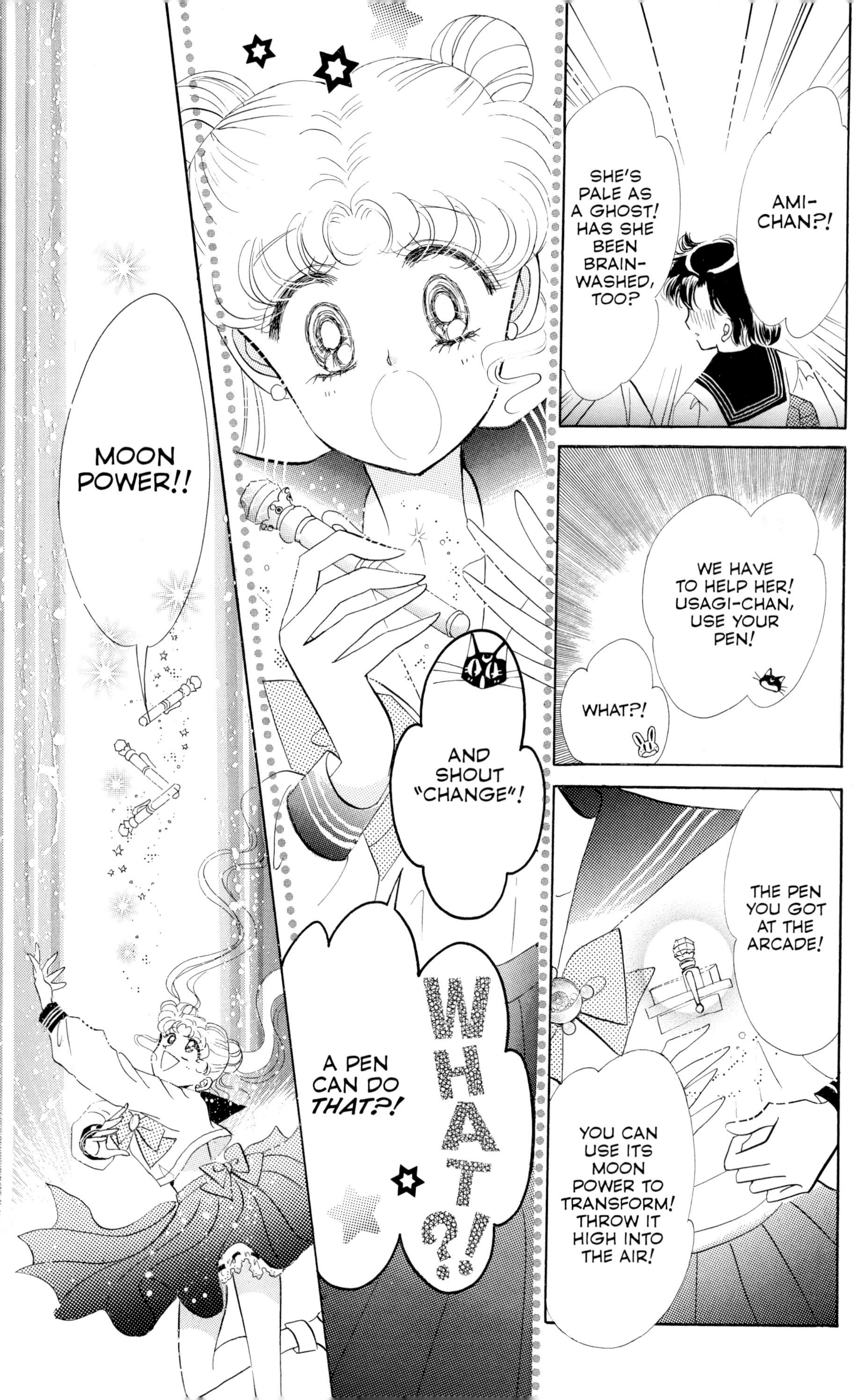
AMI-CHAN?!
SHE'S PALE AS A GHOST! HAS SHE BEEN BRAIN-WASHED, TOO?
WE HAVE TO HELP HER! USAGI-CHAN, USE YOUR PEN!
WHAT?!
THE PEN YOU GOT AT THE ARCADE!
YOU CAN USE ITS MOON POWER TO TRANSFORM! THROW IT HIGH INTO THE AIR!
AND SHOUT "CHANGE"!
WHAT?!
A PEN CAN DO *THAT?!*
MOON POWER!!

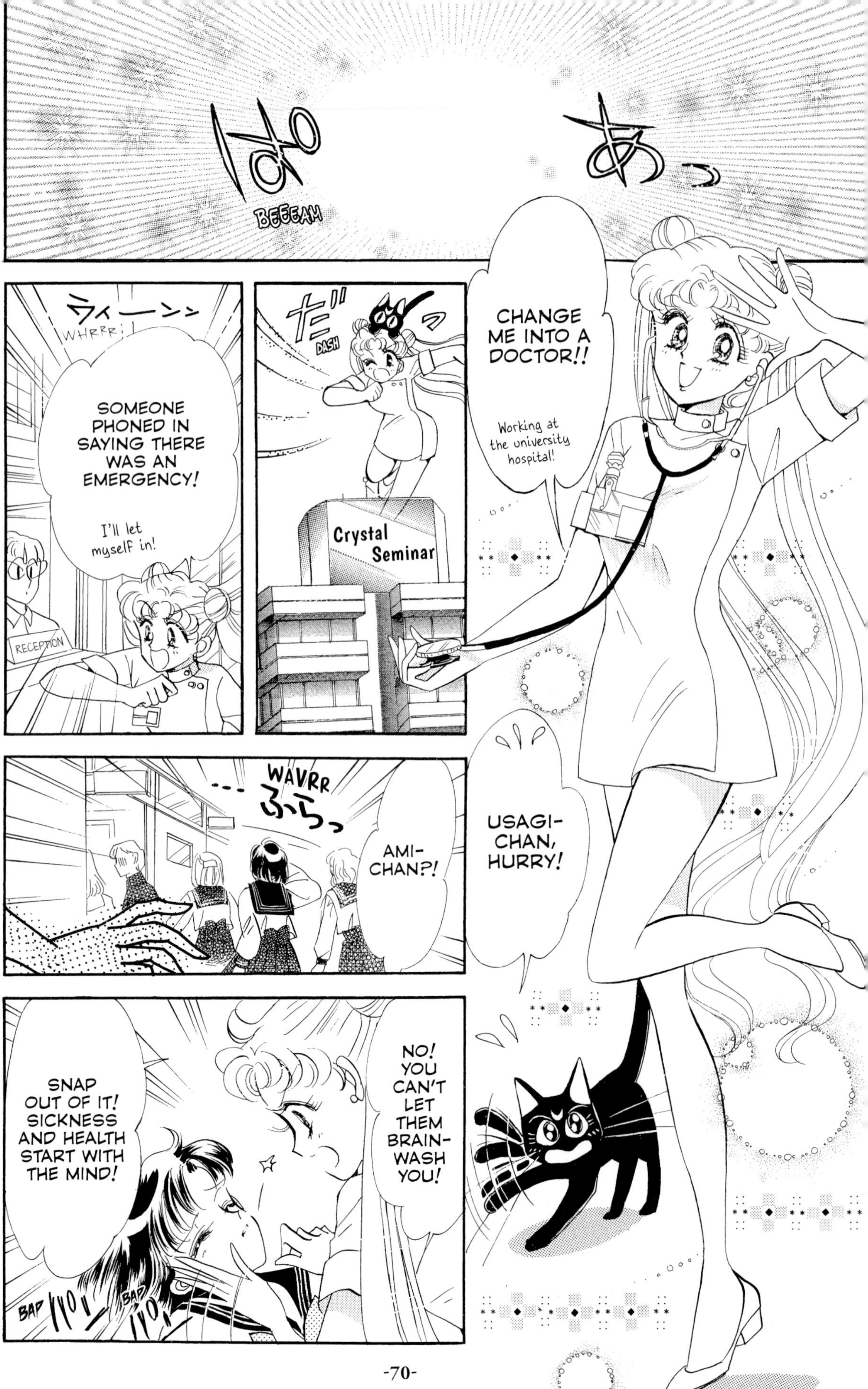

ぱ
あっ
BEEEAM
CHANGE ME INTO A DOCTOR!!
Working at the university hospital!
USAGI-CHAN, HURRY!
だっ
DASH
Crystal Seminar
ウィーンン
WHRRR
SOMEONE PHONED IN SAYING THERE WAS AN EMERGENCY!
I'll let myself in!
RECEPTION
WAVRR
...ふらっ
AMI-CHAN?!
NO! YOU CAN'T LET THEM BRAIN-WASH YOU!
SNAP OUT OF IT! SICKNESS AND HEALTH START WITH THE MIND!
BAP
BAP

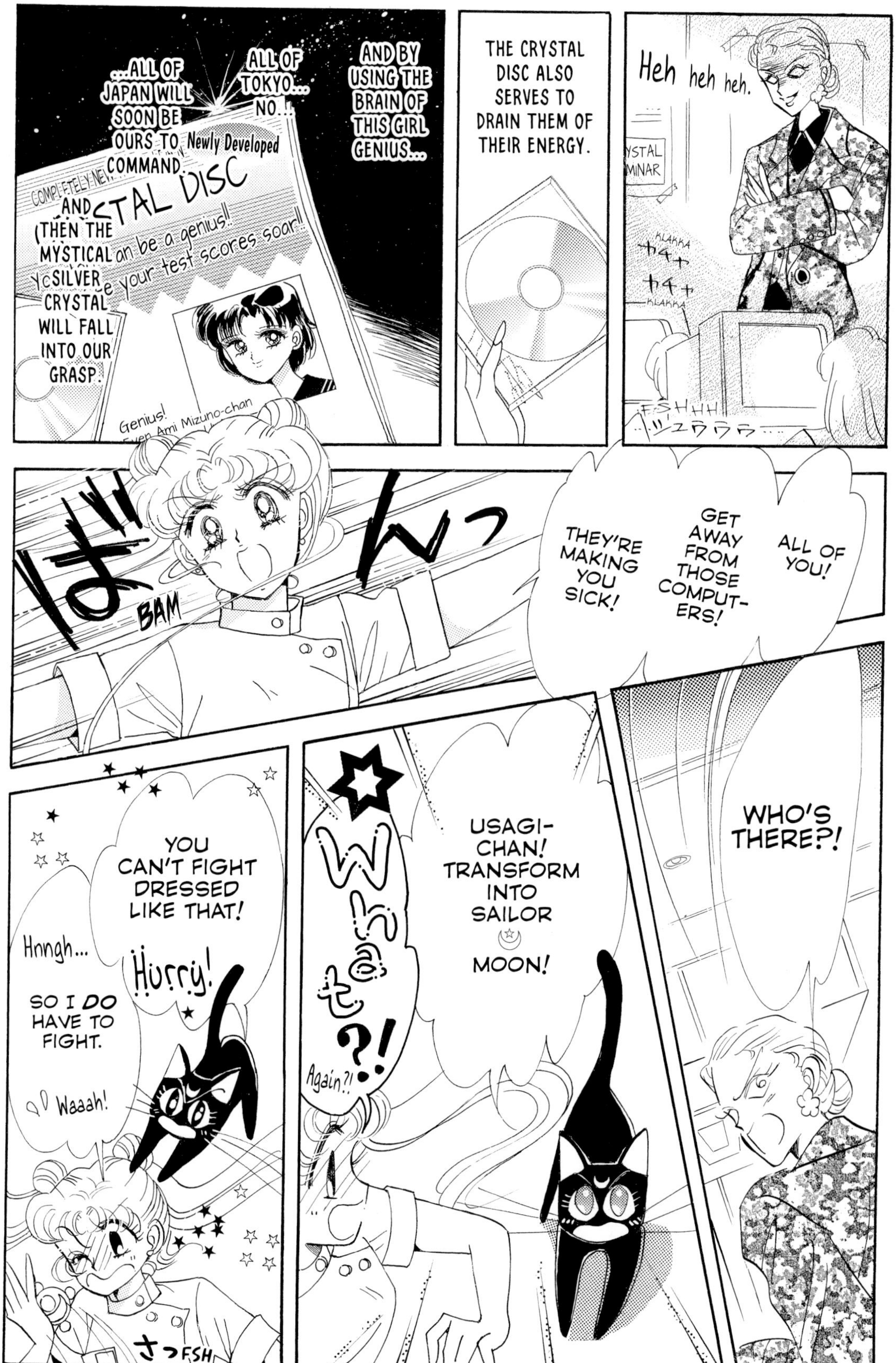
Heh heh heh.
KLAKKA
KLAKKA
FSHHH
THE CRYSTAL DISC ALSO SERVES TO DRAIN THEM OF THEIR ENERGY.
AND BY USING THE BRAIN OF THIS GIRL GENIUS...
ALL OF TOKYO... NO...
...ALL OF JAPAN WILL SOON BE OURS TO COMMAND.
Newly Developed
AND THEN THE MYSTICAL SILVER CRYSTAL WILL FALL INTO OUR GRASP.
Genius!
ALL OF YOU!
GET AWAY FROM THOSE COMPUTERS!
THEY'RE MAKING YOU SICK!
BAM
WHO'S THERE?!
USAGI-CHAN! TRANSFORM INTO SAILOR MOON!
What?!
Again?!
YOU CAN'T FIGHT DRESSED LIKE THAT!
Hurry!
Hnngh...
SO I DO HAVE TO FIGHT.
Waaah!
FSH

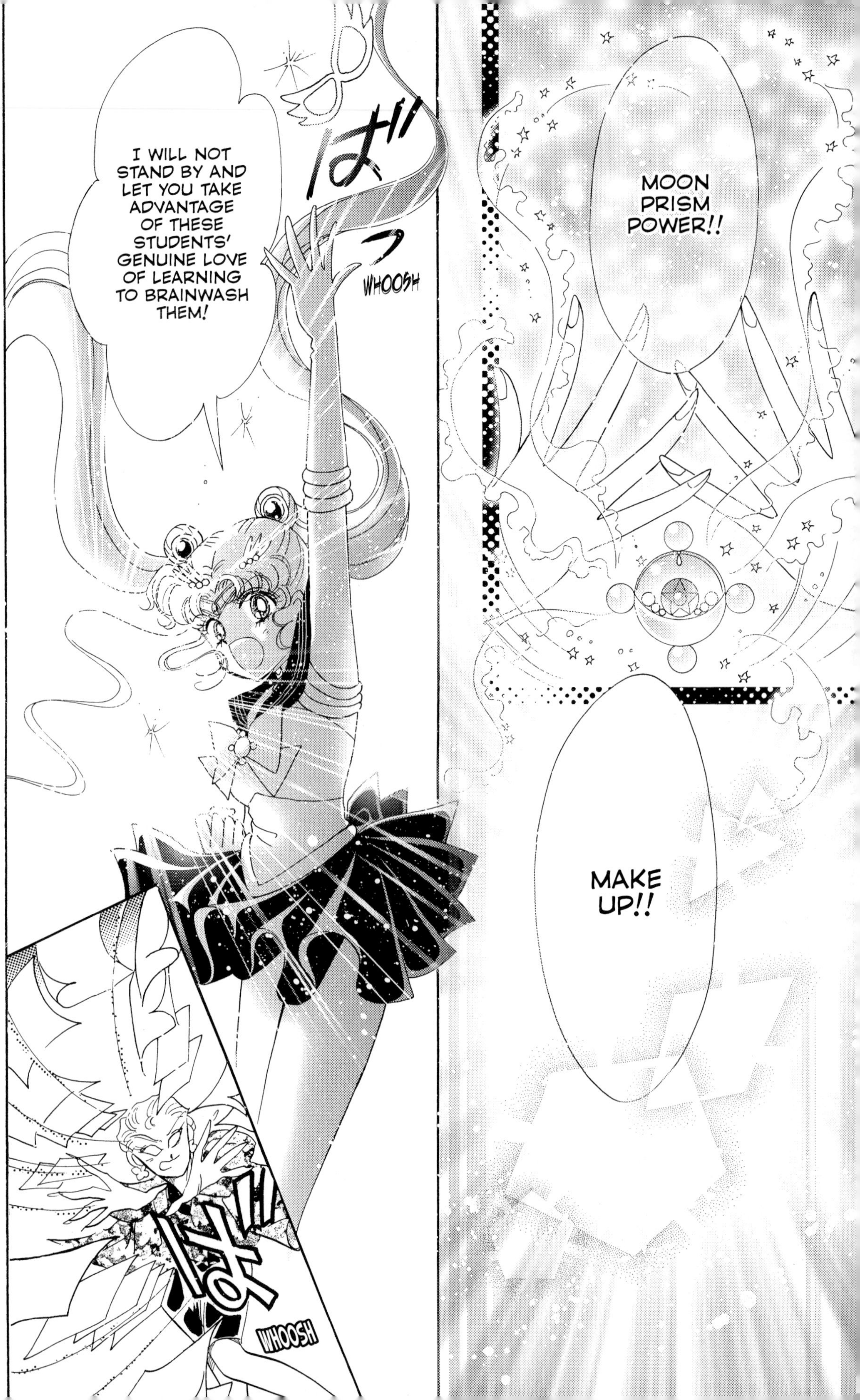
MOON PRISM POWER!!
MAKE UP!!
I WILL NOT STAND BY AND LET YOU TAKE ADVANTAGE OF THESE STUDENTS' GENUINE LOVE OF LEARNING TO BRAINWASH THEM!
ばっ
WHOOSH
ばっ
WHOOSH

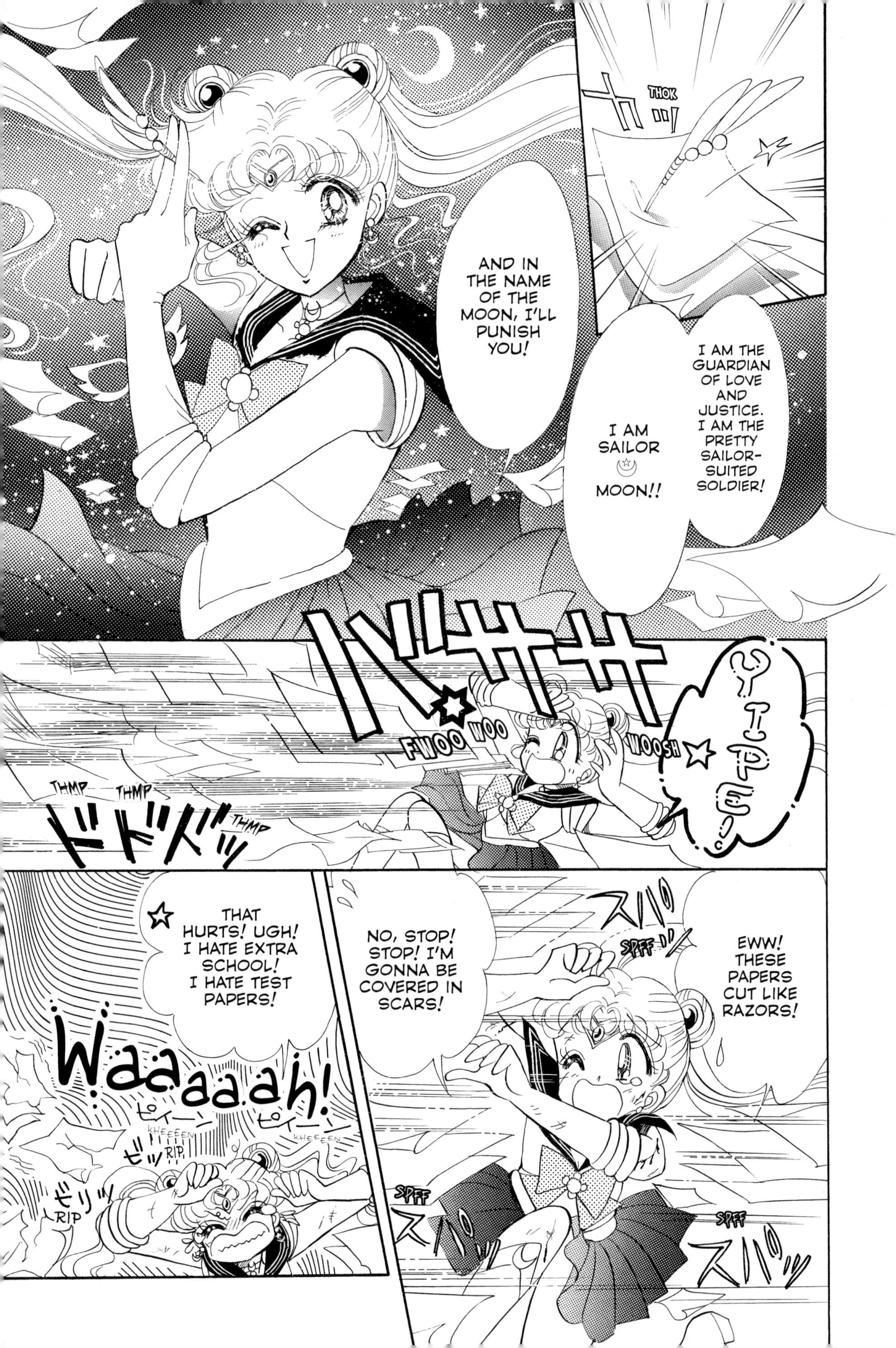
THOK
I AM THE GUARDIAN OF LOVE AND JUSTICE. I AM THE PRETTY SAILOR-SUITED SOLDIER!
I AM SAILOR MOON!!
AND IN THE NAME OF THE MOON, I'LL PUNISH YOU!
WOOSH
FWOO WOO
THMP THMP THMP
SPFF
EWW! THESE PAPERS CUT LIKE RAZORS!
NO, STOP! STOP! I'M GONNA BE COVERED IN SCARS!
SPFF
SPFF
THAT HURTS! UGH! I HATE EXTRA SCHOOL! I HATE TEST PAPERS!
Waaaaaah!
KHEEEEN
KHEEEEN
RIP
RIP

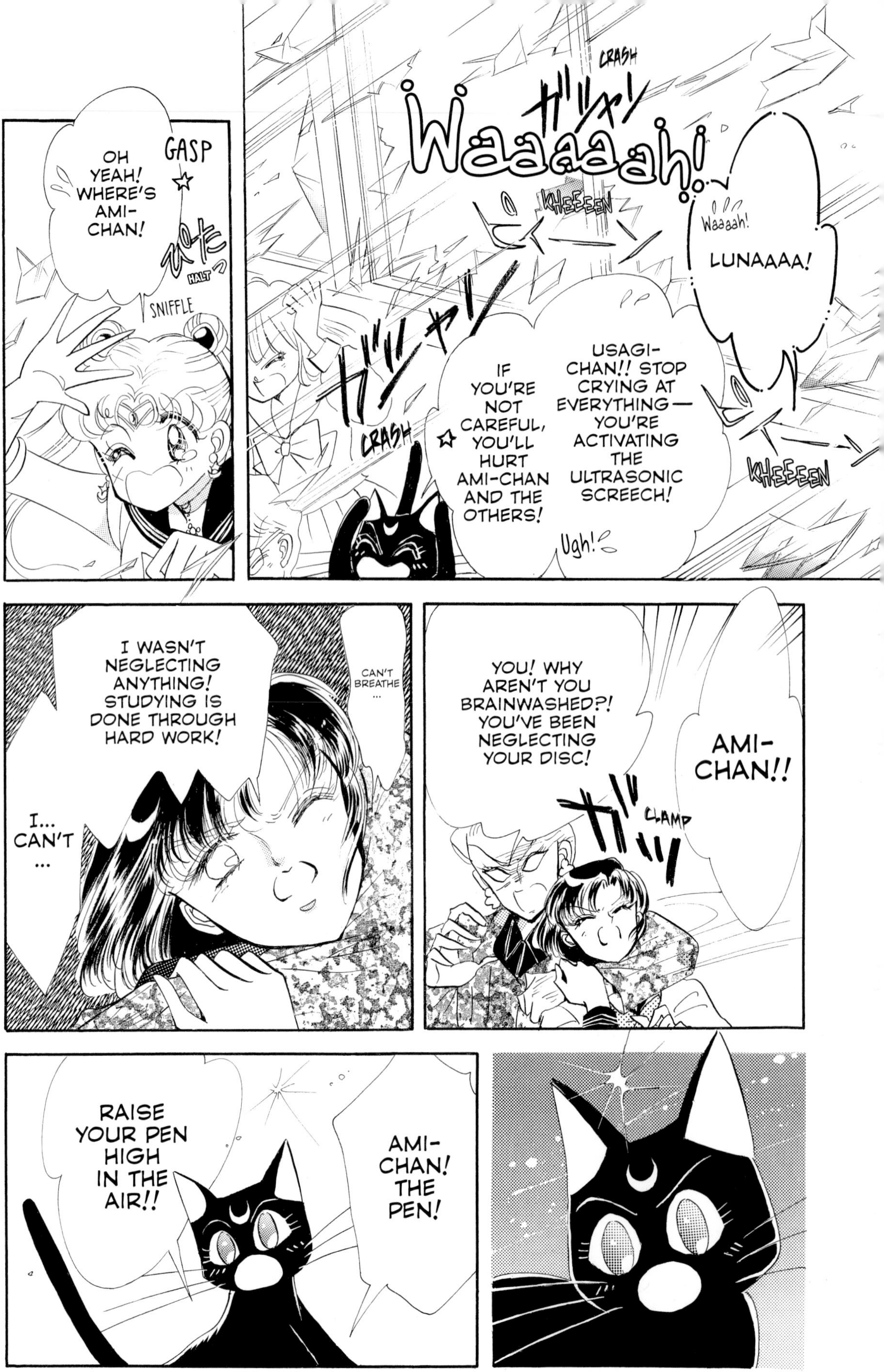
CRASH
Waaaaah!
KHEEEEN
Waaaah!
LUNAAAA!
USAGI-CHAN!! STOP CRYING AT EVERYTHING—YOU'RE ACTIVATING THE ULTRASONIC SCREECH!
IF YOU'RE NOT CAREFUL, YOU'LL HURT AMI-CHAN AND THE OTHERS!
CRASH
KHEEEEN
Ugh!
GASP
OH YEAH! WHERE'S AMI-CHAN!
HALT
SNIFFLE
AMI-CHAN!!
YOU! WHY AREN'T YOU BRAINWASHED?! YOU'VE BEEN NEGLECTING YOUR DISC!
CLAMP
CAN'T BREATHE ...
I WASN'T NEGLECTING ANYTHING! STUDYING IS DONE THROUGH HARD WORK!
I... CAN'T ...
AMI-CHAN! THE PEN!
RAISE YOUR PEN HIGH IN THE AIR!!

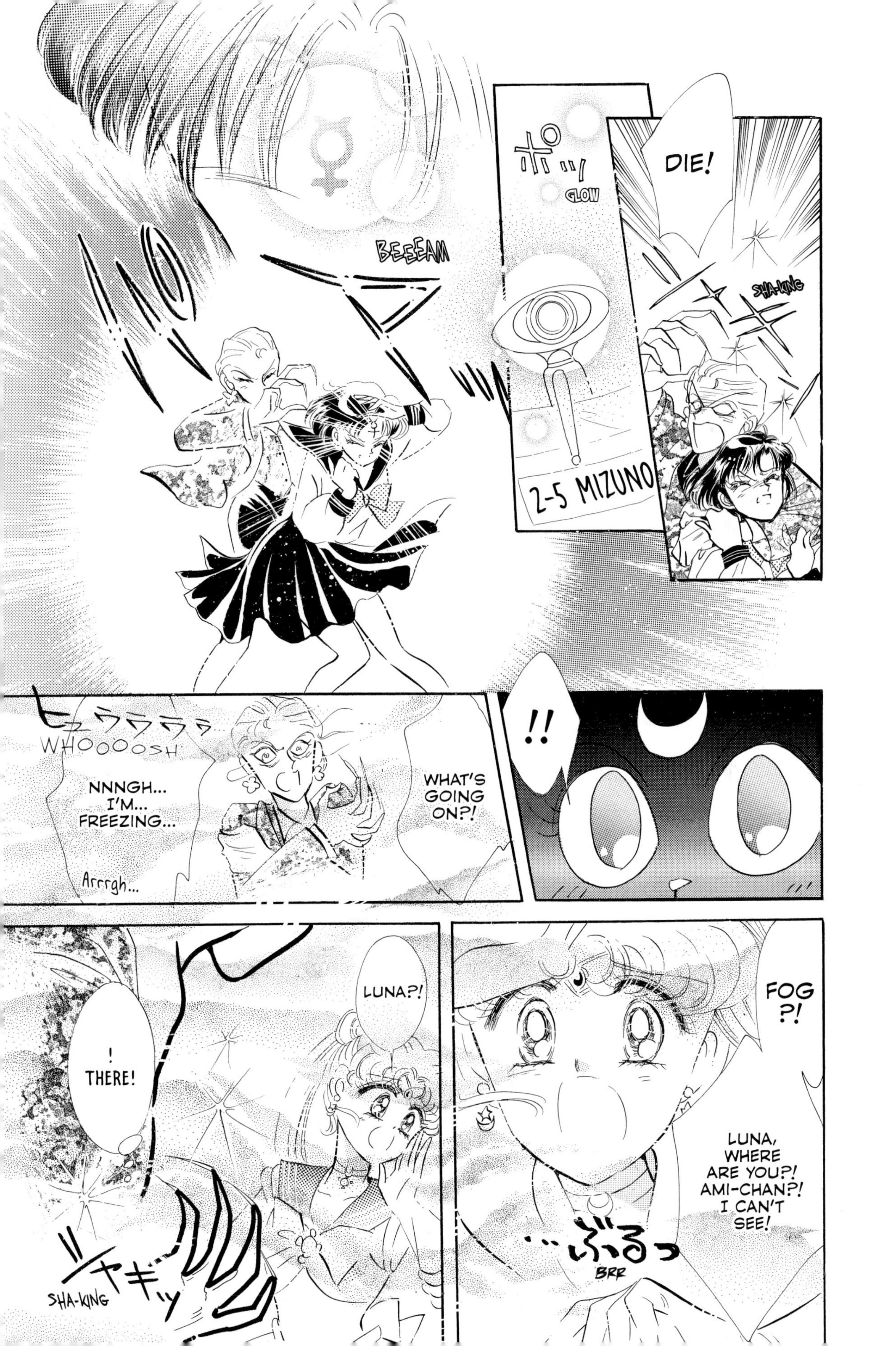
DIE!
SHA-KING
GLOW
2-5 MIZUNO
BEEEAM
!!
WHAT'S GOING ON?!
NNNGH... I'M... FREEZING...
Arrrgh...
WHOOOOOSH
FOG?!
LUNA, WHERE ARE YOU?! AMI-CHAN?! I CAN'T SEE!
...ぶるっ
BRR
LUNA?!
! THERE!
シャギッ
SHA-KING

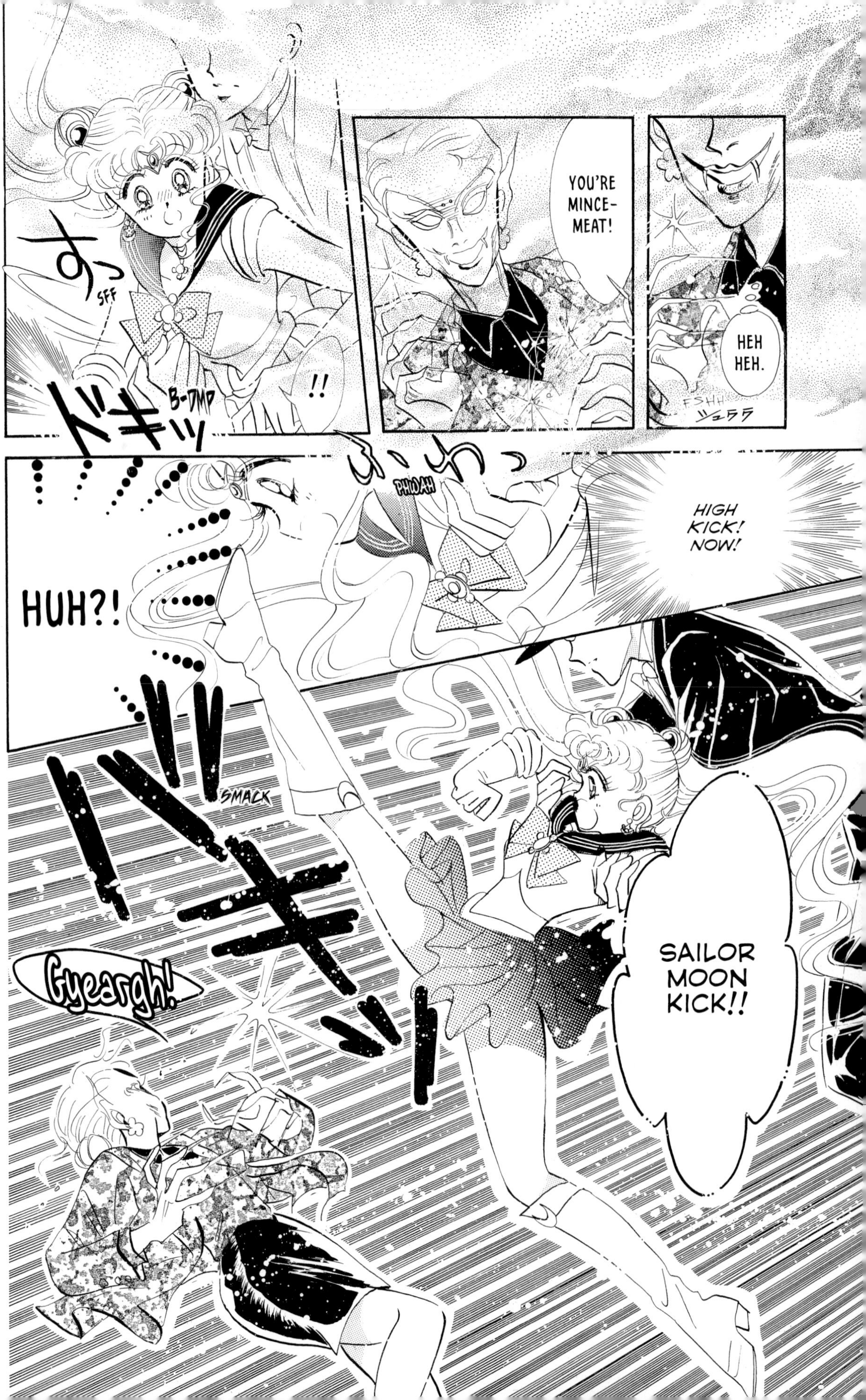
HEH HEH.
FSHH
YOU'RE MINCE-MEAT!
!!
SFF
B-DMP
HIGH KICK! NOW!
PHWAH
HUH?!
SAILOR MOON KICK!!
SMACK
Gyeargh!

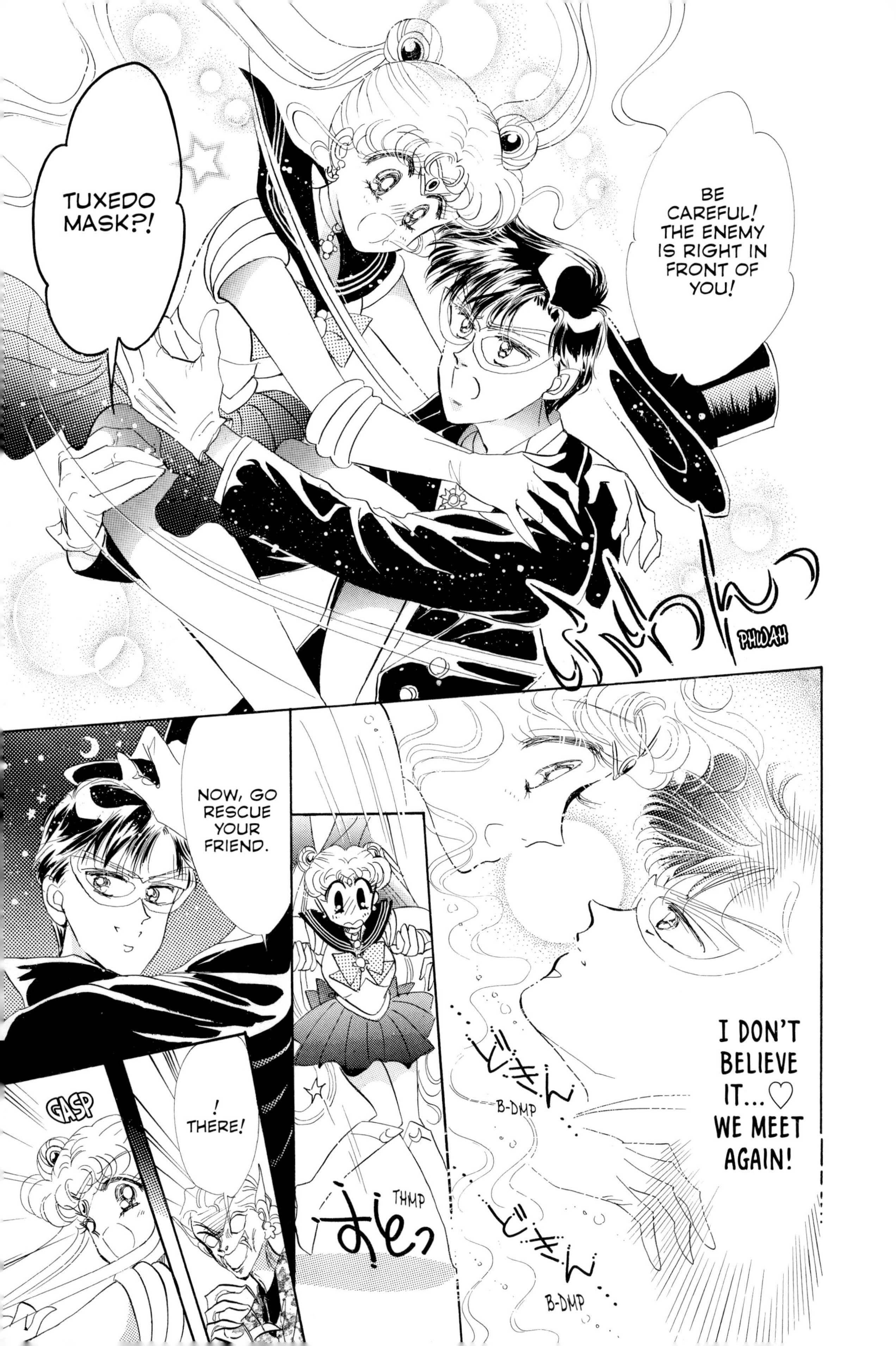
BE CAREFUL! THE ENEMY IS RIGHT IN FRONT OF YOU!
TUXEDO MASK?!
PHWAH
I DON'T BELIEVE IT...♡ WE MEET AGAIN!
どきん
B-DMP
どきん
B-DMP
すとっ
THMP
NOW, GO RESCUE YOUR FRIEND.
! THERE!
GASP

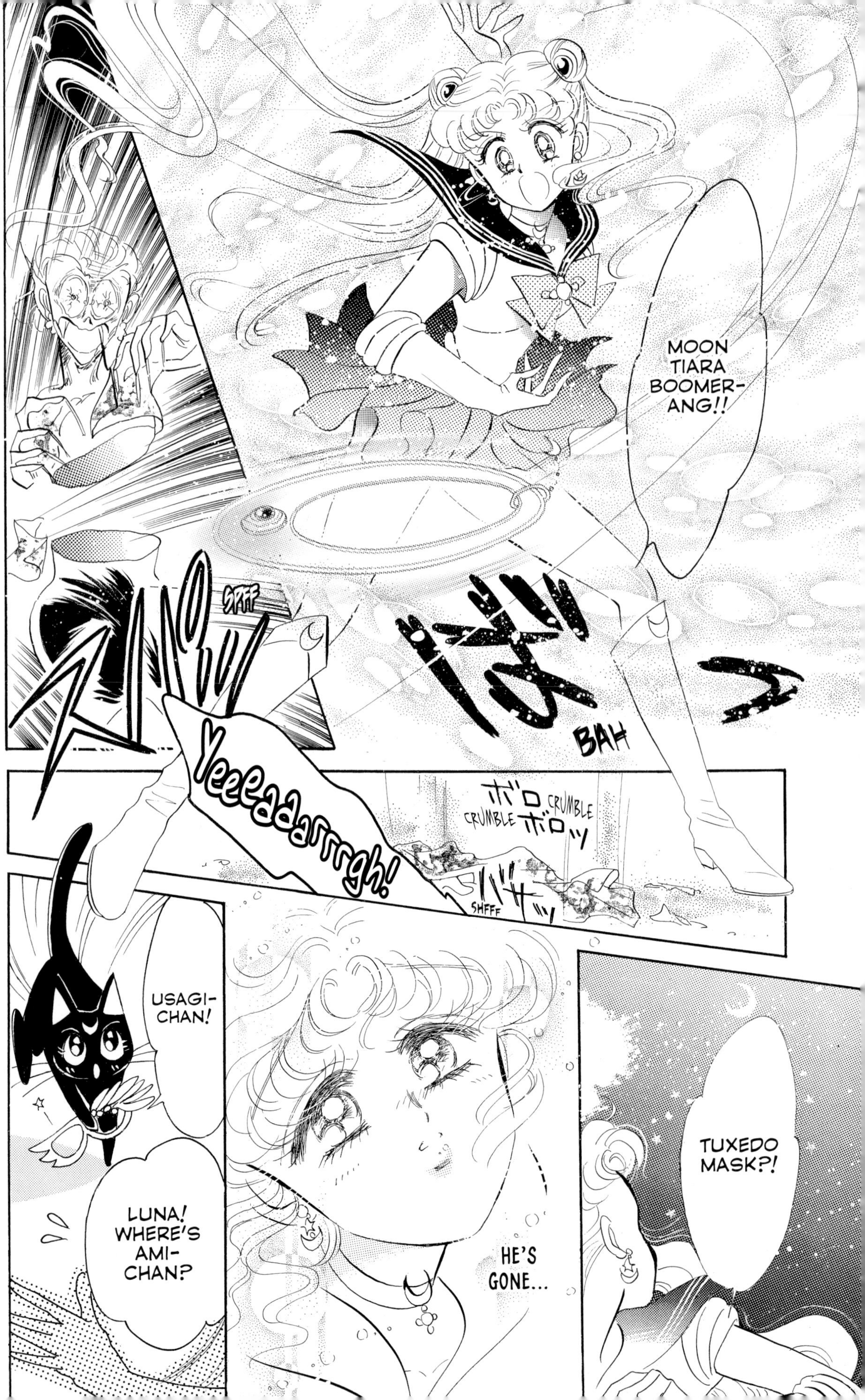
MOON TIARA BOOMER-ANG!!
BAH
SPFF
Yeeeaaarrrgh!
ボロ CRUMBLE
CRUMBLE ボロッ
バサッ
SHFFF
TUXEDO MASK?!
HE'S GONE...
USAGI-CHAN!
LUNA! WHERE'S AMI-CHAN?

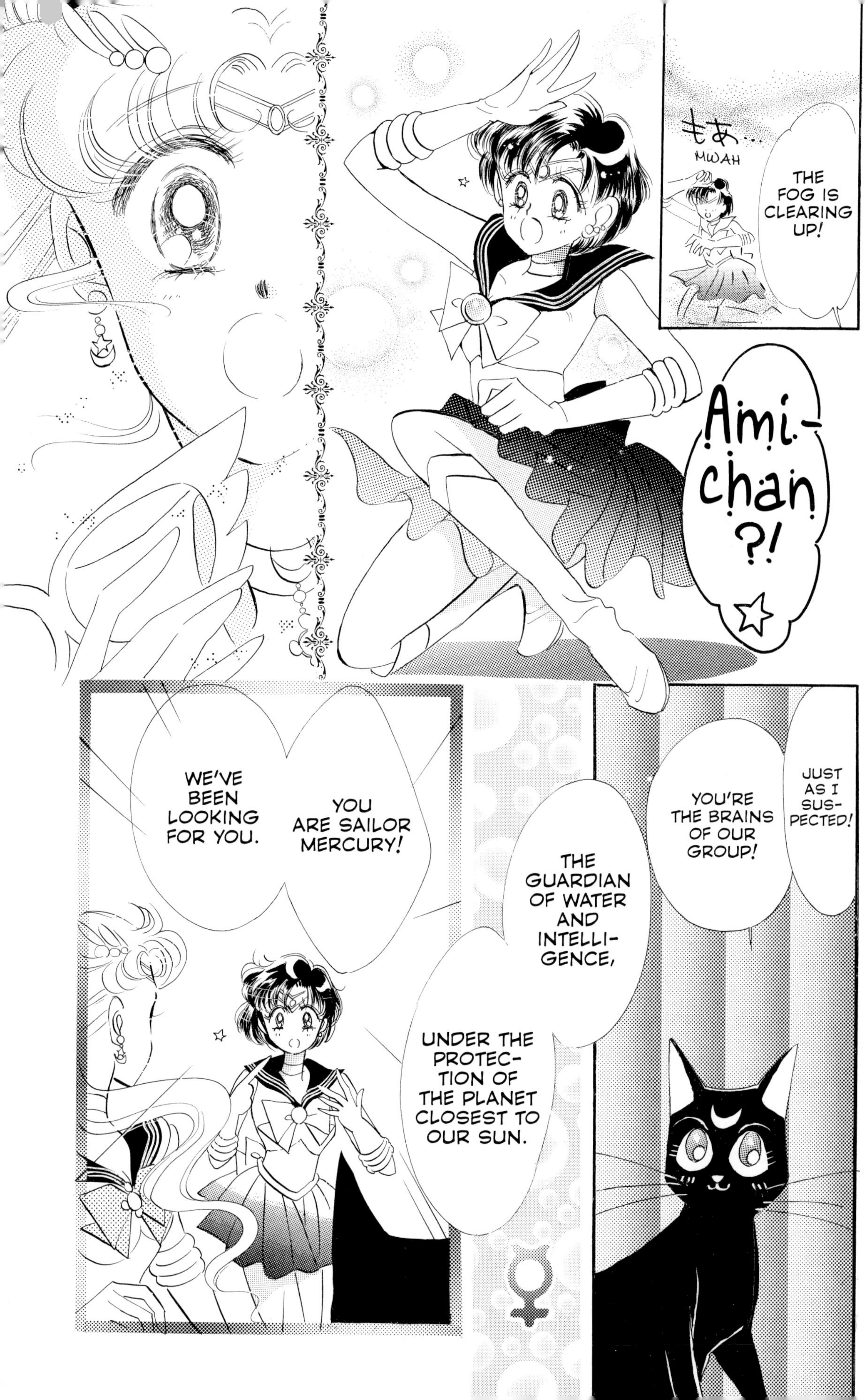
もあ…
MWAH
THE FOG IS CLEARING UP!
Ami-chan?!
JUST AS I SUS-PECTED!
YOU'RE THE BRAINS OF OUR GROUP!
THE GUARDIAN OF WATER AND INTELLI-GENCE,
UNDER THE PROTEC-TION OF THE PLANET CLOSEST TO OUR SUN.
YOU ARE SAILOR MERCURY!
WE'VE BEEN LOOKING FOR YOU.

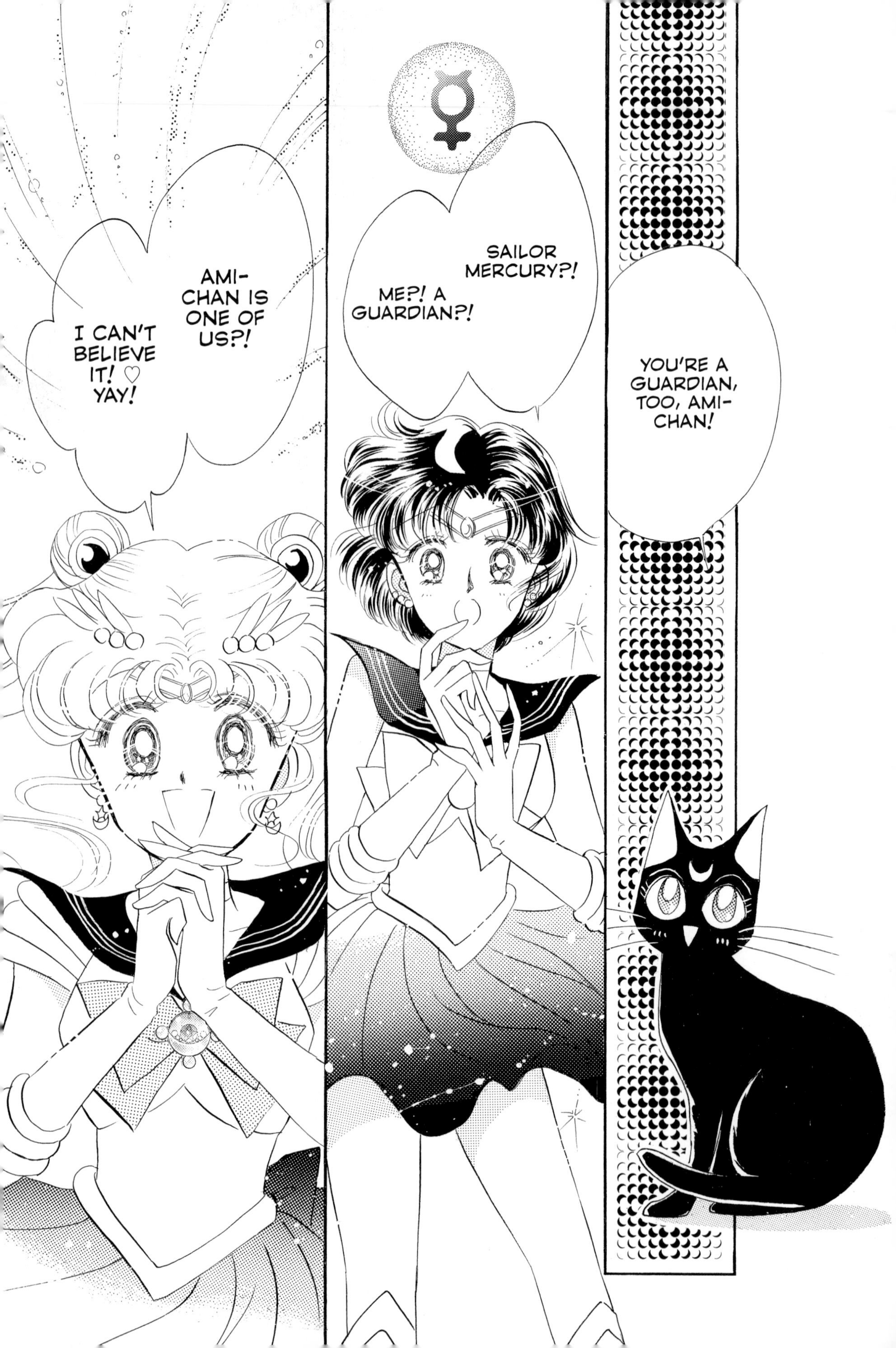
YOU'RE A GUARDIAN, TOO, AMI-CHAN!
SAILOR MERCURY?!
ME?! A GUARDIAN?!
AMI-CHAN IS ONE OF US?!
I CAN'T BELIEVE IT! ♡ YAY!

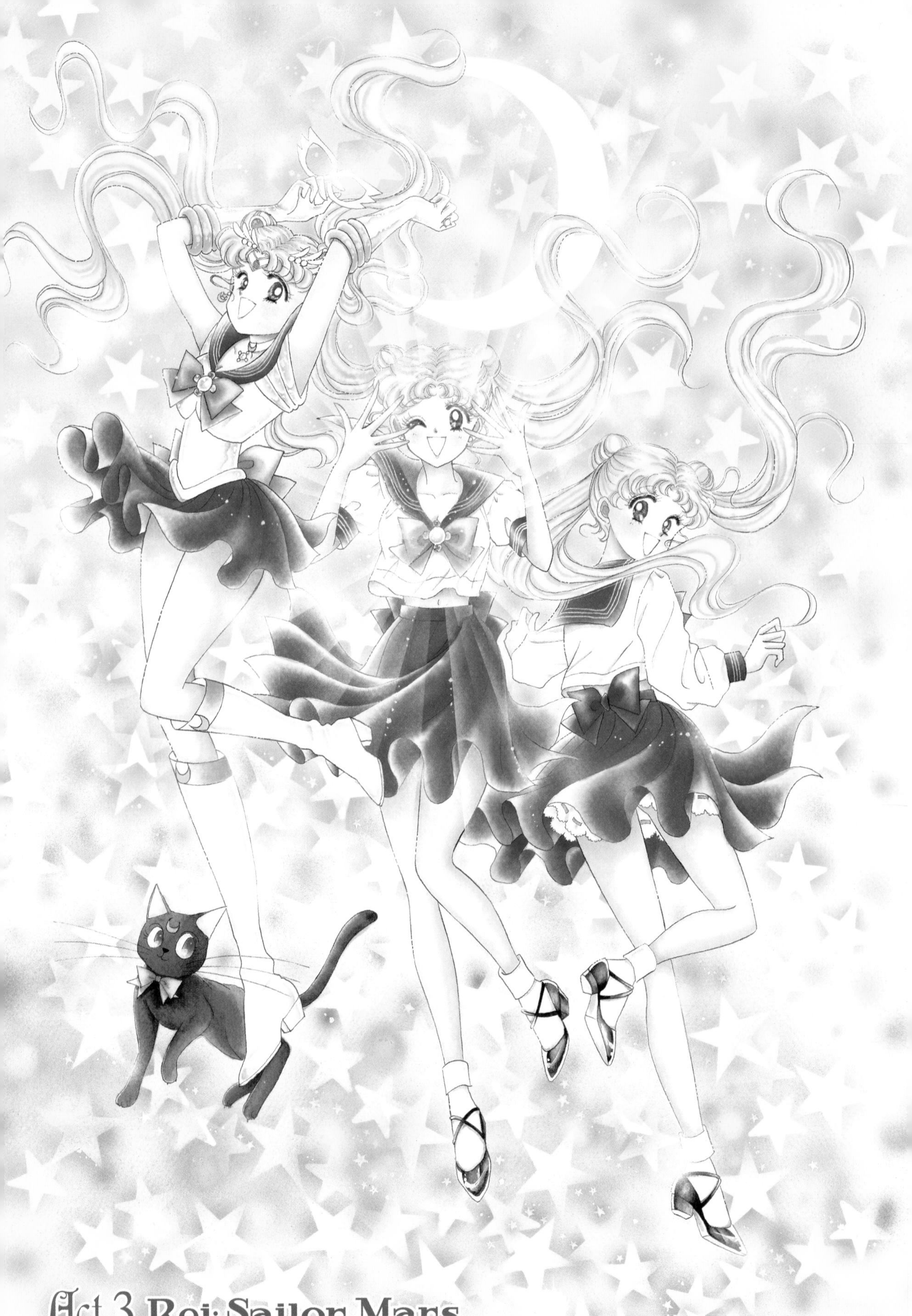

Act.3 Rei: Sailor Mars

Pretty Guardian
Sailor Moon

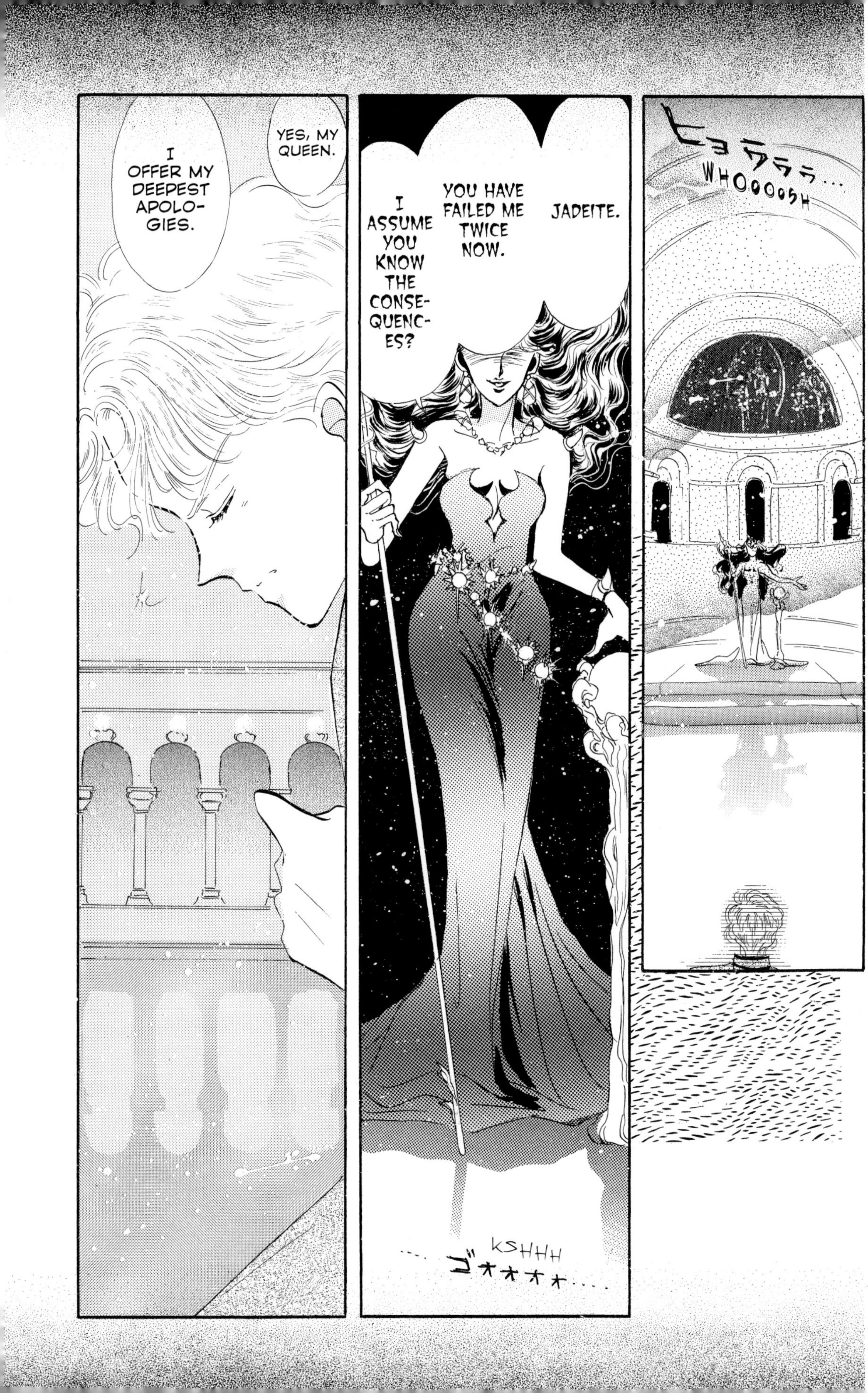
ヒョウララ…
WHOOOOOSH
JADEITE.
YOU HAVE FAILED ME TWICE NOW.
I ASSUME YOU KNOW THE CONSE-QUENC-ES?
KSHHH
…ゴォォォォ….
YES, MY QUEEN.
I OFFER MY DEEPEST APOLO-GIES.

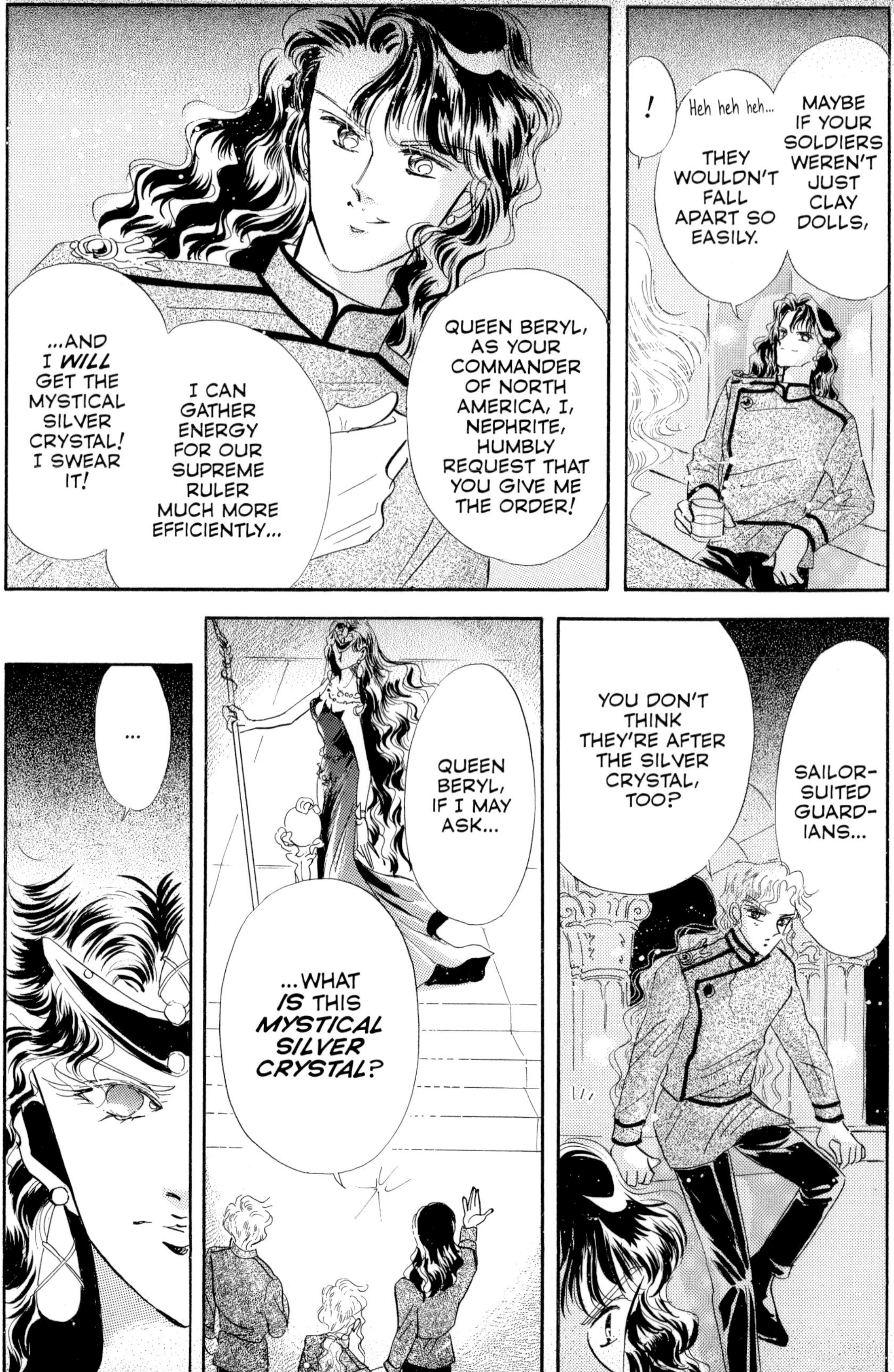
MAYBE IF YOUR SOLDIERS WEREN'T JUST CLAY DOLLS,
Heh heh heh... THEY WOULDN'T FALL APART SO EASILY.
!
QUEEN BERYL, AS YOUR COMMANDER OF NORTH AMERICA, I, NEPHRITE, HUMBLY REQUEST THAT YOU GIVE ME THE ORDER!
I CAN GATHER ENERGY FOR OUR SUPREME RULER MUCH MORE EFFICIENTLY...
...AND I *WILL* GET THE MYSTICAL SILVER CRYSTAL! I SWEAR IT!
SAILOR-SUITED GUARDIANS...
YOU DON'T THINK THEY'RE AFTER THE SILVER CRYSTAL, TOO?
QUEEN BERYL, IF I MAY ASK...
...WHAT *IS* THIS *MYSTICAL SILVER CRYSTAL*?
...

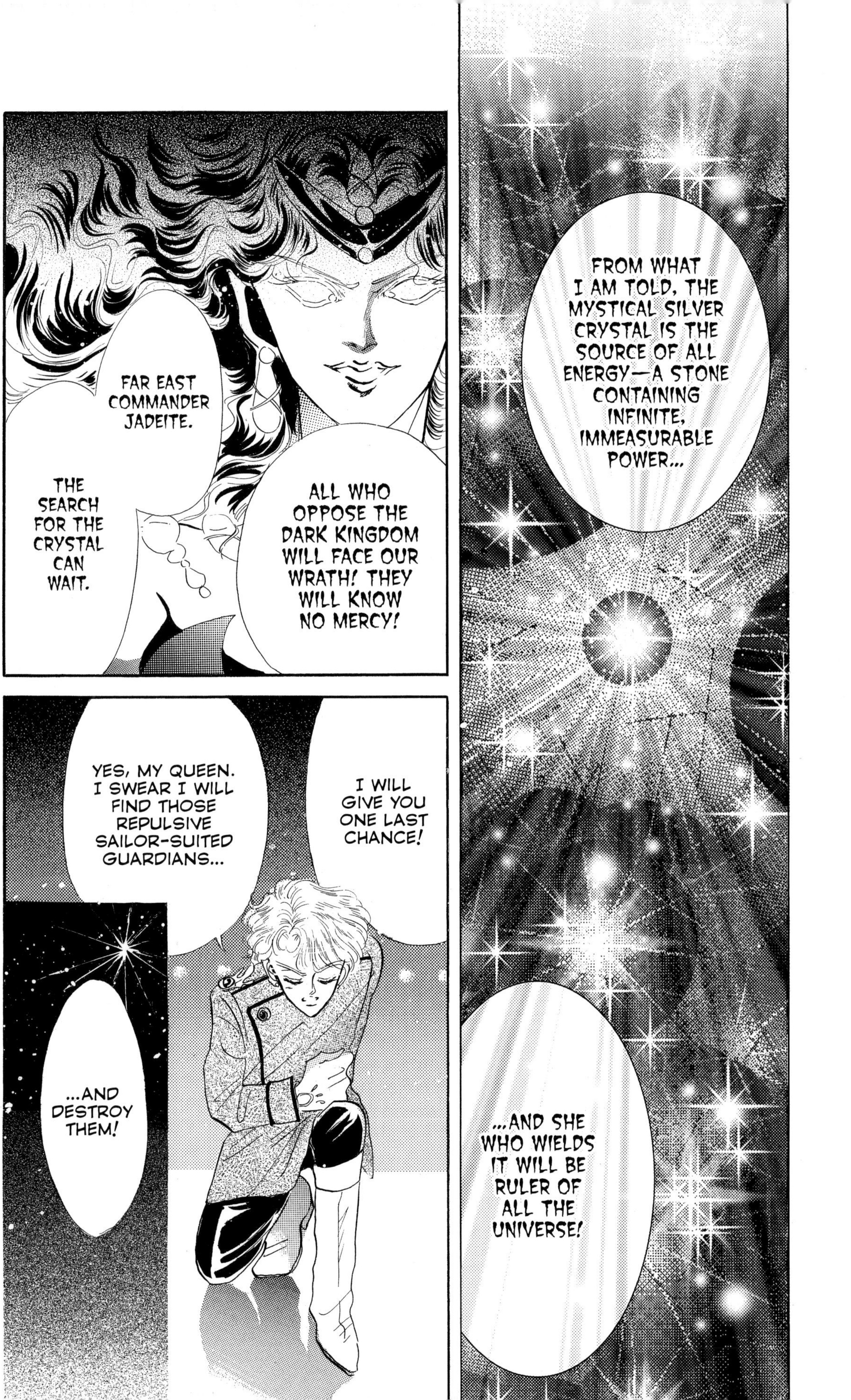
FROM WHAT I AM TOLD, THE MYSTICAL SILVER CRYSTAL IS THE SOURCE OF ALL ENERGY—A STONE CONTAINING INFINITE, IMMEASURABLE POWER...
...AND SHE WHO WIELDS IT WILL BE RULER OF ALL THE UNIVERSE!
FAR EAST COMMANDER JADEITE.
THE SEARCH FOR THE CRYSTAL CAN WAIT.
ALL WHO OPPOSE THE DARK KINGDOM WILL FACE OUR WRATH! THEY WILL KNOW NO MERCY!
I WILL GIVE YOU ONE LAST CHANCE!
YES, MY QUEEN. I SWEAR I WILL FIND THOSE REPULSIVE SAILOR-SUITED GUARDIANS...
...AND DESTROY THEM!

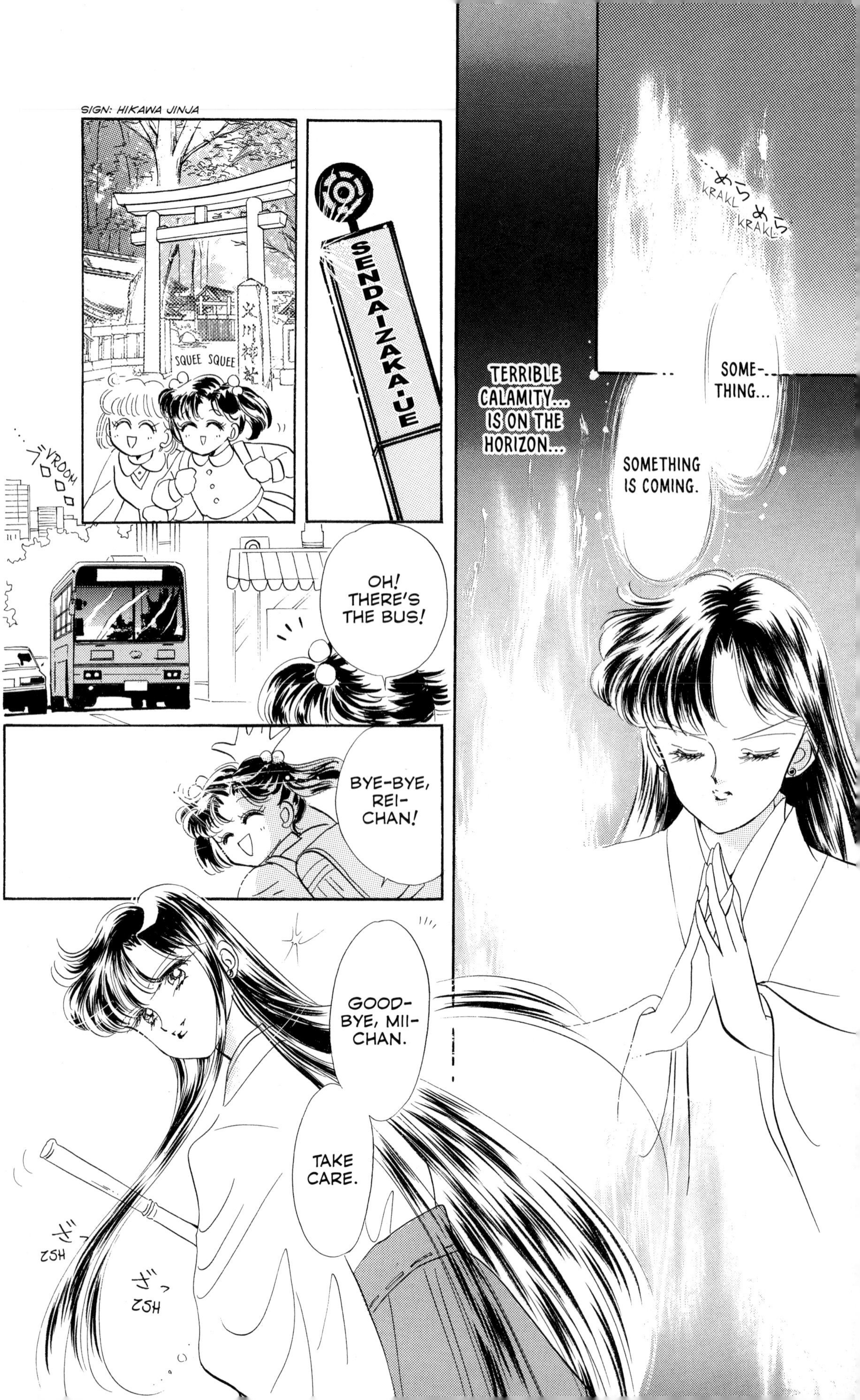

...めら めら
KRAKL KRAKL
SOME-THING...
SOMETHING IS COMING.
TERRIBLE CALAMITY... IS ON THE HORIZON...
SIGN: HIKAWA JINJA
SENDAIZAKA-UE
SQUEE SQUEE
...ブロロロ VROOM
OH! THERE'S THE BUS!
BYE-BYE, REI-CHAN!
GOOD-BYE, MII-CHAN.
TAKE CARE.
ざっ ZSH
ざっ ZSH

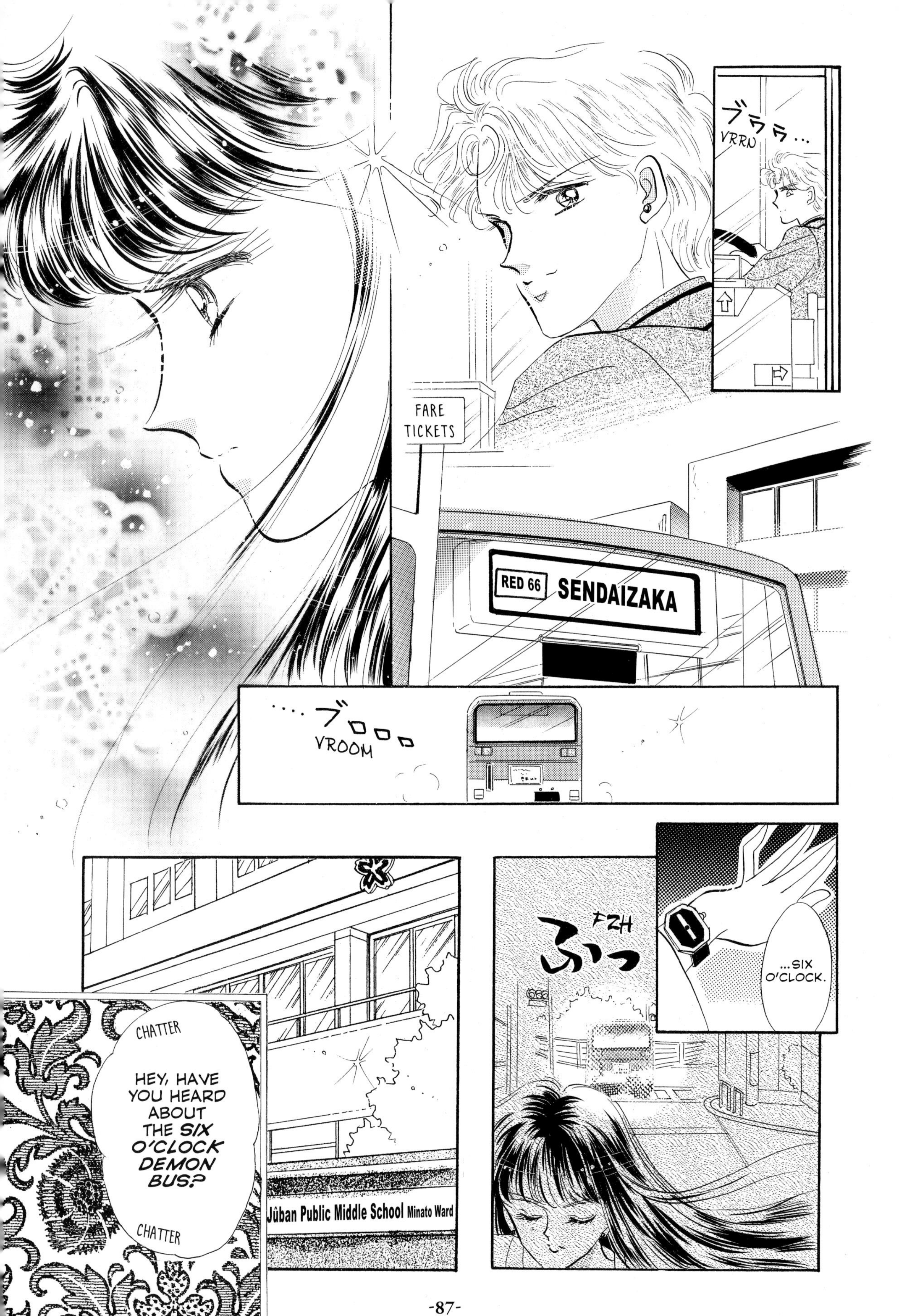

ブララ…
VRRN
FARE TICKETS
RED 66
SENDAIZAKA
…ブロロロ
VROOM
...SIX O'CLOCK.
FZH
ふっ
Jûban Public Middle School Minato Ward
CHATTER
HEY, HAVE YOU HEARD ABOUT THE SIX O'CLOCK DEMON BUS?
CHATTER

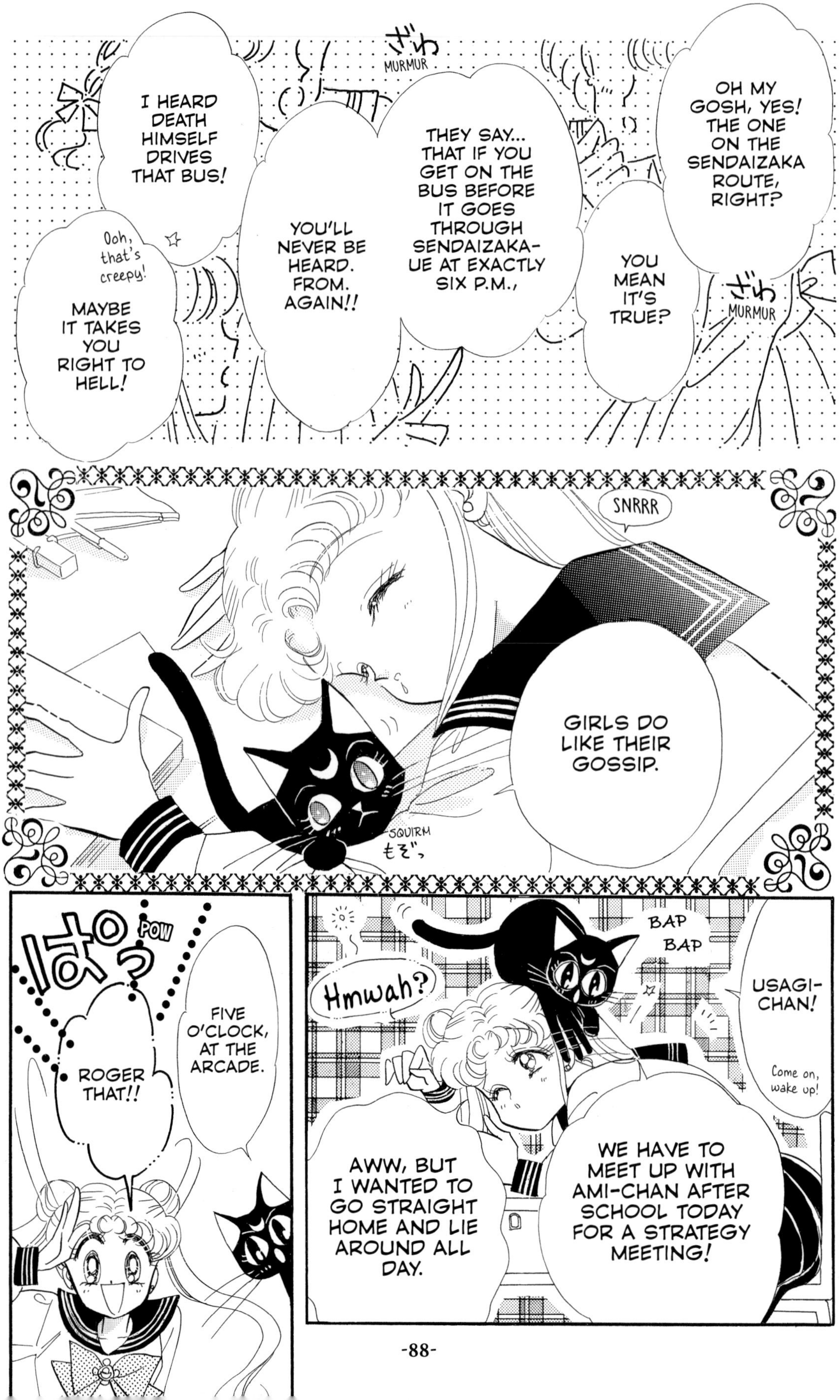
ざわ
MURMUR
OH MY GOSH, YES! THE ONE ON THE SENDAIZAKA ROUTE, RIGHT?
ざわ
MURMUR
YOU MEAN IT'S TRUE?
THEY SAY... THAT IF YOU GET ON THE BUS BEFORE IT GOES THROUGH SENDAIZAKA-UE AT EXACTLY SIX P.M.,
YOU'LL NEVER BE HEARD. FROM. AGAIN!!
I HEARD DEATH HIMSELF DRIVES THAT BUS!
Ooh, that's creepy!
MAYBE IT TAKES YOU RIGHT TO HELL!
SNRRR
GIRLS DO LIKE THEIR GOSSIP.
SQUIRM
もぞっ
USAGI-CHAN!
Come on, wake up!
BAP
BAP
Hmwah?
WE HAVE TO MEET UP WITH AMI-CHAN AFTER SCHOOL TODAY FOR A STRATEGY MEETING!
AWW, BUT I WANTED TO GO STRAIGHT HOME AND LIE AROUND ALL DAY.
はっ
POW
FIVE O'CLOCK, AT THE ARCADE.
ROGER THAT!!

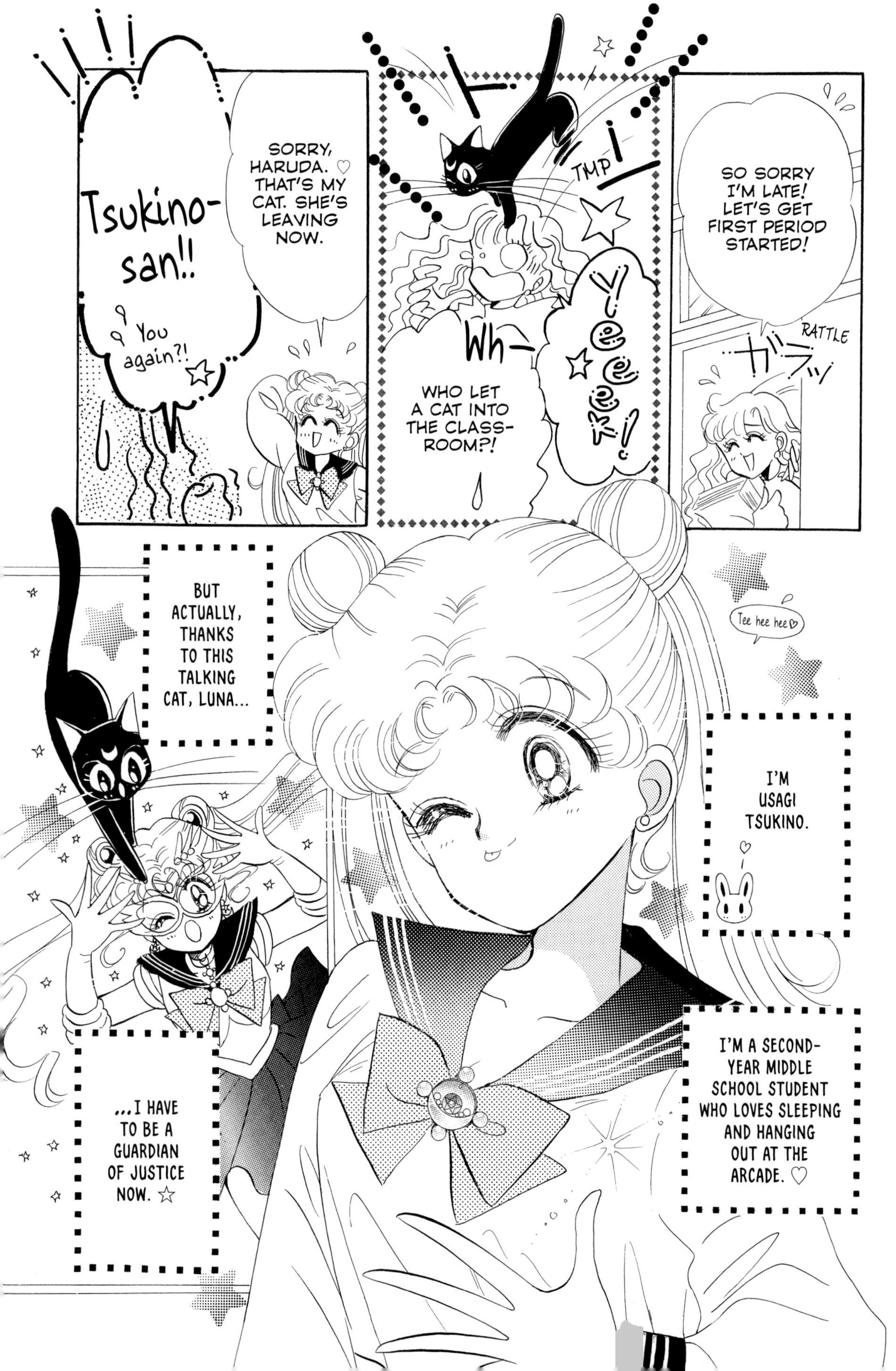
SO SORRY I'M LATE! LET'S GET FIRST PERIOD STARTED!
RATTLE
ガラッ
TMP
Yeeeek!
Wh—
WHO LET A CAT INTO THE CLASSROOM?!
Tsukino-san!!
You again?!
SORRY, HARUDA. ♡ THAT'S MY CAT. SHE'S LEAVING NOW.
Tee hee hee♡
I'M USAGI TSUKINO.
I'M A SECOND-YEAR MIDDLE SCHOOL STUDENT WHO LOVES SLEEPING AND HANGING OUT AT THE ARCADE. ♡
BUT ACTUALLY, THANKS TO THIS TALKING CAT, LUNA...
...I HAVE TO BE A GUARDIAN OF JUSTICE NOW. ☆

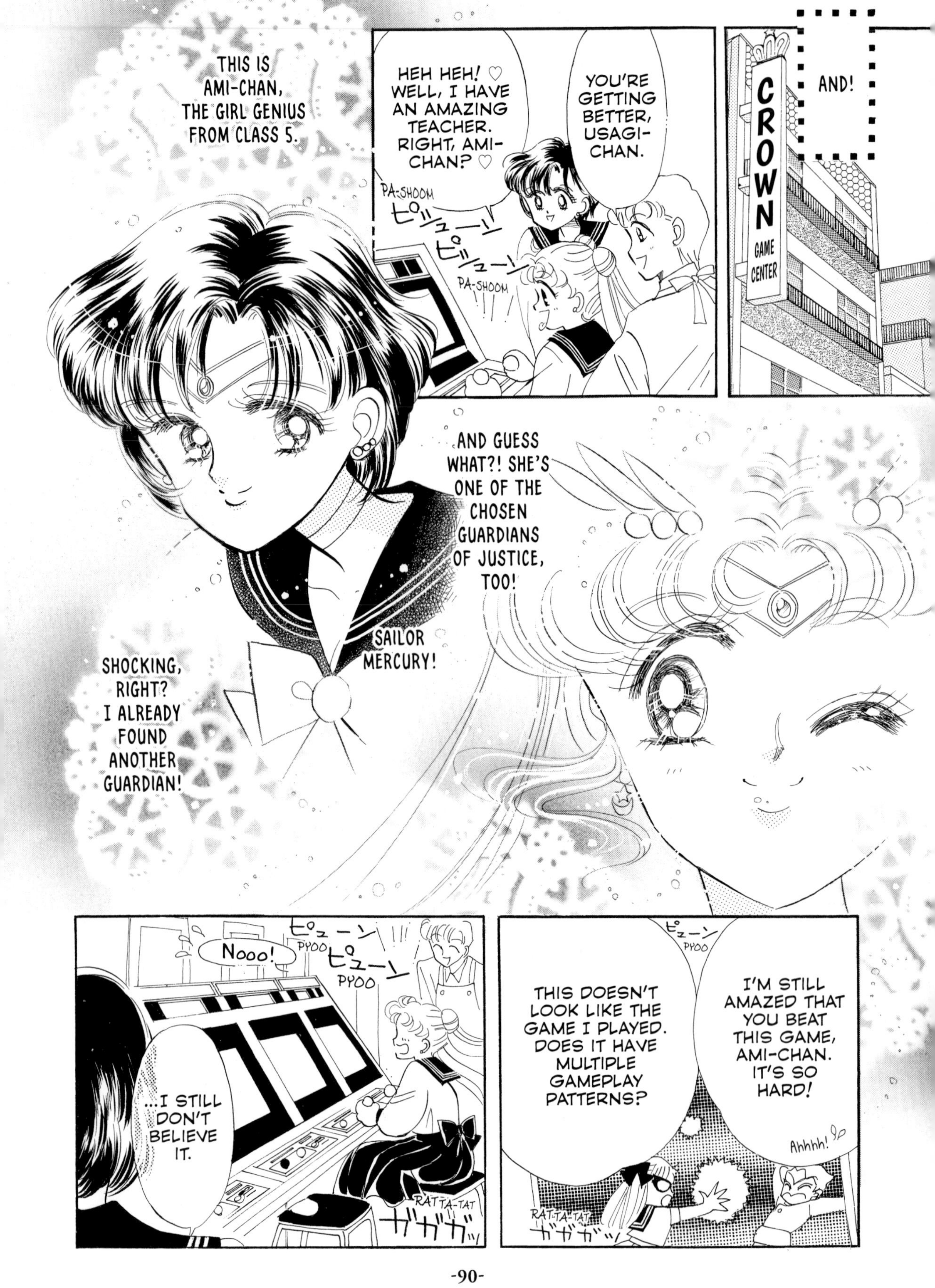
AND!
CROWN
GAME CENTER
YOU'RE GETTING BETTER, USAGI-CHAN.
HEH HEH! ♡ WELL, I HAVE AN AMAZING TEACHER. RIGHT, AMI-CHAN? ♡
PA-SHOOM
ピシューン
ピシューン
PA-SHOOM
THIS IS AMI-CHAN, THE GIRL GENIUS FROM CLASS 5.
AND GUESS WHAT?! SHE'S ONE OF THE CHOSEN GUARDIANS OF JUSTICE, TOO!
SAILOR MERCURY!
SHOCKING, RIGHT? I ALREADY FOUND ANOTHER GUARDIAN!
ピューン
PYOO
I'M STILL AMAZED THAT YOU BEAT THIS GAME, AMI-CHAN. IT'S SO HARD!
THIS DOESN'T LOOK LIKE THE GAME I PLAYED. DOES IT HAVE MULTIPLE GAMEPLAY PATTERNS?
Ahhhh!
RAT-TA-TAT
ガガガッ
ピューン
PYOO
ピューン
PYOO
Nooo!
...I STILL DON'T BELIEVE IT.
RAT-TA-TAT
ガガガッ

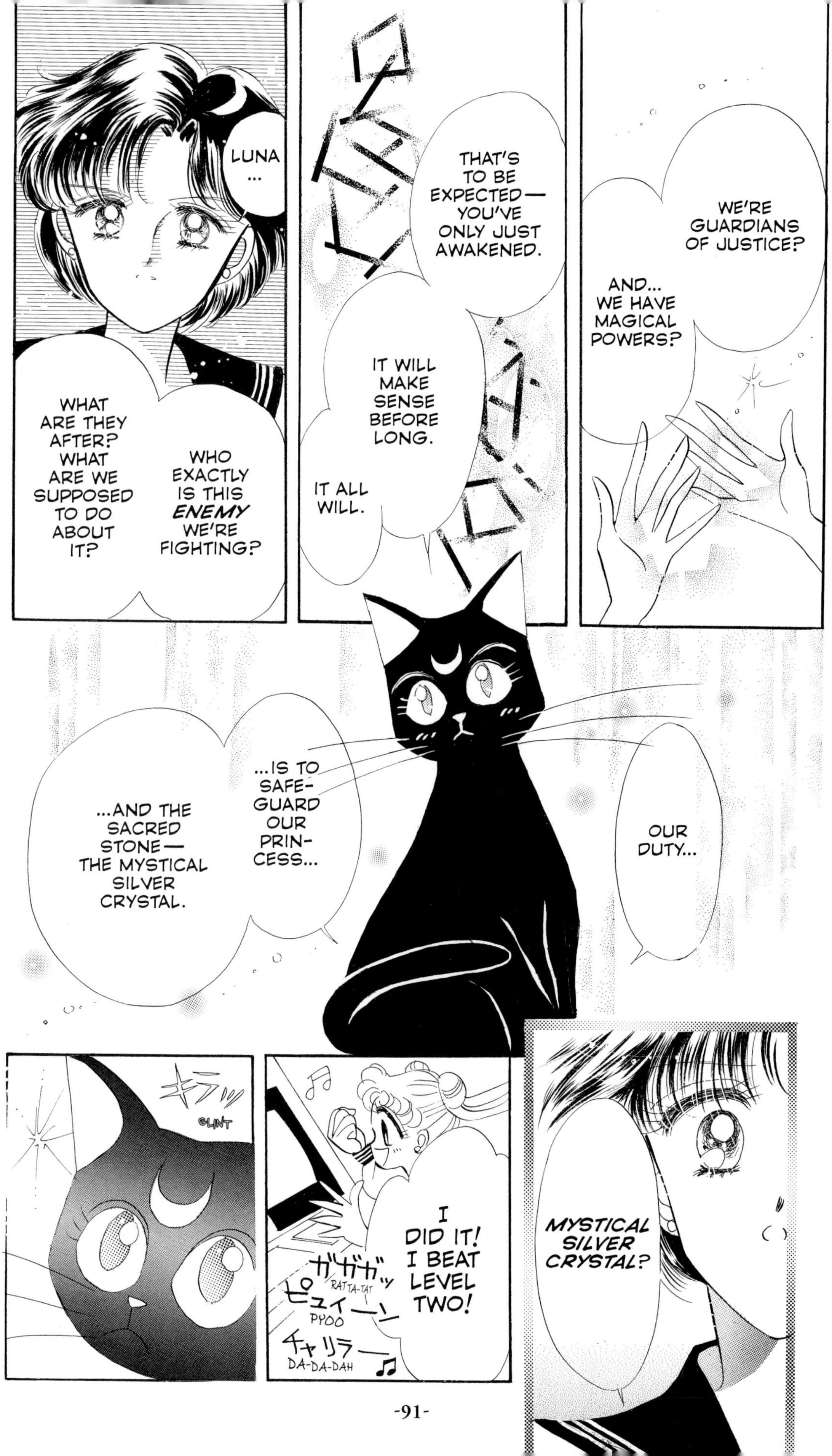
WE'RE GUARDIANS OF JUSTICE?
AND... WE HAVE MAGICAL POWERS?
THAT'S TO BE EXPECTED—YOU'VE ONLY JUST AWAKENED.
IT WILL MAKE SENSE BEFORE LONG.
IT ALL WILL.
LUNA...
WHO EXACTLY IS THIS *ENEMY* WE'RE FIGHTING?
WHAT ARE THEY AFTER? WHAT ARE WE SUPPOSED TO DO ABOUT IT?
OUR DUTY...
...IS TO SAFE-GUARD OUR PRIN-CESS...
...AND THE SACRED STONE—THE MYSTICAL SILVER CRYSTAL.
MYSTICAL SILVER CRYSTAL?
I DID IT! I BEAT LEVEL TWO!
ガガガッ
RATTA-TAT
ピュイーン
PYOO
チャリラー
DA-DA-DAH
キラッ
GLINT

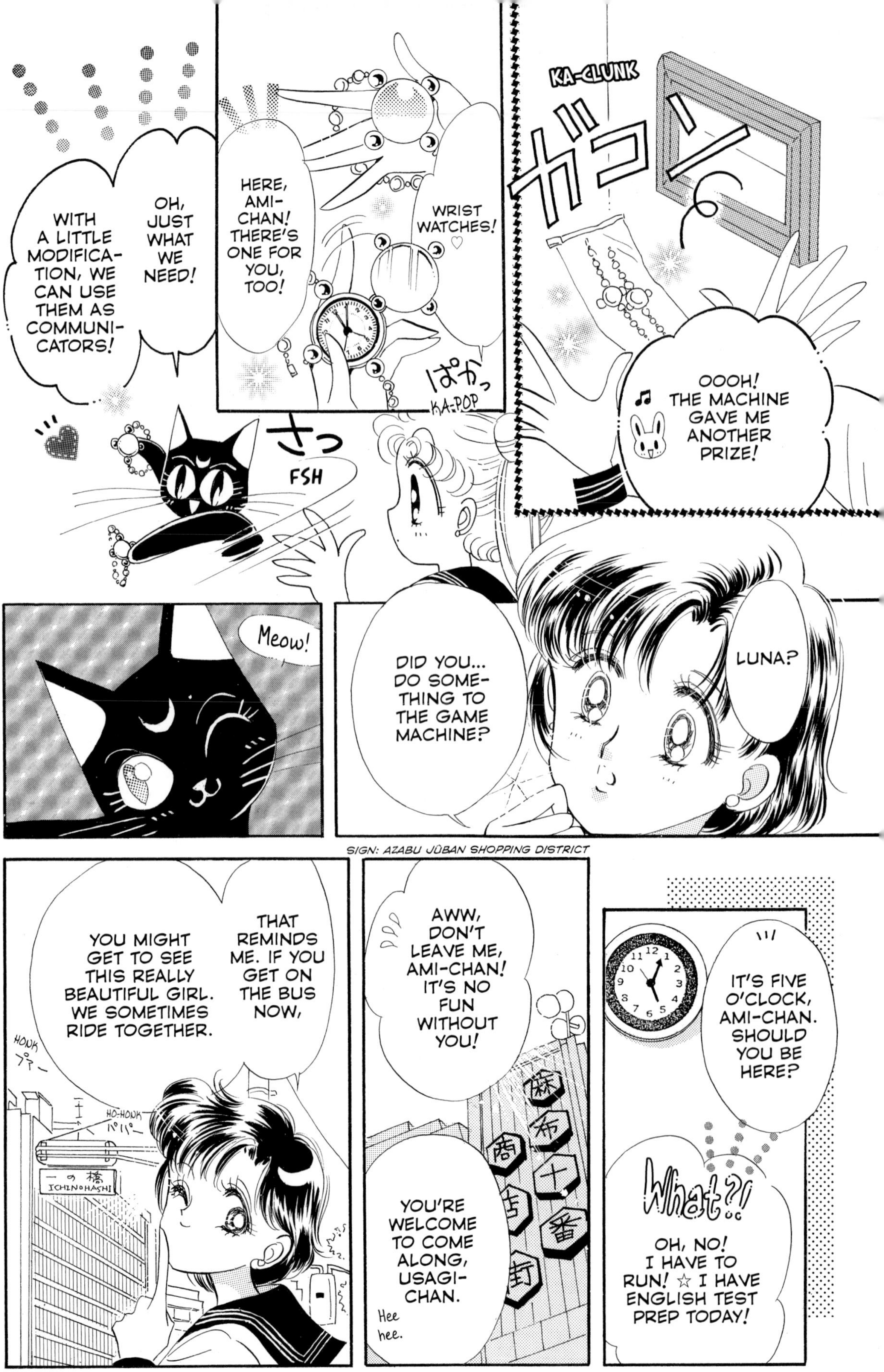
KA-CLUNK
OOOH! THE MACHINE GAVE ME ANOTHER PRIZE!
WRIST WATCHES!
HERE, AMI-CHAN! THERE'S ONE FOR YOU, TOO!
KA-POP
OH, JUST WHAT WE NEED!
WITH A LITTLE MODIFICATION, WE CAN USE THEM AS COMMUNICATORS!
FSH
LUNA?
DID YOU... DO SOMETHING TO THE GAME MACHINE?
Meow!
SIGN: AZABU JÛBAN SHOPPING DISTRICT
IT'S FIVE O'CLOCK, AMI-CHAN. SHOULD YOU BE HERE?
What?!
OH, NO! I HAVE TO RUN! ☆ I HAVE ENGLISH TEST PREP TODAY!
AWW, DON'T LEAVE ME, AMI-CHAN! IT'S NO FUN WITHOUT YOU!
YOU'RE WELCOME TO COME ALONG, USAGI-CHAN.
Hee hee.
THAT REMINDS ME. IF YOU GET ON THE BUS NOW,
YOU MIGHT GET TO SEE THIS REALLY BEAUTIFUL GIRL. WE SOMETIMES RIDE TOGETHER.
HONK
HO-HONK
ICHINOHASHI

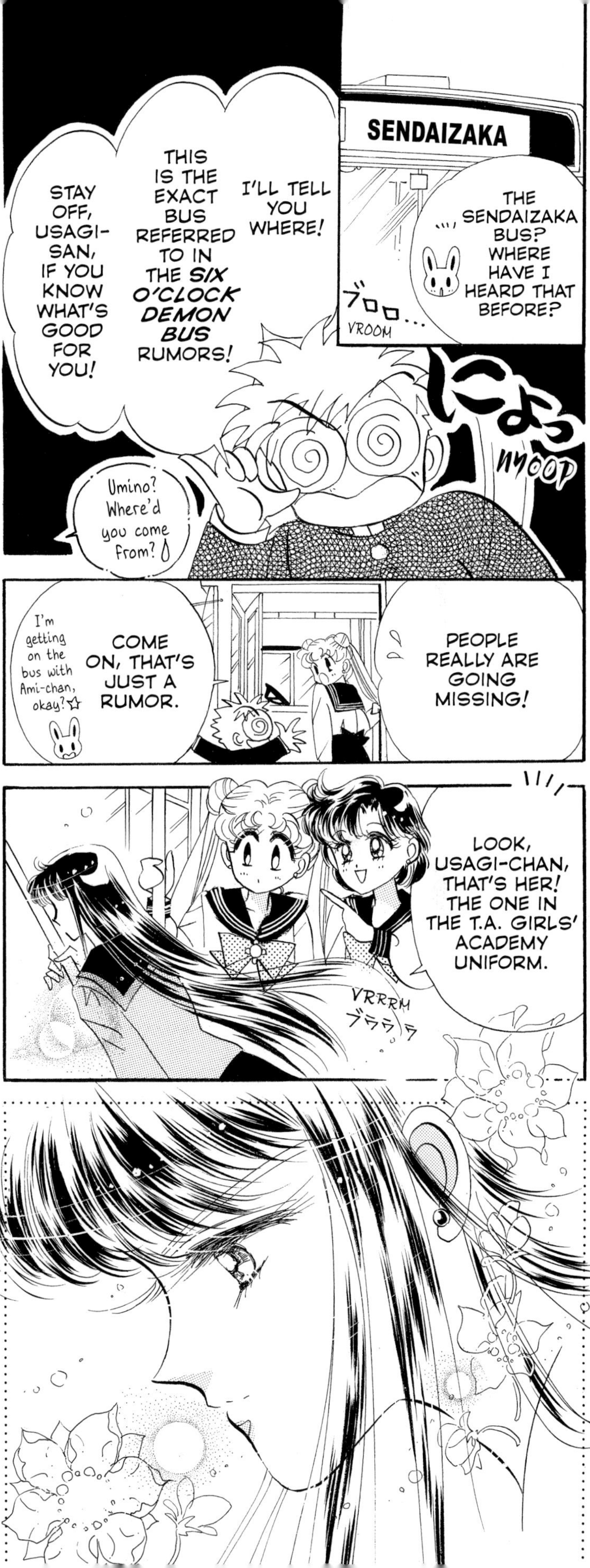
SENDAIZAKA
...THE SENDAIZAKA BUS? WHERE HAVE I HEARD THAT BEFORE?
ブロロ... VROOM
I'LL TELL YOU WHERE!
THIS IS THE EXACT BUS REFERRED TO IN THE SIX O'CLOCK DEMON BUS RUMORS!
STAY OFF, USAGI-SAN, IF YOU KNOW WHAT'S GOOD FOR YOU!
にょっ NNOOP
Umino? Where'd you come from?
PEOPLE REALLY ARE GOING MISSING!
COME ON, THAT'S JUST A RUMOR.
I'm getting on the bus with Ami-chan, okay?☆
LOOK, USAGI-CHAN, THAT'S HER! THE ONE IN THE T.A. GIRLS' ACADEMY UNIFORM.
VRRRM ブラララ
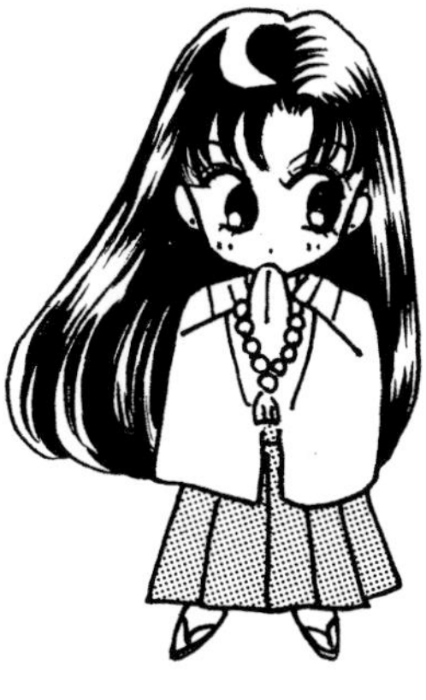

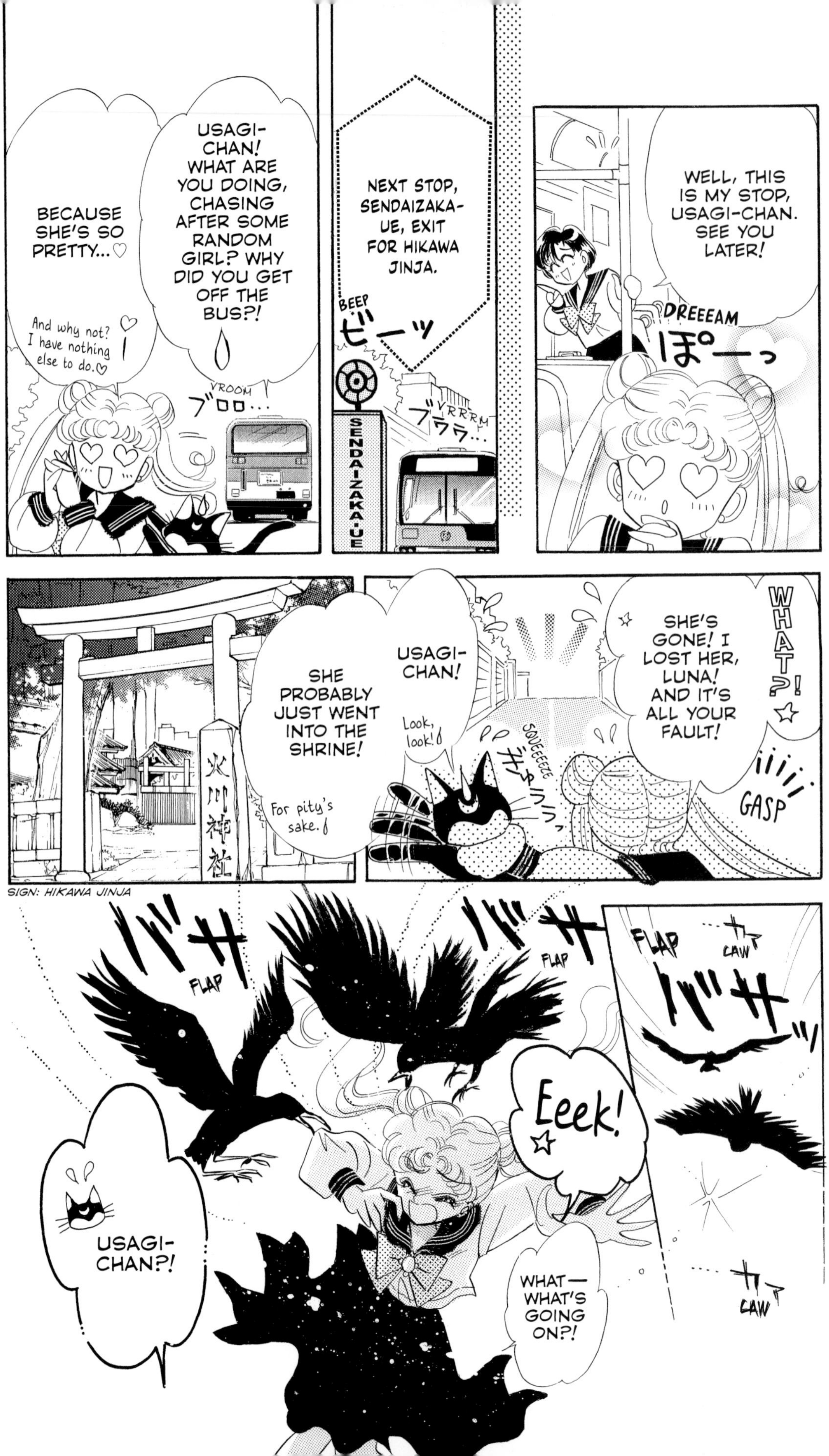
WELL, THIS IS MY STOP, USAGI-CHAN. SEE YOU LATER!
DREEEAM
ぽーっ
NEXT STOP, SENDAIZAKA-UE, EXIT FOR HIKAWA JINJA.
BEEP
ビーッ
SENDAIZAKA-UE
VRRRM
ブララ…
USAGI-CHAN! WHAT ARE YOU DOING, CHASING AFTER SOME RANDOM GIRL? WHY DID YOU GET OFF THE BUS?!
BECAUSE SHE'S SO PRETTY...♡
And why not? I have nothing else to do.♡
VROOM
ブロロ…
WHAT?!
SHE'S GONE! I LOST HER, LUNA! AND IT'S ALL YOUR FAULT!
GASP
SQUEEEEZE
ギュウウ
USAGI-CHAN!
Look, look!
SHE PROBABLY JUST WENT INTO THE SHRINE!
For pity's sake.
火川神社
SIGN: HIKAWA JINJA
FLAP
バサ
CAW
カァ
Eeek!
WHAT—WHAT'S GOING ON?!
CAW
カァ
バサ
FLAP
バサ
FLAP
USAGI-CHAN?!

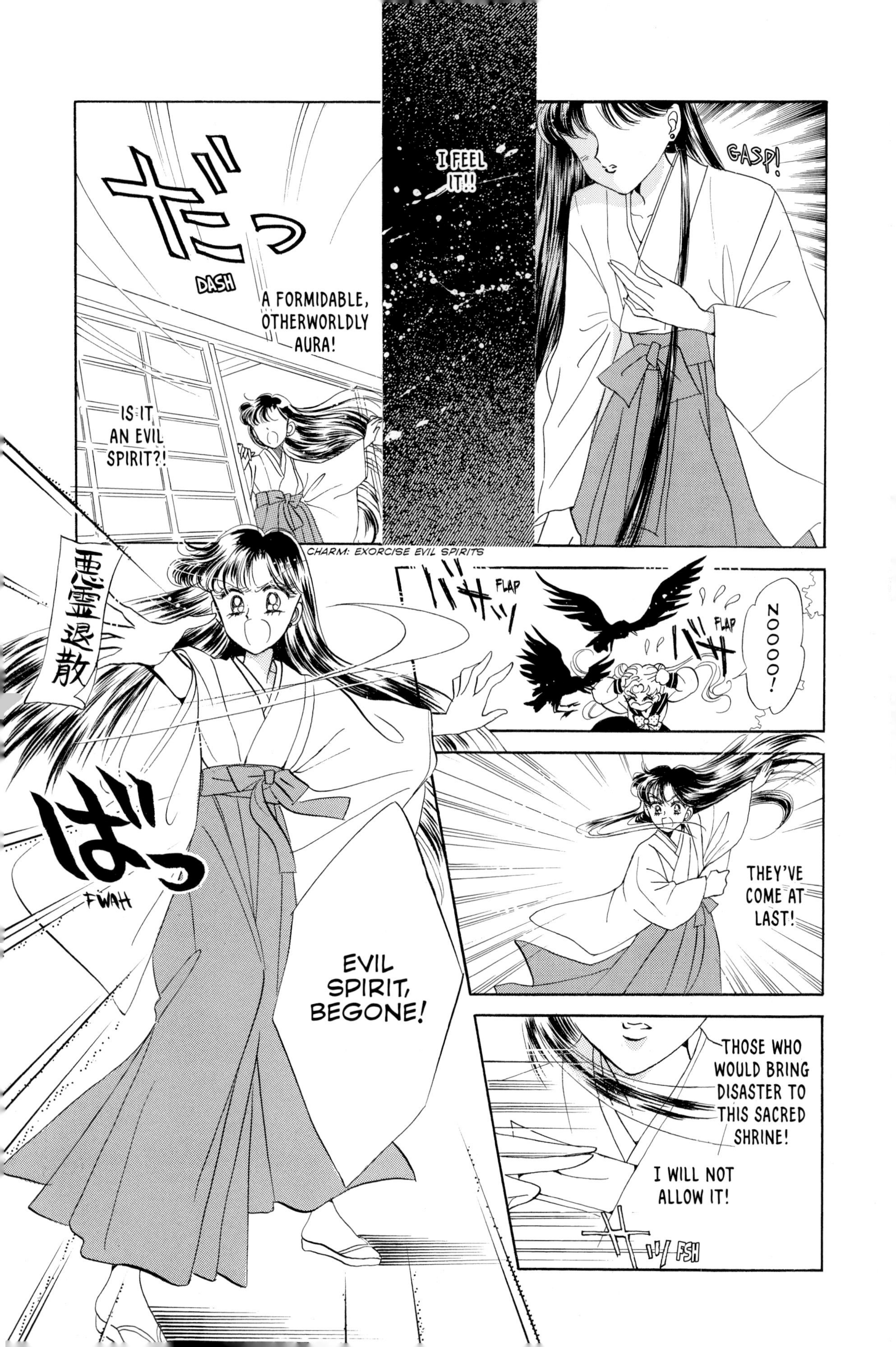
GASP!
I FEEL IT!!
だっ
DASH
A FORMIDABLE, OTHERWORLDLY AURA!
IS IT AN EVIL SPIRIT?!
バサッ
FLAP
バサ
FLAP
NOOOO!
THEY'VE COME AT LAST!
THOSE WHO WOULD BRING DISASTER TO THIS SACRED SHRINE!
I WILL NOT ALLOW IT!
サッ
FSH
悪霊退散
CHARM: EXORCISE EVIL SPIRITS
ばっ
FWAH
EVIL SPIRIT, BEGONE!

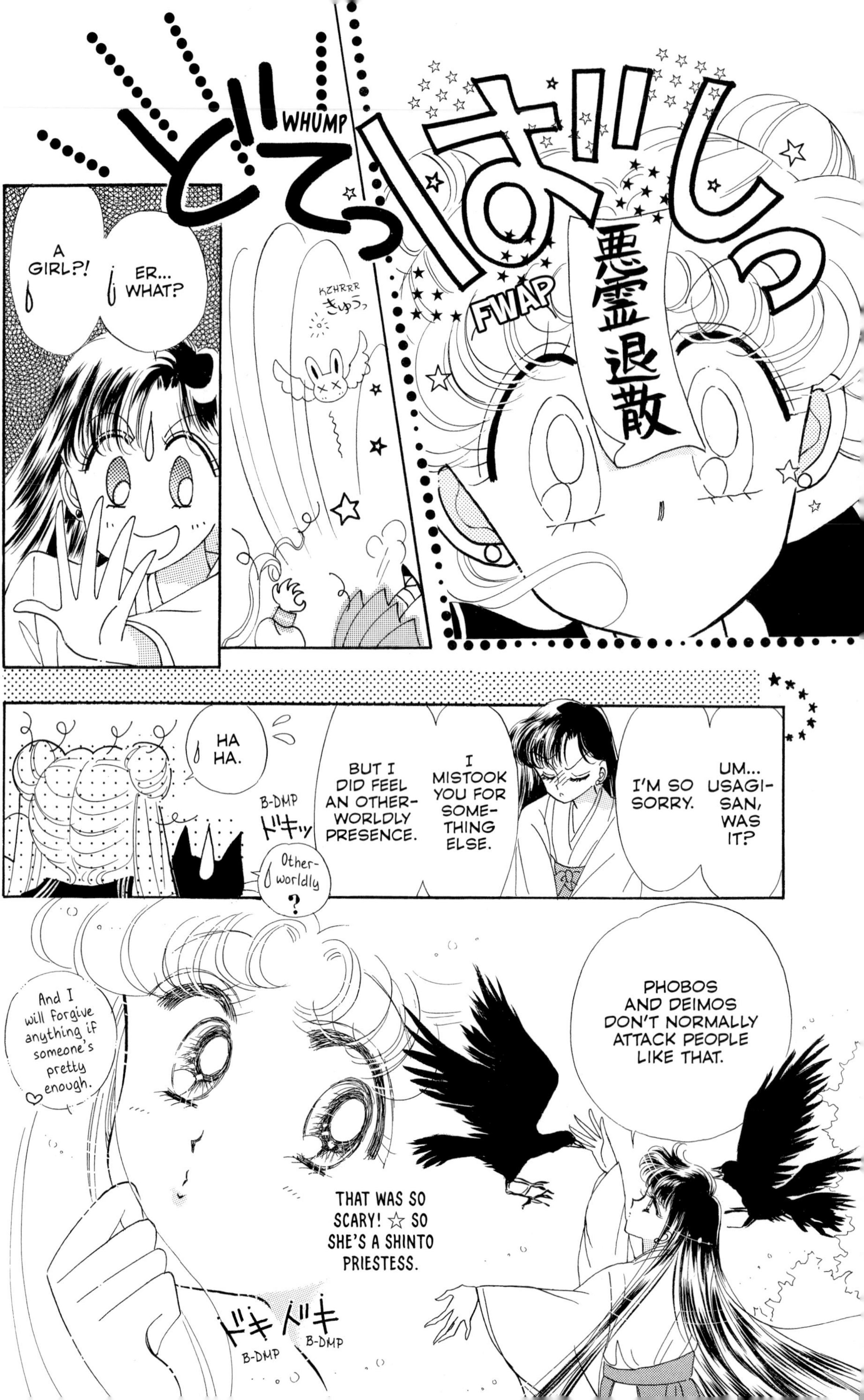
ばしっ
FWAP
悪霊退散
どてっ
WHUMP
KZHRRR
きゅうっ
ER... WHAT?
A GIRL?!
UM... USAGI-SAN, WAS IT?
I'M SO SORRY.
I MISTOOK YOU FOR SOMETHING ELSE.
BUT I DID FEEL AN OTHER-WORLDLY PRESENCE.
B-DMP
ドキッ
Other-worldly ?
HA HA.
PHOBOS AND DEIMOS DON'T NORMALLY ATTACK PEOPLE LIKE THAT.
THAT WAS SO SCARY! ☆ SO SHE'S A SHINTO PRIESTESS.
ドキドキ
B-DMP B-DMP
And I will forgive anything if someone's pretty enough. ♡

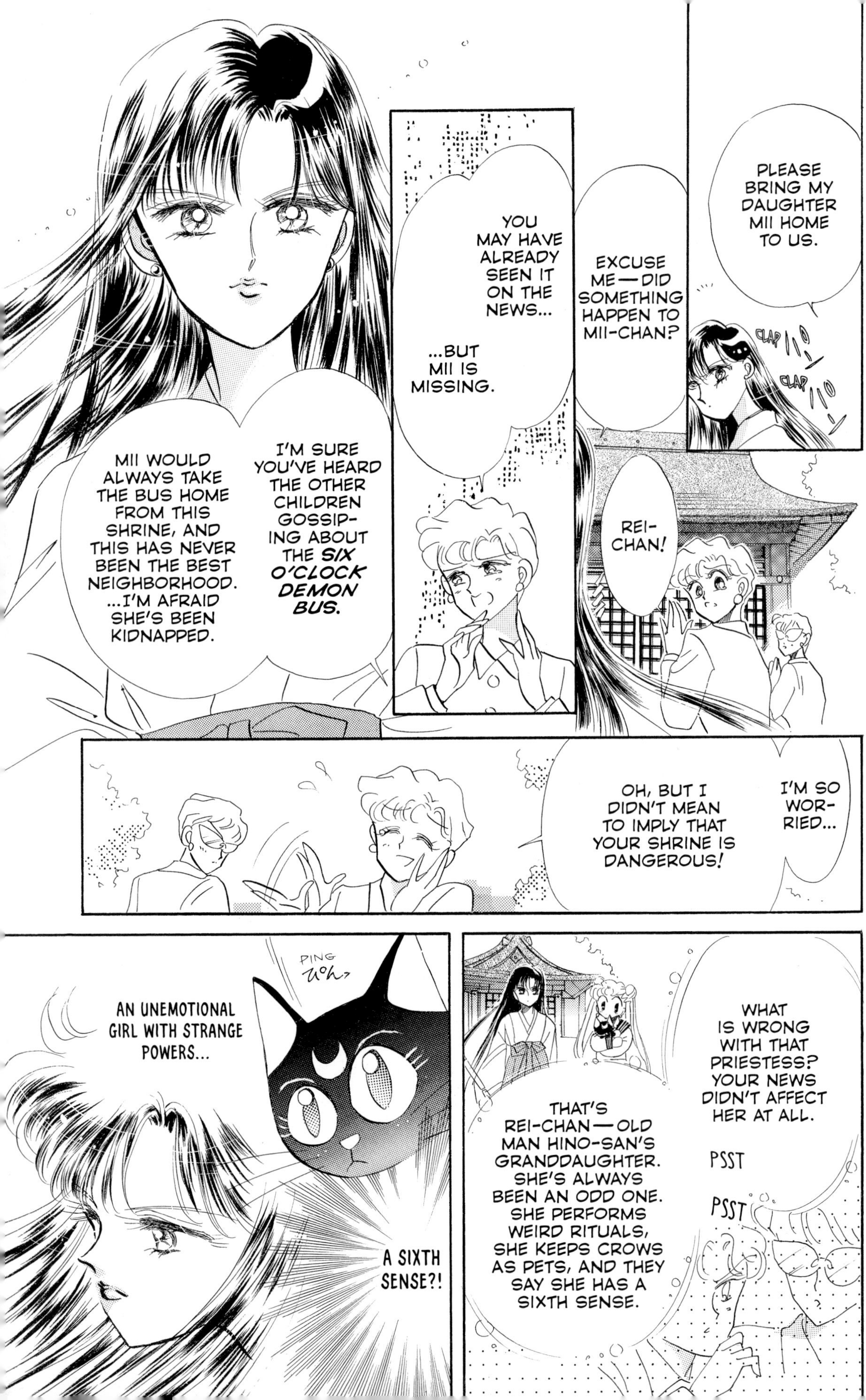
PLEASE BRING MY DAUGHTER MII HOME TO US.
CLAP
CLAP
REI-CHAN!
EXCUSE ME—DID SOMETHING HAPPEN TO MII-CHAN?
YOU MAY HAVE ALREADY SEEN IT ON THE NEWS...
...BUT MII IS MISSING.
I'M SURE YOU'VE HEARD THE OTHER CHILDREN GOSSIP-ING ABOUT THE SIX O'CLOCK DEMON BUS.
MII WOULD ALWAYS TAKE THE BUS HOME FROM THIS SHRINE, AND THIS HAS NEVER BEEN THE BEST NEIGHBORHOOD. ...I'M AFRAID SHE'S BEEN KIDNAPPED.
I'M SO WOR-RIED...
OH, BUT I DIDN'T MEAN TO IMPLY THAT YOUR SHRINE IS DANGEROUS!
WHAT IS WRONG WITH THAT PRIESTESS? YOUR NEWS DIDN'T AFFECT HER AT ALL.
PSST
PSST
THAT'S REI-CHAN—OLD MAN HINO-SAN'S GRANDDAUGHTER. SHE'S ALWAYS BEEN AN ODD ONE. SHE PERFORMS WEIRD RITUALS, SHE KEEPS CROWS AS PETS, AND THEY SAY SHE HAS A SIXTH SENSE.
PING
AN UNEMOTIONAL GIRL WITH STRANGE POWERS...
A SIXTH SENSE?!

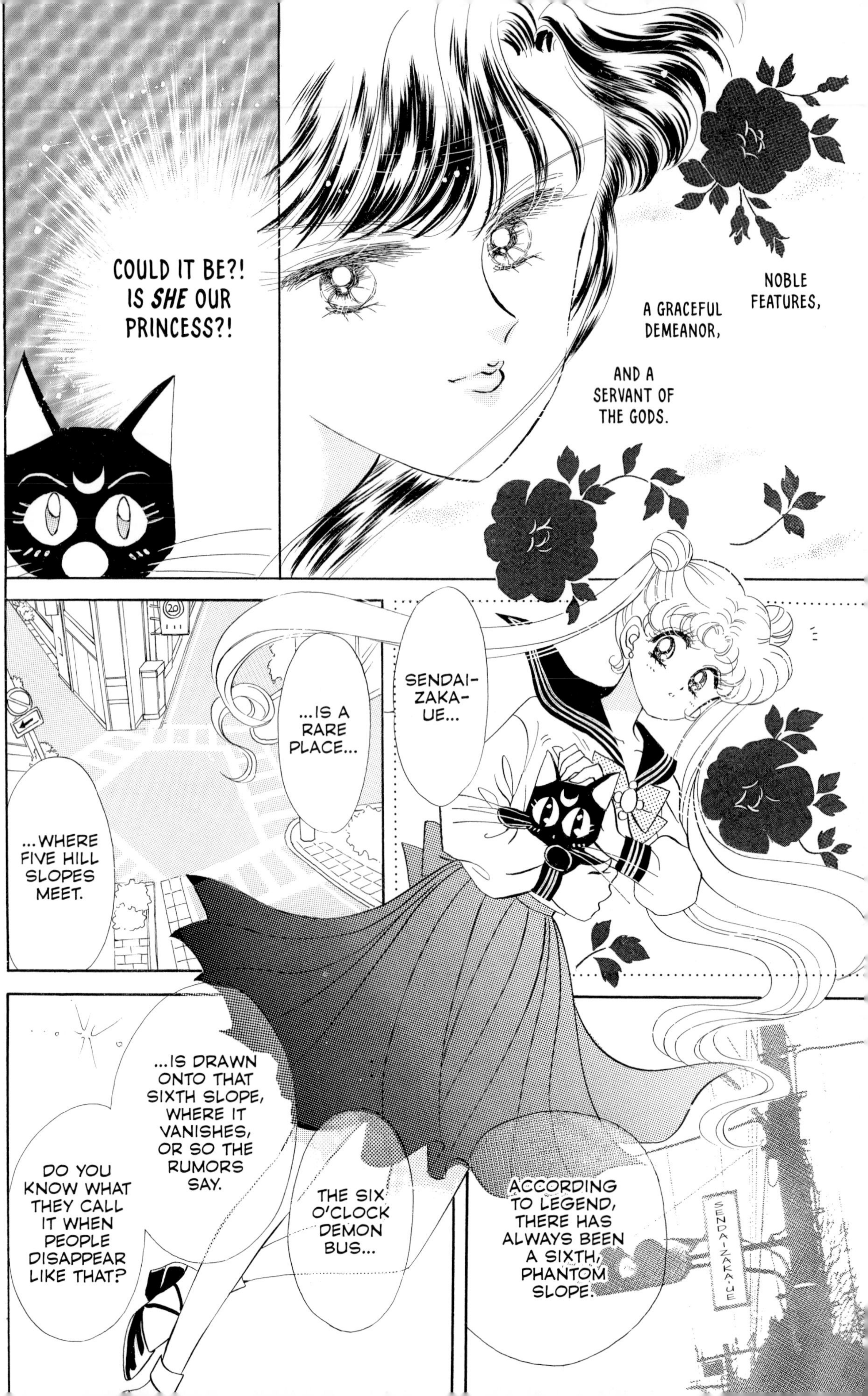
NOBLE FEATURES,
A GRACEFUL DEMEANOR,
AND A SERVANT OF THE GODS.
COULD IT BE?! IS *SHE* OUR PRINCESS?!
SENDAI-ZAKA-UE...
...IS A RARE PLACE...
...WHERE FIVE HILL SLOPES MEET.
ACCORDING TO LEGEND, THERE HAS ALWAYS BEEN A SIXTH, PHANTOM SLOPE.
SENDAI-ZAKA-UE
THE SIX O'CLOCK DEMON BUS...
...IS DRAWN ONTO THAT SIXTH SLOPE, WHERE IT VANISHES, OR SO THE RUMORS SAY.
DO YOU KNOW WHAT THEY CALL IT WHEN PEOPLE DISAPPEAR LIKE THAT?

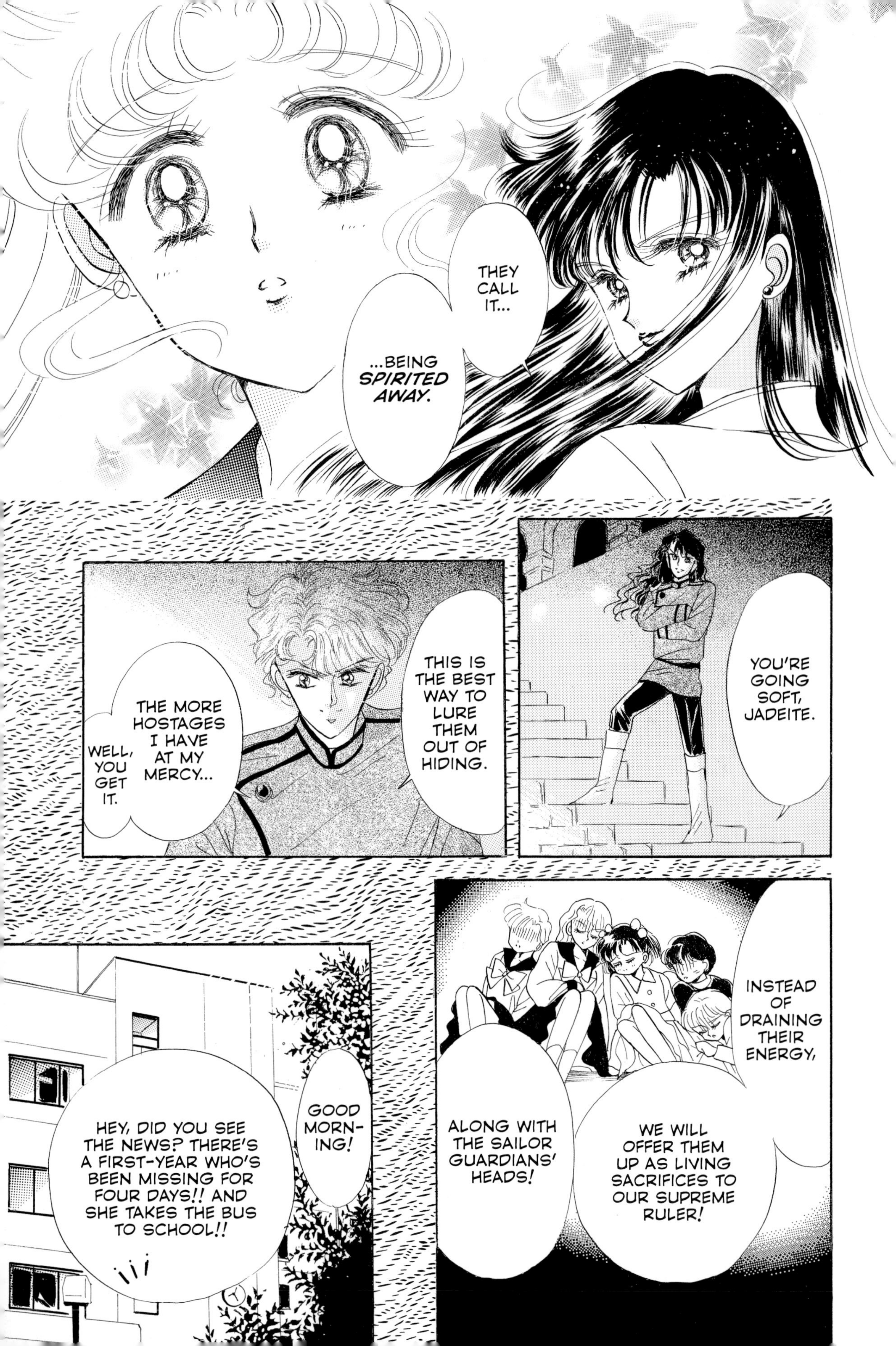
THEY CALL IT...
...BEING *SPIRITED AWAY.*
YOU'RE GOING SOFT, JADEITE.
THIS IS THE BEST WAY TO LURE THEM OUT OF HIDING.
THE MORE HOSTAGES I HAVE AT MY MERCY...
WELL, YOU GET IT.
INSTEAD OF DRAINING THEIR ENERGY,
WE WILL OFFER THEM UP AS LIVING SACRIFICES TO OUR SUPREME RULER!
ALONG WITH THE SAILOR GUARDIANS' HEADS!
GOOD MORN-ING!
HEY, DID YOU SEE THE NEWS? THERE'S A FIRST-YEAR WHO'S BEEN MISSING FOR FOUR DAYS!! AND SHE TAKES THE BUS TO SCHOOL!!

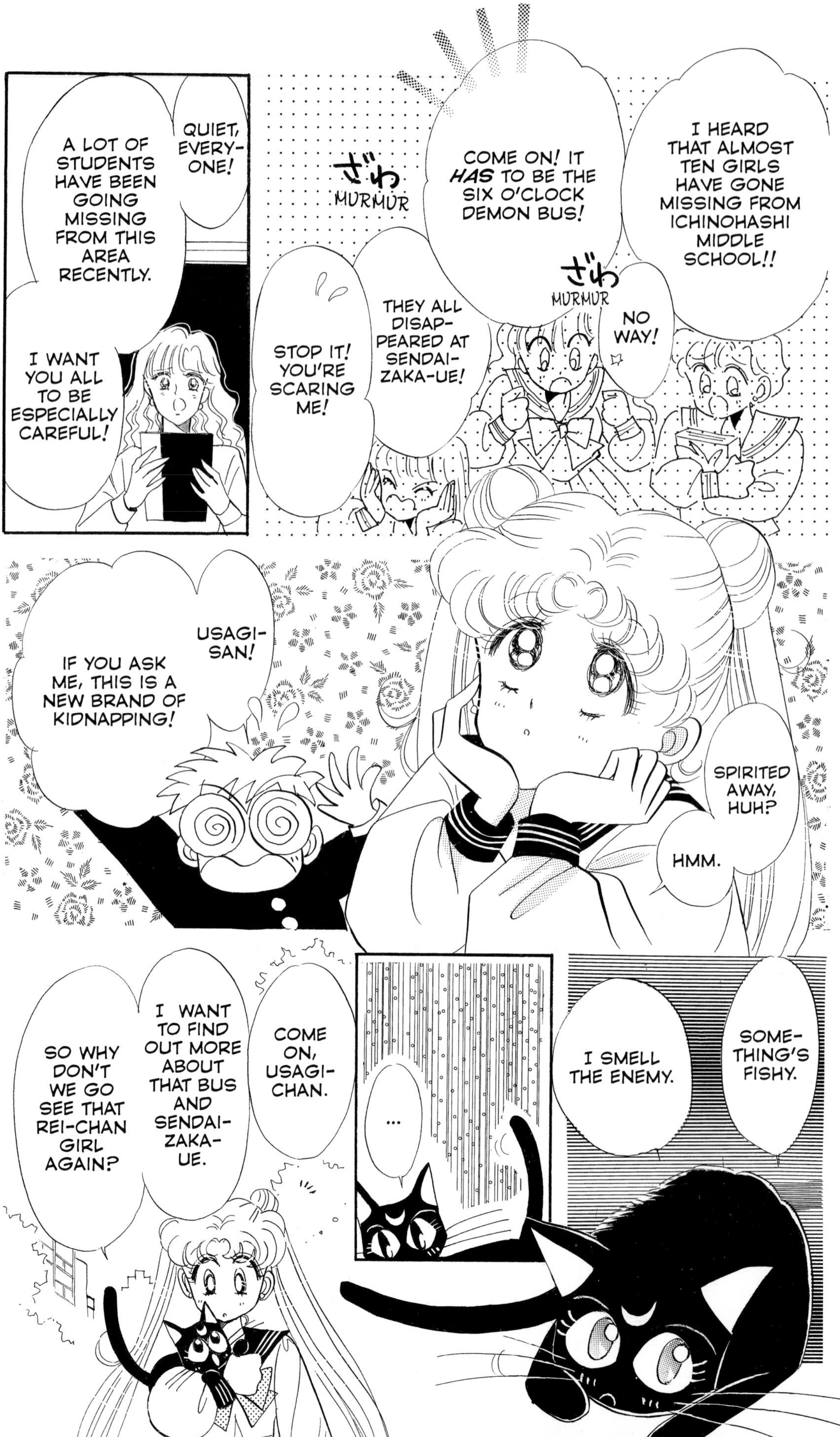
I HEARD THAT ALMOST TEN GIRLS HAVE GONE MISSING FROM ICHINOHASHI MIDDLE SCHOOL!!
COME ON! IT *HAS* TO BE THE SIX O'CLOCK DEMON BUS!
ざわ MURMUR
NO WAY!
ざわ MURMUR
THEY ALL DISAPPEARED AT SENDAI-ZAKA-UE!
STOP IT! YOU'RE SCARING ME!
QUIET, EVERYONE!
A LOT OF STUDENTS HAVE BEEN GOING MISSING FROM THIS AREA RECENTLY.
I WANT YOU ALL TO BE ESPECIALLY CAREFUL!
SPIRITED AWAY, HUH?
HMM.
USAGI-SAN!
IF YOU ASK ME, THIS IS A NEW BRAND OF KIDNAPPING!
SOMETHING'S FISHY.
I SMELL THE ENEMY.
...
COME ON, USAGI-CHAN.
I WANT TO FIND OUT MORE ABOUT THAT BUS AND SENDAI-ZAKA-UE.
SO WHY DON'T WE GO SEE THAT REI-CHAN GIRL AGAIN?

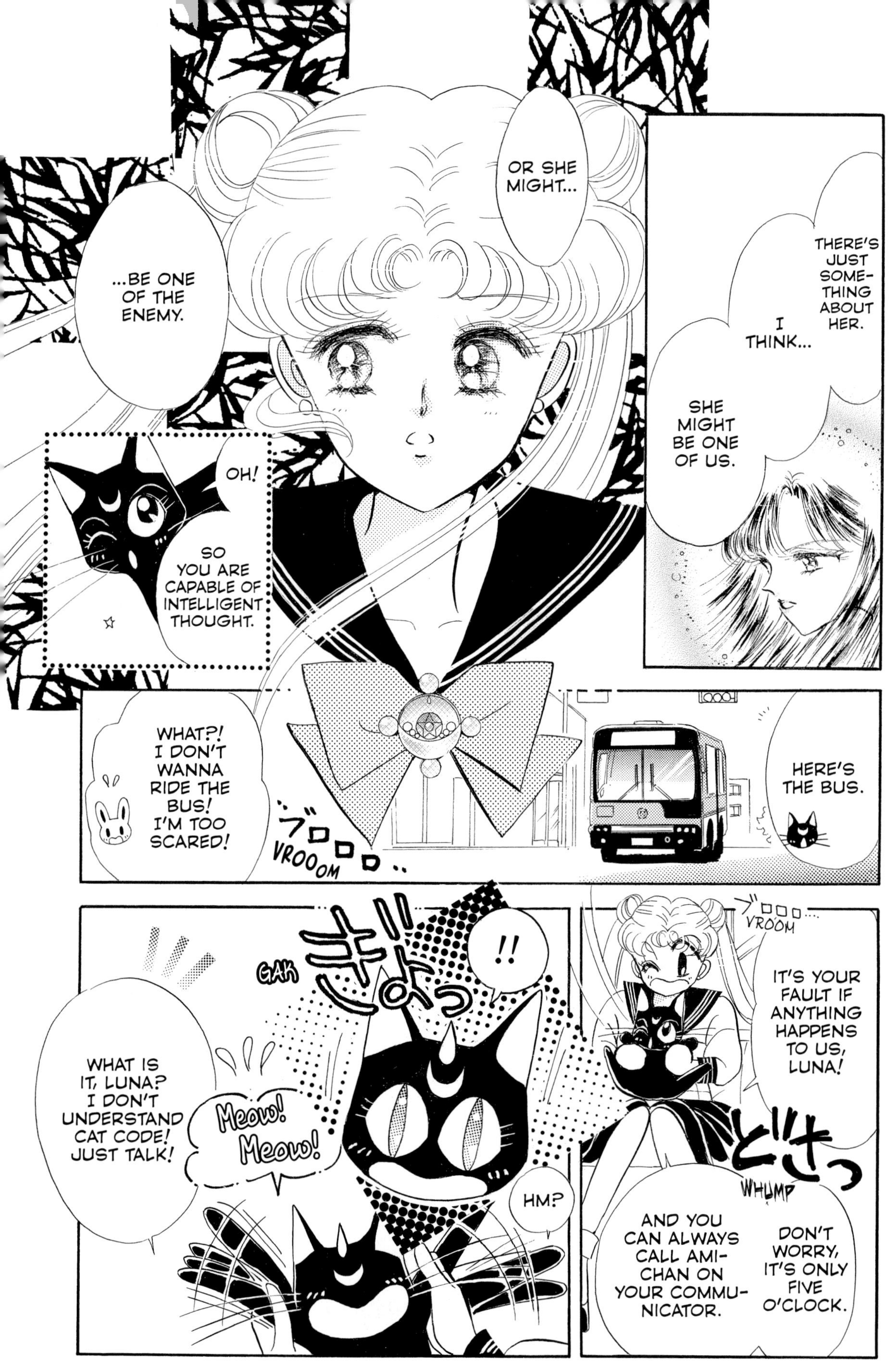
THERE'S JUST SOMETHING ABOUT HER.
I THINK...
SHE MIGHT BE ONE OF US.
OR SHE MIGHT...
...BE ONE OF THE ENEMY.
OH!
SO YOU ARE CAPABLE OF INTELLIGENT THOUGHT.
HERE'S THE BUS.
ブロロロ..
VROOOM
WHAT?! I DON'T WANNA RIDE THE BUS! I'M TOO SCARED!
ブロロロ....
VROOM
IT'S YOUR FAULT IF ANYTHING HAPPENS TO US, LUNA!
どさっ
WHUMP
DON'T WORRY, IT'S ONLY FIVE O'CLOCK.
AND YOU CAN ALWAYS CALL AMI-CHAN ON YOUR COMMUNICATOR.
!!
ぎょっ
GAK
HM?
Meow! Meow!
WHAT IS IT, LUNA? I DON'T UNDERSTAND CAT CODE! JUST TALK!

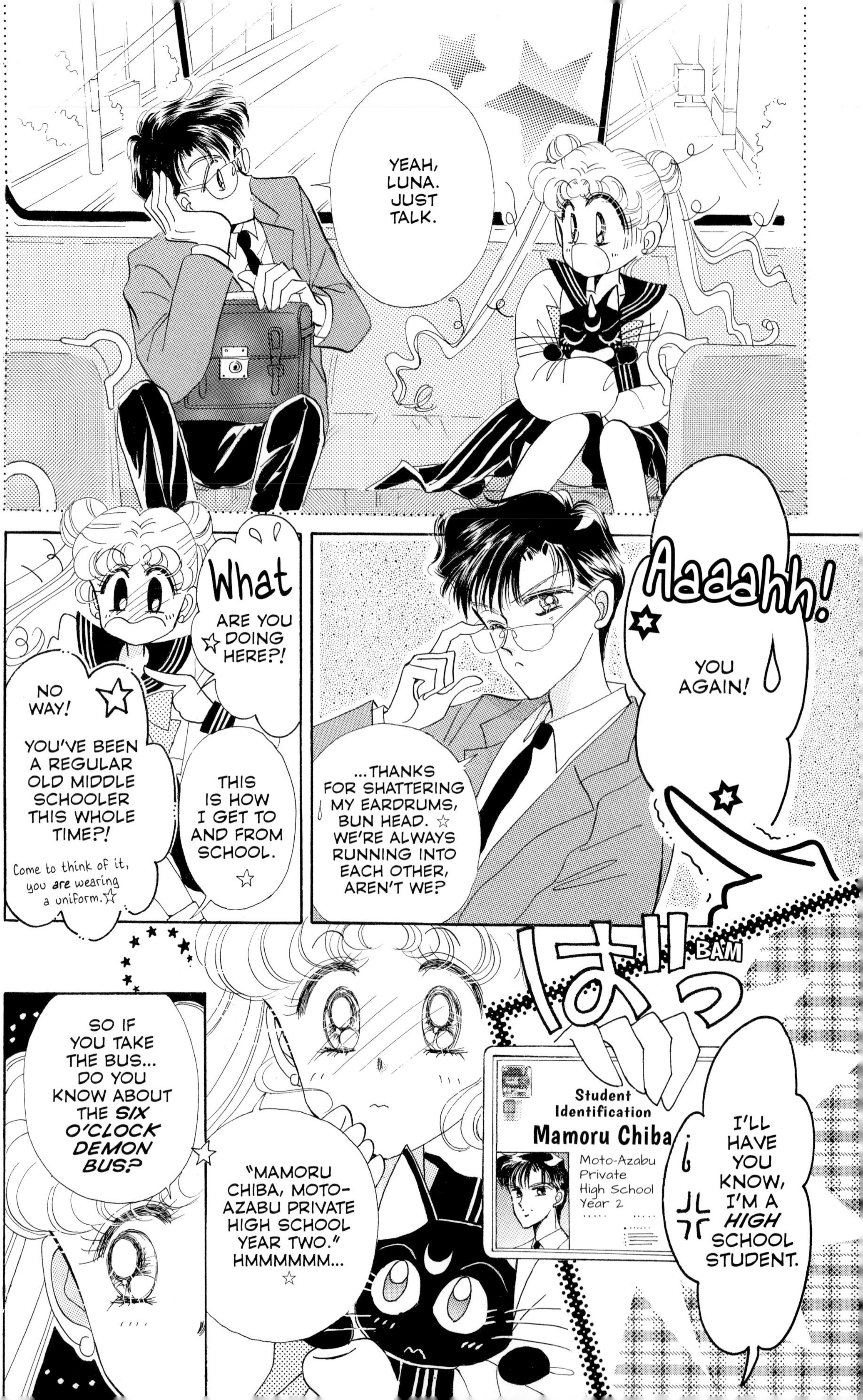
YEAH, LUNA. JUST TALK.
Aaaahh!
YOU AGAIN!
...THANKS FOR SHATTERING MY EARDRUMS, BUN HEAD. WE'RE ALWAYS RUNNING INTO EACH OTHER, AREN'T WE?
What ARE YOU DOING HERE?!
THIS IS HOW I GET TO AND FROM SCHOOL.
NO WAY! YOU'VE BEEN A REGULAR OLD MIDDLE SCHOOLER THIS WHOLE TIME?!
Come to think of it, you are wearing a uniform.
BAM
Student Identification
Mamoru Chiba
Moto-Azabu Private High School Year 2
I'LL HAVE YOU KNOW, I'M A HIGH SCHOOL STUDENT.
"MAMORU CHIBA, MOTO-AZABU PRIVATE HIGH SCHOOL YEAR TWO." HMMMMMM...
SO IF YOU TAKE THE BUS... DO YOU KNOW ABOUT THE SIX O'CLOCK DEMON BUS?

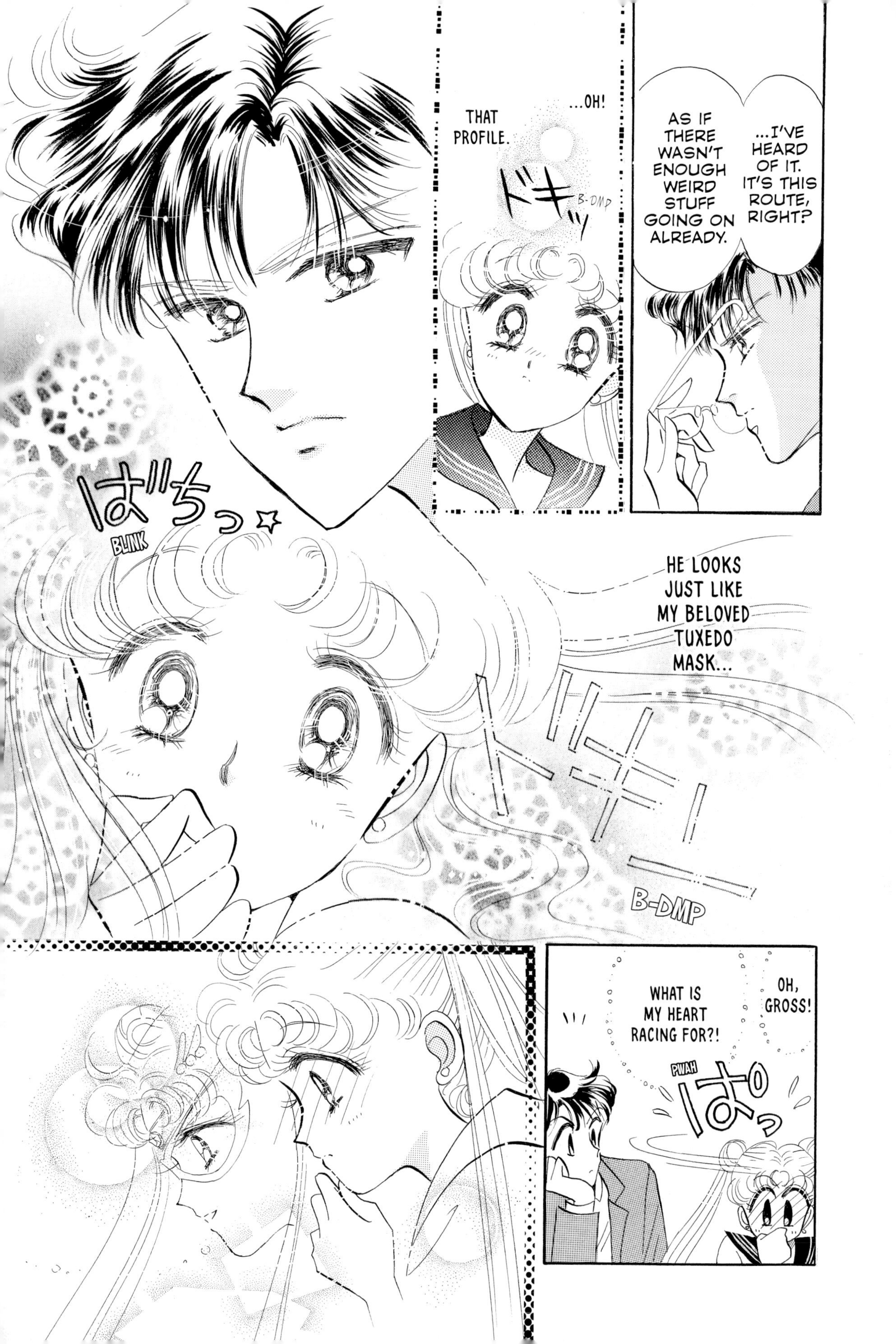
...I'VE HEARD OF IT. IT'S THIS ROUTE, RIGHT?
AS IF THERE WASN'T ENOUGH WEIRD STUFF GOING ON ALREADY.
...OH!
ドキッ
B-DMP
THAT PROFILE.
HE LOOKS JUST LIKE MY BELOVED TUXEDO MASK...
ドキー
B-DMP
ぱちっ☆
BLINK
OH, GROSS!
WHAT IS MY HEART RACING FOR?!
ぱっ
PWAH

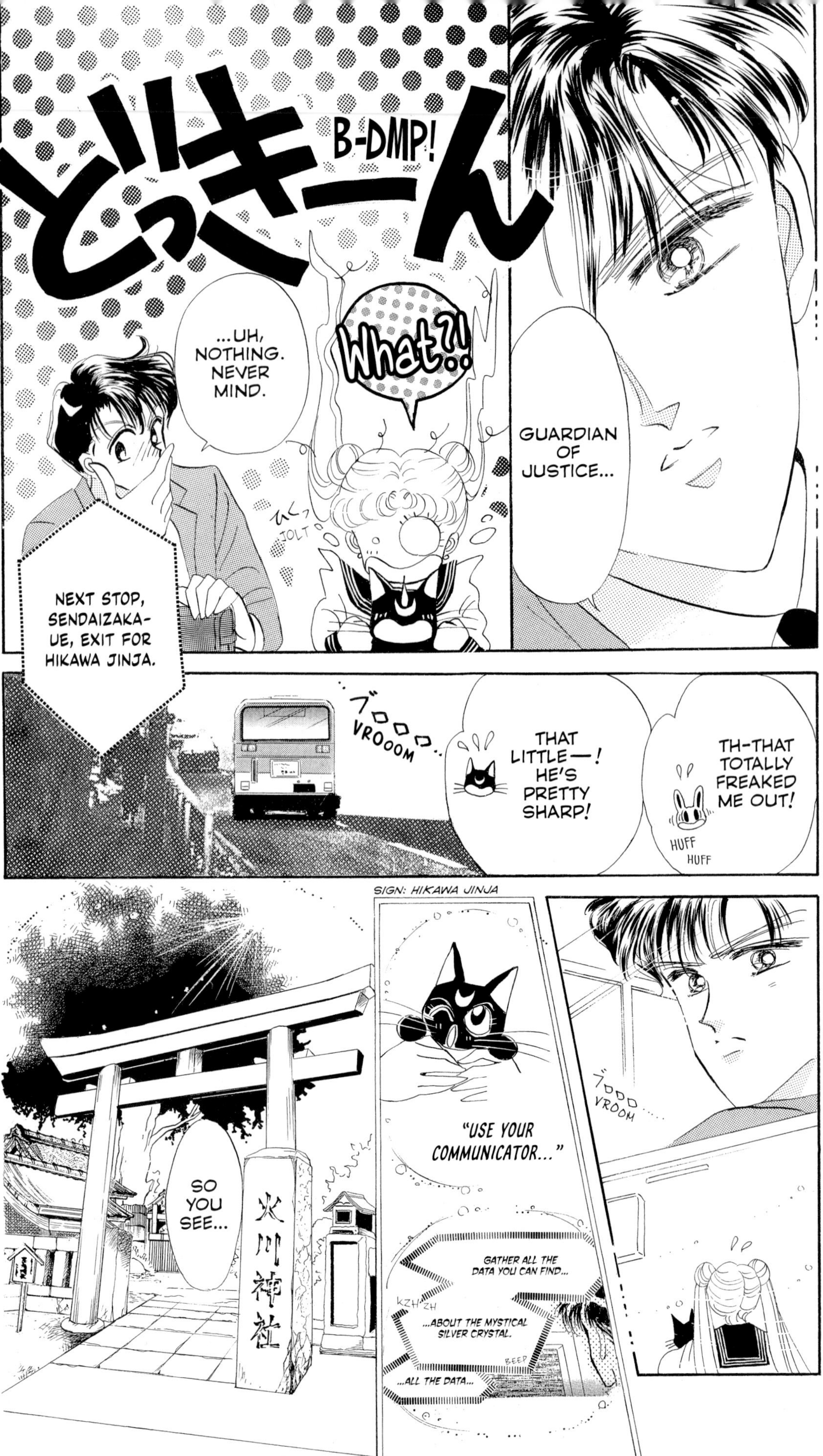
GUARDIAN OF JUSTICE...
どっきーん
B-DMP!
What?!
...UH, NOTHING. NEVER MIND.
ひくっ
JOLT
NEXT STOP, SENDAIZAKA-UE, EXIT FOR HIKAWA JINJA.
TH-THAT TOTALLY FREAKED ME OUT!
HUFF HUFF
THAT LITTLE—! HE'S PRETTY SHARP!
ブロロロ
VROOOM
ブロロロ
VROOM
SIGN: HIKAWA JINJA
"USE YOUR COMMUNICATOR..."
GATHER ALL THE DATA YOU CAN FIND...
KZH ZH
...ABOUT THE MYSTICAL SILVER CRYSTAL.
BEEP
...ALL THE DATA...
SO YOU SEE...
火川神社

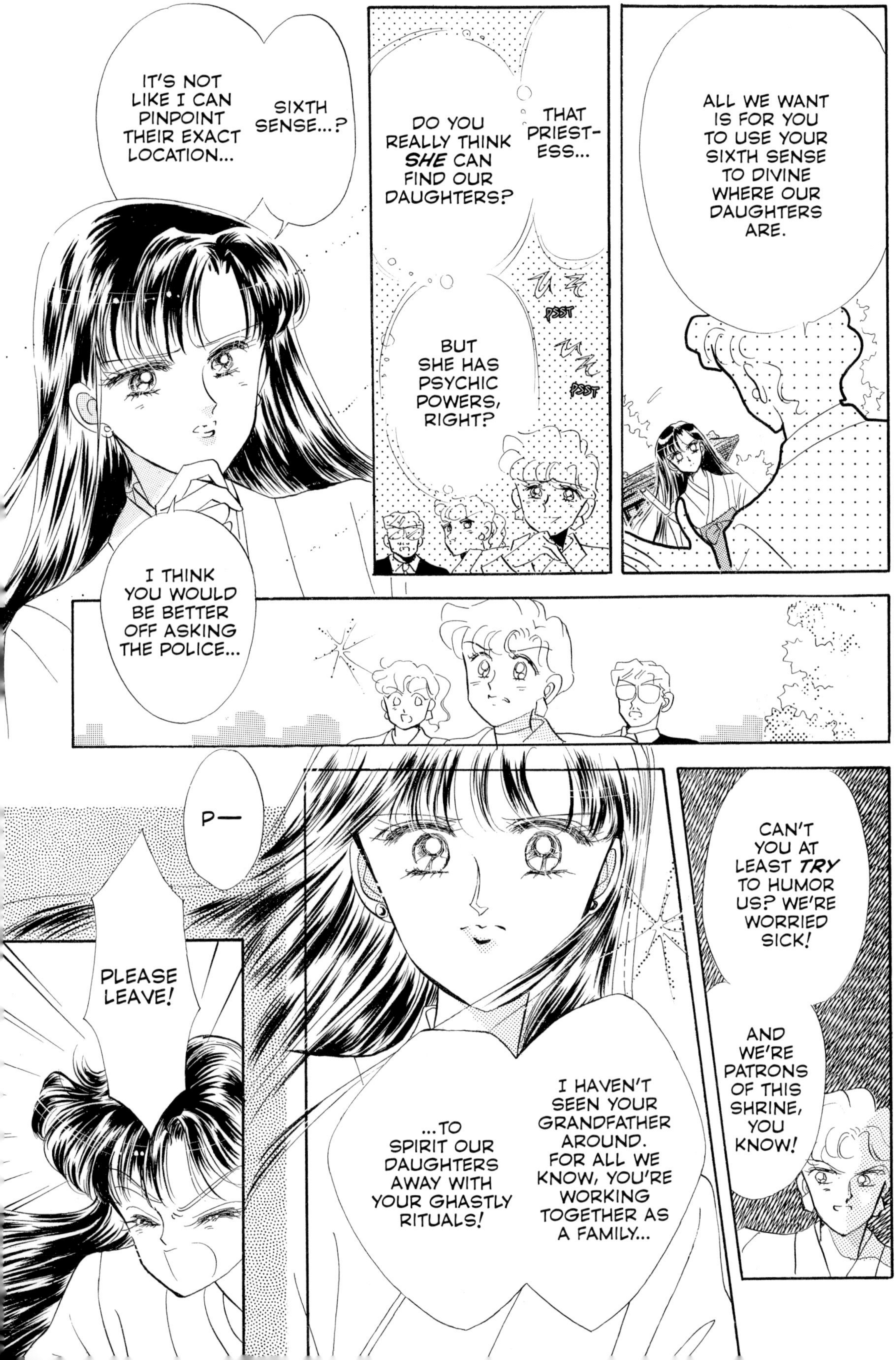
ALL WE WANT IS FOR YOU TO USE YOUR SIXTH SENSE TO DIVINE WHERE OUR DAUGHTERS ARE.
THAT PRIESTESS...
DO YOU REALLY THINK *SHE* CAN FIND OUR DAUGHTERS?
PSSST
PSSST
BUT SHE HAS PSYCHIC POWERS, RIGHT?
SIXTH SENSE...?
IT'S NOT LIKE I CAN PINPOINT THEIR EXACT LOCATION...
I THINK YOU WOULD BE BETTER OFF ASKING THE POLICE...
CAN'T YOU AT LEAST *TRY* TO HUMOR US? WE'RE WORRIED SICK!
AND WE'RE PATRONS OF THIS SHRINE, YOU KNOW!
I HAVEN'T SEEN YOUR GRANDFATHER AROUND. FOR ALL WE KNOW, YOU'RE WORKING TOGETHER AS A FAMILY...
...TO SPIRIT OUR DAUGHTERS AWAY WITH YOUR GHASTLY RITUALS!
P—
PLEASE LEAVE!

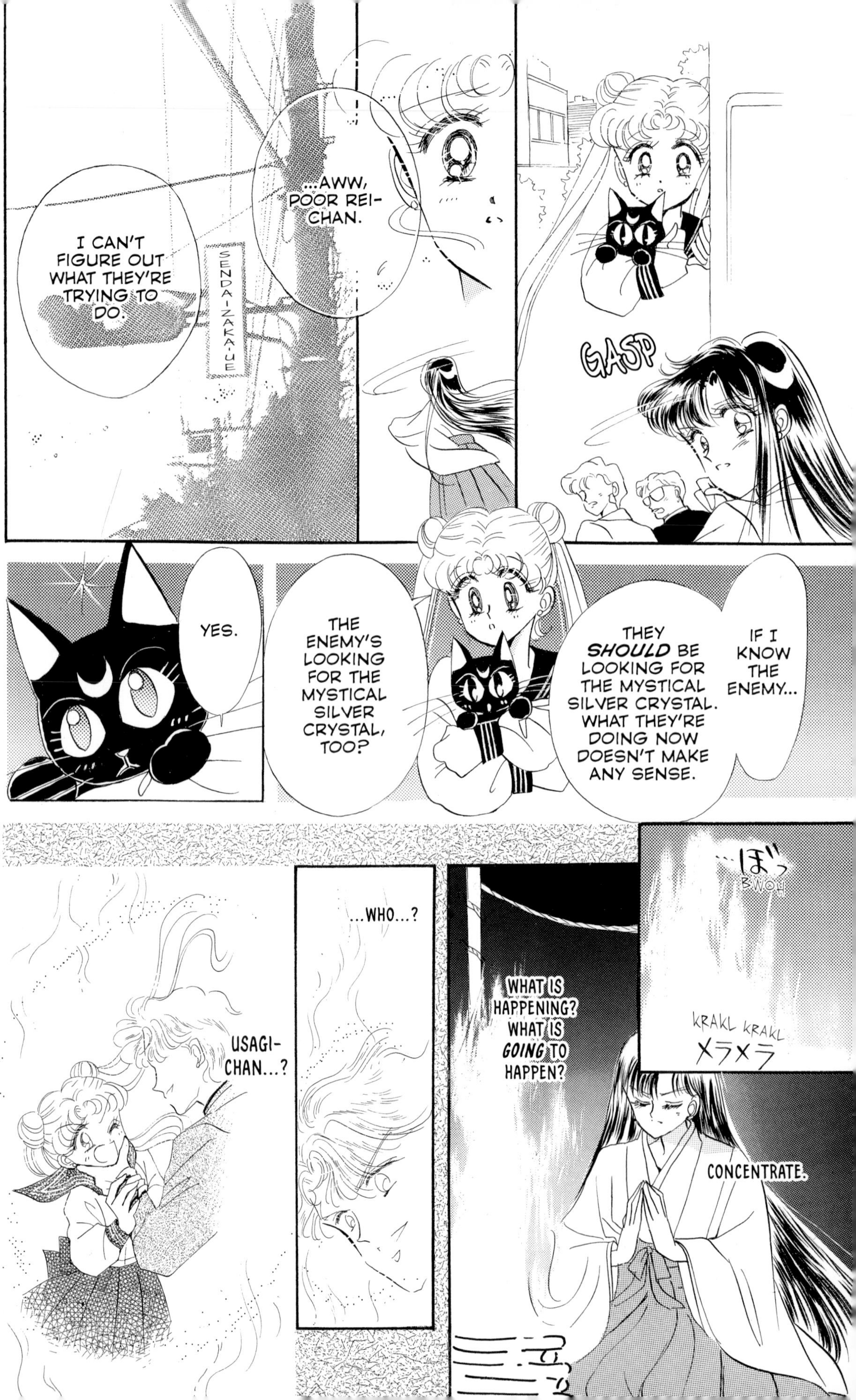

GASP
...AWW, POOR REI-CHAN.
I CAN'T FIGURE OUT WHAT THEY'RE TRYING TO DO.
SENDAI-ZAKA-UE
IF I KNOW THE ENEMY...
THEY SHOULD BE LOOKING FOR THE MYSTICAL SILVER CRYSTAL. WHAT THEY'RE DOING NOW DOESN'T MAKE ANY SENSE.
THE ENEMY'S LOOKING FOR THE MYSTICAL SILVER CRYSTAL, TOO?
YES.
...ぼっ
BWOH
KRAKL KRAKL
メラメラ
WHAT IS HAPPENING? WHAT IS GOING TO HAPPEN?
CONCENTRATE.
...WHO...?
USAGI-CHAN...?

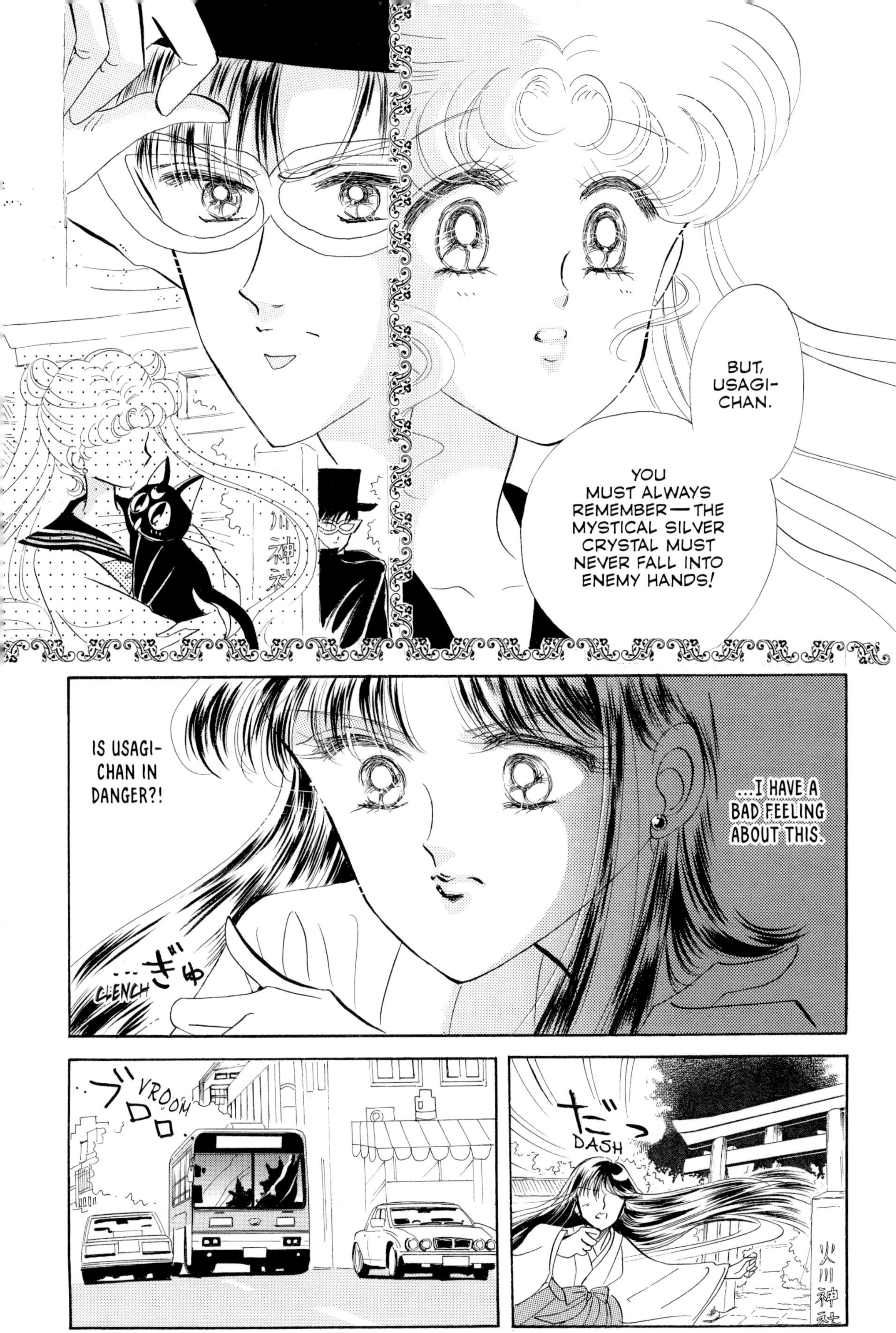
BUT, USAGI-CHAN.
YOU MUST ALWAYS REMEMBER — THE MYSTICAL SILVER CRYSTAL MUST NEVER FALL INTO ENEMY HANDS!
...I HAVE A BAD FEELING ABOUT THIS.
IS USAGI-CHAN IN DANGER?!
...ぎゅ
CLENCH
だっ
DASH
火川神社
ブロロ
VROOM

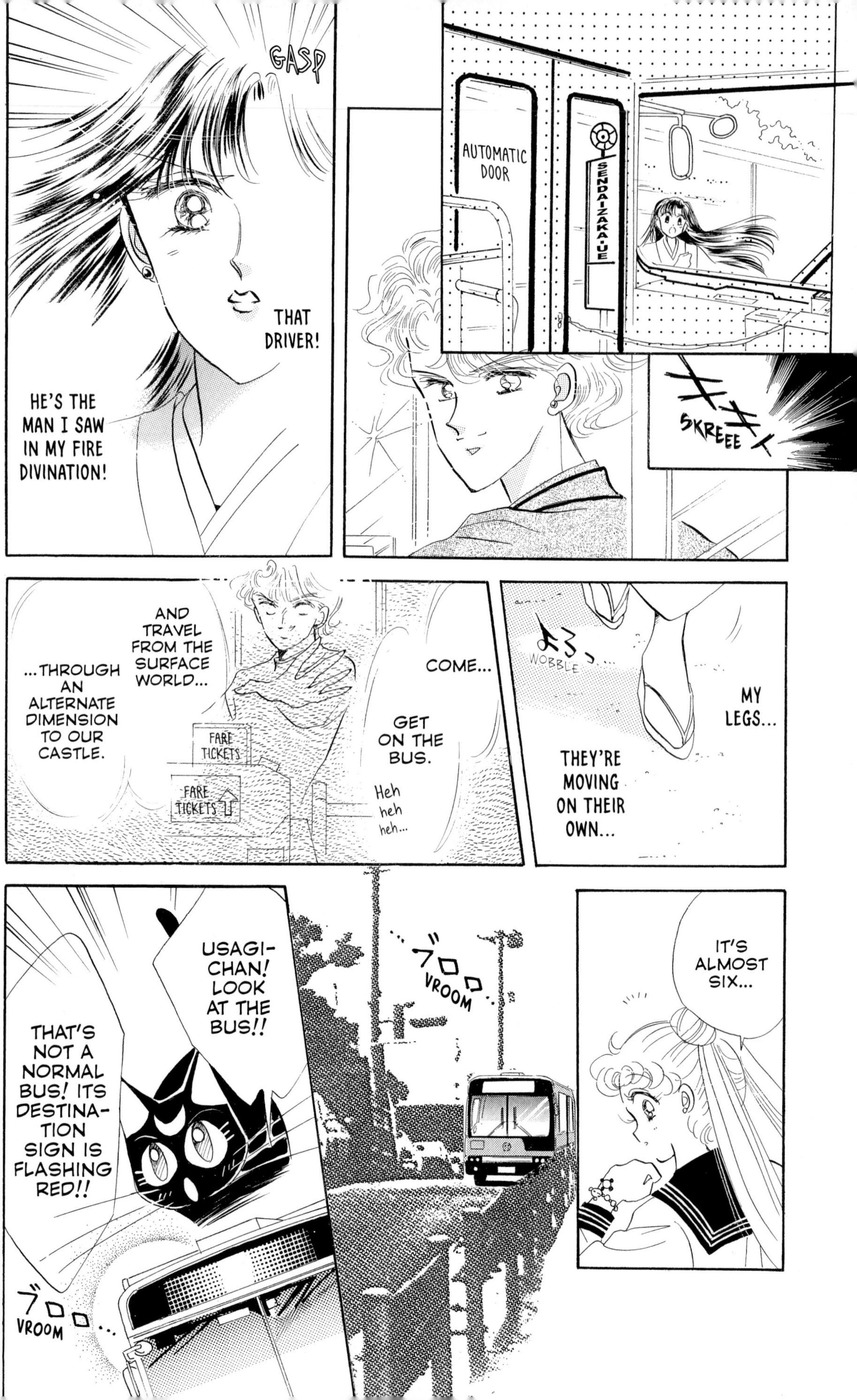
AUTOMATIC DOOR
SENDAIZAKA-UE
SKREEE
GASP
THAT DRIVER!
HE'S THE MAN I SAW IN MY FIRE DIVINATION!
よろっ…
WOBBLE
MY LEGS...
THEY'RE MOVING ON THEIR OWN...
COME...
GET ON THE BUS.
Heh heh heh...
AND TRAVEL FROM THE SURFACE WORLD...
...THROUGH AN ALTERNATE DIMENSION TO OUR CASTLE.
FARE TICKETS
FARE TICKETS
IT'S ALMOST SIX...
…ブロロ…
VROOM
USAGI-CHAN! LOOK AT THE BUS!!
THAT'S NOT A NORMAL BUS! ITS DESTINATION SIGN IS FLASHING RED!!
ブロロ…
VROOM

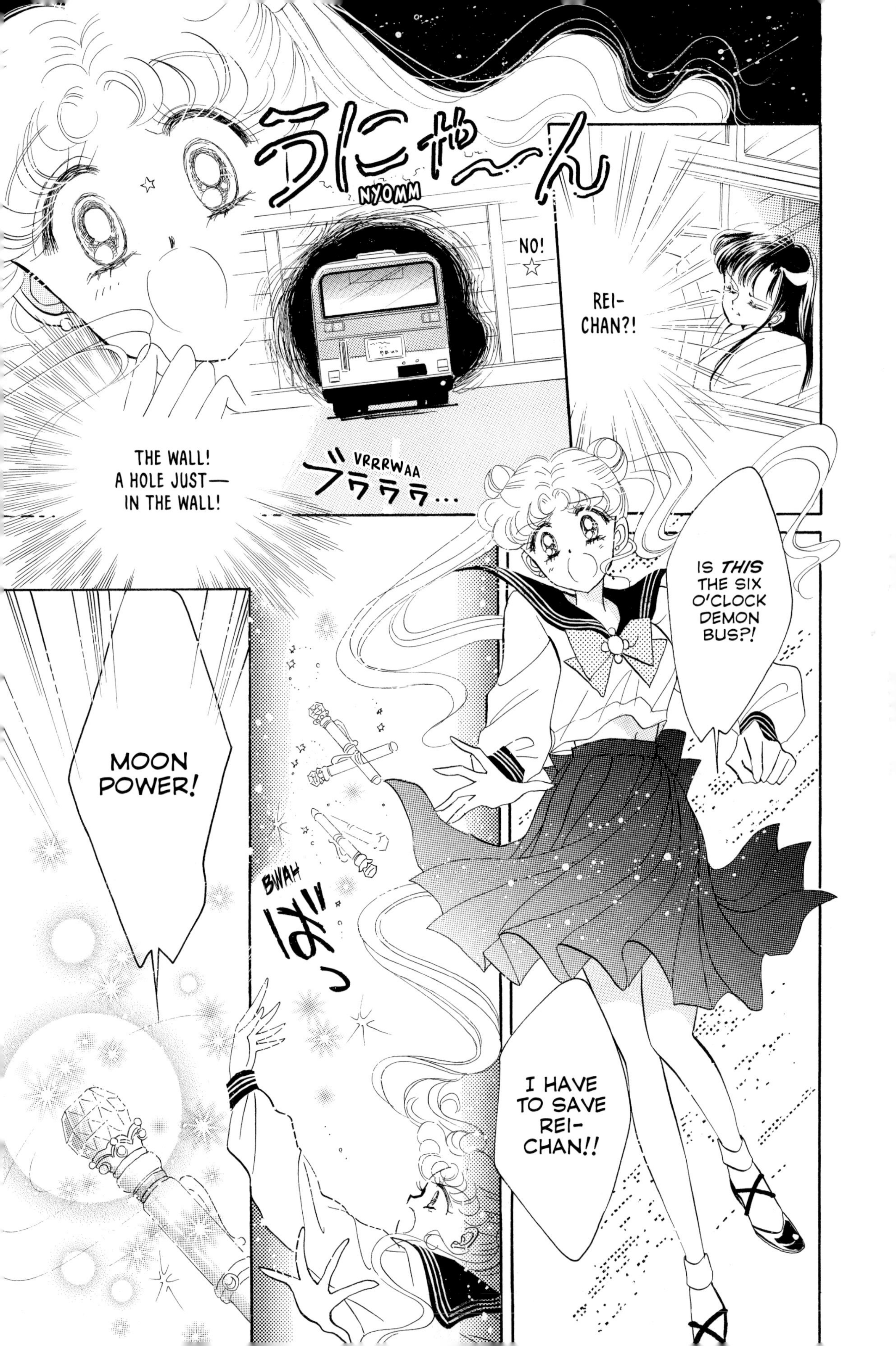
REI-CHAN?!
うにゃ〜ん
NYOMM
NO!
THE WALL! A HOLE JUST— IN THE WALL!
ブラララ…
VRRRWAA
IS *THIS* THE SIX O'CLOCK DEMON BUS?!
I HAVE TO SAVE REI-CHAN!!
ぼっ
BWAH
MOON POWER!

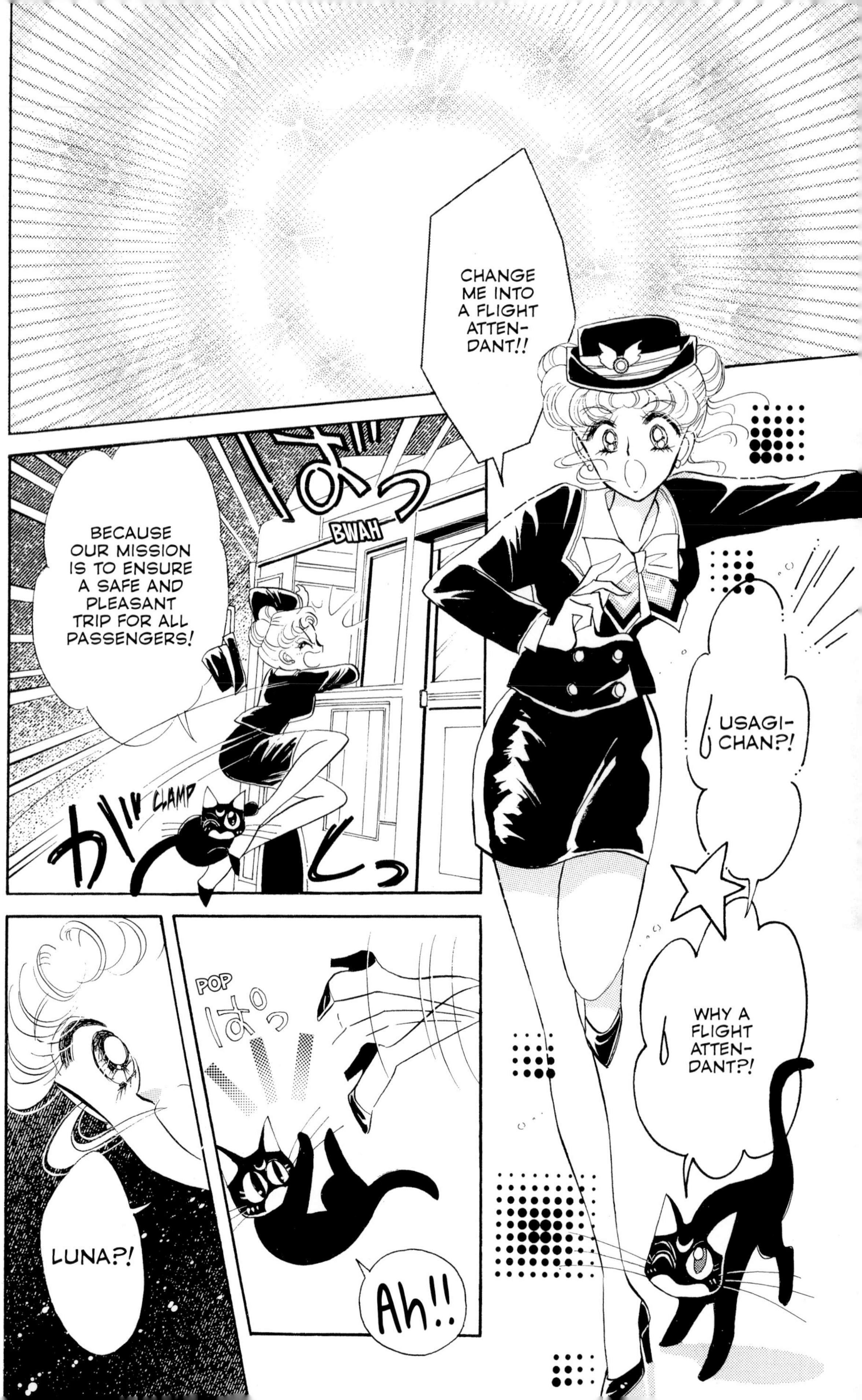
CHANGE ME INTO A FLIGHT ATTEN-DANT!!
USAGI-CHAN?!
WHY A FLIGHT ATTEN-DANT?!
BWAH
BECAUSE OUR MISSION IS TO ENSURE A SAFE AND PLEASANT TRIP FOR ALL PASSENGERS!
CLAMP
POP
Ah!!
LUNA?!

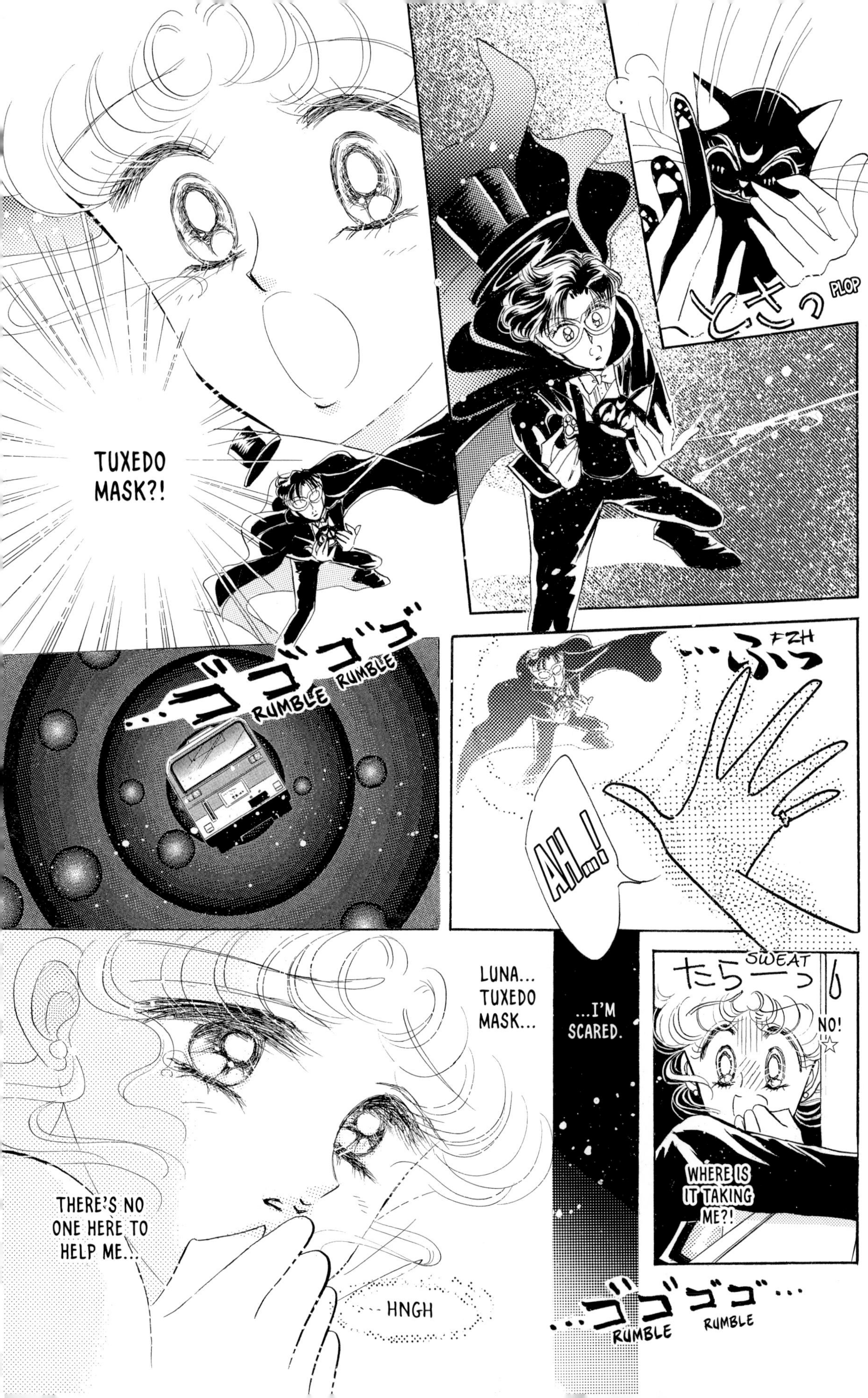

とさっ
PLOP
TUXEDO MASK?!
…ふっ
FZH
AH…!
…ゴゴゴゴ
RUMBLE RUMBLE
たらーっ
SWEAT
NO!
WHERE IS IT TAKING ME?!
…I'M SCARED.
…ゴゴゴゴ…
RUMBLE RUMBLE
LUNA… TUXEDO MASK…
THERE'S NO ONE HERE TO HELP ME…
…HNGH

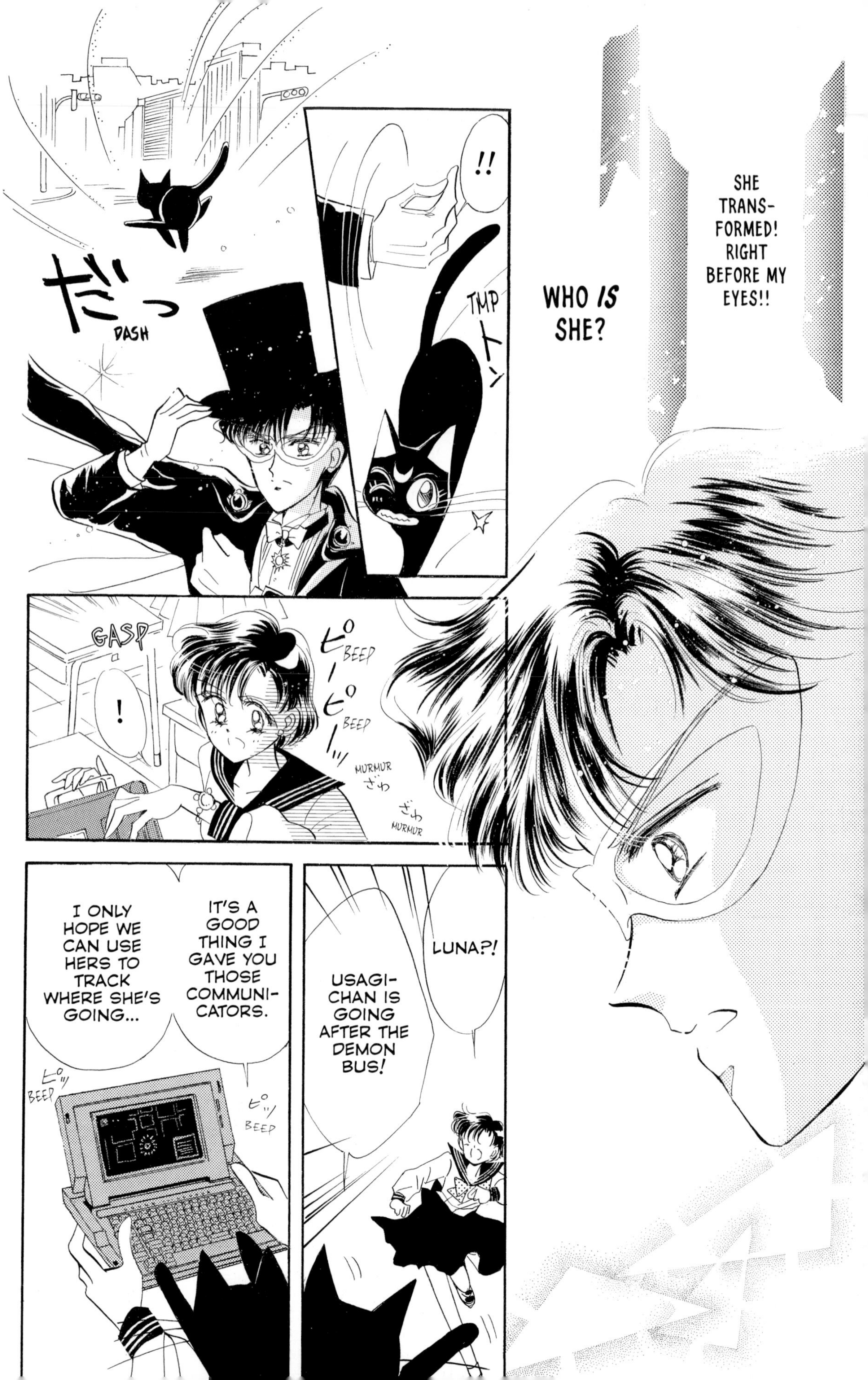
SHE TRANS-FORMED! RIGHT BEFORE MY EYES!!
WHO *IS* SHE?
!!
TMP
トン
だっ
DASH
GASP
!
ピーピーッ
BEEP BEEP
ざわ MURMUR
ざわ MURMUR
LUNA?!
USAGI-CHAN IS GOING AFTER THE DEMON BUS!
IT'S A GOOD THING I GAVE YOU THOSE COMMUNI-CATORS.
I ONLY HOPE WE CAN USE HERS TO TRACK WHERE SHE'S GOING...
ピッ BEEP
ピッ BEEP

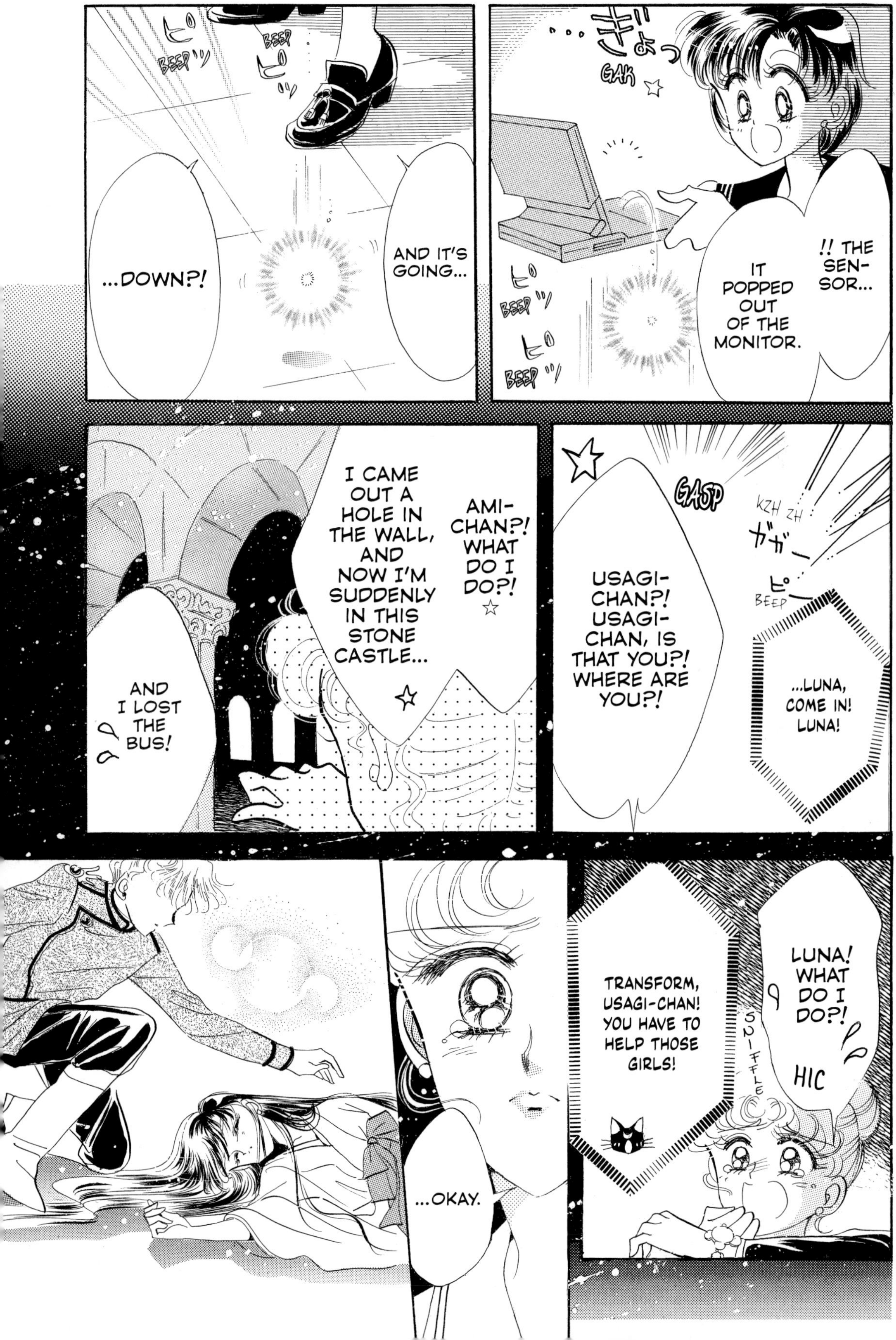
...ぎょっ
GAK
!! THE SENSOR...
IT POPPED OUT OF THE MONITOR.
ピッ BEEP
ピッ BEEP
AND IT'S GOING...
...DOWN?!
ピッ BEEP
BEEP ピッ
GASP
KZH ZH ガガー
ピー BEEP
...LUNA, COME IN! LUNA!
USAGI-CHAN?! USAGI-CHAN, IS THAT YOU?! WHERE ARE YOU?!
AMI-CHAN?! WHAT DO I DO?!
I CAME OUT A HOLE IN THE WALL, AND NOW I'M SUDDENLY IN THIS STONE CASTLE...
AND I LOST THE BUS!
LUNA! WHAT DO I DO?!
HIC
SNIFFLE
TRANSFORM, USAGI-CHAN! YOU HAVE TO HELP THOSE GIRLS!
...OKAY.

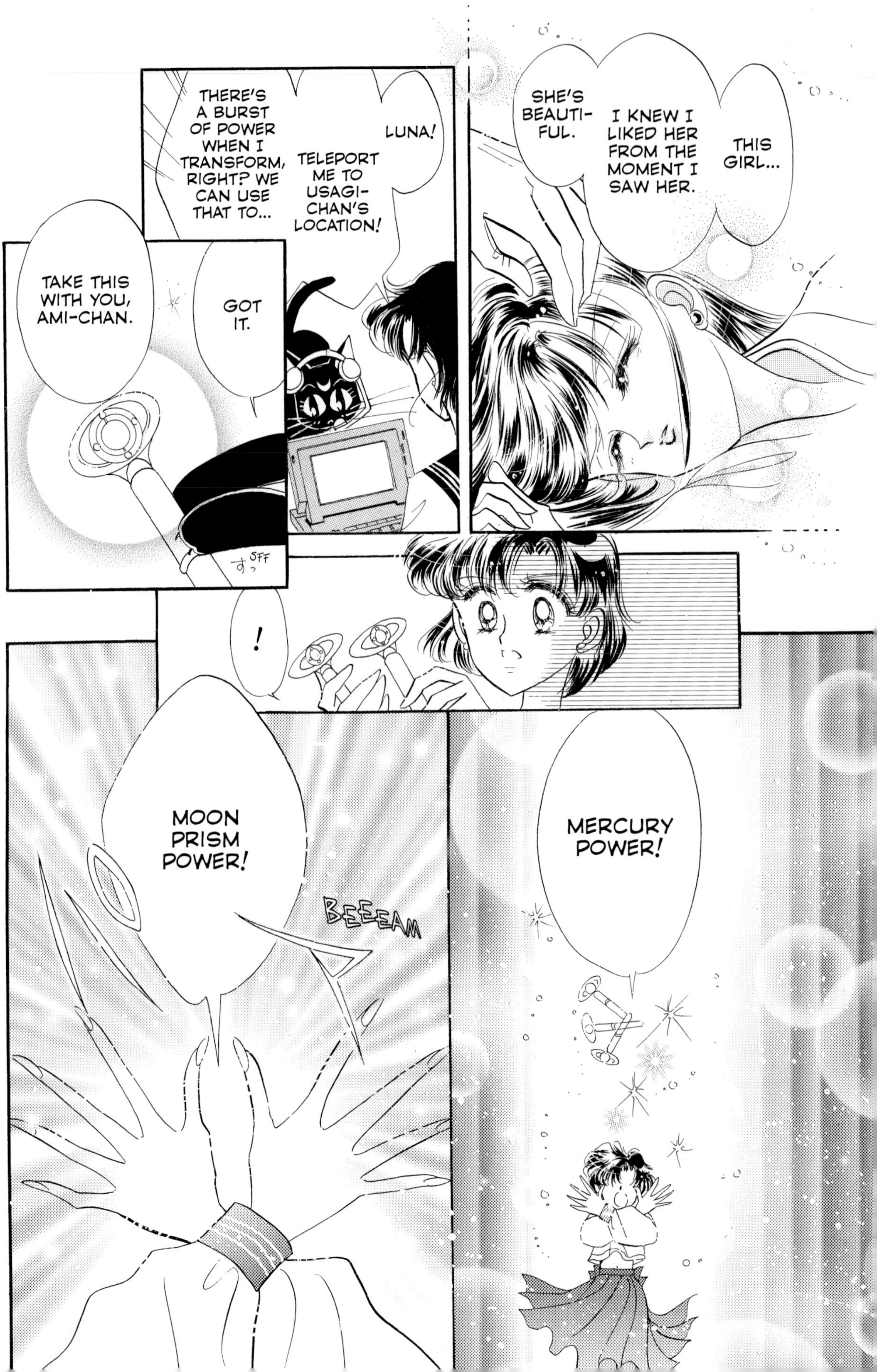
THIS GIRL...
I KNEW I LIKED HER FROM THE MOMENT I SAW HER.
SHE'S BEAUTI-FUL.
LUNA!
TELEPORT ME TO USAGI-CHAN'S LOCATION!
THERE'S A BURST OF POWER WHEN I TRANSFORM, RIGHT? WE CAN USE THAT TO...
GOT IT.
TAKE THIS WITH YOU, AMI-CHAN.
すっ SFF
!
MERCURY POWER!
MOON PRISM POWER!
BEEEAM

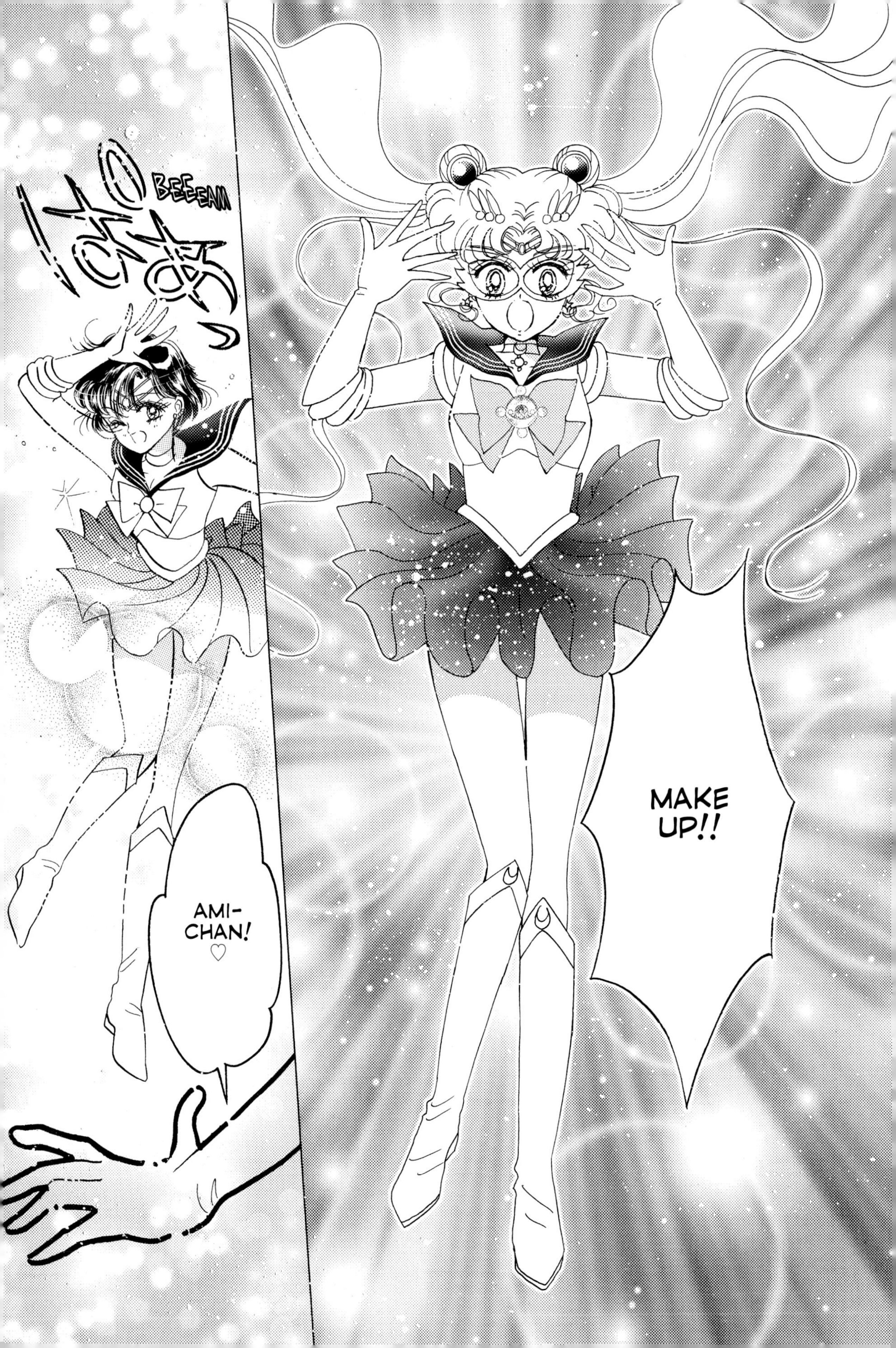
MAKE UP!!
BEEEAM
AMI-CHAN! ♡

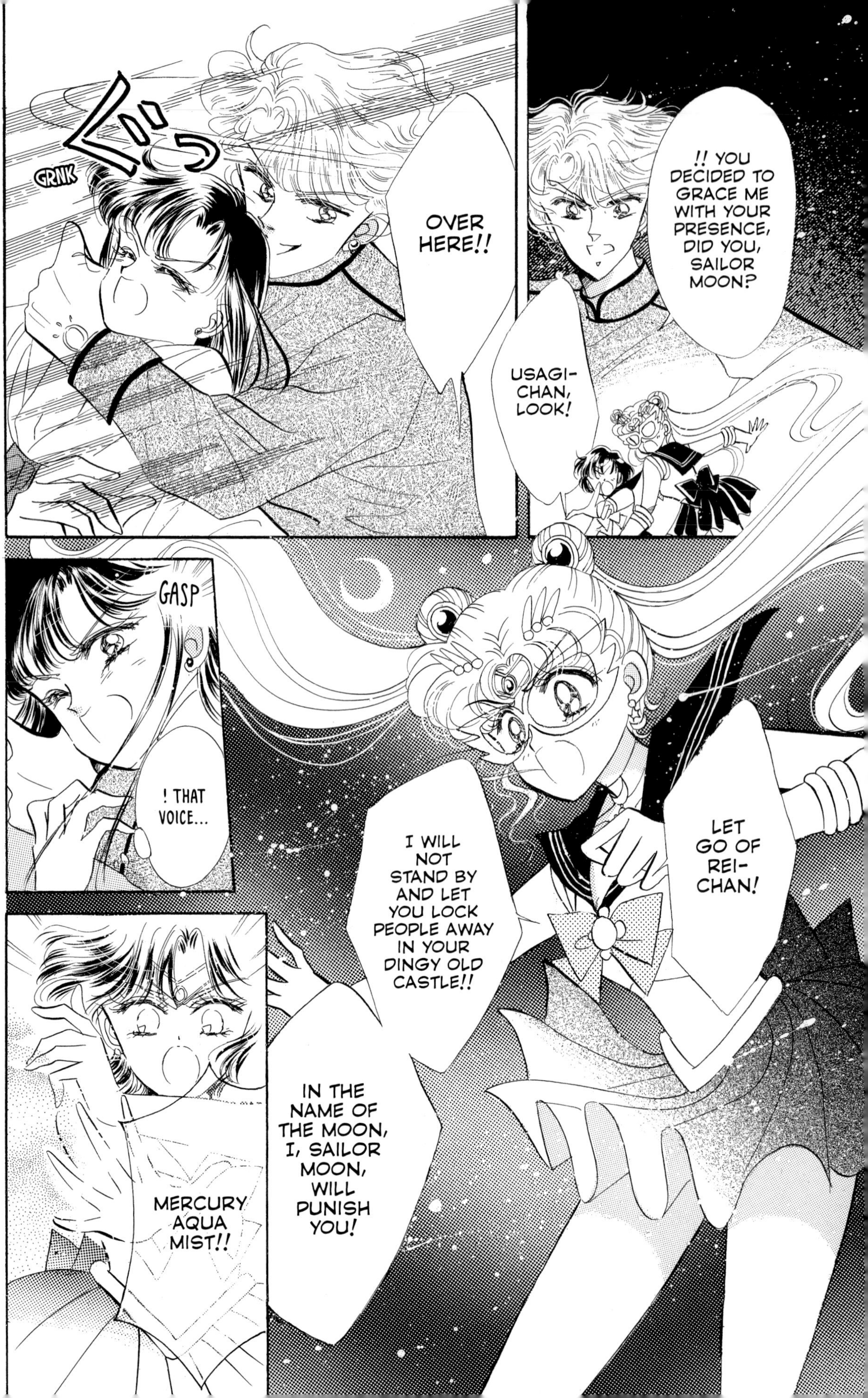
!! YOU DECIDED TO GRACE ME WITH YOUR PRESENCE, DID YOU, SAILOR MOON?
USAGI-CHAN, LOOK!
OVER HERE!!
GRNK
LET GO OF REI-CHAN!
I WILL NOT STAND BY AND LET YOU LOCK PEOPLE AWAY IN YOUR DINGY OLD CASTLE!!
IN THE NAME OF THE MOON, I, SAILOR MOON, WILL PUNISH YOU!
GASP
! THAT VOICE...
MERCURY AQUA MIST!!

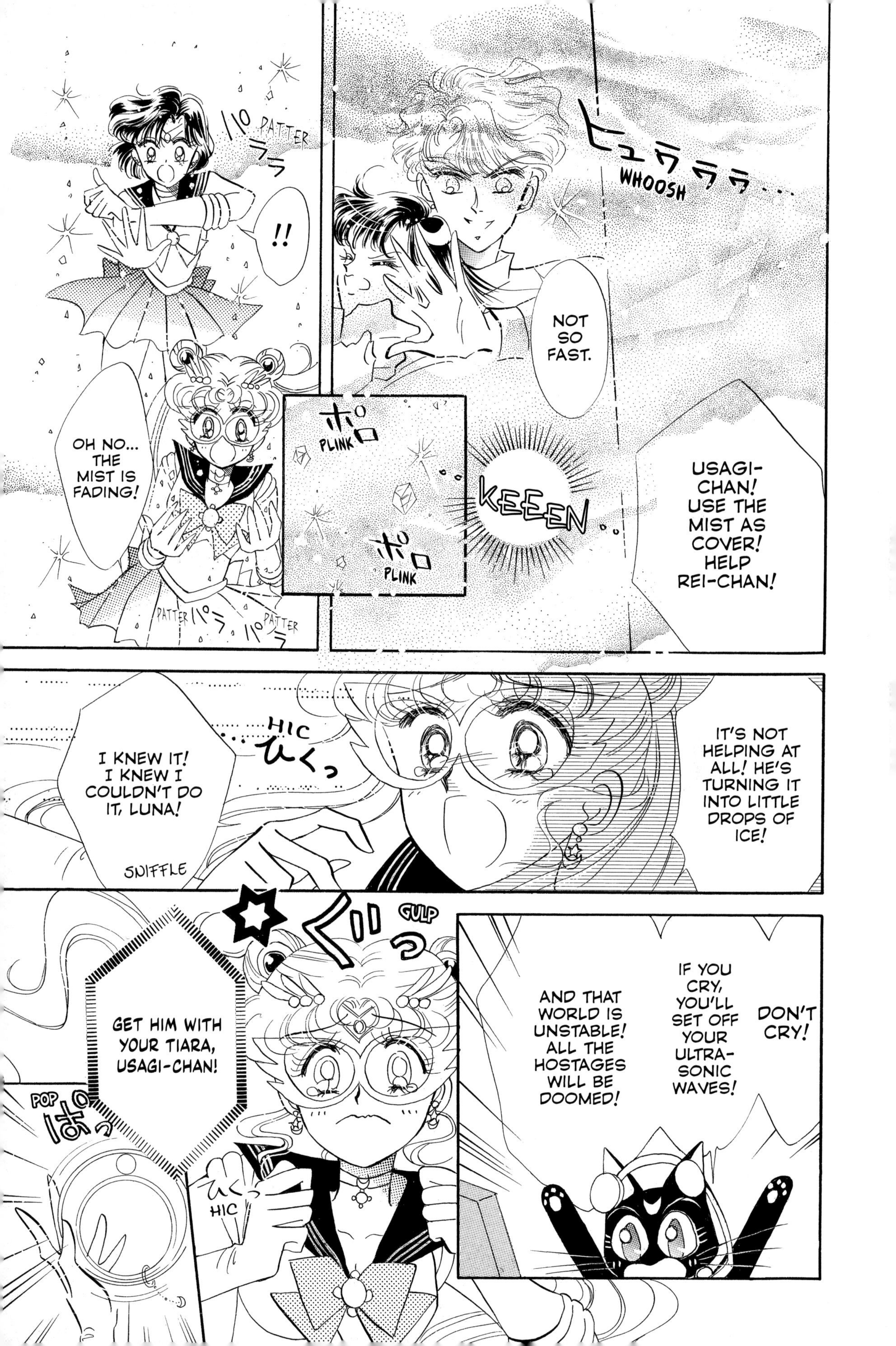

ヒュラララ…
WHOOSH
NOT SO FAST.
USAGI-CHAN! USE THE MIST AS COVER! HELP REI-CHAN!
KEEEN
ポロ
PLINK
ポロ
PLINK
パラ
PATTER
ラ
!!
OH NO... THE MIST IS FADING!
PATTER
パラ
PATTER
パラ
IT'S NOT HELPING AT ALL! HE'S TURNING IT INTO LITTLE DROPS OF ICE!
HIC
ひくっ
I KNEW IT! I KNEW I COULDN'T DO IT, LUNA!
SNIFFLE
DON'T CRY!
IF YOU CRY, YOU'LL SET OFF YOUR ULTRA-SONIC WAVES!
AND THAT WORLD IS UNSTABLE! ALL THE HOSTAGES WILL BE DOOMED!
GULP
GET HIM WITH YOUR TIARA, USAGI-CHAN!
POP
はっ
ひくっ
HIC

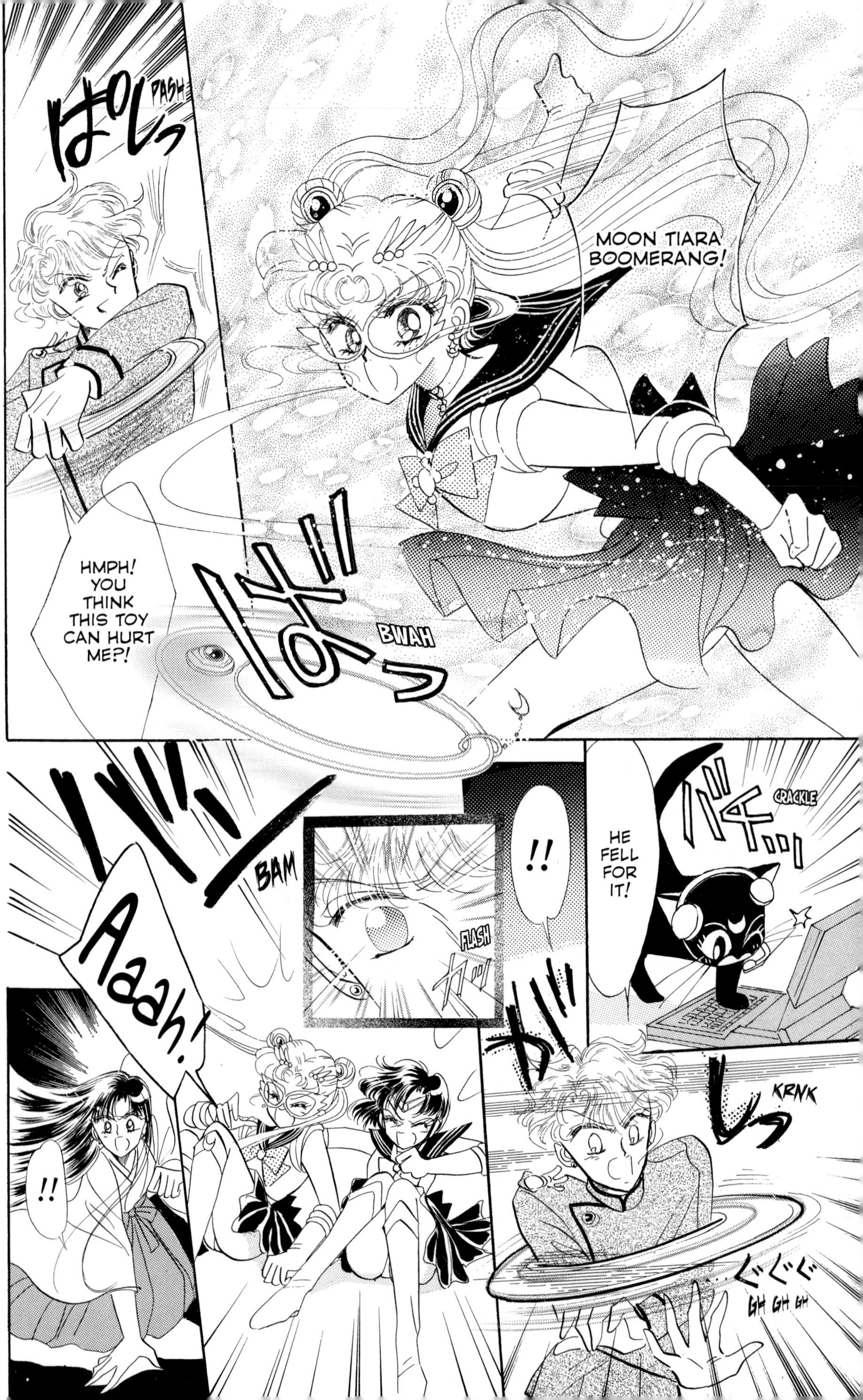
MOON TIARA BOOMERANG!
BWAH
PASH
HMPH! YOU THINK THIS TOY CAN HURT ME?!
CRACKLE
HE FELL FOR IT!
!!
FLASH
KRNK
GH GH GH
BAM
Aaah!
!!

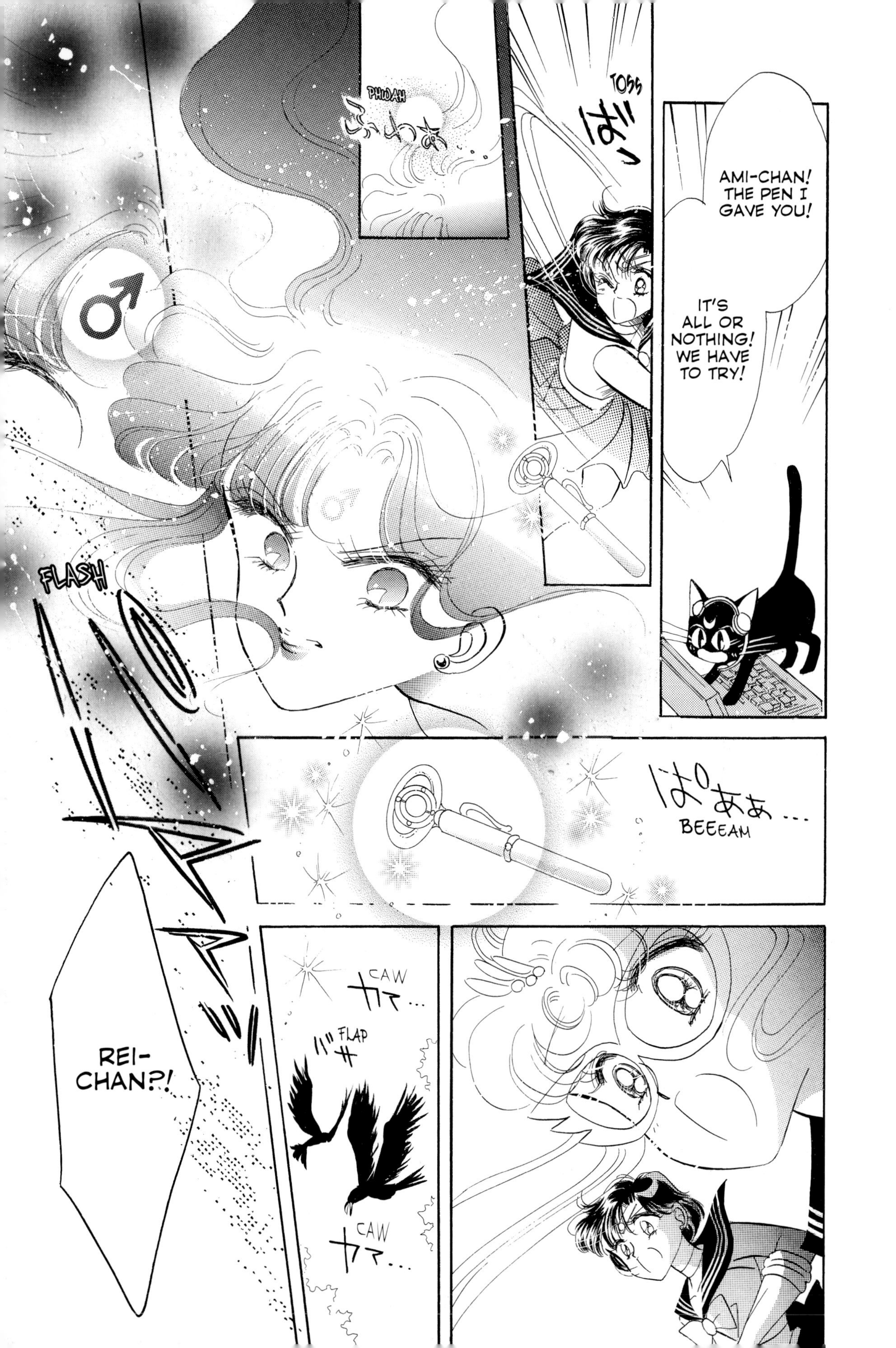
AMI-CHAN! THE PEN I GAVE YOU!
IT'S ALL OR NOTHING! WE HAVE TO TRY!
ばっ TOSS
ぶわっ PHUOAH
FLASH
ぱぁぁ… BEEEAM
カァ… CAW
バサ FLAP
カァ… CAW
REI-CHAN?!

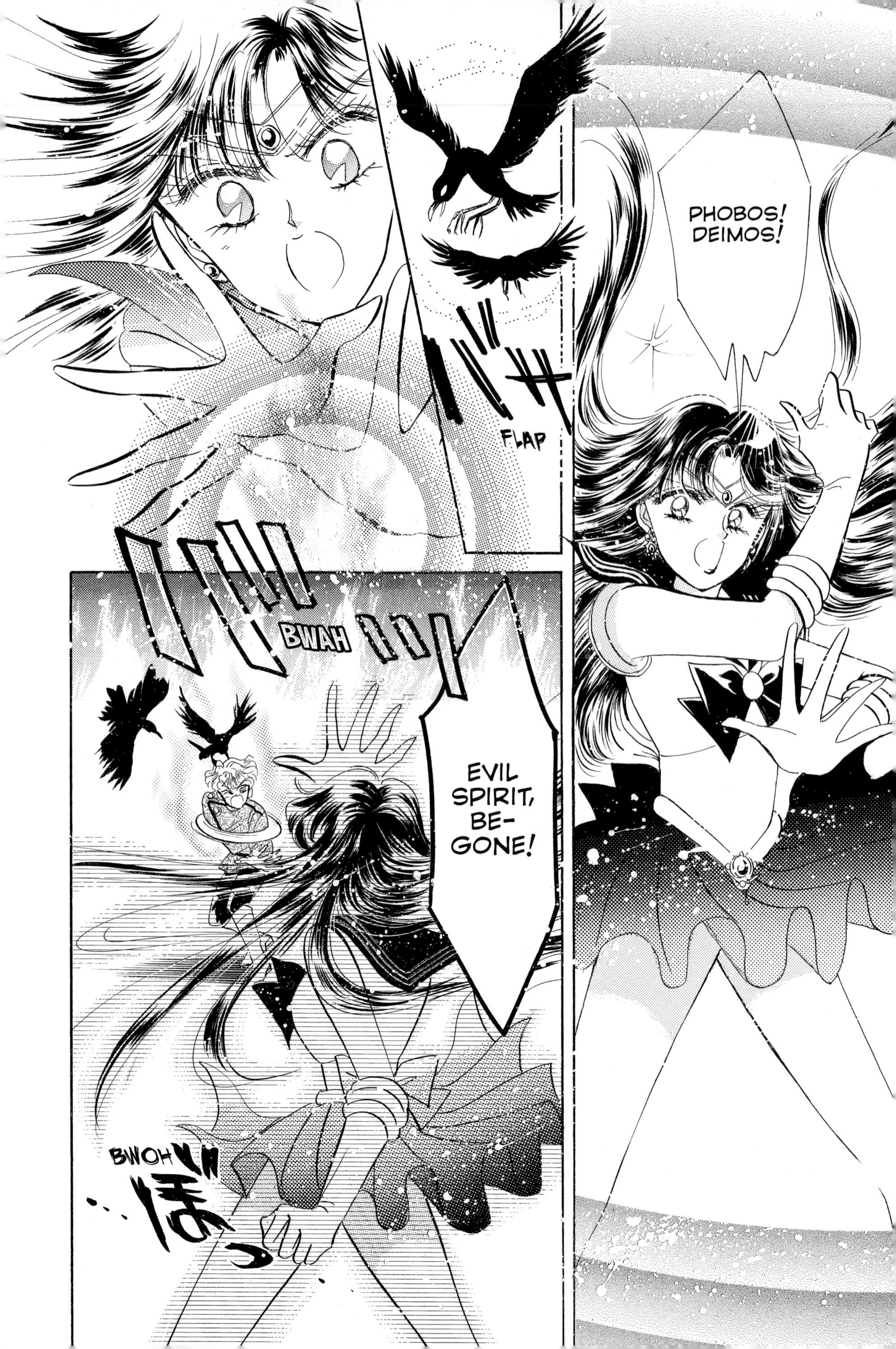
PHOBOS! DEIMOS!
FLAP
BWAH
EVIL SPIRIT, BE-GONE!
BWOH

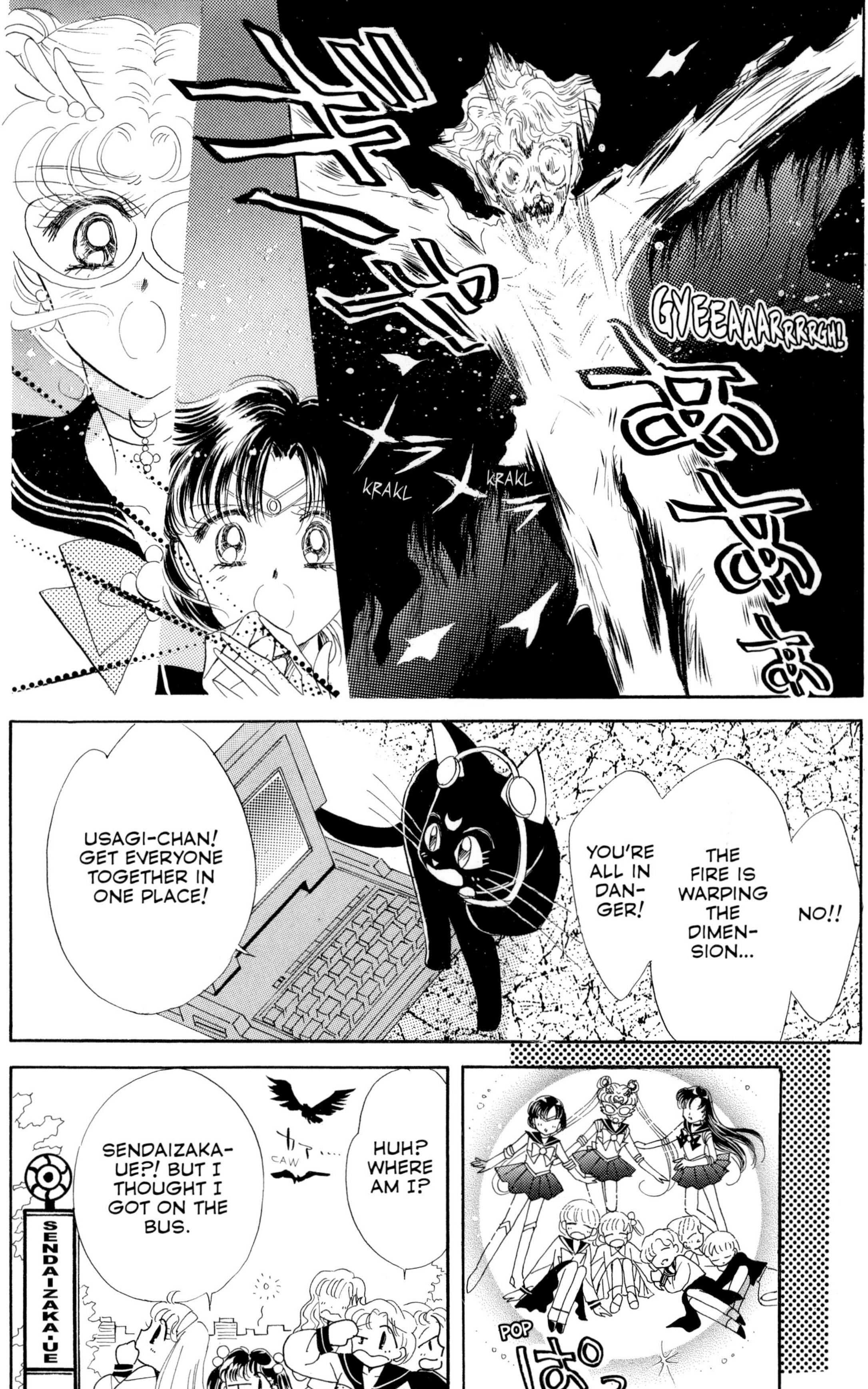
GYEEAAARRRRGH!!
KRAKL
KRAKL
NO!!
YOU'RE ALL IN DANGER!
THE FIRE IS WARPING THE DIMENSION...
USAGI-CHAN! GET EVERYONE TOGETHER IN ONE PLACE!
POP
HUH? WHERE AM I?
CAW
SENDAIZAKA-UE?! BUT I THOUGHT I GOT ON THE BUS.
SENDAIZAKA-UE

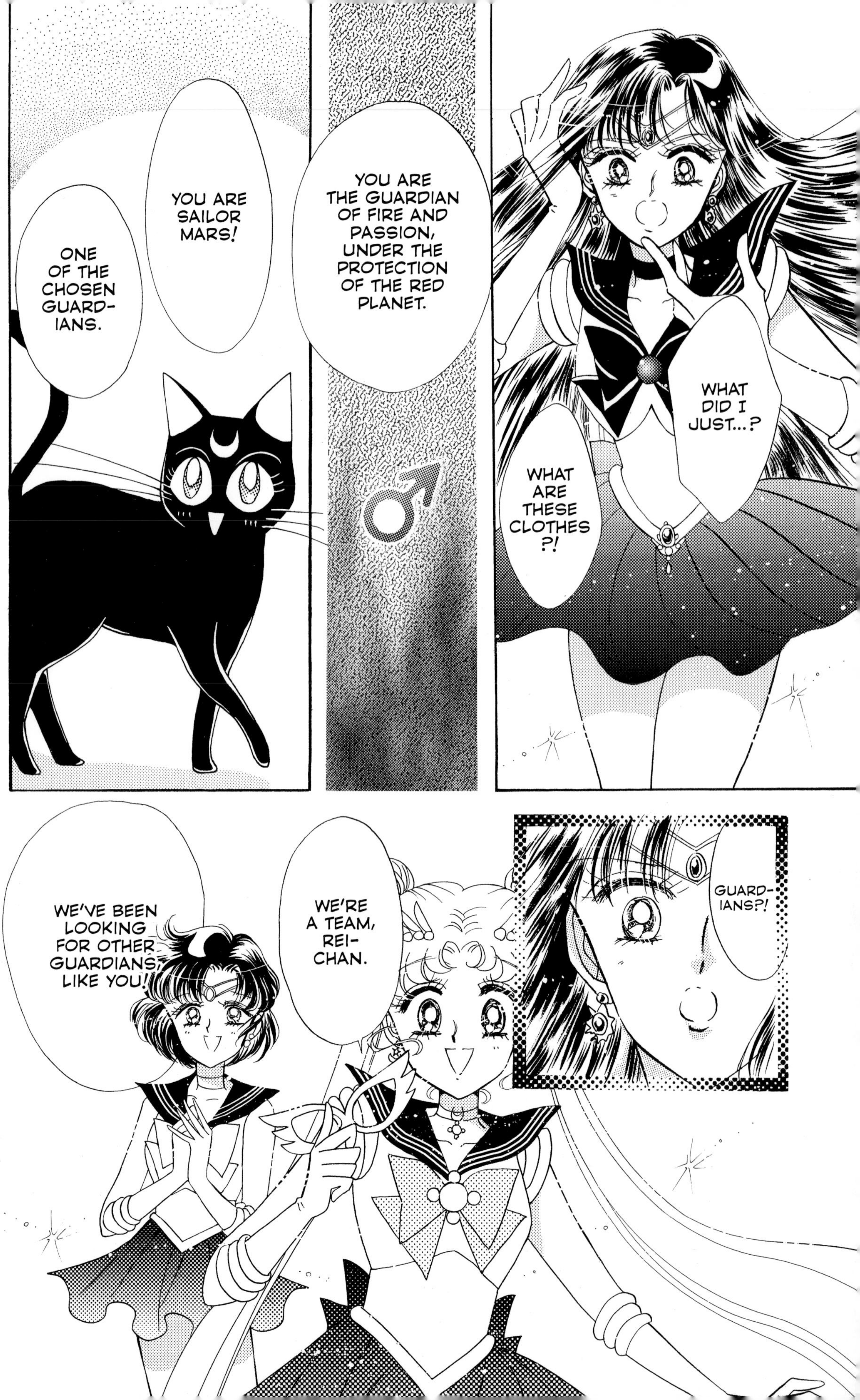
WHAT DID I JUST...?
WHAT ARE THESE CLOTHES?!
YOU ARE THE GUARDIAN OF FIRE AND PASSION, UNDER THE PROTECTION OF THE RED PLANET.
YOU ARE SAILOR MARS!
ONE OF THE CHOSEN GUARDIANS.
GUARDIANS?!
WE'RE A TEAM, REI-CHAN.
WE'VE BEEN LOOKING FOR OTHER GUARDIANS LIKE YOU!

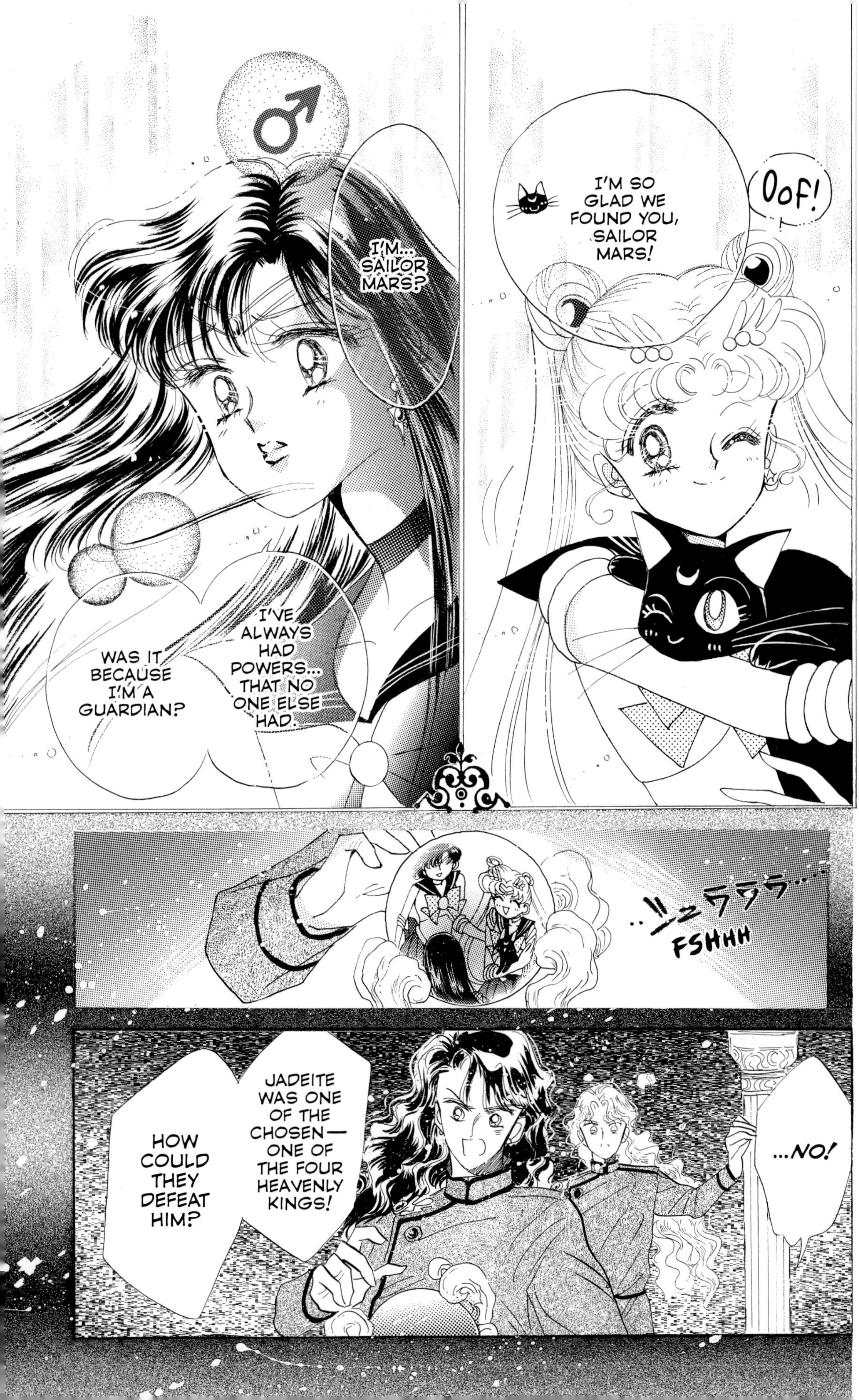
Oof!
I'M SO GLAD WE FOUND YOU, SAILOR MARS!
I'M... SAILOR MARS?
I'VE ALWAYS HAD POWERS... THAT NO ONE ELSE HAD.
WAS IT BECAUSE I'M A GUARDIAN?
FSHHH
...NO!
JADEITE WAS ONE OF THE CHOSEN—ONE OF THE FOUR HEAVENLY KINGS!
HOW COULD THEY DEFEAT HIM?

Pretty Guardian *Sailor Moon*

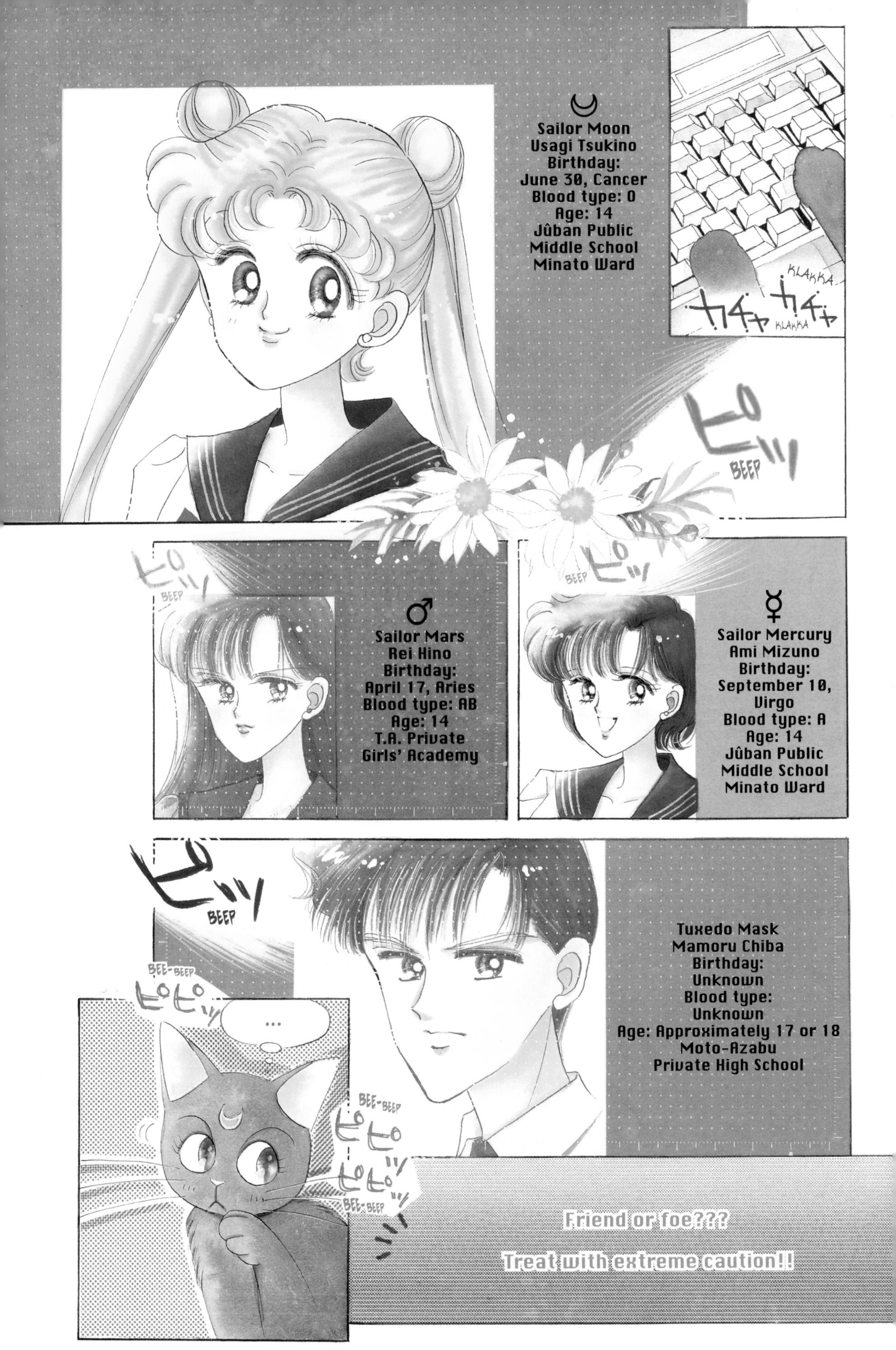

KLAKKA
KLAKKA
Sailor Moon
Usagi Tsukino
Birthday:
June 30, Cancer
Blood type: O
Age: 14
Jûban Public
Middle School
Minato Ward
BEEP
BEEP
☿
Sailor Mercury
Ami Mizuno
Birthday:
September 10,
Virgo
Blood type: A
Age: 14
Jûban Public
Middle School
Minato Ward
BEEP
♂
Sailor Mars
Rei Hino
Birthday:
April 17, Aries
Blood type: AB
Age: 14
T.A. Private
Girls' Academy
Tuxedo Mask
Mamoru Chiba
Birthday:
Unknown
Blood type:
Unknown
Age: Approximately 17 or 18
Moto-Azabu
Private High School
BEEP
BEE-BEEP
...
BEE-BEEP
BEE-BEEP
Friend or foe???
Treat with extreme caution!!

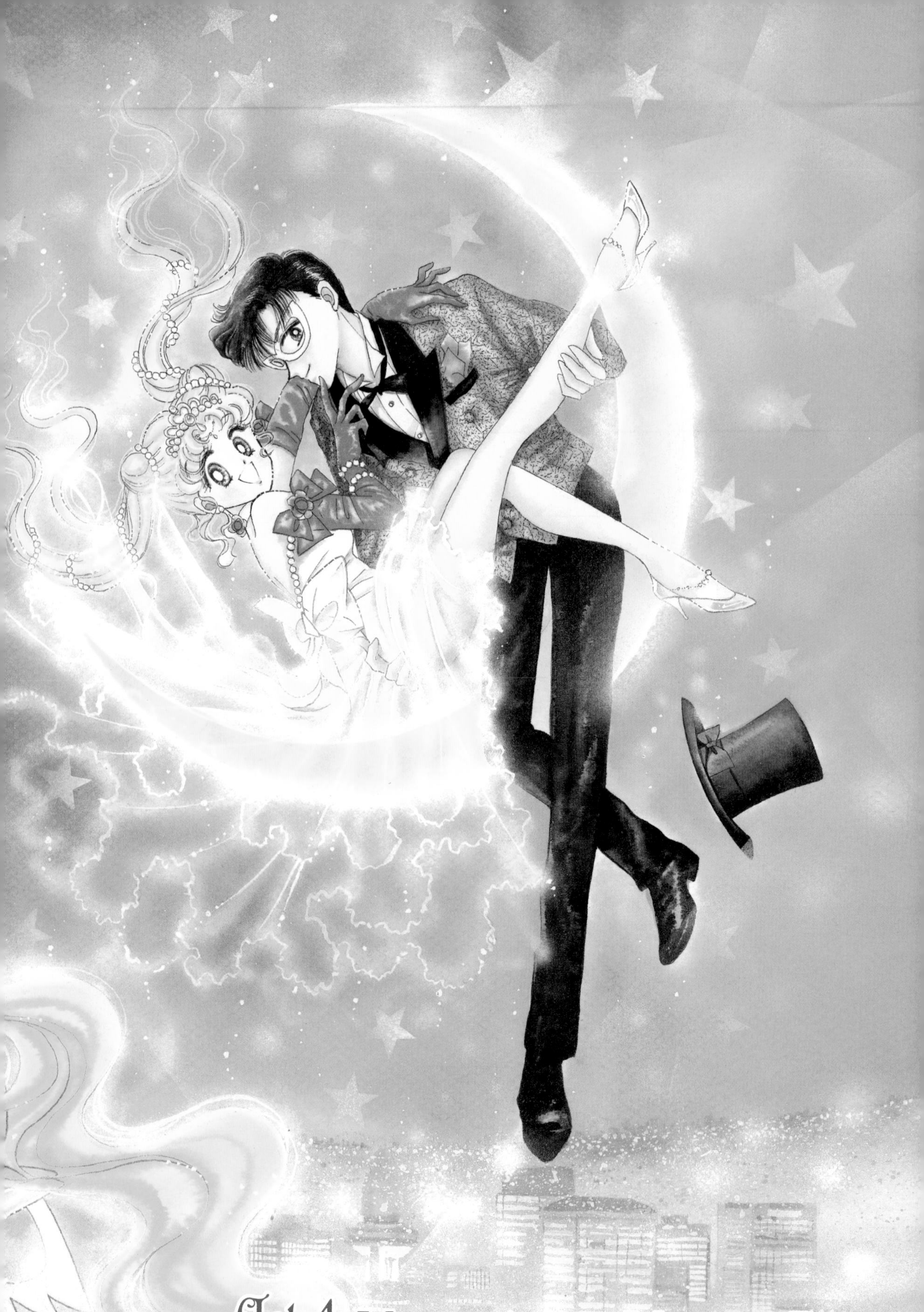

Act.4 Masquerade: Masked Ball

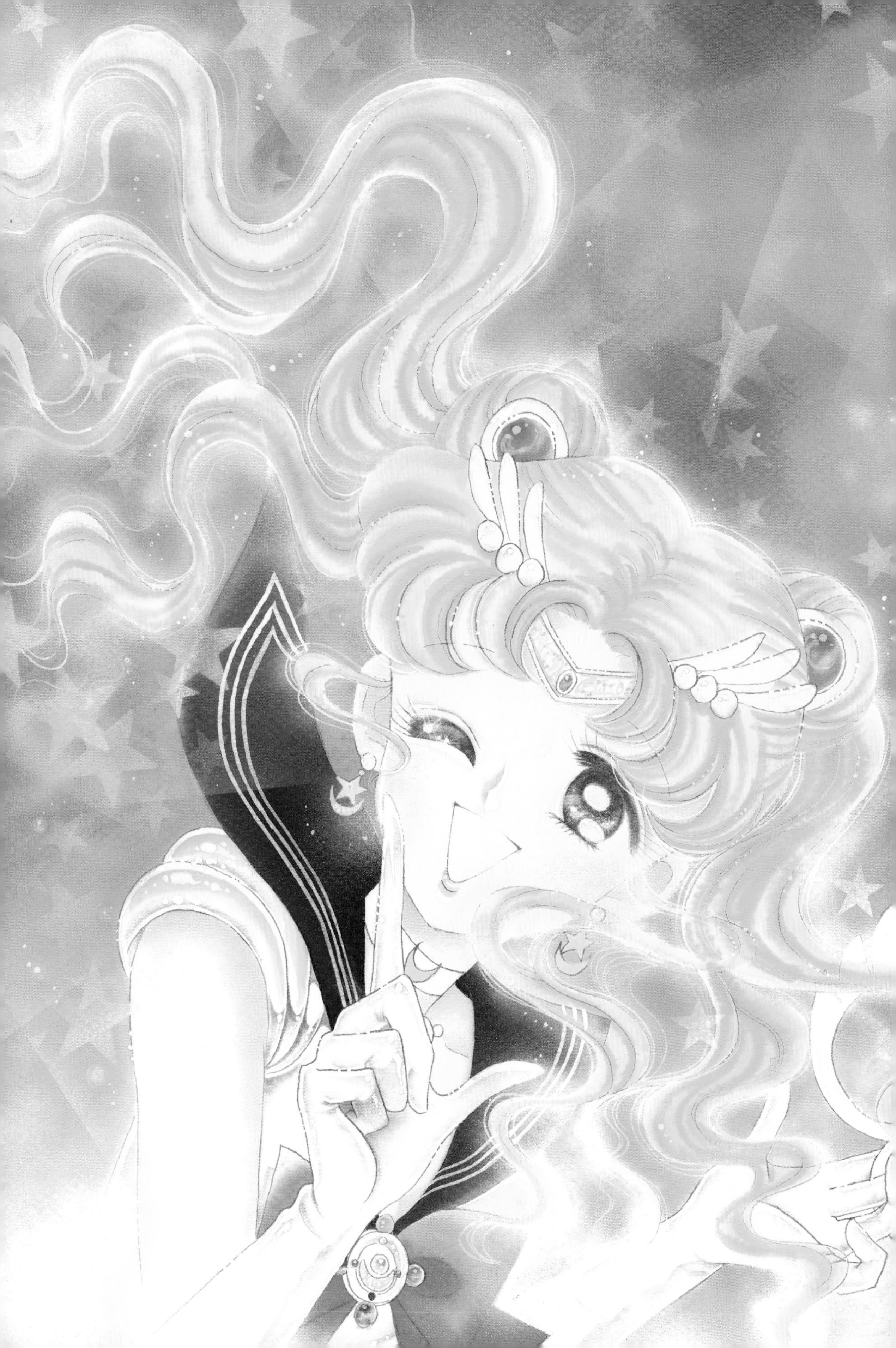

Pretty Guardian

Sailor Moon

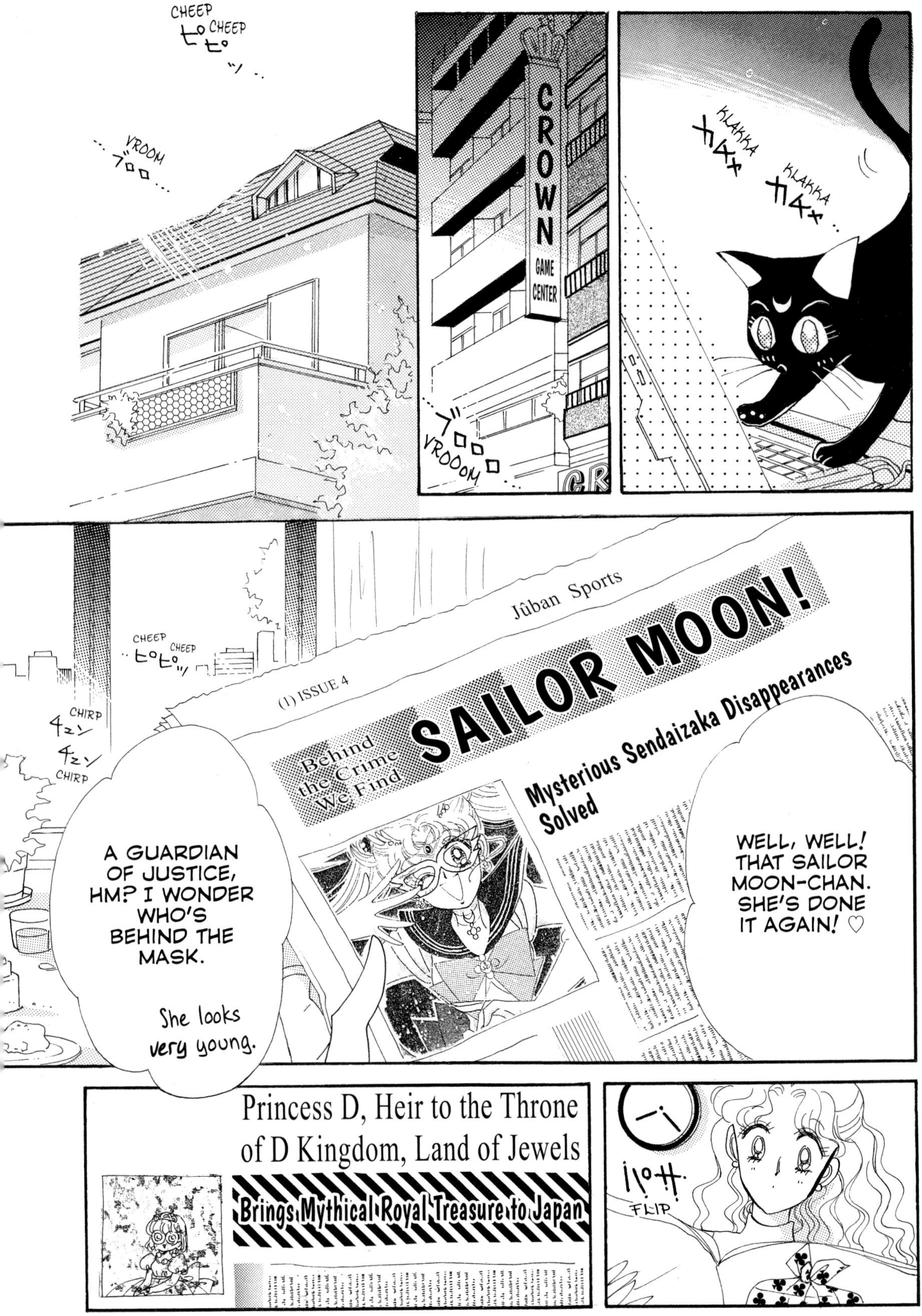
KLAKKA
KLAKKA
CROWN
GAME CENTER
VROOOM
CHEEP
CHEEP
VROOM
Jûban Sports
(1) ISSUE 4
SAILOR MOON!
Behind the Crime We Find
Mysterious Sendaizaka Disappearances Solved
CHEEP CHEEP
CHIRP
CHIRP
WELL, WELL! THAT SAILOR MOON-CHAN. SHE'S DONE IT AGAIN! ♡
A GUARDIAN OF JUSTICE, HM? I WONDER WHO'S BEHIND THE MASK.
She looks very young.
FLIP
Princess D, Heir to the Throne of D Kingdom, Land of Jewels
Brings Mythical Royal Treasure to Japan

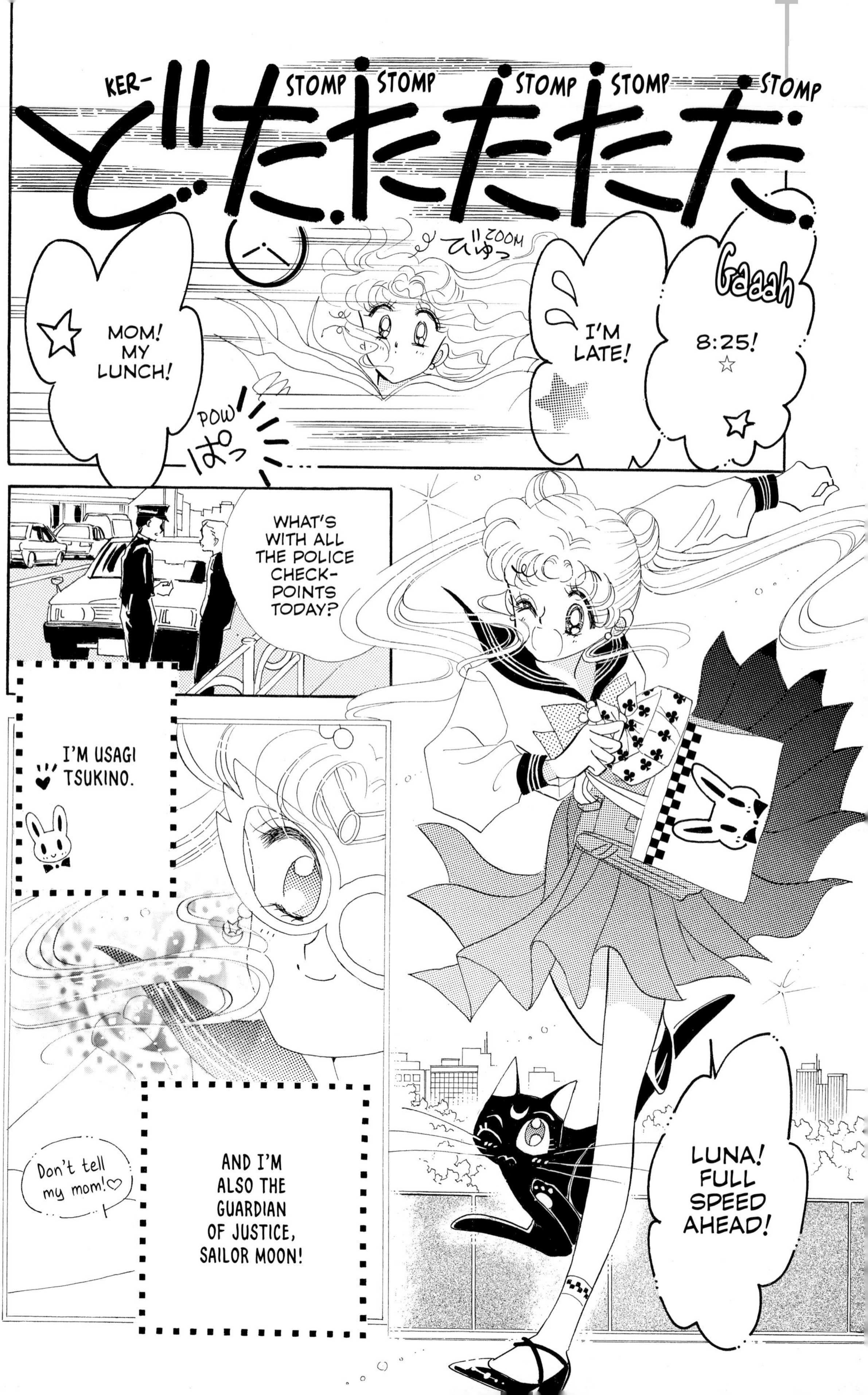

KER- STOMP STOMP STOMP STOMP STOMP
どたたたたた
Gaaah
8:25!
I'M LATE!
ZOOM ぴゅっ
MOM! MY LUNCH!
POW ぱっ
LUNA! FULL SPEED AHEAD!
WHAT'S WITH ALL THE POLICE CHECK-POINTS TODAY?
I'M USAGI TSUKINO.
AND I'M ALSO THE GUARDIAN OF JUSTICE, SAILOR MOON!
Don't tell my mom!♡

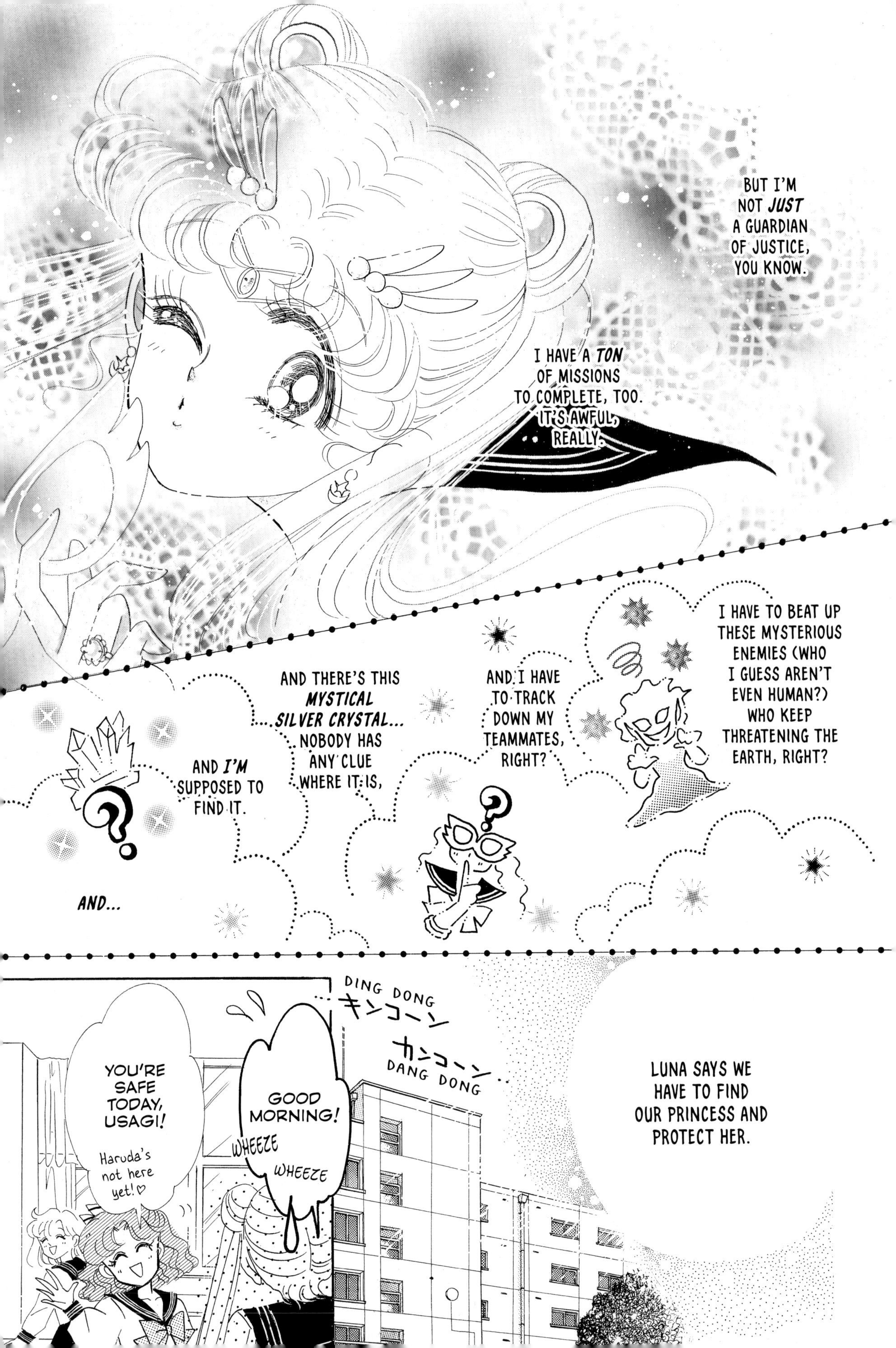

BUT I'M NOT JUST A GUARDIAN OF JUSTICE, YOU KNOW.
I HAVE A TON OF MISSIONS TO COMPLETE, TOO. IT'S AWFUL, REALLY.
I HAVE TO BEAT UP THESE MYSTERIOUS ENEMIES (WHO I GUESS AREN'T EVEN HUMAN?) WHO KEEP THREATENING THE EARTH, RIGHT?
AND I HAVE TO TRACK DOWN MY TEAMMATES, RIGHT?
AND THERE'S THIS MYSTICAL SILVER CRYSTAL... NOBODY HAS ANY CLUE WHERE IT IS,
AND I'M SUPPOSED TO FIND IT.
AND...
LUNA SAYS WE HAVE TO FIND OUR PRINCESS AND PROTECT HER.
DING DONG キンコーン
カンコーン DANG DONG
GOOD MORNING!
WHEEZE WHEEZE
YOU'RE SAFE TODAY, USAGI!
Haruda's not here yet!♡

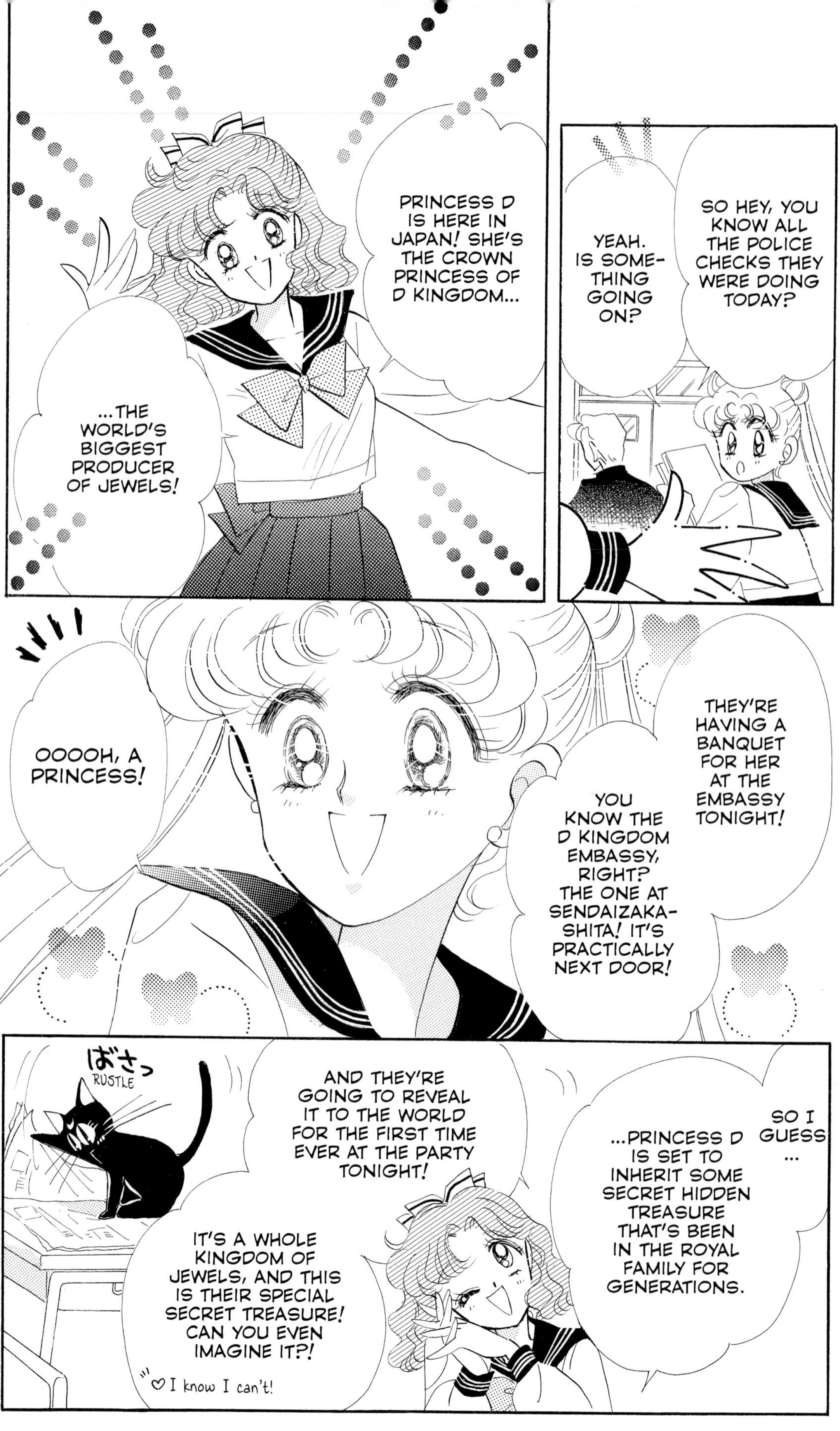
SO HEY, YOU KNOW ALL THE POLICE CHECKS THEY WERE DOING TODAY?
YEAH. IS SOME-THING GOING ON?
PRINCESS D IS HERE IN JAPAN! SHE'S THE CROWN PRINCESS OF D KINGDOM...
...THE WORLD'S BIGGEST PRODUCER OF JEWELS!
THEY'RE HAVING A BANQUET FOR HER AT THE EMBASSY TONIGHT!
YOU KNOW THE D KINGDOM EMBASSY, RIGHT? THE ONE AT SENDAIZAKA-SHITA! IT'S PRACTICALLY NEXT DOOR!
OOOOH, A PRINCESS!
SO I GUESS ...
...PRINCESS D IS SET TO INHERIT SOME SECRET HIDDEN TREASURE THAT'S BEEN IN THE ROYAL FAMILY FOR GENERATIONS.
AND THEY'RE GOING TO REVEAL IT TO THE WORLD FOR THE FIRST TIME EVER AT THE PARTY TONIGHT!
IT'S A WHOLE KINGDOM OF JEWELS, AND THIS IS THEIR SPECIAL SECRET TREASURE! CAN YOU EVEN IMAGINE IT?!
♡ I know I can't!
ばさっ
RUSTLE

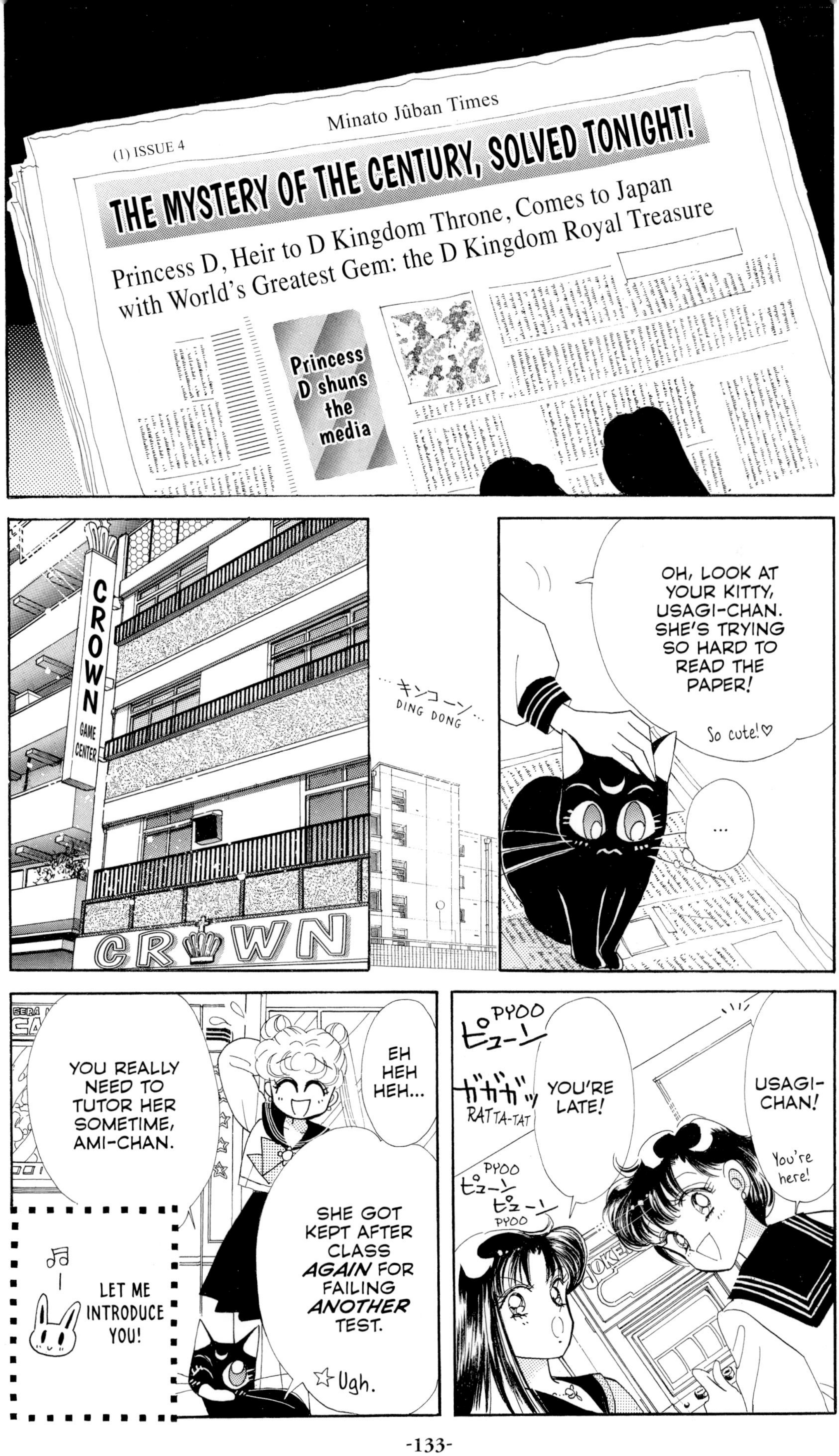

Minato Jûban Times
(1) ISSUE 4
THE MYSTERY OF THE CENTURY, SOLVED TONIGHT!
Princess D, Heir to D Kingdom Throne, Comes to Japan with World's Greatest Gem: the D Kingdom Royal Treasure
Princess D shuns the media
OH, LOOK AT YOUR KITTY, USAGI-CHAN. SHE'S TRYING SO HARD TO READ THE PAPER!
So cute!♡
...
…キンコーン… DING DONG
CROWN GAME CENTER
CROWN
USAGI-CHAN!
You're here!
YOU'RE LATE!
ピュ〜ン PYOO
ガガガッ RATTA-TAT
ピュ〜ン PYOO
ピュ〜ン PYOO
EH HEH HEH...
SHE GOT KEPT AFTER CLASS AGAIN FOR FAILING ANOTHER TEST.
Ugh.
YOU REALLY NEED TO TUTOR HER SOMETIME, AMI-CHAN.
LET ME INTRODUCE YOU!

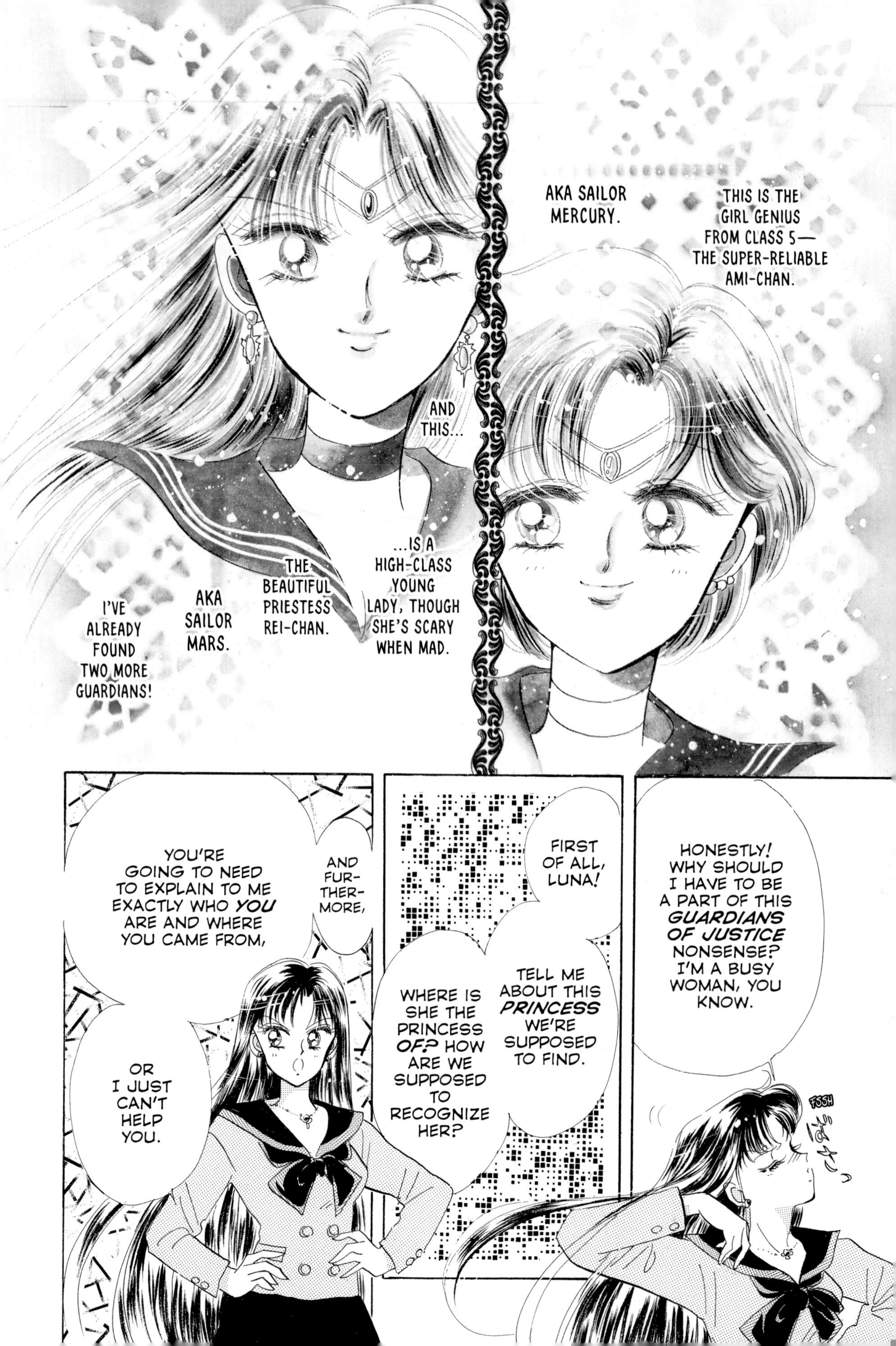
THIS IS THE GIRL GENIUS FROM CLASS 5— THE SUPER-RELIABLE AMI-CHAN.
AKA SAILOR MERCURY.
AND THIS...
...IS A HIGH-CLASS YOUNG LADY, THOUGH SHE'S SCARY WHEN MAD.
THE BEAUTIFUL PRIESTESS REI-CHAN.
AKA SAILOR MARS.
I'VE ALREADY FOUND TWO MORE GUARDIANS!
HONESTLY! WHY SHOULD I HAVE TO BE A PART OF THIS ***GUARDIANS OF JUSTICE*** NONSENSE? I'M A BUSY WOMAN, YOU KNOW.
FSSH
FIRST OF ALL, LUNA!
TELL ME ABOUT THIS ***PRINCESS*** WE'RE SUPPOSED TO FIND.
WHERE IS SHE THE PRINCESS ***OF?*** HOW ARE WE SUPPOSED TO RECOGNIZE HER?
AND FUR-THER-MORE,
YOU'RE GOING TO NEED TO EXPLAIN TO ME EXACTLY WHO ***YOU*** ARE AND WHERE YOU CAME FROM,
OR I JUST CAN'T HELP YOU.

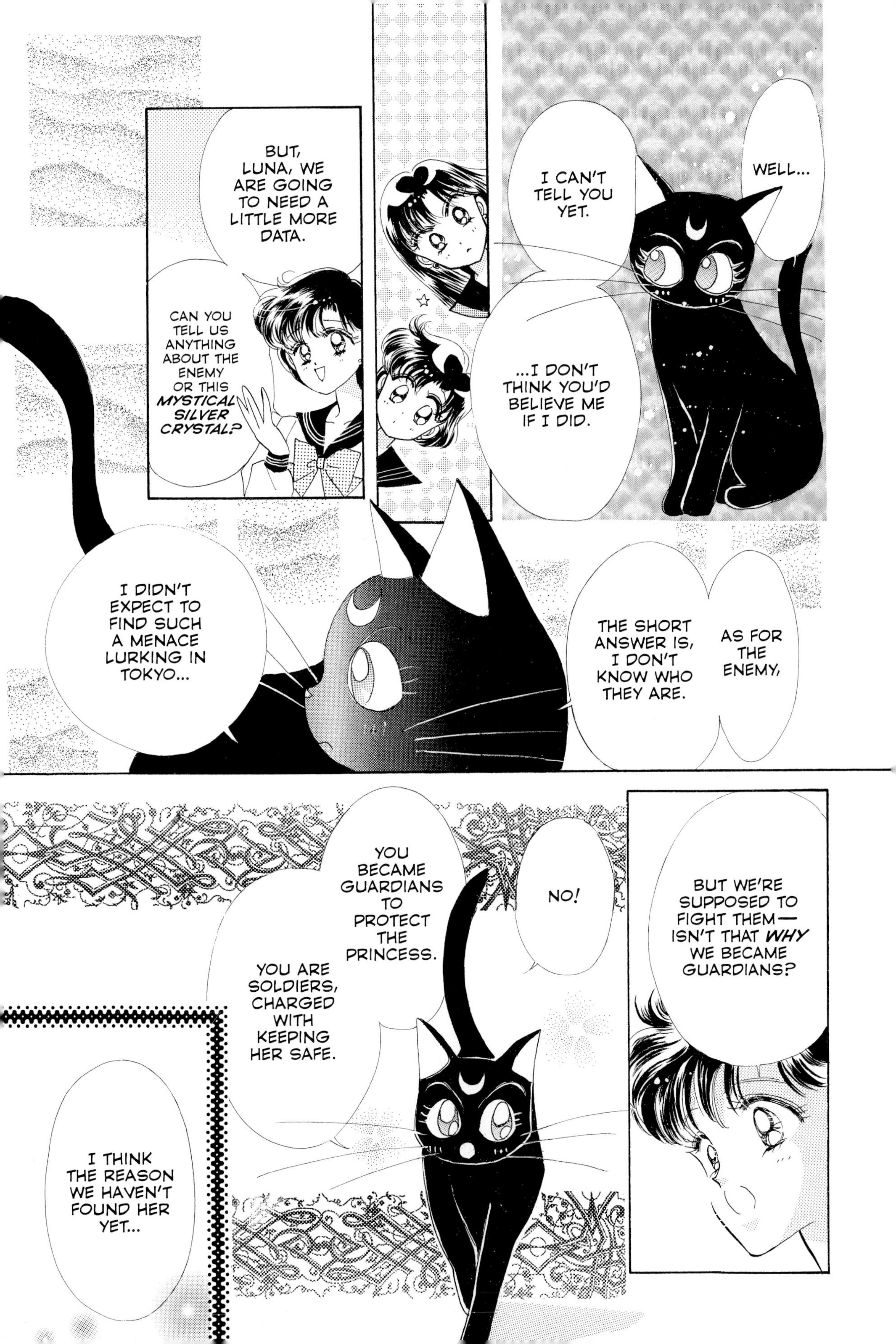
WELL...
I CAN'T TELL YOU YET.
...I DON'T THINK YOU'D BELIEVE ME IF I DID.
BUT, LUNA, WE ARE GOING TO NEED A LITTLE MORE DATA.
CAN YOU TELL US ANYTHING ABOUT THE ENEMY OR THIS *MYSTICAL SILVER CRYSTAL?*
AS FOR THE ENEMY,
THE SHORT ANSWER IS, I DON'T KNOW WHO THEY ARE.
I DIDN'T EXPECT TO FIND SUCH A MENACE LURKING IN TOKYO...
BUT WE'RE SUPPOSED TO FIGHT THEM—ISN'T THAT *WHY* WE BECAME GUARDIANS?
NO!
YOU BECAME GUARDIANS TO PROTECT THE PRINCESS.
YOU ARE SOLDIERS, CHARGED WITH KEEPING HER SAFE.
I THINK THE REASON WE HAVEN'T FOUND HER YET...

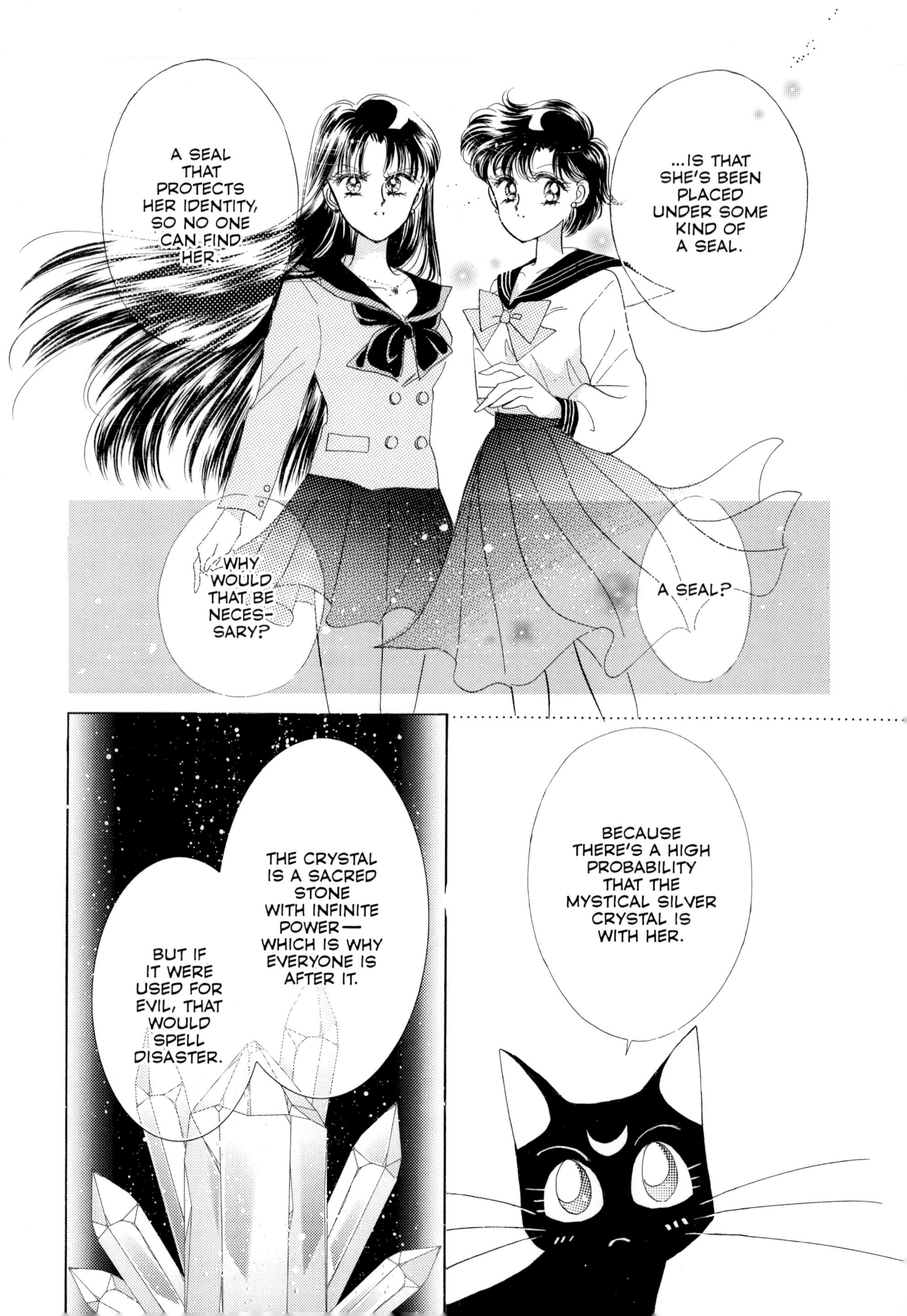
...IS THAT SHE'S BEEN PLACED UNDER SOME KIND OF A SEAL.
A SEAL THAT PROTECTS HER IDENTITY, SO NO ONE CAN FIND HER.
A SEAL?
WHY WOULD THAT BE NECES-SARY?
BECAUSE THERE'S A HIGH PROBABILITY THAT THE MYSTICAL SILVER CRYSTAL IS WITH HER.
THE CRYSTAL IS A SACRED STONE WITH INFINITE POWER— WHICH IS WHY EVERYONE IS AFTER IT.
BUT IF IT WERE USED FOR EVIL, THAT WOULD SPELL DISASTER.

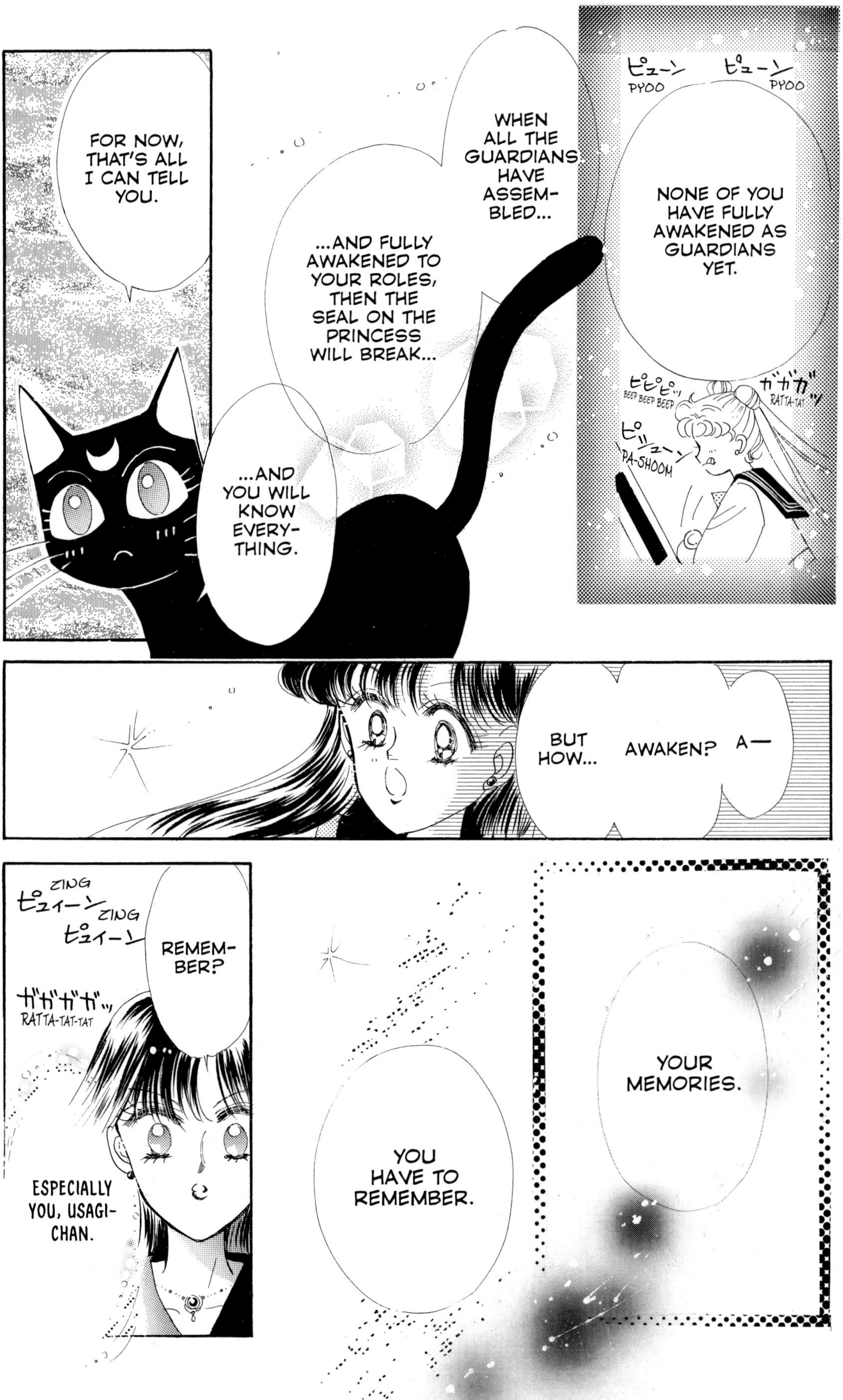
ピューン PYOO
ピューン PYOO
NONE OF YOU HAVE FULLY AWAKENED AS GUARDIANS YET.
ガガガッ RATTA-TAT
ピピピッ BEEP BEEP BEEP
ピシューン PA-SHOOM
WHEN ALL THE GUARDIANS HAVE ASSEMBLED...
...AND FULLY AWAKENED TO YOUR ROLES, THEN THE SEAL ON THE PRINCESS WILL BREAK...
...AND YOU WILL KNOW EVERYTHING.
FOR NOW, THAT'S ALL I CAN TELL YOU.
A—
AWAKEN?
BUT HOW...
YOUR MEMORIES.
YOU HAVE TO REMEMBER.
REMEMBER?
ピュイーン ZING
ピュイーン ZING
ガガガガッ RATTA-TAT-TAT
ESPECIALLY YOU, USAGI-CHAN.

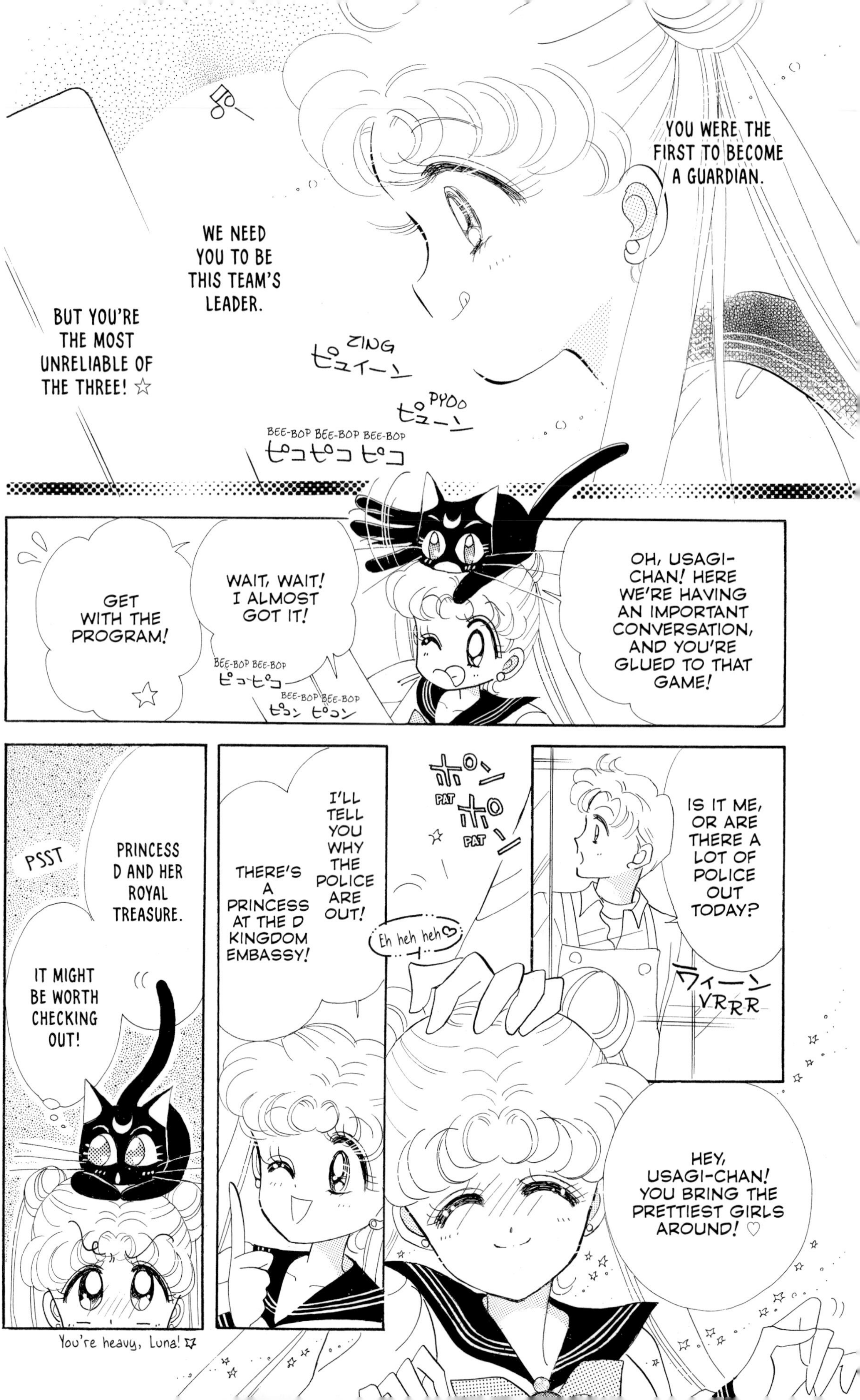
YOU WERE THE FIRST TO BECOME A GUARDIAN.
WE NEED YOU TO BE THIS TEAM'S LEADER.
BUT YOU'RE THE MOST UNRELIABLE OF THE THREE! ☆
ZING ピュイーン
PYOO ピューン
BEE-BOP BEE-BOP BEE-BOP ピコピコピコ
OH, USAGI-CHAN! HERE WE'RE HAVING AN IMPORTANT CONVERSATION, AND YOU'RE GLUED TO THAT GAME!
WAIT, WAIT! I ALMOST GOT IT!
BEE-BOP BEE-BOP ピコピコ
BEE-BOP BEE-BOP ピコンピコン
GET WITH THE PROGRAM!
IS IT ME, OR ARE THERE A LOT OF POLICE OUT TODAY?
ウィーン VRRR
ポン PAT ポン PAT
Eh heh heh♡
HEY, USAGI-CHAN! YOU BRING THE PRETTIEST GIRLS AROUND! ♡
I'LL TELL YOU WHY THE POLICE ARE OUT!
THERE'S A PRINCESS AT THE D KINGDOM EMBASSY!
PRINCESS D AND HER ROYAL TREASURE.
PSST
IT MIGHT BE WORTH CHECKING OUT!
You're heavy, Luna! ☆

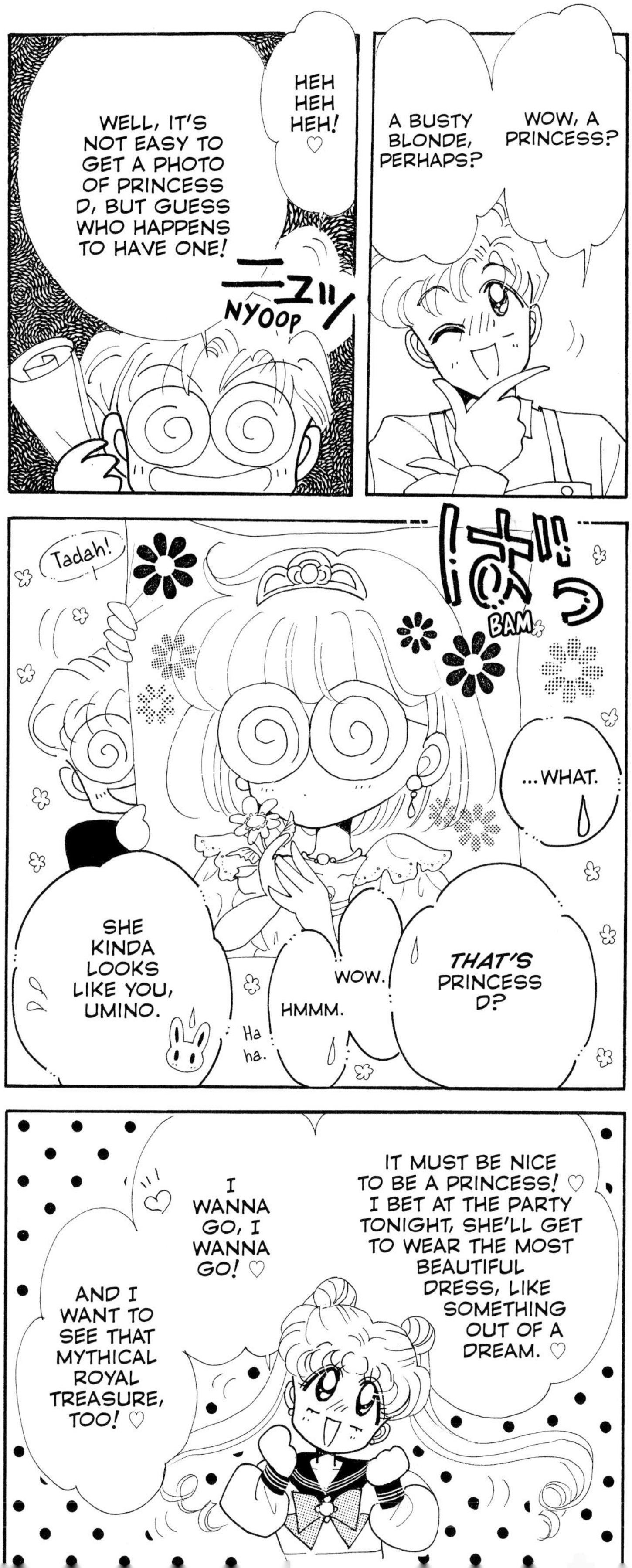
WOW, A PRINCESS?
A BUSTY BLONDE, PERHAPS?
HEH HEH HEH! ♡
WELL, IT'S NOT EASY TO GET A PHOTO OF PRINCESS D, BUT GUESS WHO HAPPENS TO HAVE ONE!
ニュッ
NYOOP
ぱっ
BAM
Tadah!
...WHAT.
THAT'S PRINCESS D?
WOW.
HMMM.
Ha ha.
SHE KINDA LOOKS LIKE YOU, UMINO.
IT MUST BE NICE TO BE A PRINCESS! ♡ I BET AT THE PARTY TONIGHT, SHE'LL GET TO WEAR THE MOST BEAUTIFUL DRESS, LIKE SOMETHING OUT OF A DREAM. ♡
I WANNA GO, I WANNA GO! ♡
AND I WANT TO SEE THAT MYTHICAL ROYAL TREASURE, TOO! ♡
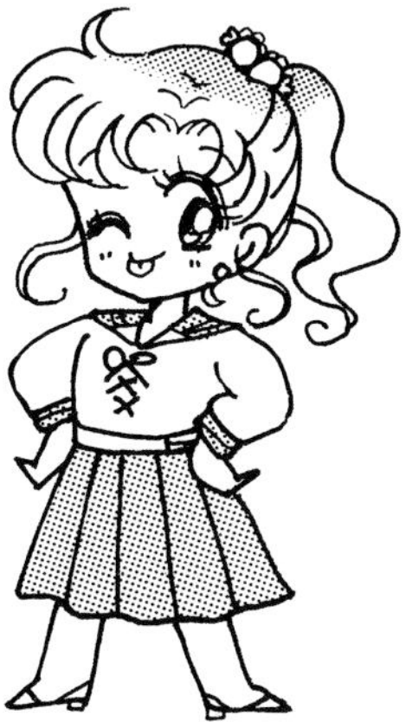

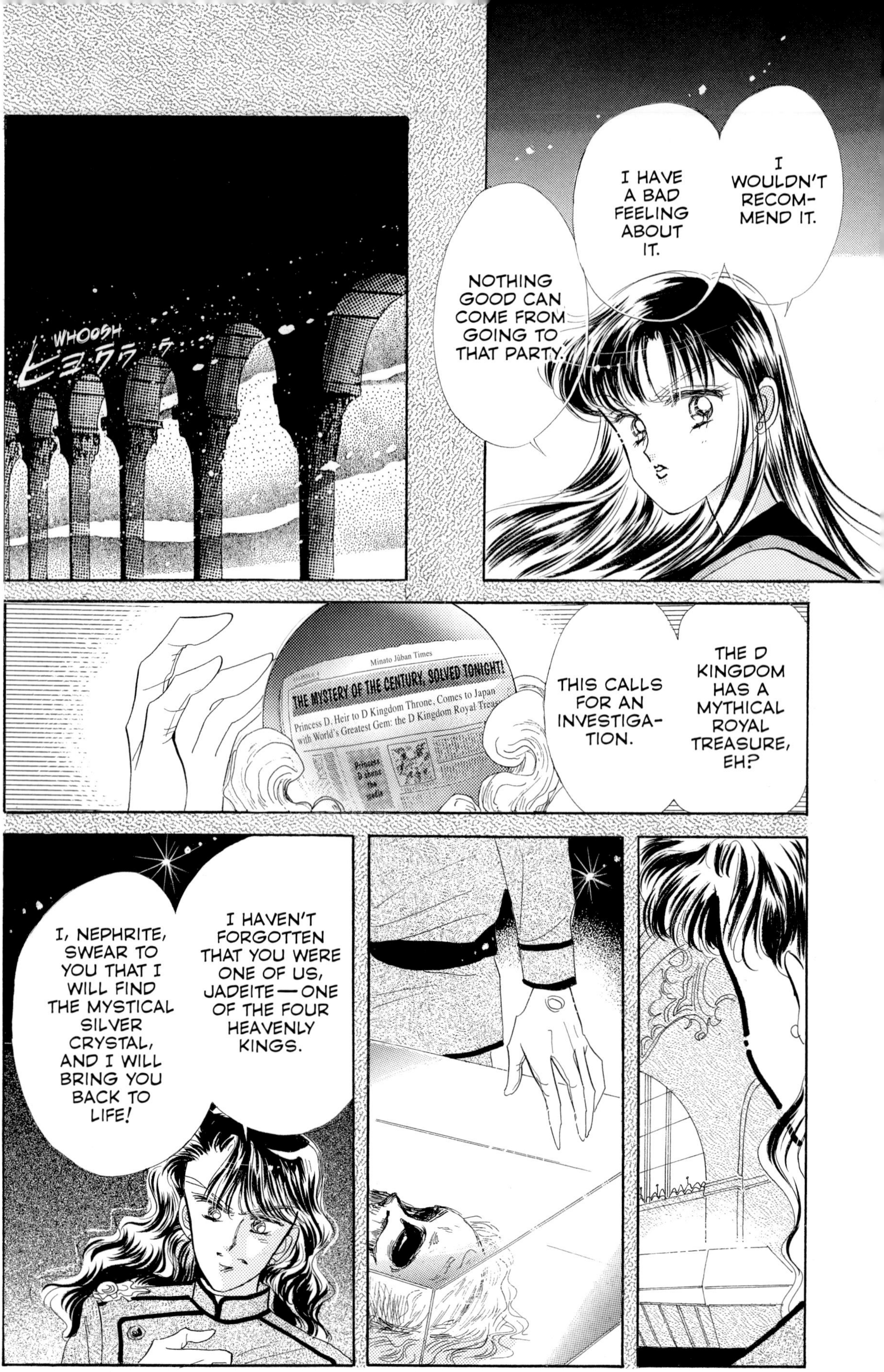
I WOULDN'T RECOMMEND IT.
I HAVE A BAD FEELING ABOUT IT.
NOTHING GOOD CAN COME FROM GOING TO THAT PARTY.
WHOOSH
ヒョウウウ
THE D KINGDOM HAS A MYTHICAL ROYAL TREASURE, EH?
THIS CALLS FOR AN INVESTIGATION.
Minato Jūban Times
THE MYSTERY OF THE CENTURY, SOLVED TONIGHT!
Princess D, Heir to D Kingdom Throne, Comes to Japan with World's Greatest Gem: the D Kingdom Royal Treas
I HAVEN'T FORGOTTEN THAT YOU WERE ONE OF US, JADEITE—ONE OF THE FOUR HEAVENLY KINGS.
I, NEPHRITE, SWEAR TO YOU THAT I WILL FIND THE MYSTICAL SILVER CRYSTAL, AND I WILL BRING YOU BACK TO LIFE!

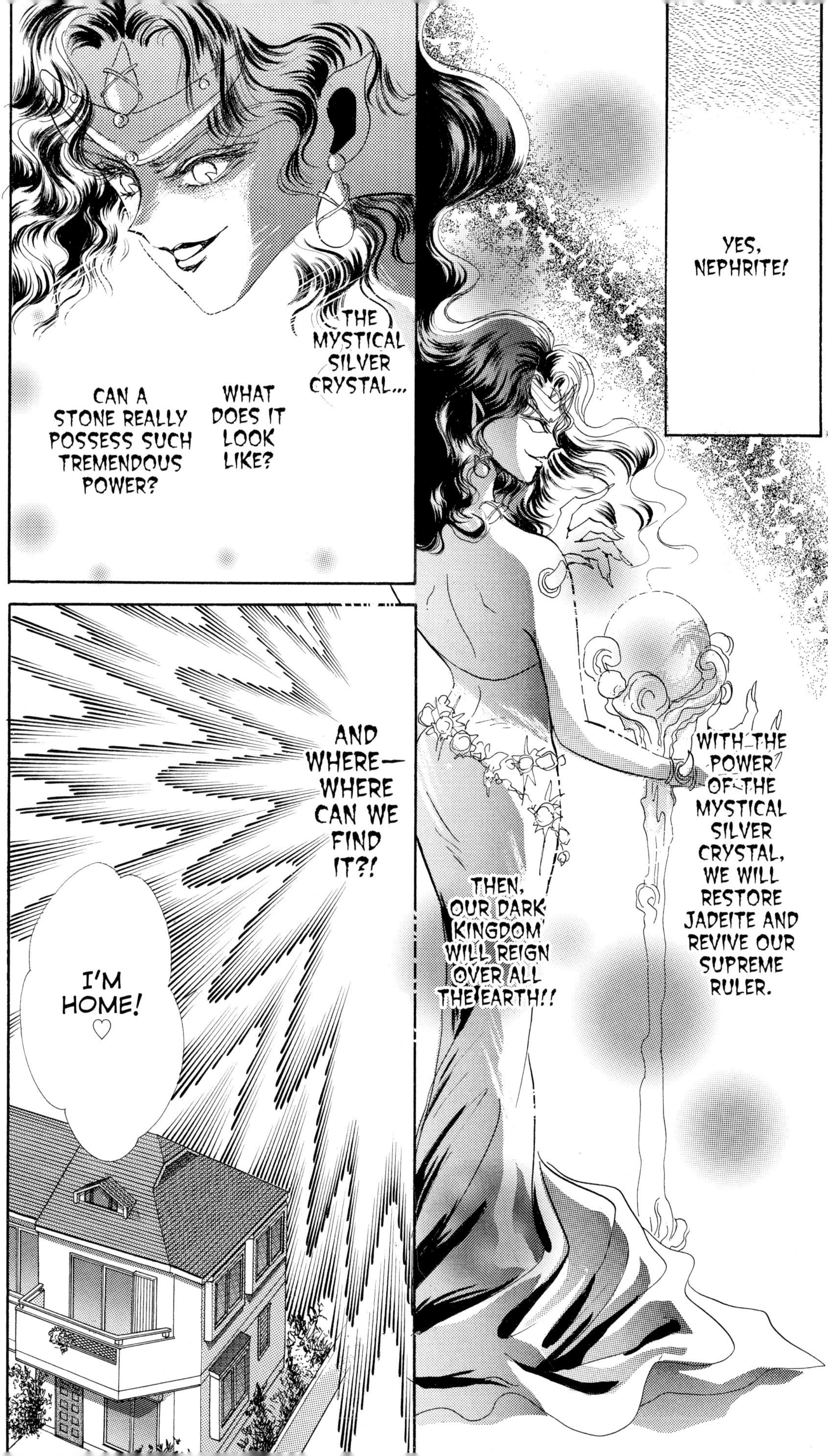
YES, NEPHRITE!
WITH THE POWER OF THE MYSTICAL SILVER CRYSTAL, WE WILL RESTORE JADEITE AND REVIVE OUR SUPREME RULER.
THEN, OUR DARK KINGDOM WILL REIGN OVER ALL THE EARTH!!
THE MYSTICAL SILVER CRYSTAL...
WHAT DOES IT LOOK LIKE?
CAN A STONE REALLY POSSESS SUCH TREMENDOUS POWER?
AND WHERE—WHERE CAN WE FIND IT?!
I'M HOME! ♡

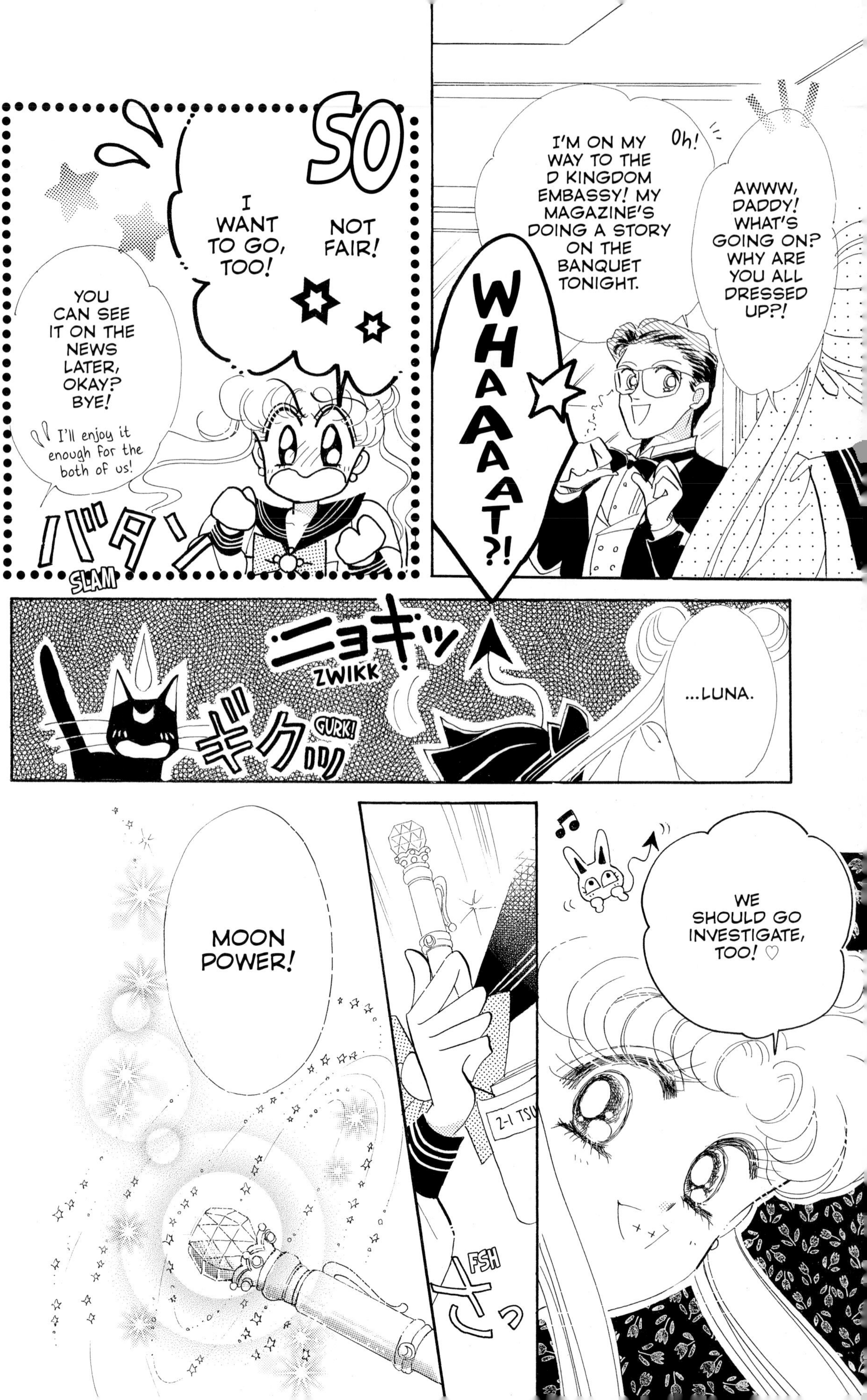
AWWW, DADDY! WHAT'S GOING ON? WHY ARE YOU ALL DRESSED UP?!
Oh!
I'M ON MY WAY TO THE D KINGDOM EMBASSY! MY MAGAZINE'S DOING A STORY ON THE BANQUET TONIGHT.
WHAAAAT?!
SO
NOT FAIR!
I WANT TO GO, TOO!
YOU CAN SEE IT ON THE NEWS LATER, OKAY? BYE!
I'll enjoy it enough for the both of us!
バタン
SLAM
...LUNA.
ニョキッ
ZWIKK
ギクッ
GURK!
WE SHOULD GO INVESTIGATE, TOO! ♡
2-1 TSU
さっ
FSH
MOON POWER!

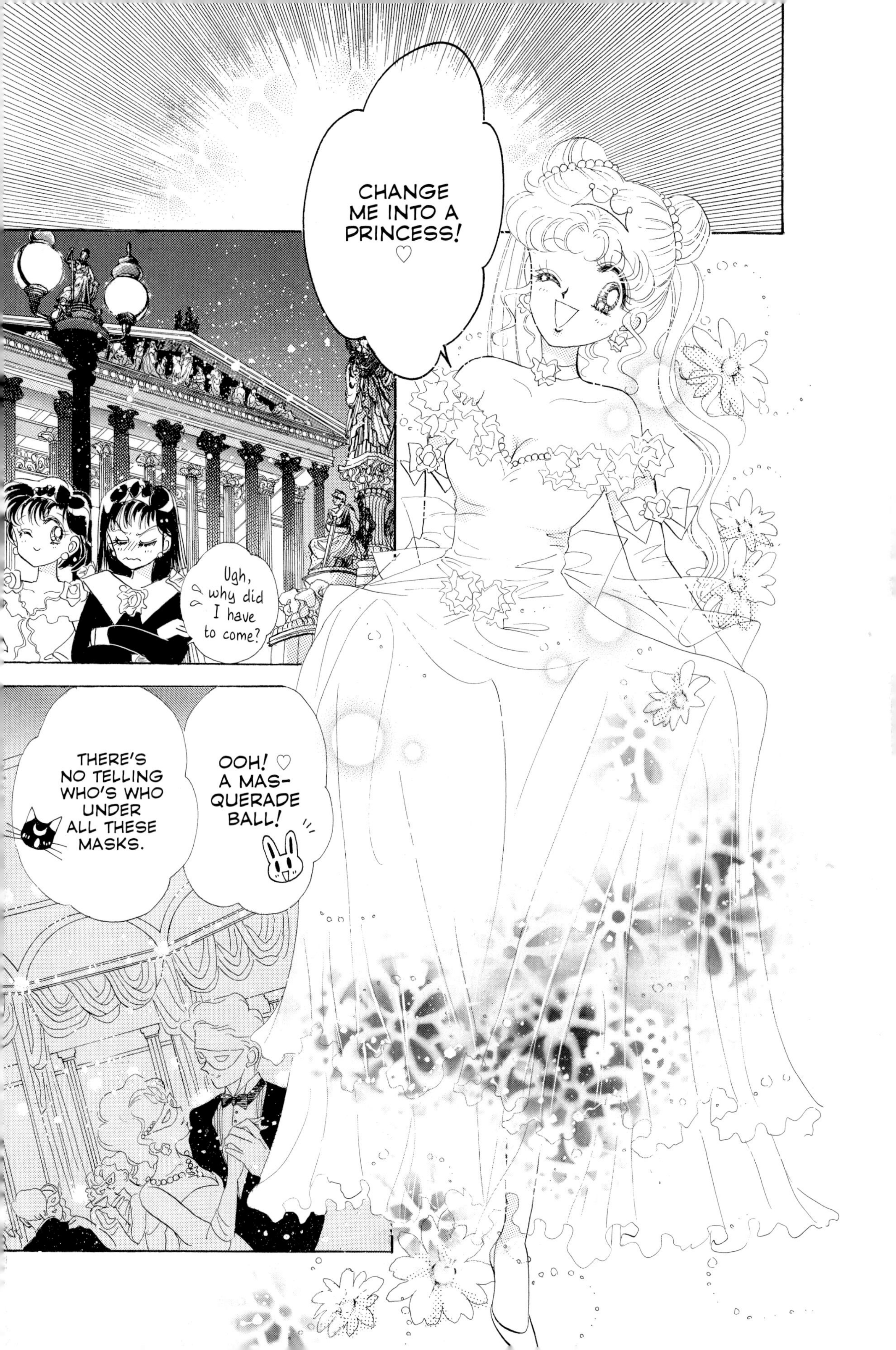
CHANGE ME INTO A PRINCESS! ♡
Ugh, why did I have to come?
OOH! ♡ A MAS-QUERADE BALL!
THERE'S NO TELLING WHO'S WHO UNDER ALL THESE MASKS.

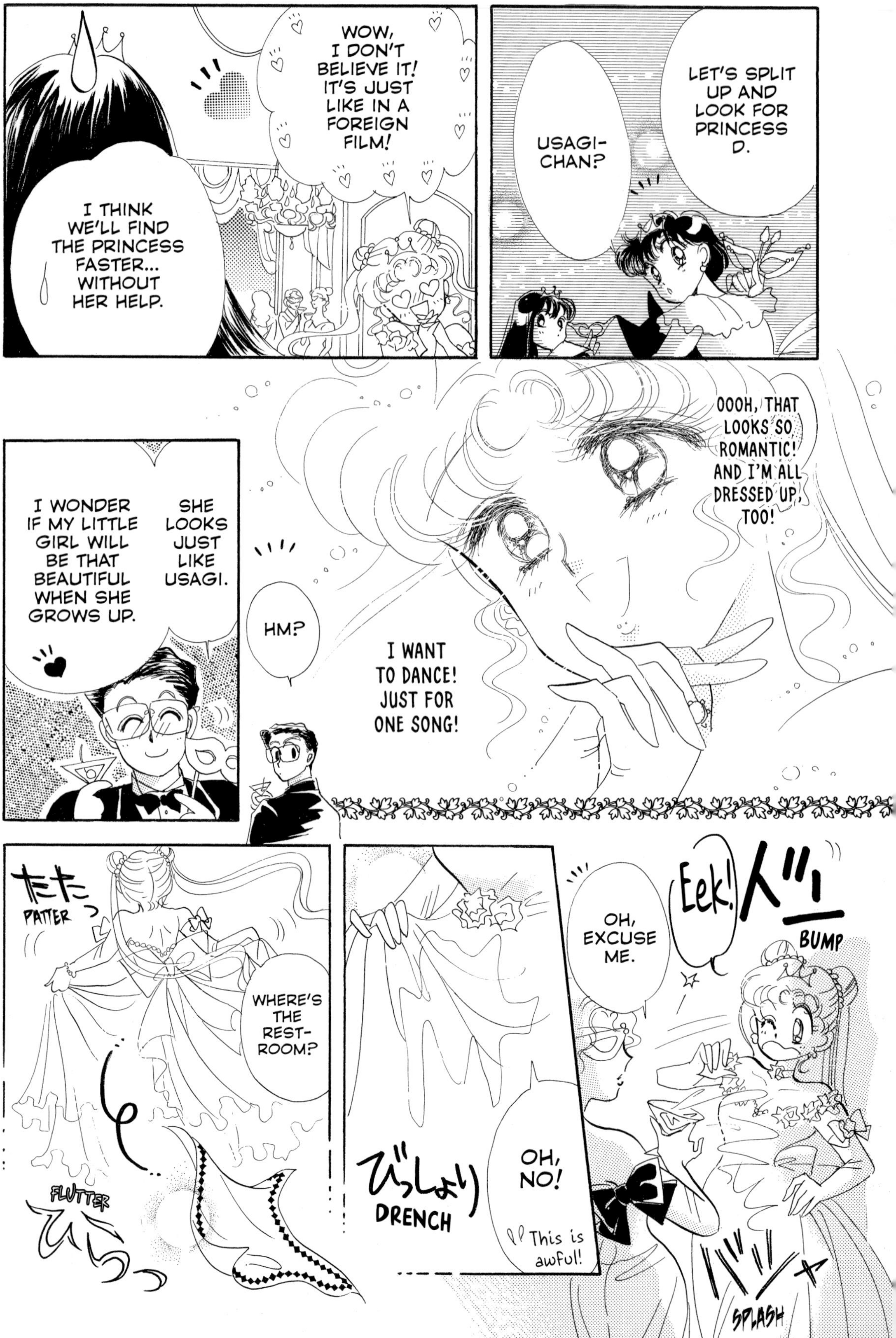
LET'S SPLIT UP AND LOOK FOR PRINCESS D.
USAGI-CHAN?
WOW, I DON'T BELIEVE IT! IT'S JUST LIKE IN A FOREIGN FILM!
I THINK WE'LL FIND THE PRINCESS FASTER... WITHOUT HER HELP.
OOOH, THAT LOOKS SO ROMANTIC! AND I'M ALL DRESSED UP, TOO!
I WANT TO DANCE! JUST FOR ONE SONG!
HM?
SHE LOOKS JUST LIKE USAGI.
I WONDER IF MY LITTLE GIRL WILL BE THAT BEAUTIFUL WHEN SHE GROWS UP.
Eek!
BUMP
OH, EXCUSE ME.
SPLASH
びっしょり
DRENCH
OH, NO!
This is awful!
PATTER
WHERE'S THE REST-ROOM?
FLUTTER

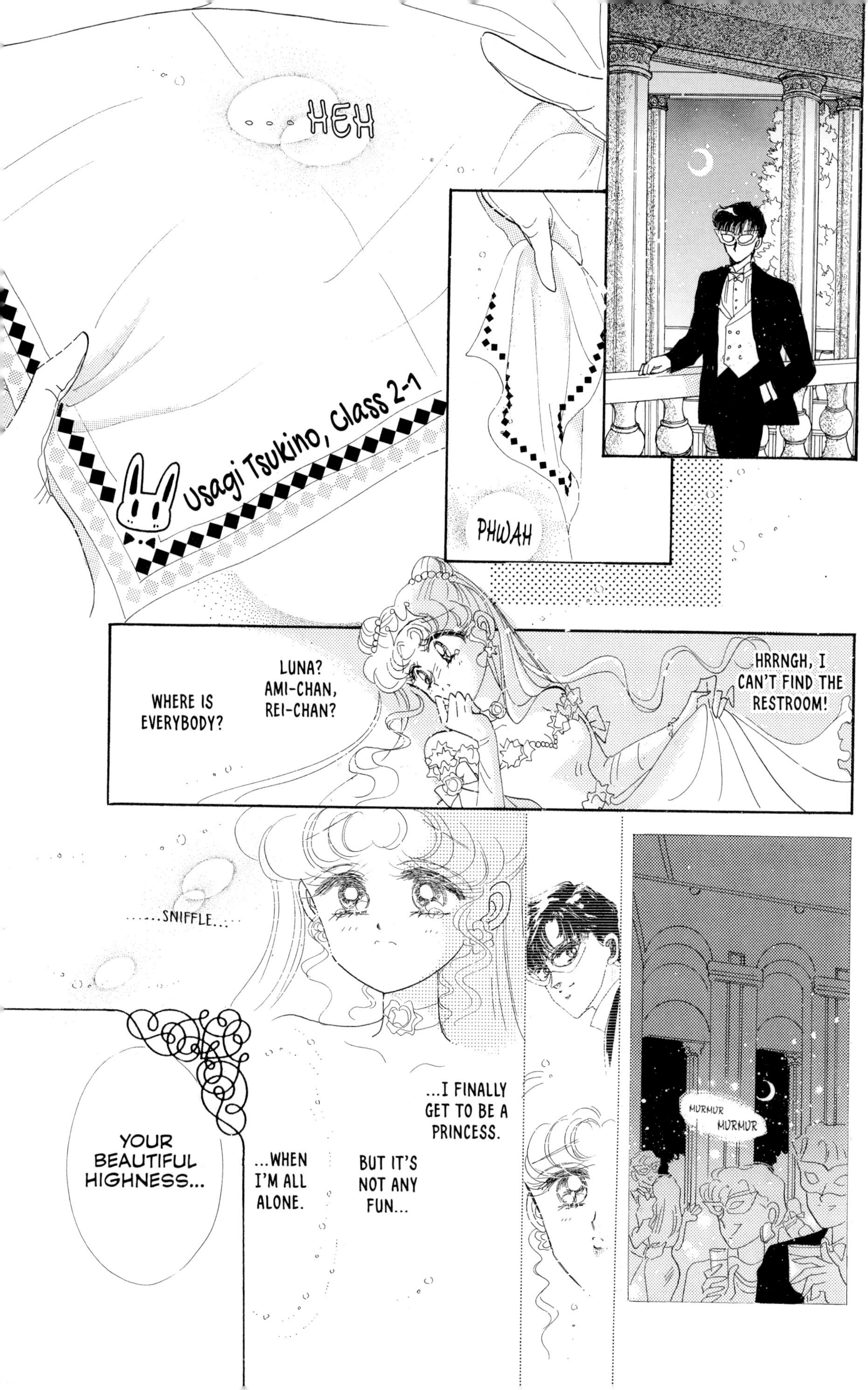
PHWAH
...HEH
Usagi Tsukino, Class 2-1
HRRNGH, I CAN'T FIND THE RESTROOM!
LUNA? AMI-CHAN, REI-CHAN?
WHERE IS EVERYBODY?
MURMUR
MURMUR
...SNIFFLE...
...I FINALLY GET TO BE A PRINCESS.
BUT IT'S NOT ANY FUN...
...WHEN I'M ALL ALONE.
YOUR BEAUTIFUL HIGHNESS...

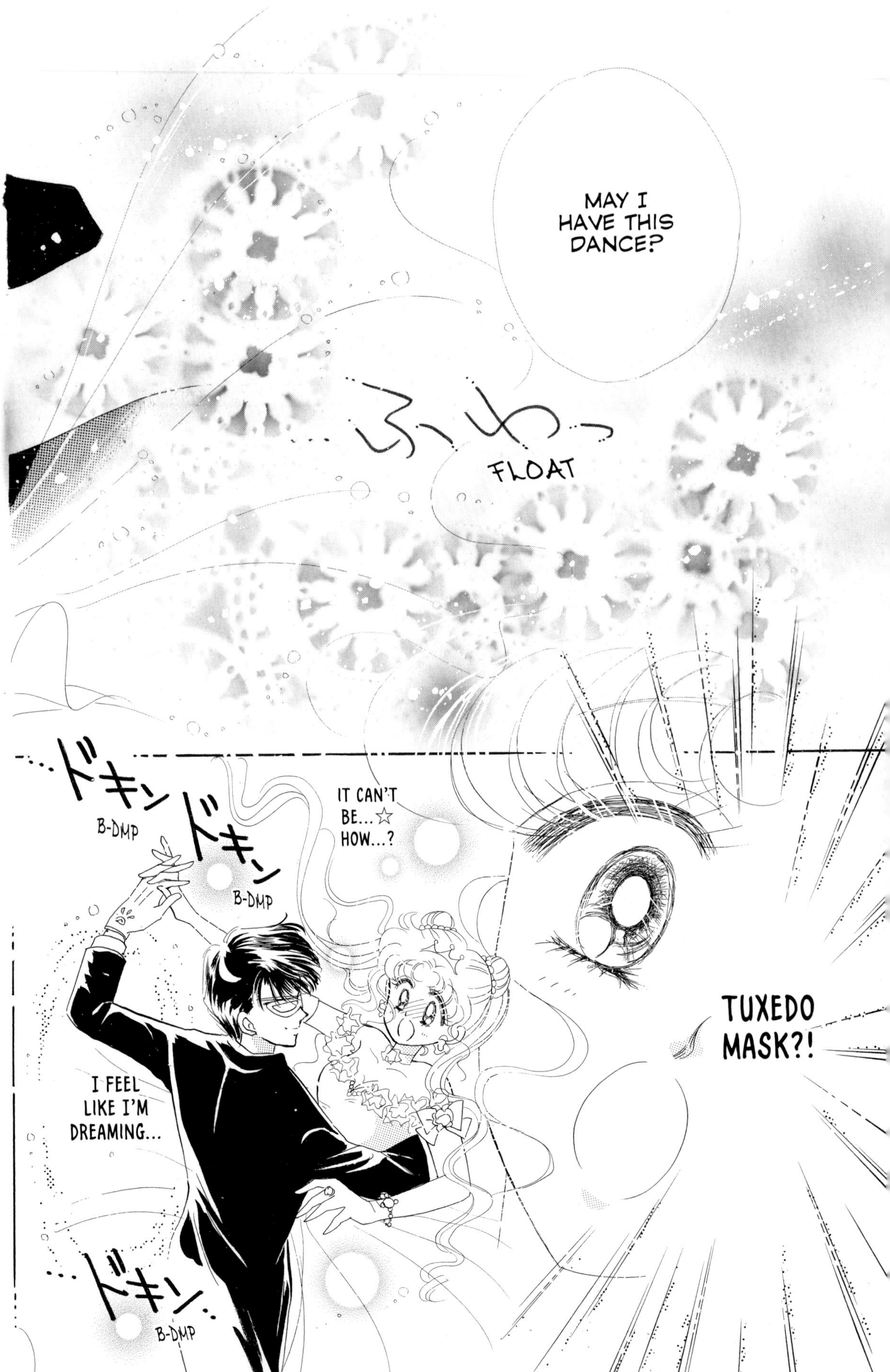
MAY I HAVE THIS DANCE?
ふわっ
FLOAT
TUXEDO MASK?!
IT CAN'T BE...☆ HOW...?
ドキン
B-DMP
ドキン
B-DMP
I FEEL LIKE I'M DREAMING...
ドキン
B-DMP

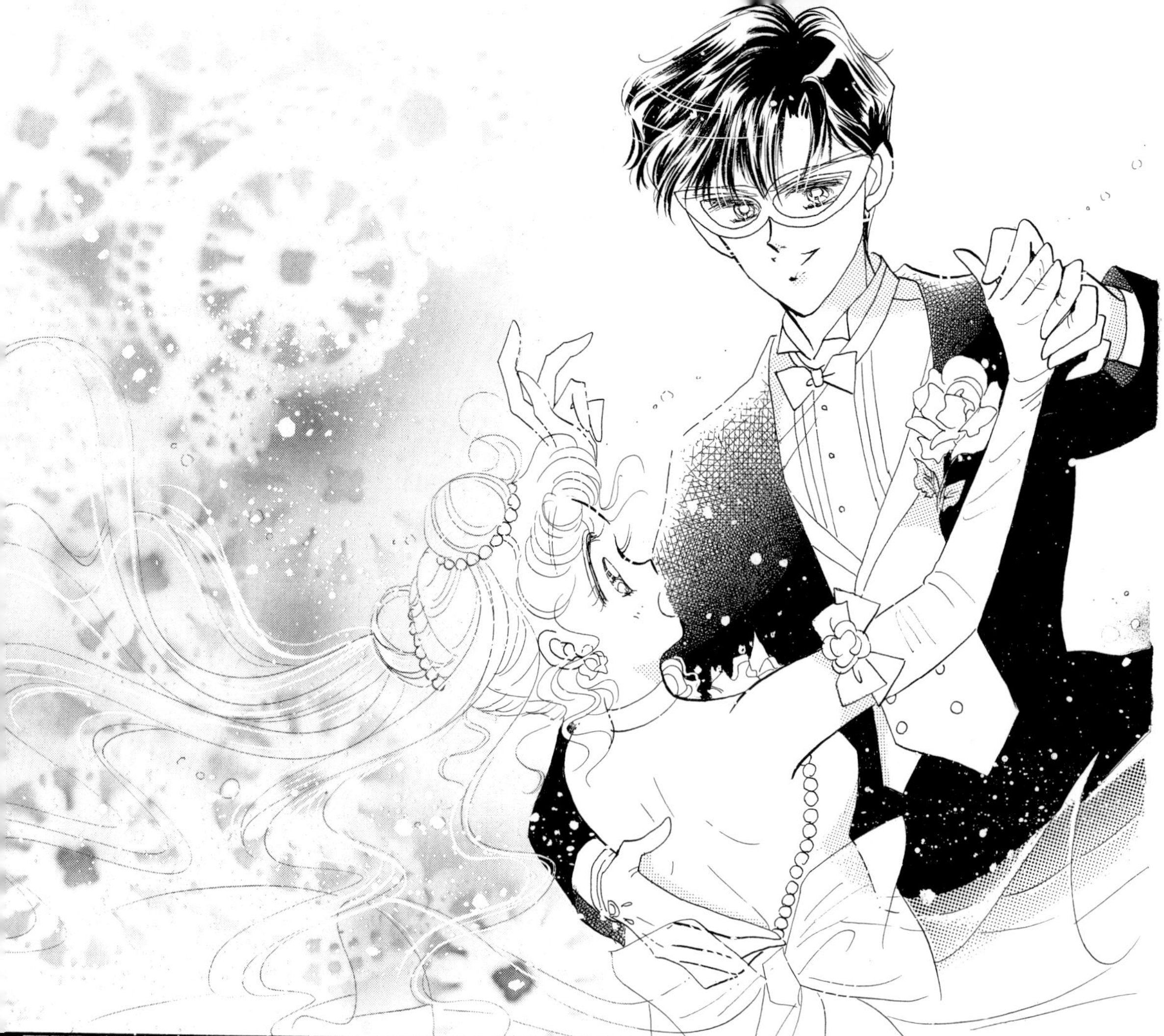

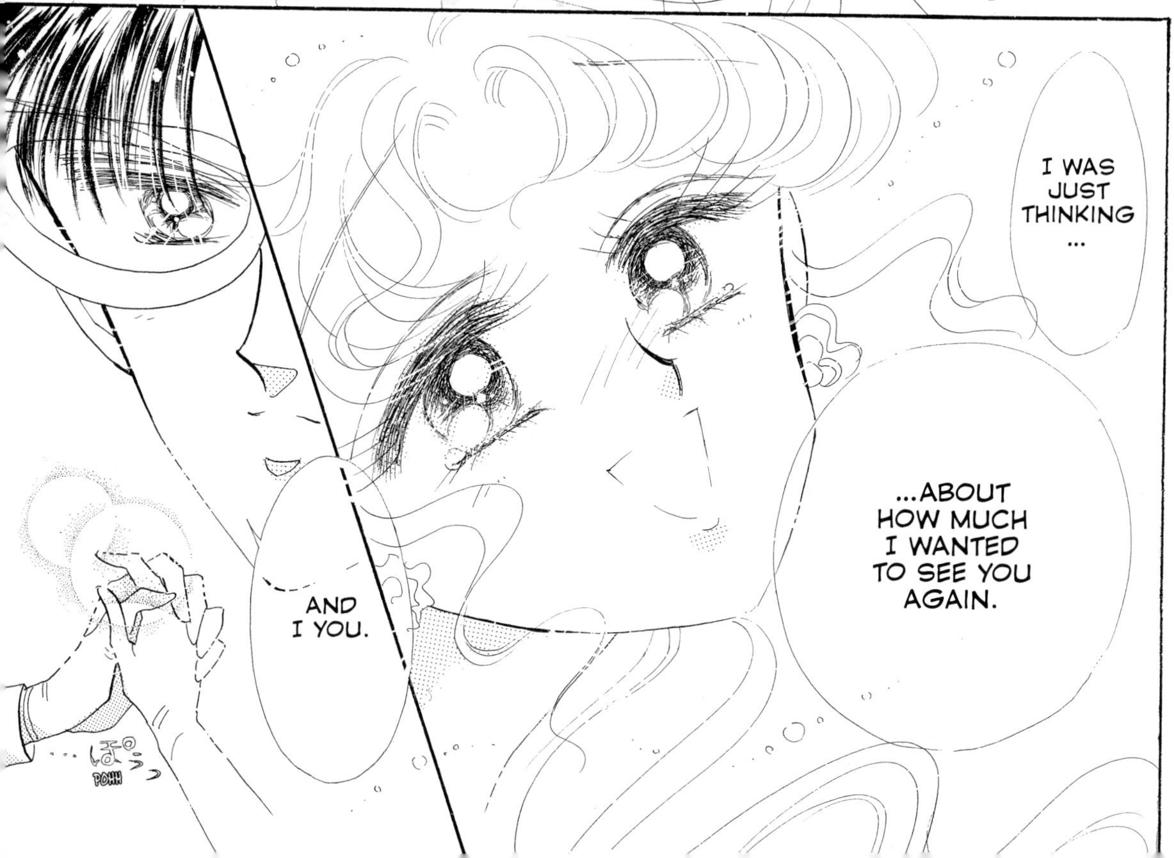
I WAS JUST THINKING ...
...ABOUT HOW MUCH I WANTED TO SEE YOU AGAIN.
AND I YOU.
POHH

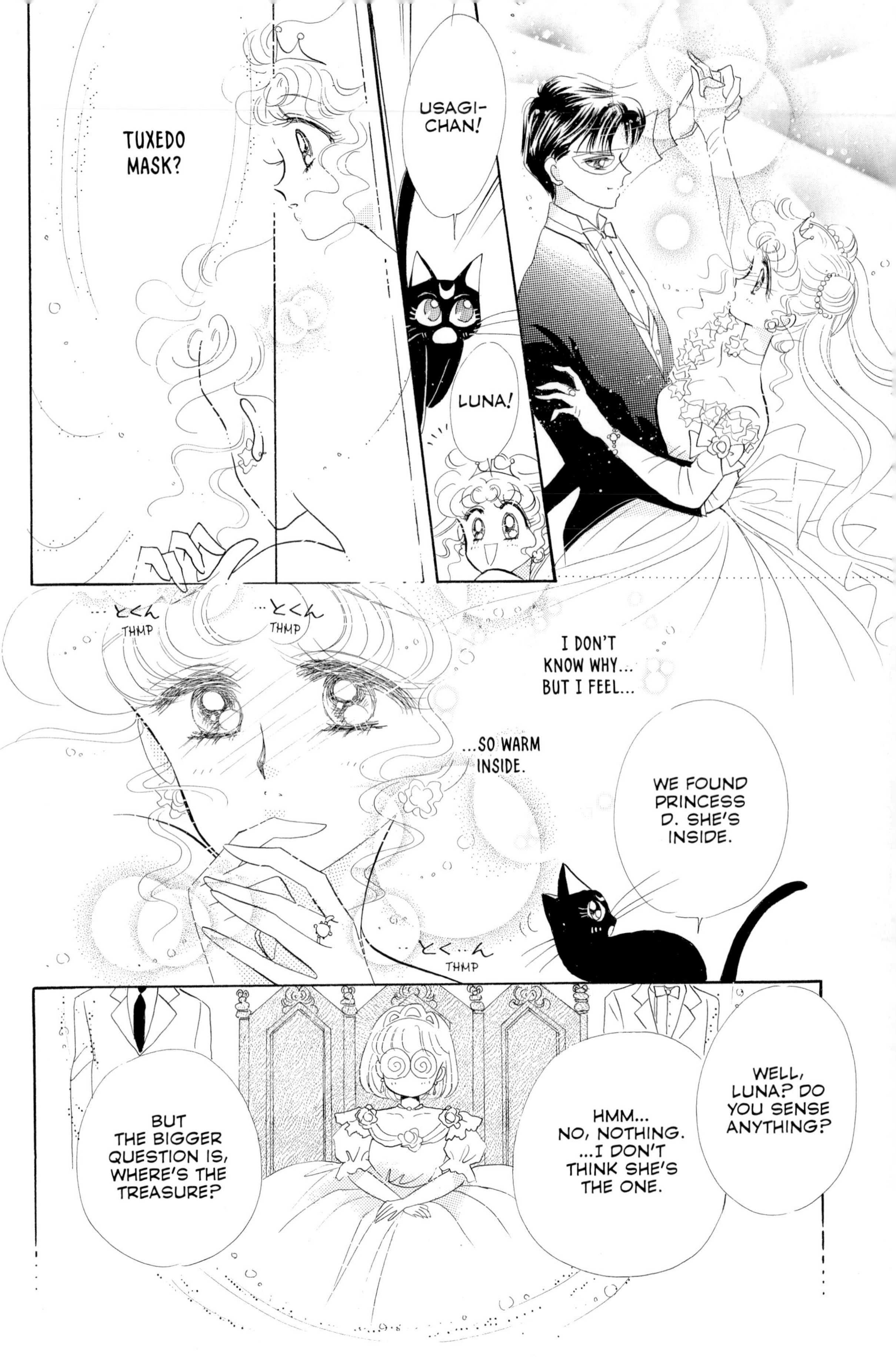
USAGI-CHAN!
LUNA!
TUXEDO MASK?
I DON'T KNOW WHY... BUT I FEEL...
...とくん THMP
...とくん THMP
...SO WARM INSIDE.
WE FOUND PRINCESS D. SHE'S INSIDE.
...とく...ん THMP
WELL, LUNA? DO YOU SENSE ANYTHING?
HMM... NO, NOTHING. ...I DON'T THINK SHE'S THE ONE.
BUT THE BIGGER QUESTION IS, WHERE'S THE TREASURE?

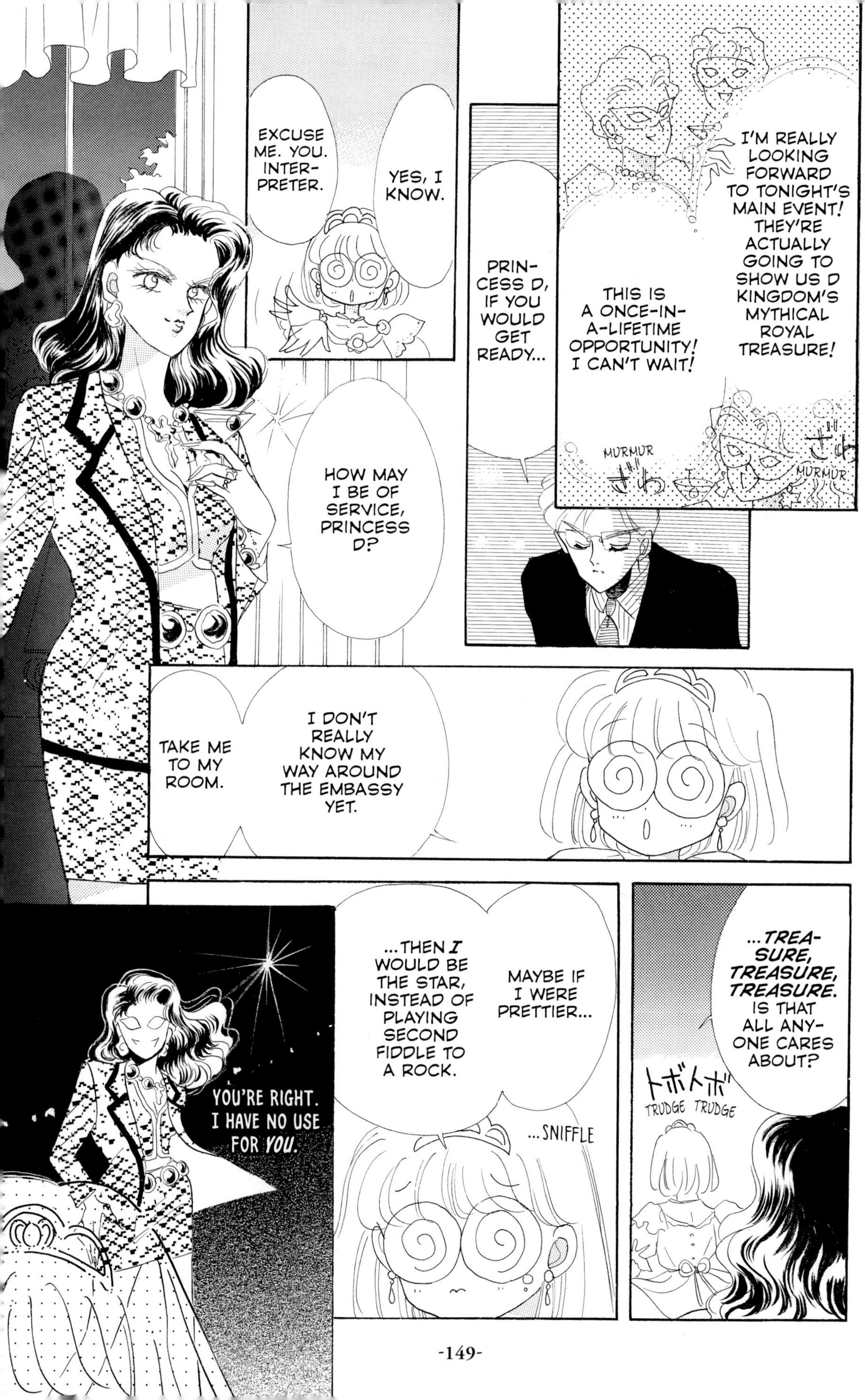
I'M REALLY LOOKING FORWARD TO TONIGHT'S MAIN EVENT! THEY'RE ACTUALLY GOING TO SHOW US D KINGDOM'S MYTHICAL ROYAL TREASURE!
THIS IS A ONCE-IN-A-LIFETIME OPPORTUNITY! I CAN'T WAIT!
MURMUR
MURMUR
PRIN-CESS D, IF YOU WOULD GET READY...
YES, I KNOW.
EXCUSE ME. YOU. INTER-PRETER.
HOW MAY I BE OF SERVICE, PRINCESS D?
I DON'T REALLY KNOW MY WAY AROUND THE EMBASSY YET.
TAKE ME TO MY ROOM.
...*TREA-SURE, TREASURE, TREASURE.* IS THAT ALL ANY-ONE CARES ABOUT?
トボトボ
TRUDGE TRUDGE
MAYBE IF I WERE PRETTIER...
...THEN *I* WOULD BE THE STAR, INSTEAD OF PLAYING SECOND FIDDLE TO A ROCK.
...SNIFFLE
YOU'RE RIGHT. I HAVE NO USE FOR *YOU*.

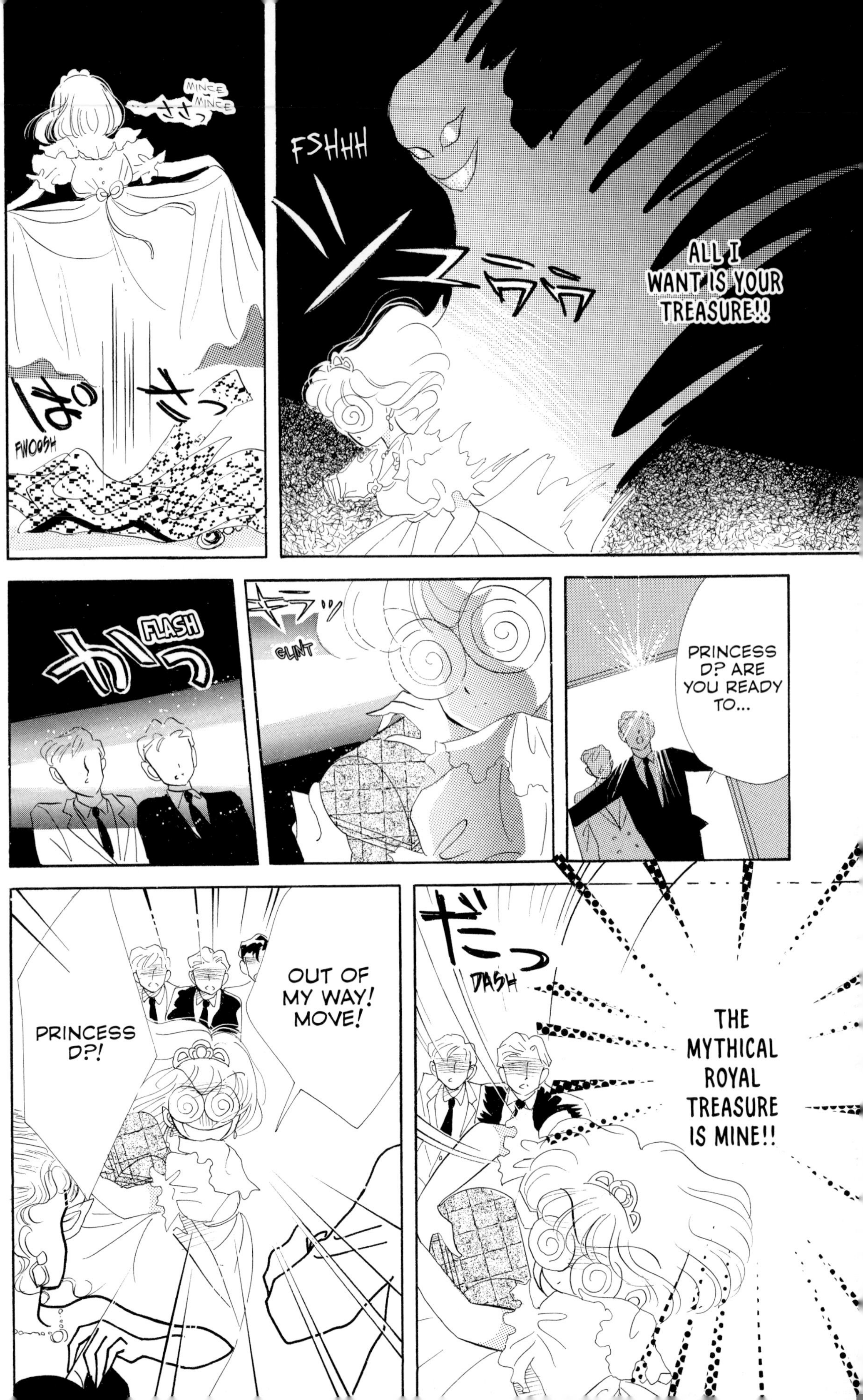
FSHHH
ALL I WANT IS YOUR TREASURE!!
MINCE MINCE
FWOOSH
PRINCESS D? ARE YOU READY TO...
GLINT
FLASH
DASH
THE MYTHICAL ROYAL TREASURE IS MINE!!
OUT OF MY WAY! MOVE!
PRINCESS D?!

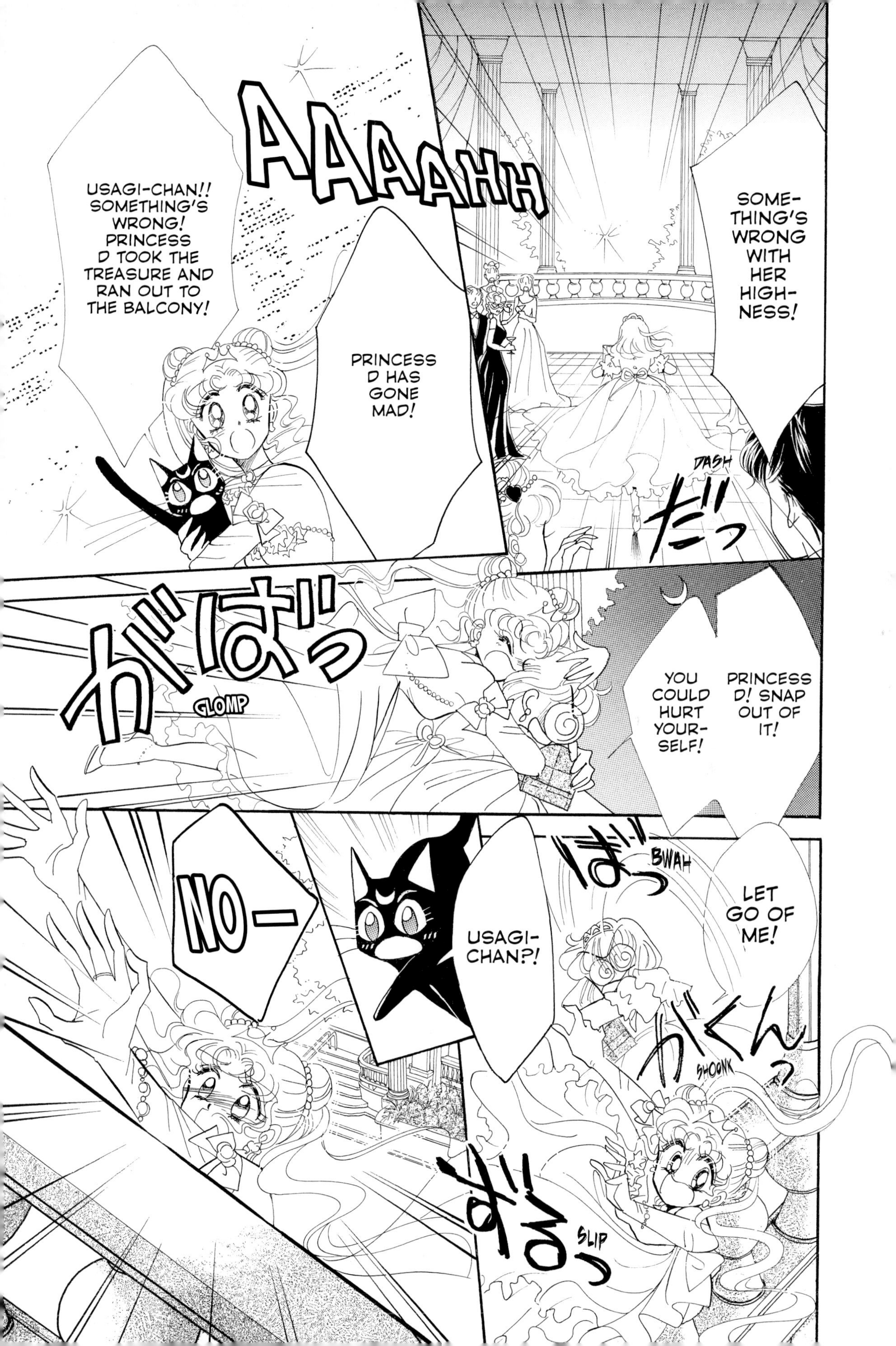
SOME-THING'S WRONG WITH HER HIGH-NESS!
だっ
DASH
AAAAHH
USAGI-CHAN!! SOMETHING'S WRONG! PRINCESS D TOOK THE TREASURE AND RAN OUT TO THE BALCONY!
PRINCESS D HAS GONE MAD!
PRINCESS D! SNAP OUT OF IT!
YOU COULD HURT YOUR-SELF!
がばっ
GLOMP
ばっ
BWAH
LET GO OF ME!
がくんっ
SHOONK
ずるっ
SLIP
USAGI-CHAN?!
NO-

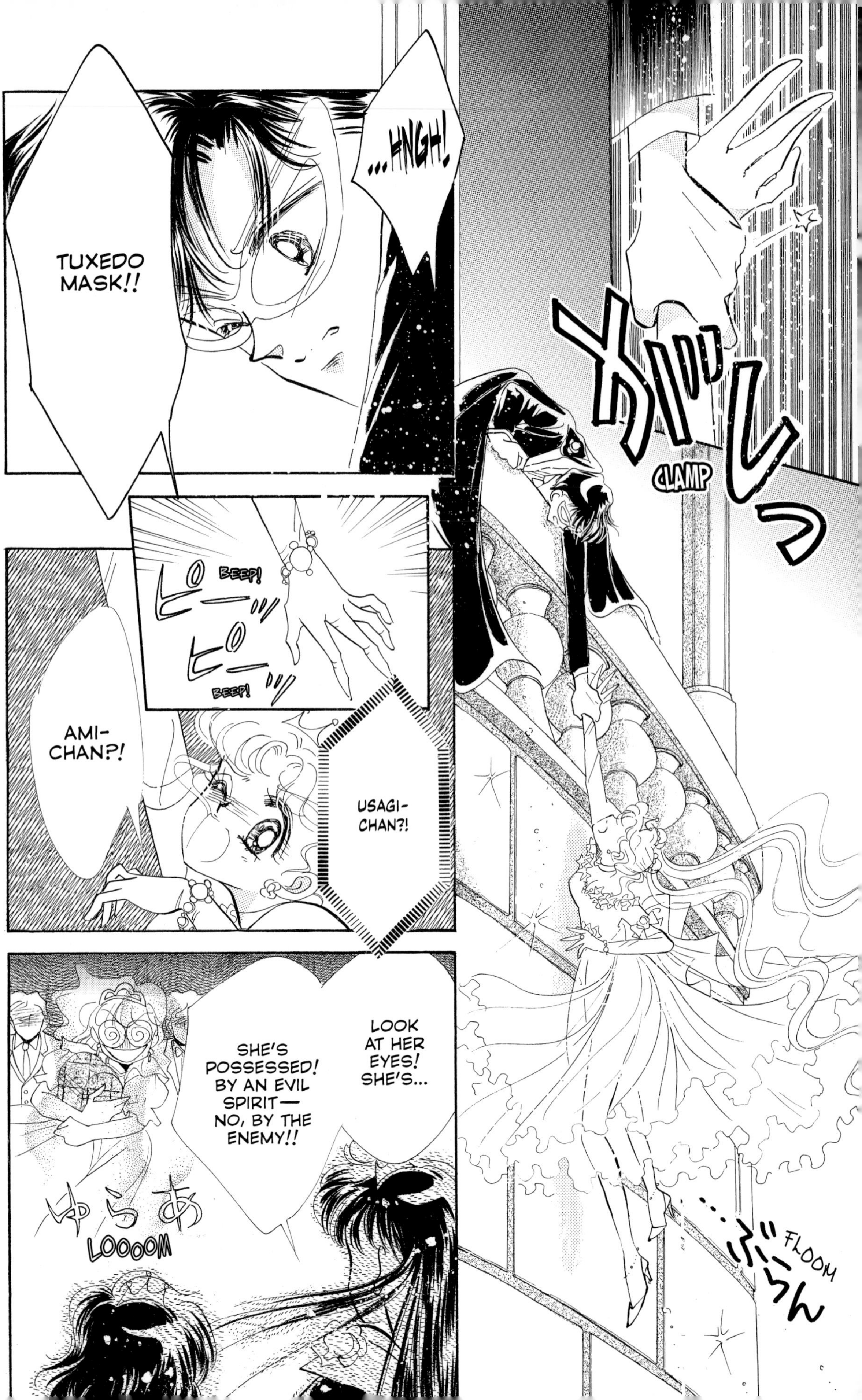

...HNGH!
ガシッ
CLAMP
...ぶらん
FLOOM
TUXEDO MASK!!
ピーッ BEEP!
ピーッ BEEP!
USAGI-CHAN?!
AMI-CHAN?!
LOOK AT HER EYES! SHE'S...
SHE'S POSSESSED! BY AN EVIL SPIRIT— NO, BY THE ENEMY!!
ゆらぁ
LOOOOM

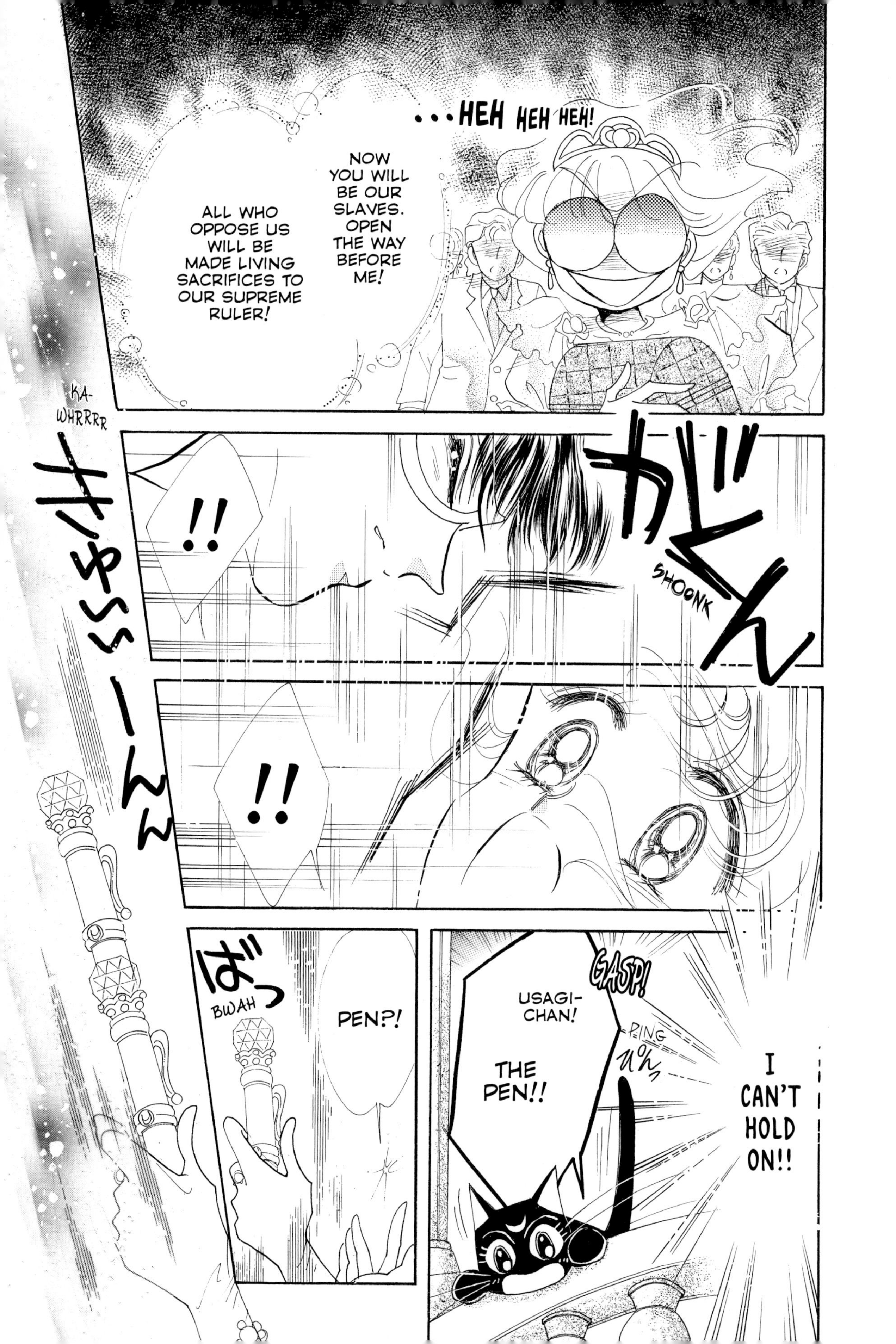
...HEH HEH HEH!
NOW YOU WILL BE OUR SLAVES. OPEN THE WAY BEFORE ME!
ALL WHO OPPOSE US WILL BE MADE LIVING SACRIFICES TO OUR SUPREME RULER!
がどん
SHOONK
!!
!!
きゃいいーんん
KA-WHRRRR
GASP!
I CAN'T HOLD ON!!
ぴん
PING
USAGI-CHAN!
THE PEN!!
PEN?!
ばっ
BWAH

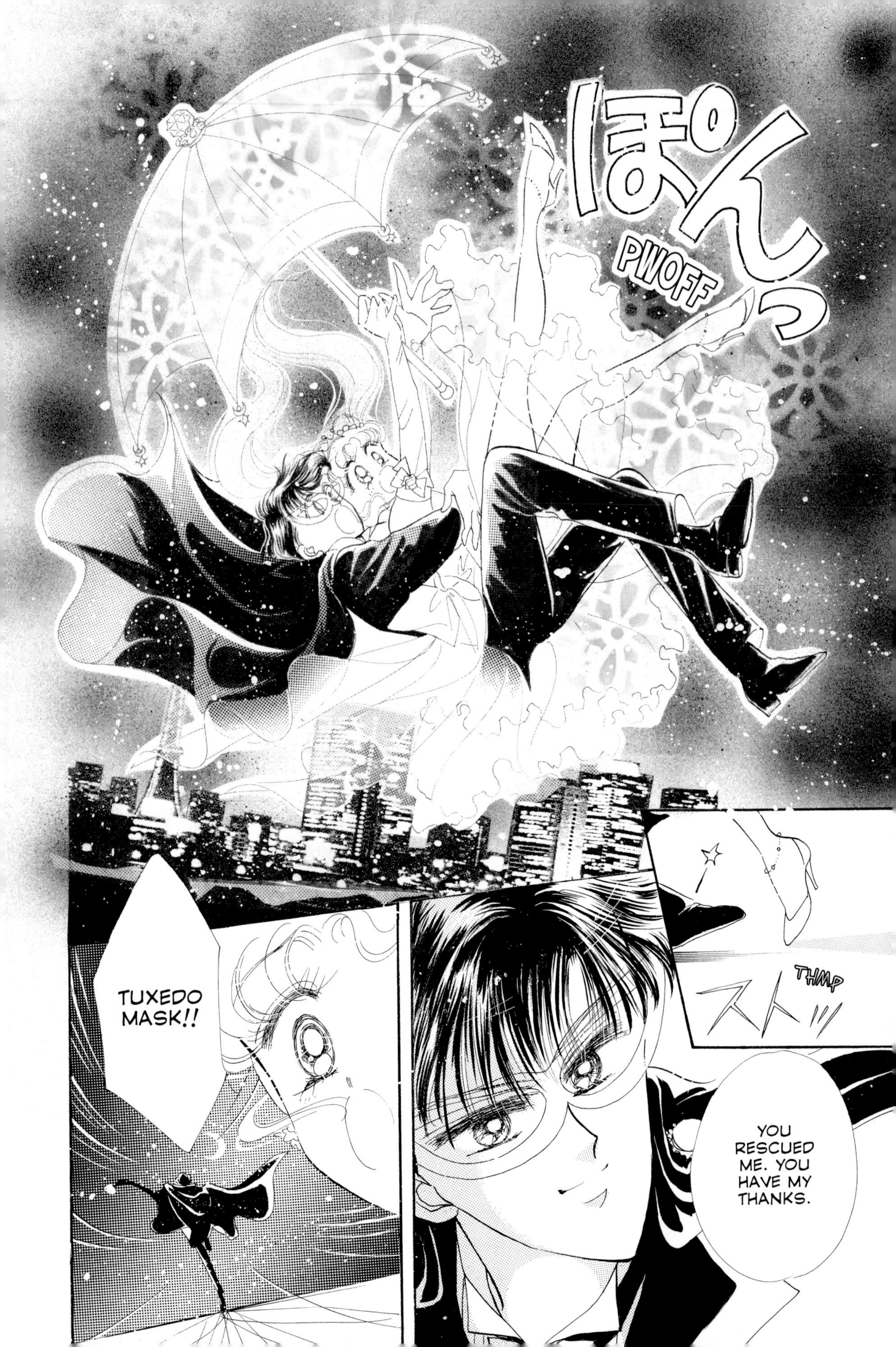
ぽんっ
PWOFF
ストッ
THMP
YOU RESCUED ME. YOU HAVE MY THANKS.
TUXEDO MASK!!

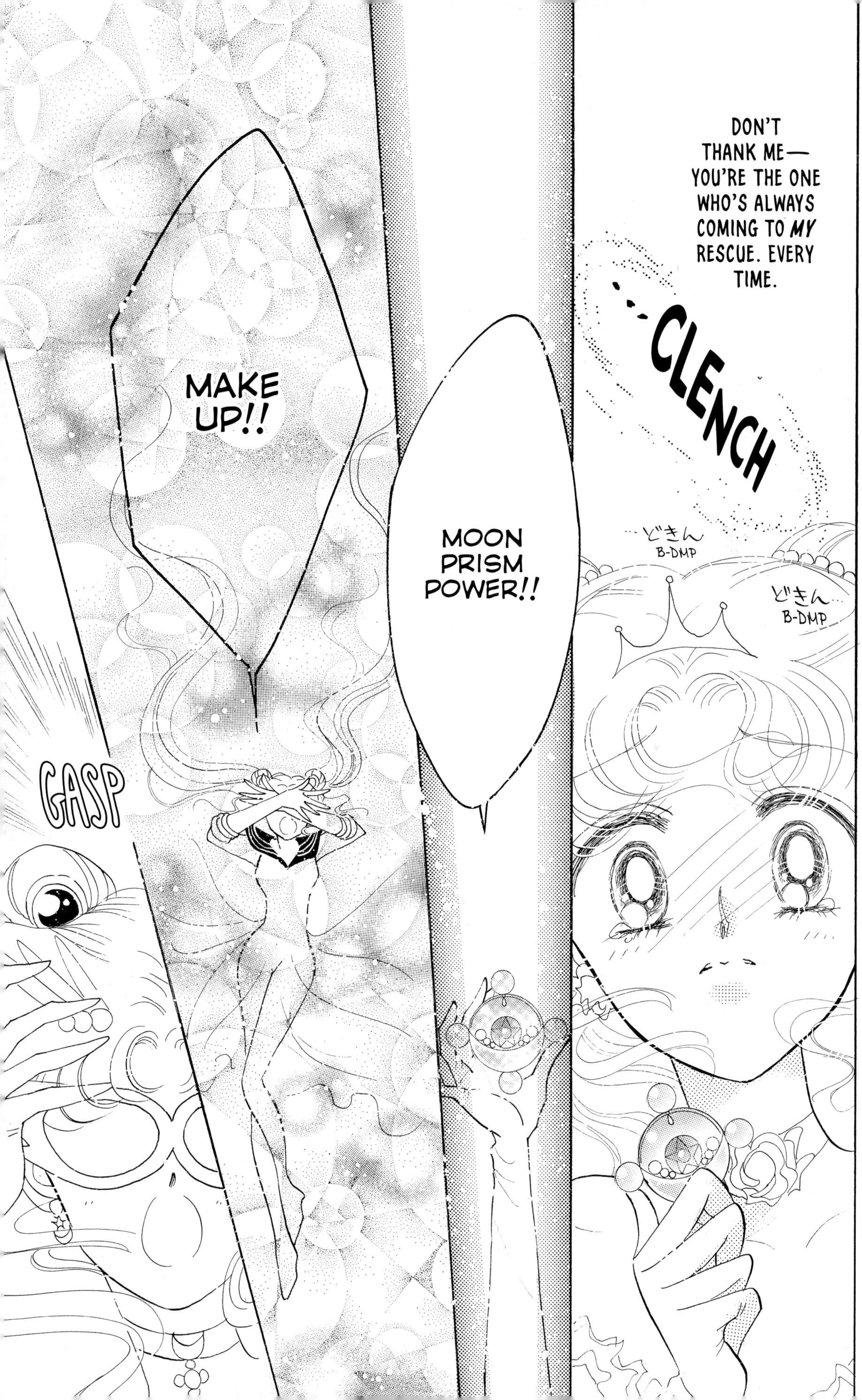
DON'T THANK ME— YOU'RE THE ONE WHO'S ALWAYS COMING TO *MY* RESCUE. EVERY TIME.
...CLENCH
...どきん
B-DMP
どきん...
B-DMP
MOON PRISM POWER!!
MAKE UP!!
GASP

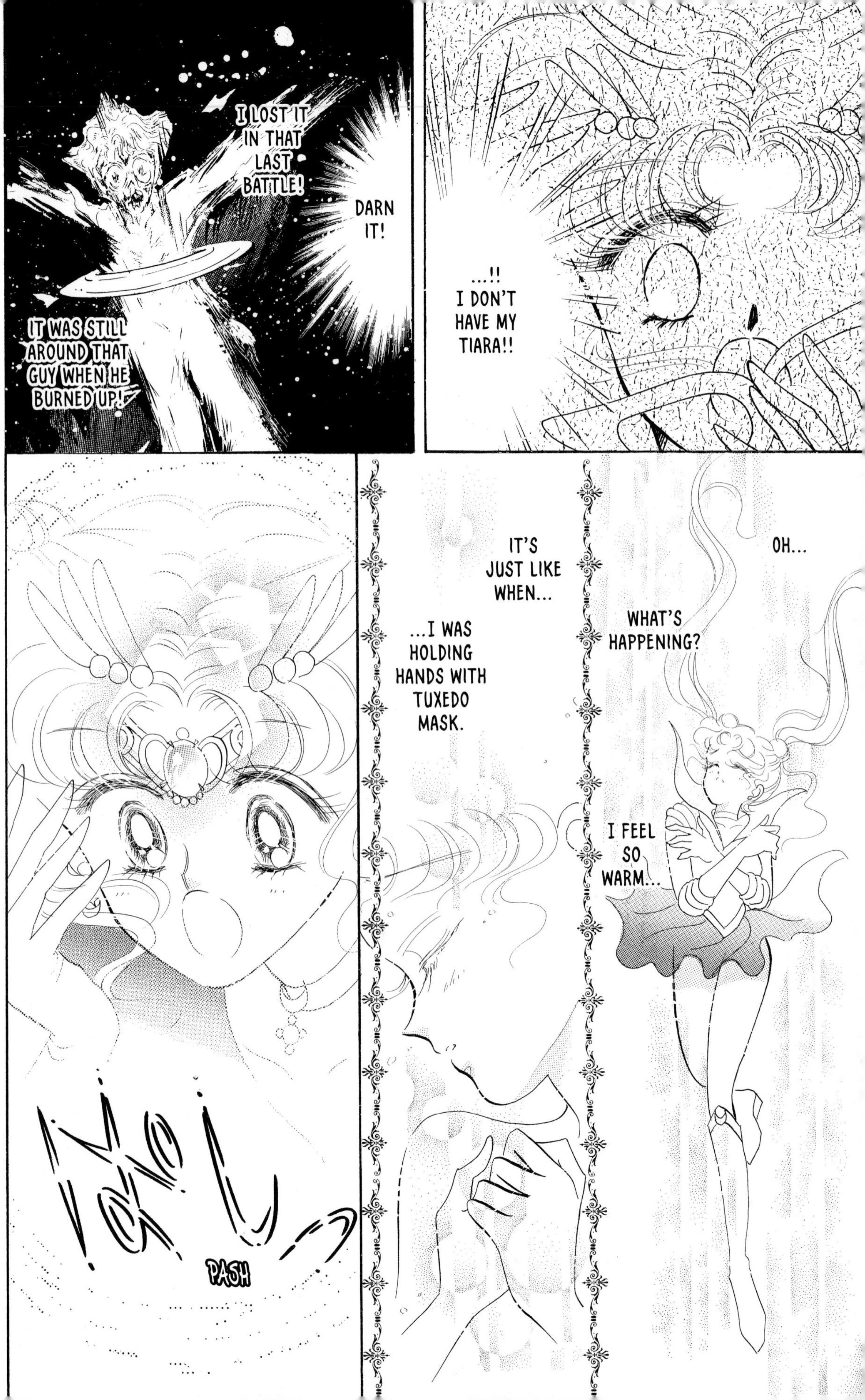
...!!
I DON'T HAVE MY TIARA!!
DARN IT!
I LOST IT IN THAT LAST BATTLE!
IT WAS STILL AROUND THAT GUY WHEN HE BURNED UP!
OH...
WHAT'S HAPPENING?
I FEEL SO WARM...
IT'S JUST LIKE WHEN...
...I WAS HOLDING HANDS WITH TUXEDO MASK.
No!
PASH

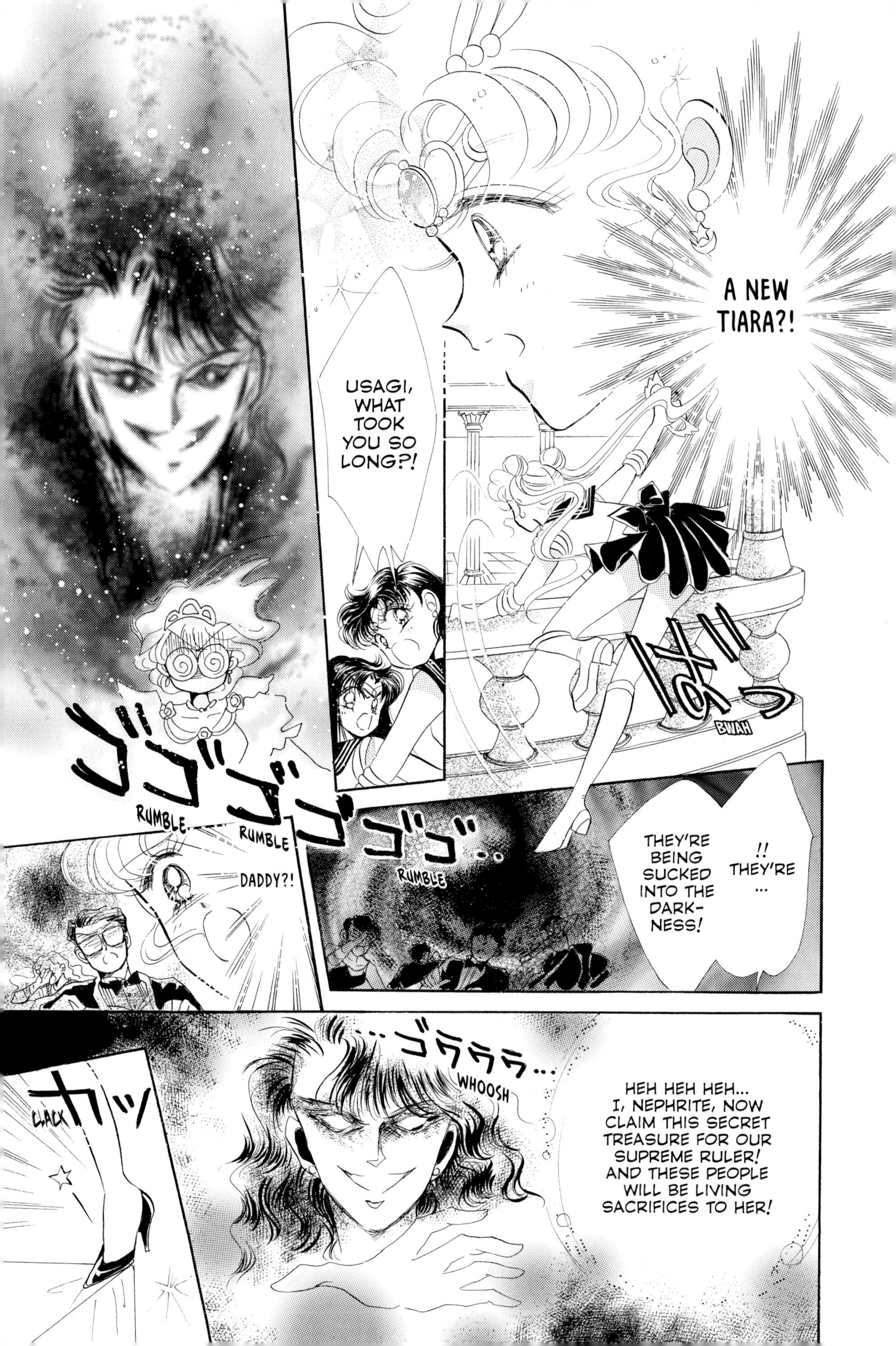

A NEW TIARA?!
BWAH
USAGI, WHAT TOOK YOU SO LONG?!
RUMBLE
RUMBLE
!! THEY'RE ...
THEY'RE BEING SUCKED INTO THE DARK-NESS!
RUMBLE
DADDY?!
WHOOSH
HEH HEH HEH... I, NEPHRITE, NOW CLAIM THIS SECRET TREASURE FOR OUR SUPREME RULER! AND THESE PEOPLE WILL BE LIVING SACRIFICES TO HER!
CLACK

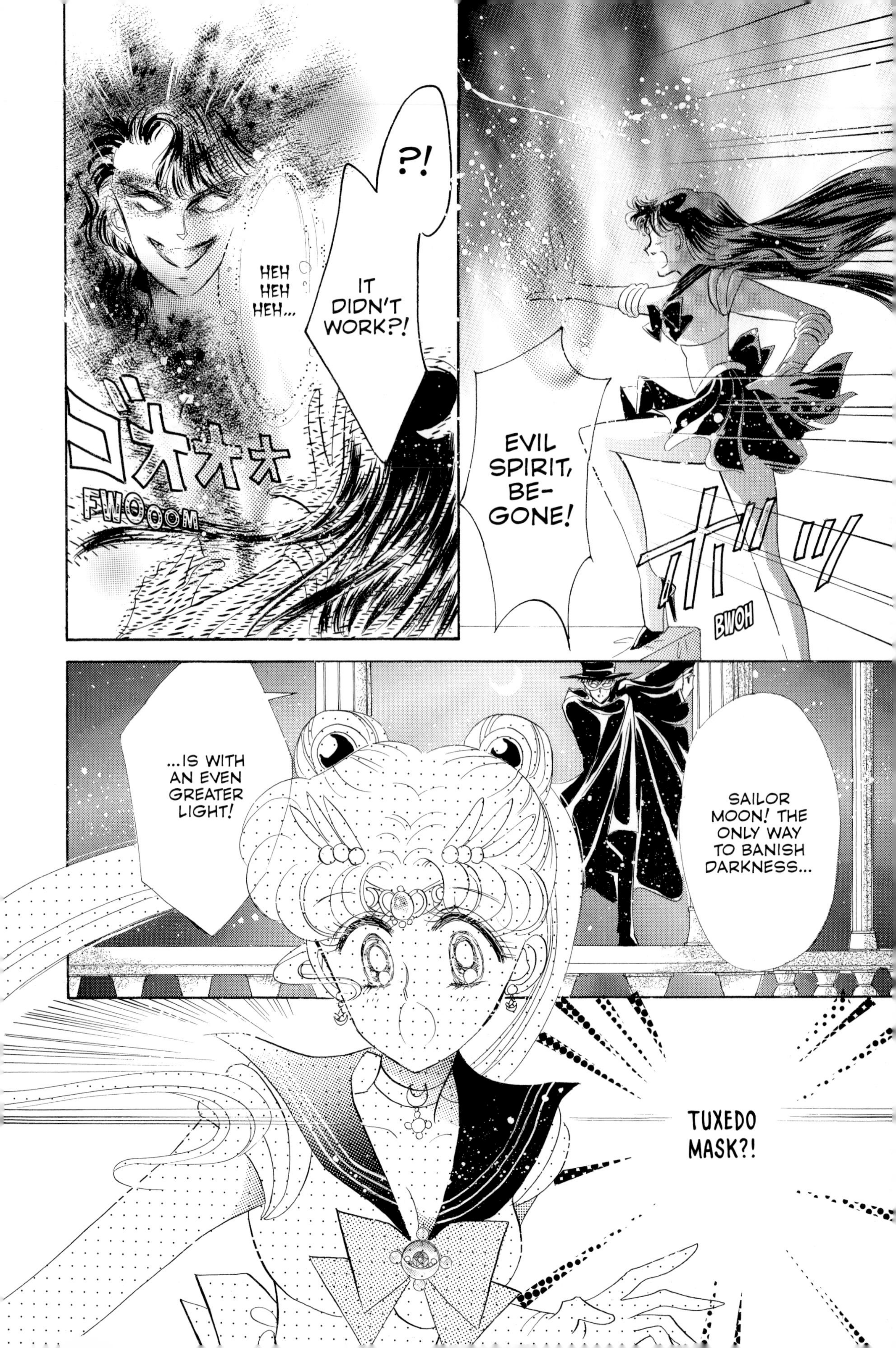
EVIL SPIRIT, BE-GONE!
BWOH
?!
IT DIDN'T WORK?!
HEH HEH HEH...
ゴオオオ
FWOOOM
SAILOR MOON! THE ONLY WAY TO BANISH DARKNESS...
...IS WITH AN EVEN GREATER LIGHT!
TUXEDO MASK?!

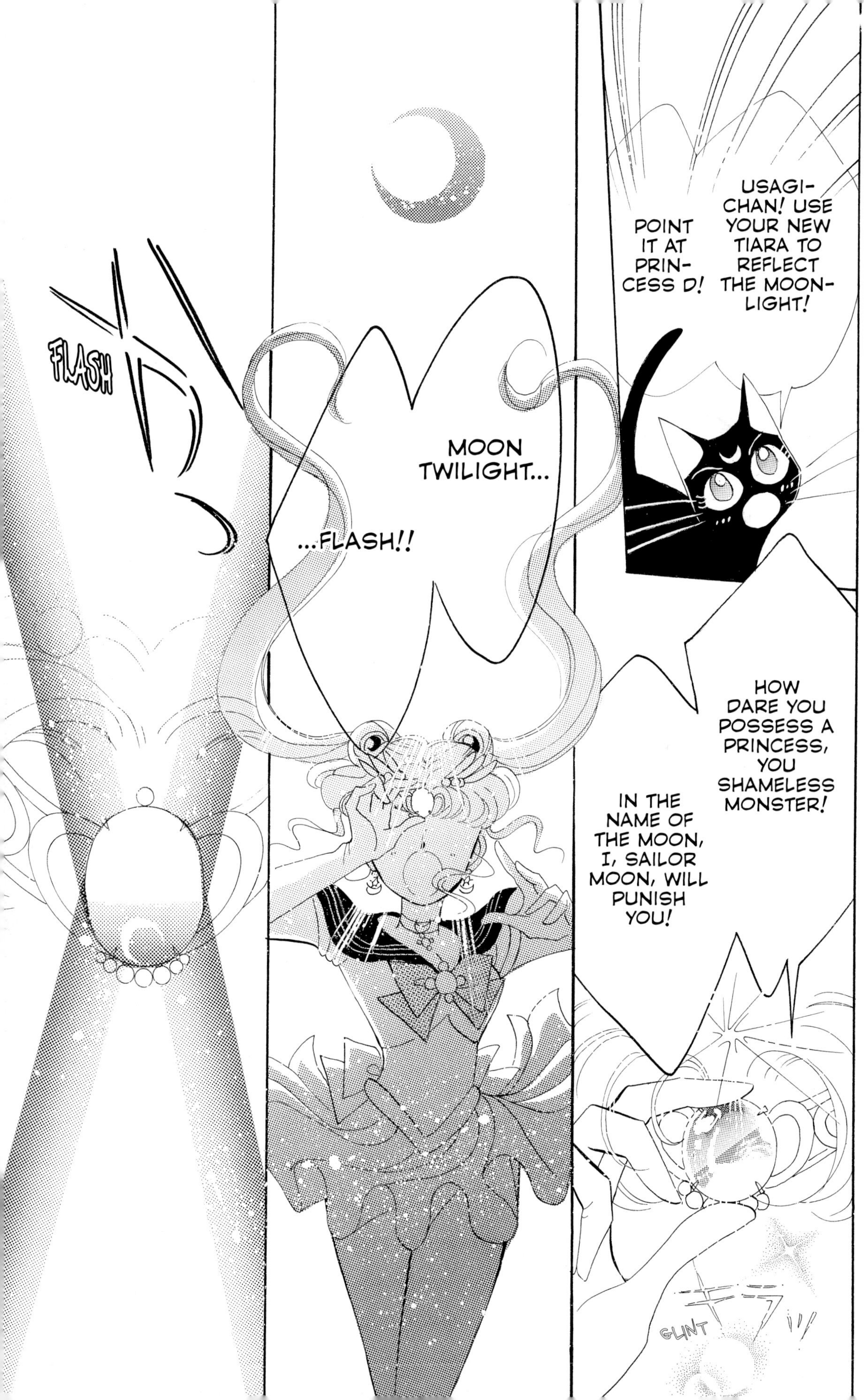

USAGI-CHAN! USE YOUR NEW TIARA TO REFLECT THE MOONLIGHT!
POINT IT AT PRINCESS D!
HOW DARE YOU POSSESS A PRINCESS, YOU SHAMELESS MONSTER!
IN THE NAME OF THE MOON, I, SAILOR MOON, WILL PUNISH YOU!
GLINT
MOON TWILIGHT...
...FLASH!!
FLASH

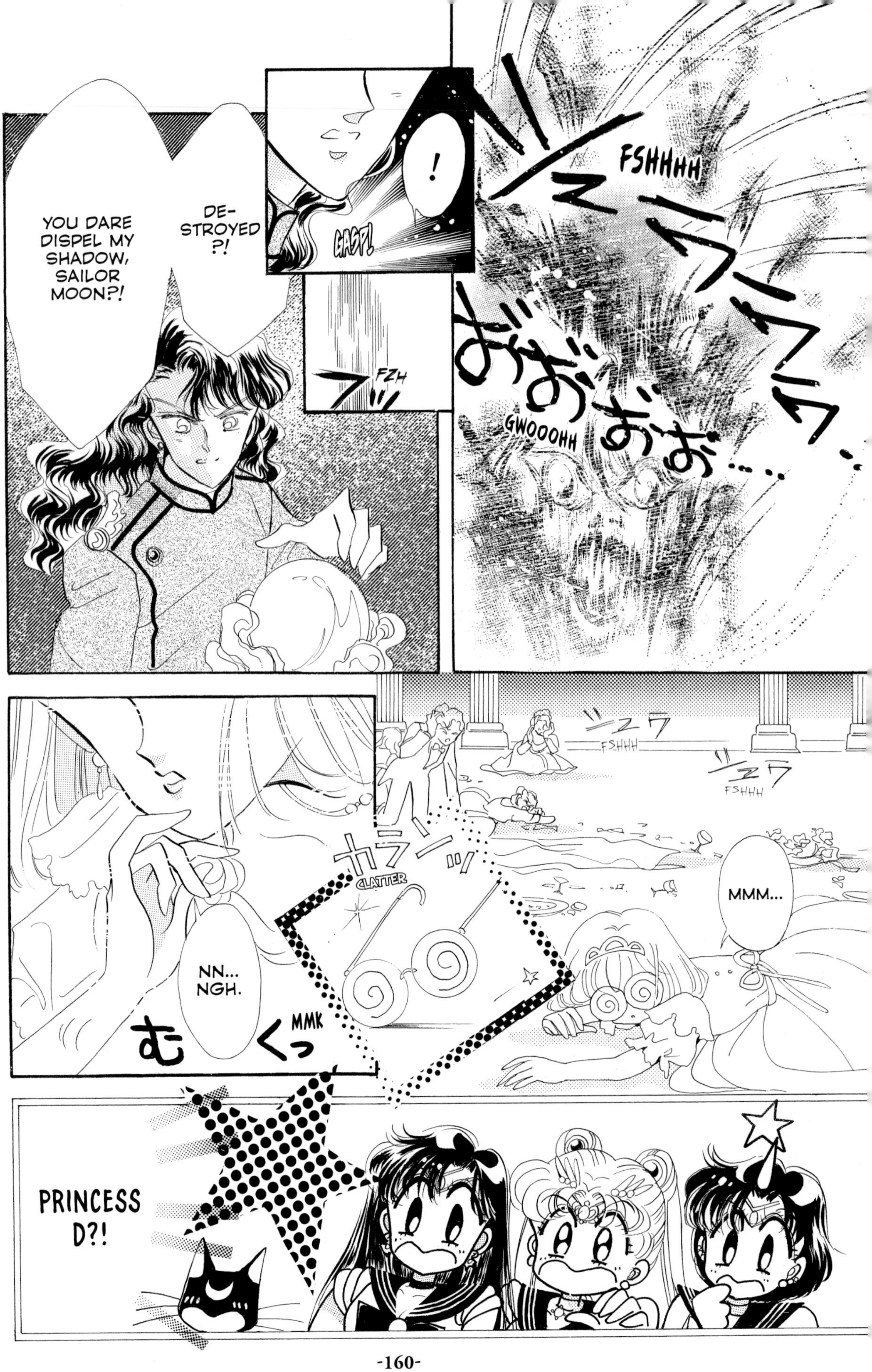
FSHHHH
GWOOOHH
!
GASP!
FZH
DE-STROYED?!
YOU DARE DISPEL MY SHADOW, SAILOR MOON?!
FSHHH
FSHHH
MMM...
カラーンッ
CLATTER
NN... NGH.
むくっ
MMK
PRINCESS D?!

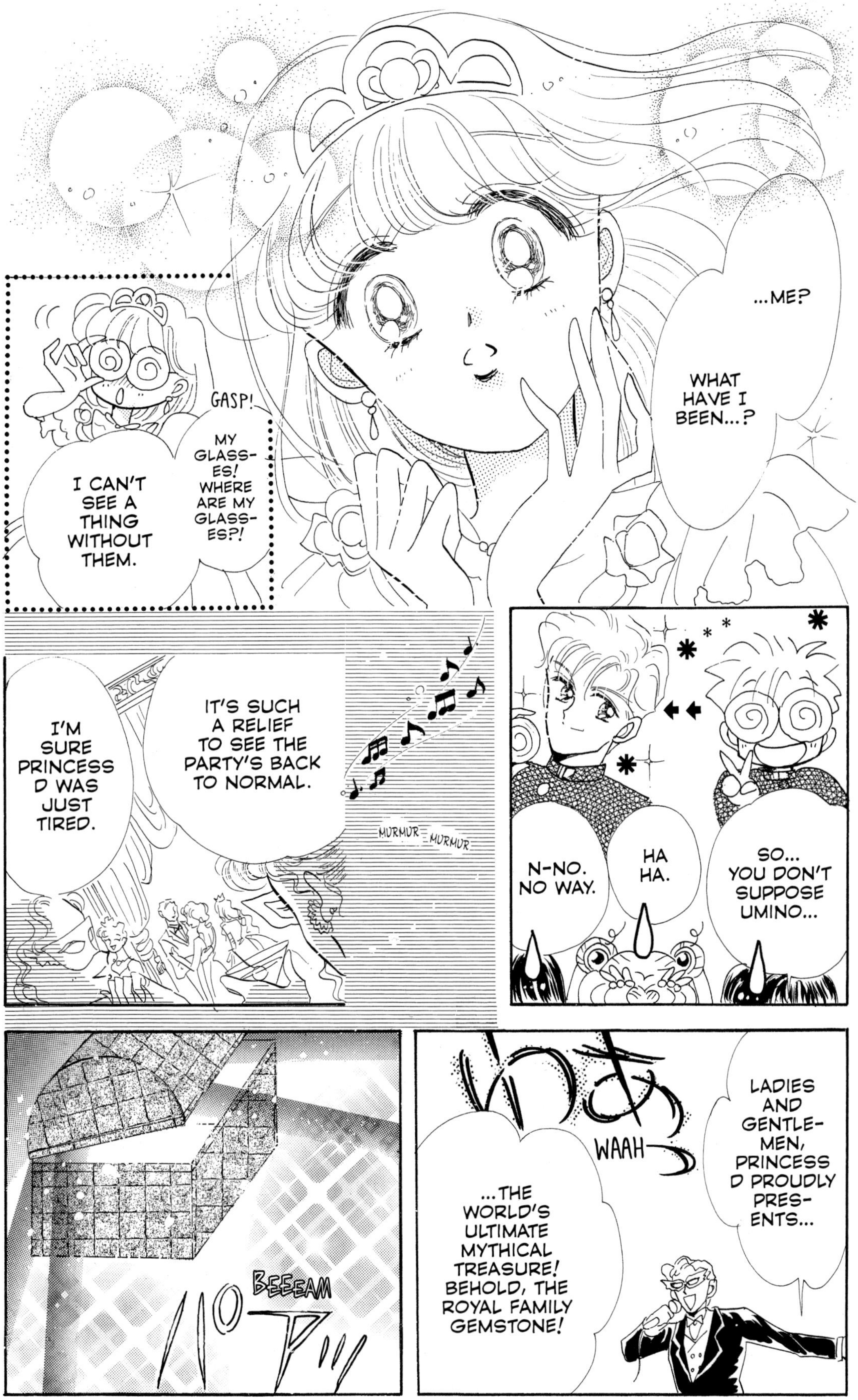
...ME?
WHAT HAVE I BEEN...?
GASP!
MY GLASSES! WHERE ARE MY GLASSES?!
I CAN'T SEE A THING WITHOUT THEM.
SO... YOU DON'T SUPPOSE UMINO...
HA HA.
N-NO. NO WAY.
IT'S SUCH A RELIEF TO SEE THE PARTY'S BACK TO NORMAL.
I'M SURE PRINCESS D WAS JUST TIRED.
MURMUR MURMUR
LADIES AND GENTLEMEN, PRINCESS D PROUDLY PRESENTS...
WAAH
...THE WORLD'S ULTIMATE MYTHICAL TREASURE! BEHOLD, THE ROYAL FAMILY GEMSTONE!
BEEEAM

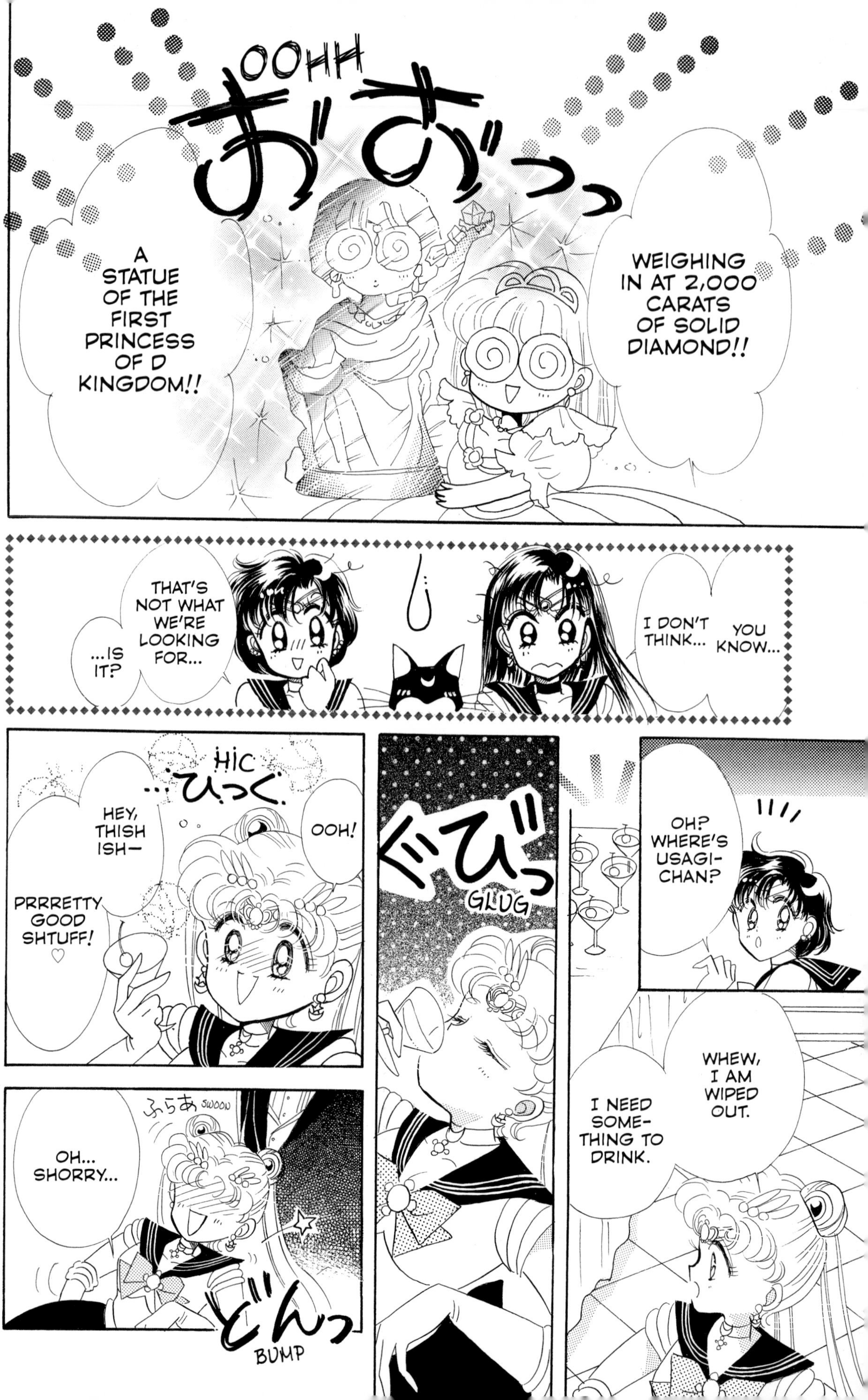

おおっっ
OOHH
WEIGHING IN AT 2,000 CARATS OF SOLID DIAMOND!!
A STATUE OF THE FIRST PRINCESS OF D KINGDOM!!
YOU KNOW... I DON'T THINK...
THAT'S NOT WHAT WE'RE LOOKING FOR...
...IS IT?
OH? WHERE'S USAGI-CHAN?
WHEW, I AM WIPED OUT.
I NEED SOME-THING TO DRINK.
ぐびっ
GLUG
ひっく
HIC
OOH!
HEY, THISH ISH—
PRRRETTY GOOD SHTUFF! ♡
ふらあ SWOON
OH... SHORRY...
どんっ
BUMP

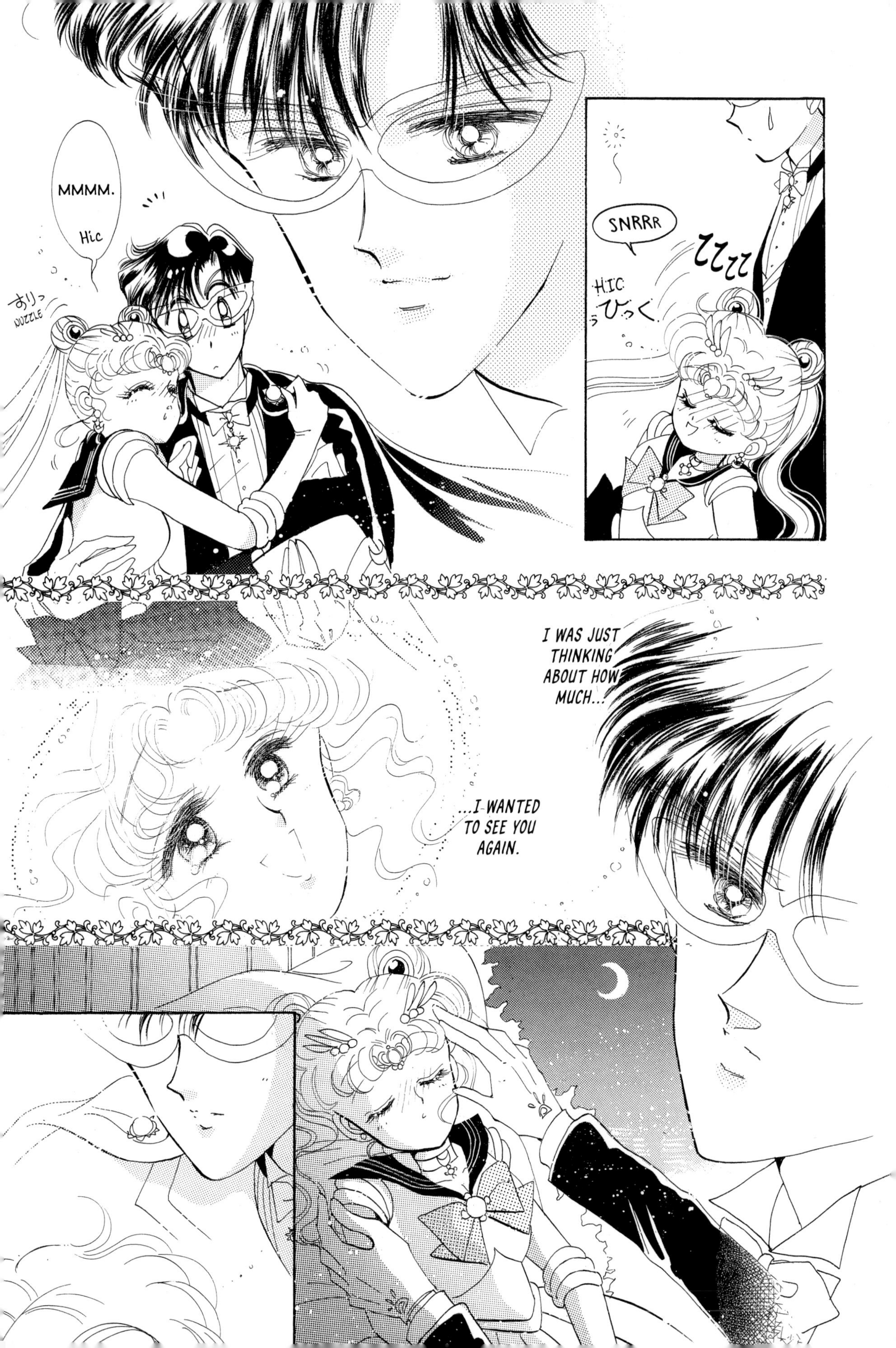
SNRRR
ZZZZ
HIC
ひっく
MMMM.
Hic
おりっ
NUZZLE
I WAS JUST THINKING ABOUT HOW MUCH...
...I WANTED TO SEE YOU AGAIN.

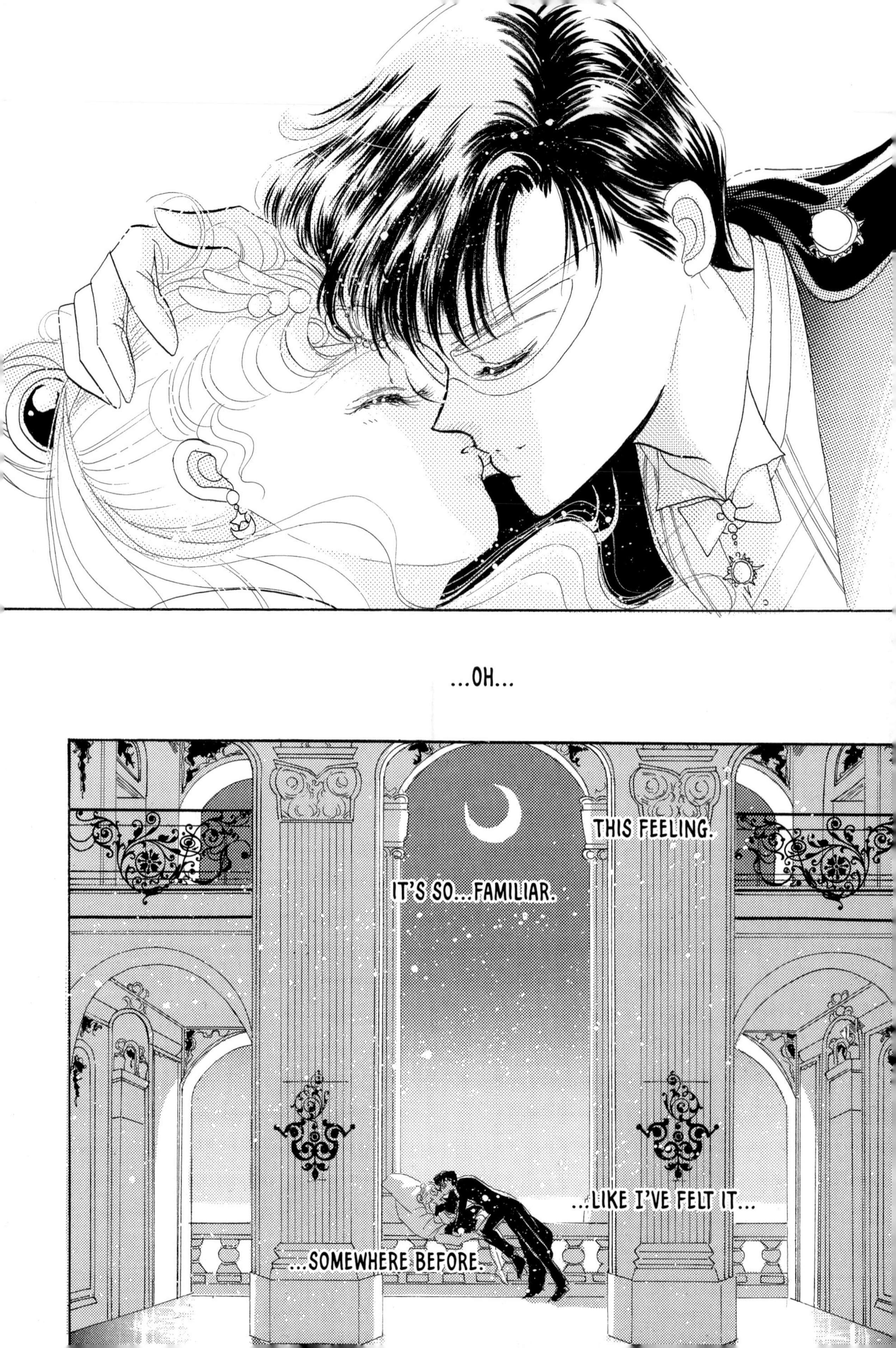
...OH...
THIS FEELING.
IT'S SO...FAMILIAR.
...LIKE I'VE FELT IT...
...SOMEWHERE BEFORE.

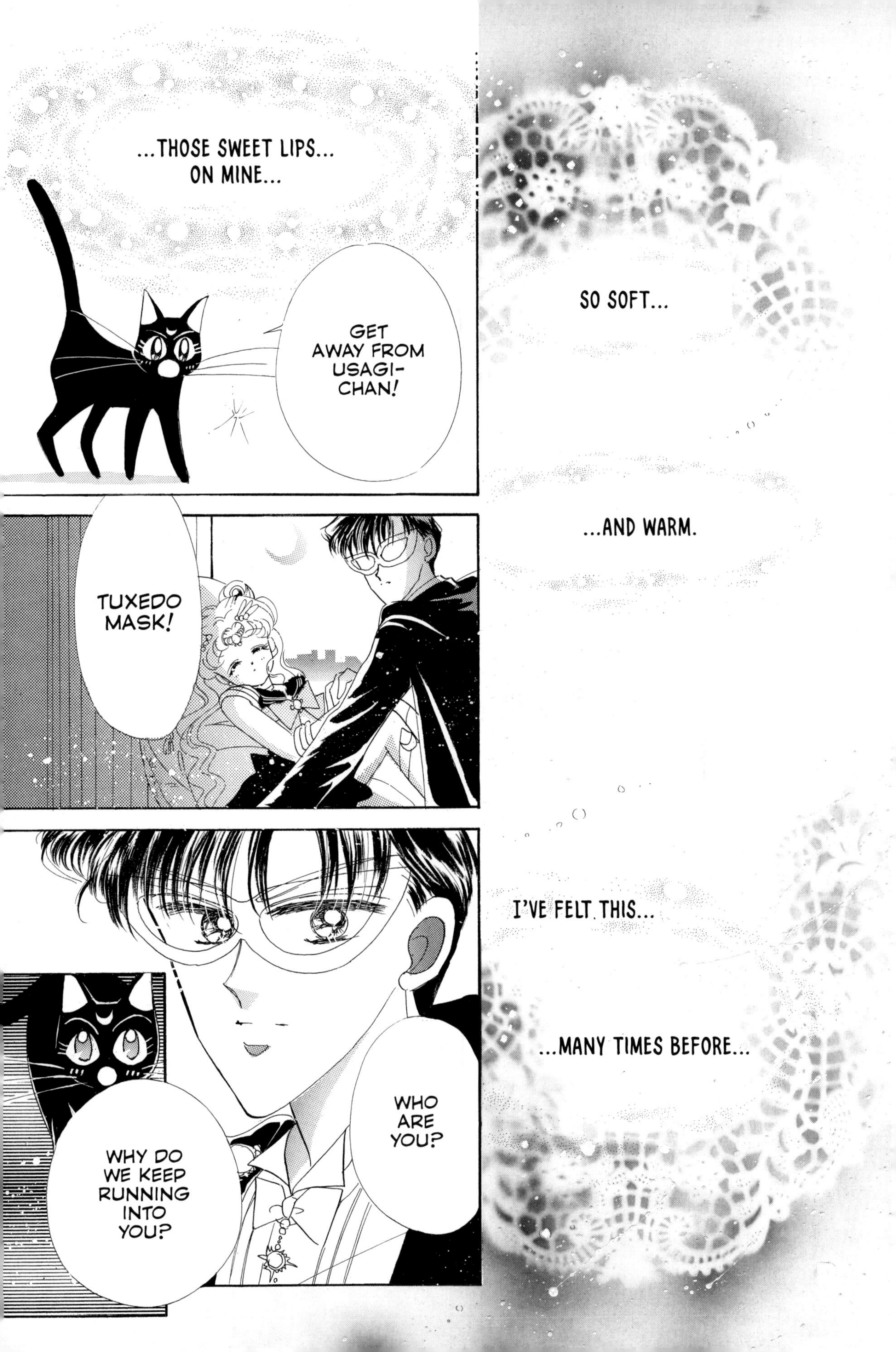
SO SOFT...
...AND WARM.
I'VE FELT THIS...
...MANY TIMES BEFORE...
...THOSE SWEET LIPS... ON MINE...
GET AWAY FROM USAGI-CHAN!
TUXEDO MASK!
WHO ARE YOU?
WHY DO WE KEEP RUNNING INTO YOU?

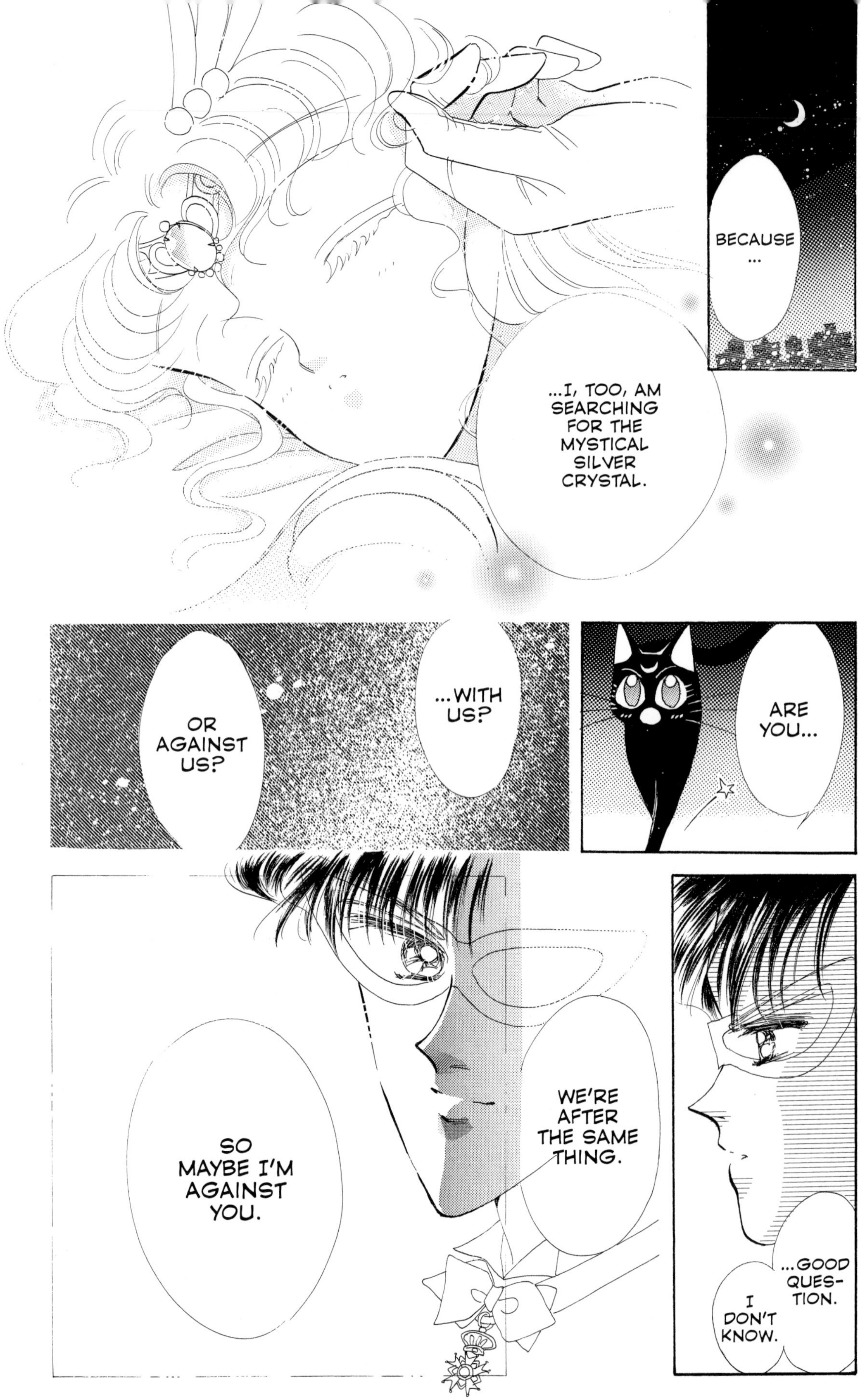
BECAUSE ...
...I, TOO, AM SEARCHING FOR THE MYSTICAL SILVER CRYSTAL.
ARE YOU...
...WITH US?
OR AGAINST US?
...GOOD QUES-TION.
I DON'T KNOW.
WE'RE AFTER THE SAME THING.
SO MAYBE I'M AGAINST YOU.

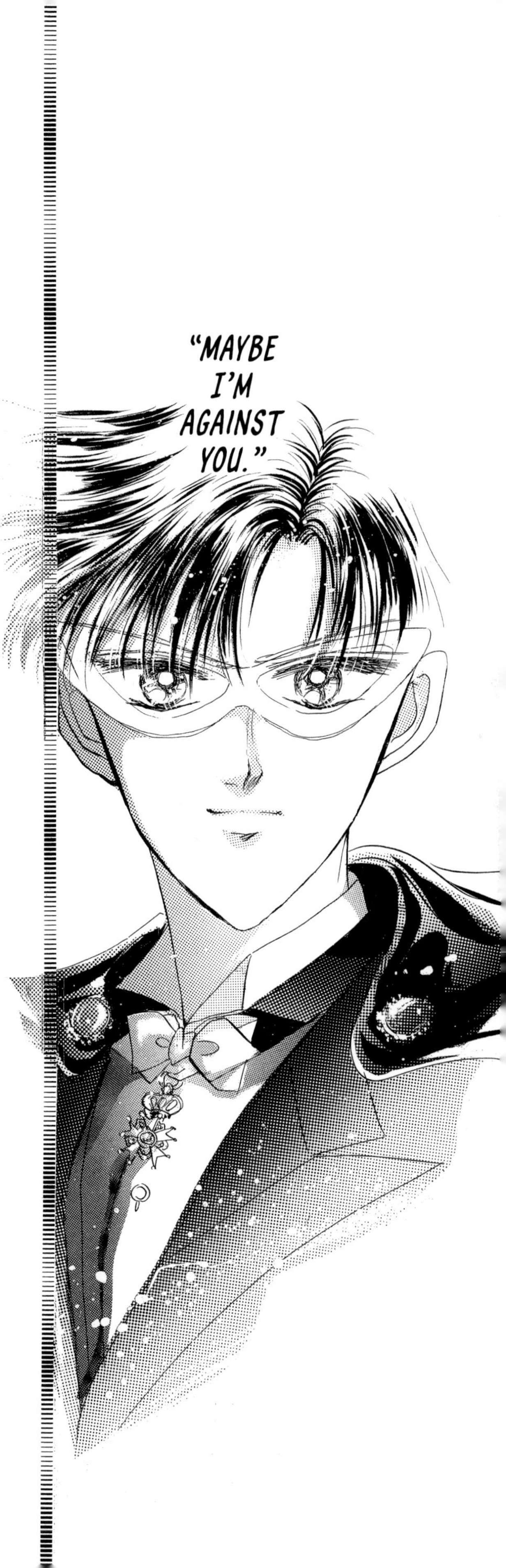
"MAYBE I'M AGAINST YOU."

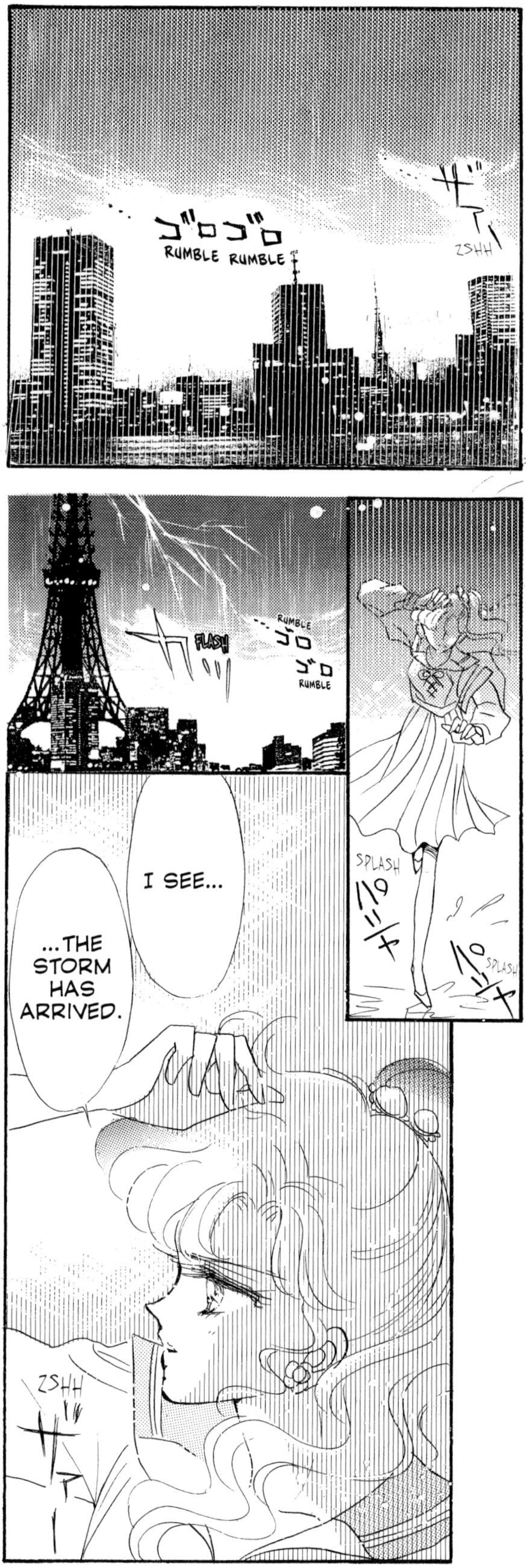
ザァ
ZSHH
ゴロゴロ
RUMBLE RUMBLE
パシャ
SPLASH
パシャ
SPLASH
ゴロゴロ
RUMBLE
RUMBLE
FLASH
I SEE...
...THE STORM HAS ARRIVED.
ZSHH
ザァ

Pretty Guardian
Sailor Moon

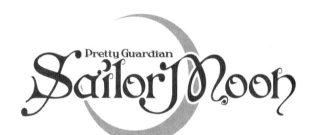

Act.5 Makoto: Sailor Jupiter

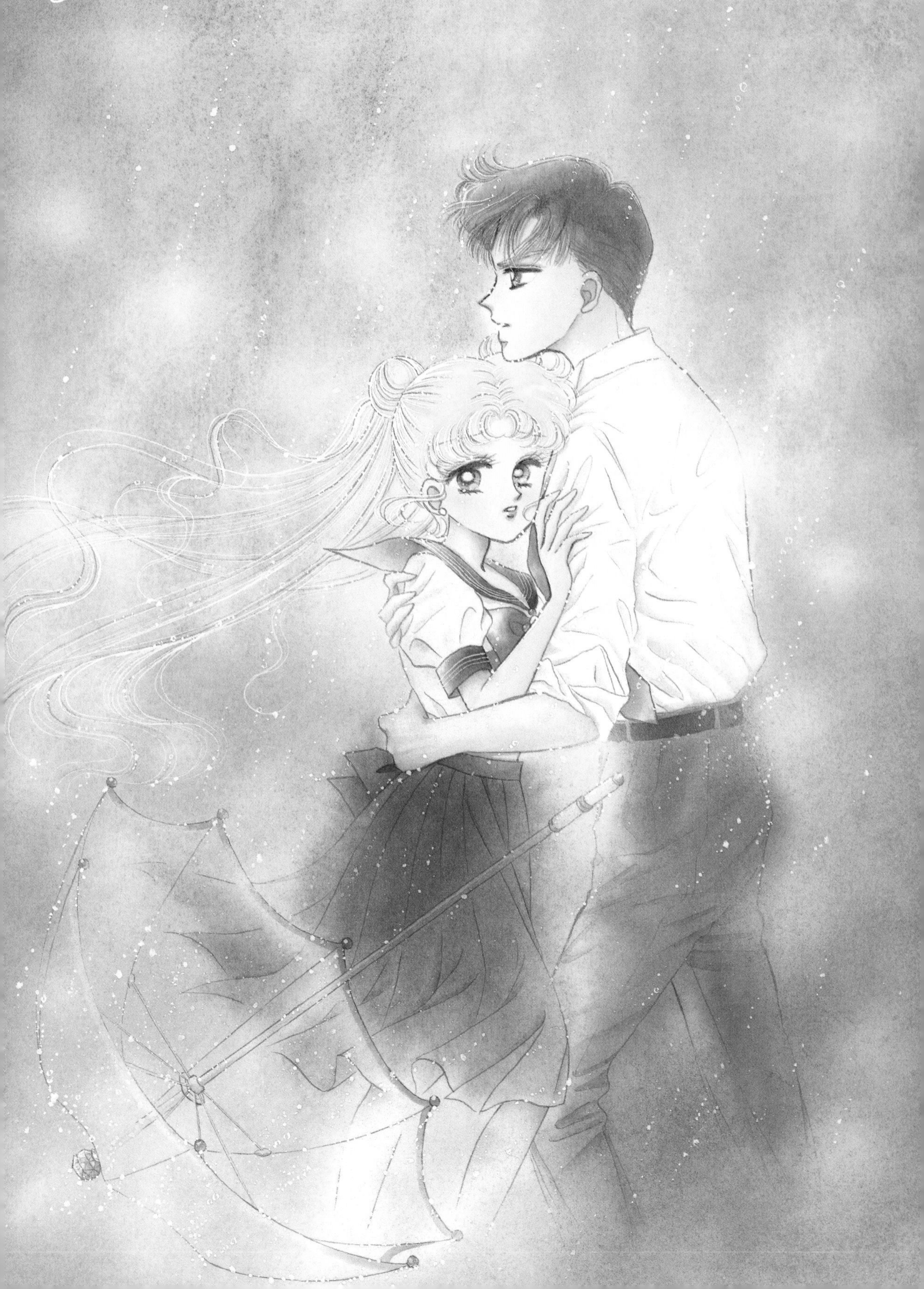

Pretty Guardian Sailor Moon

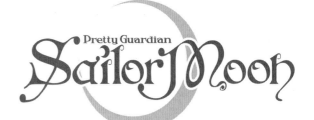

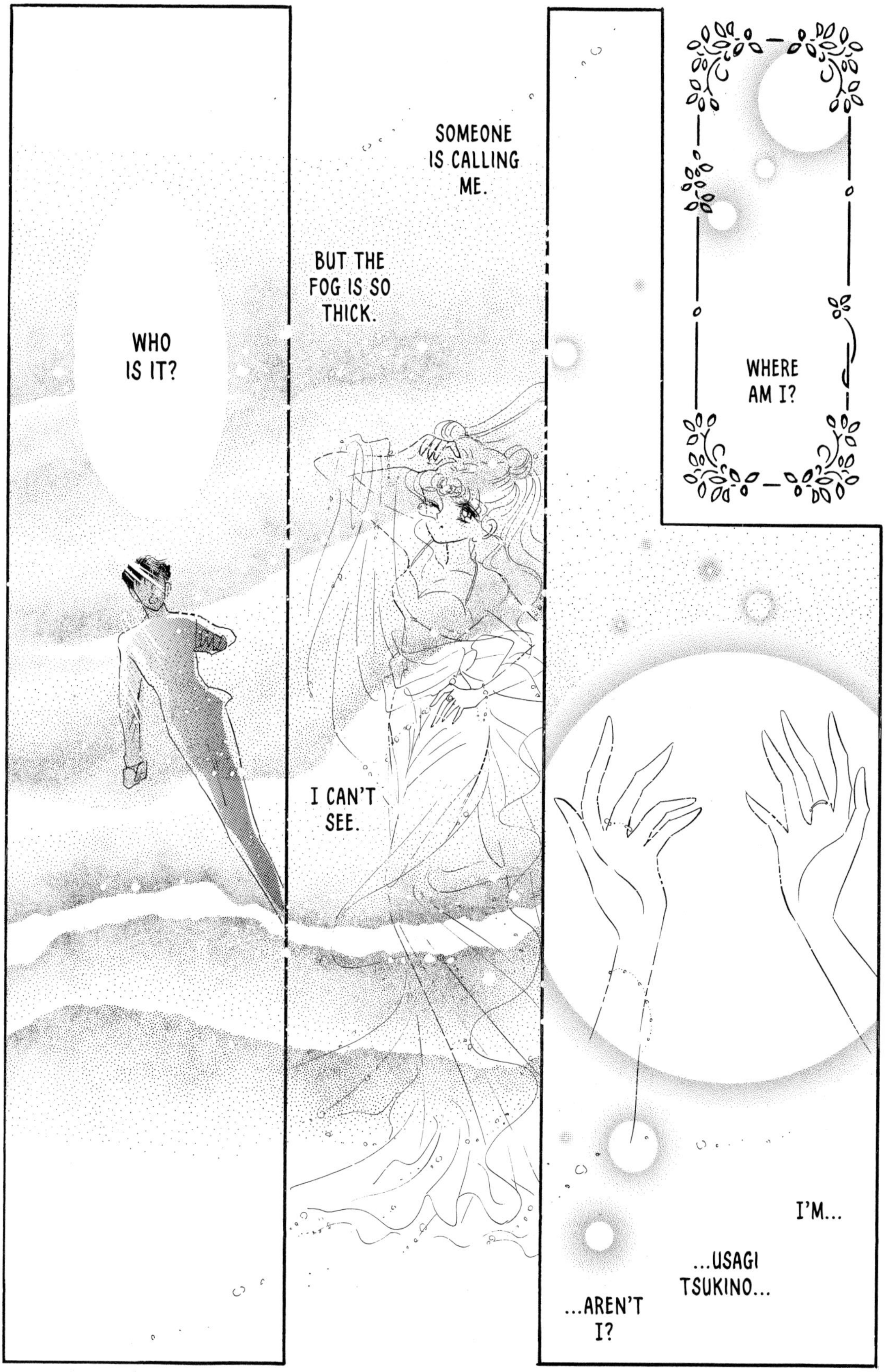
WHERE AM I?
I'M...
...USAGI TSUKINO...
...AREN'T I?
SOMEONE IS CALLING ME.
BUT THE FOG IS SO THICK.
I CAN'T SEE.
WHO IS IT?

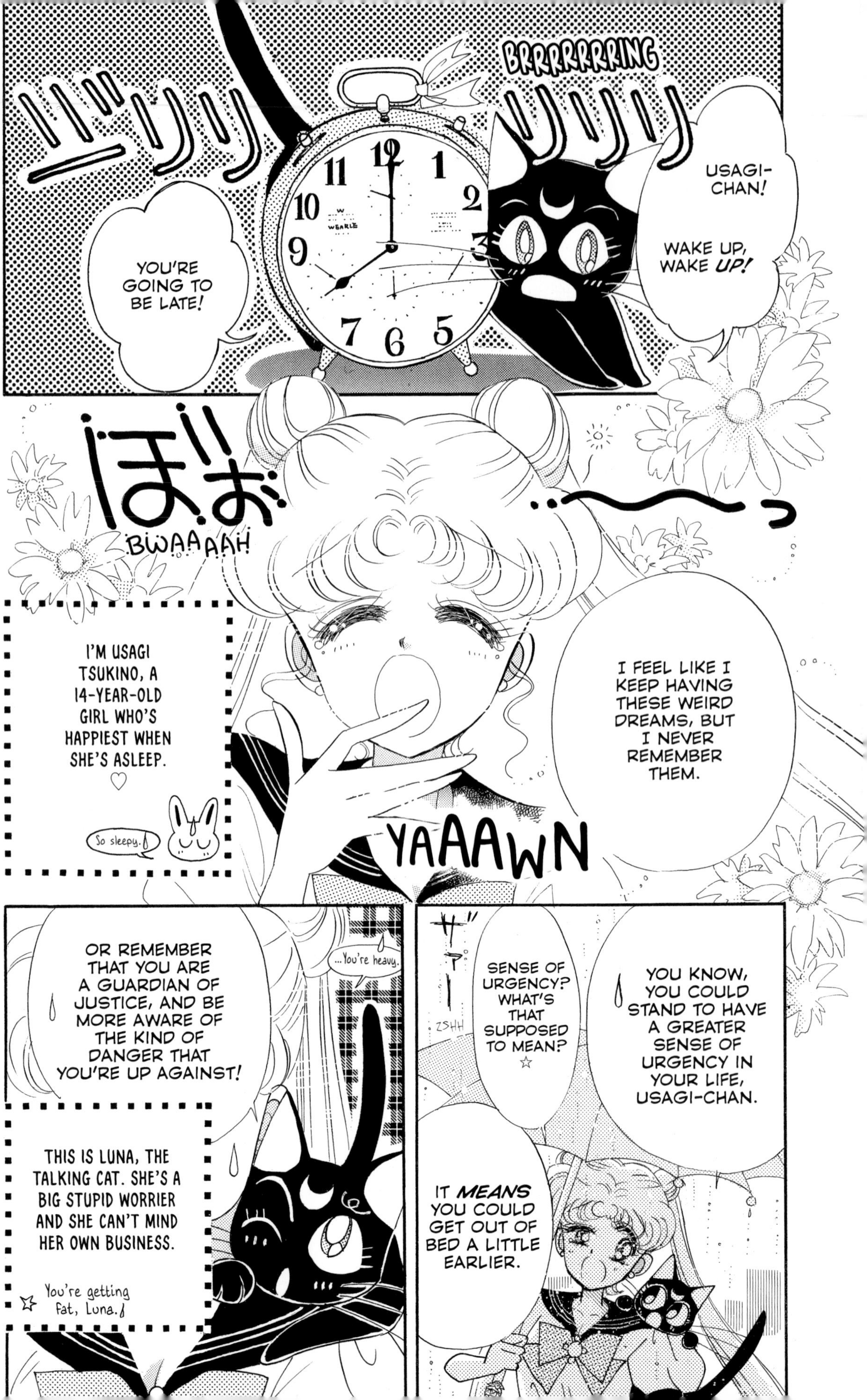
BRRRRRRRING
USAGI-CHAN!
WAKE UP, WAKE *UP!*
YOU'RE GOING TO BE LATE!
BWAAAAH
I FEEL LIKE I KEEP HAVING THESE WEIRD DREAMS, BUT I NEVER REMEMBER THEM.
YAAAWN
I'M USAGI TSUKINO, A 14-YEAR-OLD GIRL WHO'S HAPPIEST WHEN SHE'S ASLEEP. ♡
So sleepy.
YOU KNOW, YOU COULD STAND TO HAVE A GREATER SENSE OF URGENCY IN YOUR LIFE, USAGI-CHAN.
SENSE OF URGENCY? WHAT'S THAT SUPPOSED TO MEAN? ☆
ZSHH
IT *MEANS* YOU COULD GET OUT OF BED A LITTLE EARLIER.
OR REMEMBER THAT YOU ARE A GUARDIAN OF JUSTICE, AND BE MORE AWARE OF THE KIND OF DANGER THAT YOU'RE UP AGAINST!
...You're heavy.
THIS IS LUNA, THE TALKING CAT. SHE'S A BIG STUPID WORRIER AND SHE CAN'T MIND HER OWN BUSINESS.
You're getting fat, Luna.

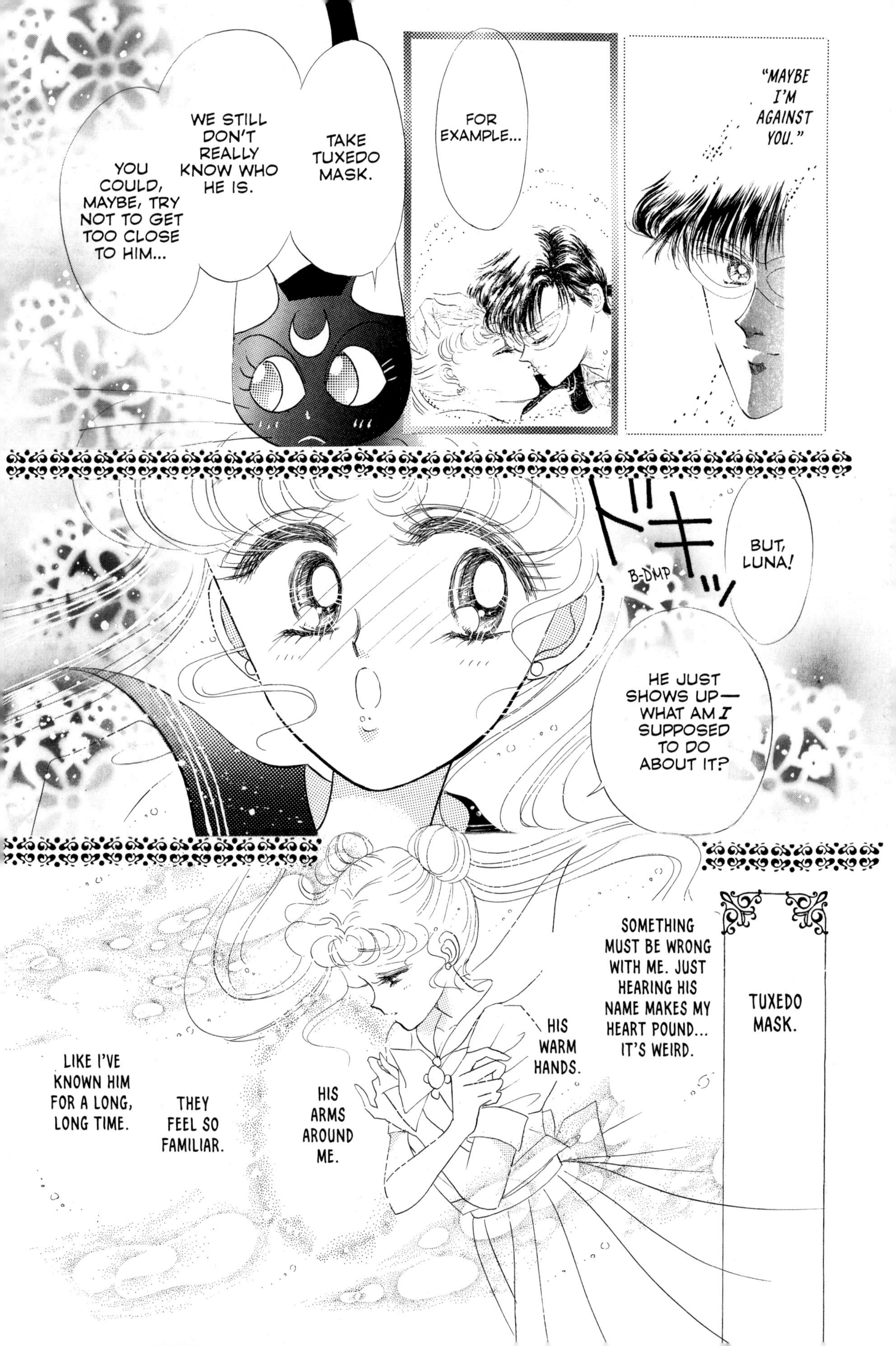
"MAYBE I'M AGAINST YOU."
FOR EXAMPLE...
TAKE TUXEDO MASK.
WE STILL DON'T REALLY KNOW WHO HE IS.
YOU COULD, MAYBE, TRY NOT TO GET TOO CLOSE TO HIM...
BUT, LUNA!
ドキッ
B-DMP
HE JUST SHOWS UP—WHAT AM *I* SUPPOSED TO DO ABOUT IT?
TUXEDO MASK.
SOMETHING MUST BE WRONG WITH ME. JUST HEARING HIS NAME MAKES MY HEART POUND... IT'S WEIRD.
HIS WARM HANDS.
HIS ARMS AROUND ME.
THEY FEEL SO FAMILIAR.
LIKE I'VE KNOWN HIM FOR A LONG, LONG TIME.

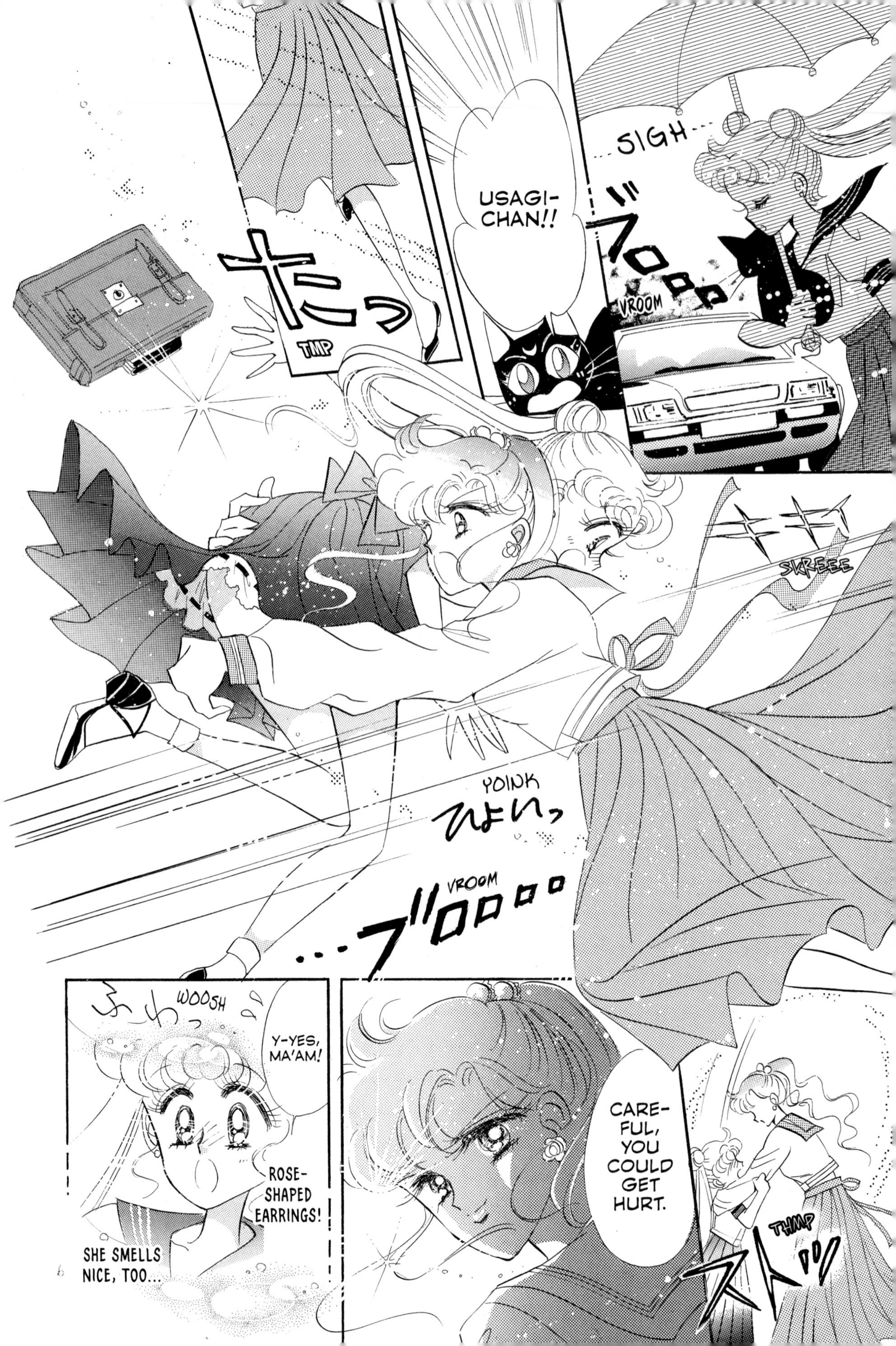

SIGH
VROOM
USAGI-CHAN!!
TMP
SKREEE
YOINK
VROOM
THMP
CARE-FUL, YOU COULD GET HURT.
WOOSH
Y-YES, MA'AM!
ROSE-SHAPED EARRINGS!
SHE SMELLS NICE, TOO...

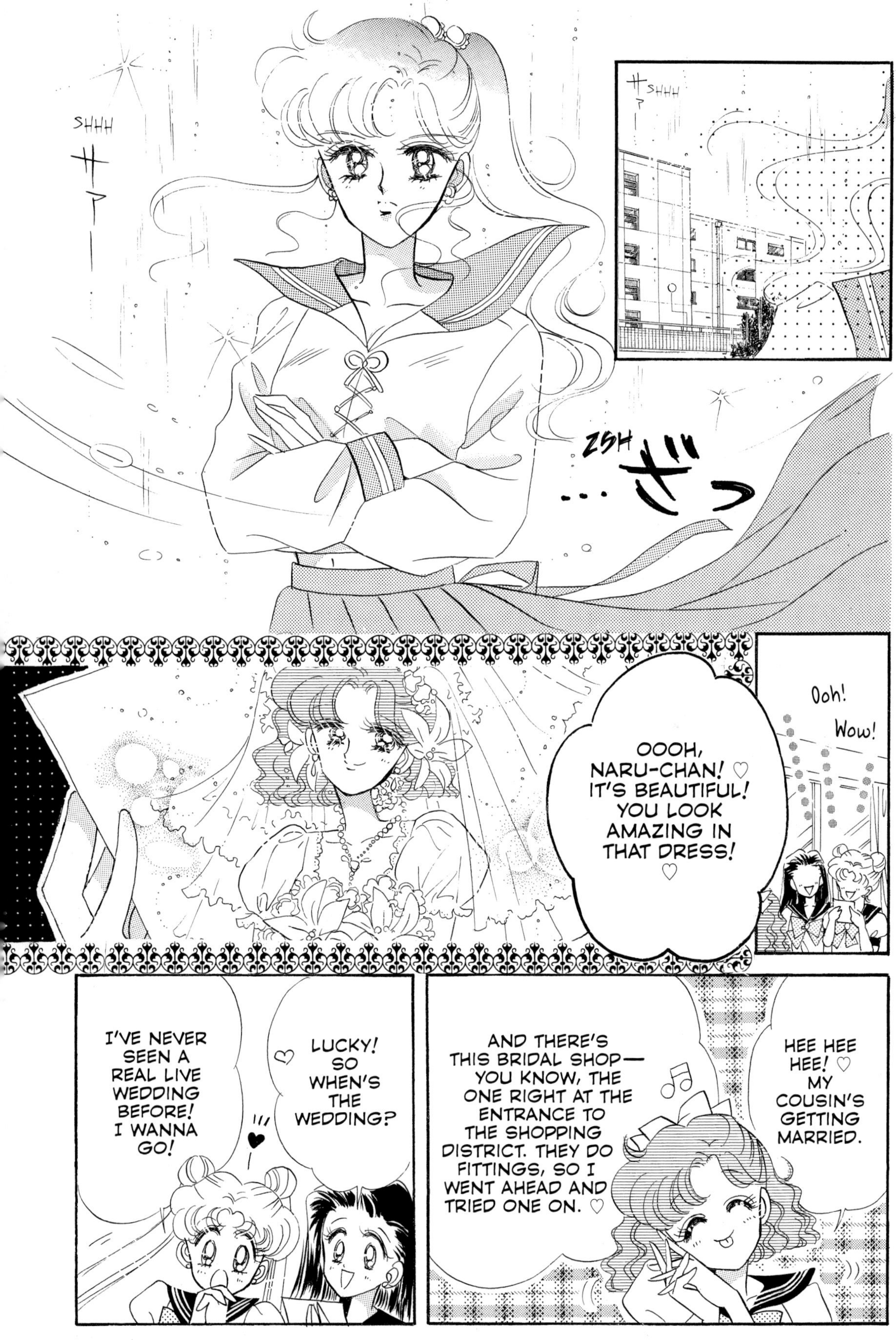
SHHH サァー
SHHH サァー
...ZSH ざっ
Ooh!
Wow!
OOOH, NARU-CHAN! ♡ IT'S BEAUTIFUL! YOU LOOK AMAZING IN THAT DRESS! ♡
HEE HEE HEE! ♡ MY COUSIN'S GETTING MARRIED.
AND THERE'S THIS BRIDAL SHOP—YOU KNOW, THE ONE RIGHT AT THE ENTRANCE TO THE SHOPPING DISTRICT. THEY DO FITTINGS, SO I WENT AHEAD AND TRIED ONE ON. ♡
LUCKY! SO WHEN'S THE WEDDING?
I'VE NEVER SEEN A REAL LIVE WEDDING BEFORE! I WANNA GO!

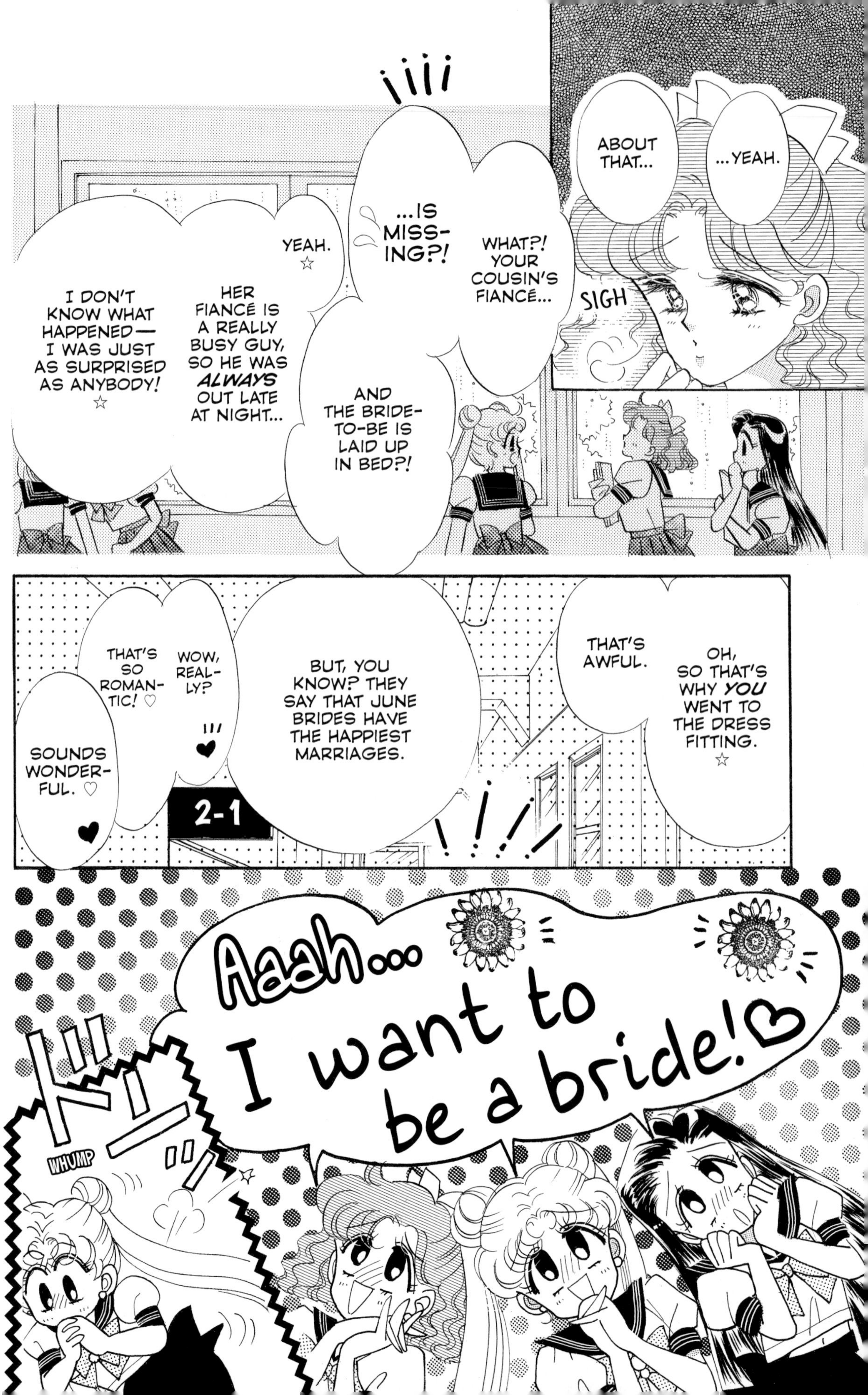

...YEAH.
ABOUT THAT...
SIGH
WHAT?! YOUR COUSIN'S FIANCE...
...IS MISSING?!
AND THE BRIDE-TO-BE IS LAID UP IN BED?!
YEAH. ☆
HER FIANCÉ IS A REALLY BUSY GUY, SO HE WAS *ALWAYS* OUT LATE AT NIGHT...
I DON'T KNOW WHAT HAPPENED— I WAS JUST AS SURPRISED AS ANYBODY! ☆
OH, SO THAT'S WHY *YOU* WENT TO THE DRESS FITTING. ☆
THAT'S AWFUL.
BUT, YOU KNOW? THEY SAY THAT JUNE BRIDES HAVE THE HAPPIEST MARRIAGES.
WOW, REALLY?
THAT'S SO ROMANTIC! ♡
SOUNDS WONDERFUL. ♡
2-1
Aaah... I want to be a bride!♡
WHUMP

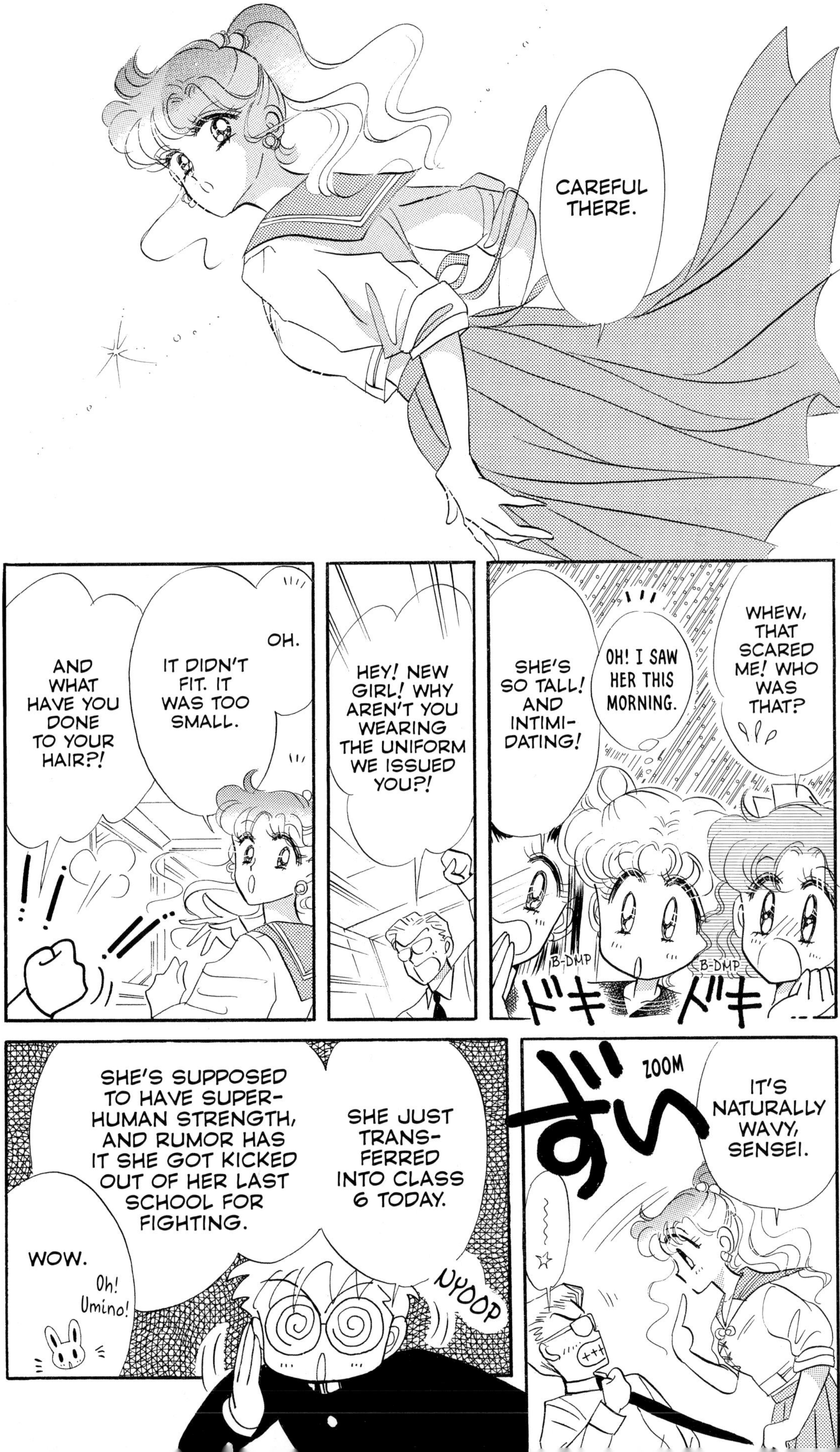

CAREFUL THERE.
WHEW, THAT SCARED ME! WHO WAS THAT?
OH! I SAW HER THIS MORNING.
SHE'S SO TALL! AND INTIMIDATING!
B-DMP
ドキ
B-DMP
ドキ
HEY! NEW GIRL! WHY AREN'T YOU WEARING THE UNIFORM WE ISSUED YOU?!
OH.
IT DIDN'T FIT. IT WAS TOO SMALL.
AND WHAT HAVE YOU DONE TO YOUR HAIR?!
ずい
ZOOM
IT'S NATURALLY WAVY, SENSEI.
SHE JUST TRANSFERRED INTO CLASS 6 TODAY.
SHE'S SUPPOSED TO HAVE SUPERHUMAN STRENGTH, AND RUMOR HAS IT SHE GOT KICKED OUT OF HER LAST SCHOOL FOR FIGHTING.
NYOOP
WOW.
Oh! Umino!

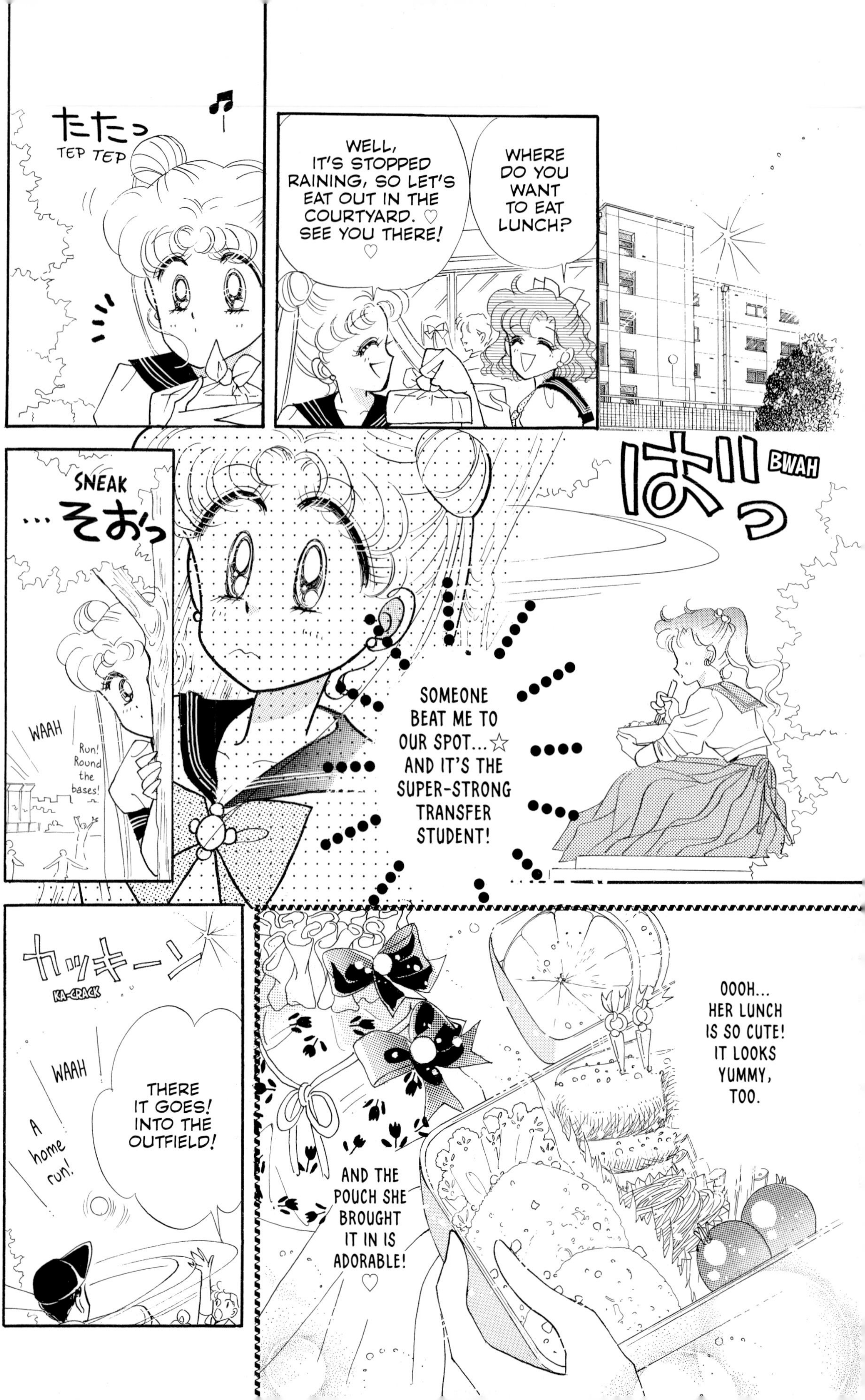
WHERE DO YOU WANT TO EAT LUNCH?
WELL, IT'S STOPPED RAINING, SO LET'S EAT OUT IN THE COURTYARD. ♡ SEE YOU THERE! ♡
たたっ
TEP TEP
はっ
BWAH
SOMEONE BEAT ME TO OUR SPOT...☆ AND IT'S THE SUPER-STRONG TRANSFER STUDENT!
SNEAK
...そおっ
WAAH
Run! Round the bases!
OOOH... HER LUNCH IS SO CUTE! IT LOOKS YUMMY, TOO.
AND THE POUCH SHE BROUGHT IT IN IS ADORABLE! ♡
カッキーン
KA-CRACK
WAAH
THERE IT GOES! INTO THE OUTFIELD!
A home run!

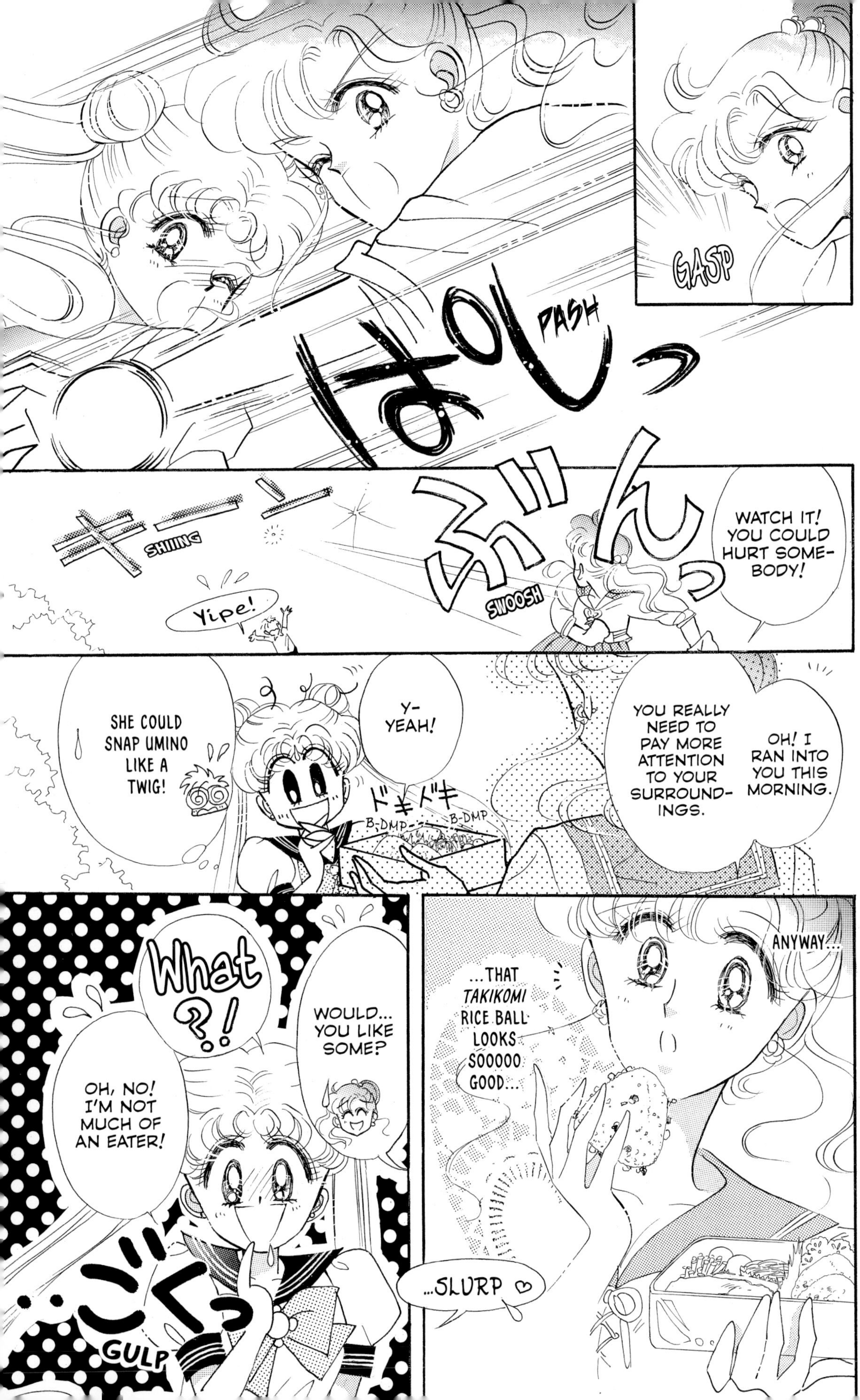
GASP
ぱしっ
PASH
WATCH IT! YOU COULD HURT SOME-BODY!
ぶんっ
SWOOSH
キーン
SHIIING
Yipe!
OH! I RAN INTO YOU THIS MORNING.
YOU REALLY NEED TO PAY MORE ATTENTION TO YOUR SURROUND-INGS.
Y-YEAH!
ドキドキ
B-DMP B-DMP
SHE COULD SNAP UMINO LIKE A TWIG!
ANYWAY...
...THAT *TAKIKOMI* RICE BALL LOOKS SOOOOO GOOD...
...SLURP
WOULD... YOU LIKE SOME?
What?!
OH, NO! I'M NOT MUCH OF AN EATER!
ごくっ
GULP

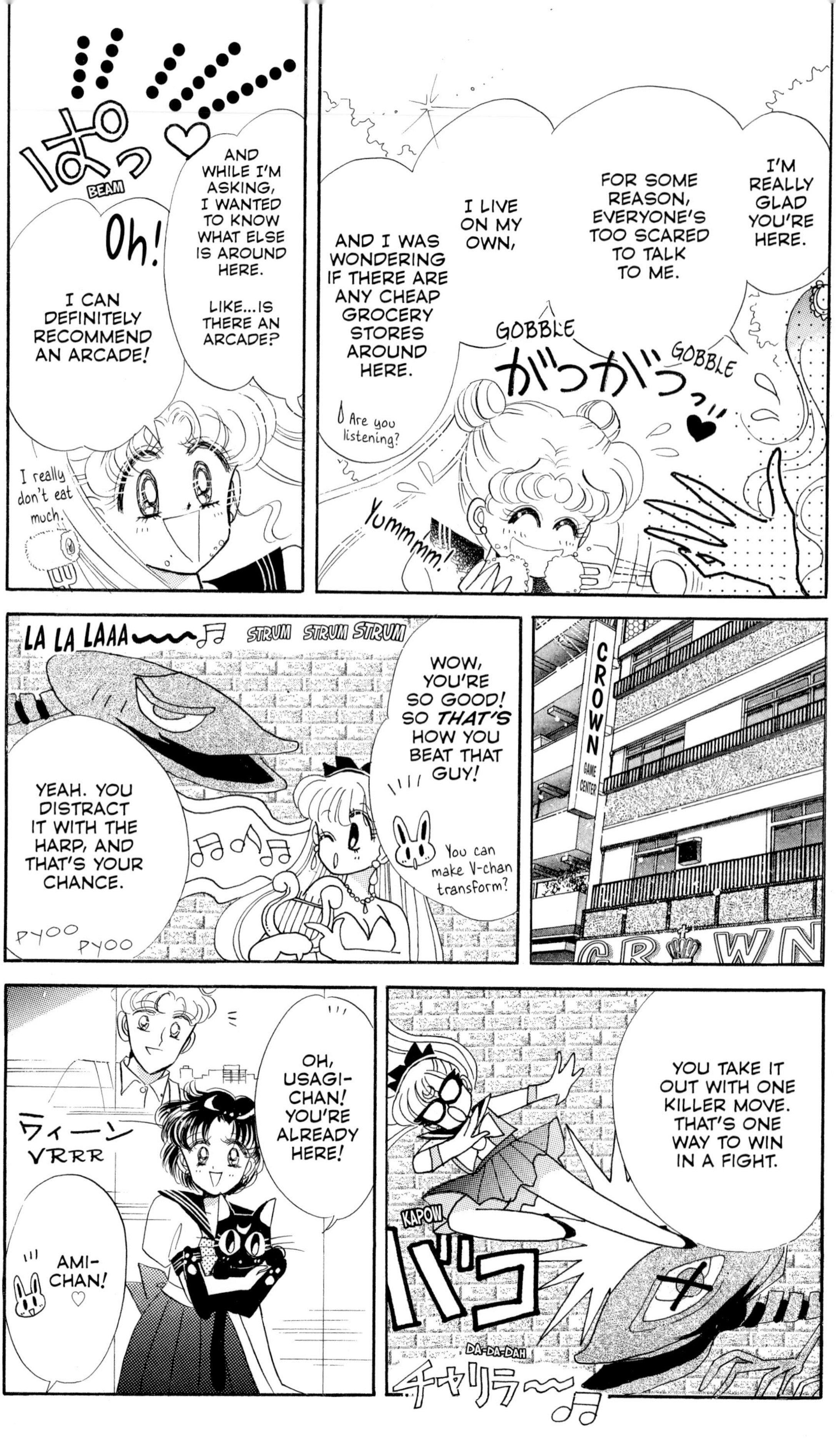
I'M REALLY GLAD YOU'RE HERE.
FOR SOME REASON, EVERYONE'S TOO SCARED TO TALK TO ME.
I LIVE ON MY OWN,
AND I WAS WONDERING IF THERE ARE ANY CHEAP GROCERY STORES AROUND HERE.
がつがつっ
GOBBLE GOBBLE
Are you listening?
Yummmm!
ぱっ
BEAM
AND WHILE I'M ASKING, I WANTED TO KNOW WHAT ELSE IS AROUND HERE.
LIKE...IS THERE AN ARCADE?
Oh!
I CAN DEFINITELY RECOMMEND AN ARCADE!
I really don't eat much.
CROWN GAME CENTER
CROWN
LA LA LAAA
STRUM STRUM STRUM
WOW, YOU'RE SO GOOD! SO *THAT'S* HOW YOU BEAT THAT GUY!
You can make V-chan transform?
YEAH. YOU DISTRACT IT WITH THE HARP, AND THAT'S YOUR CHANCE.
PYOO PYOO
YOU TAKE IT OUT WITH ONE KILLER MOVE. THAT'S ONE WAY TO WIN IN A FIGHT.
KAPOW
バコ
DA-DA-DAH
チャリラ〜
OH, USAGI-CHAN! YOU'RE ALREADY HERE!
ウィーン
VRRR
AMI-CHAN!

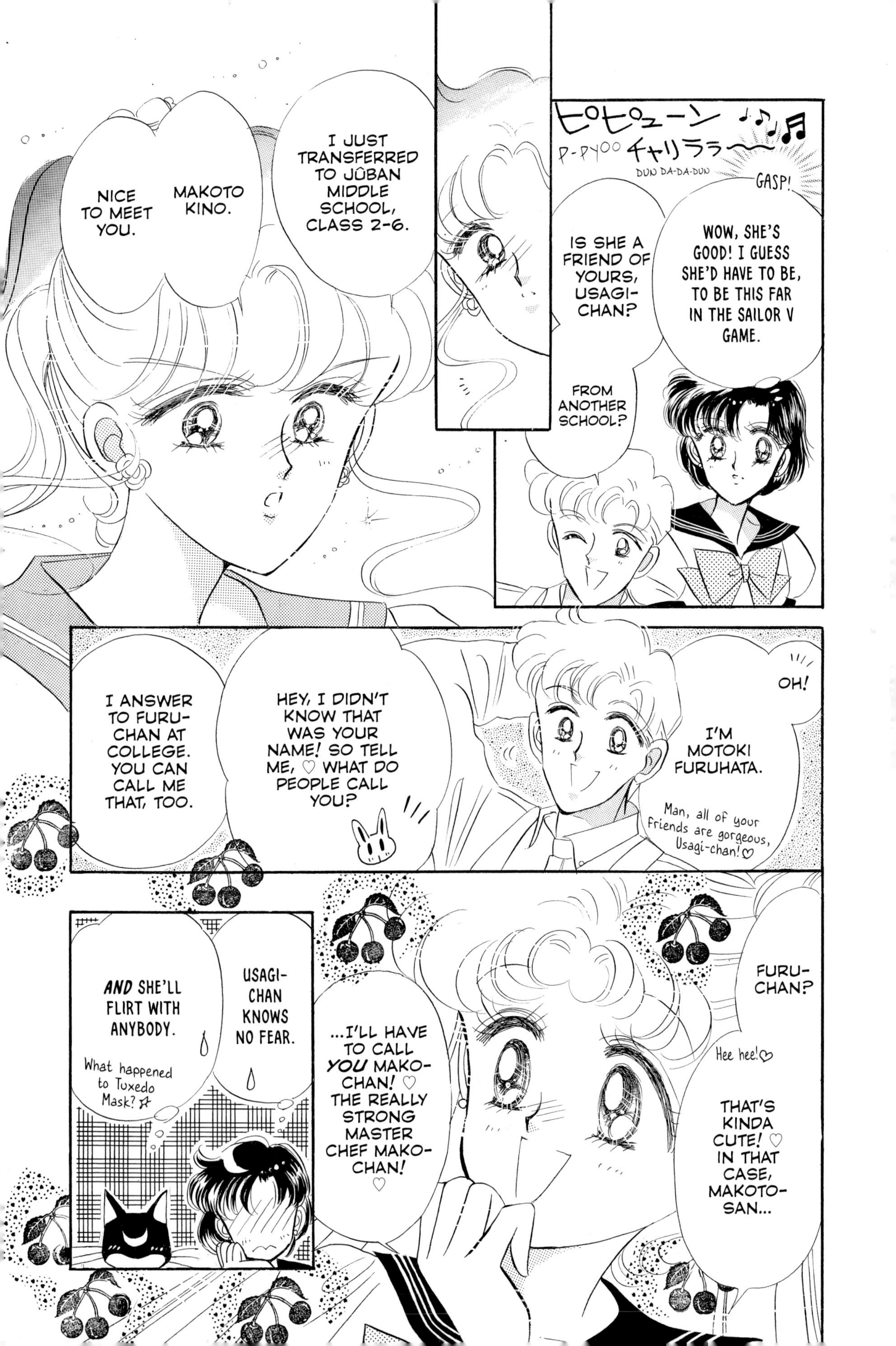
ピピューン ♪♫
P-PYOO チャリララ〜
DUN DA-DA-DUN
GASP!
WOW, SHE'S GOOD! I GUESS SHE'D HAVE TO BE, TO BE THIS FAR IN THE SAILOR V GAME.
IS SHE A FRIEND OF YOURS, USAGI-CHAN?
FROM ANOTHER SCHOOL?
I JUST TRANSFERRED TO JÛBAN MIDDLE SCHOOL, CLASS 2-6.
MAKOTO KINO.
NICE TO MEET YOU.
OH!
I'M MOTOKI FURUHATA.
Man, all of your friends are gorgeous, Usagi-chan! ♡
HEY, I DIDN'T KNOW THAT WAS YOUR NAME! SO TELL ME, ♡ WHAT DO PEOPLE CALL YOU?
I ANSWER TO FURU-CHAN AT COLLEGE. YOU CAN CALL ME THAT, TOO.
FURU-CHAN?
Hee hee! ♡
THAT'S KINDA CUTE! ♡ IN THAT CASE, MAKOTO-SAN...
...I'LL HAVE TO CALL *YOU* MAKO-CHAN! ♡ THE REALLY STRONG MASTER CHEF MAKO-CHAN! ♡
USAGI-CHAN KNOWS NO FEAR.
AND SHE'LL FLIRT WITH ANYBODY.
What happened to Tuxedo Mask? ☆

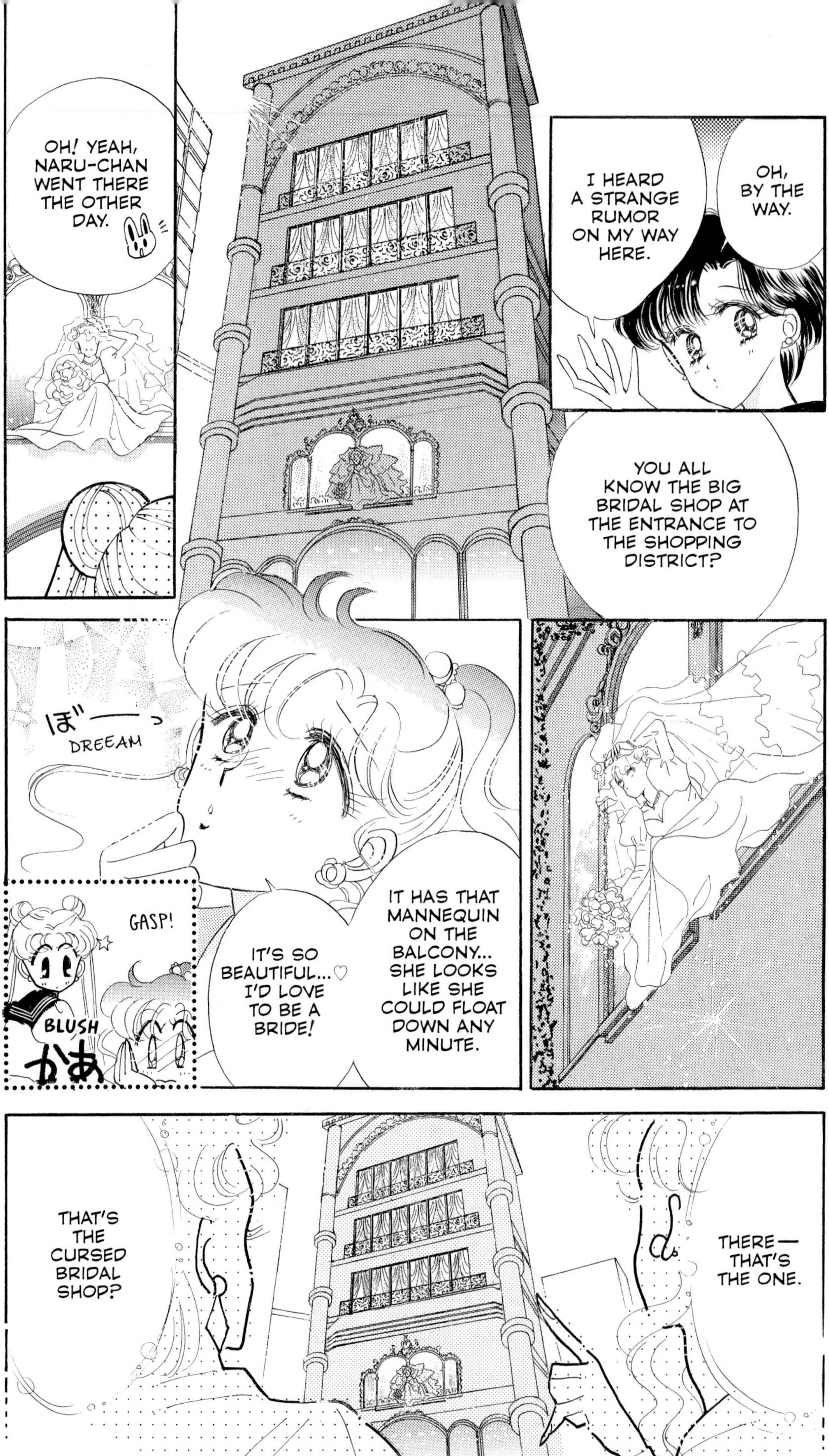
OH, BY THE WAY.
I HEARD A STRANGE RUMOR ON MY WAY HERE.
YOU ALL KNOW THE BIG BRIDAL SHOP AT THE ENTRANCE TO THE SHOPPING DISTRICT?
OH! YEAH, NARU-CHAN WENT THERE THE OTHER DAY.
IT HAS THAT MANNEQUIN ON THE BALCONY... SHE LOOKS LIKE SHE COULD FLOAT DOWN ANY MINUTE.
IT'S SO BEAUTIFUL...♡ I'D LOVE TO BE A BRIDE!
ぼーーっ
DREEAM
GASP!
BLUSH
かあ
THERE—THAT'S THE ONE.
THAT'S THE CURSED BRIDAL SHOP?

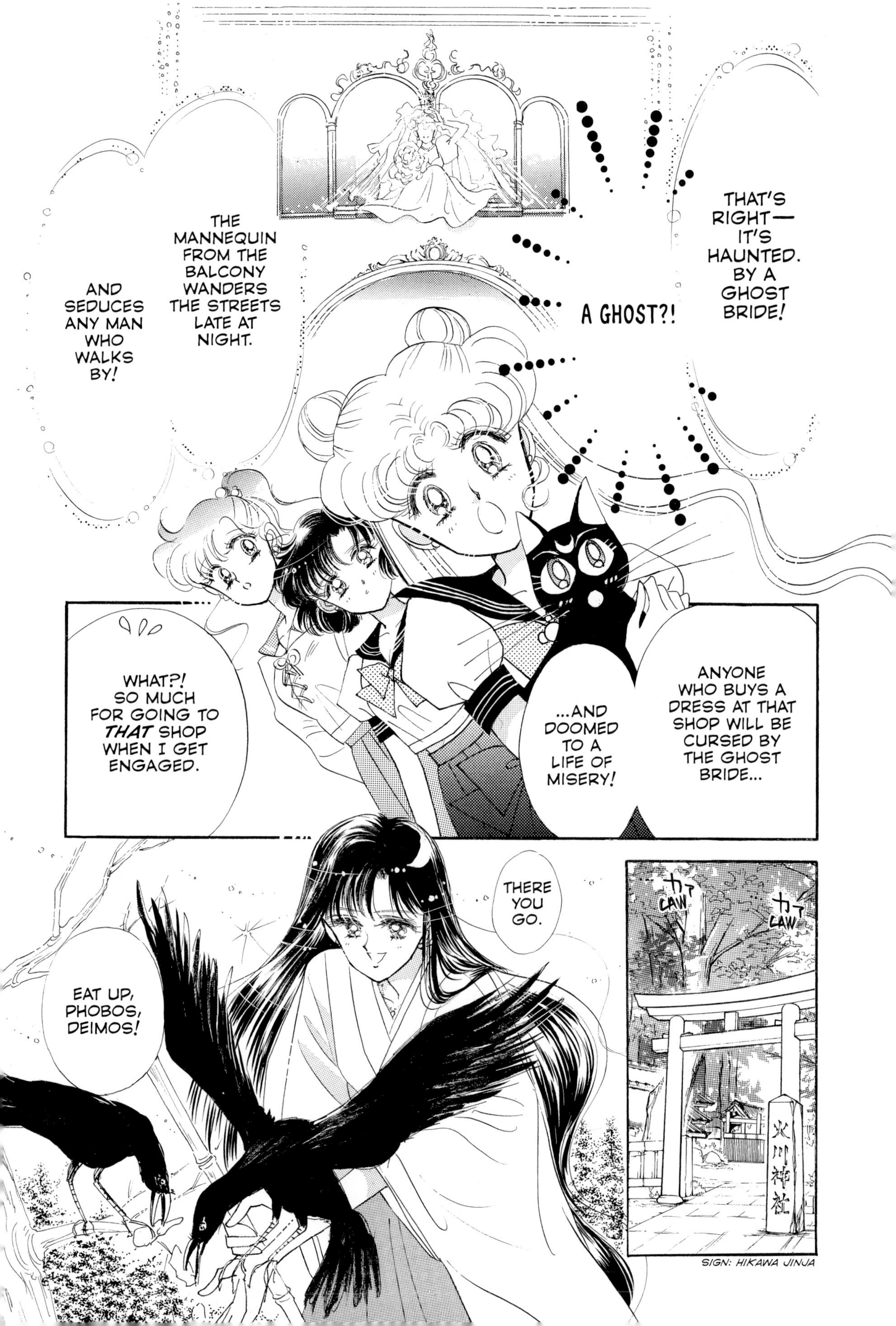
THAT'S RIGHT—IT'S HAUNTED. BY A GHOST BRIDE!
A GHOST?!
THE MANNEQUIN FROM THE BALCONY WANDERS THE STREETS LATE AT NIGHT.
AND SEDUCES ANY MAN WHO WALKS BY!
ANYONE WHO BUYS A DRESS AT THAT SHOP WILL BE CURSED BY THE GHOST BRIDE...
...AND DOOMED TO A LIFE OF MISERY!
WHAT?! SO MUCH FOR GOING TO *THAT* SHOP WHEN I GET ENGAGED.
カァ CAW
カァ CAW
火川神社
SIGN: HIKAWA JINJA
THERE YOU GO.
EAT UP, PHOBOS, DEIMOS!

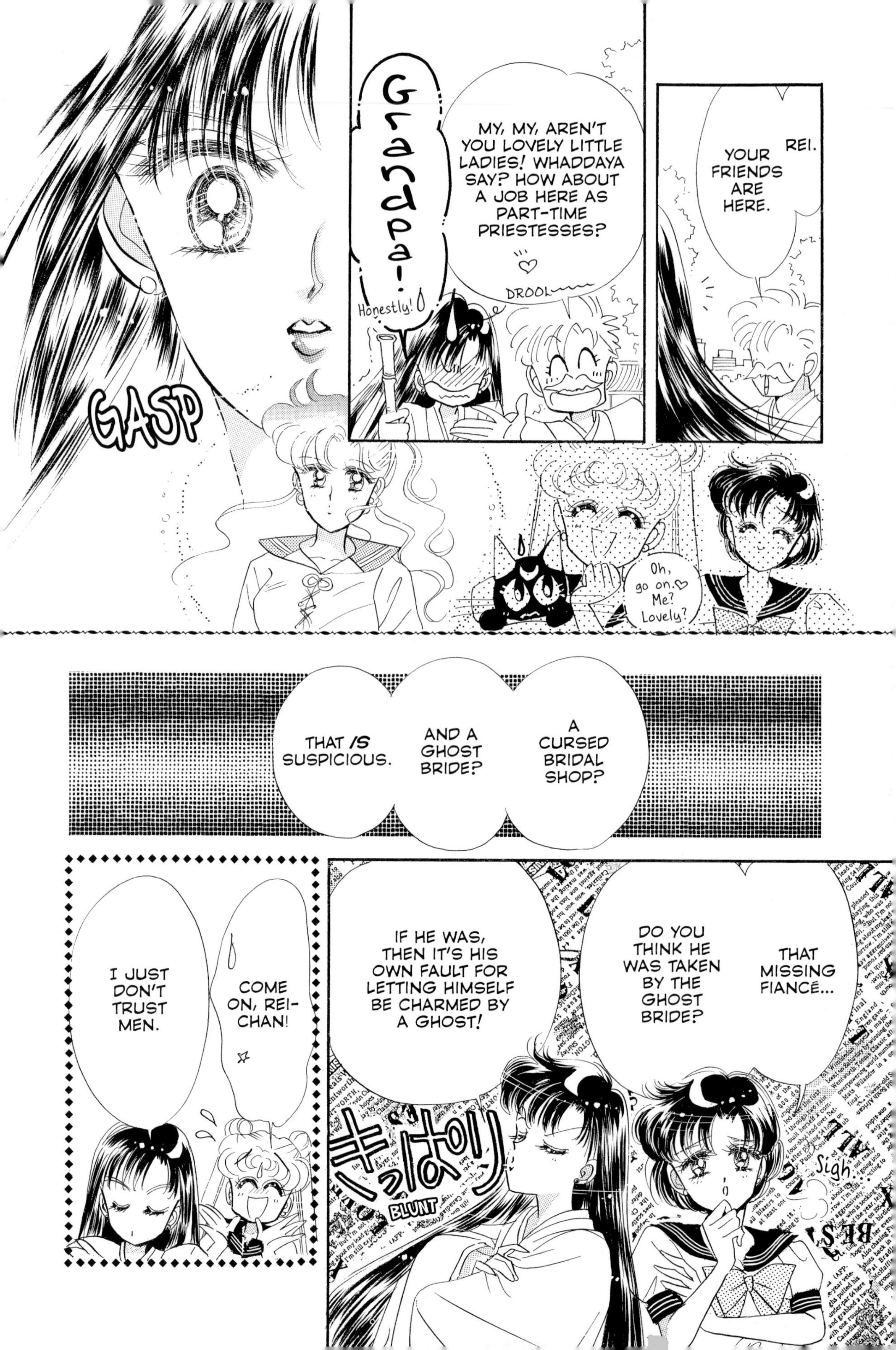
REI.
YOUR FRIENDS ARE HERE.
MY, MY, AREN'T YOU LOVELY LITTLE LADIES! WHADDAYA SAY? HOW ABOUT A JOB HERE AS PART-TIME PRIESTESSES?
DROOL
Grandpa!
Honestly!
GASP
Oh, go on. Me? Lovely?
A CURSED BRIDAL SHOP?
AND A GHOST BRIDE?
THAT *IS* SUSPICIOUS.
THAT MISSING FIANCÉ...
DO YOU THINK HE WAS TAKEN BY THE GHOST BRIDE?
Sigh
IF HE WAS, THEN IT'S HIS OWN FAULT FOR LETTING HIMSELF BE CHARMED BY A GHOST!
きっぱり
BLUNT
COME ON, REI-CHAN!
I JUST DON'T TRUST MEN.

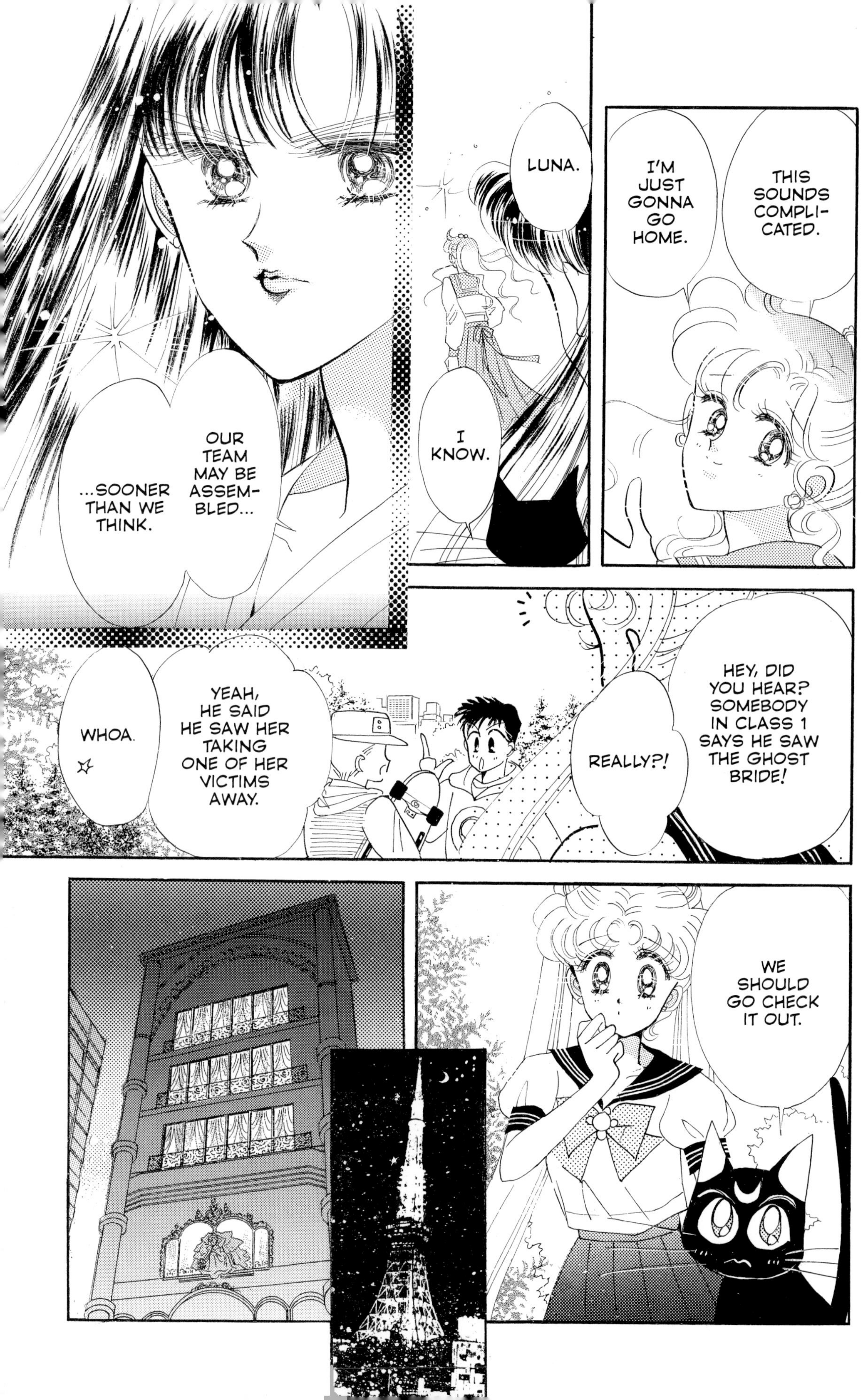
THIS SOUNDS COMPLICATED.
I'M JUST GONNA GO HOME.
LUNA.
I KNOW.
OUR TEAM MAY BE ASSEMBLED...
...SOONER THAN WE THINK.
HEY, DID YOU HEAR? SOMEBODY IN CLASS 1 SAYS HE SAW THE GHOST BRIDE!
REALLY?!
YEAH, HE SAID HE SAW HER TAKING ONE OF HER VICTIMS AWAY.
WHOA.
WE SHOULD GO CHECK IT OUT.

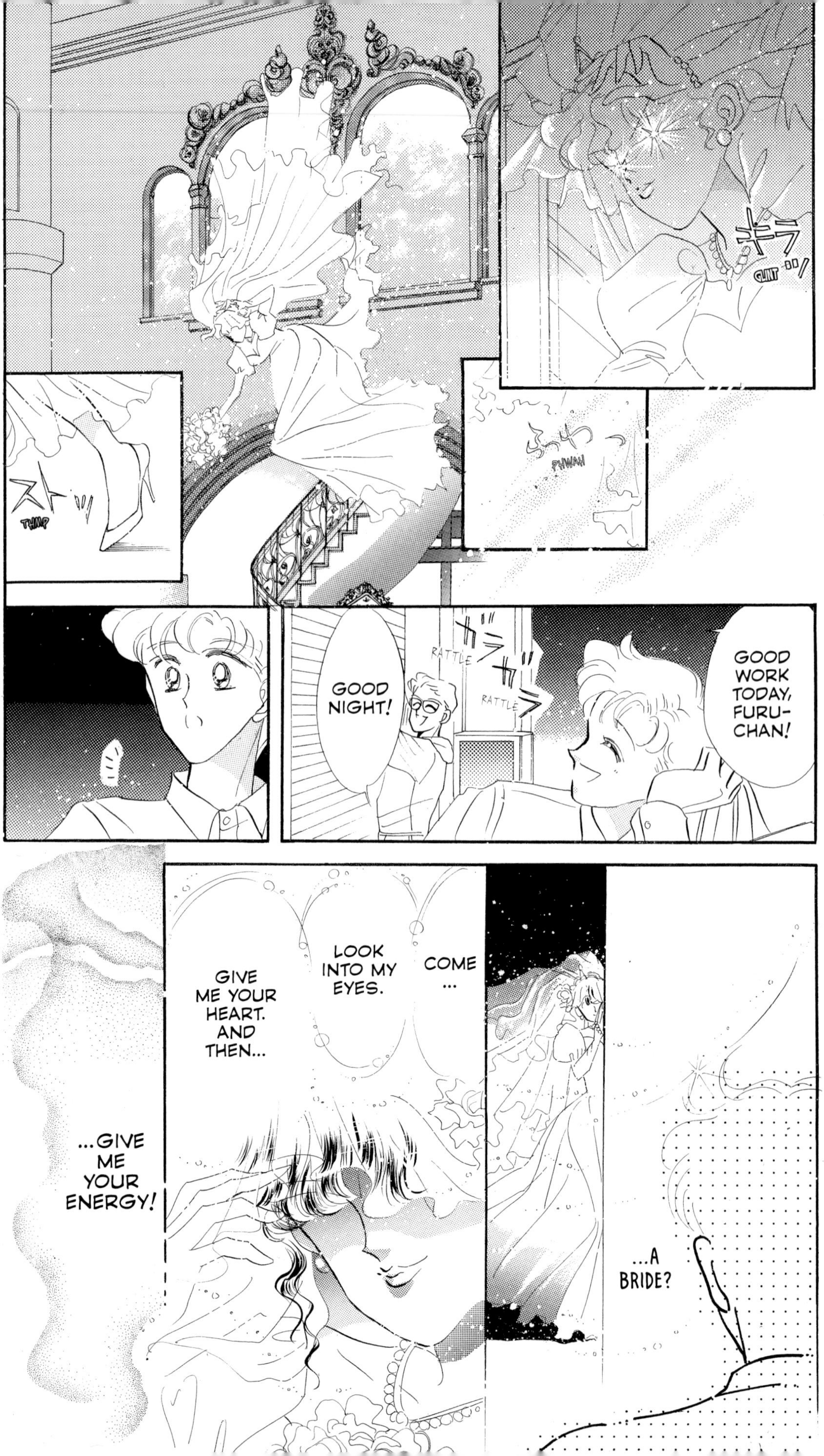
キラッ
GLINT
ふわっ
PHWAH
スト
THMP
GOOD WORK TODAY, FURU-CHAN!
ガラ ガラ
RATTLE
RATTLE
GOOD NIGHT!
...A BRIDE?
COME...
LOOK INTO MY EYES.
GIVE ME YOUR HEART. AND THEN...
...GIVE ME YOUR ENERGY!

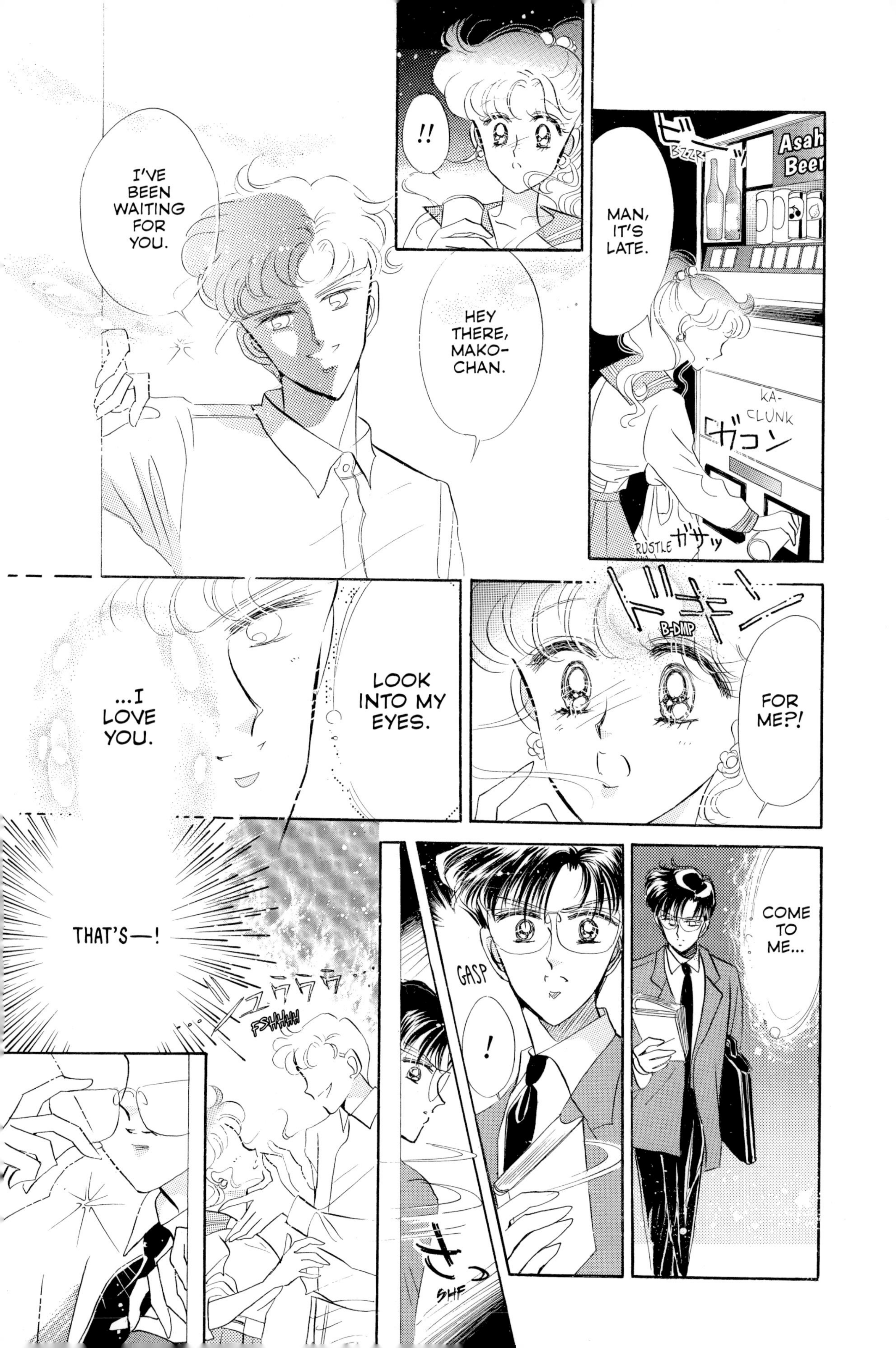

Asah
Beer
BZZR
MAN, IT'S LATE.
KA-CLUNK
RUSTLE
!!
HEY THERE, MAKO-CHAN.
I'VE BEEN WAITING FOR YOU.
B-DMP
FOR ME?!
LOOK INTO MY EYES.
...I LOVE YOU.
COME TO ME...
GASP
!
SHF
THAT'S—!
FSHHHH

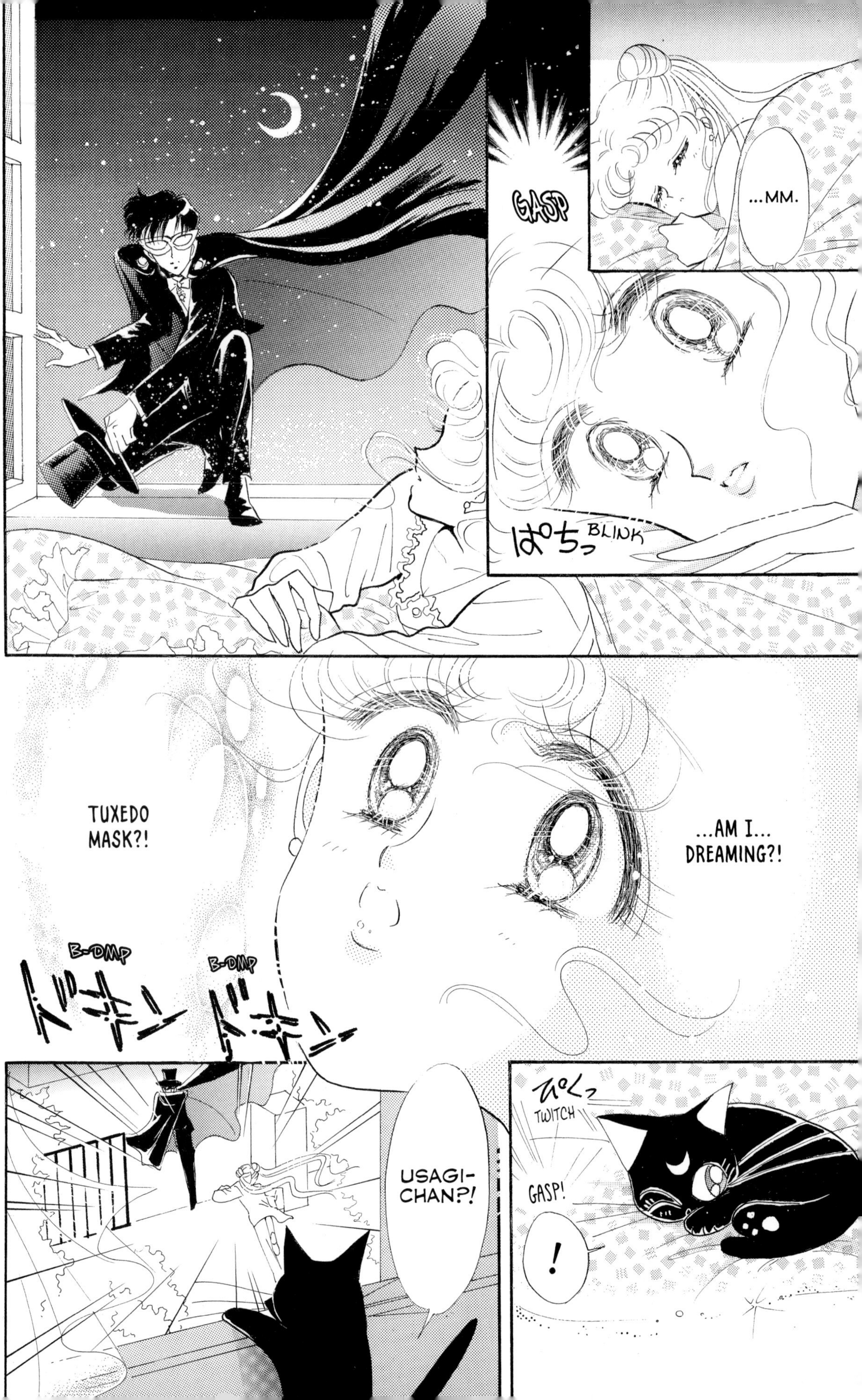
...MM.
GASP
ぱちっ BLINK
...AM I... DREAMING?!
TUXEDO MASK?!
B-DMP
B-DMP
ぴくっ TWITCH
GASP!
!
USAGI-CHAN?!

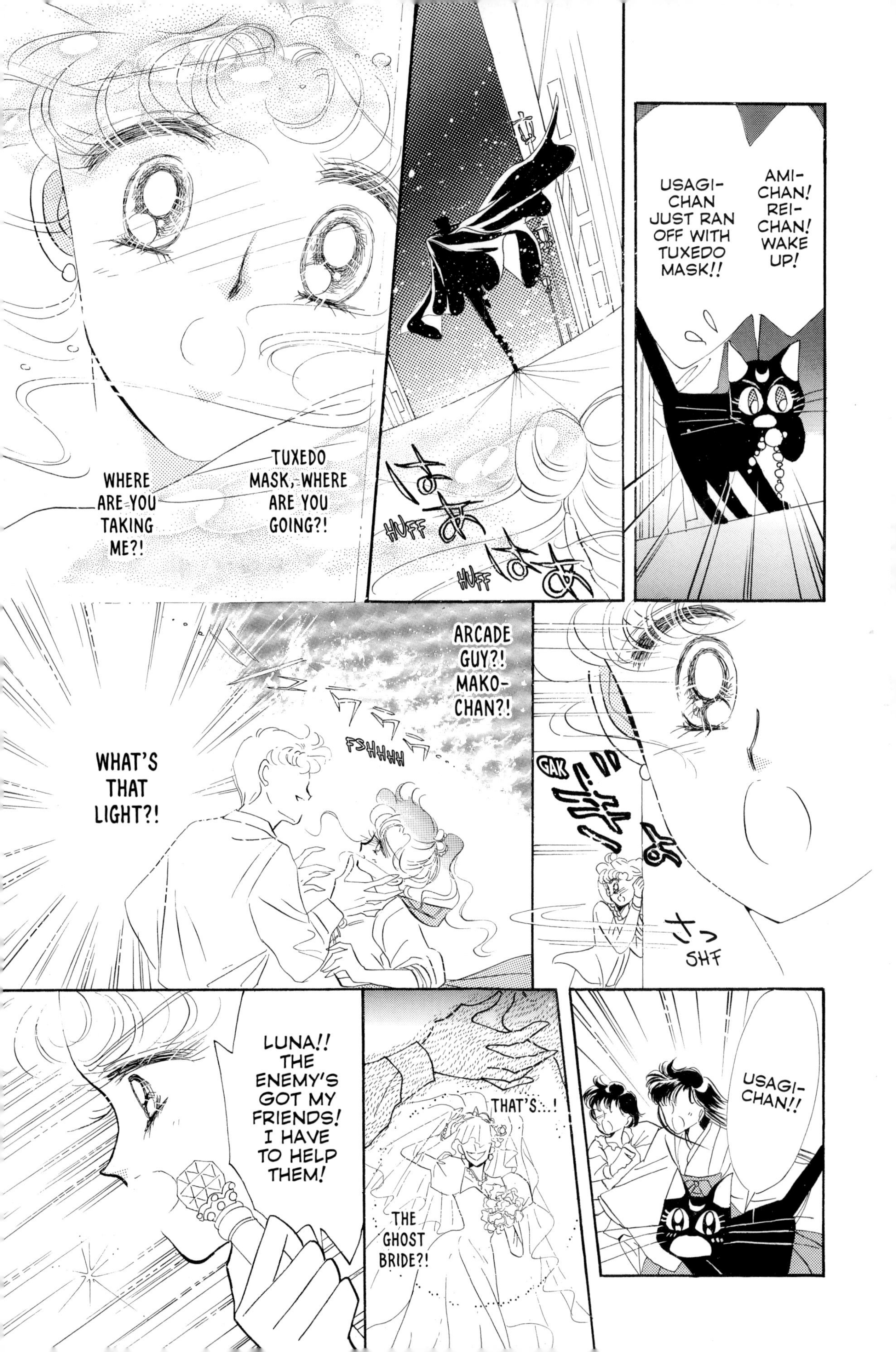
AMI-CHAN! REI-CHAN! WAKE UP!
USAGI-CHAN JUST RAN OFF WITH TUXEDO MASK!!
HUFF
HUFF
TUXEDO MASK, WHERE ARE YOU GOING?!
WHERE ARE YOU TAKING ME?!
GAK
SHF
ARCADE GUY?! MAKO-CHAN?!
FSHHHH
WHAT'S THAT LIGHT?!
USAGI-CHAN!!
THAT'S...!
THE GHOST BRIDE?!
LUNA!! THE ENEMY'S GOT MY FRIENDS! I HAVE TO HELP THEM!

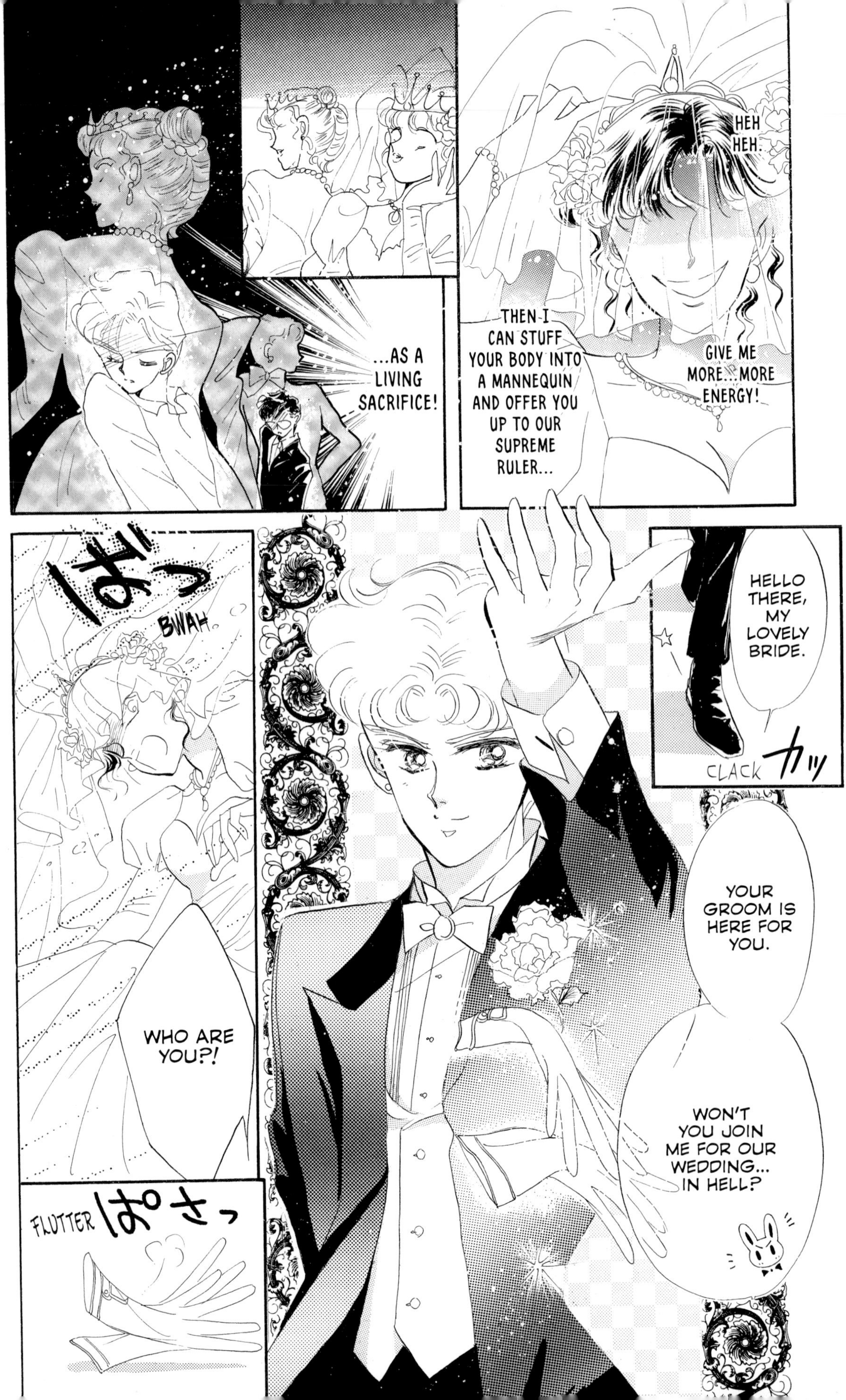
HEH HEH.
GIVE ME MORE...MORE ENERGY!
THEN I CAN STUFF YOUR BODY INTO A MANNEQUIN AND OFFER YOU UP TO OUR SUPREME RULER...
...AS A LIVING SACRIFICE!
HELLO THERE, MY LOVELY BRIDE.
CLACK カッ
YOUR GROOM IS HERE FOR YOU.
WON'T YOU JOIN ME FOR OUR WEDDING... IN HELL?
ばっ BWAH
WHO ARE YOU?!
FLUTTER ぱさっ

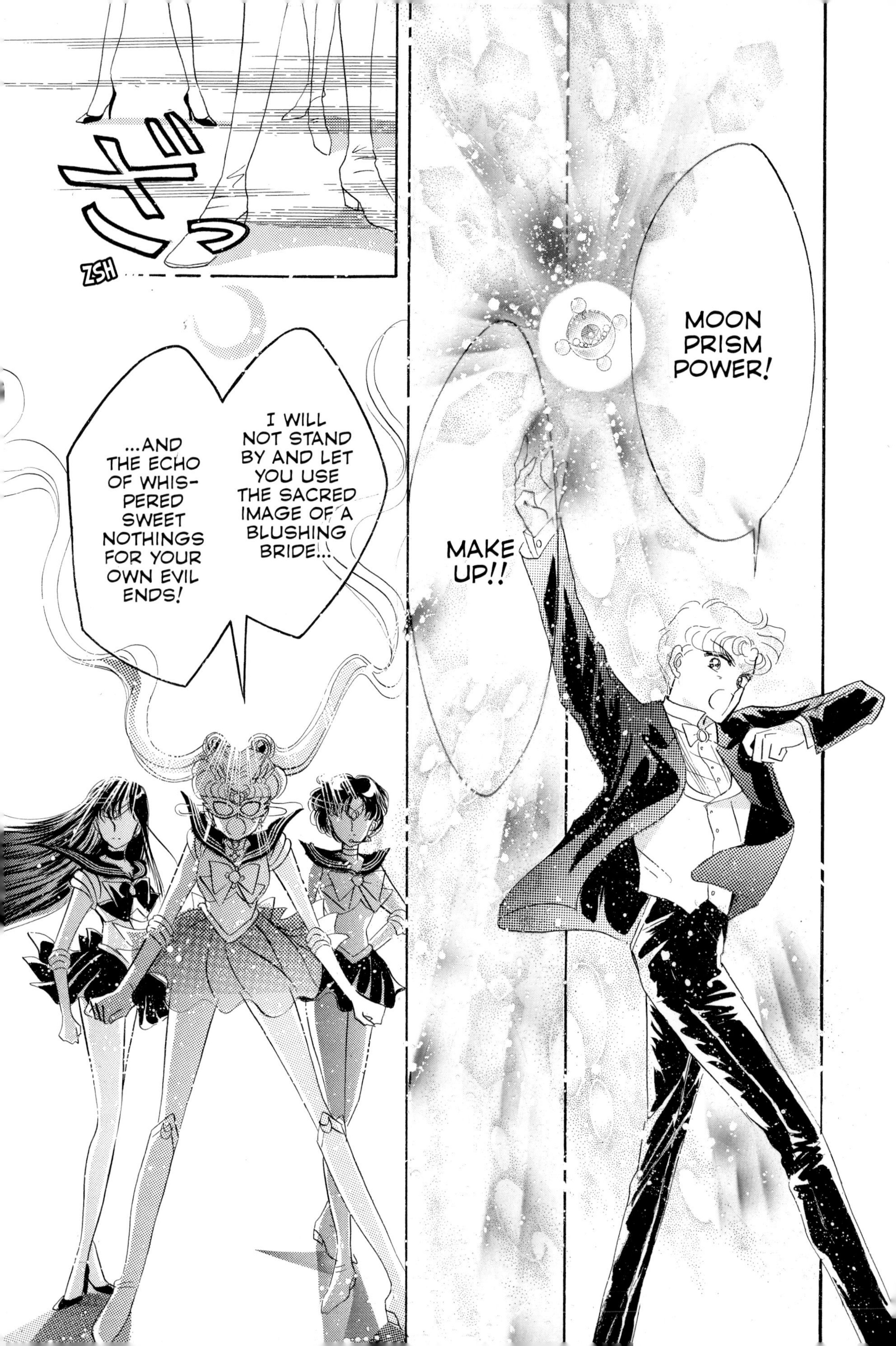
MOON PRISM POWER!
MAKE UP!!
ZSH
I WILL NOT STAND BY AND LET YOU USE THE SACRED IMAGE OF A BLUSHING BRIDE...
...AND THE ECHO OF WHIS-PERED SWEET NOTHINGS FOR YOUR OWN EVIL ENDS!

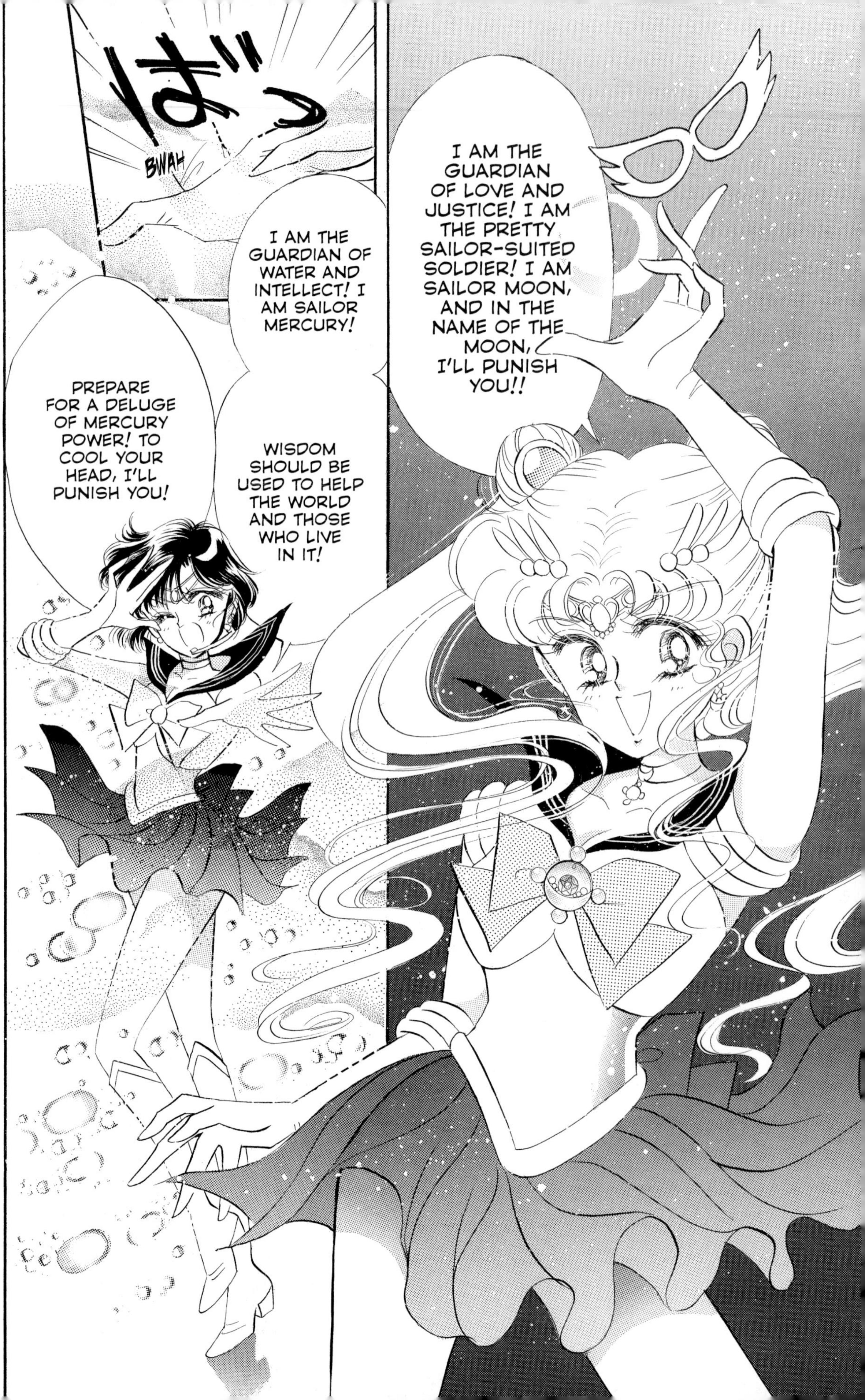

I AM THE GUARDIAN OF LOVE AND JUSTICE! I AM THE PRETTY SAILOR-SUITED SOLDIER! I AM SAILOR MOON, AND IN THE NAME OF THE MOON, I'LL PUNISH YOU!!
ばっ
BWAH
I AM THE GUARDIAN OF WATER AND INTELLECT! I AM SAILOR MERCURY!
WISDOM SHOULD BE USED TO HELP THE WORLD AND THOSE WHO LIVE IN IT!
PREPARE FOR A DELUGE OF MERCURY POWER! TO COOL YOUR HEAD, I'LL PUNISH YOU!

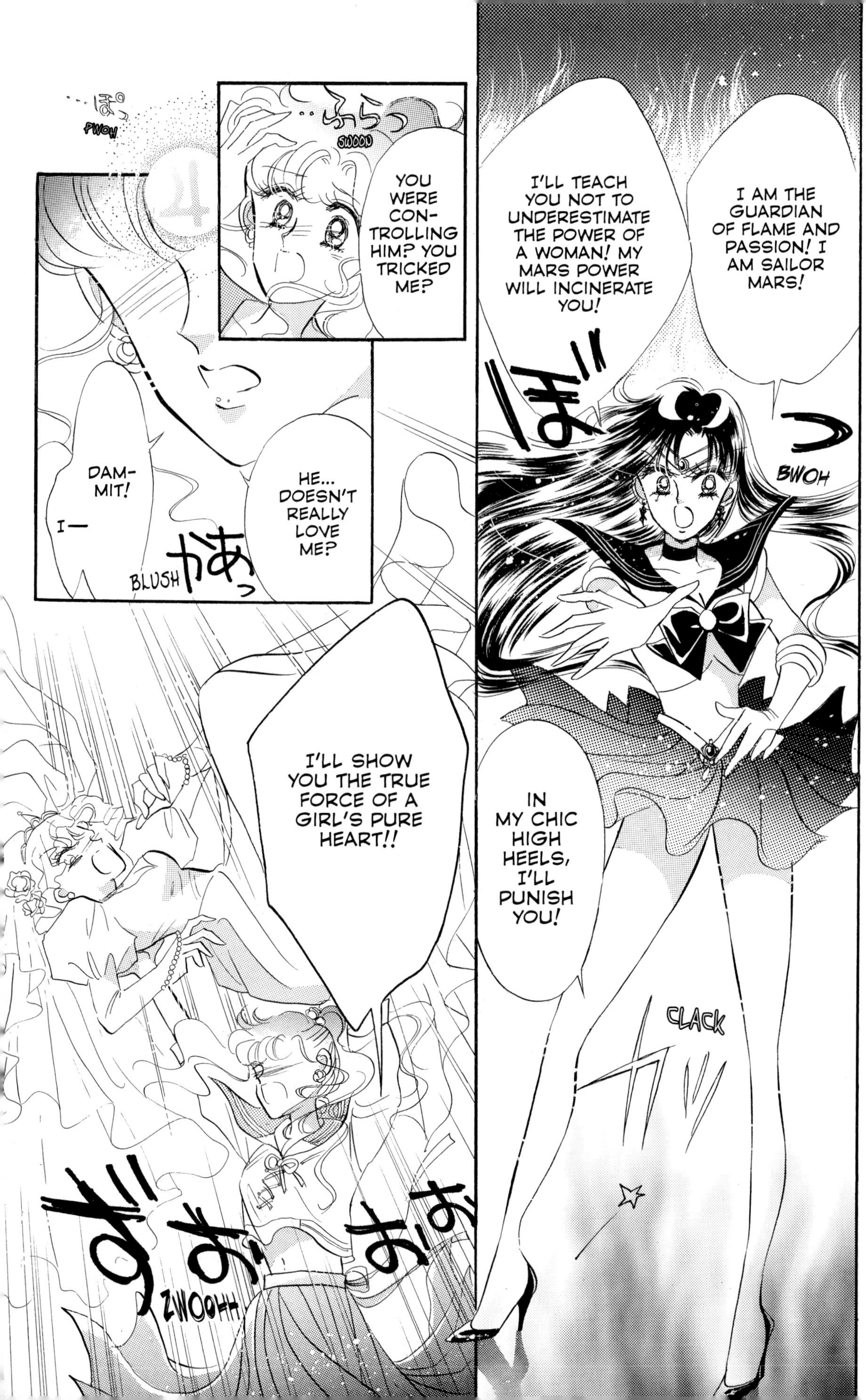
I AM THE GUARDIAN OF FLAME AND PASSION! I AM SAILOR MARS!
I'LL TEACH YOU NOT TO UNDERESTIMATE THE POWER OF A WOMAN! MY MARS POWER WILL INCINERATE YOU!
ぼっ
BWOH
IN MY CHIC HIGH HEELS, I'LL PUNISH YOU!
カツ
CLACK
…ふらっ
SWOON
YOU WERE CON-TROLLING HIM? YOU TRICKED ME?
…ぽっ
PWOH
HE... DOESN'T REALLY LOVE ME?
かあっ
BLUSH
DAM-MIT!
I—
I'LL SHOW YOU THE TRUE FORCE OF A GIRL'S PURE HEART!!
ずおおおお
ZWOOHH

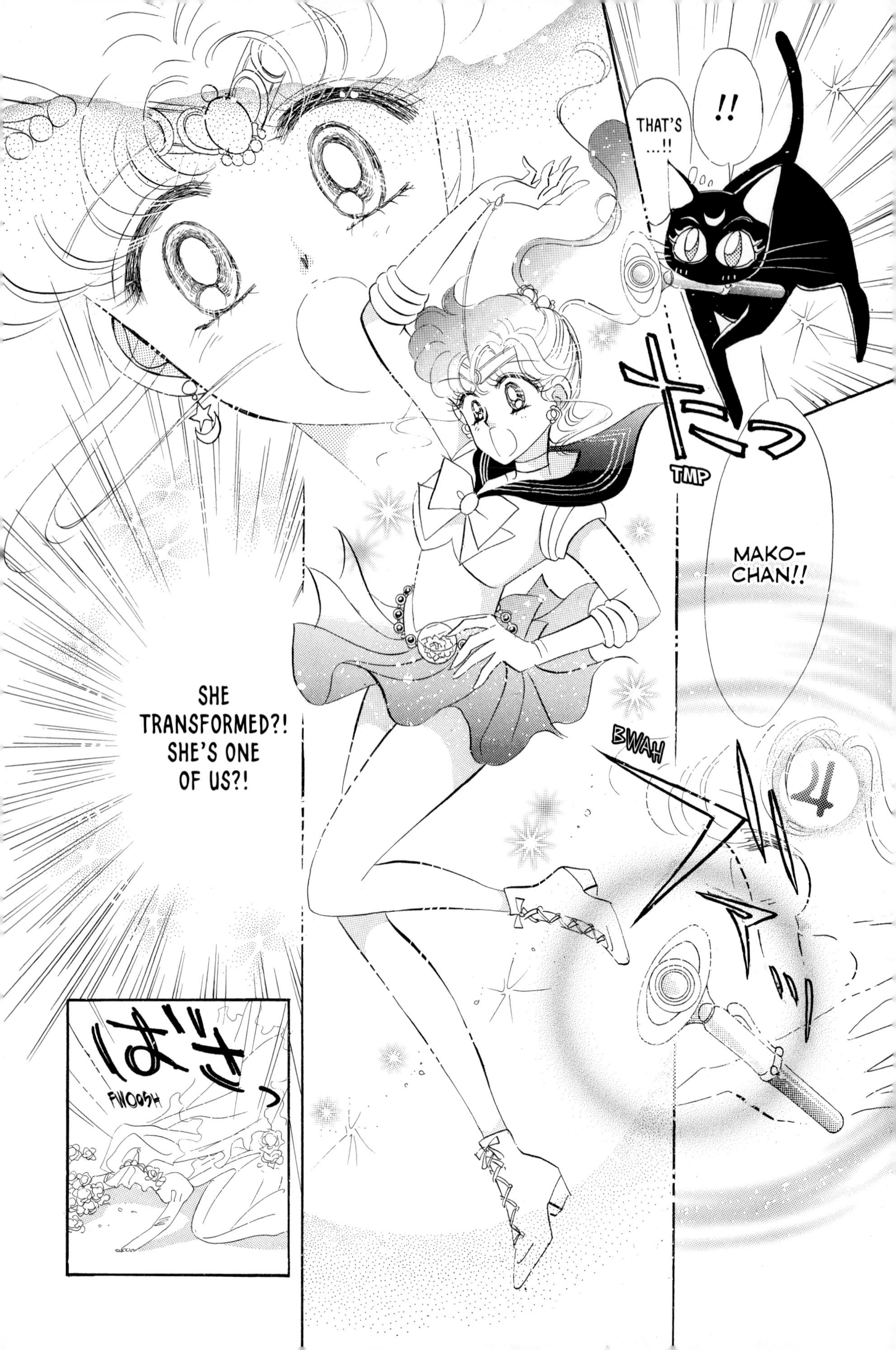
!!
THAT'S ...!!
TMP
MAKO-CHAN!!
BWAH
SHE TRANSFORMED?! SHE'S ONE OF US?!
ばさっ
FWOOSH

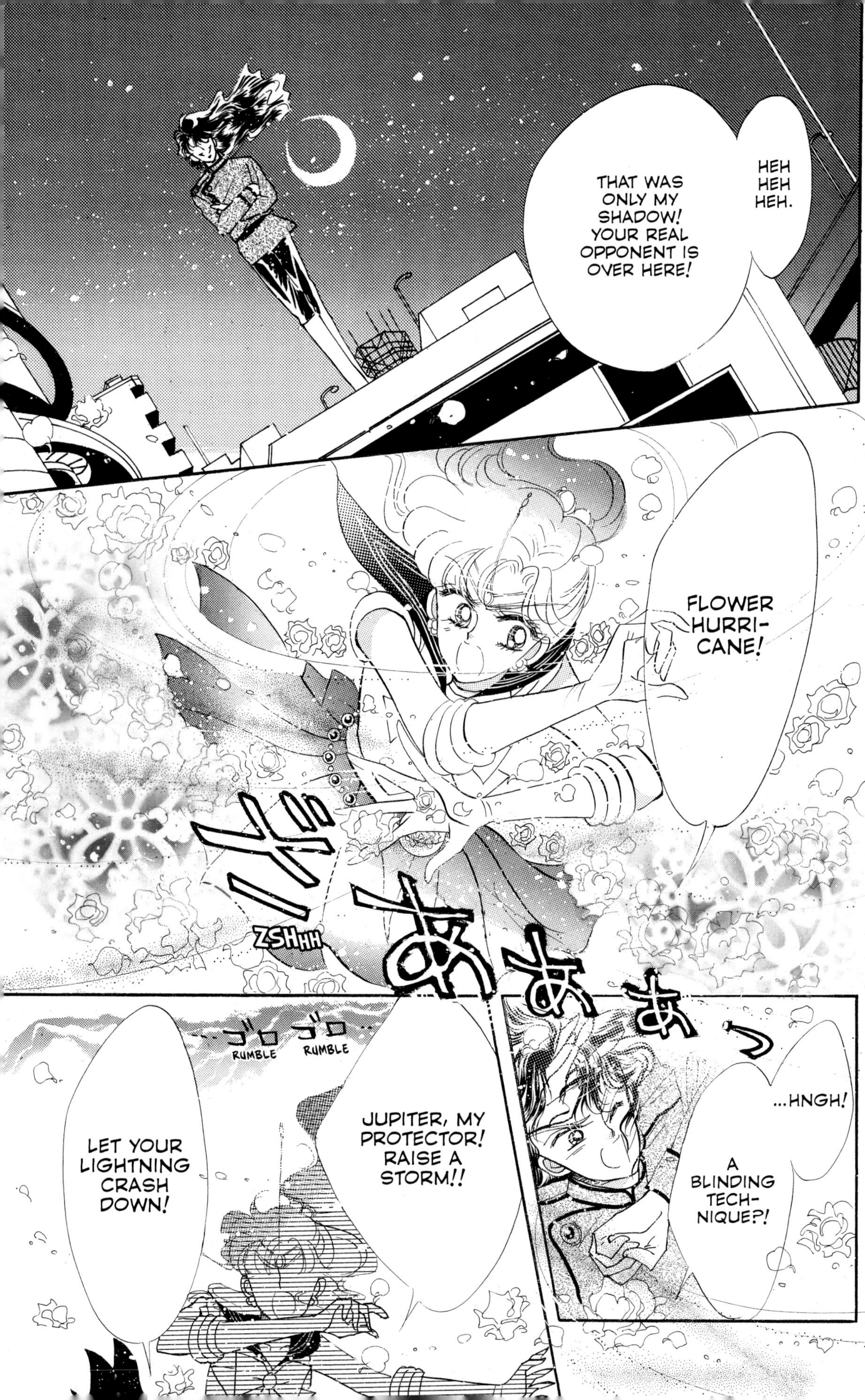
HEH HEH HEH.
THAT WAS ONLY MY SHADOW! YOUR REAL OPPONENT IS OVER HERE!
FLOWER HURRI-CANE!
ザッ
ZSHHH
あああっ
...HNGH!
A BLINDING TECH-NIQUE?!
ゴロゴロ
RUMBLE RUMBLE
JUPITER, MY PROTECTOR! RAISE A STORM!!
LET YOUR LIGHTNING CRASH DOWN!

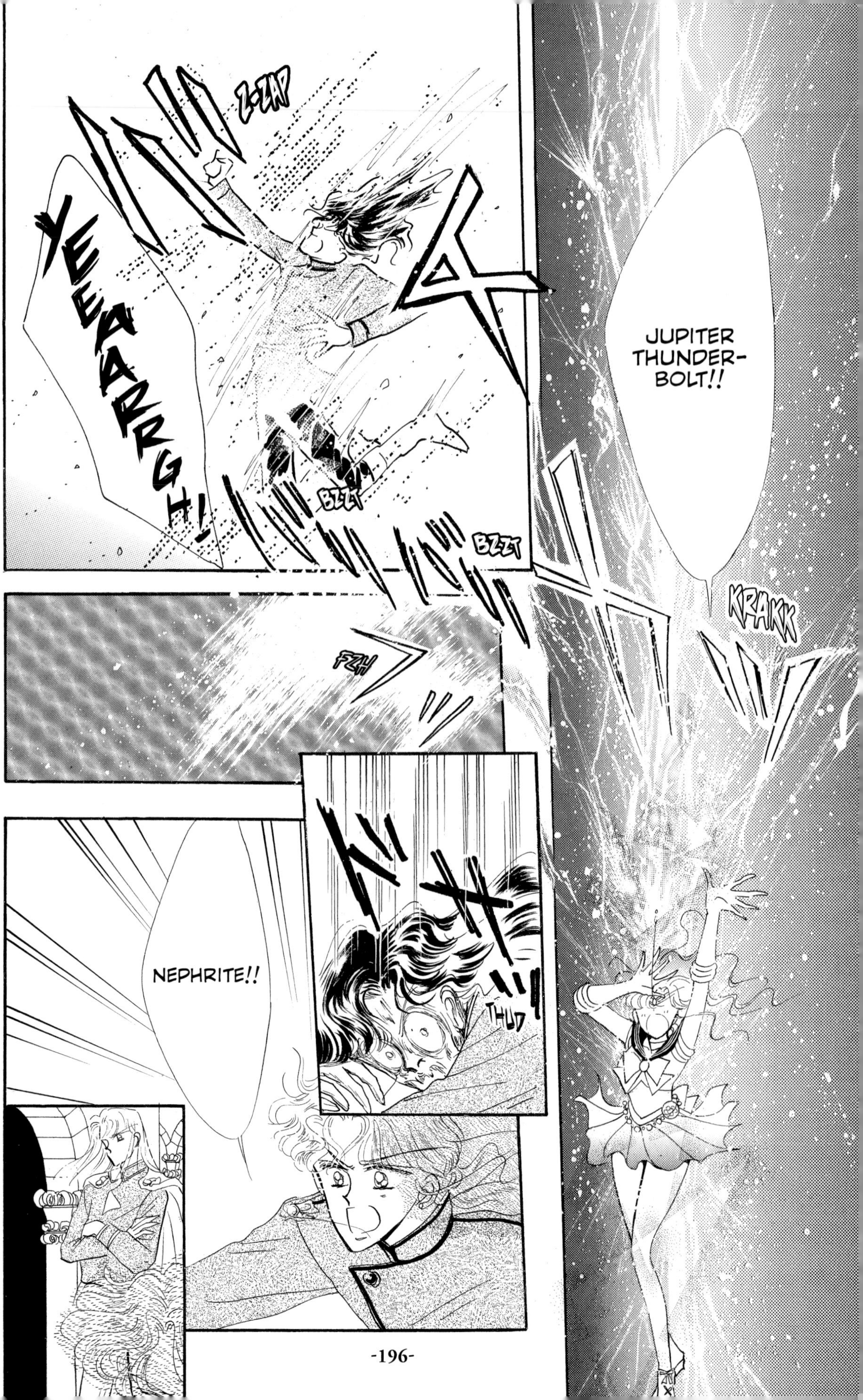
JUPITER THUNDER-BOLT!!
KRAKK
Z-ZAP
YEEAARRGH!
BZZT
BZZT
FZH
THUD
NEPHRITE!!

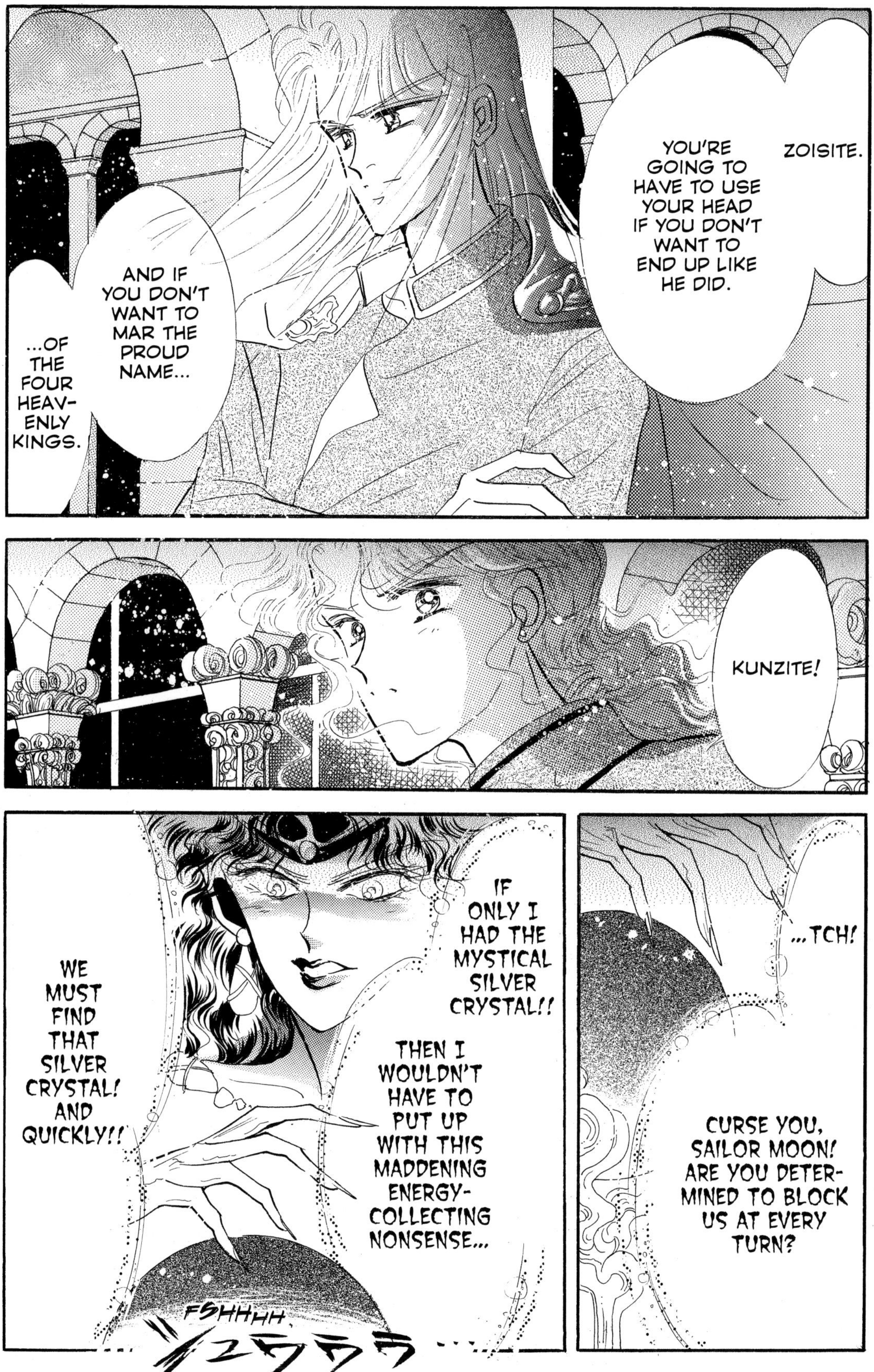
ZOISITE.
YOU'RE GOING TO HAVE TO USE YOUR HEAD IF YOU DON'T WANT TO END UP LIKE HE DID.
AND IF YOU DON'T WANT TO MAR THE PROUD NAME...
...OF THE FOUR HEAVENLY KINGS.
KUNZITE!
...TCH!
CURSE YOU, SAILOR MOON! ARE YOU DETERMINED TO BLOCK US AT EVERY TURN?
IF ONLY I HAD THE MYSTICAL SILVER CRYSTAL!!
THEN I WOULDN'T HAVE TO PUT UP WITH THIS MADDENING ENERGY-COLLECTING NONSENSE...
WE MUST FIND THAT SILVER CRYSTAL! AND QUICKLY!!
FSHHHH

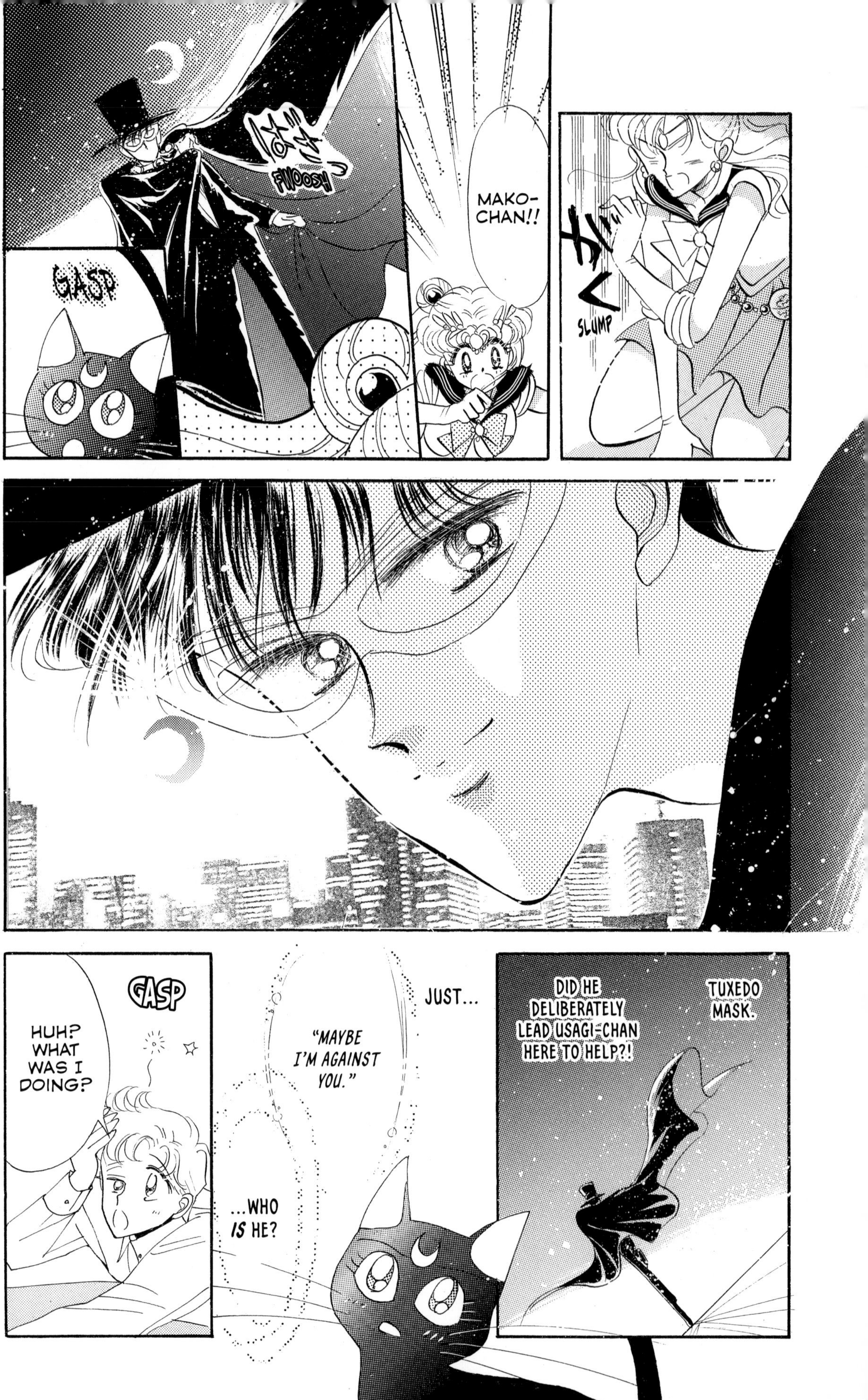
SLUMP
MAKO-CHAN!!
FWOOSH
GASP
TUXEDO MASK.
DID HE DELIBERATELY LEAD USAGI-CHAN HERE TO HELP?!
JUST...
"MAYBE I'M AGAINST YOU."
...WHO *IS* HE?
GASP
HUH? WHAT WAS I DOING?

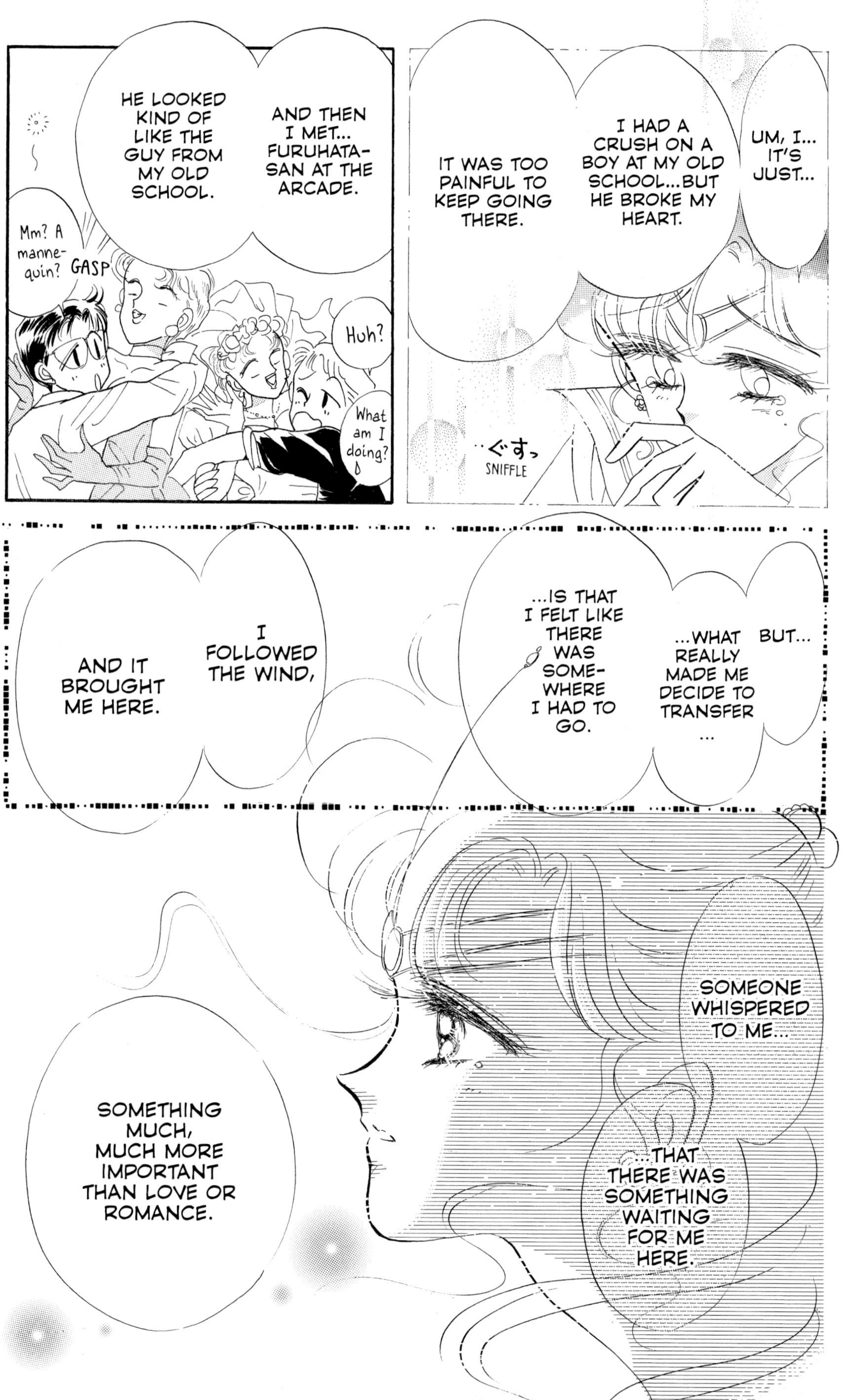
UM, I... IT'S JUST...
I HAD A CRUSH ON A BOY AT MY OLD SCHOOL...BUT HE BROKE MY HEART.
IT WAS TOO PAINFUL TO KEEP GOING THERE.
…ぐすっ
SNIFFLE
AND THEN I MET... FURUHATA-SAN AT THE ARCADE.
HE LOOKED KIND OF LIKE THE GUY FROM MY OLD SCHOOL.
Huh?
What am I doing?
GASP
Mm? A manne-quin?
BUT...
...WHAT REALLY MADE ME DECIDE TO TRANSFER ...
...IS THAT I FELT LIKE THERE WAS SOME-WHERE I HAD TO GO.
I FOLLOWED THE WIND,
AND IT BROUGHT ME HERE.
SOMEONE WHISPERED TO ME...
...THAT THERE WAS SOMETHING WAITING FOR ME HERE.
SOMETHING MUCH, MUCH MORE IMPORTANT THAN LOVE OR ROMANCE.

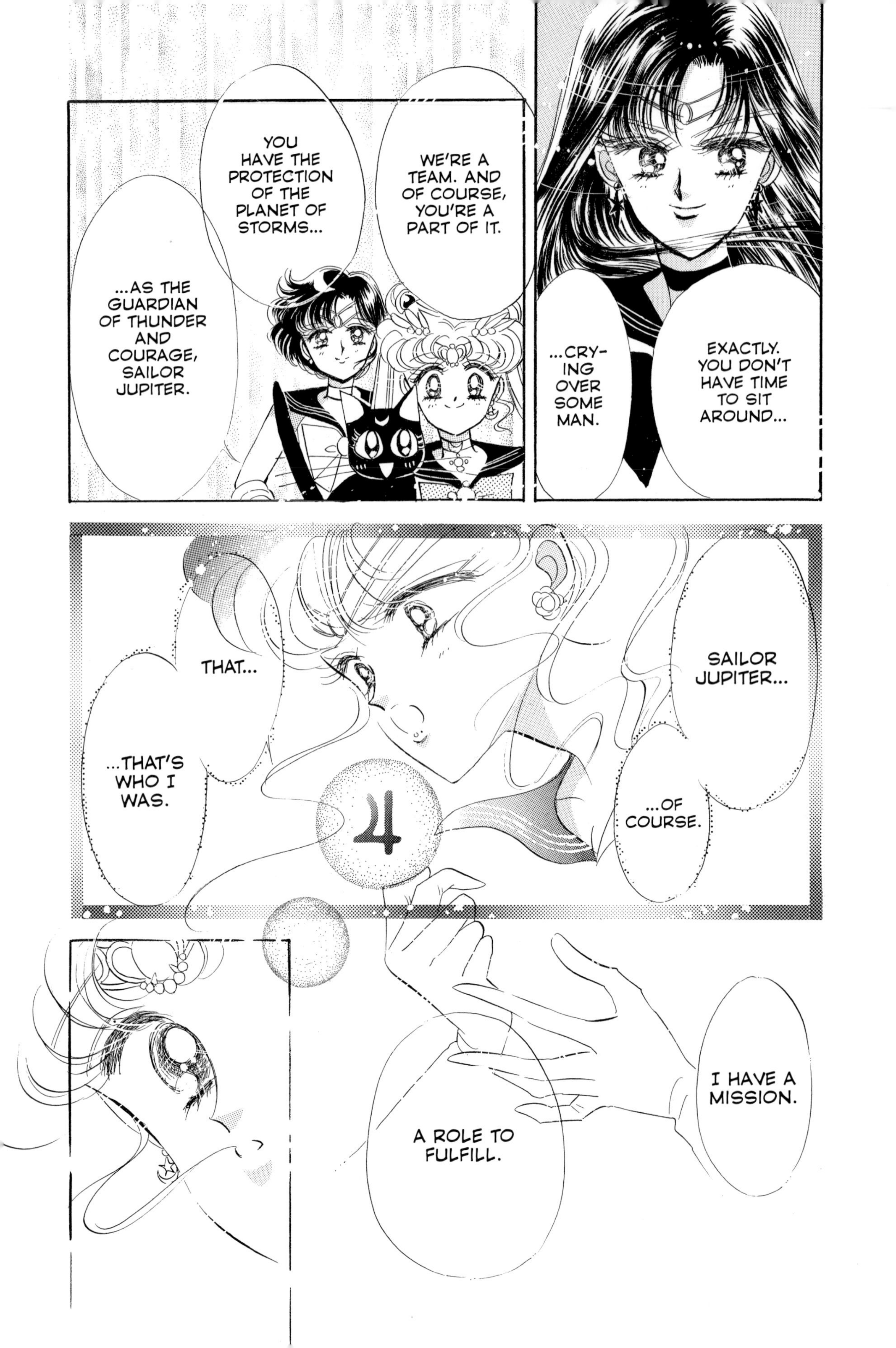
EXACTLY. YOU DON'T HAVE TIME TO SIT AROUND...
...CRY-ING OVER SOME MAN.
WE'RE A TEAM. AND OF COURSE, YOU'RE A PART OF IT.
YOU HAVE THE PROTECTION OF THE PLANET OF STORMS...
...AS THE GUARDIAN OF THUNDER AND COURAGE, SAILOR JUPITER.
SAILOR JUPITER...
...OF COURSE.
THAT...
...THAT'S WHO I WAS.
I HAVE A MISSION.
A ROLE TO FULFILL.

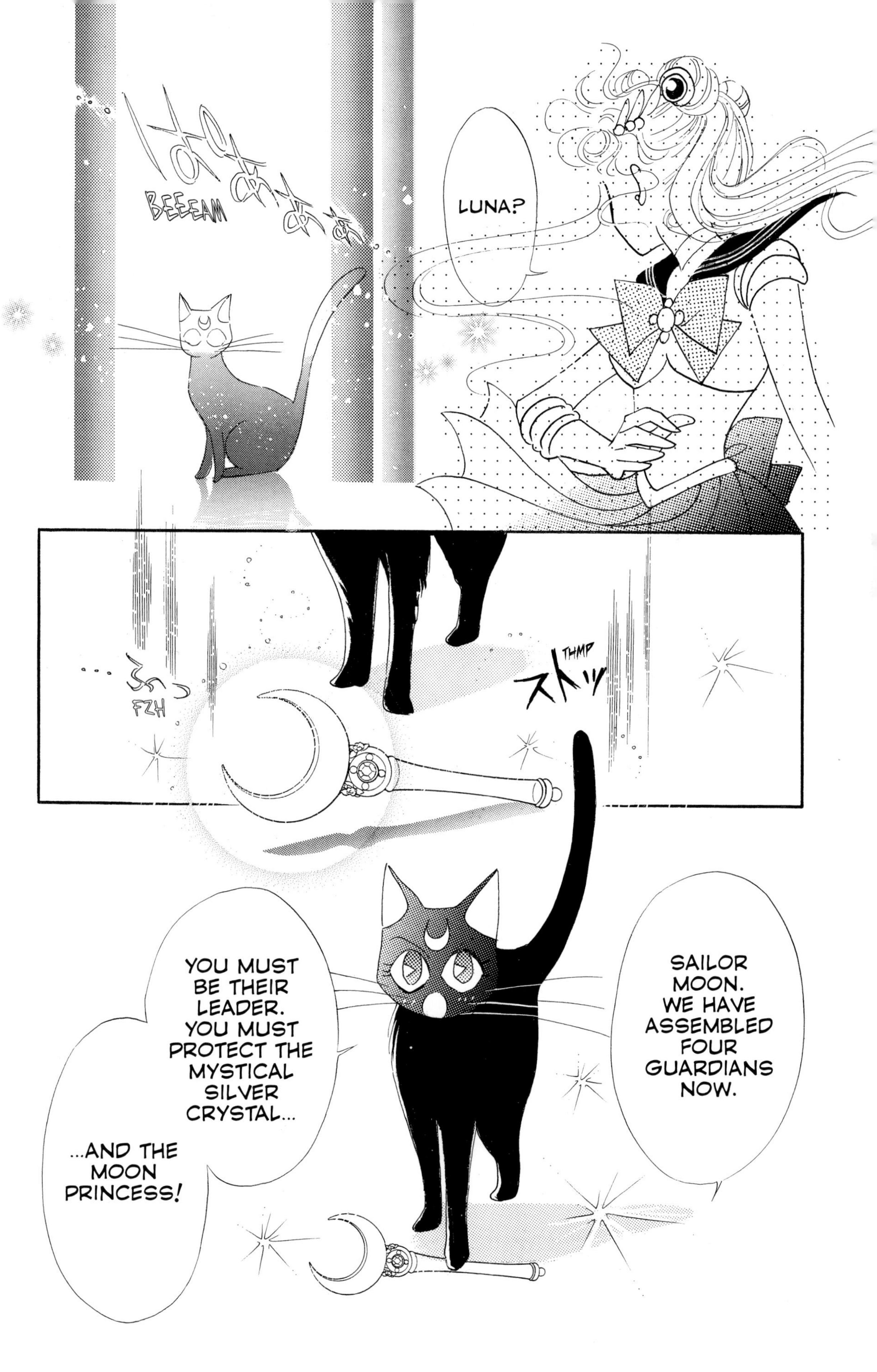
LUNA?
BEEEAM
THMP
ストッ
FZH
SAILOR MOON. WE HAVE ASSEMBLED FOUR GUARDIANS NOW.
YOU MUST BE THEIR LEADER. YOU MUST PROTECT THE MYSTICAL SILVER CRYSTAL...
...AND THE MOON PRINCESS!

Pretty Guardian

Sailor Moon

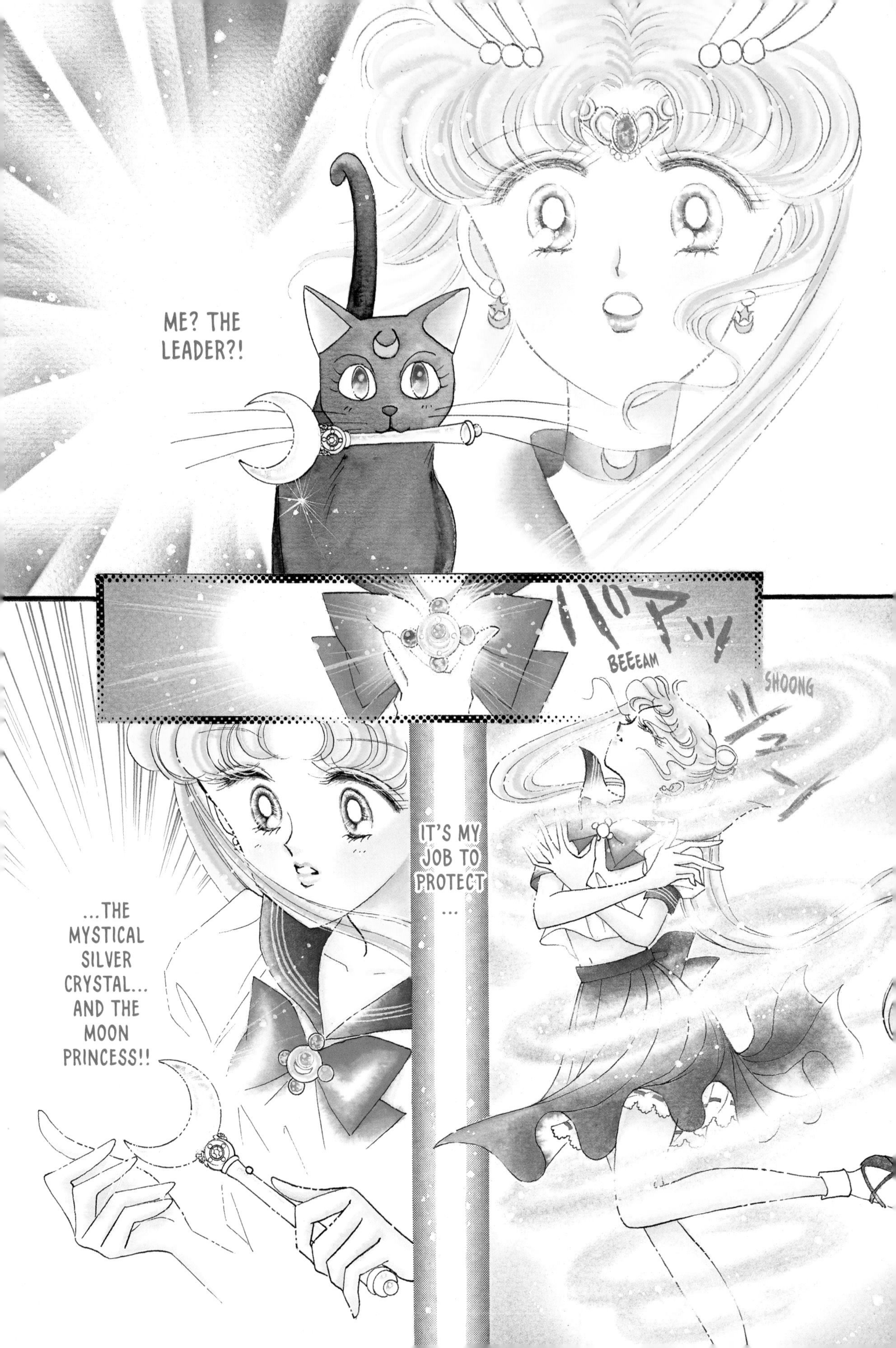
ME? THE LEADER?!
BEEEAM
SHOONG
IT'S MY JOB TO PROTECT ...
...THE MYSTICAL SILVER CRYSTAL... AND THE MOON PRINCESS!!

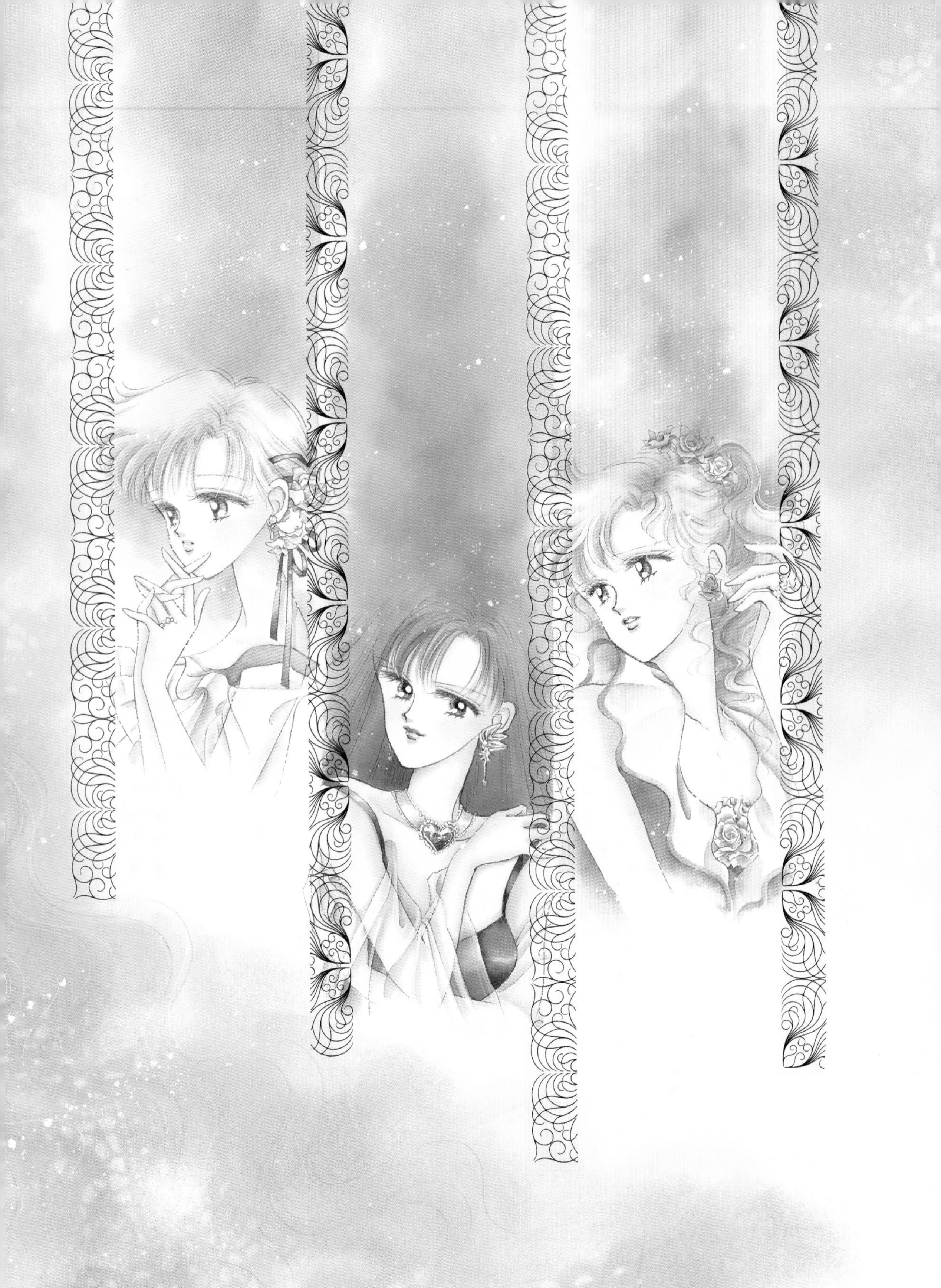

Act.6 Tuxedo Kamen: Tuxedo Mask

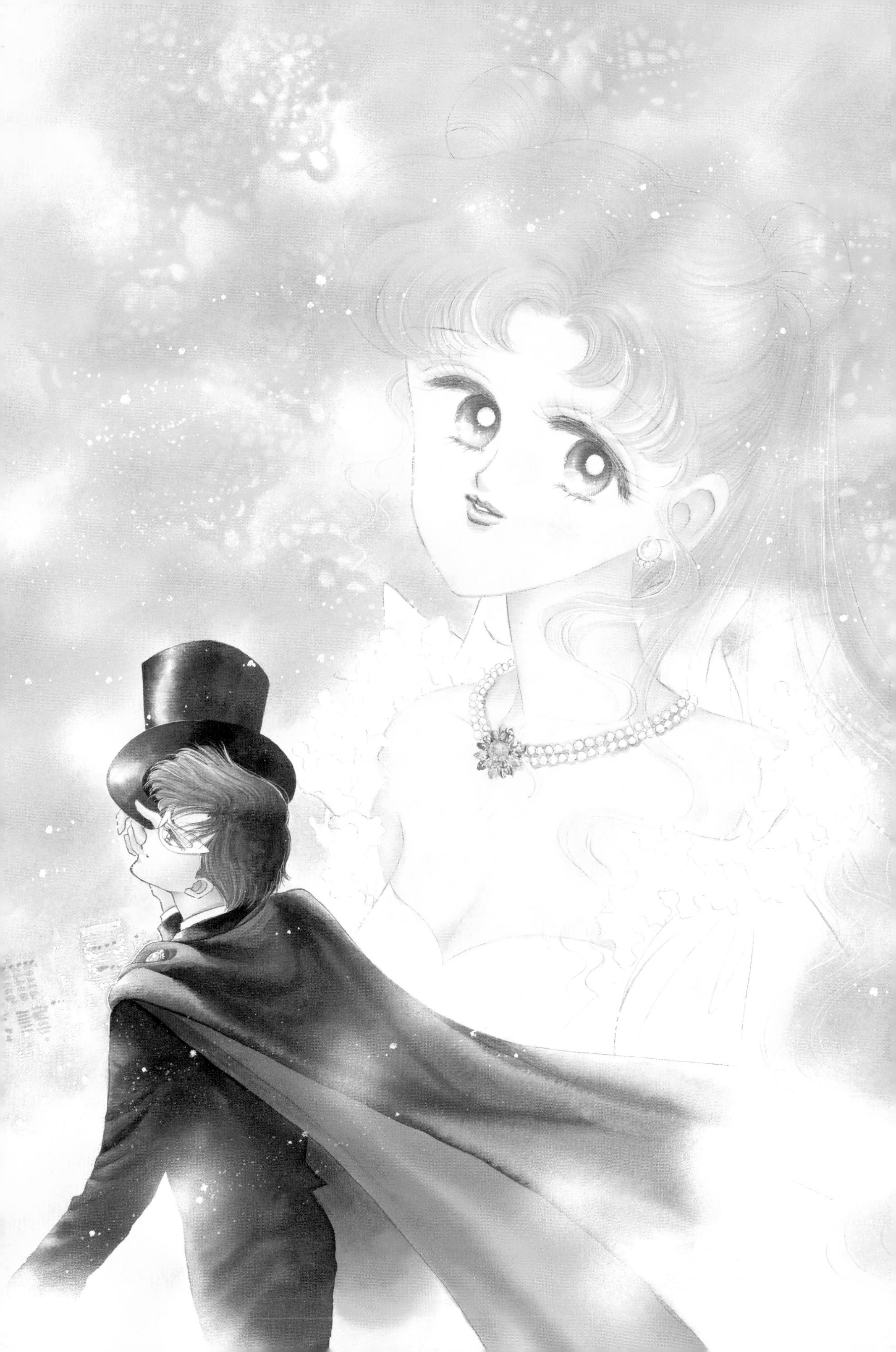

Pretty Guardian Sailor Moon

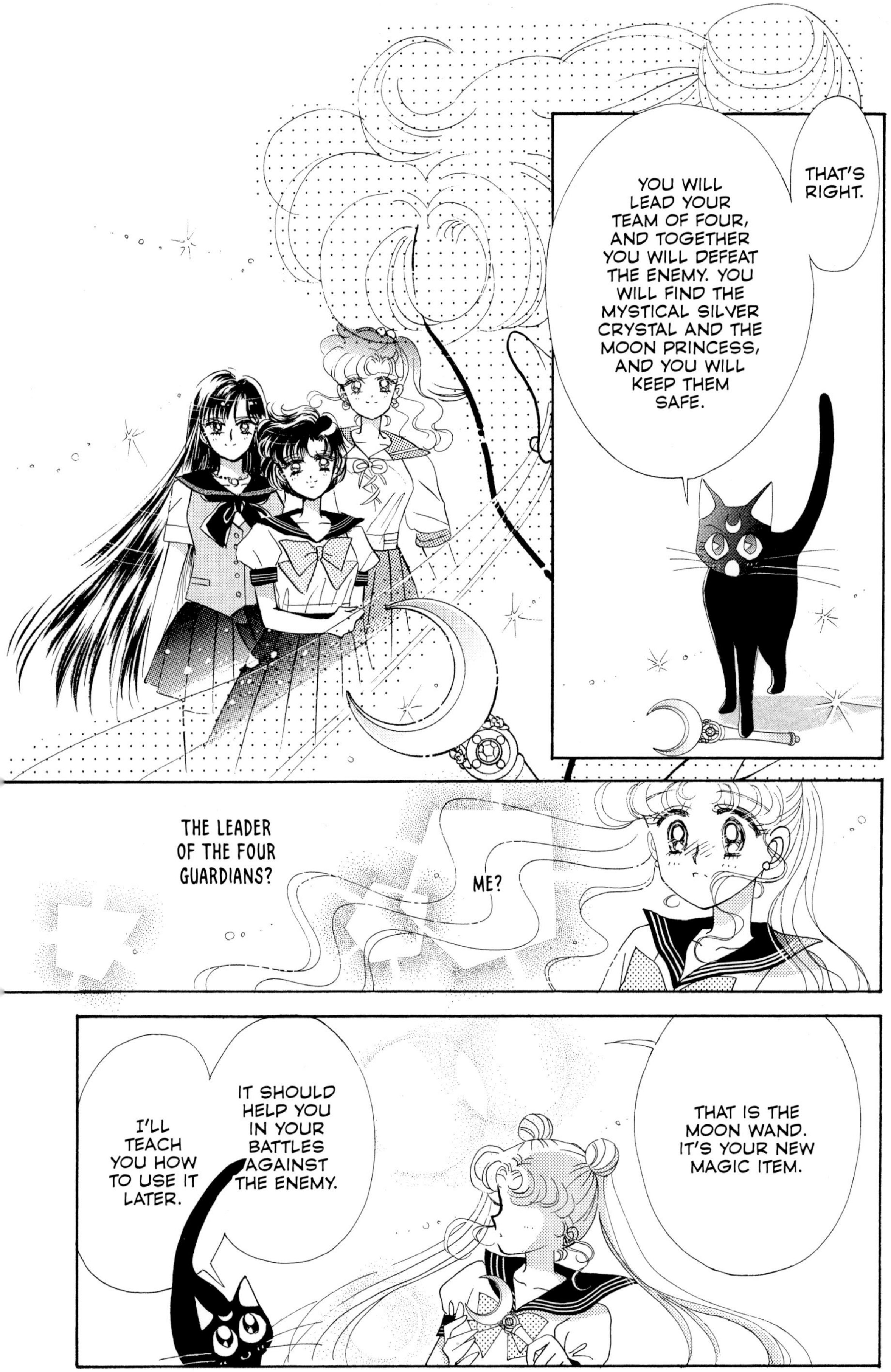
THAT'S RIGHT.
YOU WILL LEAD YOUR TEAM OF FOUR, AND TOGETHER YOU WILL DEFEAT THE ENEMY. YOU WILL FIND THE MYSTICAL SILVER CRYSTAL AND THE MOON PRINCESS, AND YOU WILL KEEP THEM SAFE.
THE LEADER OF THE FOUR GUARDIANS?
ME?
THAT IS THE MOON WAND. IT'S YOUR NEW MAGIC ITEM.
IT SHOULD HELP YOU IN YOUR BATTLES AGAINST THE ENEMY.
I'LL TEACH YOU HOW TO USE IT LATER.

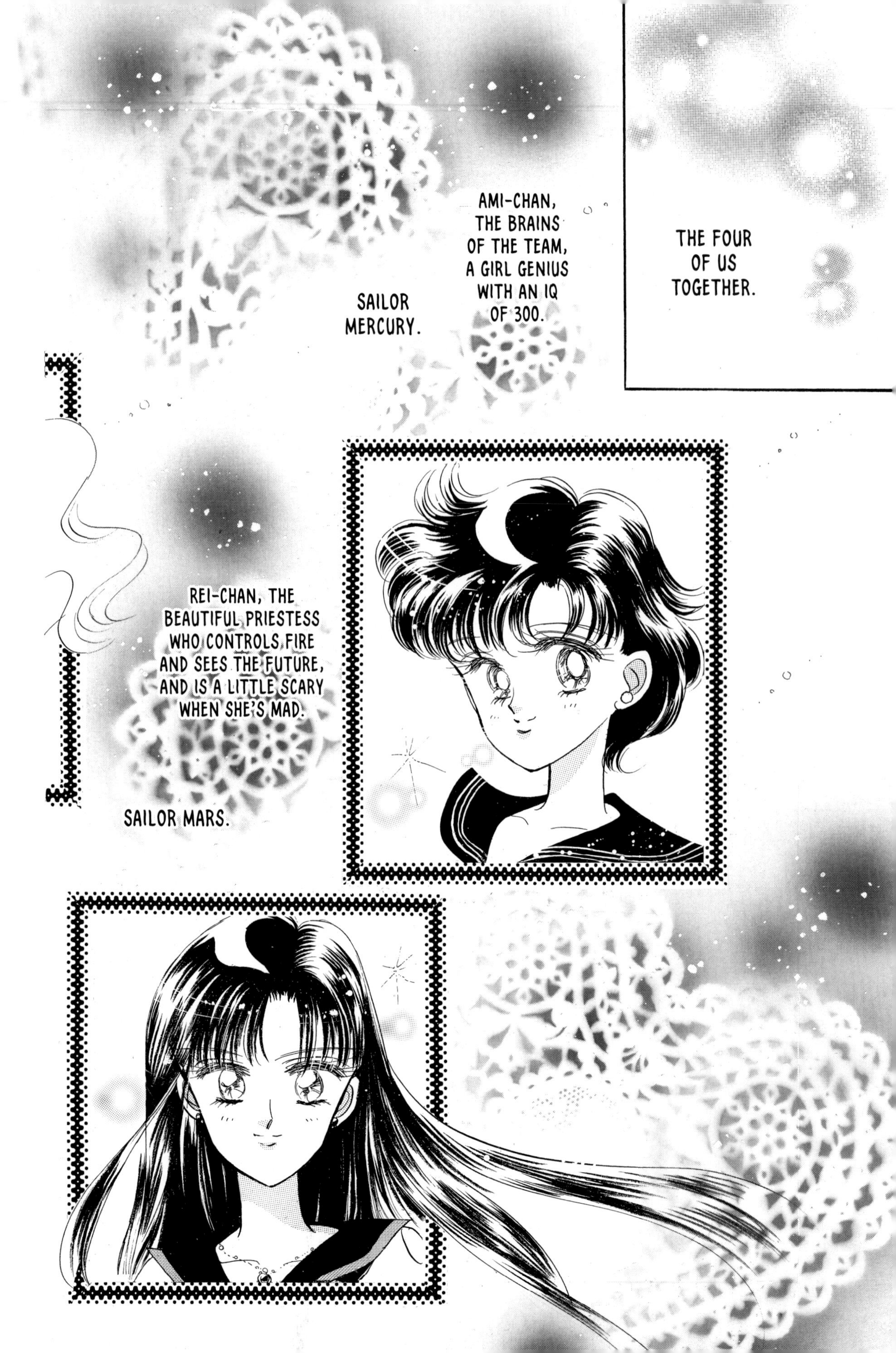
THE FOUR OF US TOGETHER.
AMI-CHAN, THE BRAINS OF THE TEAM, A GIRL GENIUS WITH AN IQ OF 300.
SAILOR MERCURY.
REI-CHAN, THE BEAUTIFUL PRIESTESS WHO CONTROLS FIRE AND SEES THE FUTURE, AND IS A LITTLE SCARY WHEN SHE'S MAD.
SAILOR MARS.

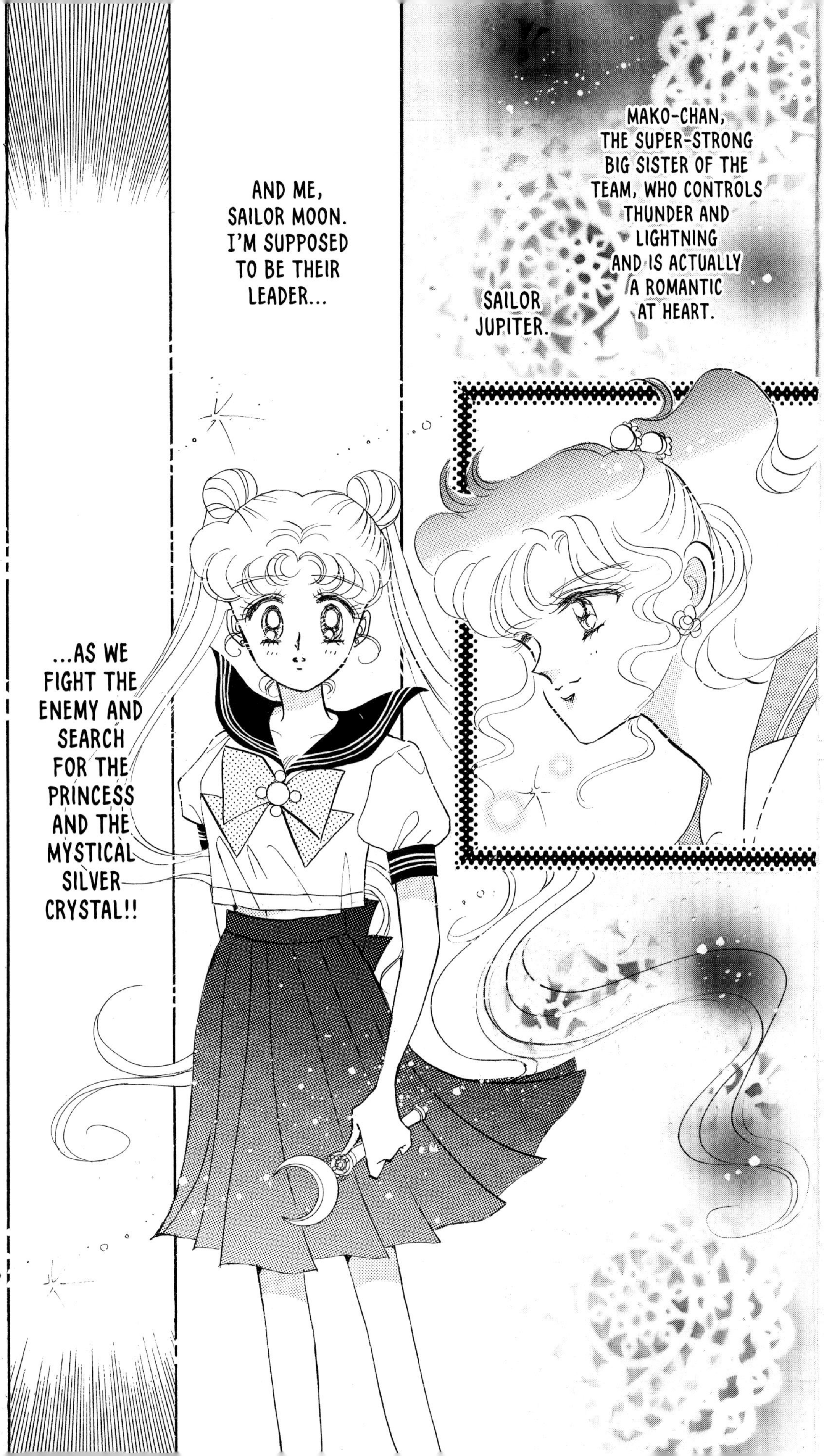
MAKO-CHAN, THE SUPER-STRONG BIG SISTER OF THE TEAM, WHO CONTROLS THUNDER AND LIGHTNING AND IS ACTUALLY A ROMANTIC AT HEART.
SAILOR JUPITER.
AND ME, SAILOR MOON. I'M SUPPOSED TO BE THEIR LEADER...
...AS WE FIGHT THE ENEMY AND SEARCH FOR THE PRINCESS AND THE MYSTICAL SILVER CRYSTAL!!

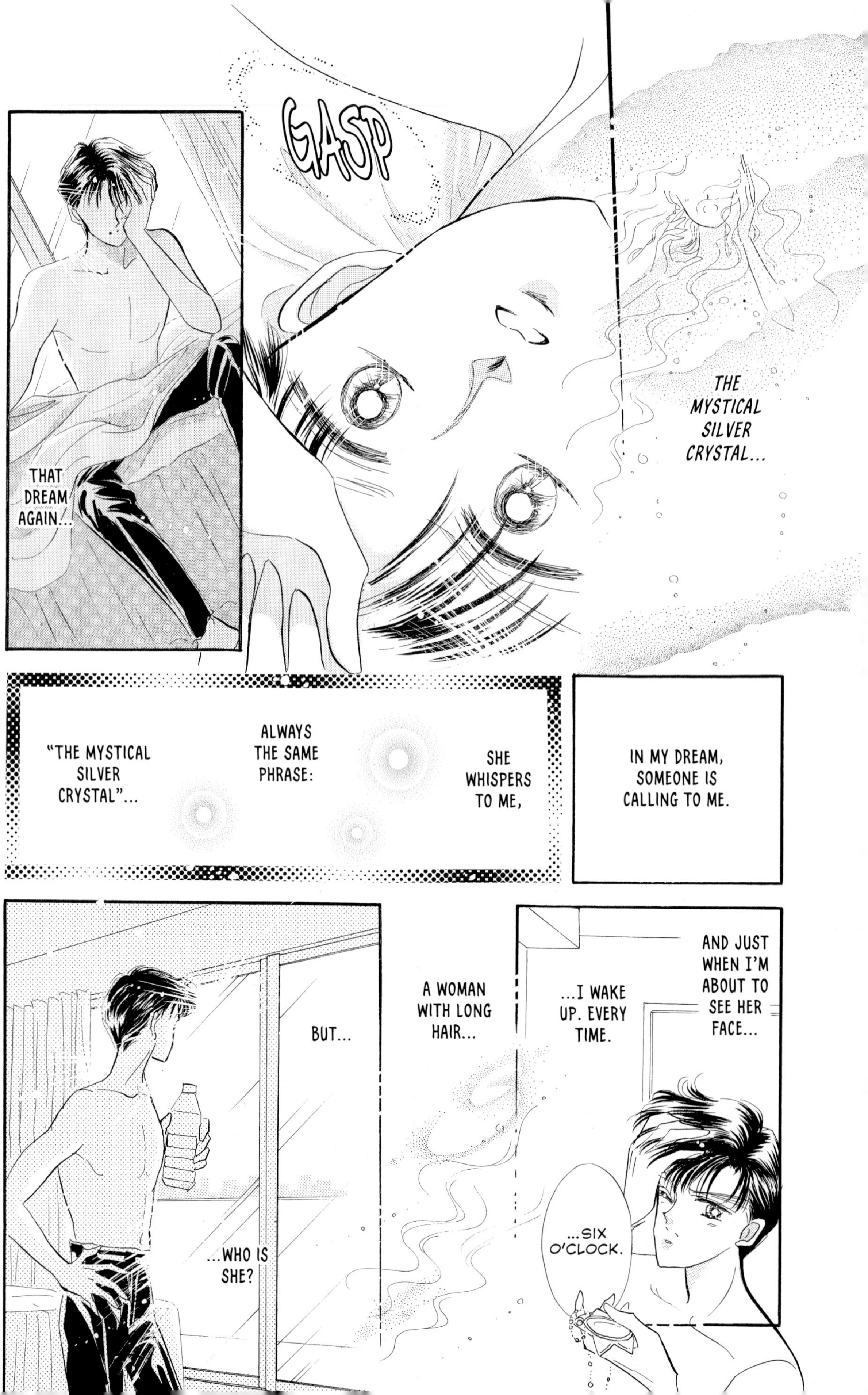
THE MYSTICAL SILVER CRYSTAL...
GASP
THAT DREAM AGAIN...
IN MY DREAM, SOMEONE IS CALLING TO ME.
SHE WHISPERS TO ME,
ALWAYS THE SAME PHRASE:
“THE MYSTICAL SILVER CRYSTAL”...
AND JUST WHEN I’M ABOUT TO SEE HER FACE...
...I WAKE UP. EVERY TIME.
...SIX O’CLOCK.
A WOMAN WITH LONG HAIR...
BUT...
...WHO IS SHE?

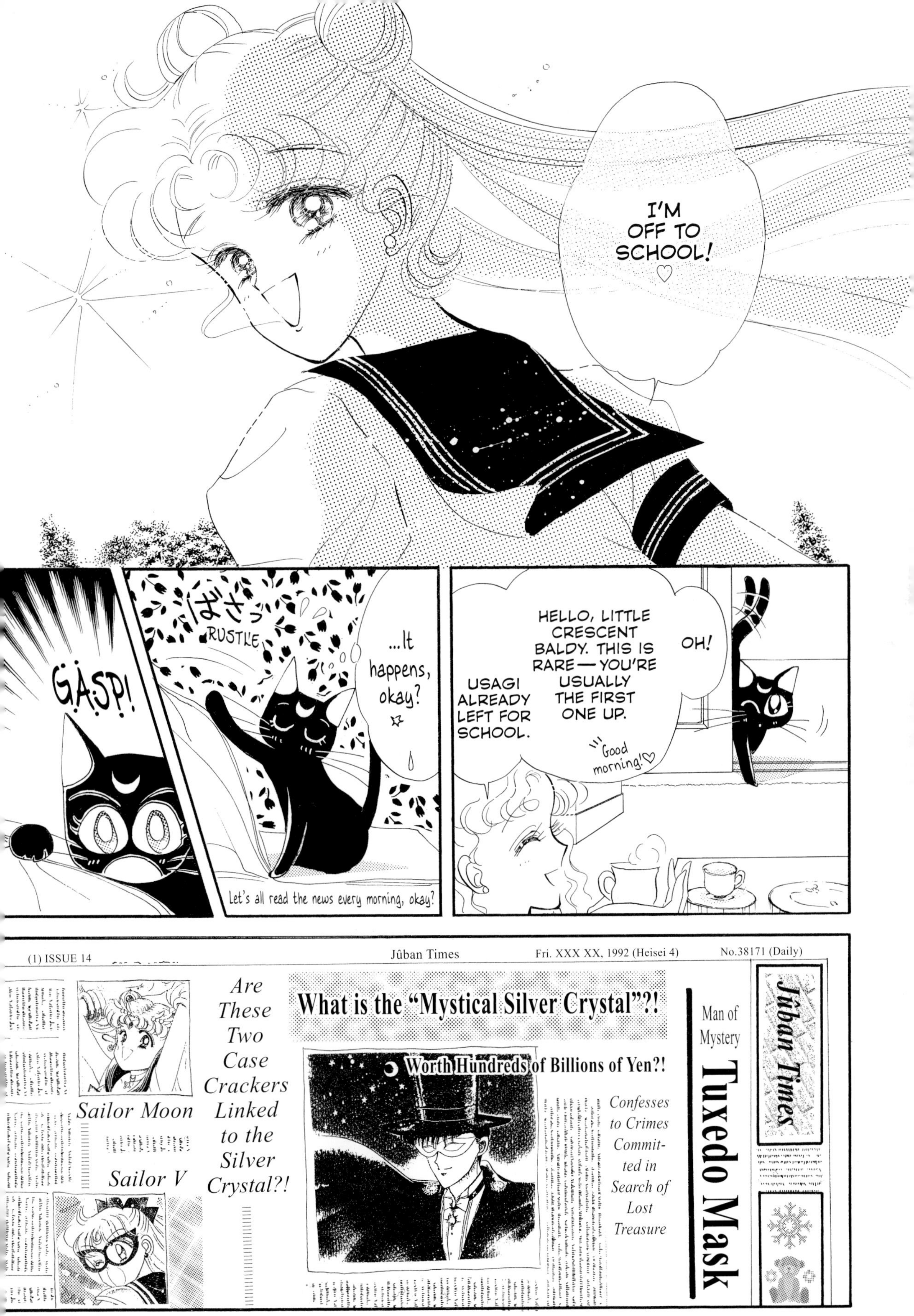
I'M OFF TO SCHOOL! ♡
OH!
HELLO, LITTLE CRESCENT BALDY. THIS IS RARE — YOU'RE USUALLY THE FIRST ONE UP.
USAGI ALREADY LEFT FOR SCHOOL.
Good morning!♡
...It happens, okay?
ばさっ
RUSTLE
Let's all read the news every morning, okay?
GASP!
(1) ISSUE 14
Jûban Times
Fri. XXX XX, 1992 (Heisei 4)
No.38171 (Daily)
Jûban Times
Man of Mystery
Tuxedo Mask
Confesses to Crimes Committed in Search of Lost Treasure
What is the "Mystical Silver Crystal"?!
Worth Hundreds of Billions of Yen?!
Are These Two Case Crackers Linked to the Silver Crystal?!
Sailor Moon
Sailor V

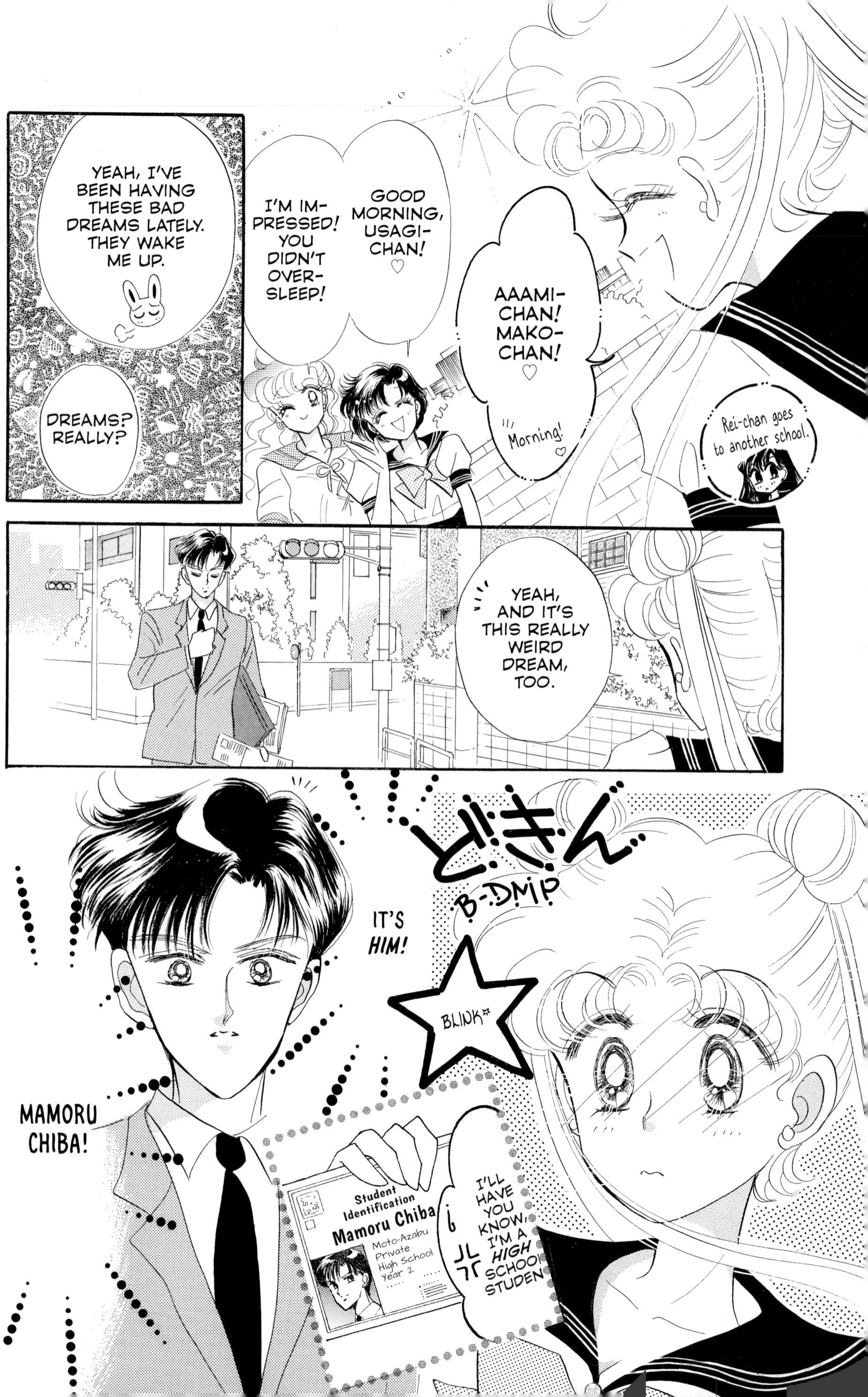
AAAMI-CHAN! MAKO-CHAN! ♡
Rei-chan goes to another school.
GOOD MORNING, USAGI-CHAN! ♡
I'M IM-PRESSED! YOU DIDN'T OVER-SLEEP!
Morning! ♡
YEAH, I'VE BEEN HAVING THESE BAD DREAMS LATELY. THEY WAKE ME UP.
DREAMS? REALLY?
YEAH, AND IT'S THIS REALLY WEIRD DREAM, TOO.
どきん
B-DMP
IT'S HIM!
BLINK
MAMORU CHIBA!
I'LL HAVE YOU KNOW, I'M A HIGH SCHOOL STUDEN
Student Identification
Mamoru Chiba
Moto-Azabu Private High School Year 2

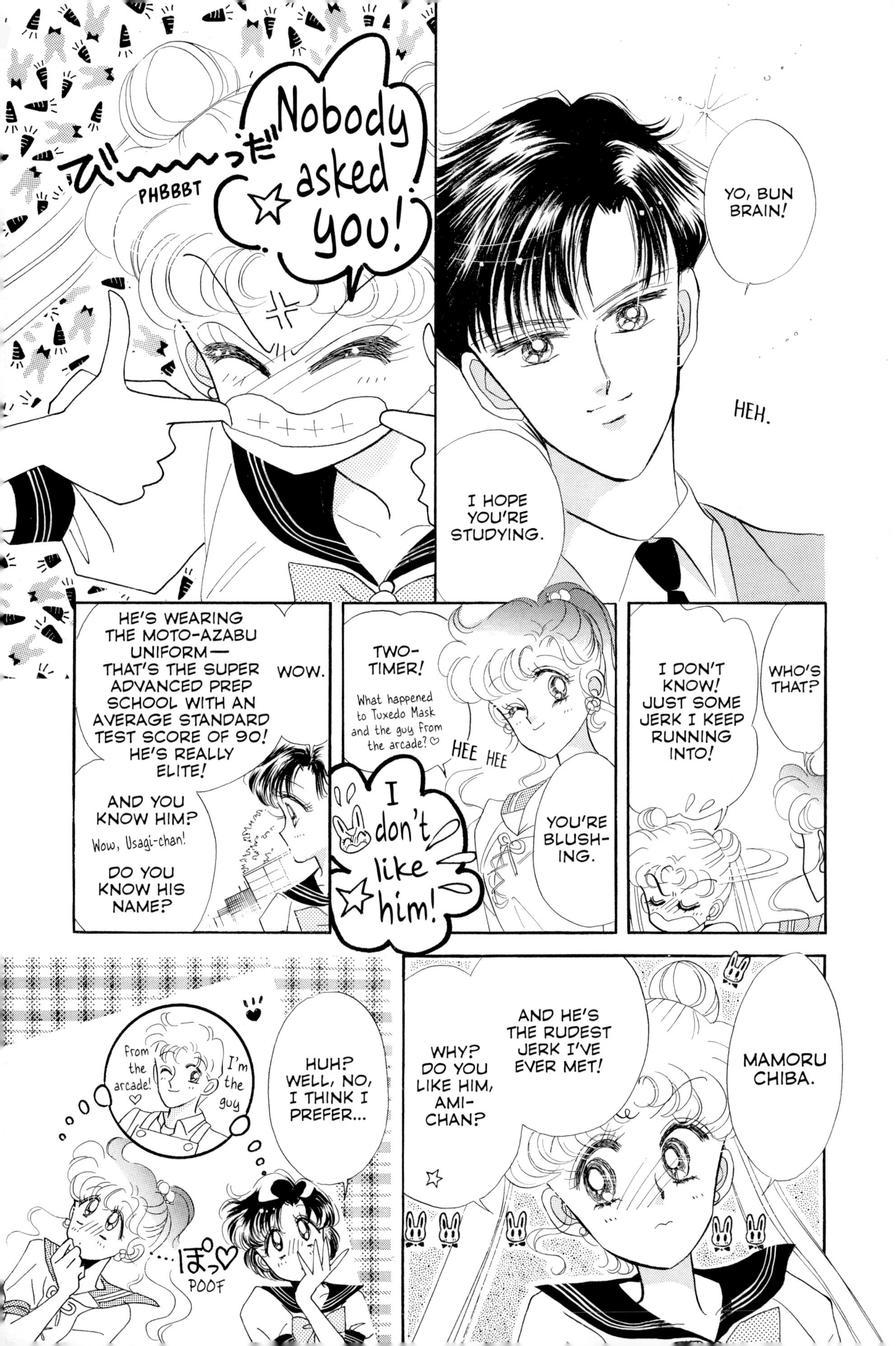
YO, BUN BRAIN!
HEH.
I HOPE YOU'RE STUDYING.
び～～っだ
PHBBBT
Nobody asked ☆ you!
WHO'S THAT?
I DON'T KNOW! JUST SOME JERK I KEEP RUNNING INTO!
TWO-TIMER!
What happened to Tuxedo Mask and the guy from the arcade? ♡
HEE HEE
YOU'RE BLUSH-ING.
I don't ☆ like him!
WOW.
HE'S WEARING THE MOTO-AZABU UNIFORM— THAT'S THE SUPER ADVANCED PREP SCHOOL WITH AN AVERAGE STANDARD TEST SCORE OF 90! HE'S REALLY ELITE!
AND YOU KNOW HIM?
Wow, Usagi-chan!
DO YOU KNOW HIS NAME?
MAMORU CHIBA.
AND HE'S THE RUDEST JERK I'VE EVER MET!
WHY? DO YOU LIKE HIM, AMI-CHAN?
HUH? WELL, NO, I THINK I PREFER...
I'm the guy from the arcade! ♡
…ぽっ♡
POOF

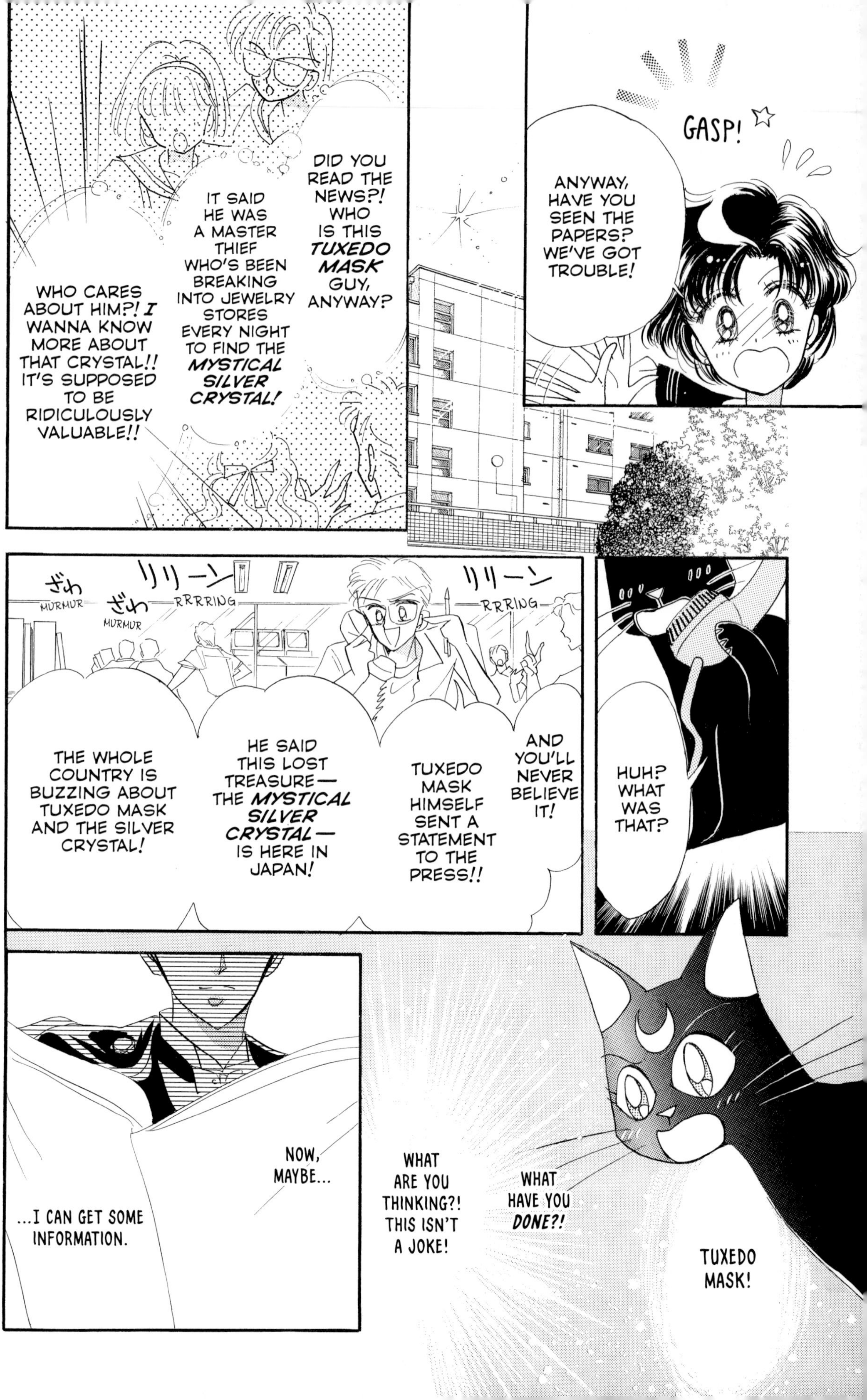
GASP!
ANYWAY, HAVE YOU SEEN THE PAPERS? WE'VE GOT TROUBLE!
DID YOU READ THE NEWS?! WHO IS THIS TUXEDO MASK GUY, ANYWAY?
IT SAID HE WAS A MASTER THIEF WHO'S BEEN BREAKING INTO JEWELRY STORES EVERY NIGHT TO FIND THE MYSTICAL SILVER CRYSTAL!
WHO CARES ABOUT HIM?! I WANNA KNOW MORE ABOUT THAT CRYSTAL!! IT'S SUPPOSED TO BE RIDICULOUSLY VALUABLE!!
HUH? WHAT WAS THAT?
リリーン RRRING
リリーン RRRRING
ざわ MURMUR
ざわ MURMUR
AND YOU'LL NEVER BELIEVE IT!
TUXEDO MASK HIMSELF SENT A STATEMENT TO THE PRESS!!
HE SAID THIS LOST TREASURE—THE MYSTICAL SILVER CRYSTAL—IS HERE IN JAPAN!
THE WHOLE COUNTRY IS BUZZING ABOUT TUXEDO MASK AND THE SILVER CRYSTAL!
TUXEDO MASK!
WHAT HAVE YOU DONE?!
WHAT ARE YOU THINKING?! THIS ISN'T A JOKE!
NOW, MAYBE...
...I CAN GET SOME INFORMATION.

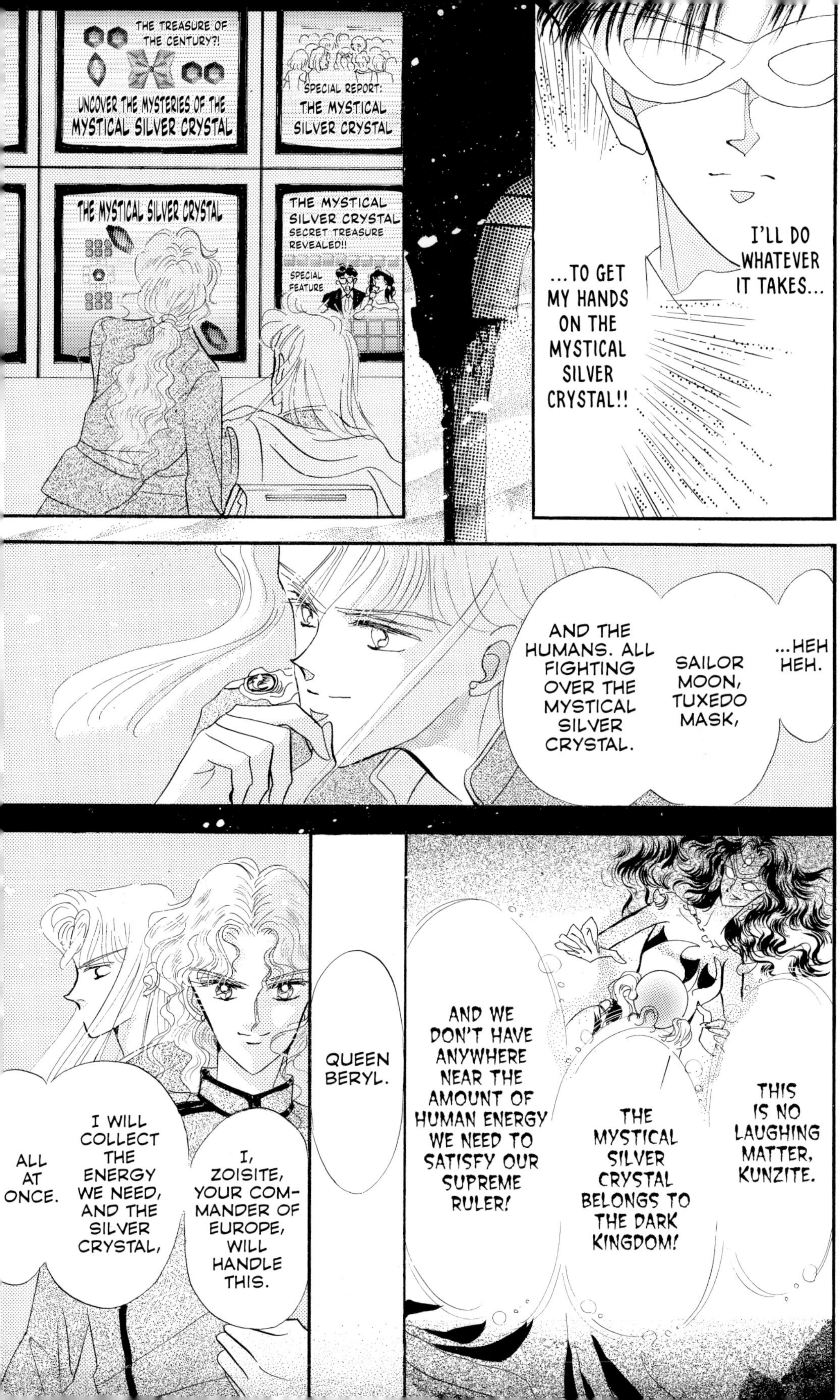
I'LL DO WHATEVER IT TAKES...
...TO GET MY HANDS ON THE MYSTICAL SILVER CRYSTAL!!
SPECIAL REPORT: THE MYSTICAL SILVER CRYSTAL
THE TREASURE OF THE CENTURY?!
UNCOVER THE MYSTERIES OF THE MYSTICAL SILVER CRYSTAL
THE MYSTICAL SILVER CRYSTAL SECRET TREASURE REVEALED!!
SPECIAL FEATURE
THE MYSTICAL SILVER CRYSTAL
...HEH HEH.
SAILOR MOON, TUXEDO MASK,
AND THE HUMANS. ALL FIGHTING OVER THE MYSTICAL SILVER CRYSTAL.
THIS IS NO LAUGHING MATTER, KUNZITE.
THE MYSTICAL SILVER CRYSTAL BELONGS TO THE DARK KINGDOM!
AND WE DON'T HAVE ANYWHERE NEAR THE AMOUNT OF HUMAN ENERGY WE NEED TO SATISFY OUR SUPREME RULER!
QUEEN BERYL.
I, ZOISITE, YOUR COMMANDER OF EUROPE, WILL HANDLE THIS.
I WILL COLLECT THE ENERGY WE NEED, AND THE SILVER CRYSTAL,
ALL AT ONCE.

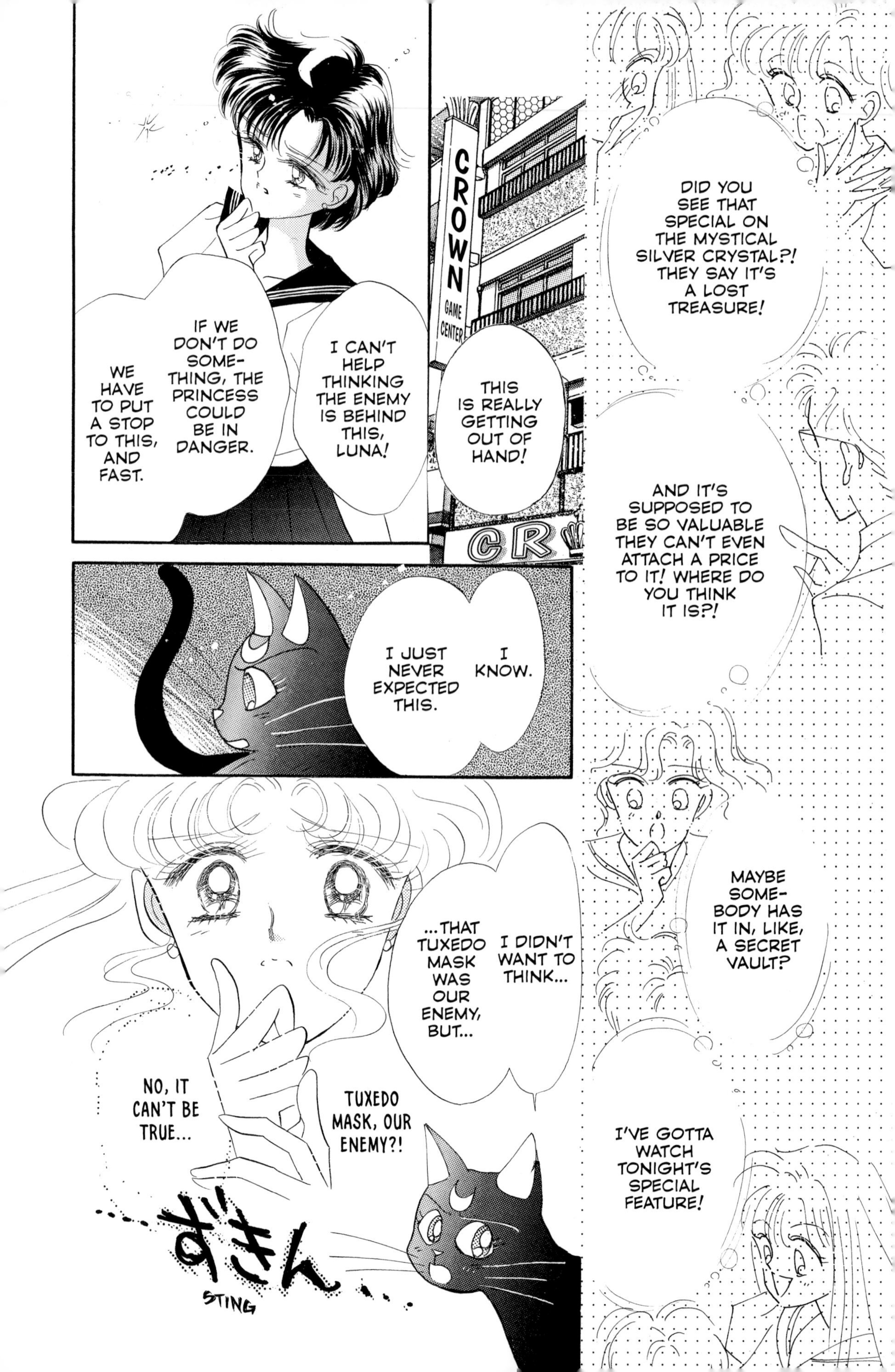
DID YOU SEE THAT SPECIAL ON THE MYSTICAL SILVER CRYSTAL?! THEY SAY IT'S A LOST TREASURE!
AND IT'S SUPPOSED TO BE SO VALUABLE THEY CAN'T EVEN ATTACH A PRICE TO IT! WHERE DO YOU THINK IT IS?!
MAYBE SOMEBODY HAS IT IN, LIKE, A SECRET VAULT?
I'VE GOTTA WATCH TONIGHT'S SPECIAL FEATURE!
CROWN GAME CENTER
THIS IS REALLY GETTING OUT OF HAND!
I CAN'T HELP THINKING THE ENEMY IS BEHIND THIS, LUNA!
IF WE DON'T DO SOMETHING, THE PRINCESS COULD BE IN DANGER.
WE HAVE TO PUT A STOP TO THIS, AND FAST.
I KNOW.
I JUST NEVER EXPECTED THIS.
I DIDN'T WANT TO THINK...
...THAT TUXEDO MASK WAS OUR ENEMY, BUT...
TUXEDO MASK, OUR ENEMY?!
NO, IT CAN'T BE TRUE...
ずきん
STING

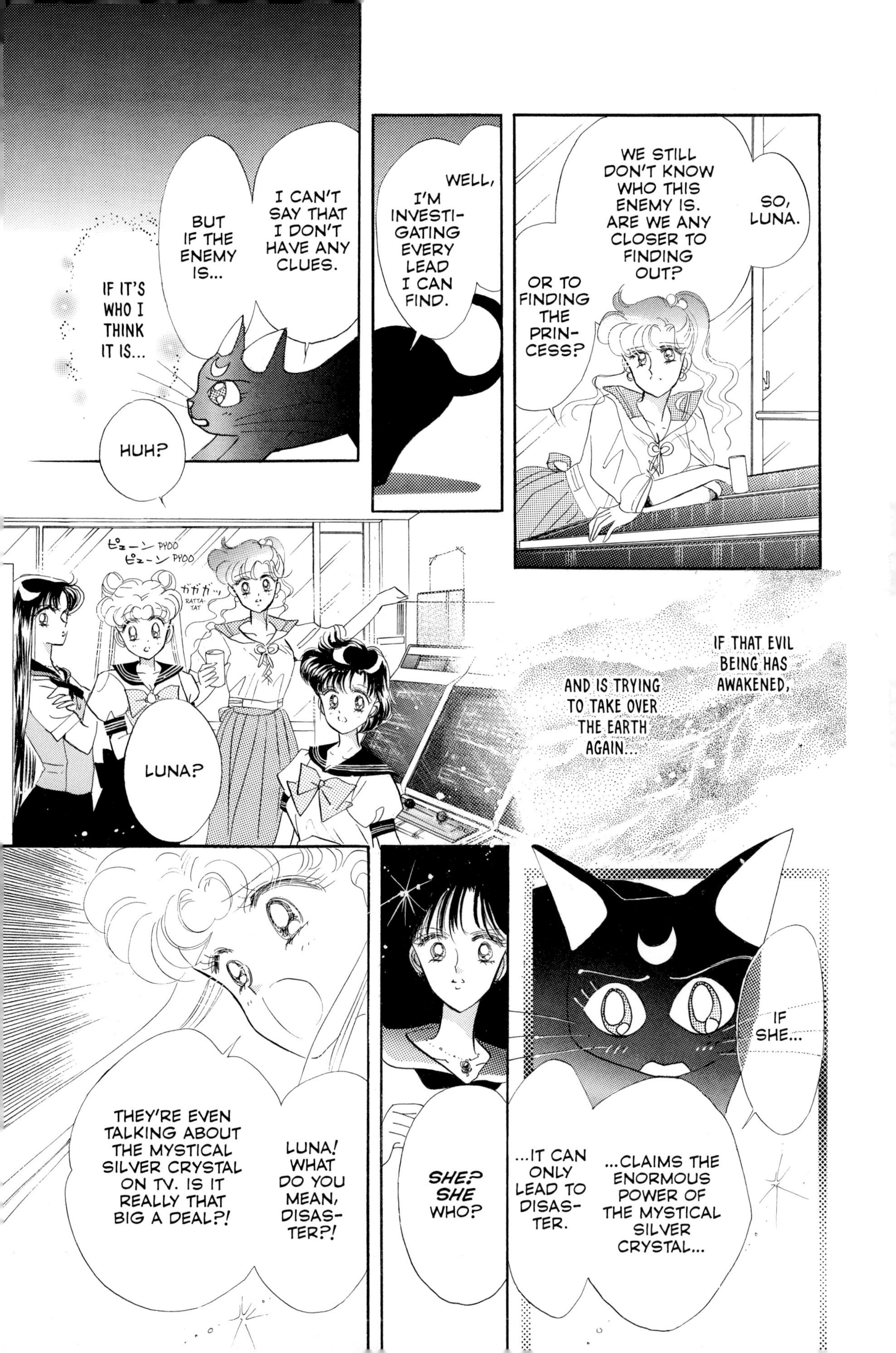
SO, LUNA.
WE STILL DON'T KNOW WHO THIS ENEMY IS. ARE WE ANY CLOSER TO FINDING OUT?
OR TO FINDING THE PRINCESS?
WELL, I'M INVESTIGATING EVERY LEAD I CAN FIND.
I CAN'T SAY THAT I DON'T HAVE ANY CLUES.
BUT IF THE ENEMY IS...
IF IT'S WHO I THINK IT IS...
HUH?
IF THAT EVIL BEING HAS AWAKENED,
AND IS TRYING TO TAKE OVER THE EARTH AGAIN...
ピューン PYOO
ピューン PYOO
ガガガッ RATTA-TAT
LUNA?
IF SHE...
...CLAIMS THE ENORMOUS POWER OF THE MYSTICAL SILVER CRYSTAL...
...IT CAN ONLY LEAD TO DISASTER.
SHE? SHE WHO?
LUNA! WHAT DO YOU MEAN, DISASTER?!
THEY'RE EVEN TALKING ABOUT THE MYSTICAL SILVER CRYSTAL ON TV. IS IT REALLY THAT BIG A DEAL?!

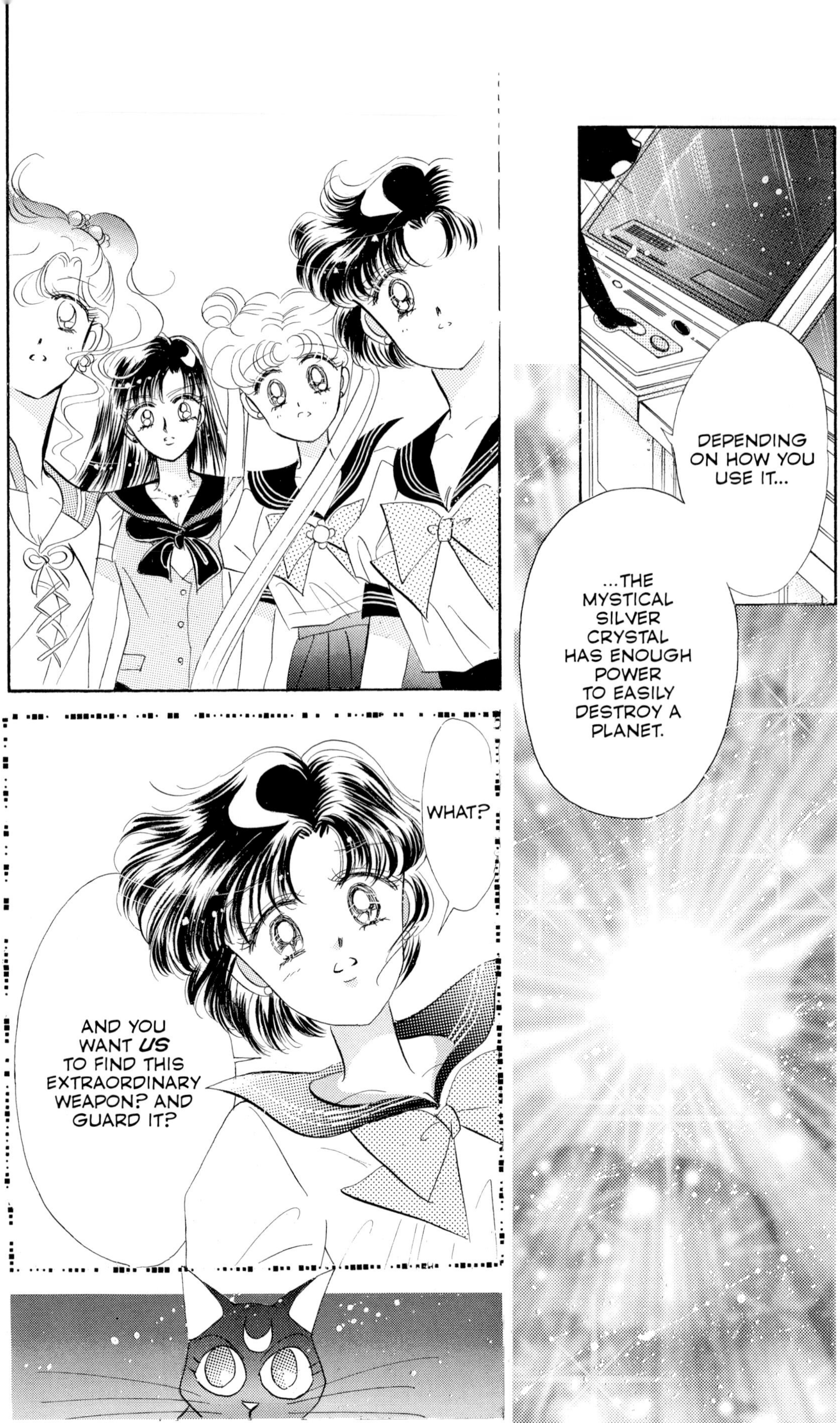
DEPENDING ON HOW YOU USE IT...
...THE MYSTICAL SILVER CRYSTAL HAS ENOUGH POWER TO EASILY DESTROY A PLANET.
WHAT?
AND YOU WANT *US* TO FIND THIS EXTRAORDINARY WEAPON? AND GUARD IT?

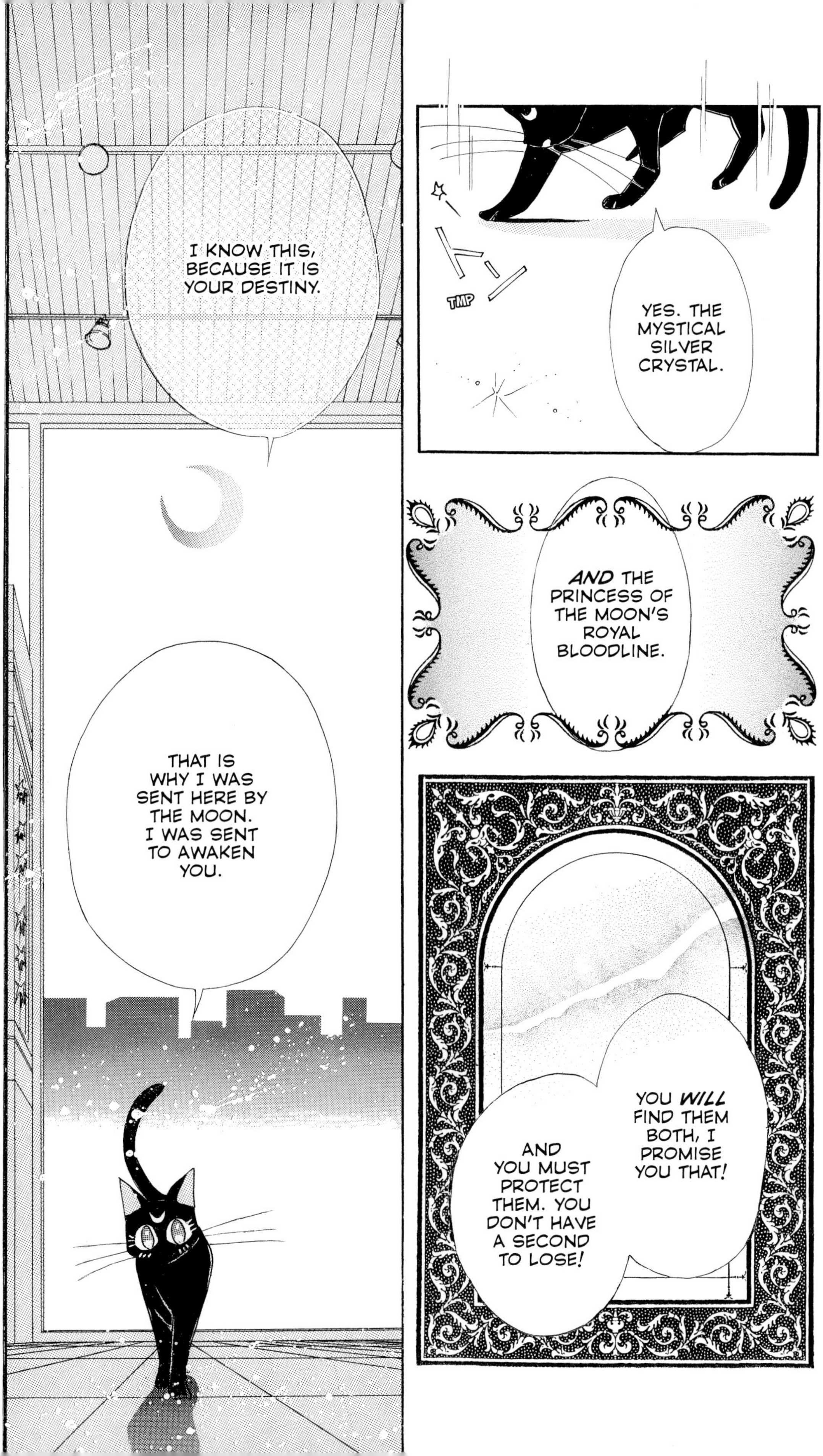
TMP
YES. THE MYSTICAL SILVER CRYSTAL.
AND THE PRINCESS OF THE MOON'S ROYAL BLOODLINE.
YOU WILL FIND THEM BOTH, I PROMISE YOU THAT!
AND YOU MUST PROTECT THEM. YOU DON'T HAVE A SECOND TO LOSE!
I KNOW THIS, BECAUSE IT IS YOUR DESTINY.
THAT IS WHY I WAS SENT HERE BY THE MOON. I WAS SENT TO AWAKEN YOU.

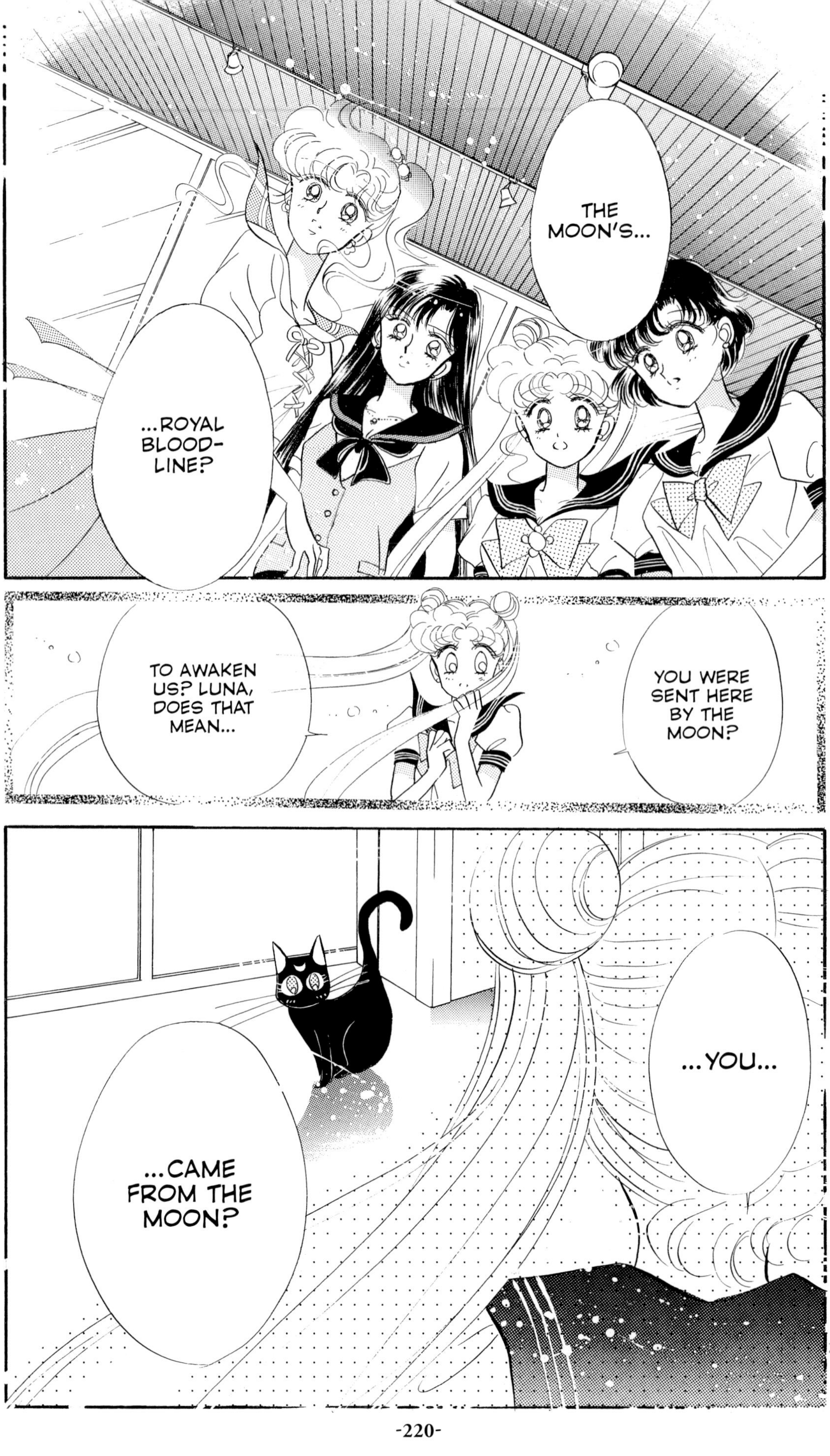
THE MOON'S...
...ROYAL BLOOD-LINE?
YOU WERE SENT HERE BY THE MOON?
TO AWAKEN US? LUNA, DOES THAT MEAN...
...YOU...
...CAME FROM THE MOON?

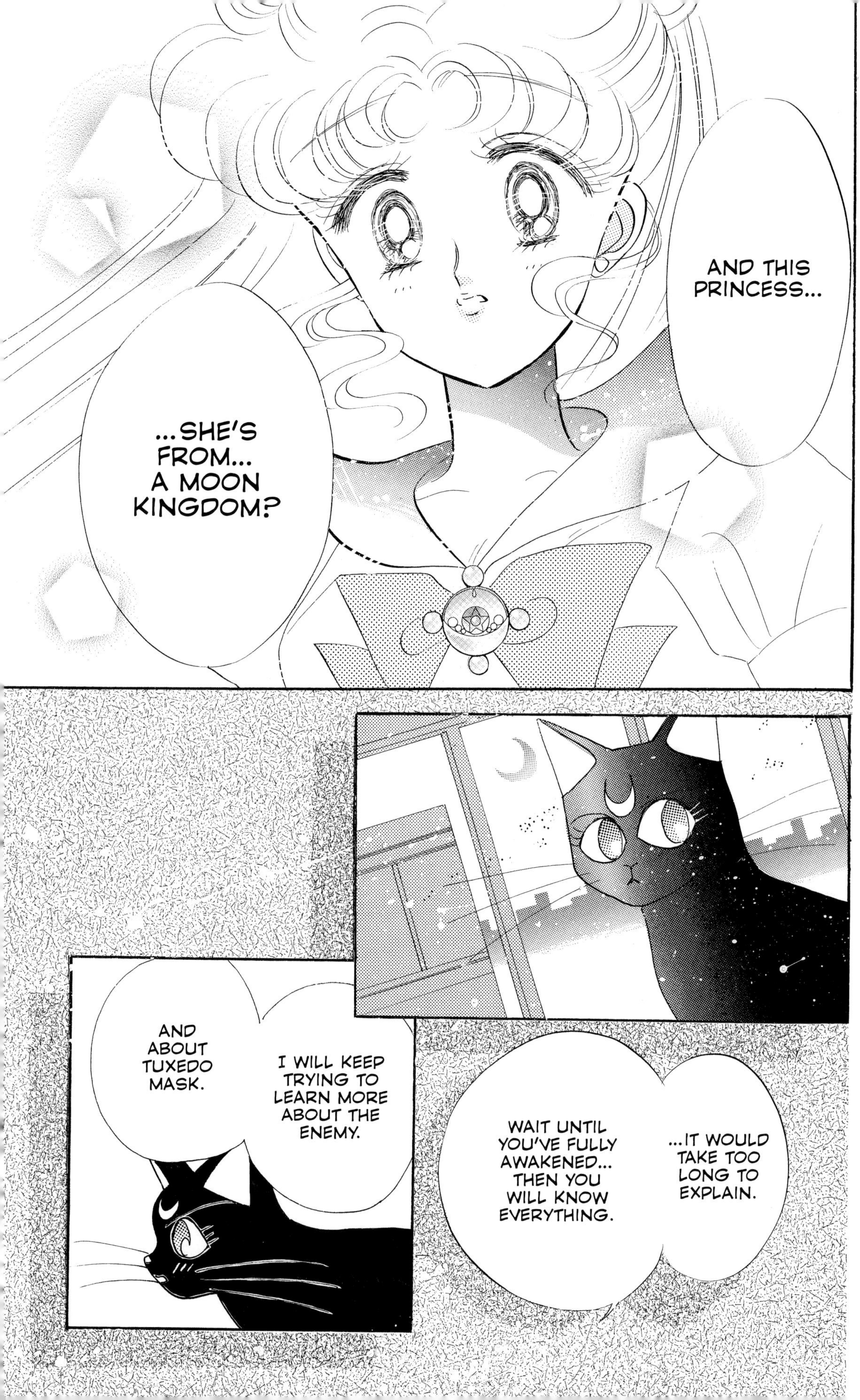
AND THIS PRINCESS...
...SHE'S FROM... A MOON KINGDOM?
...IT WOULD TAKE TOO LONG TO EXPLAIN.
WAIT UNTIL YOU'VE FULLY AWAKENED... THEN YOU WILL KNOW EVERYTHING.
I WILL KEEP TRYING TO LEARN MORE ABOUT THE ENEMY.
AND ABOUT TUXEDO MASK.

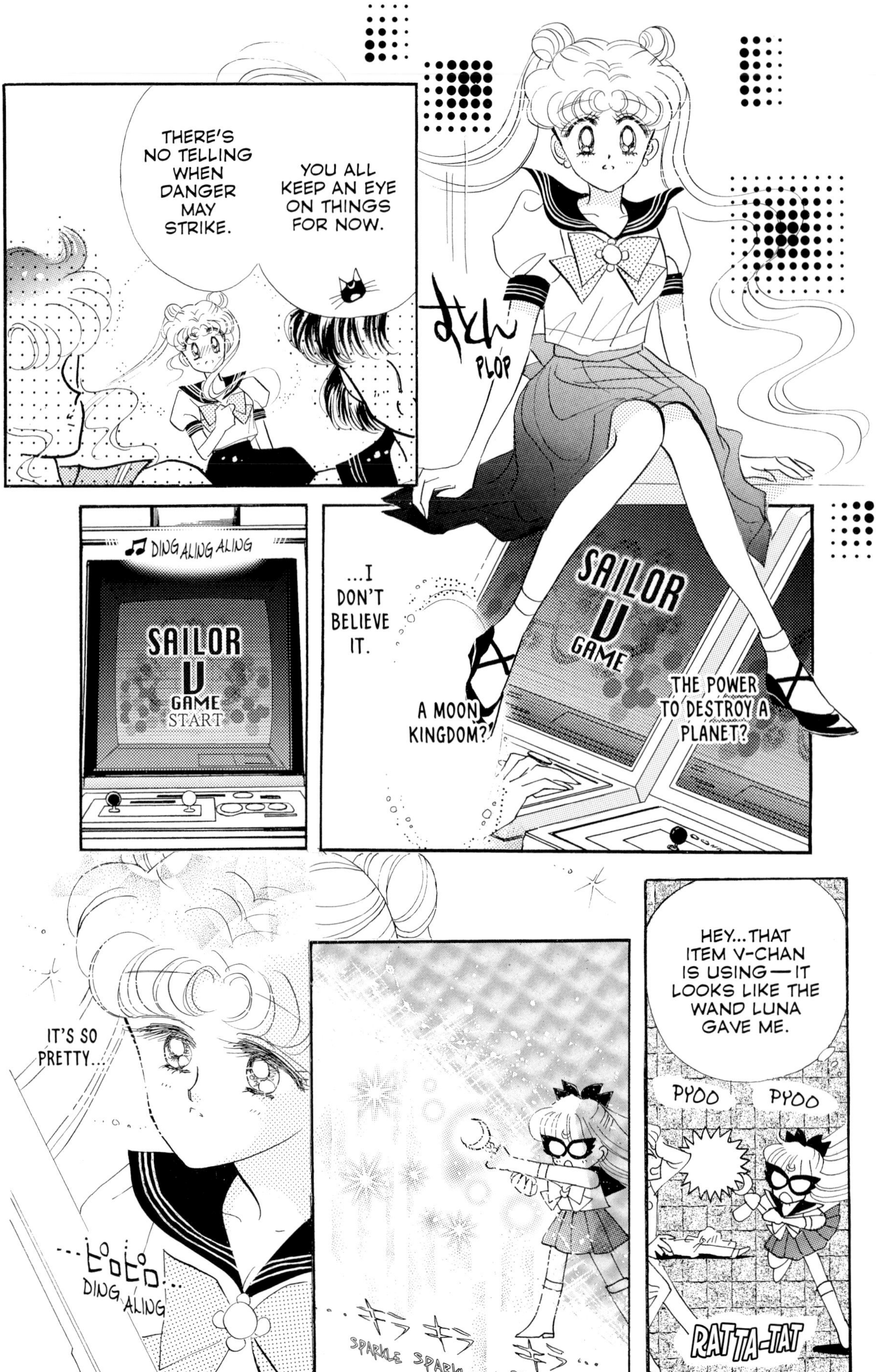
THERE'S NO TELLING WHEN DANGER MAY STRIKE.
YOU ALL KEEP AN EYE ON THINGS FOR NOW.
むとん
PLOP
THE POWER TO DESTROY A PLANET?
A MOON KINGDOM?
...I DON'T BELIEVE IT.
♫ DING ALING ALING
SAILOR V GAME START
SAILOR V GAME
HEY...THAT ITEM V-CHAN IS USING—IT LOOKS LIKE THE WAND LUNA GAVE ME.
PYOO PYOO
RATTA-TAT
キラ キラ キラ...
SPARKLE SPARKLE SPARKLE
IT'S SO PRETTY...
...ピロピロ...
DING ALING

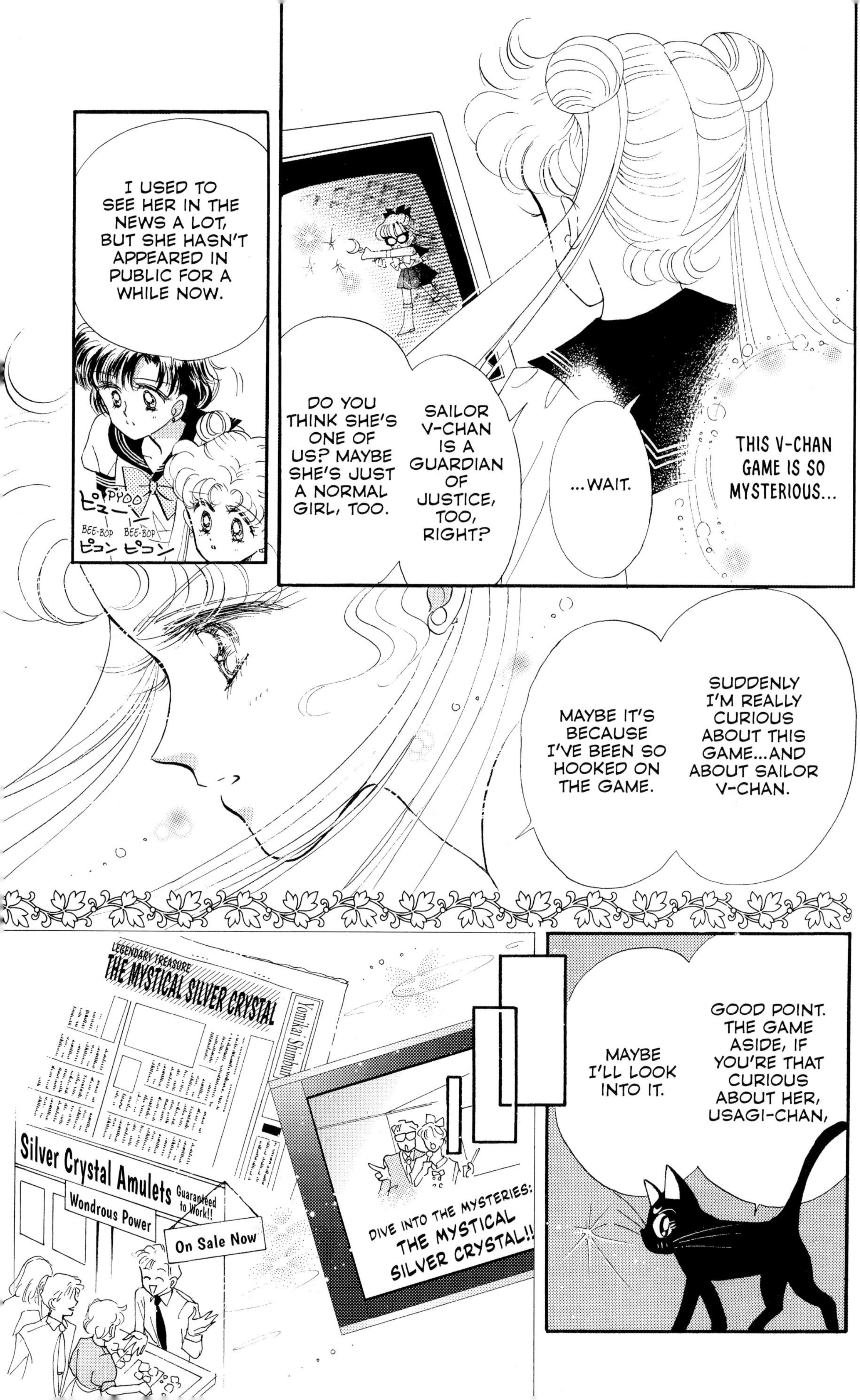
THIS V-CHAN GAME IS SO MYSTERIOUS...
...WAIT.
SAILOR V-CHAN IS A GUARDIAN OF JUSTICE, TOO, RIGHT?
DO YOU THINK SHE'S ONE OF US? MAYBE SHE'S JUST A NORMAL GIRL, TOO.
I USED TO SEE HER IN THE NEWS A LOT, BUT SHE HASN'T APPEARED IN PUBLIC FOR A WHILE NOW.
ピューー PYOO
ピコン BEE-BOP ピコン BEE-BOP
SUDDENLY I'M REALLY CURIOUS ABOUT THIS GAME...AND ABOUT SAILOR V-CHAN.
MAYBE IT'S BECAUSE I'VE BEEN SO HOOKED ON THE GAME.
GOOD POINT. THE GAME ASIDE, IF YOU'RE THAT CURIOUS ABOUT HER, USAGI-CHAN,
MAYBE I'LL LOOK INTO IT.
LEGENDARY TREASURE
THE MYSTICAL SILVER CRYSTAL
Yomikai Shimbun
Silver Crystal Amulets
Guaranteed to Work!!
Wondrous Power
On Sale Now
DIVE INTO THE MYSTERIES: THE MYSTICAL SILVER CRYSTAL!!

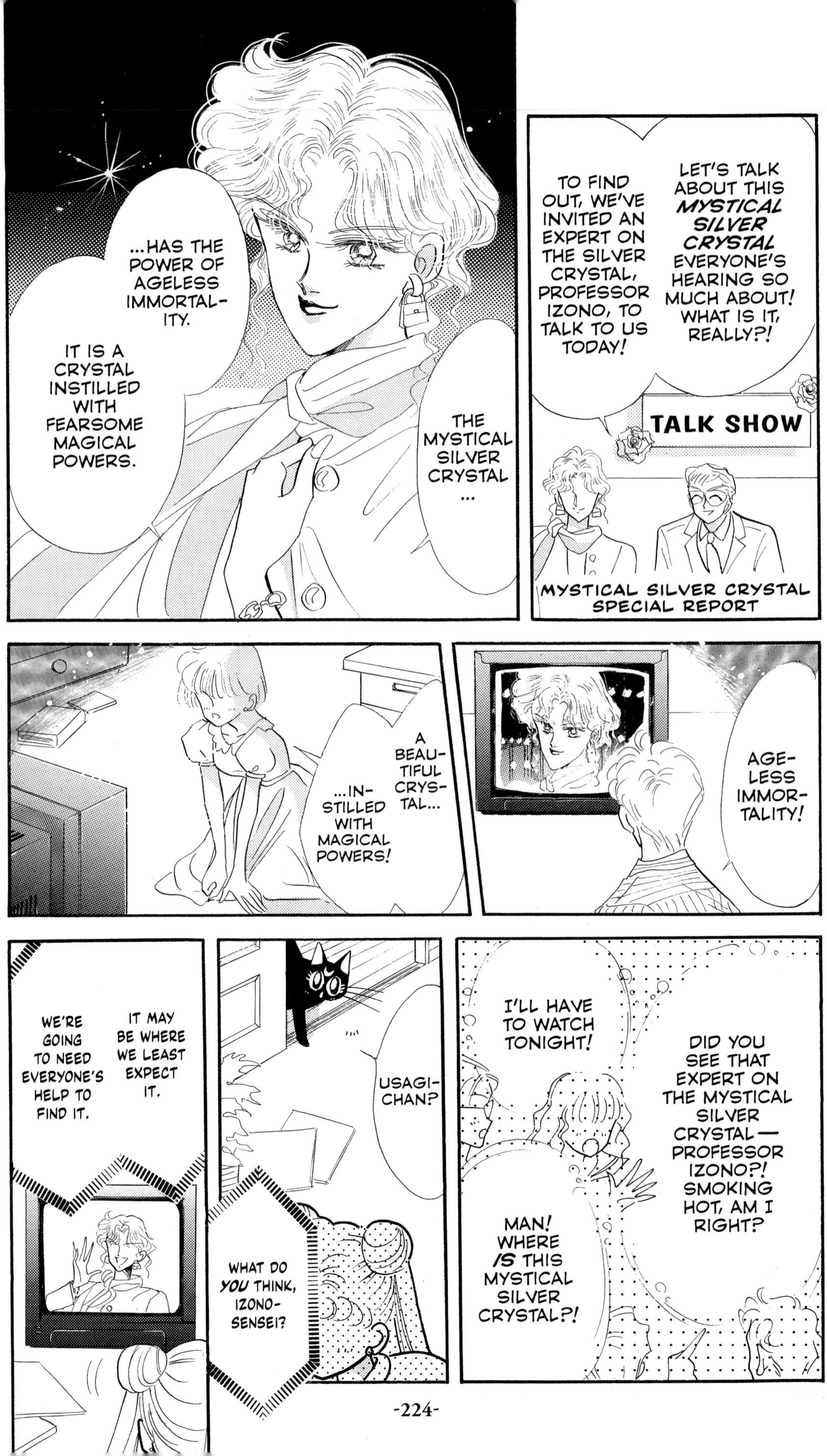
LET'S TALK ABOUT THIS *MYSTICAL SILVER CRYSTAL* EVERYONE'S HEARING SO MUCH ABOUT! WHAT IS IT, REALLY?!
TO FIND OUT, WE'VE INVITED AN EXPERT ON THE SILVER CRYSTAL, PROFESSOR IZONO, TO TALK TO US TODAY!
TALK SHOW
MYSTICAL SILVER CRYSTAL SPECIAL REPORT
THE MYSTICAL SILVER CRYSTAL...
...HAS THE POWER OF AGELESS IMMORTALITY.
IT IS A CRYSTAL INSTILLED WITH FEARSOME MAGICAL POWERS.
AGELESS IMMORTALITY!
A BEAUTIFUL CRYSTAL...
...INSTILLED WITH MAGICAL POWERS!
DID YOU SEE THAT EXPERT ON THE MYSTICAL SILVER CRYSTAL—PROFESSOR IZONO?! SMOKING HOT, AM I RIGHT?
I'LL HAVE TO WATCH TONIGHT!
MAN! WHERE *IS* THIS MYSTICAL SILVER CRYSTAL?!
USAGI-CHAN?
WHAT DO *YOU* THINK, IZONO-SENSEI?
IT MAY BE WHERE WE LEAST EXPECT IT.
WE'RE GOING TO NEED EVERYONE'S HELP TO FIND IT.

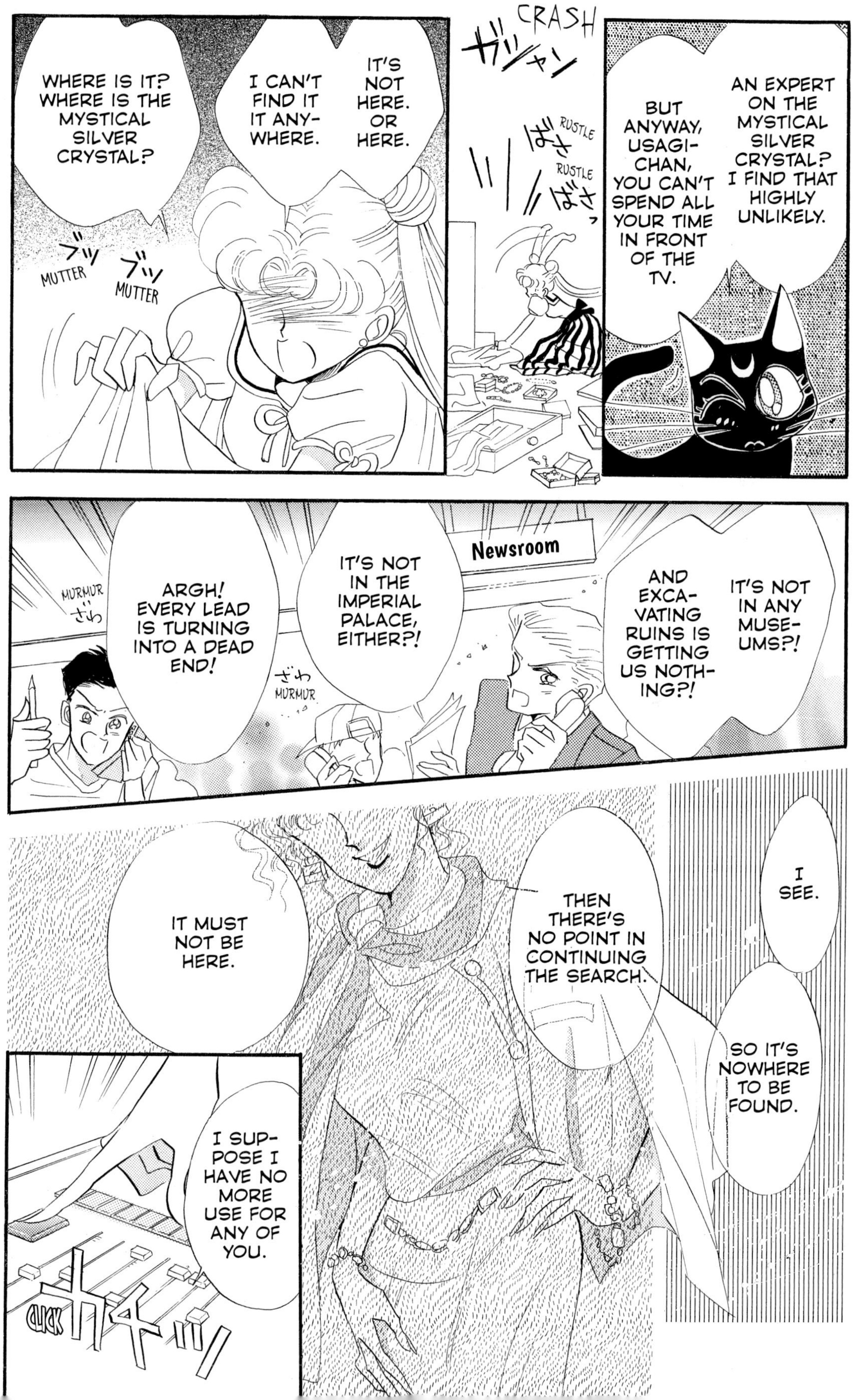
AN EXPERT ON THE MYSTICAL SILVER CRYSTAL? I FIND THAT HIGHLY UNLIKELY.
BUT ANYWAY, USAGI-CHAN, YOU CAN'T SPEND ALL YOUR TIME IN FRONT OF THE TV.
ガシャン
CRASH
ばさ
RUSTLE
ばさ
RUSTLE
IT'S NOT HERE. OR HERE.
I CAN'T FIND IT IT ANY-WHERE.
WHERE IS IT? WHERE IS THE MYSTICAL SILVER CRYSTAL?
ブツ
MUTTER
ブツ
MUTTER
IT'S NOT IN ANY MUSE-UMS?!
AND EXCA-VATING RUINS IS GETTING US NOTH-ING?!
Newsroom
IT'S NOT IN THE IMPERIAL PALACE, EITHER?!
ざわ
MURMUR
ARGH! EVERY LEAD IS TURNING INTO A DEAD END!
ざわ
MURMUR
I SEE.
SO IT'S NOWHERE TO BE FOUND.
THEN THERE'S NO POINT IN CONTINUING THE SEARCH.
IT MUST NOT BE HERE.
I SUP-POSE I HAVE NO MORE USE FOR ANY OF YOU.
カチッ
CLICK

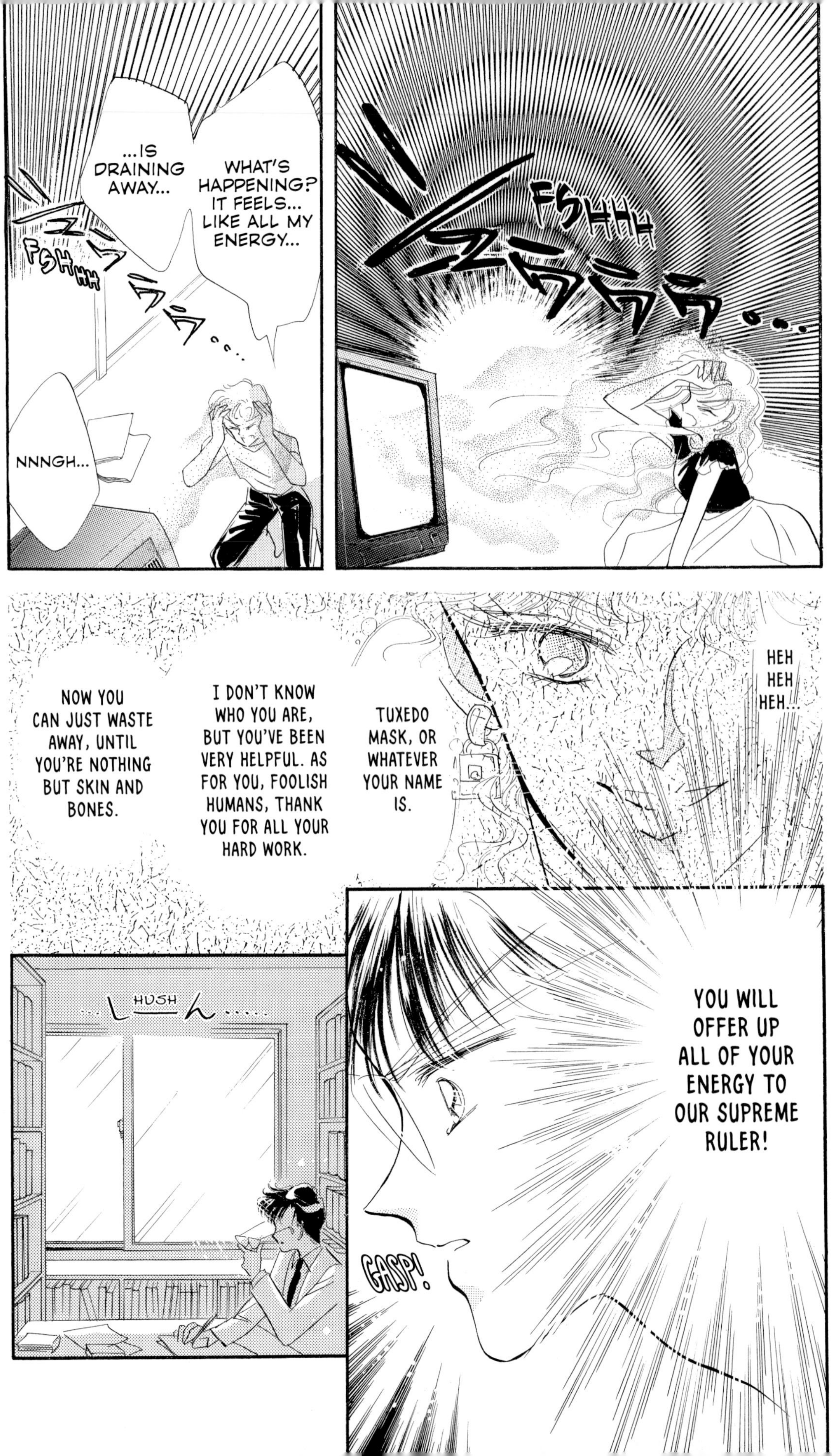
FSHHH
WHAT'S HAPPENING? IT FEELS... LIKE ALL MY ENERGY...
...IS DRAINING AWAY...
FSHHH
NNNGH...
HEH HEH HEH...
TUXEDO MASK, OR WHATEVER YOUR NAME IS.
I DON'T KNOW WHO YOU ARE, BUT YOU'VE BEEN VERY HELPFUL. AS FOR YOU, FOOLISH HUMANS, THANK YOU FOR ALL YOUR HARD WORK.
NOW YOU CAN JUST WASTE AWAY, UNTIL YOU'RE NOTHING BUT SKIN AND BONES.
YOU WILL OFFER UP ALL OF YOUR ENERGY TO OUR SUPREME RULER!
GASP!
HUSH

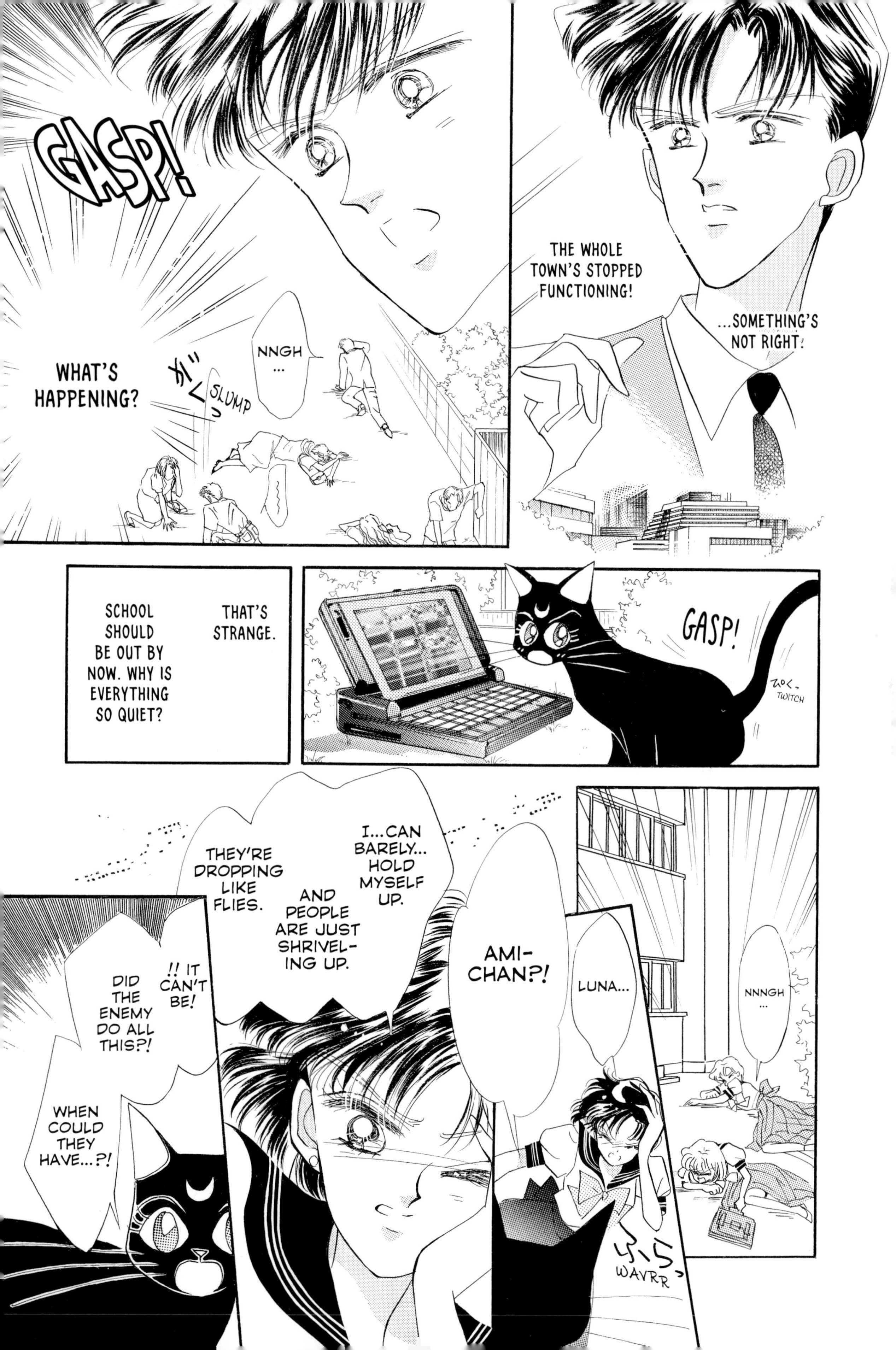
THE WHOLE TOWN'S STOPPED FUNCTIONING!
...SOMETHING'S NOT RIGHT!
GASP!
NNGH ...
SLUMP
WHAT'S HAPPENING?
GASP!
TWITCH
THAT'S STRANGE.
SCHOOL SHOULD BE OUT BY NOW. WHY IS EVERYTHING SO QUIET?
NNNGH ...
WAVRR
LUNA...
AMI-CHAN?!
I...CAN BARELY... HOLD MYSELF UP.
AND PEOPLE ARE JUST SHRIVEL-ING UP.
THEY'RE DROPPING LIKE FLIES.
!! IT CAN'T BE!
DID THE ENEMY DO ALL THIS?!
WHEN COULD THEY HAVE...?!

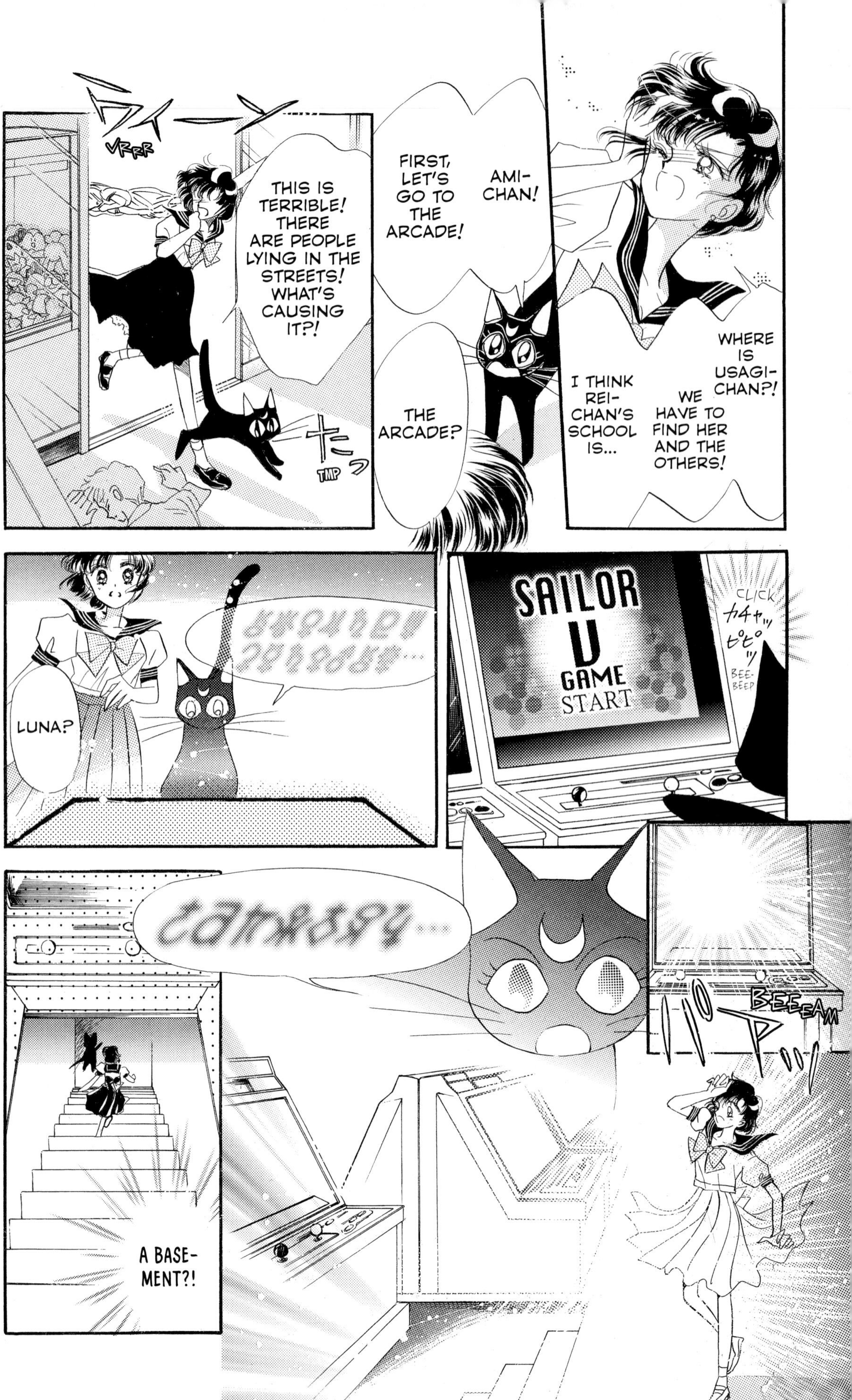
WHERE IS USAGI-CHAN?!
WE HAVE TO FIND HER AND THE OTHERS!
I THINK REI-CHAN'S SCHOOL IS...
AMI-CHAN!
FIRST, LET'S GO TO THE ARCADE!
THE ARCADE?
VRRR
THIS IS TERRIBLE! THERE ARE PEOPLE LYING IN THE STREETS! WHAT'S CAUSING IT?!
TMP
SAILOR V GAME START
CLICK
BEE-BEEP
LUNA?
BEEEAM
A BASE-MENT?!

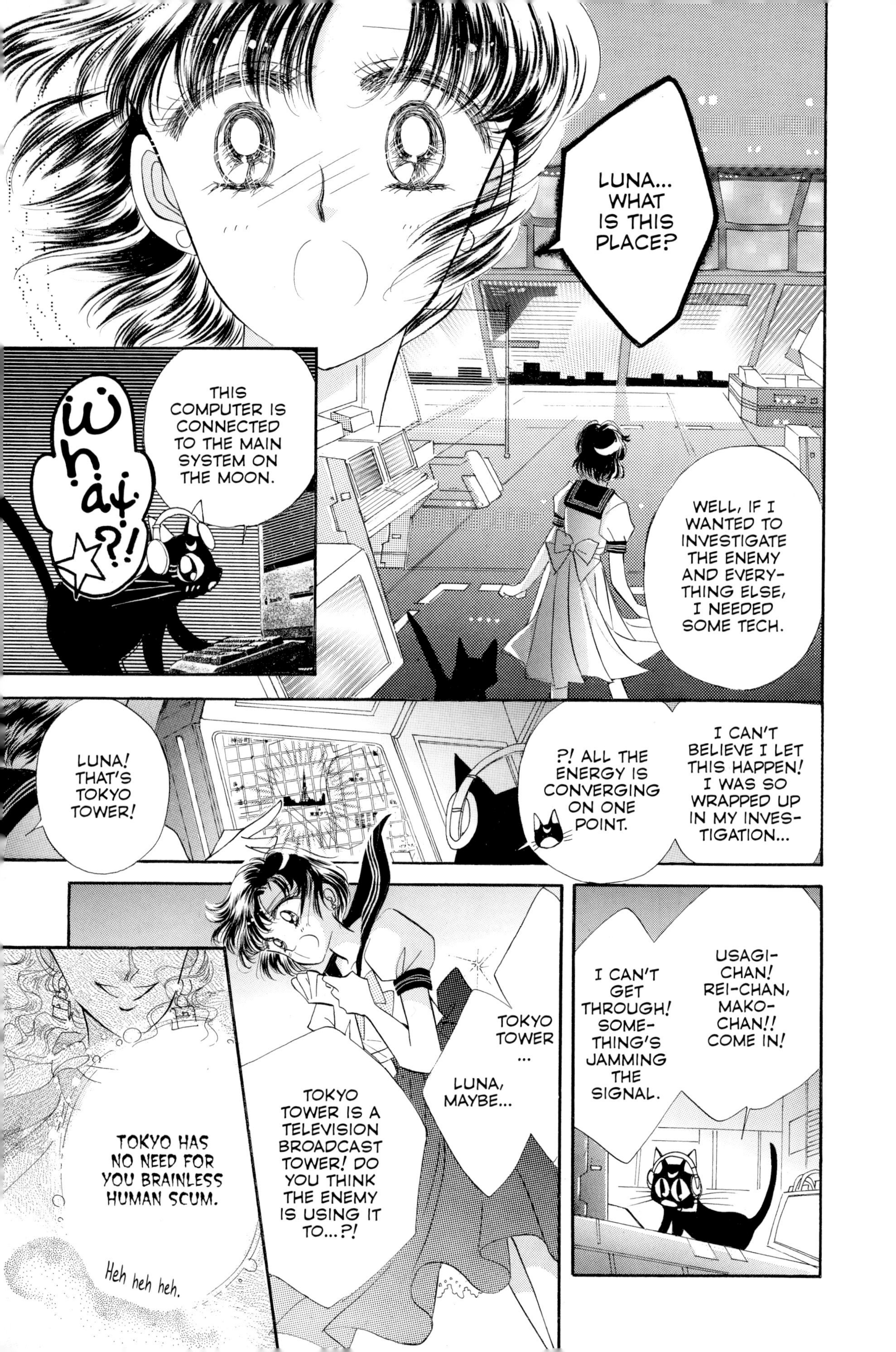
LUNA... WHAT IS THIS PLACE?
THIS COMPUTER IS CONNECTED TO THE MAIN SYSTEM ON THE MOON.
What?!
WELL, IF I WANTED TO INVESTIGATE THE ENEMY AND EVERYTHING ELSE, I NEEDED SOME TECH.
I CAN'T BELIEVE I LET THIS HAPPEN! I WAS SO WRAPPED UP IN MY INVESTIGATION...
?! ALL THE ENERGY IS CONVERGING ON ONE POINT.
LUNA! THAT'S TOKYO TOWER!
USAGI-CHAN! REI-CHAN, MAKO-CHAN!! COME IN!
I CAN'T GET THROUGH! SOMETHING'S JAMMING THE SIGNAL.
TOKYO TOWER ...
LUNA, MAYBE...
TOKYO TOWER IS A TELEVISION BROADCAST TOWER! DO YOU THINK THE ENEMY IS USING IT TO...?!
TOKYO HAS NO NEED FOR YOU BRAINLESS HUMAN SCUM.
Heh heh heh.

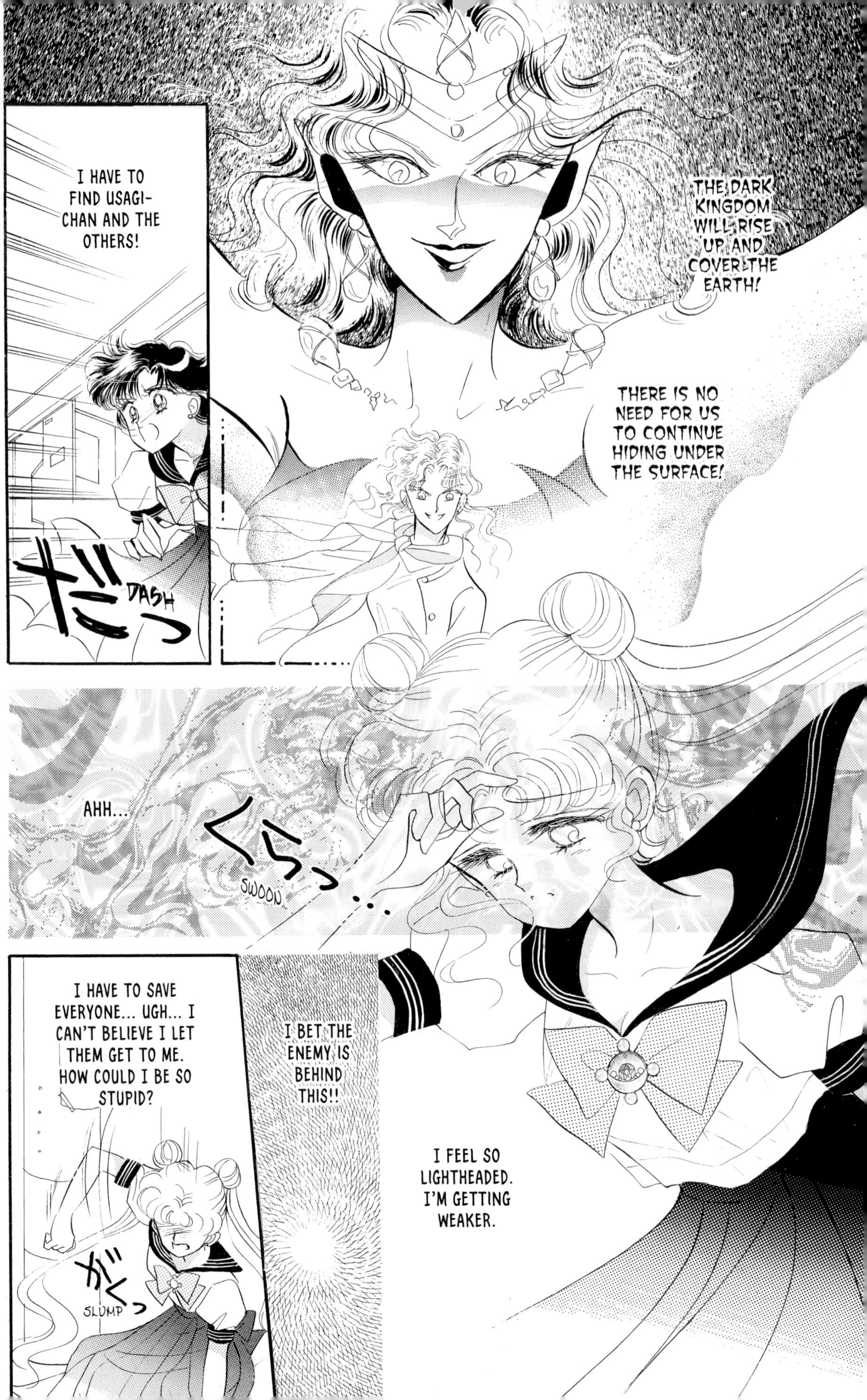
THE DARK KINGDOM WILL RISE UP AND COVER THE EARTH!
THERE IS NO NEED FOR US TO CONTINUE HIDING UNDER THE SURFACE!
I HAVE TO FIND USAGI-CHAN AND THE OTHERS!
DASH
AHH...
SWOON
I FEEL SO LIGHTHEADED. I'M GETTING WEAKER.
I BET THE ENEMY IS BEHIND THIS!!
I HAVE TO SAVE EVERYONE... UGH... I CAN'T BELIEVE I LET THEM GET TO ME. HOW COULD I BE SO STUPID?
SLUMP

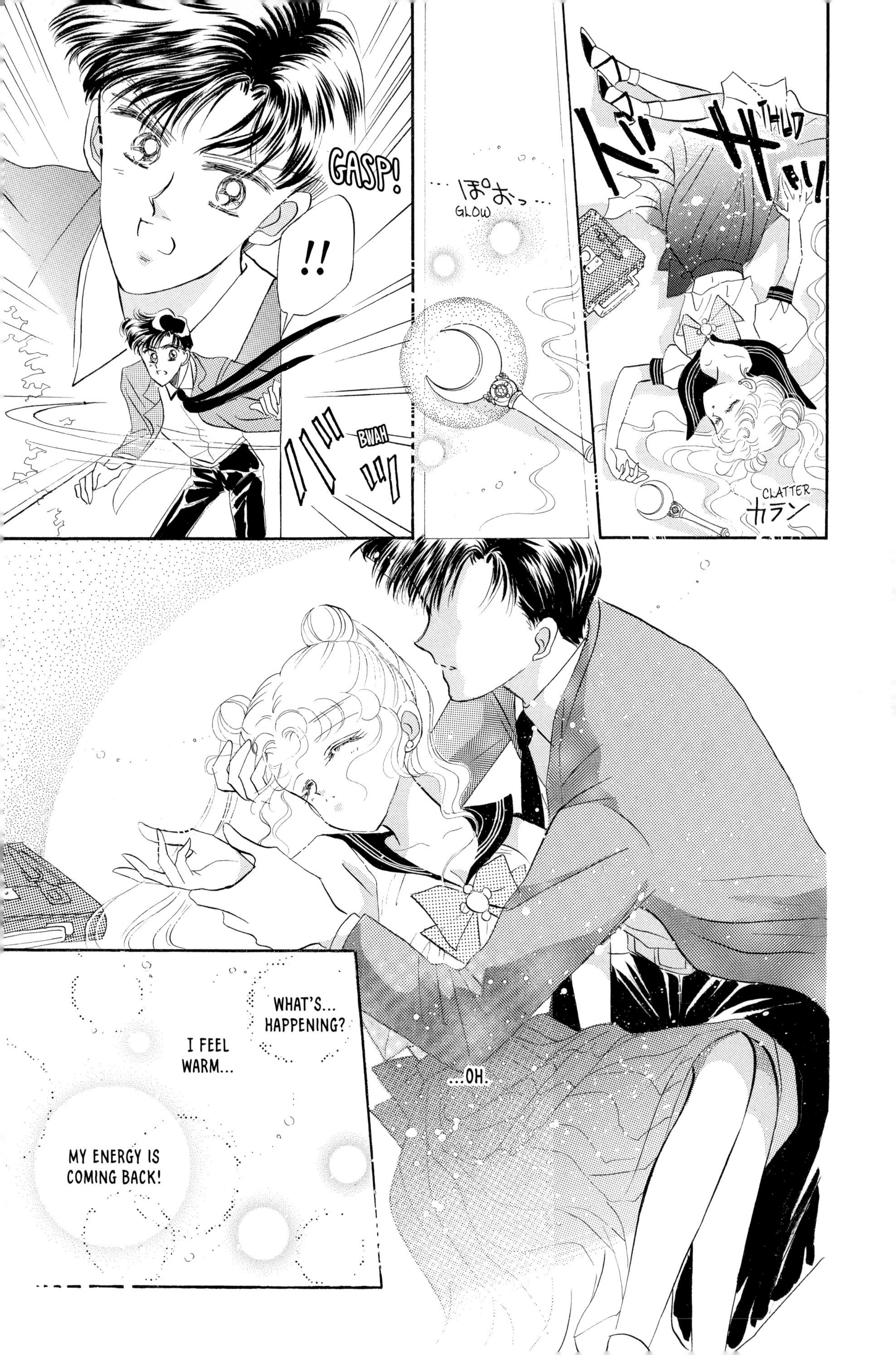

THUD
CLATTER
カラン
…ぽおっ…
GLOW
GASP!
!!
BWAH
WHAT'S... HAPPENING?
I FEEL WARM...
MY ENERGY IS COMING BACK!
...OH.

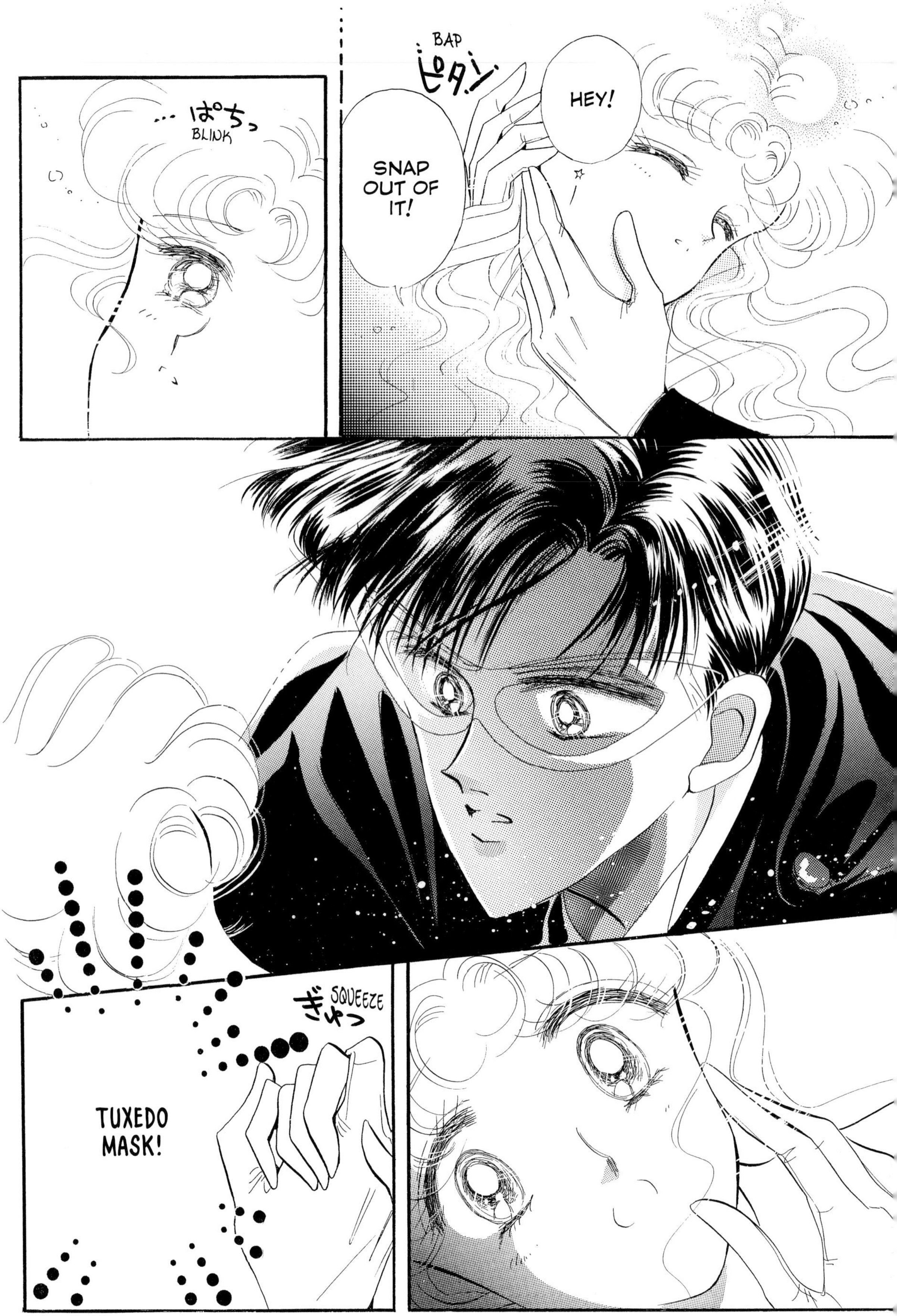
ピタン
BAP
HEY!
SNAP OUT OF IT!
…ぱちっ
BLINK
ぎゅっ
SQUEEZE
TUXEDO MASK!

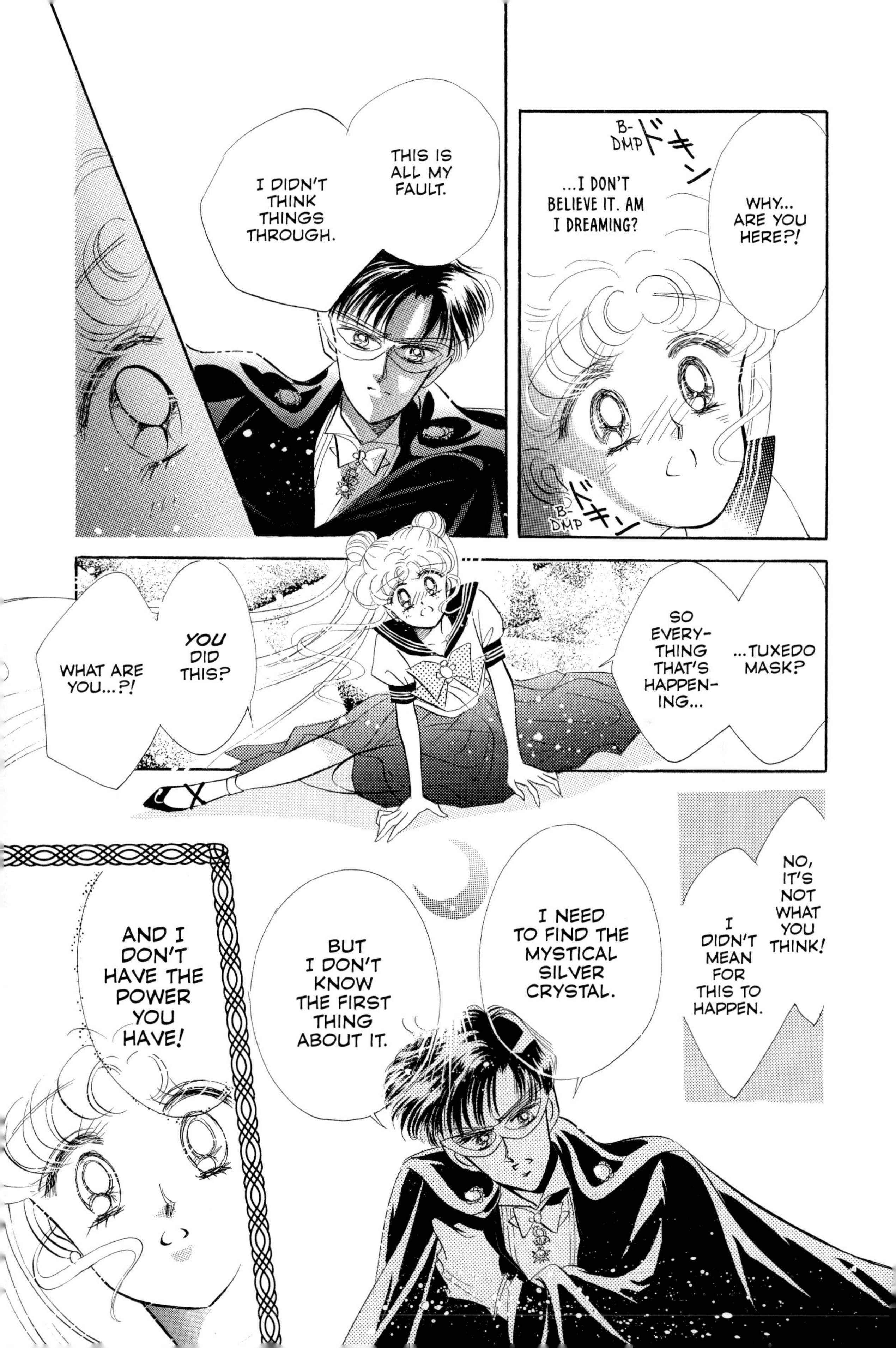
WHY... ARE YOU HERE?!
B-DMP ドキン
...I DON'T BELIEVE IT. AM I DREAMING?
B-DMP ドキン
THIS IS ALL MY FAULT.
I DIDN'T THINK THINGS THROUGH.
...TUXEDO MASK?
SO EVERYTHING THAT'S HAPPENING...
YOU DID THIS?
WHAT ARE YOU...?!
NO, IT'S NOT WHAT YOU THINK!
I DIDN'T MEAN FOR THIS TO HAPPEN.
I NEED TO FIND THE MYSTICAL SILVER CRYSTAL.
BUT I DON'T KNOW THE FIRST THING ABOUT IT.
AND I DON'T HAVE THE POWER YOU HAVE!

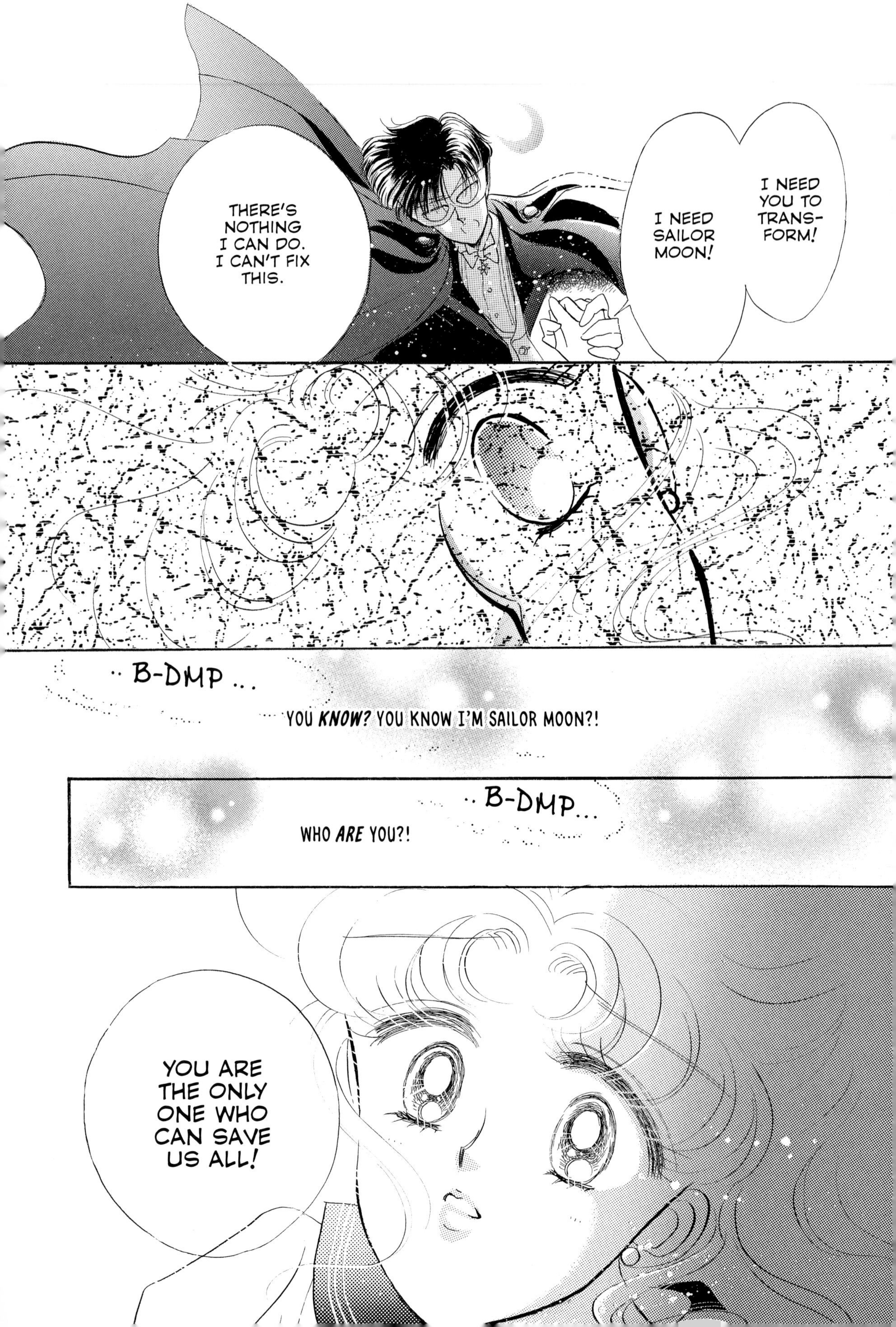

I NEED SAILOR MOON!
I NEED YOU TO TRANS-FORM!
THERE'S NOTHING I CAN DO. I CAN'T FIX THIS.
..B-DMP...
YOU *KNOW?* YOU KNOW I'M SAILOR MOON?!
..B-DMP...
WHO *ARE* YOU?!
YOU ARE THE ONLY ONE WHO CAN SAVE US ALL!

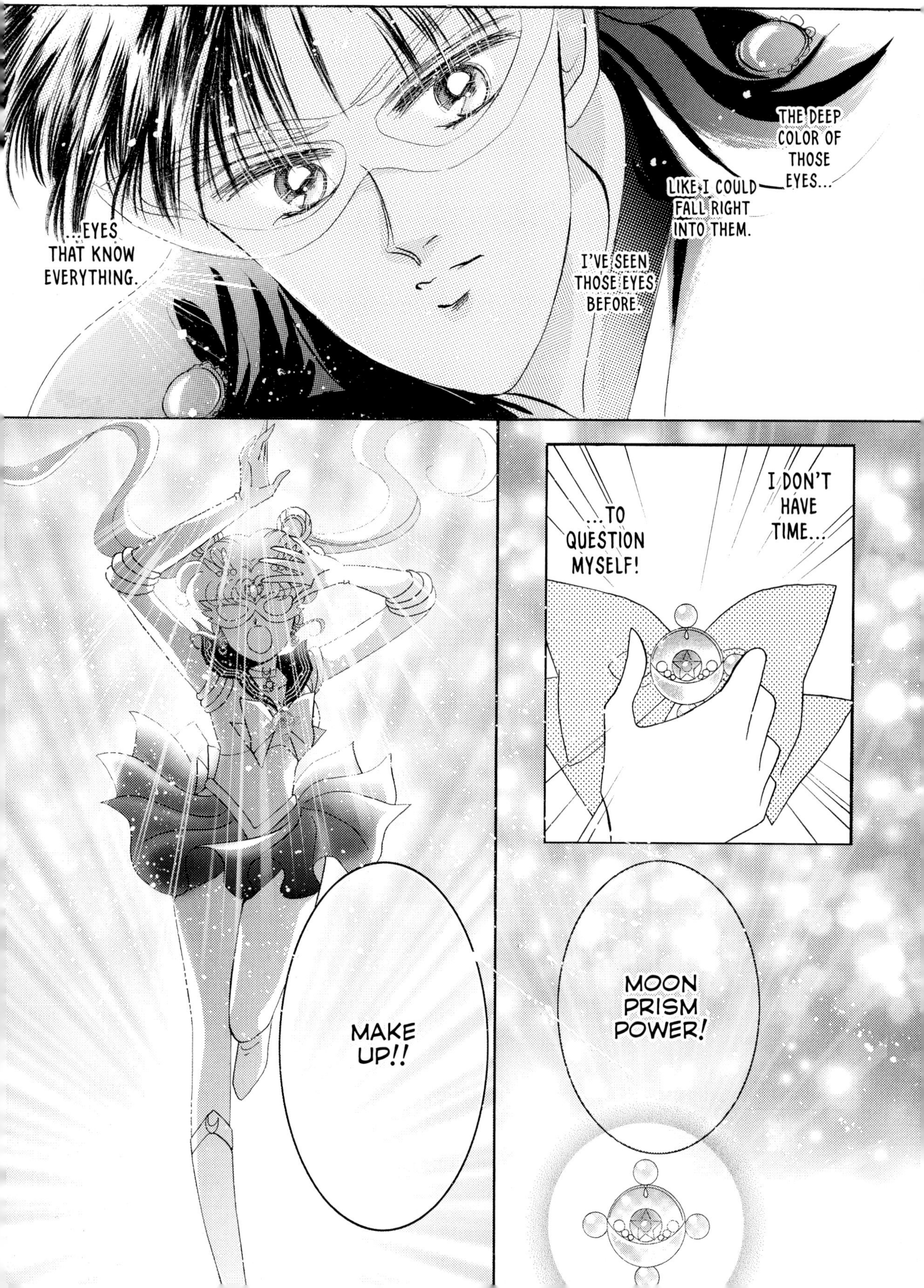
THE DEEP COLOR OF THOSE EYES...
LIKE I COULD FALL RIGHT INTO THEM.
I'VE SEEN THOSE EYES BEFORE.
...EYES THAT KNOW EVERYTHING.
I DON'T HAVE TIME...
...TO QUESTION MYSELF!
MOON PRISM POWER!
MAKE UP!!

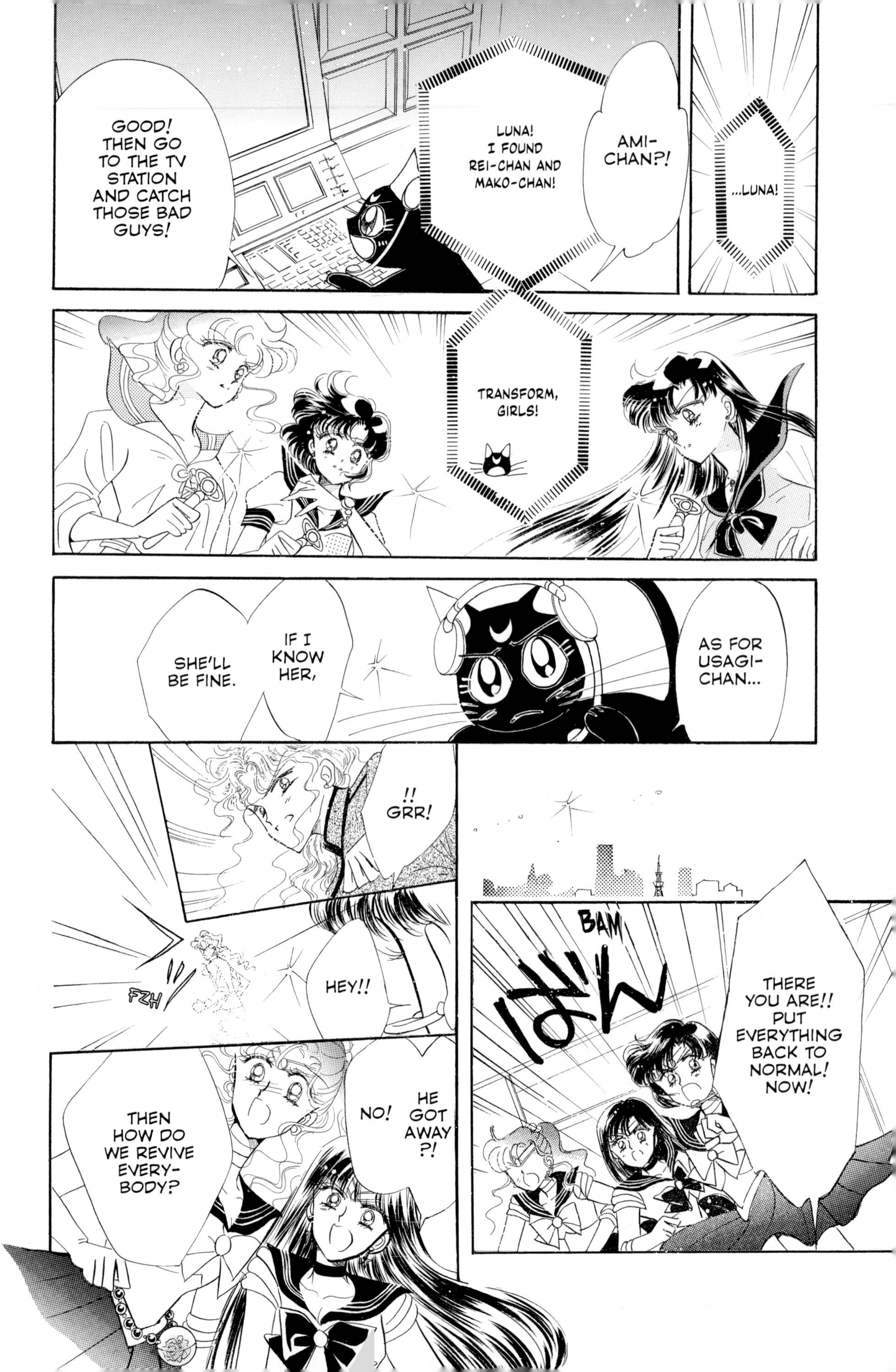
...LUNA!
AMI-CHAN?!
LUNA! I FOUND REI-CHAN AND MAKO-CHAN!
GOOD! THEN GO TO THE TV STATION AND CATCH THOSE BAD GUYS!
TRANSFORM, GIRLS!
AS FOR USAGI-CHAN...
IF I KNOW HER,
SHE'LL BE FINE.
BAM
ばん
THERE YOU ARE!! PUT EVERYTHING BACK TO NORMAL! NOW!
!! GRR!
HEY!!
FZH
HE GOT AWAY?!
NO!
THEN HOW DO WE REVIVE EVERYBODY?

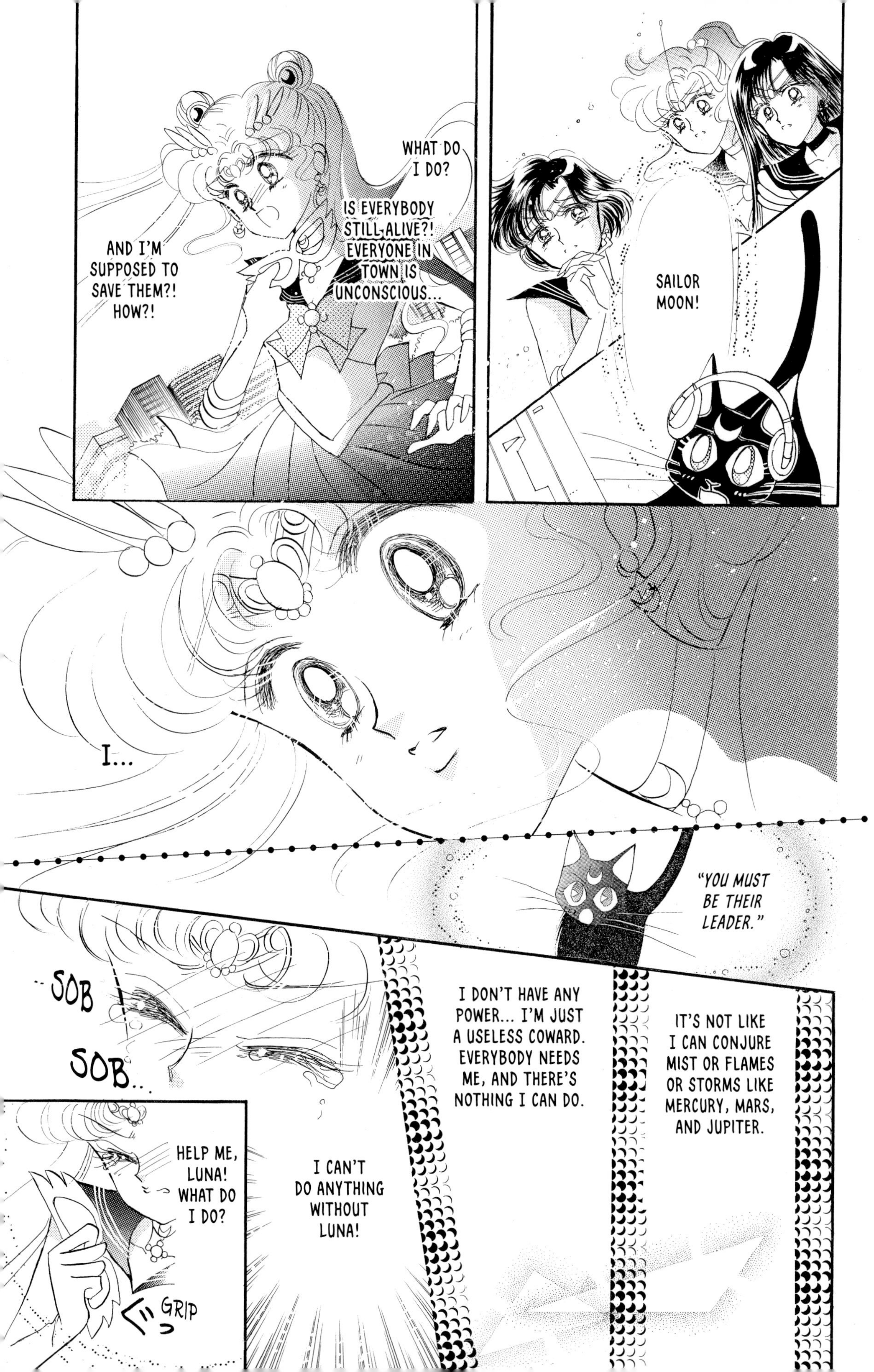
SAILOR MOON!
WHAT DO I DO?
IS EVERYBODY STILL ALIVE?! EVERYONE IN TOWN IS UNCONSCIOUS...
AND I'M SUPPOSED TO SAVE THEM?! HOW?!
"YOU MUST BE THEIR LEADER."
I...
IT'S NOT LIKE I CAN CONJURE MIST OR FLAMES OR STORMS LIKE MERCURY, MARS, AND JUPITER.
I DON'T HAVE ANY POWER... I'M JUST A USELESS COWARD. EVERYBODY NEEDS ME, AND THERE'S NOTHING I CAN DO.
SOB
SOB...
I CAN'T DO ANYTHING WITHOUT LUNA!
HELP ME, LUNA! WHAT DO I DO?
GRIP

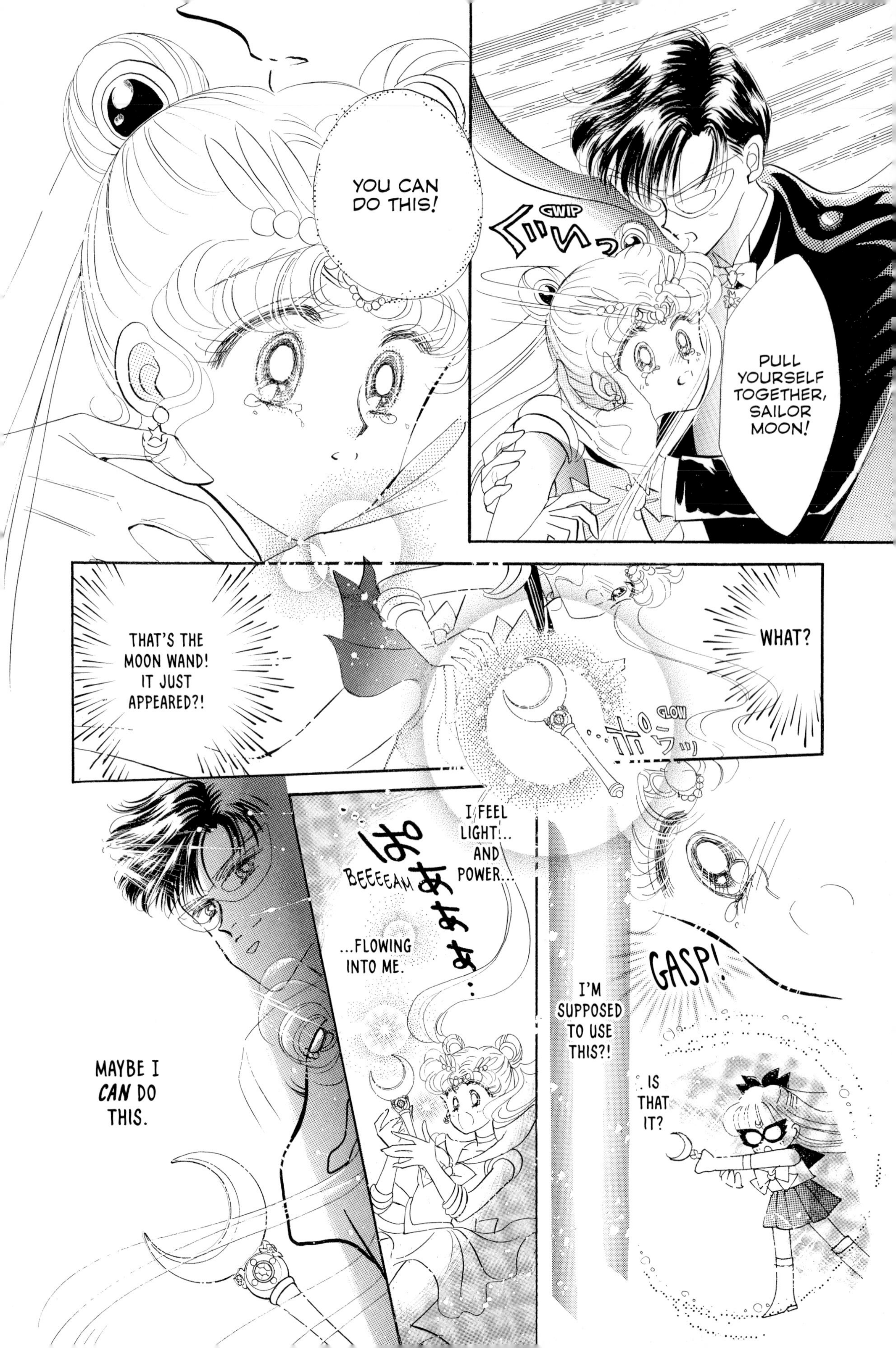
GWIP
PULL YOURSELF TOGETHER, SAILOR MOON!
YOU CAN DO THIS!
WHAT?
GLOW
THAT'S THE MOON WAND! IT JUST APPEARED?!
GASP!
IS THAT IT?
I'M SUPPOSED TO USE THIS?!
I FEEL LIGHT... AND POWER...
BEEEEAM
...FLOWING INTO ME.
MAYBE I *CAN* DO THIS.

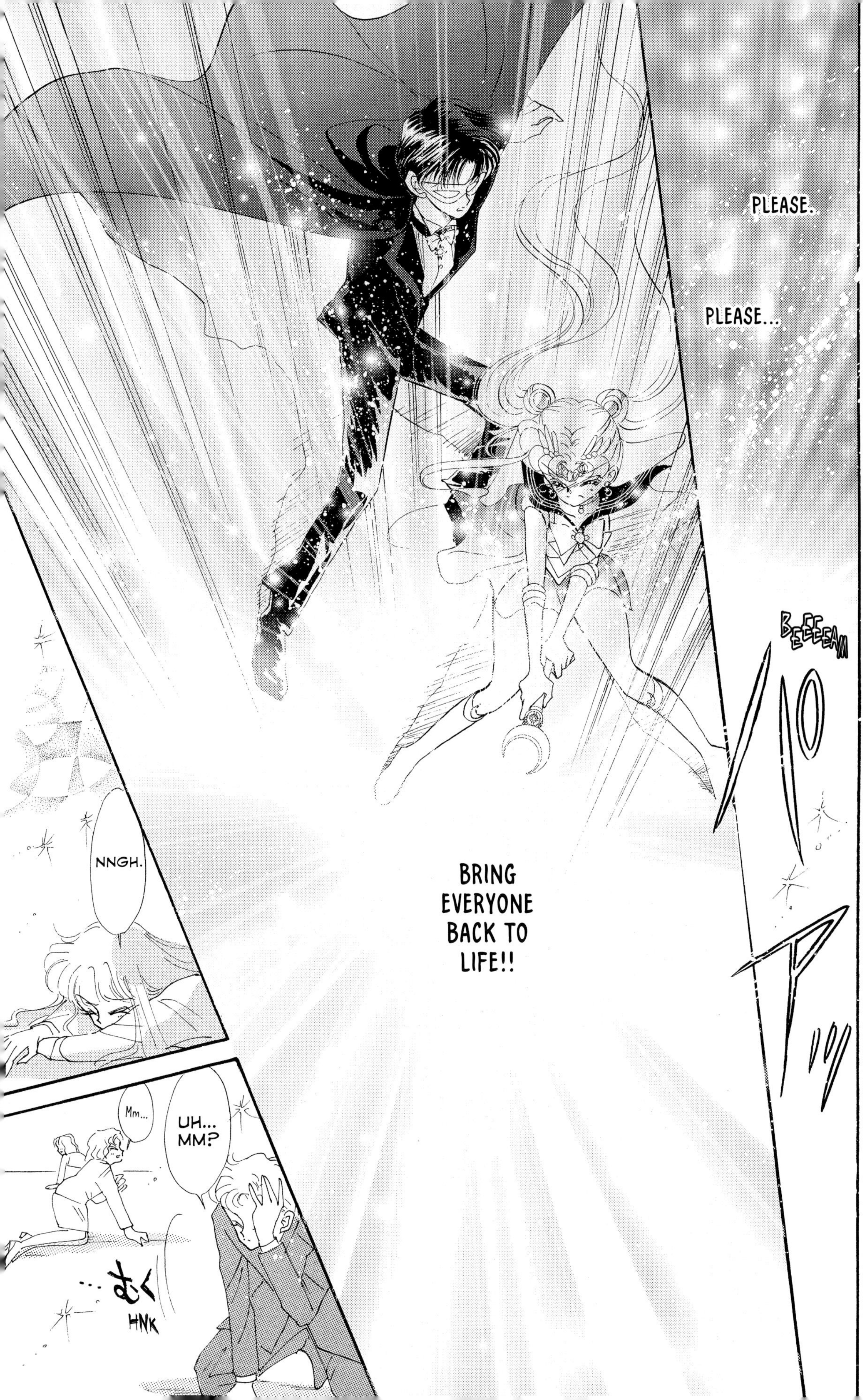
PLEASE.
PLEASE...
BEEEEAM
BRING EVERYONE BACK TO LIFE!!
NNGH.
UH... MM?
Mm...
むく
HNK

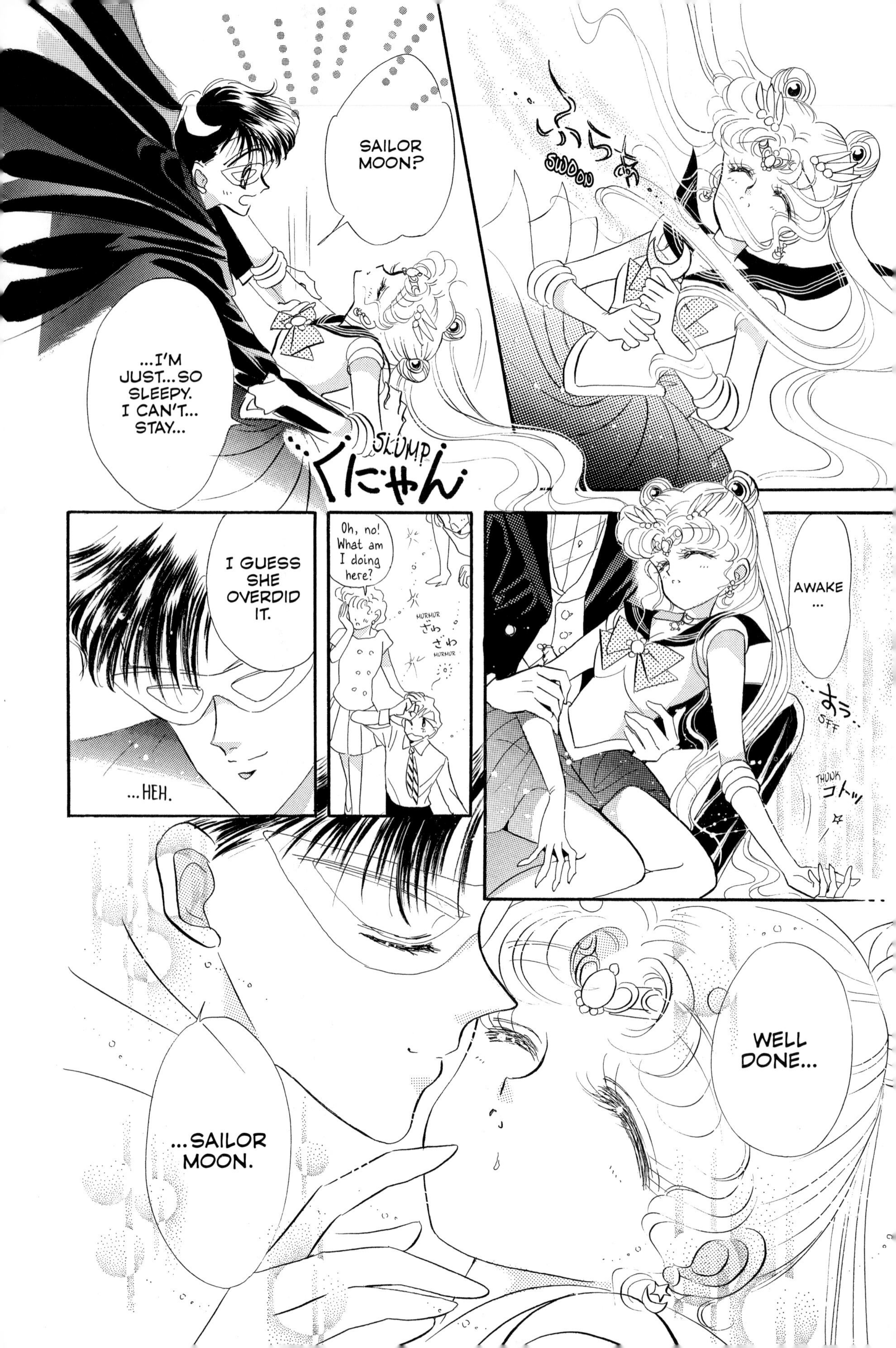
ふら
SWOON
SAILOR MOON?
...I'M JUST...SO SLEEPY. I CAN'T... STAY...
SLUMP
くにゃん
AWAKE ...
すっ
SFF
THUNK
コトッ
Oh, no! What am I doing here?
MURMUR
ざわ
ざわ
MURMUR
I GUESS SHE OVERDID IT.
...HEH.
WELL DONE...
...SAILOR MOON.

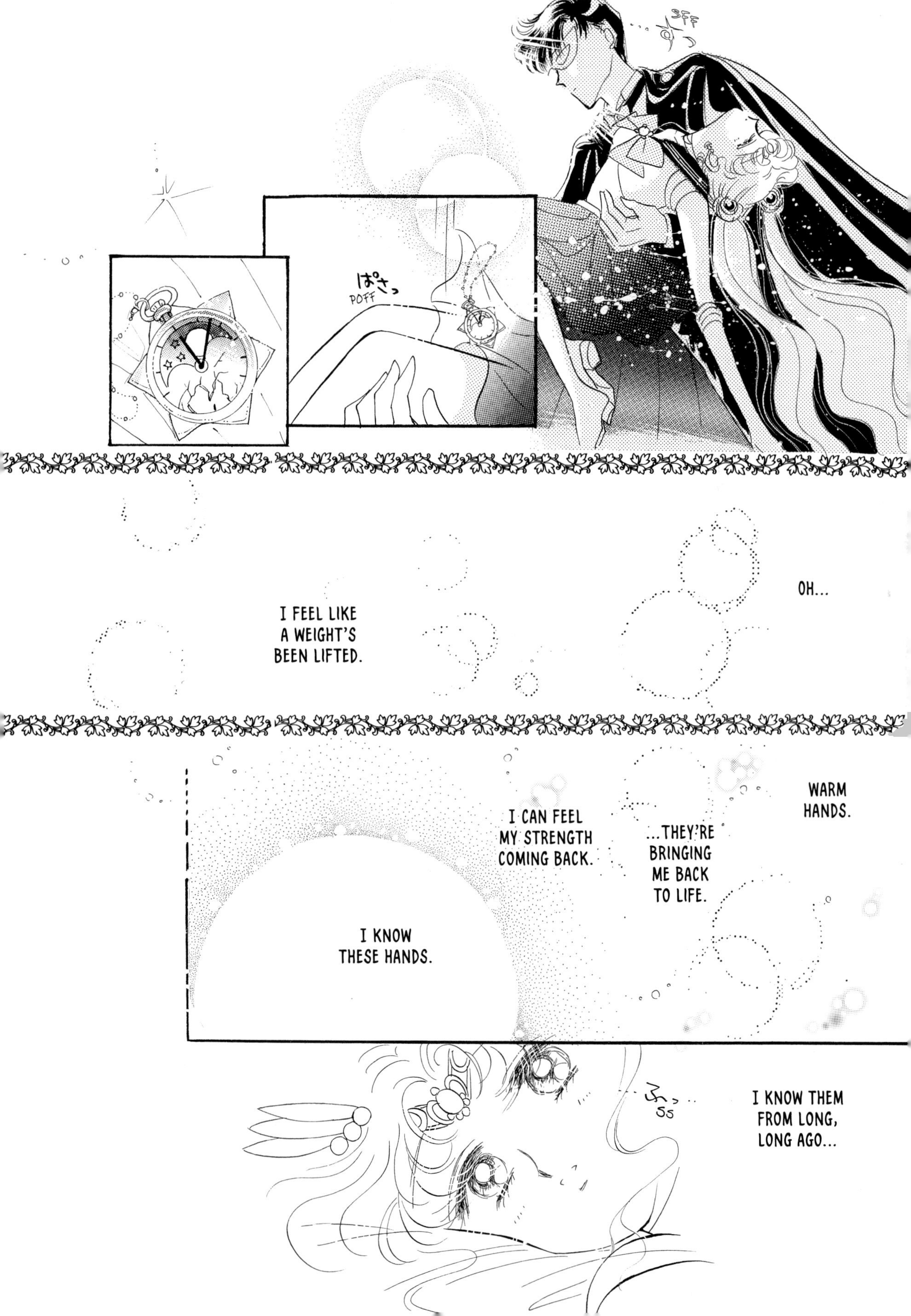

...すっ
SFF
ぱさっ
POFF
OH...
I FEEL LIKE A WEIGHT'S BEEN LIFTED.
WARM HANDS.
...THEY'RE BRINGING ME BACK TO LIFE.
I CAN FEEL MY STRENGTH COMING BACK.
I KNOW THESE HANDS.
...ふっ...
SS
I KNOW THEM FROM LONG, LONG AGO...

WHERE...
...AM I?
I FEEL LIKE...
...I WAS DREAMING.
IT WAS THAT SAME DREAM AGAIN.
A VOICE...
...CALLING ME.
A MAN'S VOICE...
WHO...
...IS HE?
SPARKLE
A POCKET WATCH...
...SHOWING THE PHASES OF THE MOON.
...IT'S BROKEN.
...WHOSE IS IT?
COULD IT BE...
B-DMP

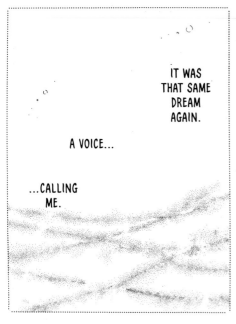

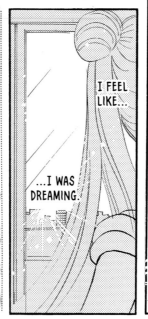

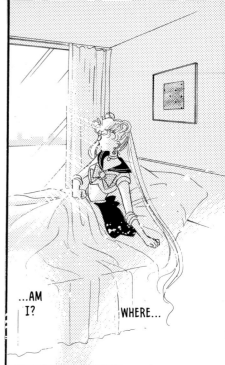

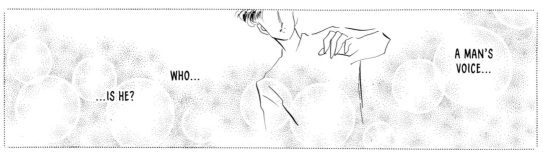

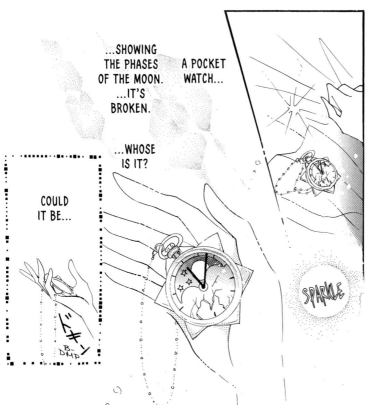

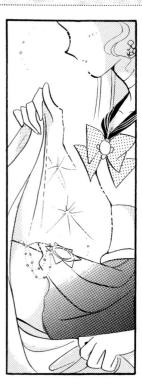

...TUXEDO MASK'S?

BEEEAM

ドキン
B-DMP

...OH YEAH.

I TRANS-FORMED...

...RIGHT IN FRONT OF HIM.

HE'S NOT MY ENEMY.

SHOONG

...HE CAN'T BE. HE'S ALWAYS RESCUING ME.

I WANT TO KNOW.

WHY?

IT'S LIKE... HE KNOWS EVERYTHING ABOUT ME.

WHO ARE YOU?

...KA-CHAK

WHY ARE YOU ALWAYS HELPING ME?

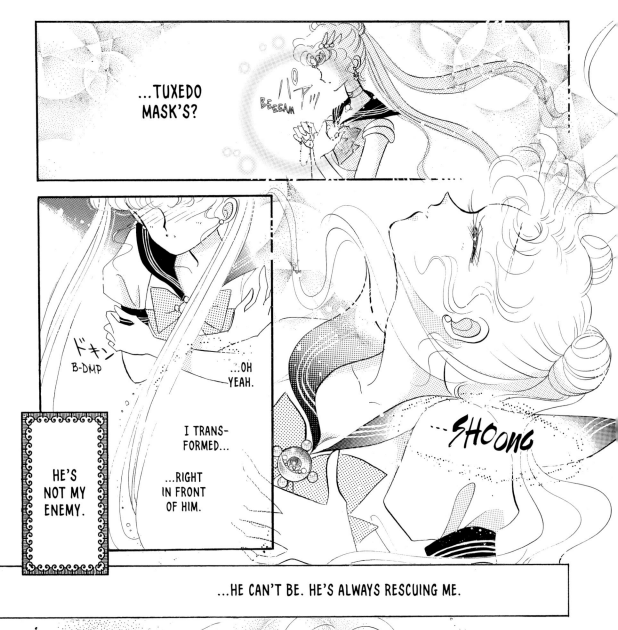

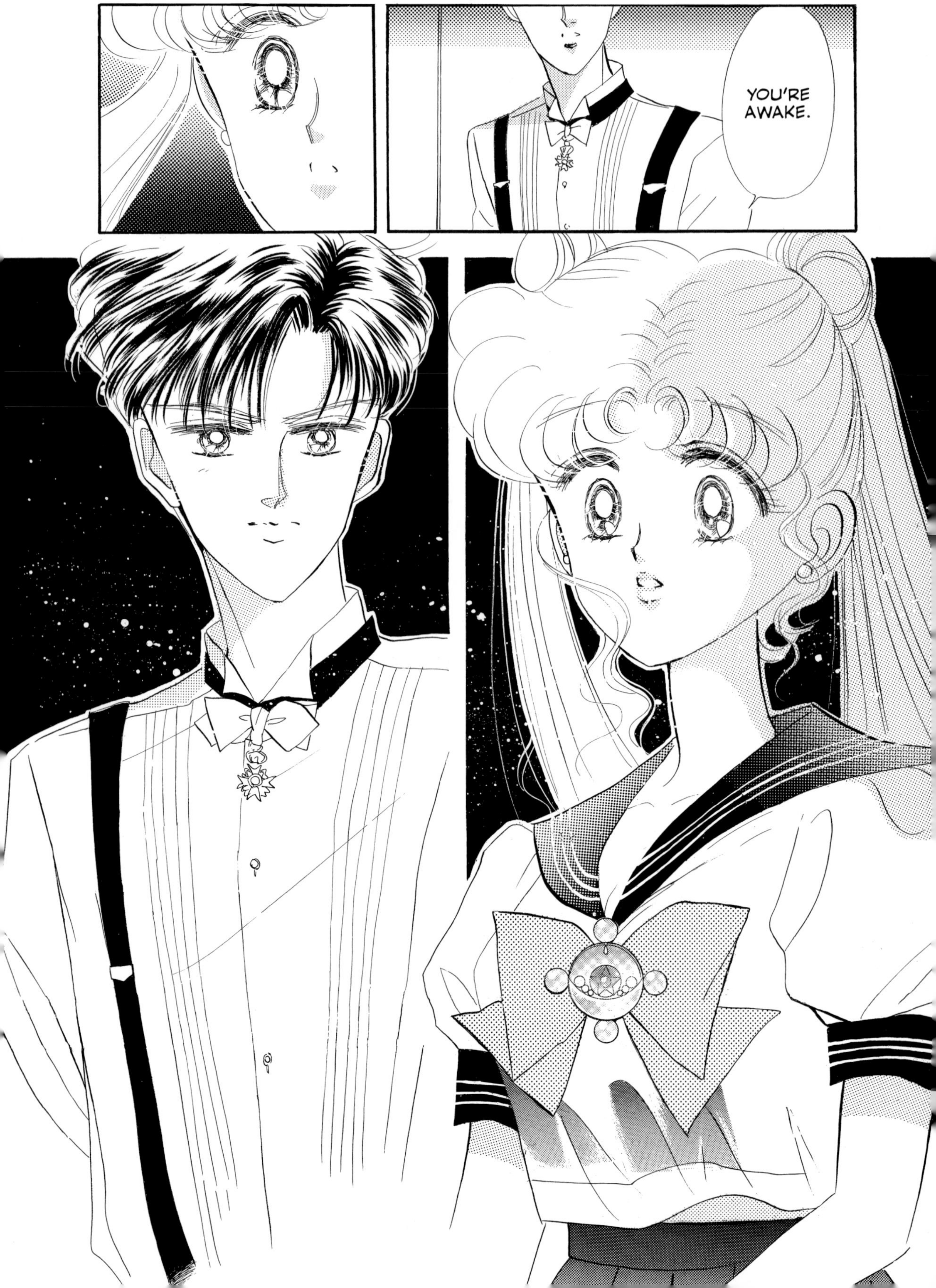
YOU'RE AWAKE.

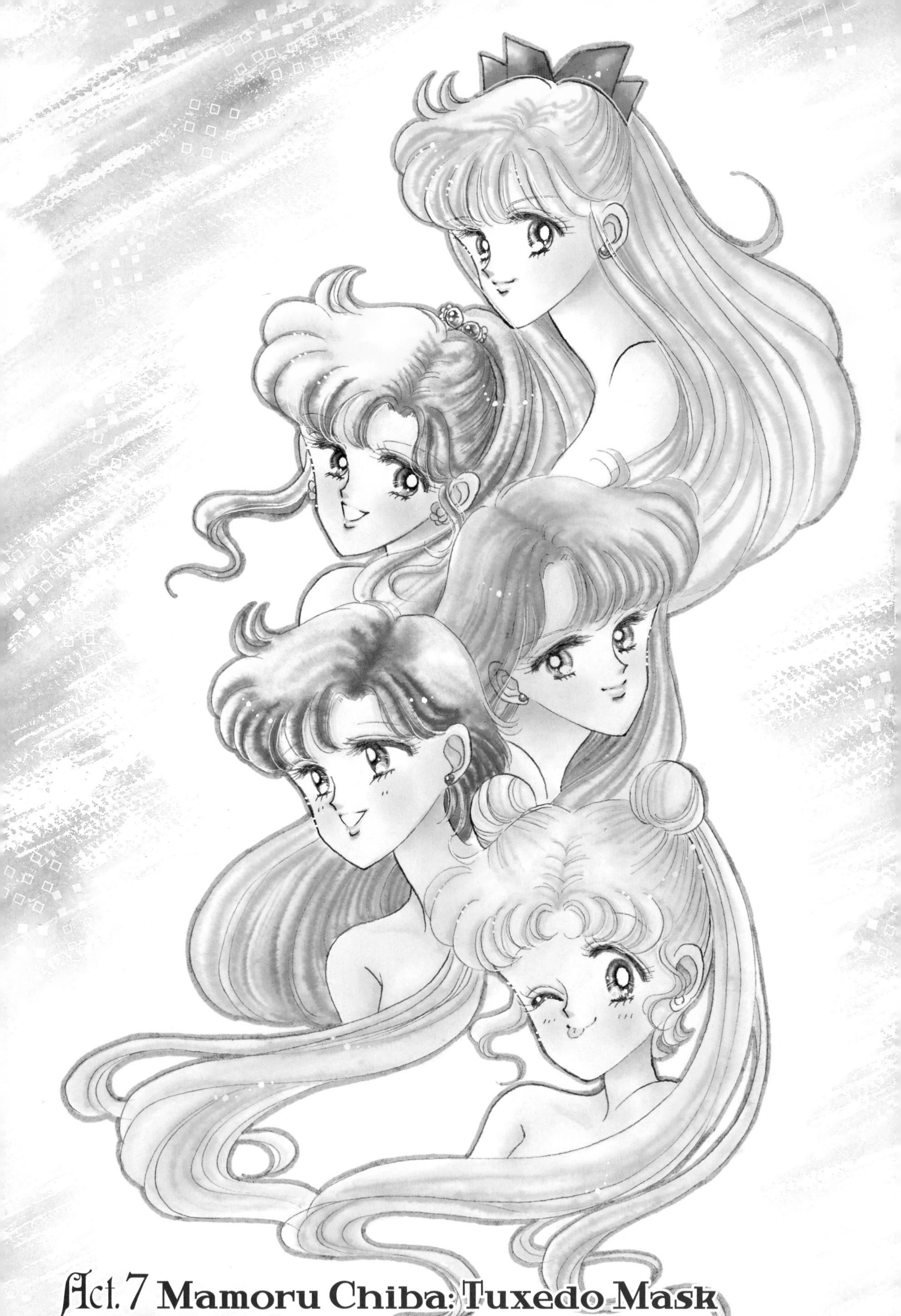

Act. 7 Mamoru Chiba: Tuxedo Mask

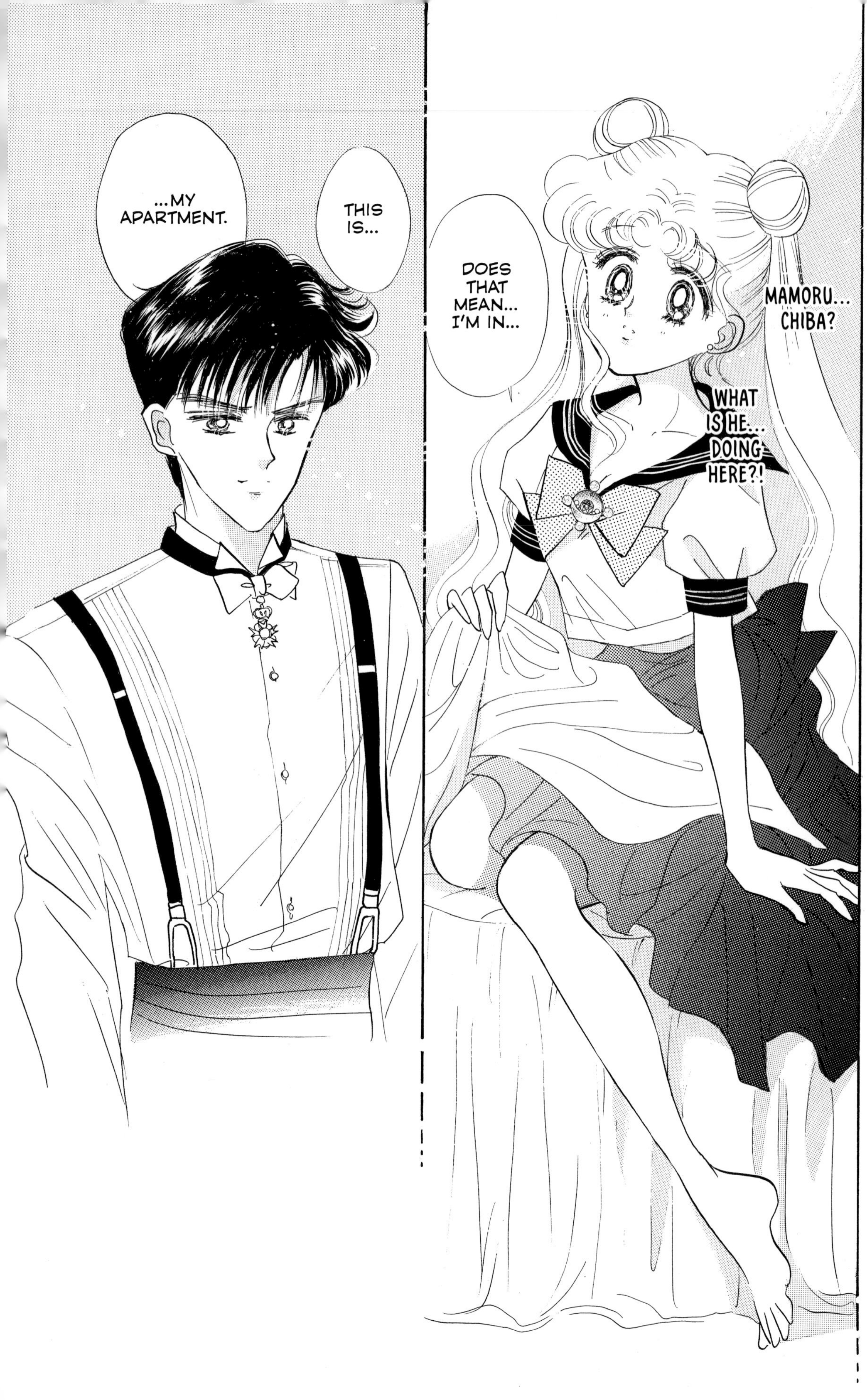
MAMORU... CHIBA?
WHAT IS HE... DOING HERE?!
DOES THAT MEAN... I'M IN...
THIS IS...
...MY APARTMENT.

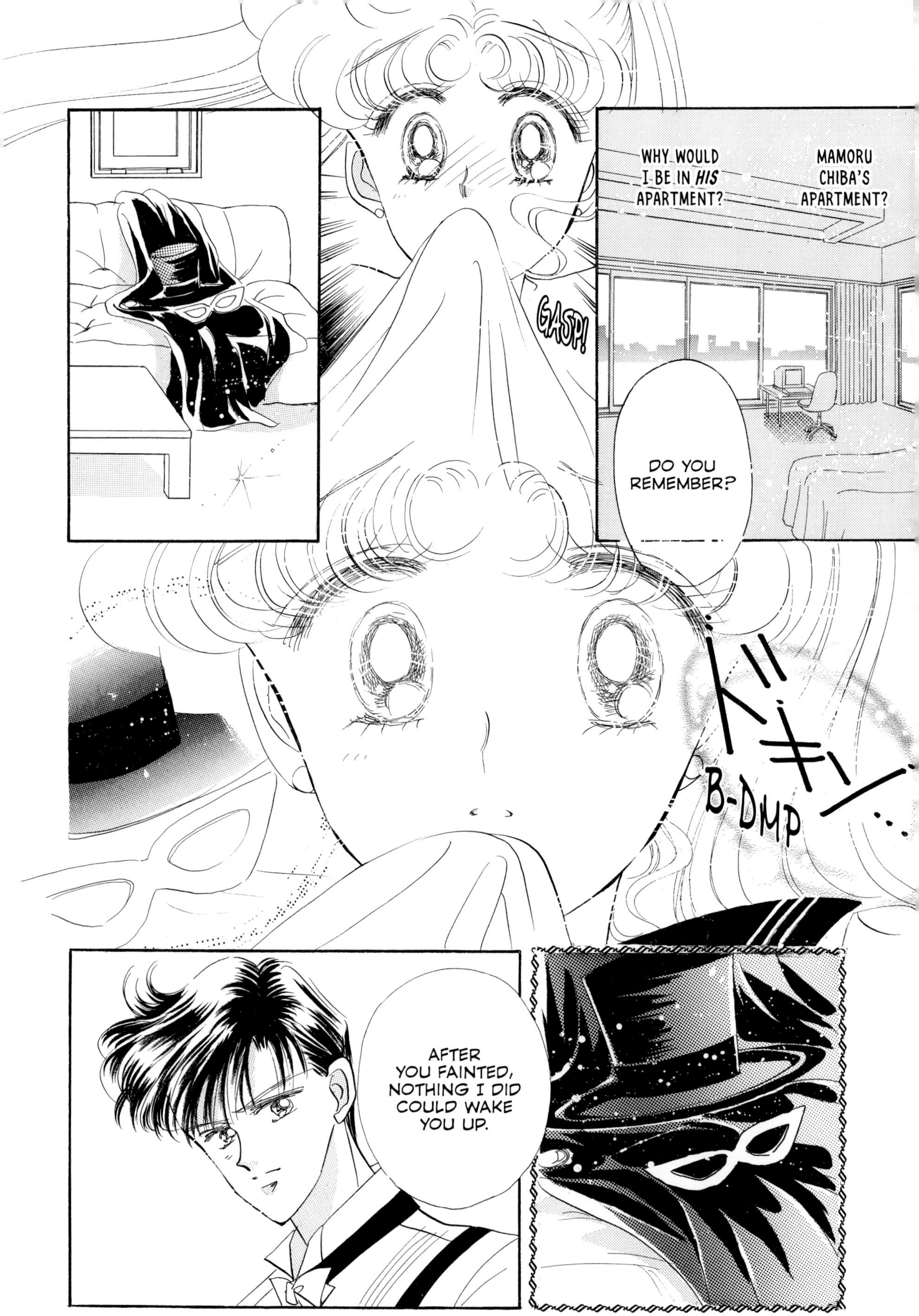
MAMORU CHIBA'S APARTMENT?
WHY WOULD I BE IN *HIS* APARTMENT?
GASP!
DO YOU REMEMBER?
———
B-DMP
AFTER YOU FAINTED, NOTHING I DID COULD WAKE YOU UP.

AND THAT...

...MEDALLION.

B-DMP

...THAT VOICE.

IT'S THE SAME...

...LOW VOICE.

I RECOGNIZE...

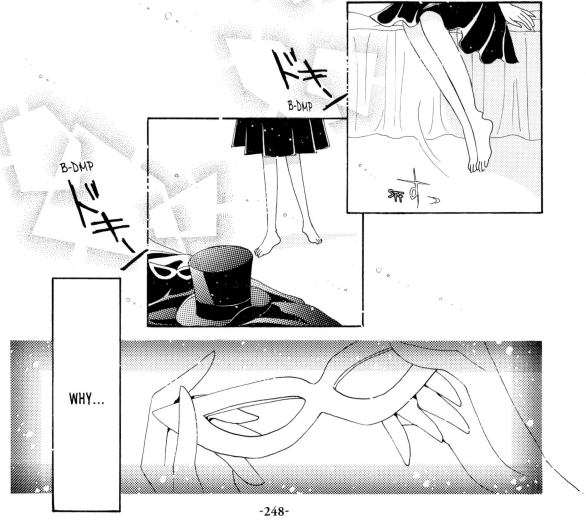

B-DMP

B-DMP

SFF

WHY...

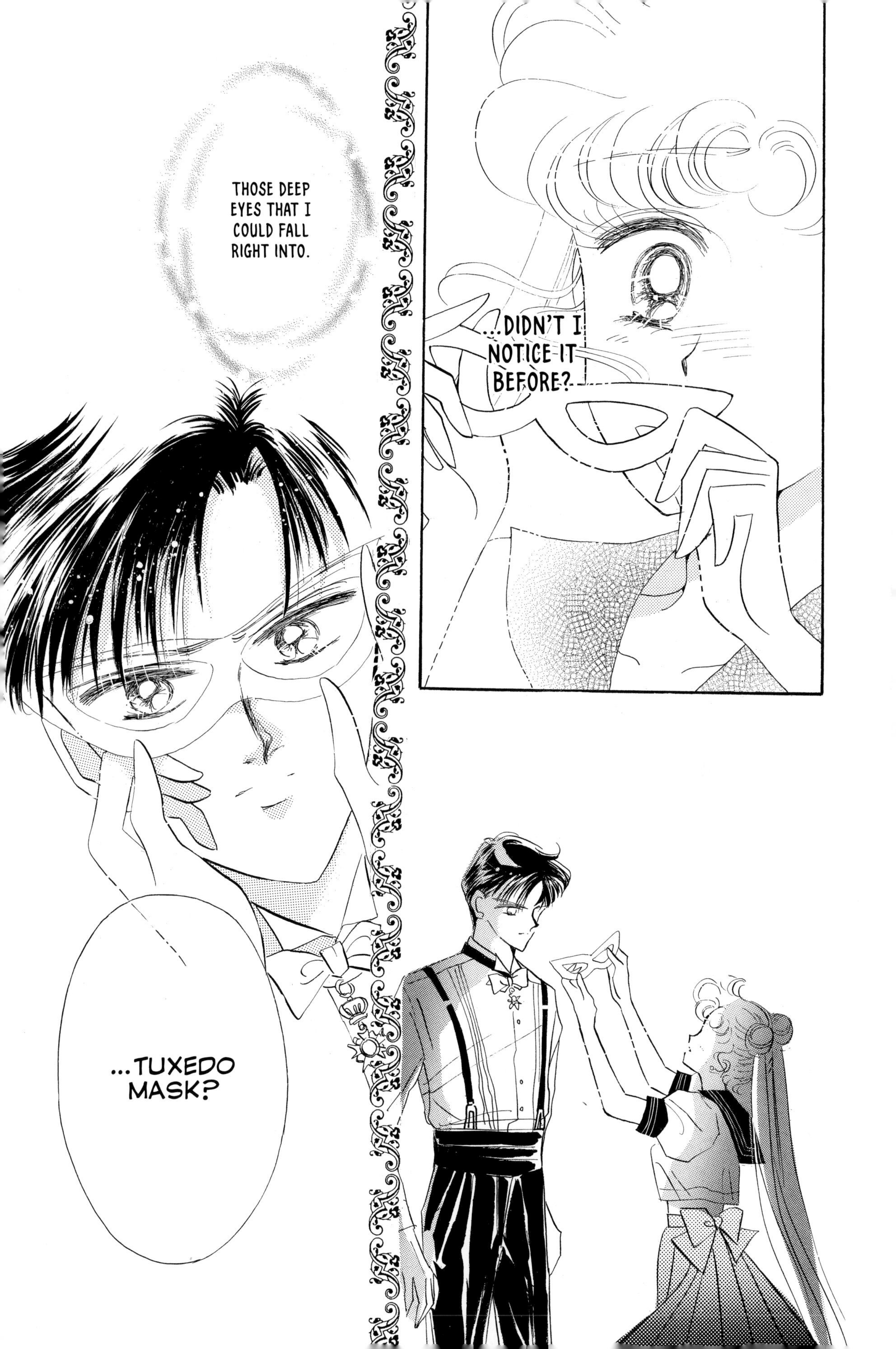
...DIDN'T I NOTICE IT BEFORE?
THOSE DEEP EYES THAT I COULD FALL RIGHT INTO.
...TUXEDO MASK?

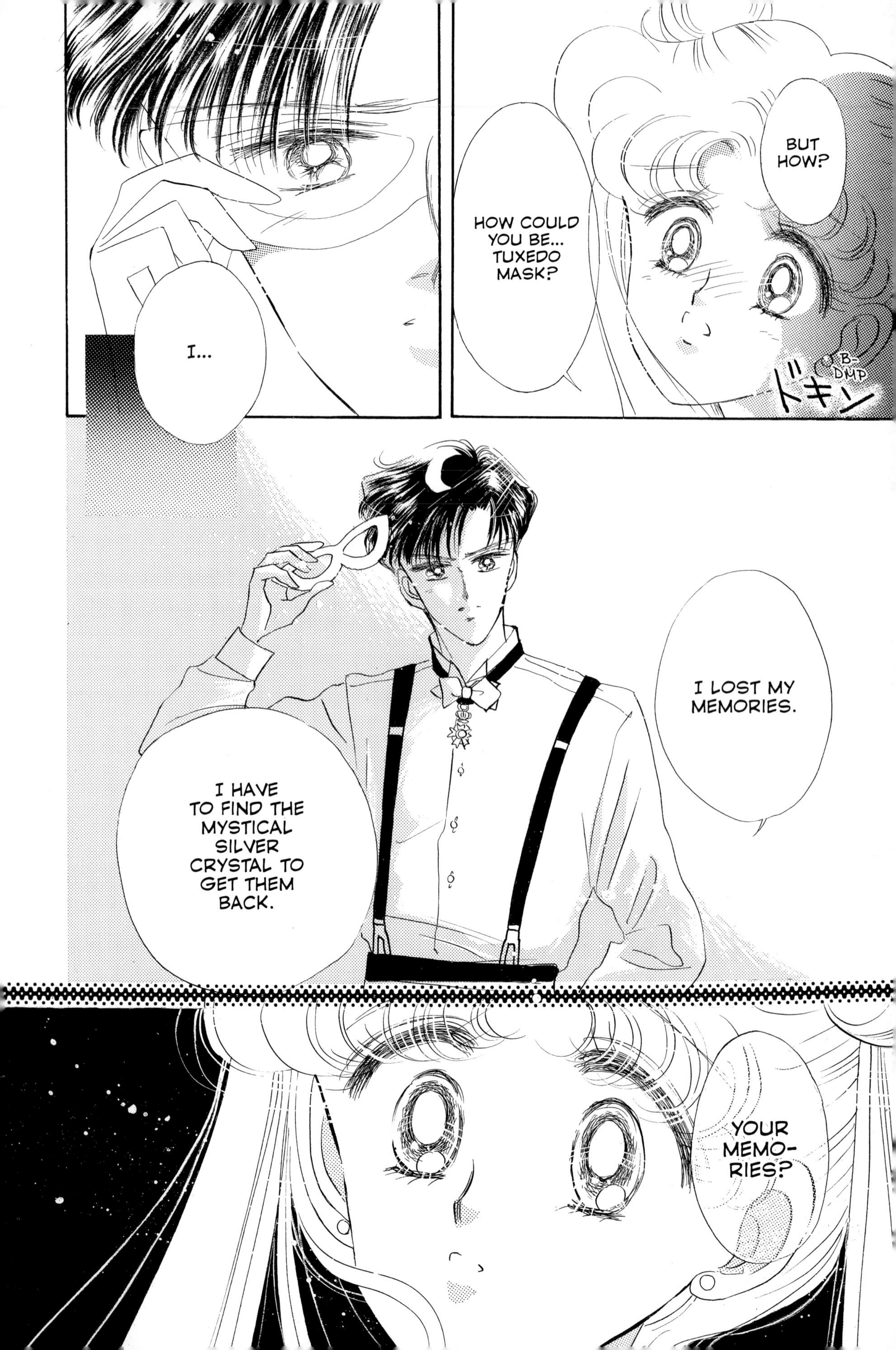
BUT HOW?
HOW COULD YOU BE... TUXEDO MASK?
B-DMP
ドキン
I...
I LOST MY MEMORIES.
I HAVE TO FIND THE MYSTICAL SILVER CRYSTAL TO GET THEM BACK.
YOUR MEMO-RIES?

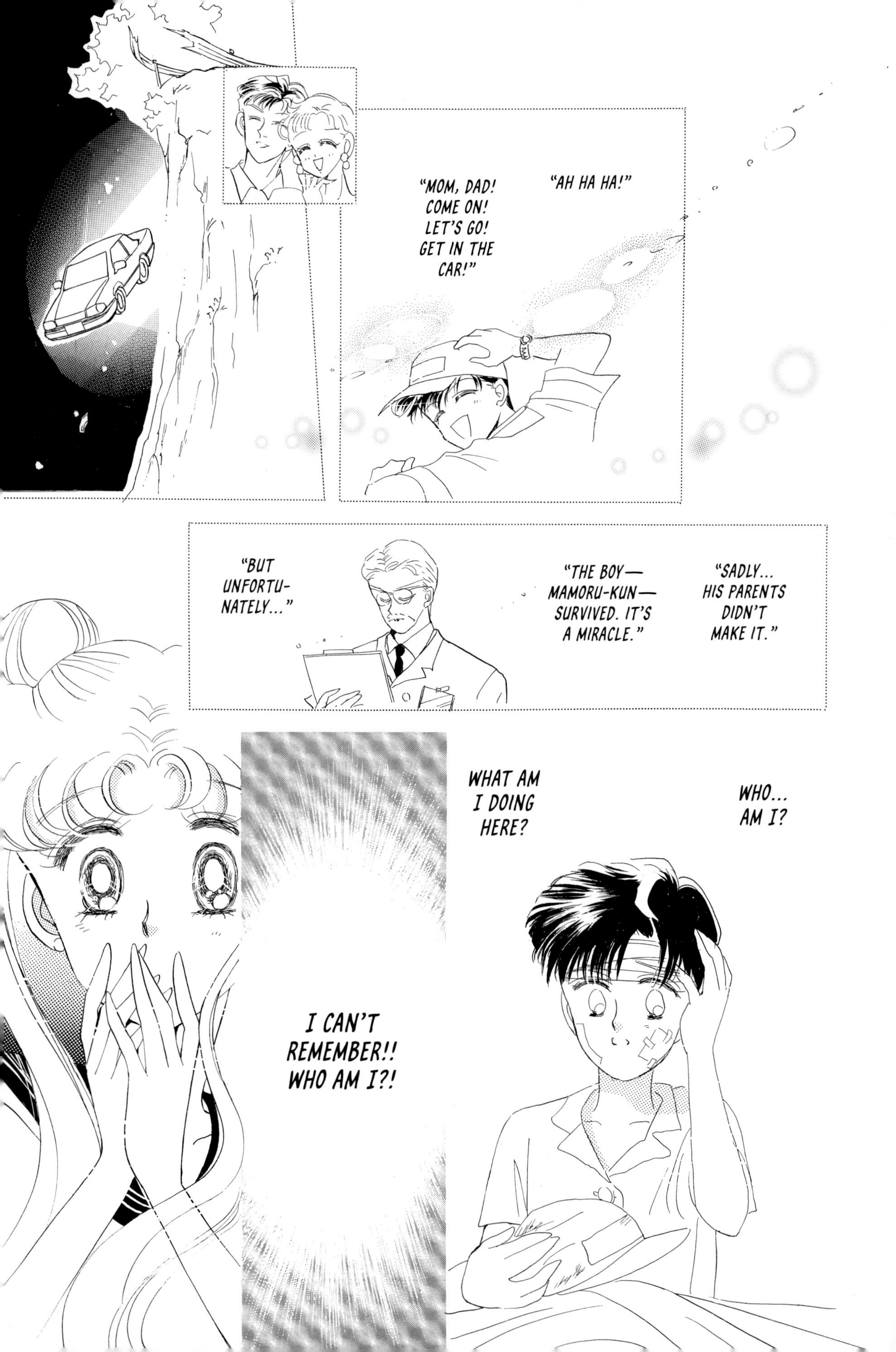
"AH HA HA!"
"MOM, DAD! COME ON! LET'S GO! GET IN THE CAR!"
"SADLY... HIS PARENTS DIDN'T MAKE IT."
"THE BOY—MAMORU-KUN—SURVIVED. IT'S A MIRACLE."
"BUT UNFORTU-NATELY..."
WHO... AM I?
WHAT AM I DOING HERE?
I CAN'T REMEMBER!! WHO AM I?!

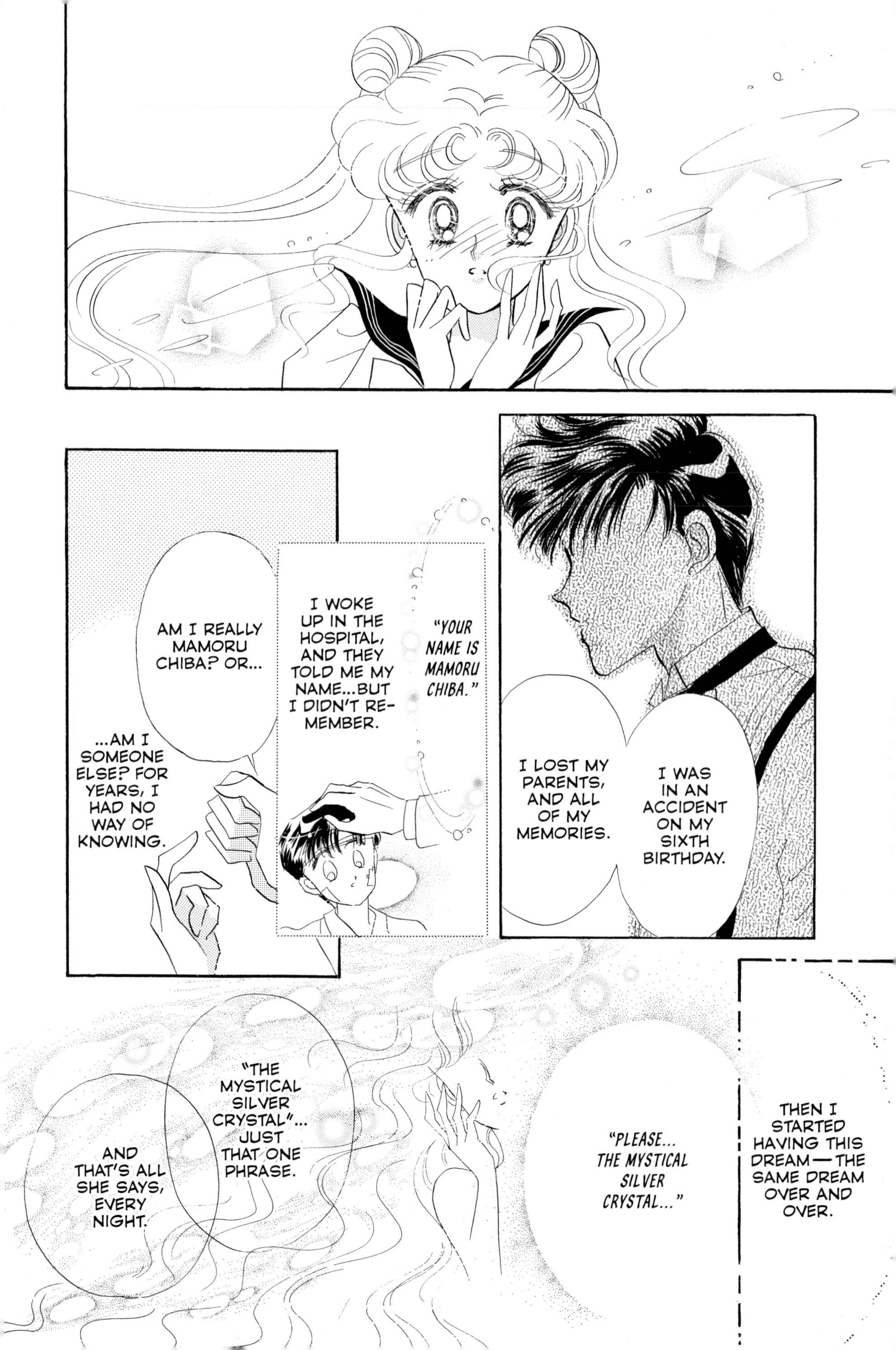
I WAS IN AN ACCIDENT ON MY SIXTH BIRTHDAY.
I LOST MY PARENTS, AND ALL OF MY MEMORIES.
"YOUR NAME IS MAMORU CHIBA."
I WOKE UP IN THE HOSPITAL, AND THEY TOLD ME MY NAME...BUT I DIDN'T RE-MEMBER.
AM I REALLY MAMORU CHIBA? OR...
...AM I SOMEONE ELSE? FOR YEARS, I HAD NO WAY OF KNOWING.
THEN I STARTED HAVING THIS DREAM—THE SAME DREAM OVER AND OVER.
"PLEASE... THE MYSTICAL SILVER CRYSTAL..."
"THE MYSTICAL SILVER CRYSTAL"... JUST THAT ONE PHRASE.
AND THAT'S ALL SHE SAYS, EVERY NIGHT.

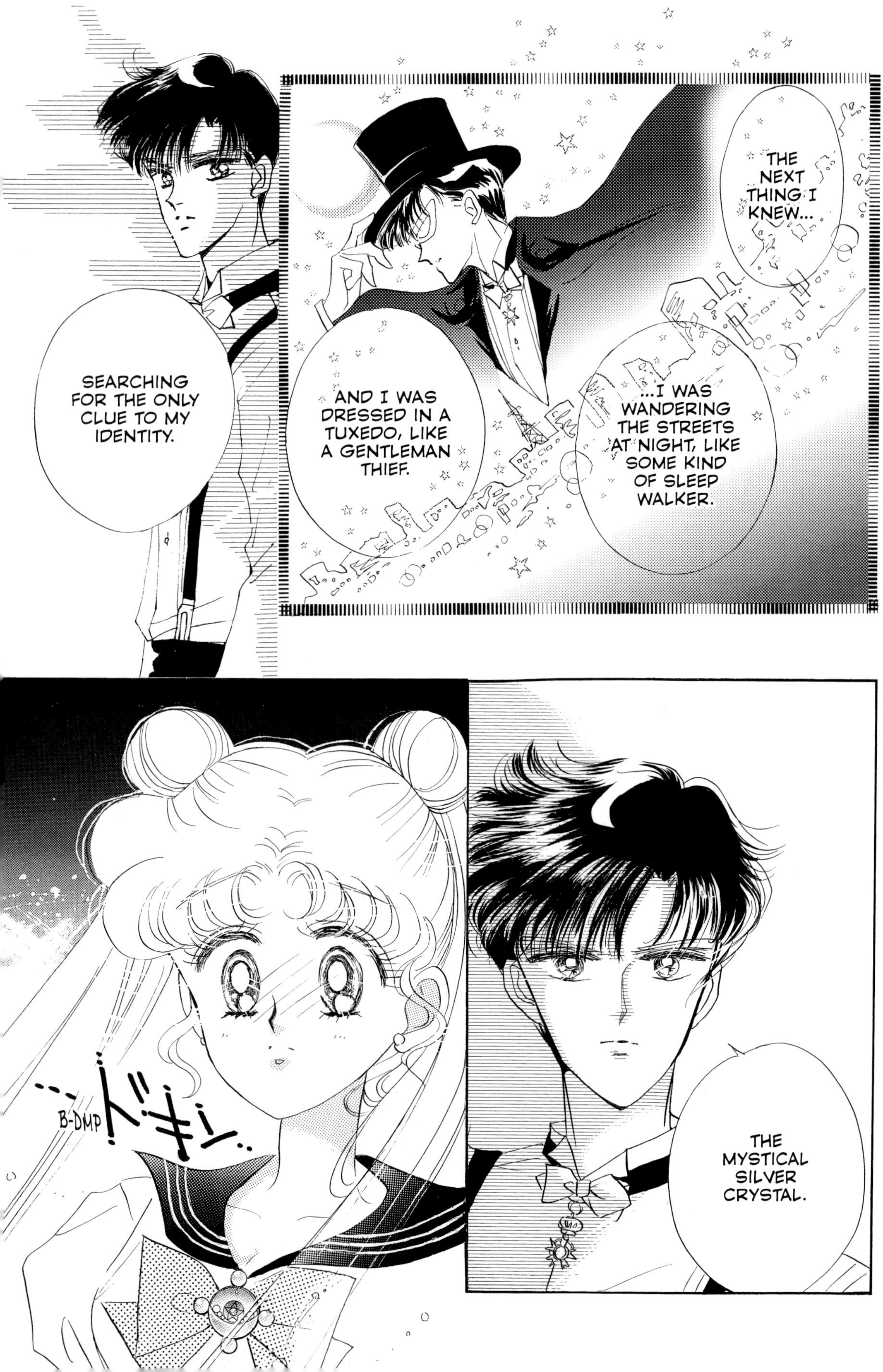
THE NEXT THING I KNEW...
...I WAS WANDERING THE STREETS AT NIGHT, LIKE SOME KIND OF SLEEP WALKER.
AND I WAS DRESSED IN A TUXEDO, LIKE A GENTLEMAN THIEF.
SEARCHING FOR THE ONLY CLUE TO MY IDENTITY.
THE MYSTICAL SILVER CRYSTAL.
B-DMP
ドキン

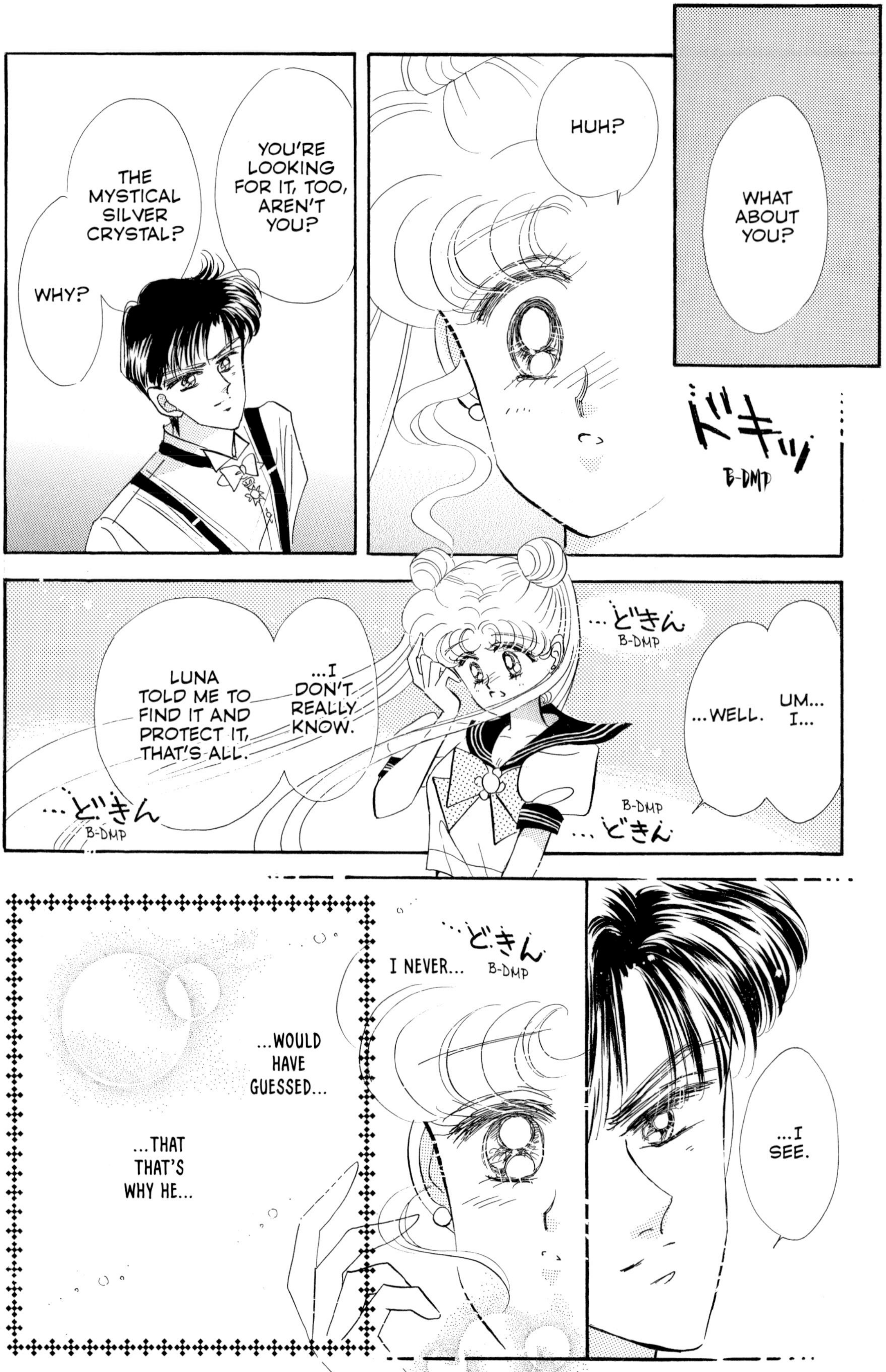
WHAT ABOUT YOU?
HUH?
ドキッ
B-DMP
YOU'RE LOOKING FOR IT, TOO, AREN'T YOU?
THE MYSTICAL SILVER CRYSTAL?
WHY?
UM... I...
...WELL.
...どきん
B-DMP
...どきん
B-DMP
...I DON'T REALLY KNOW.
LUNA TOLD ME TO FIND IT AND PROTECT IT, THAT'S ALL.
...どきん
B-DMP
...I SEE.
...どきん
B-DMP
I NEVER...
...WOULD HAVE GUESSED...
...THAT THAT'S WHY HE...

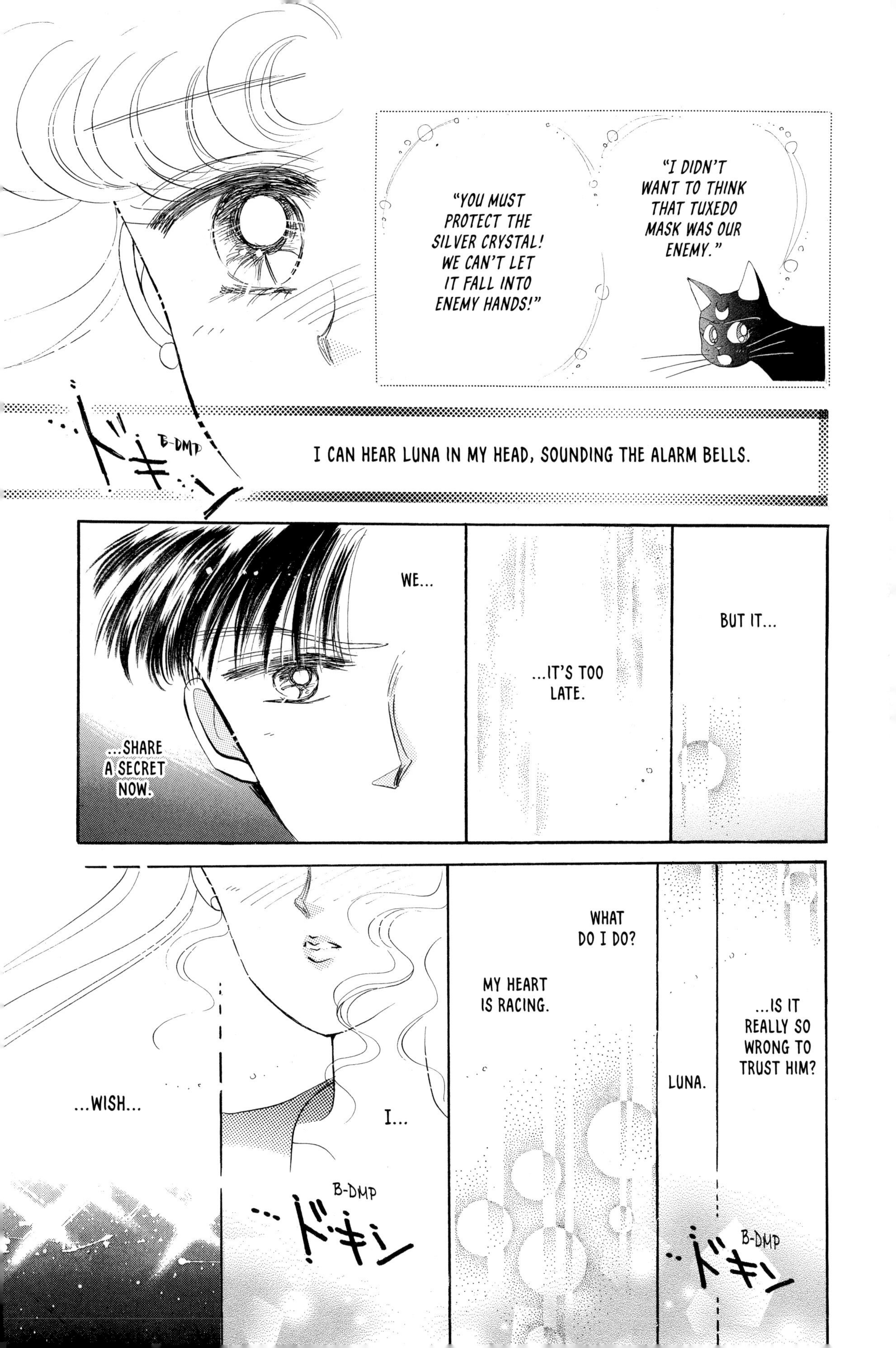
"I DIDN'T WANT TO THINK THAT TUXEDO MASK WAS OUR ENEMY."
"YOU MUST PROTECT THE SILVER CRYSTAL! WE CAN'T LET IT FALL INTO ENEMY HANDS!"
I CAN HEAR LUNA IN MY HEAD, SOUNDING THE ALARM BELLS.
B-DMP
BUT IT...
...IT'S TOO LATE.
WE...
...SHARE A SECRET NOW.
...IS IT REALLY SO WRONG TO TRUST HIM?
LUNA.
B-DMP
WHAT DO I DO?
MY HEART IS RACING.
I...
...WISH...
B-DMP

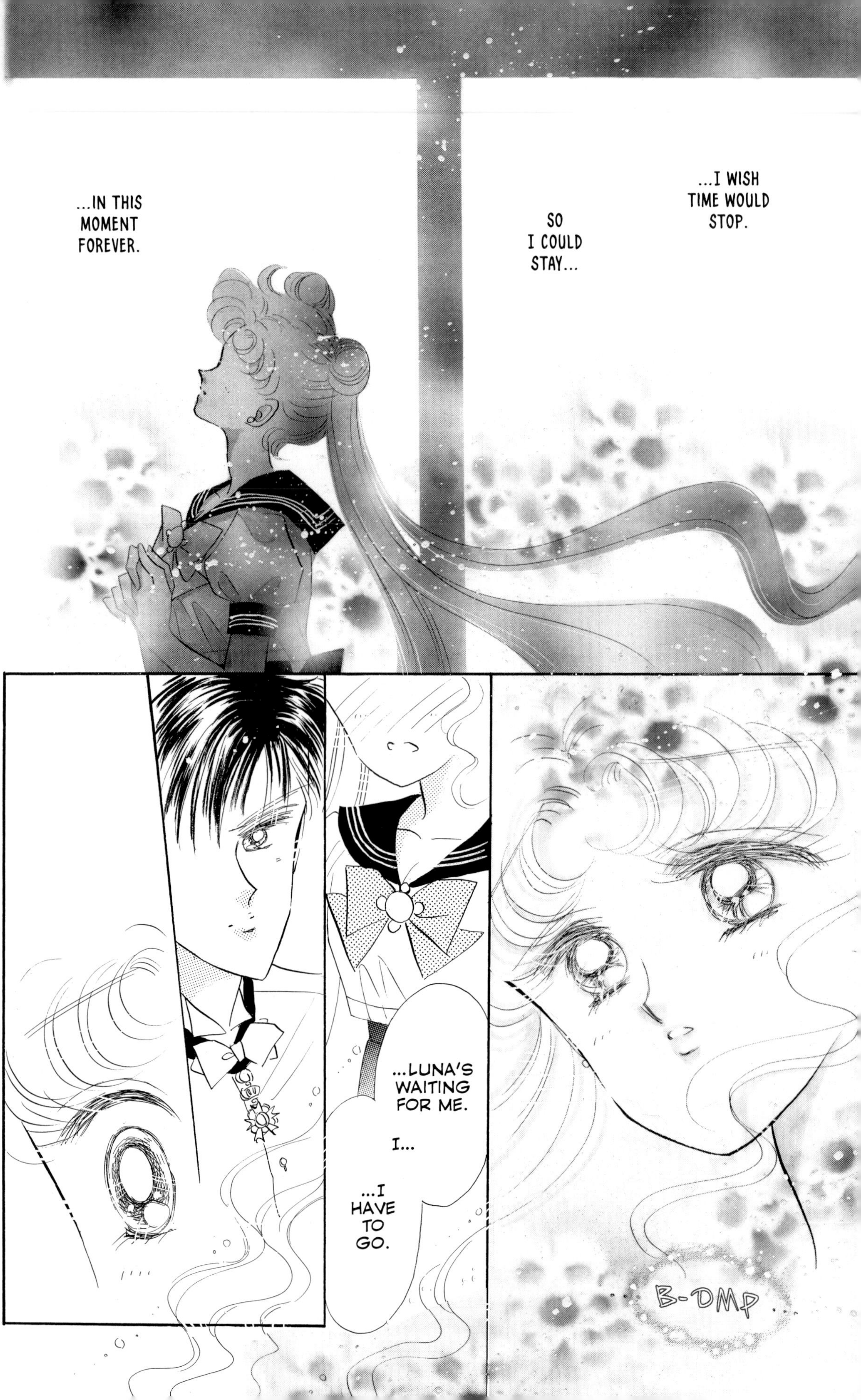

...I WISH TIME WOULD STOP.
SO I COULD STAY...
...IN THIS MOMENT FOREVER.
B-DMP
...LUNA'S WAITING FOR ME.
I...
...I HAVE TO GO.

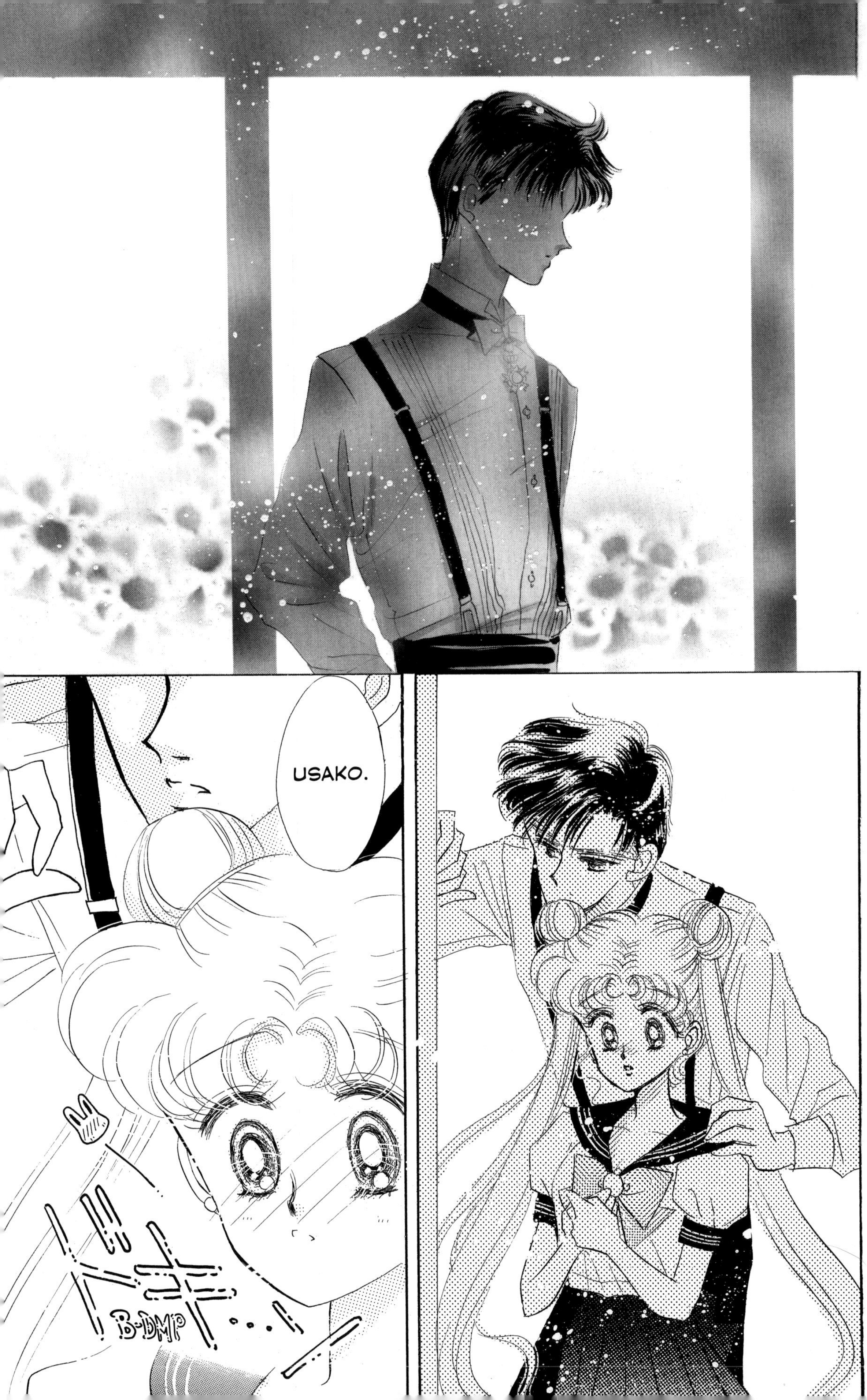
USAKO.
B-DMP

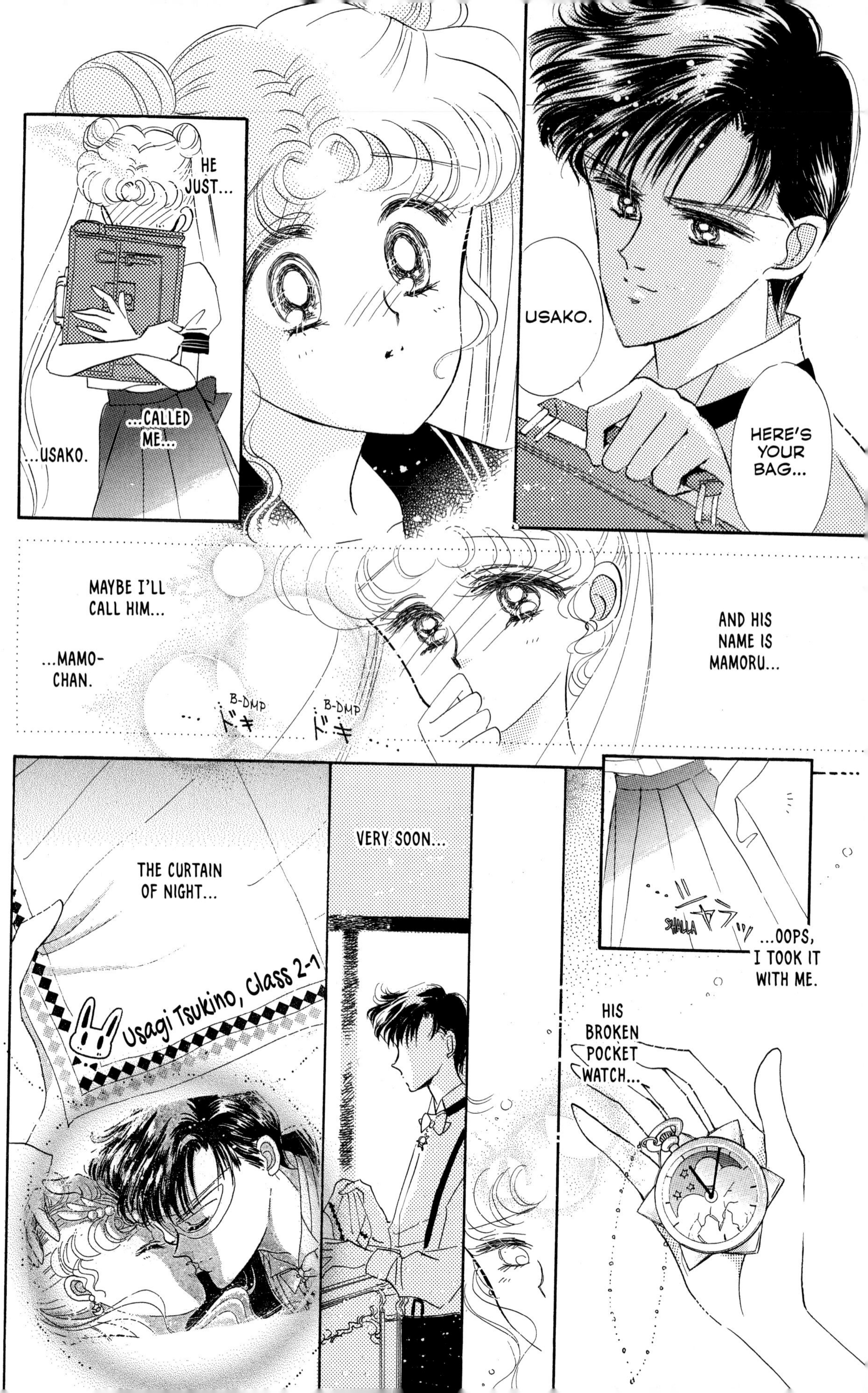
USAKO.
HERE'S YOUR BAG...
HE JUST...
...CALLED ME...
...USAKO.
AND HIS NAME IS MAMORU...
MAYBE I'LL CALL HIM...
...MAMO-CHAN.
B-DMP
ドキ
B-DMP
ドキ
SHALLA
...OOPS, I TOOK IT WITH ME.
HIS BROKEN POCKET WATCH...
VERY SOON...
THE CURTAIN OF NIGHT...
Usagi Tsukino, Class 2-1

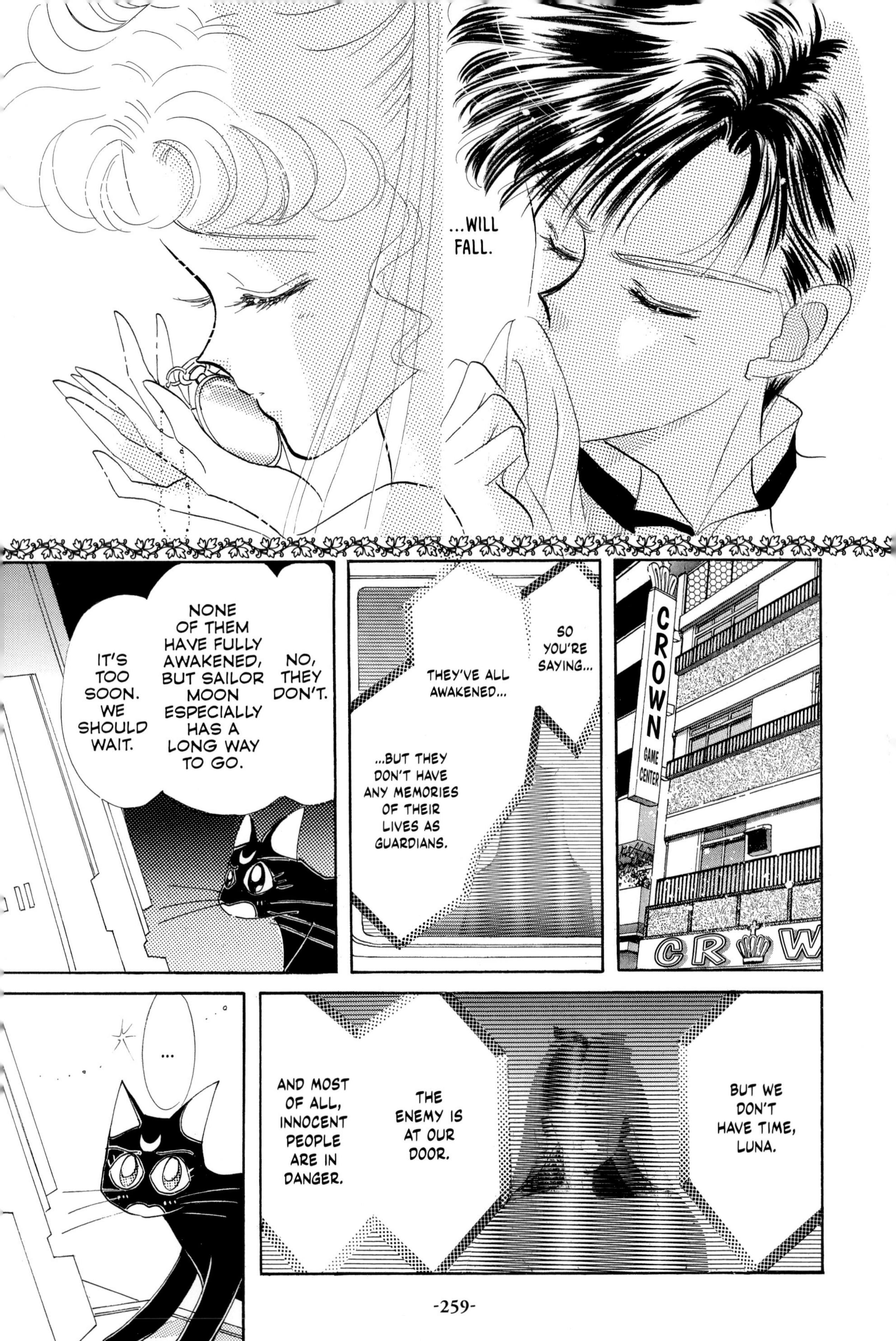
...WILL FALL.
CROWN
GAME CENTER
CROWN
SO YOU'RE SAYING...
THEY'VE ALL AWAKENED...
...BUT THEY DON'T HAVE ANY MEMORIES OF THEIR LIVES AS GUARDIANS.
NO, THEY DON'T.
NONE OF THEM HAVE FULLY AWAKENED, BUT SAILOR MOON ESPECIALLY HAS A LONG WAY TO GO.
IT'S TOO SOON. WE SHOULD WAIT.
BUT WE DON'T HAVE TIME, LUNA.
THE ENEMY IS AT OUR DOOR.
AND MOST OF ALL, INNOCENT PEOPLE ARE IN DANGER.
...

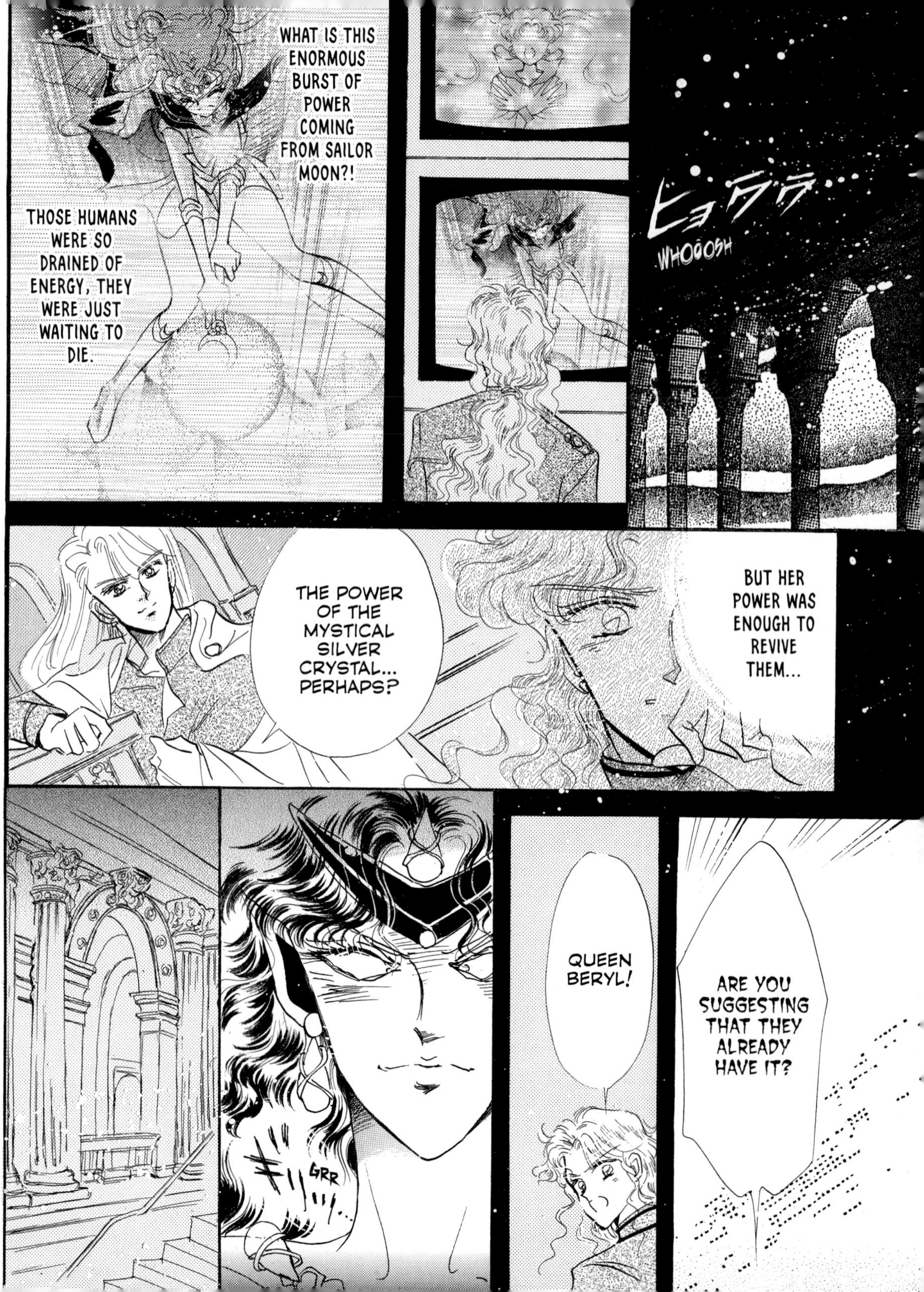
WHOOOSH
WHAT IS THIS ENORMOUS BURST OF POWER COMING FROM SAILOR MOON?!
THOSE HUMANS WERE SO DRAINED OF ENERGY, THEY WERE JUST WAITING TO DIE.
BUT HER POWER WAS ENOUGH TO REVIVE THEM...
THE POWER OF THE MYSTICAL SILVER CRYSTAL... PERHAPS?
ARE YOU SUGGESTING THAT THEY ALREADY HAVE IT?
QUEEN BERYL!
GRR

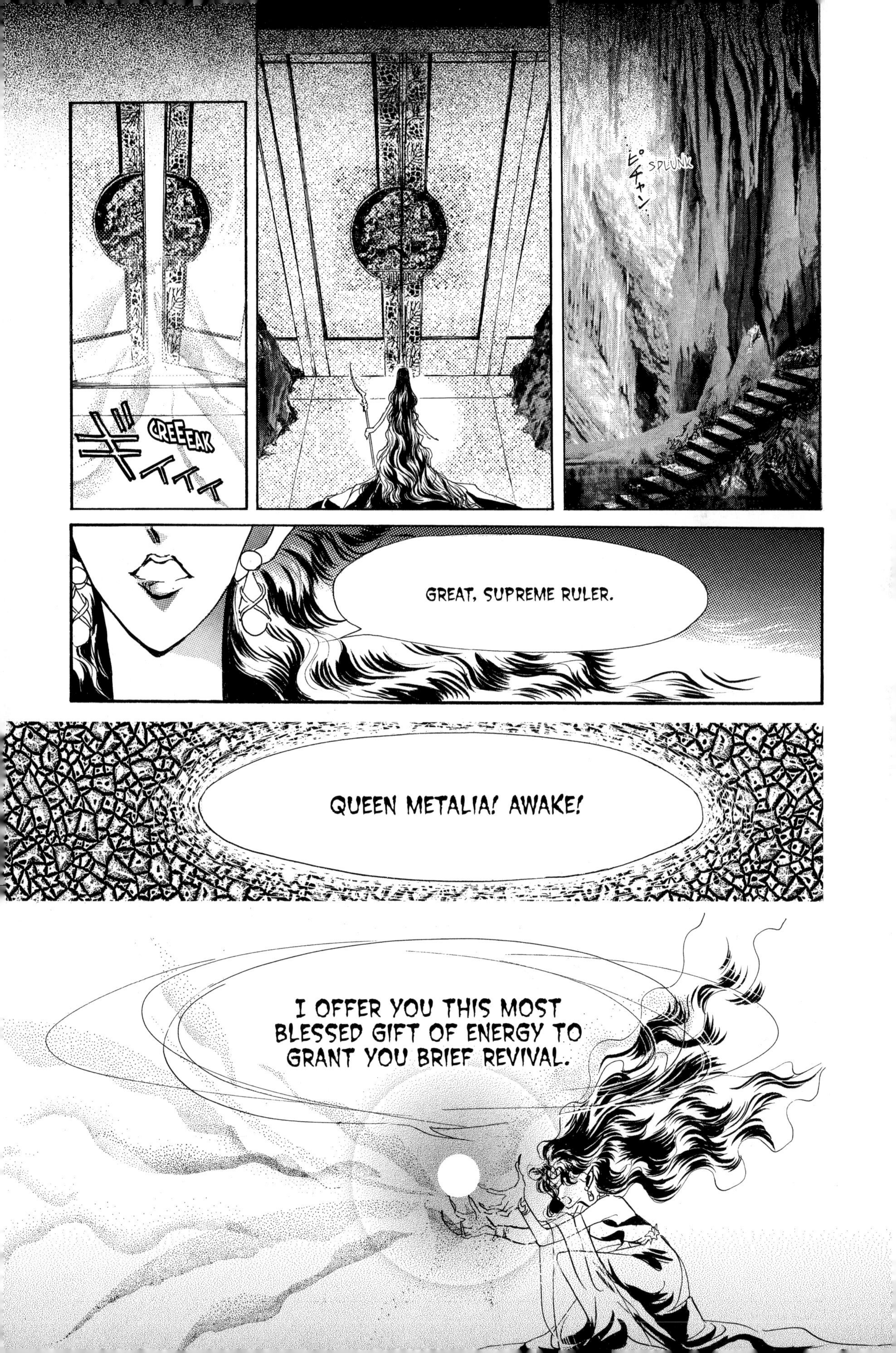

ピチャン
SPLUNK
ギイイイ
CREEEAK
GREAT, SUPREME RULER.
QUEEN METALIA! AWAKE!
I OFFER YOU THIS MOST BLESSED GIFT OF ENERGY TO GRANT YOU BRIEF REVIVAL.

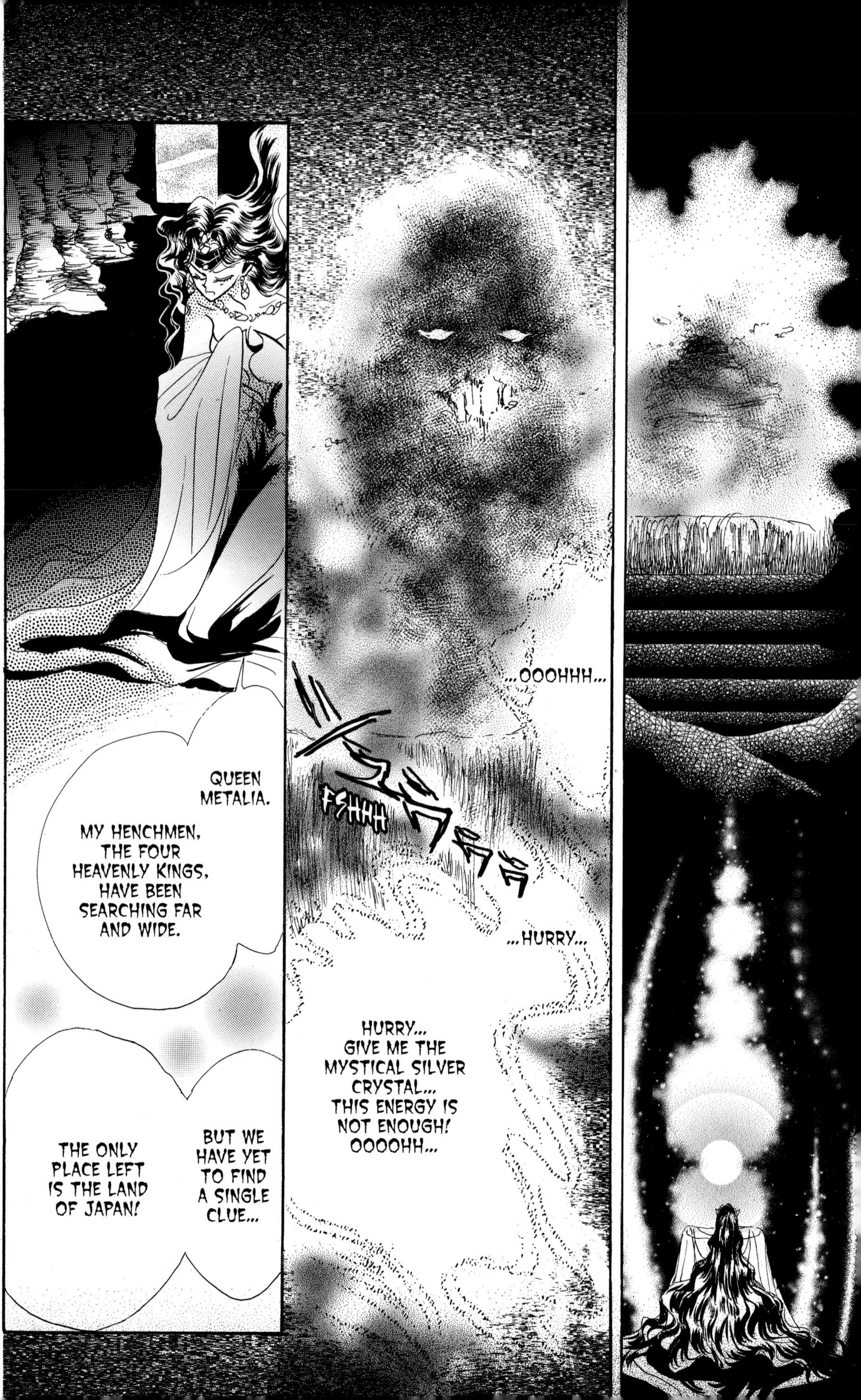
...OOOHHH...
FSHHH
...HURRY...
HURRY... GIVE ME THE MYSTICAL SILVER CRYSTAL... THIS ENERGY IS NOT ENOUGH! OOOOHH...
QUEEN METALIA.
MY HENCHMEN, THE FOUR HEAVENLY KINGS, HAVE BEEN SEARCHING FAR AND WIDE.
BUT WE HAVE YET TO FIND A SINGLE CLUE...
THE ONLY PLACE LEFT IS THE LAND OF JAPAN!

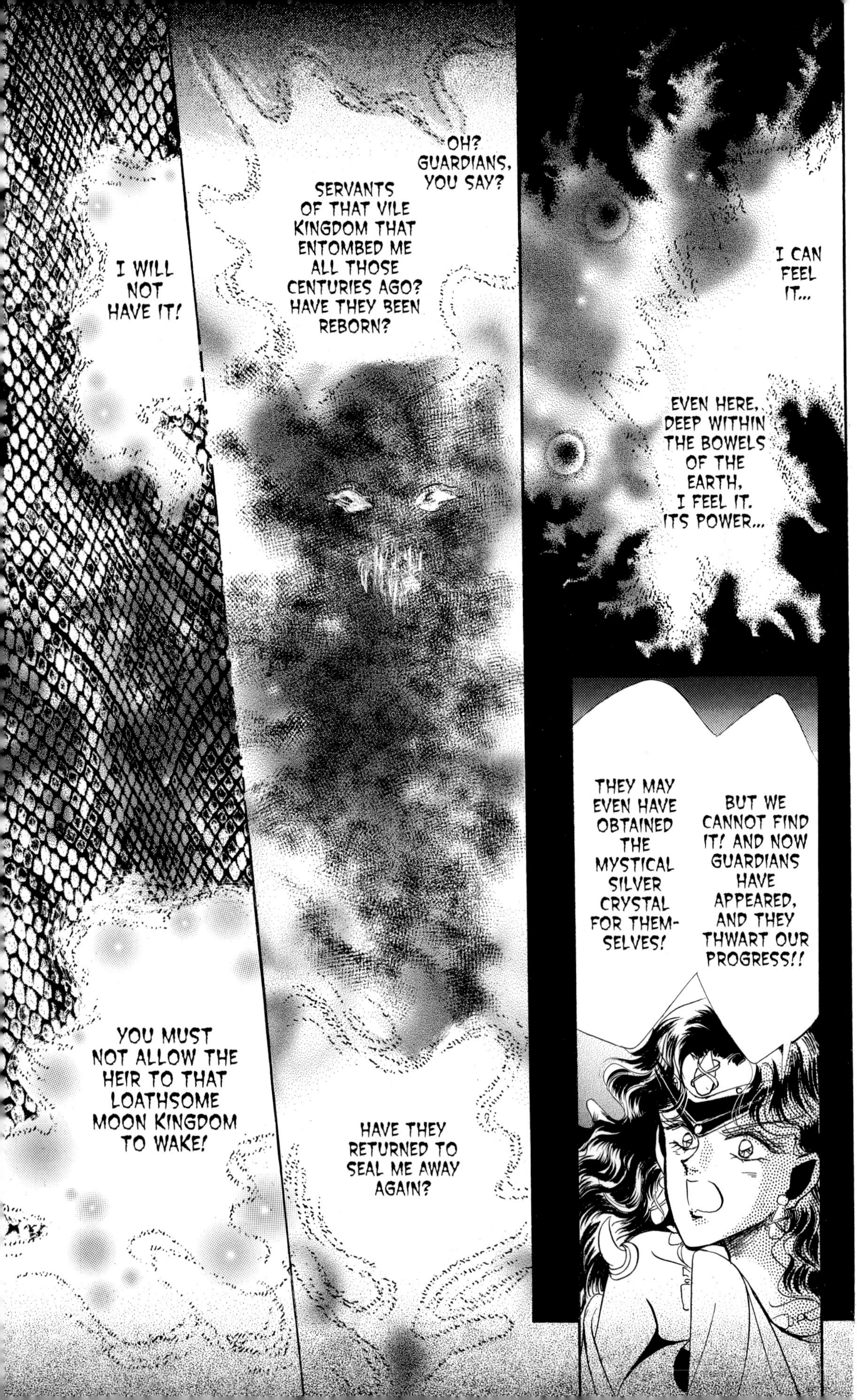
I CAN FEEL IT...
EVEN HERE, DEEP WITHIN THE BOWELS OF THE EARTH, I FEEL IT. ITS POWER...
BUT WE CANNOT FIND IT! AND NOW GUARDIANS HAVE APPEARED, AND THEY THWART OUR PROGRESS!!
THEY MAY EVEN HAVE OBTAINED THE MYSTICAL SILVER CRYSTAL FOR THEM-SELVES!
OH? GUARDIANS, YOU SAY?
SERVANTS OF THAT VILE KINGDOM THAT ENTOMBED ME ALL THOSE CENTURIES AGO? HAVE THEY BEEN REBORN?
HAVE THEY RETURNED TO SEAL ME AWAY AGAIN?
I WILL NOT HAVE IT!
YOU MUST NOT ALLOW THE HEIR TO THAT LOATHSOME MOON KINGDOM TO WAKE!

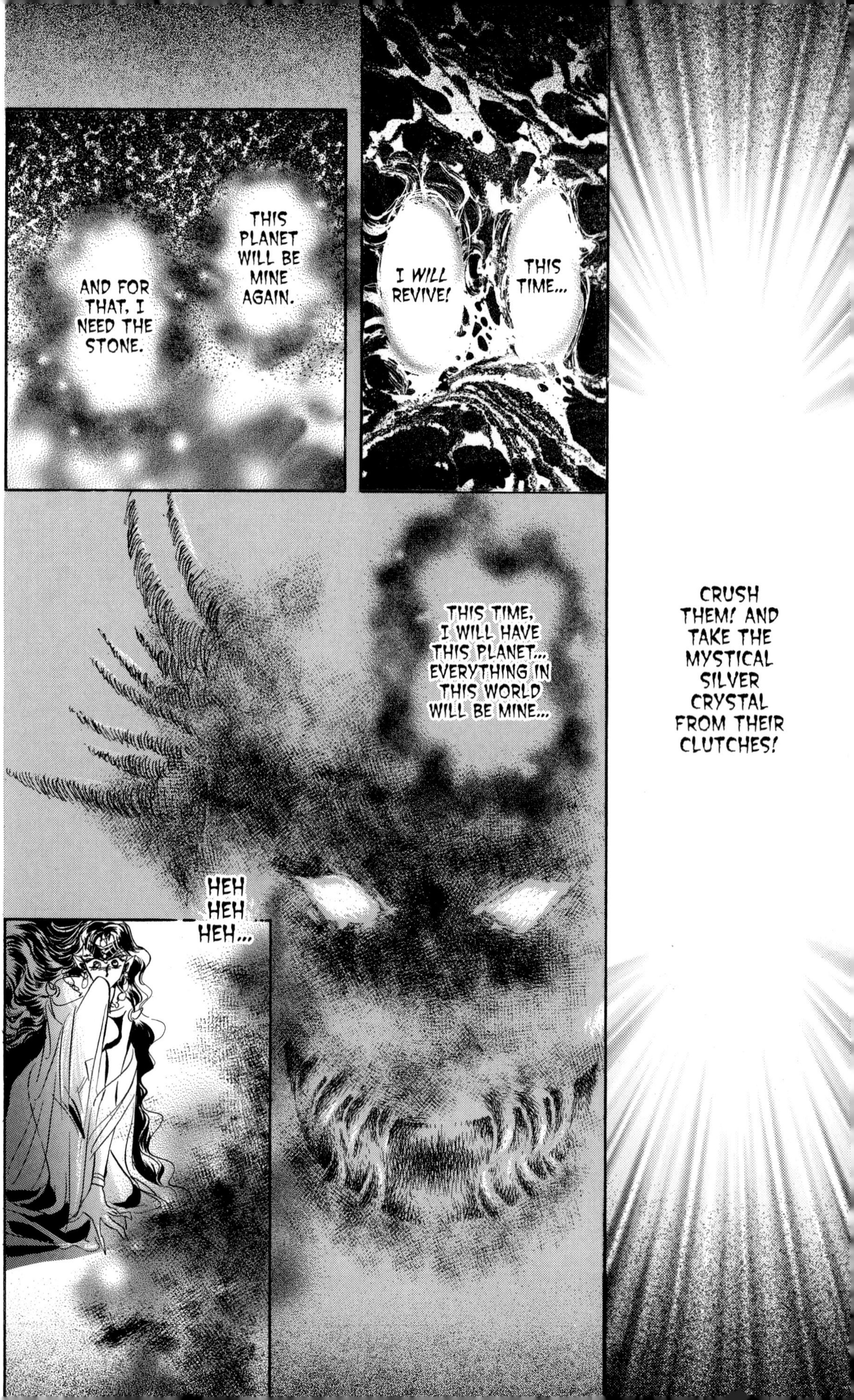
CRUSH THEM! AND TAKE THE MYSTICAL SILVER CRYSTAL FROM THEIR CLUTCHES!
THIS TIME...
I *WILL* REVIVE!
THIS PLANET WILL BE MINE AGAIN.
AND FOR THAT, I NEED THE STONE.
THIS TIME, I WILL HAVE THIS PLANET... EVERYTHING IN THIS WORLD WILL BE MINE...
HEH HEH HEH...

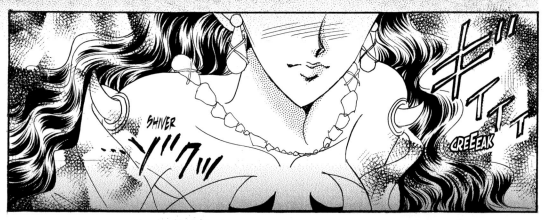

ギィィィ
CREEEAK
ゾクッ
SHIVER
EVERY TIME I SEE HER, SHE HAS GROWN DARKER AND MORE MASSIVE...
IF I TRULY AWAKEN QUEEN METALIA,
SHE MAY DEVOUR THIS ENTIRE PLANET.
BUT THERE'S NO TURNING BACK.
ONCE I BROKE THAT SEAL... MY FATE WAS SET.

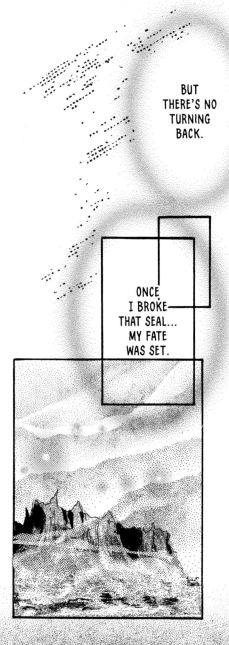

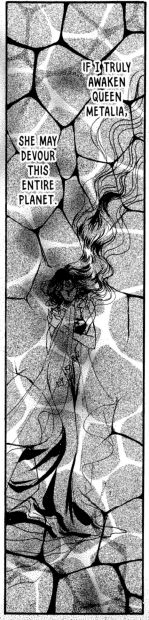

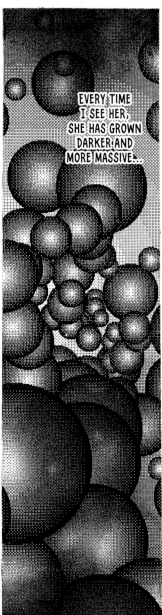

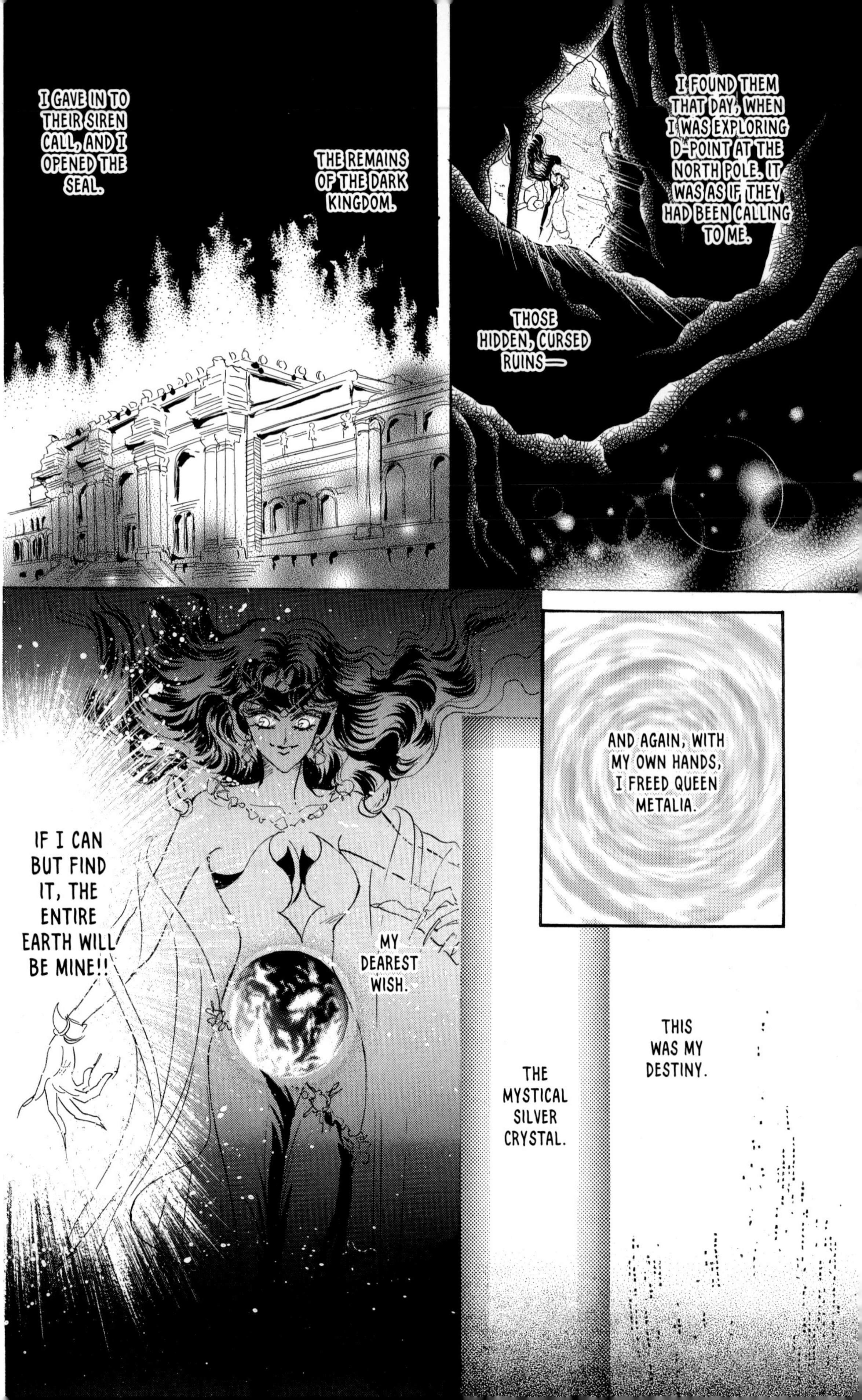
I FOUND THEM THAT DAY, WHEN I WAS EXPLORING D-POINT AT THE NORTH POLE. IT WAS AS IF THEY HAD BEEN CALLING TO ME.
THOSE HIDDEN, CURSED RUINS—
THE REMAINS OF THE DARK KINGDOM.
I GAVE IN TO THEIR SIREN CALL, AND I OPENED THE SEAL.
AND AGAIN, WITH MY OWN HANDS, I FREED QUEEN METALIA.
THIS WAS MY DESTINY.
THE MYSTICAL SILVER CRYSTAL.
MY DEAREST WISH.
IF I CAN BUT FIND IT, THE ENTIRE EARTH WILL BE MINE!!

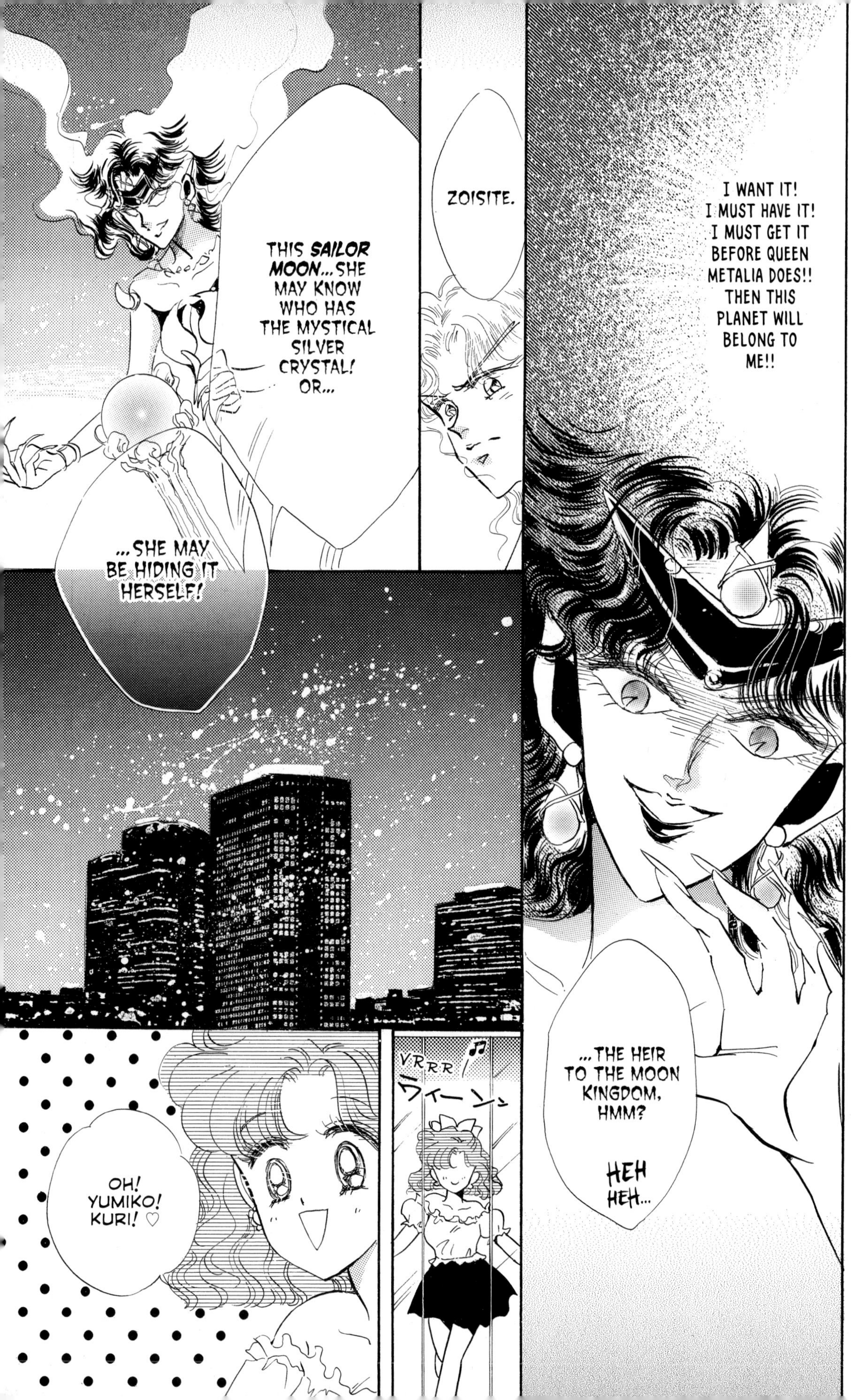

I WANT IT! I MUST HAVE IT! I MUST GET IT BEFORE QUEEN METALIA DOES!! THEN THIS PLANET WILL BELONG TO ME!!
...THE HEIR TO THE MOON KINGDOM, HMM?
HEH HEH...
ZOISITE.
THIS *SAILOR MOON*...SHE MAY KNOW WHO HAS THE MYSTICAL SILVER CRYSTAL! OR...
...SHE MAY BE HIDING IT HERSELF!
VRRR ♪
ウィーン
OH! YUMIKO! KURI! ♡

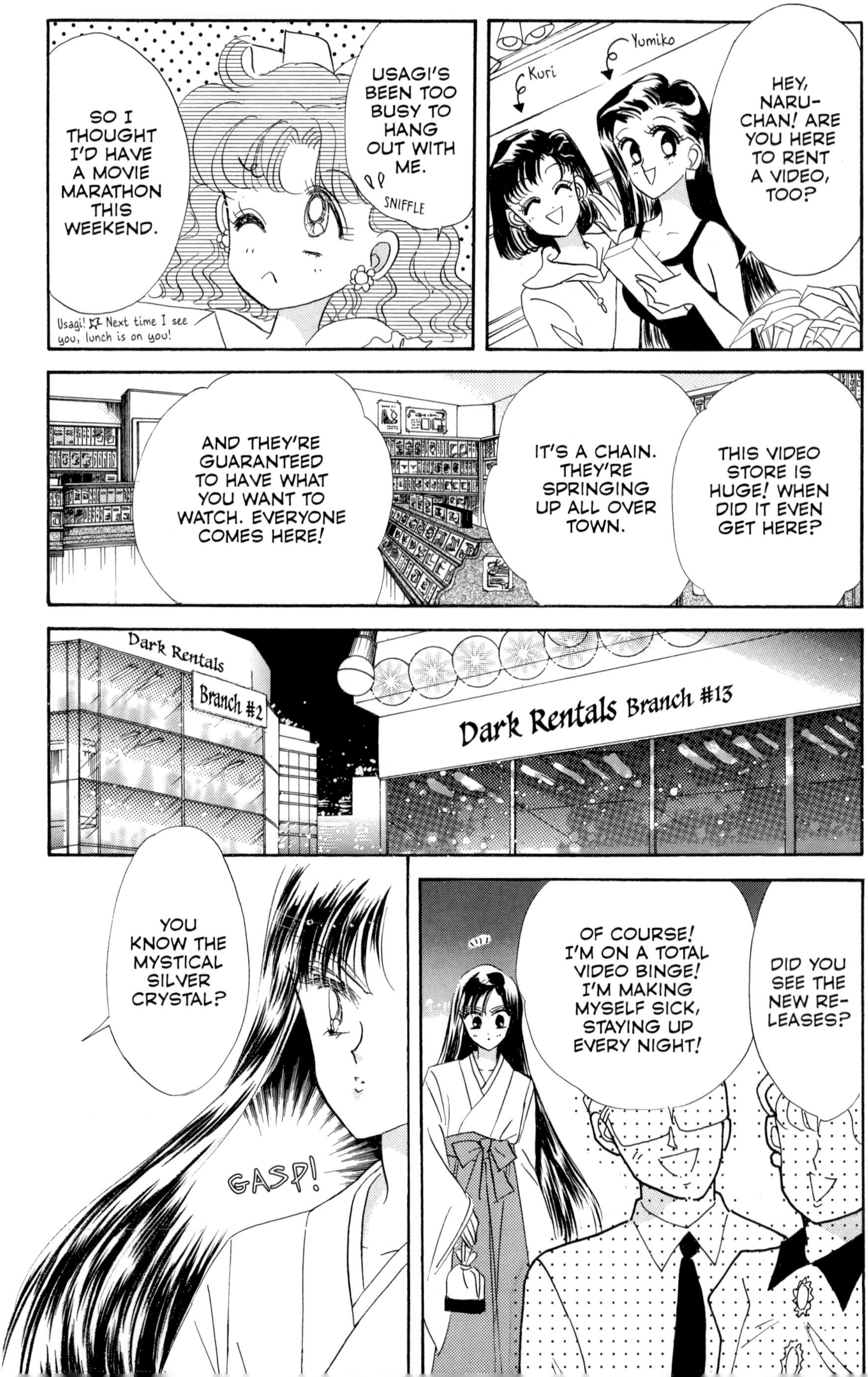
Yumiko
Kuri
HEY, NARU-CHAN! ARE YOU HERE TO RENT A VIDEO, TOO?
USAGI'S BEEN TOO BUSY TO HANG OUT WITH ME.
SNIFFLE
SO I THOUGHT I'D HAVE A MOVIE MARATHON THIS WEEKEND.
Usagi! ☆ Next time I see you, lunch is on you!
THIS VIDEO STORE IS HUGE! WHEN DID IT EVEN GET HERE?
IT'S A CHAIN. THEY'RE SPRINGING UP ALL OVER TOWN.
AND THEY'RE GUARANTEED TO HAVE WHAT YOU WANT TO WATCH. EVERYONE COMES HERE!
Dark Rentals Branch #13
Dark Rentals
Branch #2
DID YOU SEE THE NEW RE-LEASES?
OF COURSE! I'M ON A TOTAL VIDEO BINGE! I'M MAKING MYSELF SICK, STAYING UP EVERY NIGHT!
YOU KNOW THE MYSTICAL SILVER CRYSTAL?
GASP!

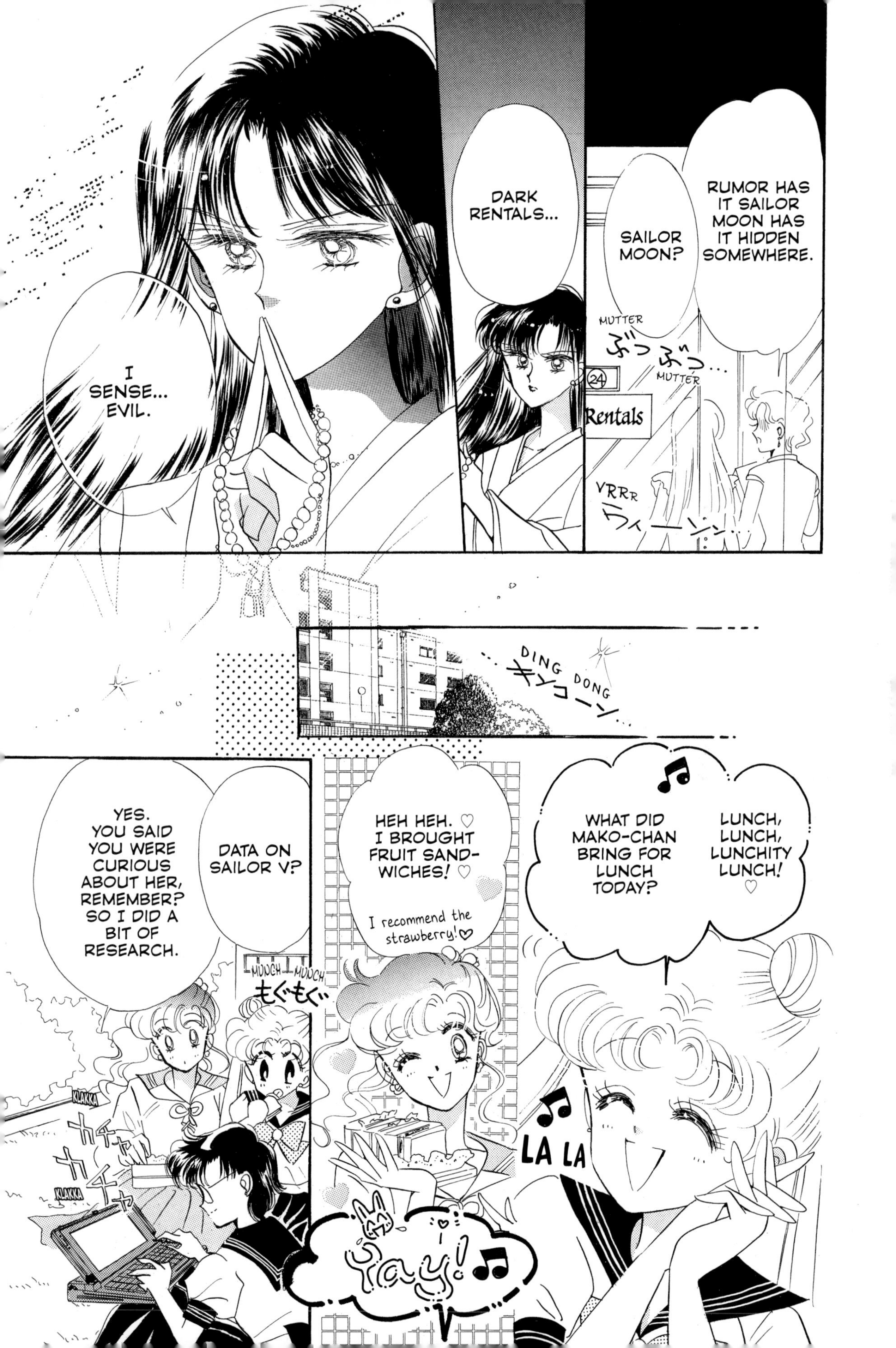
RUMOR HAS IT SAILOR MOON HAS IT HIDDEN SOMEWHERE.
SAILOR MOON?
MUTTER
ぶつぶつ…
MUTTER
24
Rentals
VRRR
ウィーン…
DARK RENTALS...
I SENSE... EVIL.
DING DONG
キンコーン…
LUNCH, LUNCH, LUNCHITY LUNCH! ♡
WHAT DID MAKO-CHAN BRING FOR LUNCH TODAY?
HEH HEH. ♡ I BROUGHT FRUIT SAND-WICHES! ♡
I recommend the strawberry!♡
LA LA
Yay!
DATA ON SAILOR V?
YES. YOU SAID YOU WERE CURIOUS ABOUT HER, REMEMBER? SO I DID A BIT OF RESEARCH.
MUNCH MUNCH
もぐもぐ
KLAKKA
カチャ
KLAKKA
カチャ

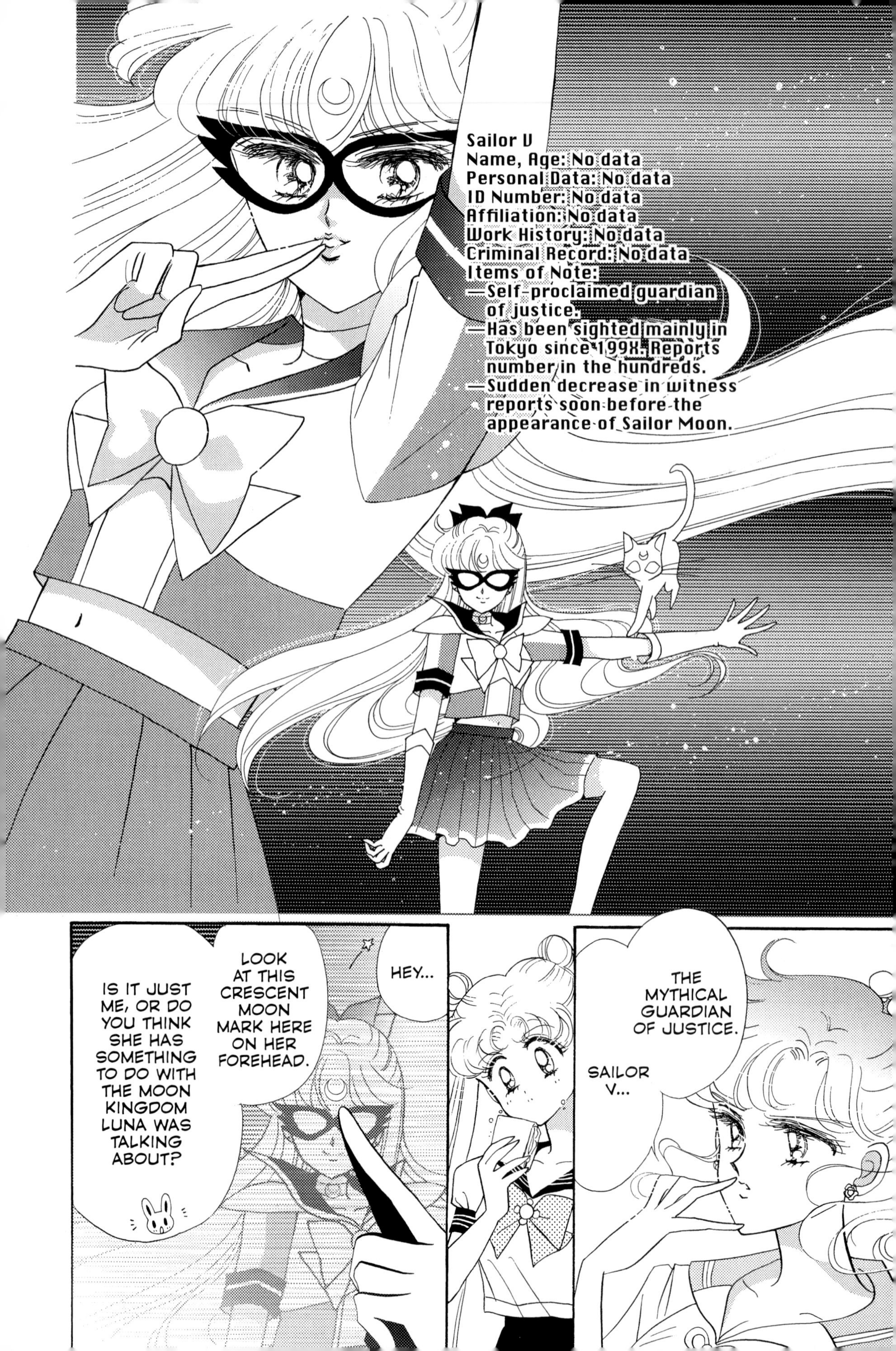
Sailor V
Name, Age: No data
Personal Data: No data
ID Number: No data
Affiliation: No data
Work History: No data
Criminal Record: No data
Items of Note:
—Self-proclaimed guardian of justice.
—Has been sighted mainly in Tokyo since 199X. Reports number in the hundreds.
—Sudden decrease in witness reports soon before the appearance of Sailor Moon.
THE MYTHICAL GUARDIAN OF JUSTICE.
SAILOR V...
HEY...
LOOK AT THIS CRESCENT MOON MARK HERE ON HER FOREHEAD.
IS IT JUST ME, OR DO YOU THINK SHE HAS SOMETHING TO DO WITH THE MOON KINGDOM LUNA WAS TALKING ABOUT?

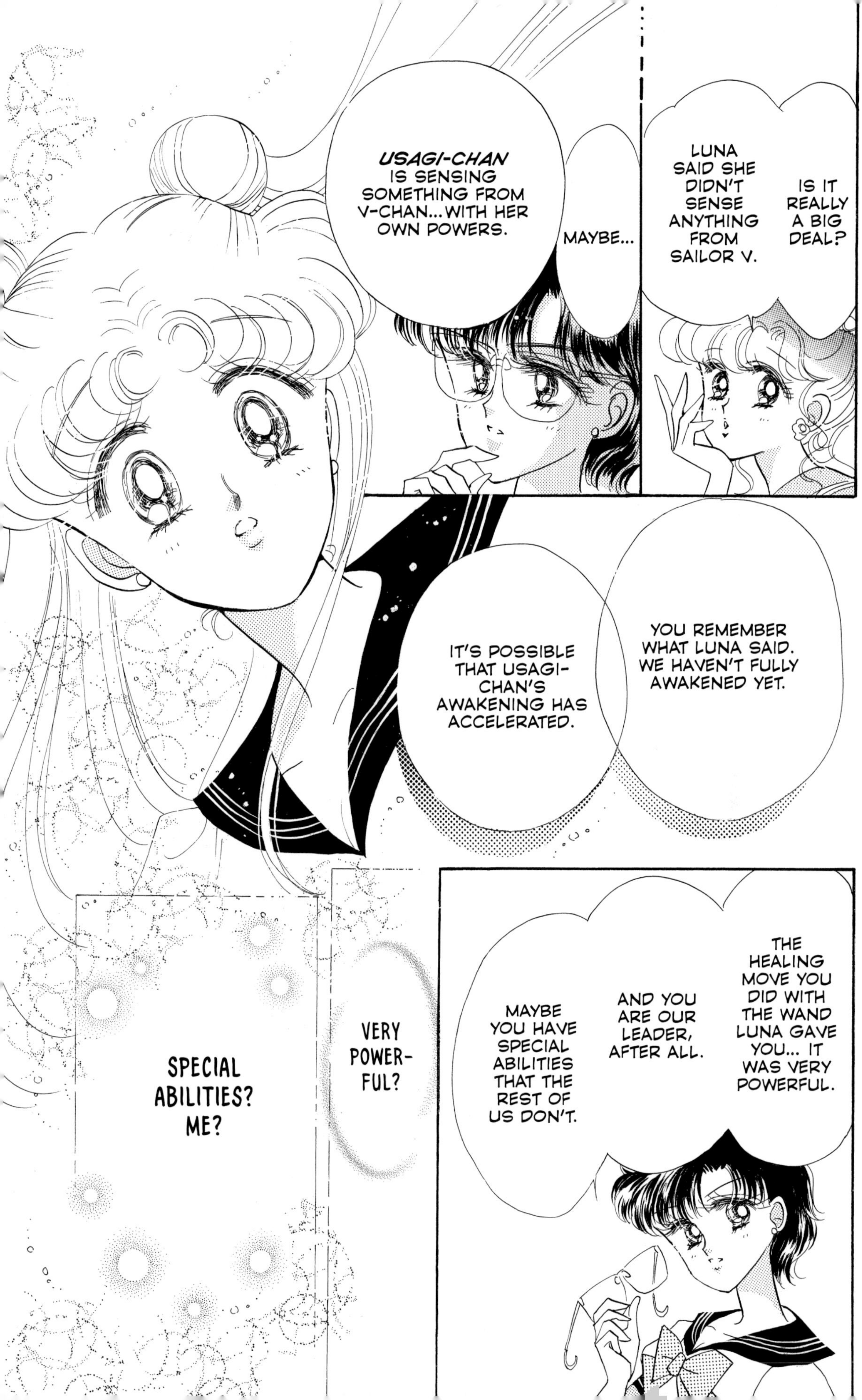
LUNA SAID SHE DIDN'T SENSE ANYTHING FROM SAILOR V.
IS IT REALLY A BIG DEAL?
MAYBE...
USAGI-CHAN IS SENSING SOMETHING FROM V-CHAN...WITH HER OWN POWERS.
YOU REMEMBER WHAT LUNA SAID. WE HAVEN'T FULLY AWAKENED YET.
IT'S POSSIBLE THAT USAGI-CHAN'S AWAKENING HAS ACCELERATED.
THE HEALING MOVE YOU DID WITH THE WAND LUNA GAVE YOU... IT WAS VERY POWERFUL.
AND YOU ARE OUR LEADER, AFTER ALL.
MAYBE YOU HAVE SPECIAL ABILITIES THAT THE REST OF US DON'T.
VERY POWER-FUL?
SPECIAL ABILITIES? ME?

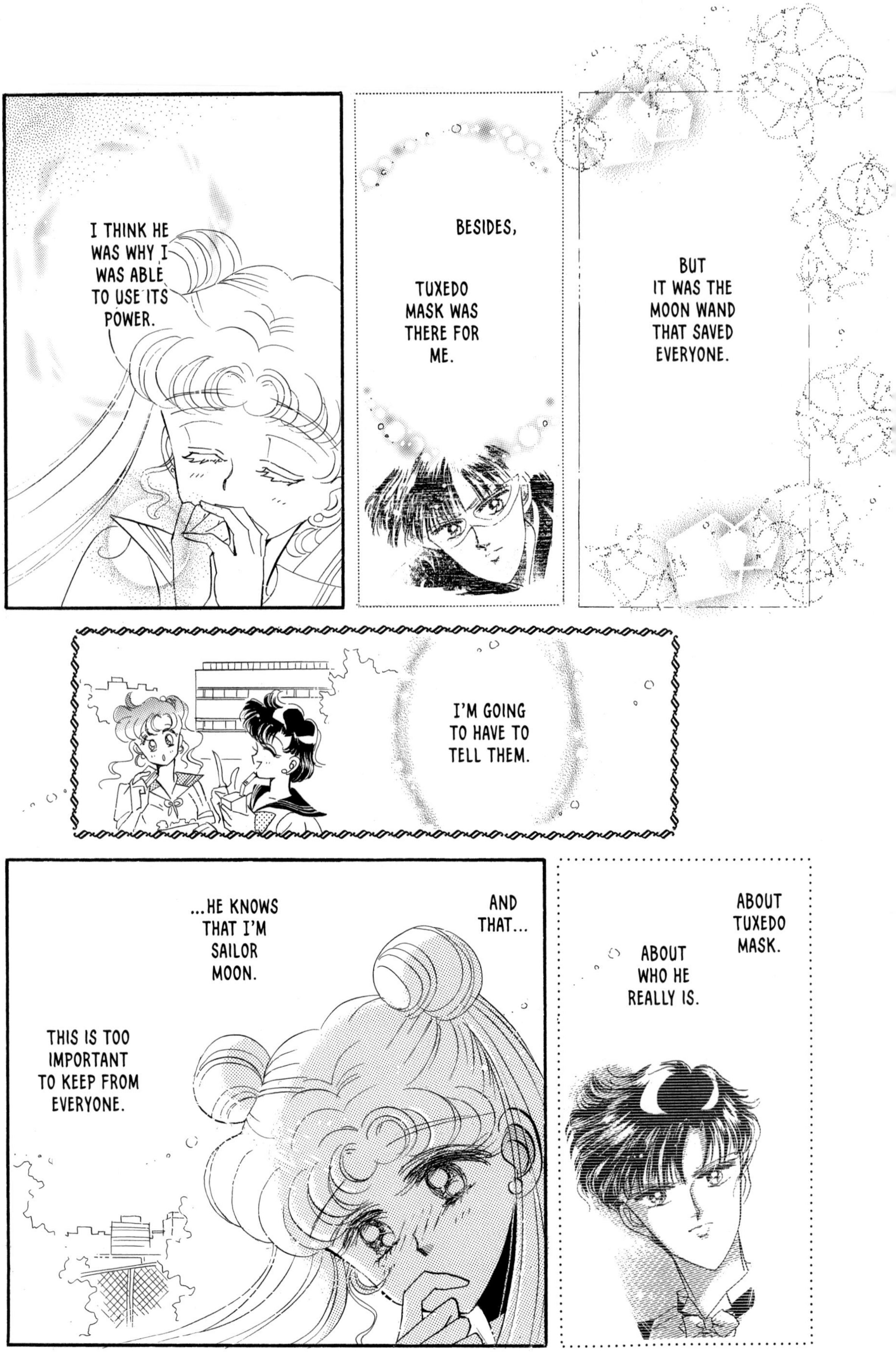
BUT IT WAS THE MOON WAND THAT SAVED EVERYONE.
BESIDES,
TUXEDO MASK WAS THERE FOR ME.
I THINK HE WAS WHY I WAS ABLE TO USE ITS POWER.
I'M GOING TO HAVE TO TELL THEM.
ABOUT TUXEDO MASK.
ABOUT WHO HE REALLY IS.
AND THAT...
...HE KNOWS THAT I'M SAILOR MOON.
THIS IS TOO IMPORTANT TO KEEP FROM EVERYONE.

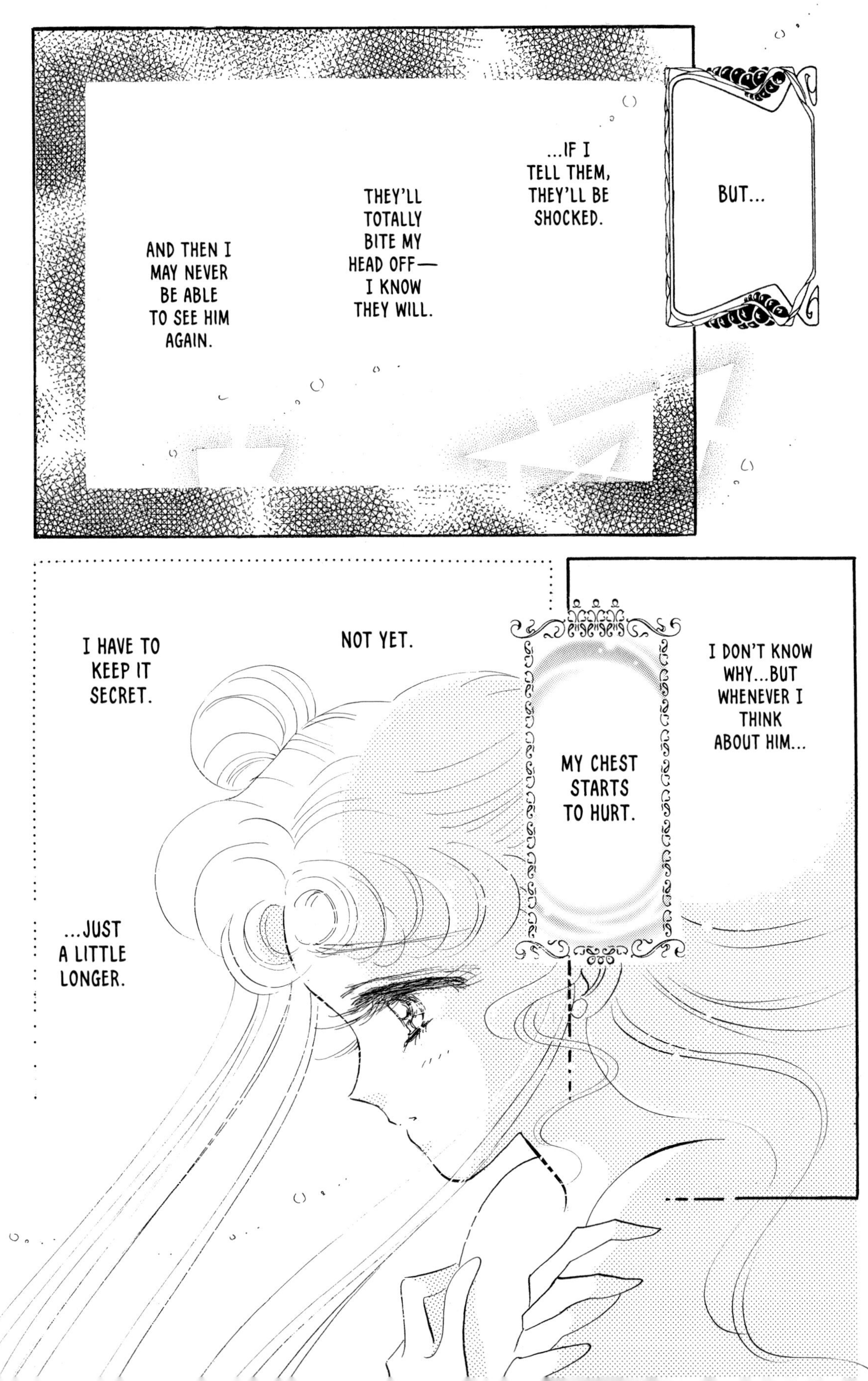
BUT...
...IF I TELL THEM, THEY'LL BE SHOCKED.
THEY'LL TOTALLY BITE MY HEAD OFF— I KNOW THEY WILL.
AND THEN I MAY NEVER BE ABLE TO SEE HIM AGAIN.
I DON'T KNOW WHY...BUT WHENEVER I THINK ABOUT HIM...
MY CHEST STARTS TO HURT.
NOT YET.
I HAVE TO KEEP IT SECRET.
...JUST A LITTLE LONGER.

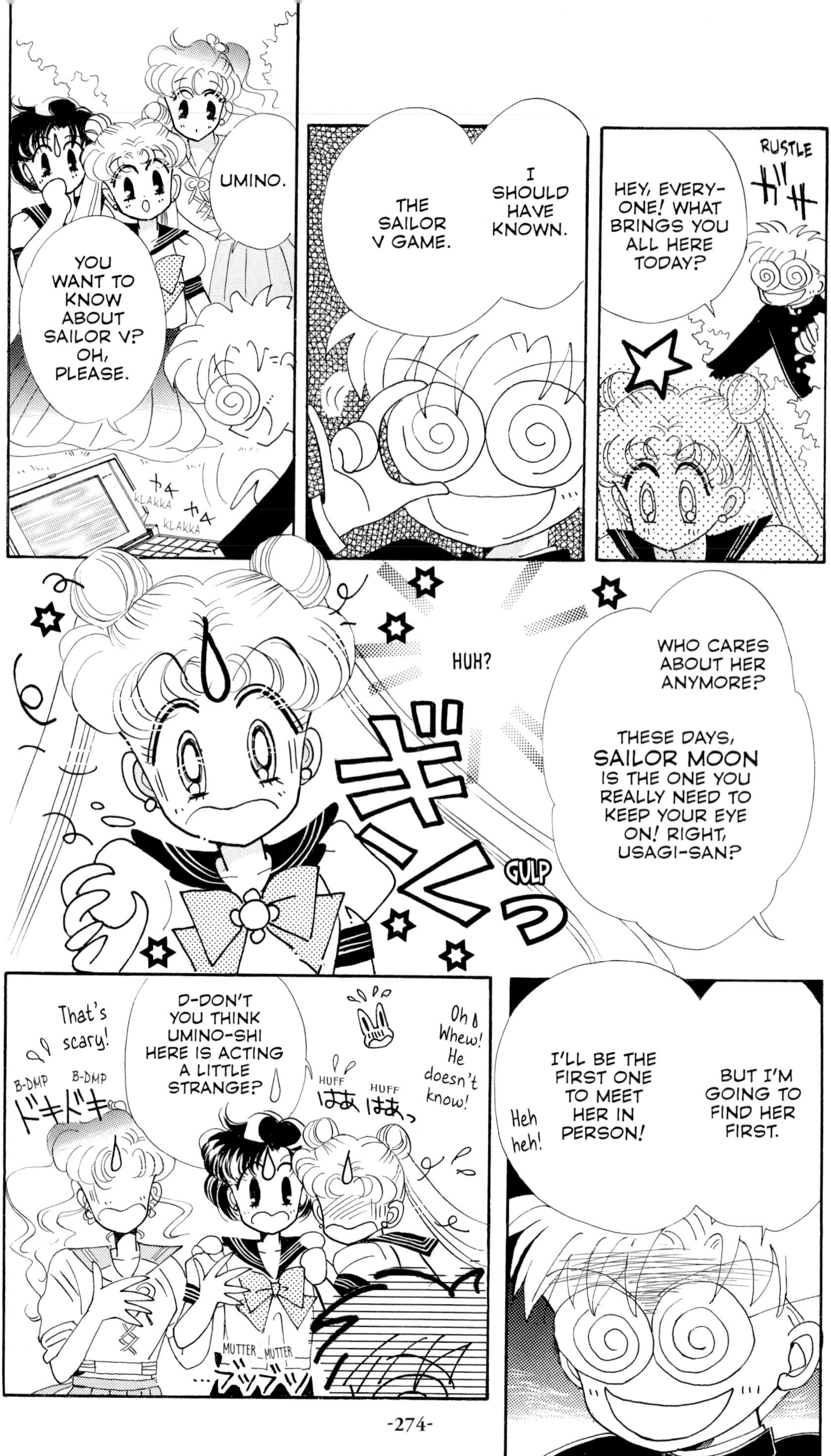
RUSTLE
ガサ
HEY, EVERY-ONE! WHAT BRINGS YOU ALL HERE TODAY?
I SHOULD HAVE KNOWN.
THE SAILOR V GAME.
UMINO.
YOU WANT TO KNOW ABOUT SAILOR V? OH, PLEASE.
KLAKKA
KLAKKA
WHO CARES ABOUT HER ANYMORE?
THESE DAYS, SAILOR MOON IS THE ONE YOU REALLY NEED TO KEEP YOUR EYE ON! RIGHT, USAGI-SAN?
HUH?
GULP
ギくっ
BUT I'M GOING TO FIND HER FIRST.
I'LL BE THE FIRST ONE TO MEET HER IN PERSON!
Heh heh!
Oh Whew! He doesn't know!
HUFF HUFF
はあ はあっ
D-DON'T YOU THINK UMINO-SHI HERE IS ACTING A LITTLE STRANGE?
That's scary!
B-DMP B-DMP
ドキドキ
MUTTER MUTTER
…ブツブツ

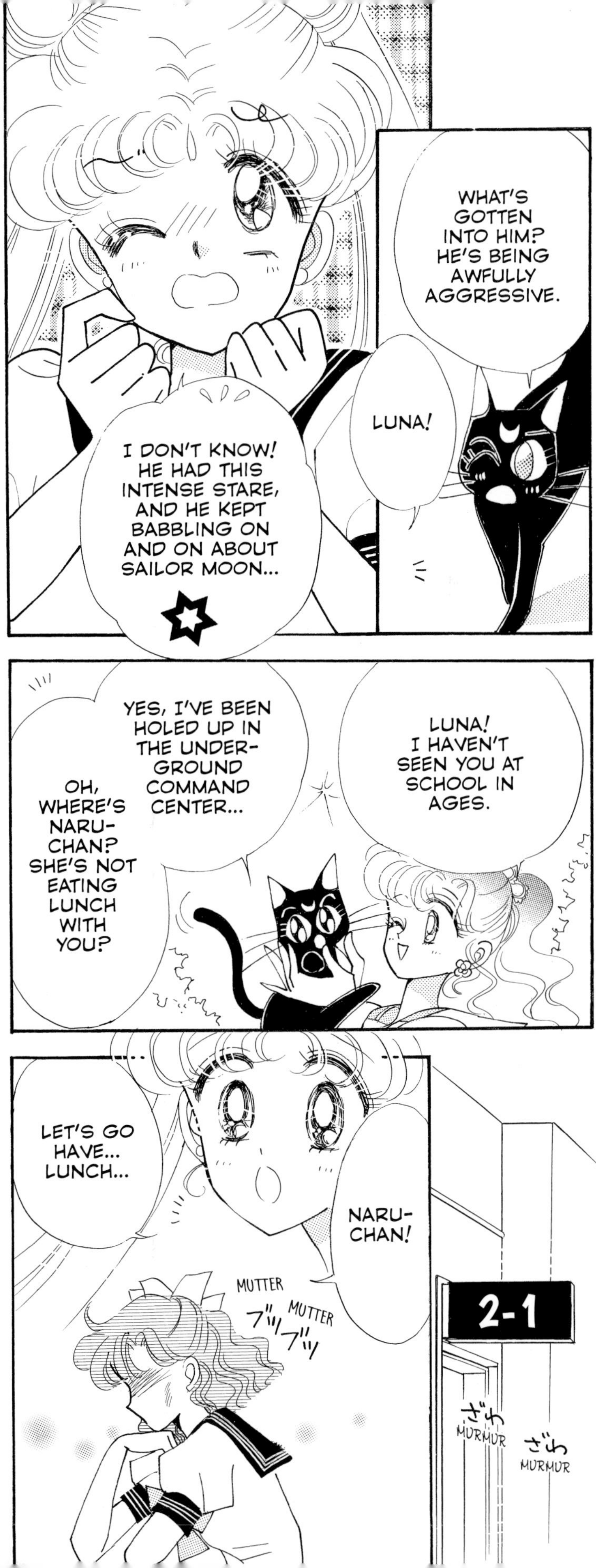
WHAT'S GOTTEN INTO HIM? HE'S BEING AWFULLY AGGRESSIVE.
LUNA!
I DON'T KNOW! HE HAD THIS INTENSE STARE, AND HE KEPT BABBLING ON AND ON ABOUT SAILOR MOON...
LUNA! I HAVEN'T SEEN YOU AT SCHOOL IN AGES.
YES, I'VE BEEN HOLED UP IN THE UNDER-GROUND COMMAND CENTER...
OH, WHERE'S NARU-CHAN? SHE'S NOT EATING LUNCH WITH YOU?
LET'S GO HAVE... LUNCH...
NARU-CHAN!
ブツブツ MUTTER MUTTER
2-1
ざわ MURMUR
ざわ MURMUR

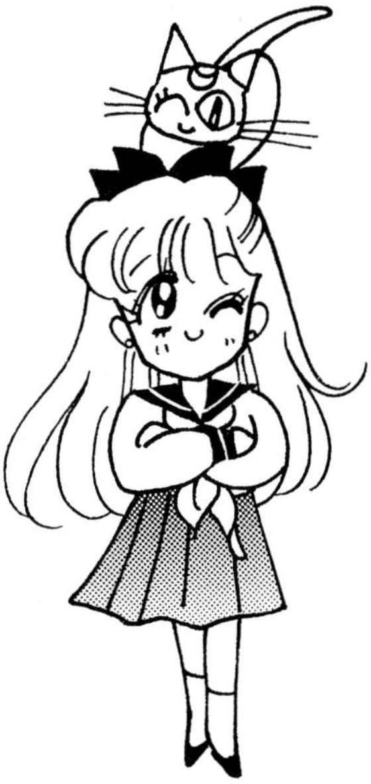

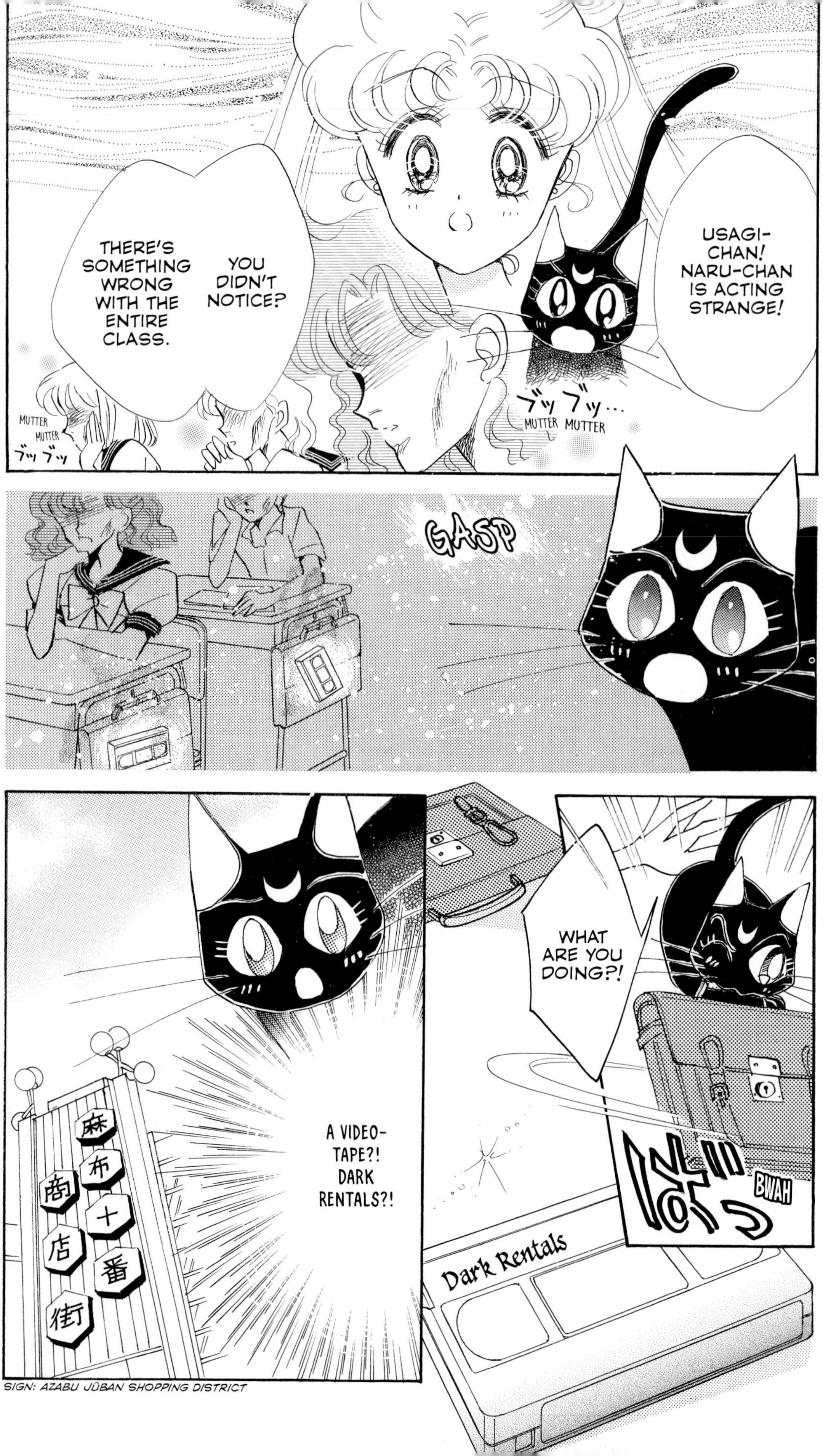
USAGI-CHAN! NARU-CHAN IS ACTING STRANGE!
YOU DIDN'T NOTICE?
THERE'S SOMETHING WRONG WITH THE ENTIRE CLASS.
ブツブツ…
MUTTER MUTTER
ブツブツ
MUTTER MUTTER
GASP
WHAT ARE YOU DOING?!
BWAH
Dark Rentals
A VIDEO-TAPE?! DARK RENTALS?!
麻布十番商店街

SIGN: AZABU JŪBAN SHOPPING DISTRICT

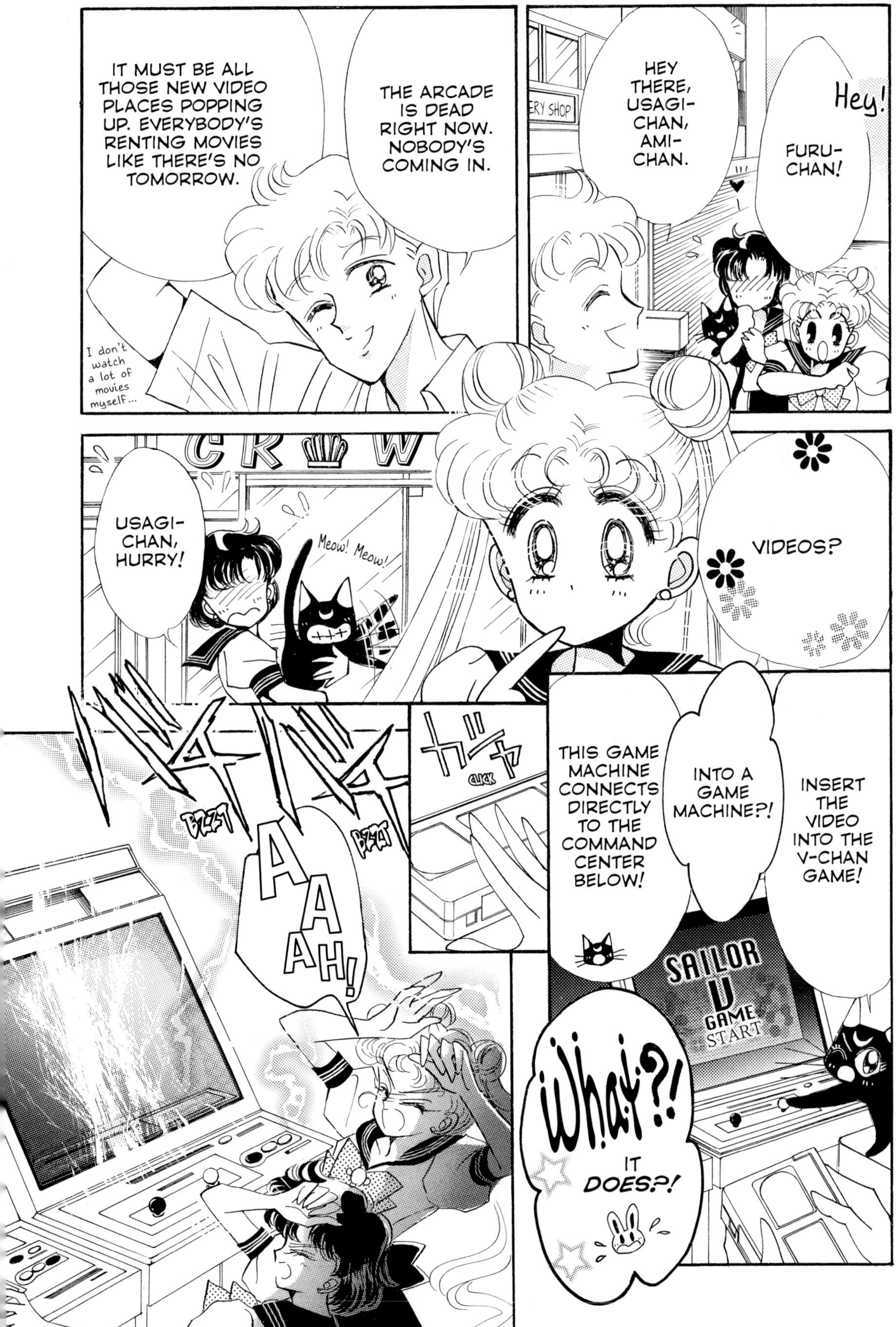
Hey!
FURU-CHAN!
HEY THERE, USAGI-CHAN, AMI-CHAN.
THE ARCADE IS DEAD RIGHT NOW. NOBODY'S COMING IN.
IT MUST BE ALL THOSE NEW VIDEO PLACES POPPING UP. EVERYBODY'S RENTING MOVIES LIKE THERE'S NO TOMORROW.
I don't watch a lot of movies myself...
VIDEOS?
Meow! Meow!
USAGI-CHAN, HURRY!
INSERT THE VIDEO INTO THE V-CHAN GAME!
INTO A GAME MACHINE?!
THIS GAME MACHINE CONNECTS DIRECTLY TO THE COMMAND CENTER BELOW!
SAILOR V GAME START
What?!
IT DOES?!
ガシャ
CLICK
BZZT
BZZT
AAAAH!

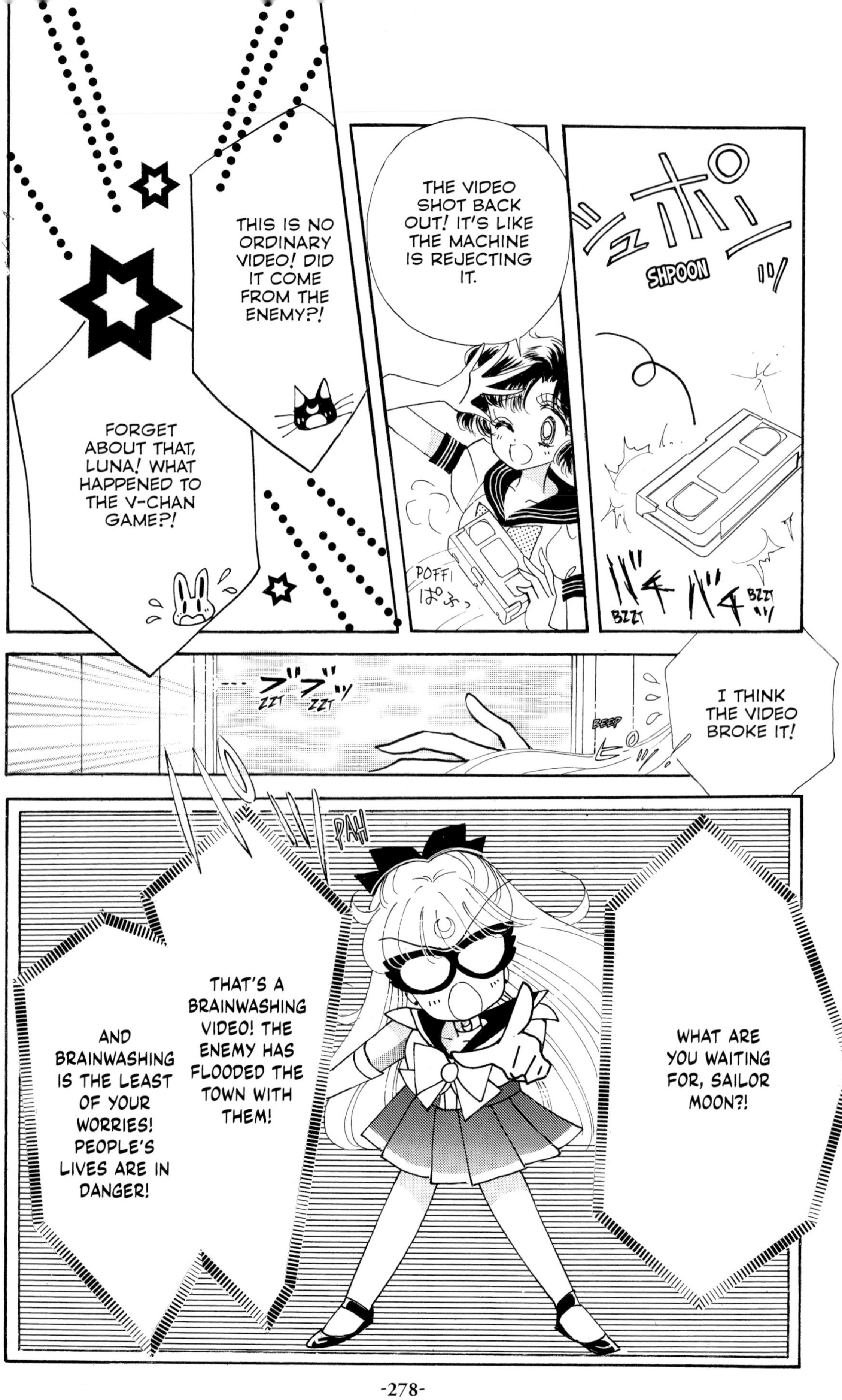
SHPOON
BZZT
BZZT
THE VIDEO SHOT BACK OUT! IT'S LIKE THE MACHINE IS REJECTING IT.
POFF!
ぱふっ
THIS IS NO ORDINARY VIDEO! DID IT COME FROM THE ENEMY?!
FORGET ABOUT THAT, LUNA! WHAT HAPPENED TO THE V-CHAN GAME?!
I THINK THE VIDEO BROKE IT!
BEEP
ZZT
ZZT
PAH
WHAT ARE YOU WAITING FOR, SAILOR MOON?!
THAT'S A BRAINWASHING VIDEO! THE ENEMY HAS FLOODED THE TOWN WITH THEM!
AND BRAINWASHING IS THE LEAST OF YOUR WORRIES! PEOPLE'S LIVES ARE IN DANGER!

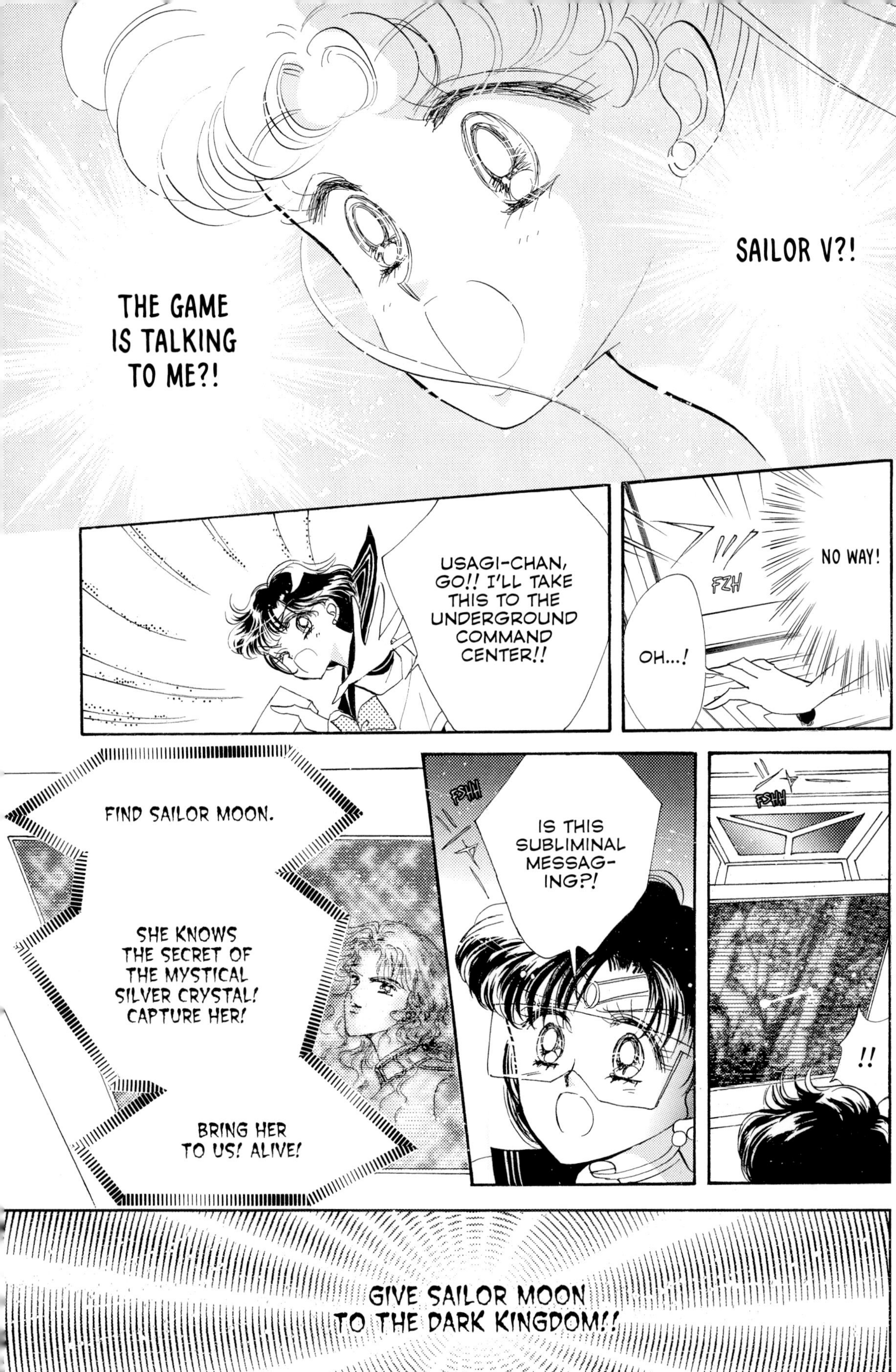
SAILOR V?!
THE GAME IS TALKING TO ME?!
NO WAY!
FZH
OH...!
USAGI-CHAN, GO!! I'LL TAKE THIS TO THE UNDERGROUND COMMAND CENTER!!
FSHH
!!
FSHH
IS THIS SUBLIMINAL MESSAG-ING?!
FIND SAILOR MOON.
SHE KNOWS THE SECRET OF THE MYSTICAL SILVER CRYSTAL! CAPTURE HER!
BRING HER TO US! ALIVE!
GIVE SAILOR MOON TO THE DARK KINGDOM!!

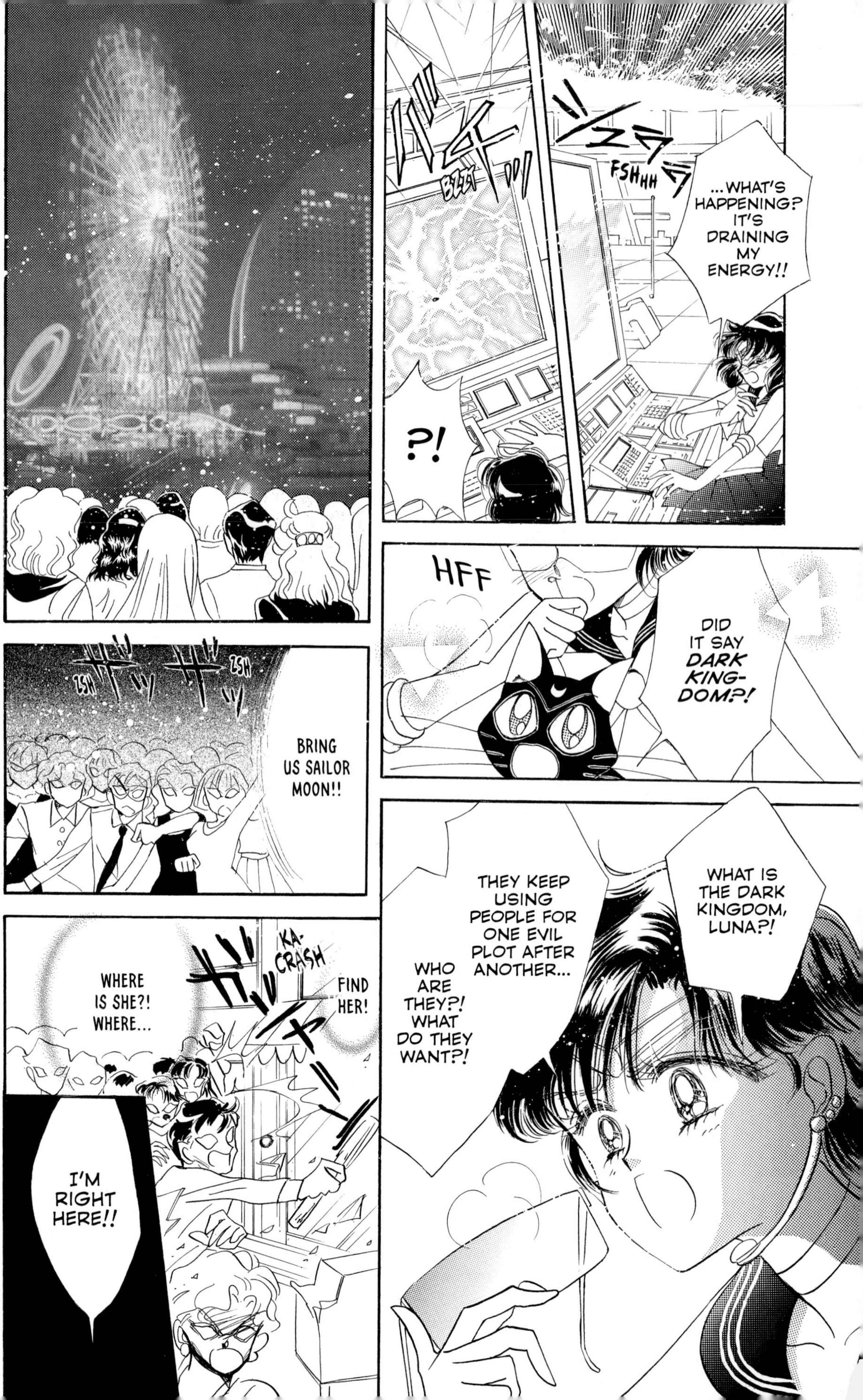
FSHHH
...WHAT'S HAPPENING? IT'S DRAINING MY ENERGY!!
BZZT
?!
HFF
DID IT SAY DARK KINGDOM?!
WHAT IS THE DARK KINGDOM, LUNA?!
THEY KEEP USING PEOPLE FOR ONE EVIL PLOT AFTER ANOTHER...
WHO ARE THEY?! WHAT DO THEY WANT?!
ZSH
ZSH
BRING US SAILOR MOON!!
KA-CRASH
FIND HER!
WHERE IS SHE?! WHERE...
I'M RIGHT HERE!!

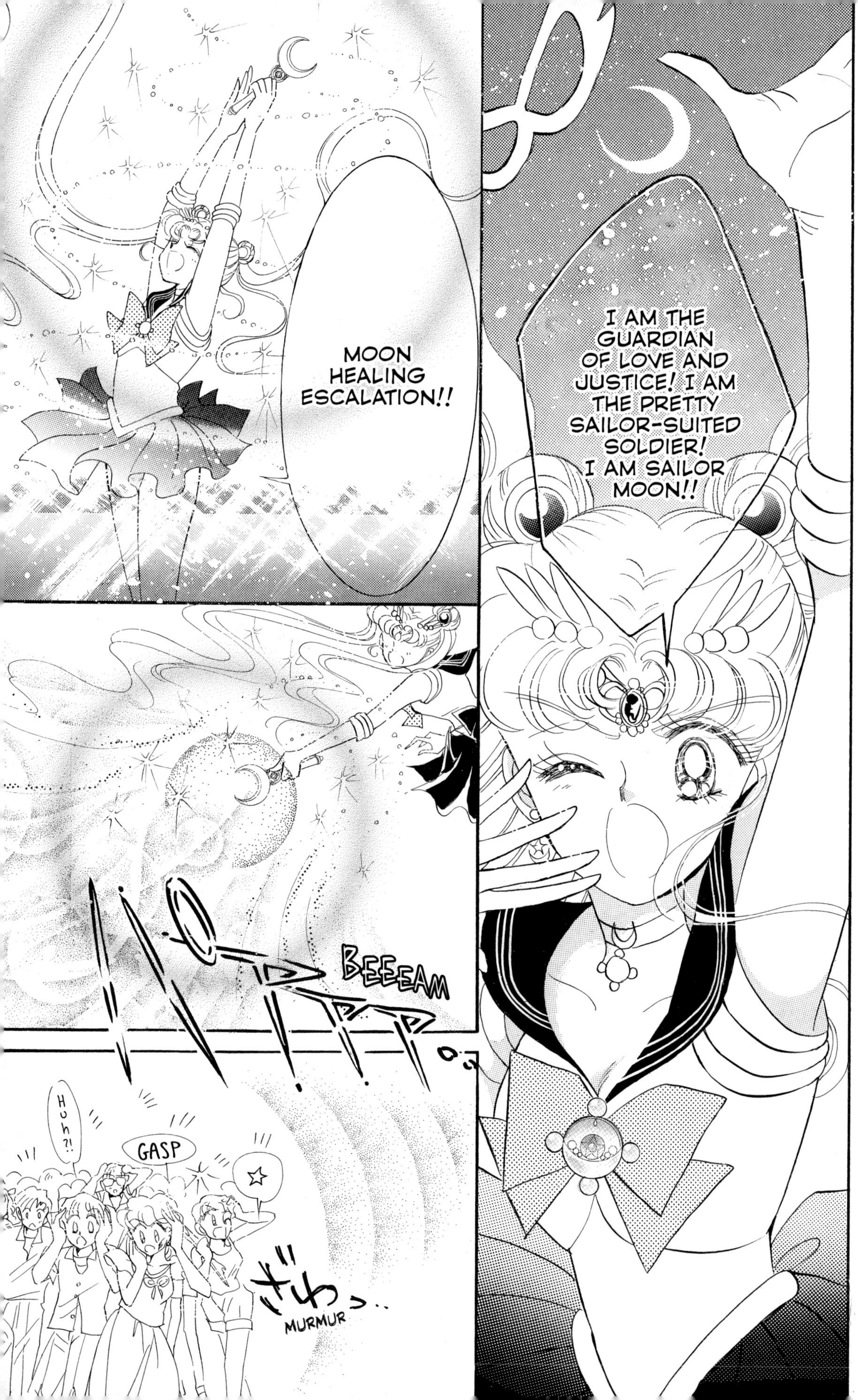
I AM THE GUARDIAN OF LOVE AND JUSTICE! I AM THE PRETTY SAILOR-SUITED SOLDIER! I AM SAILOR MOON!!
MOON HEALING ESCALATION!!
BEEEAM
Huh?!
GASP
★
ざわっ..
MURMUR

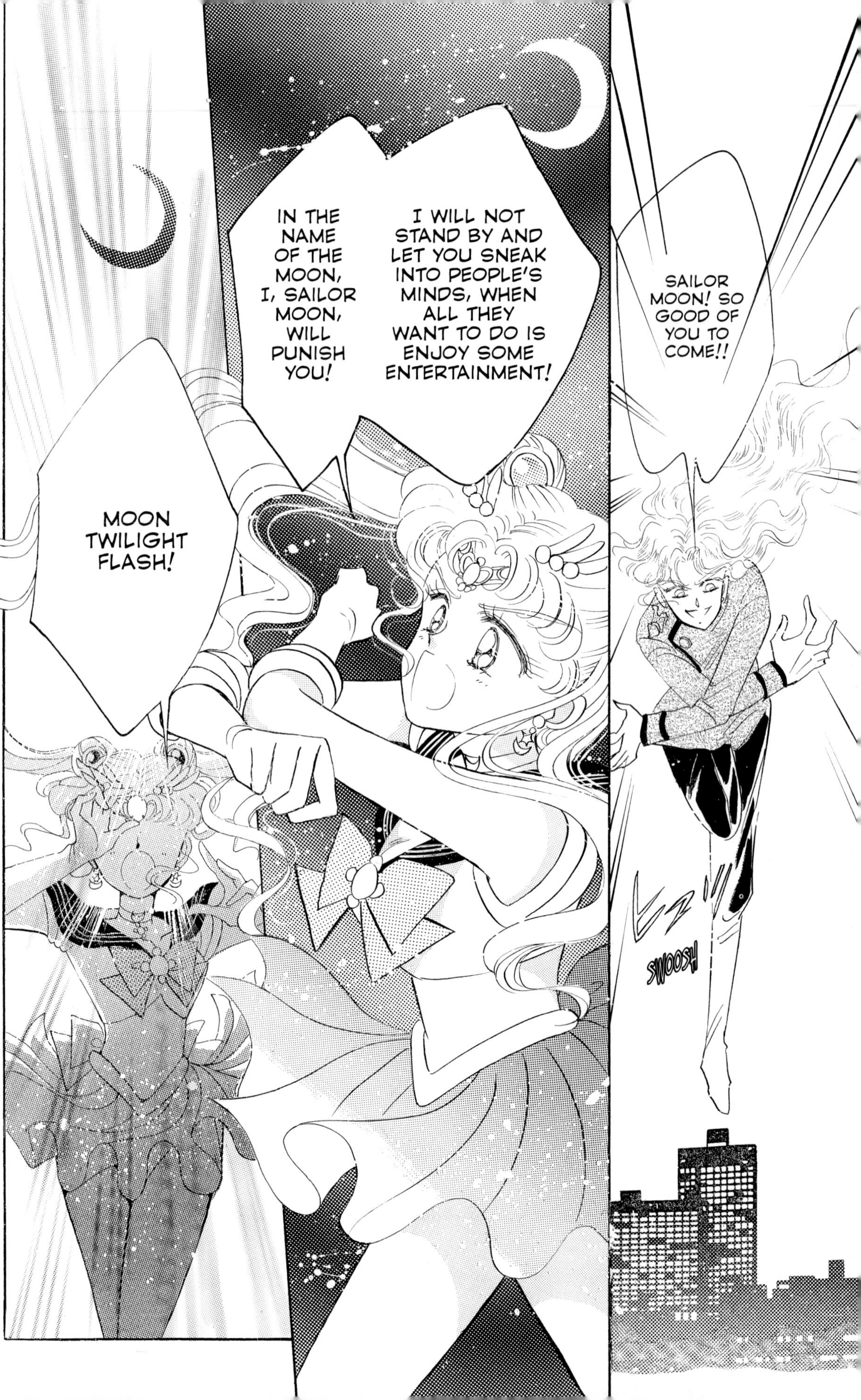
SAILOR MOON! SO GOOD OF YOU TO COME!!
SWOOSH
I WILL NOT STAND BY AND LET YOU SNEAK INTO PEOPLE'S MINDS, WHEN ALL THEY WANT TO DO IS ENJOY SOME ENTERTAINMENT!
IN THE NAME OF THE MOON, I, SAILOR MOON, WILL PUNISH YOU!
MOON TWILIGHT FLASH!

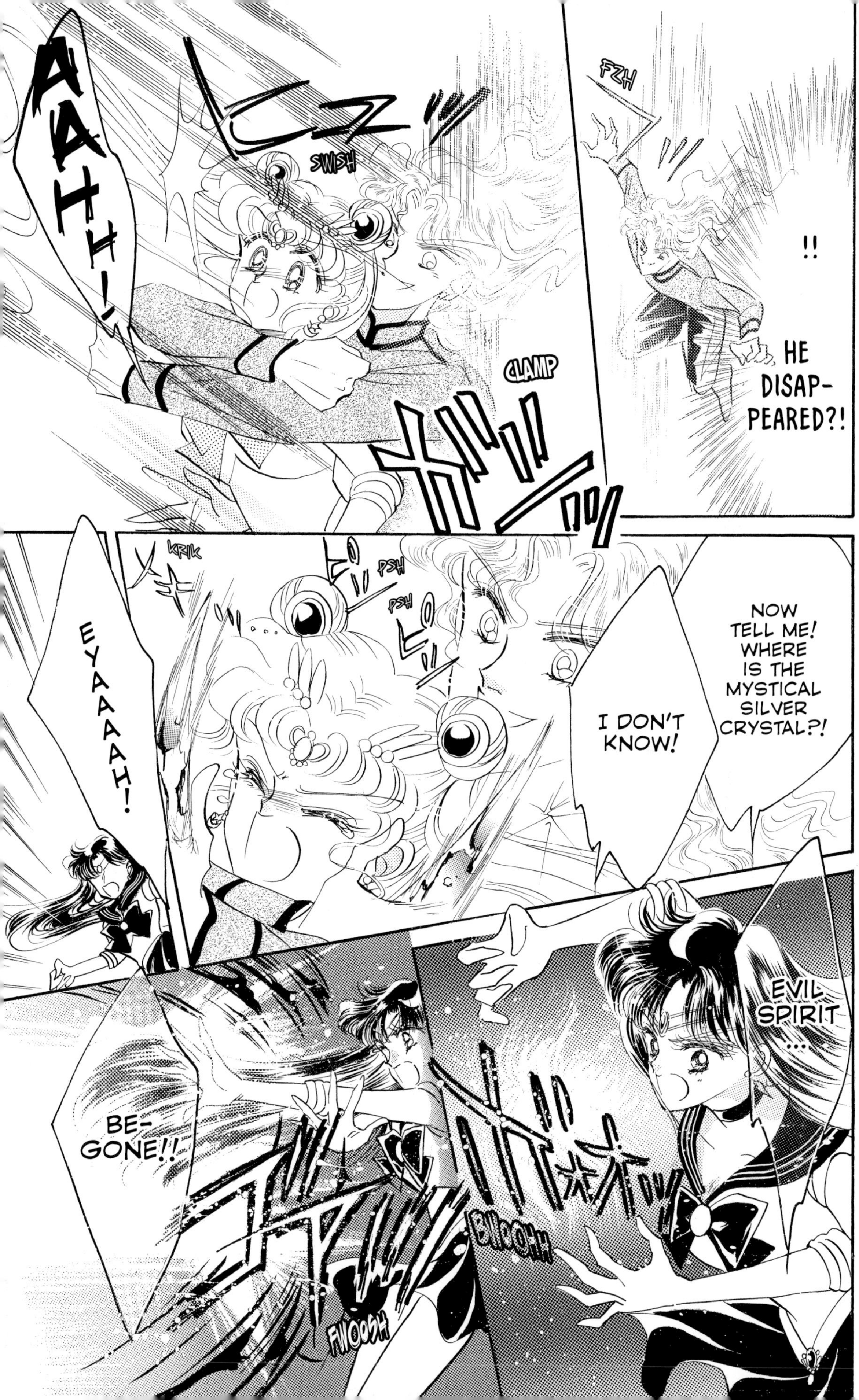

FZH
!!
HE DISAP-PEARED?!
AAHH!
SWISH
CLAMP
NOW TELL ME! WHERE IS THE MYSTICAL SILVER CRYSTAL?!
I DON'T KNOW!
PSH
PSH
KRIK
EYAAAAAH!
EVIL SPIRIT...
BWOOHH
BE-GONE!!
FWOOSH

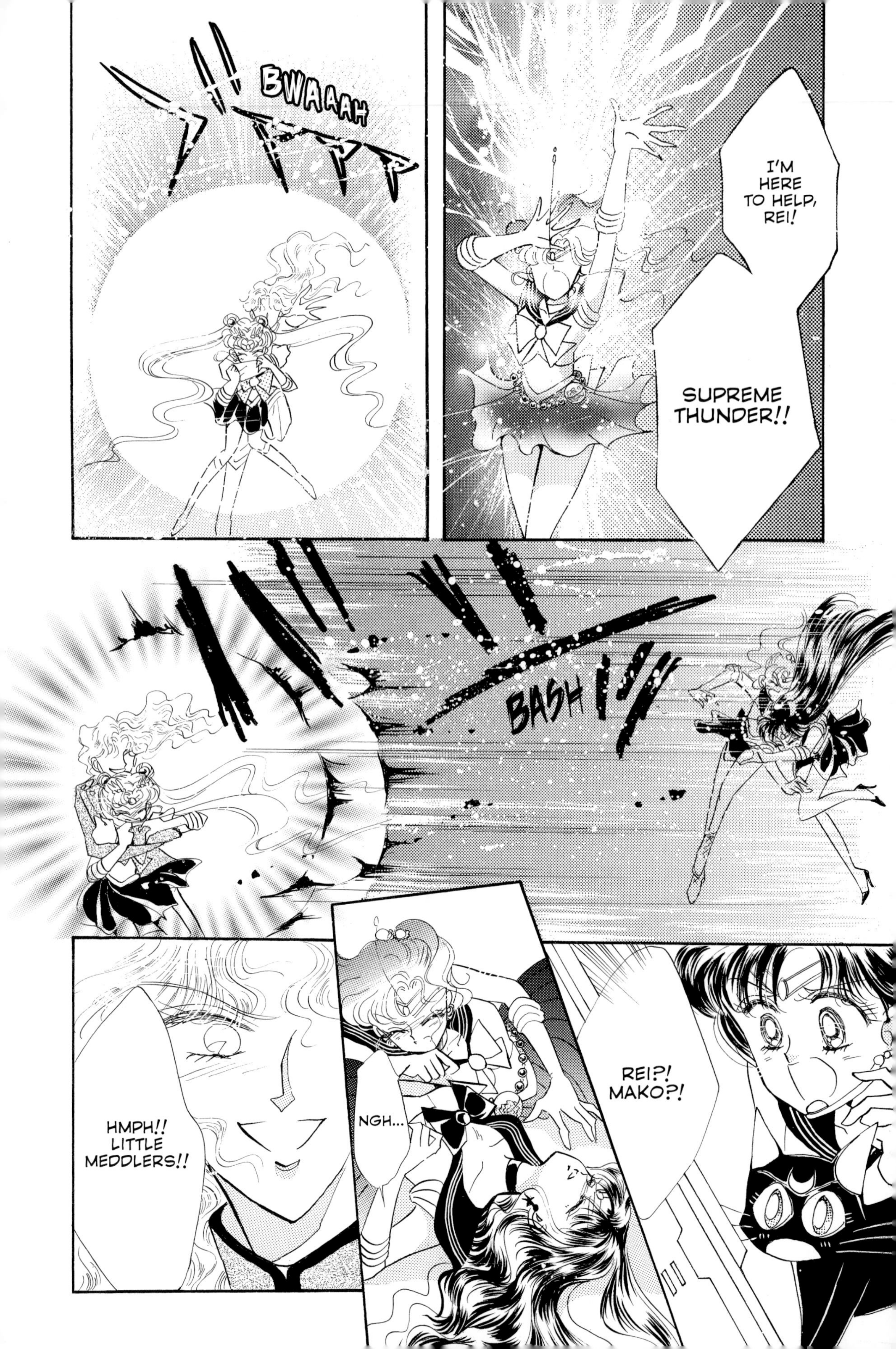
I'M HERE TO HELP, REI!
SUPREME THUNDER!!
BWAAAH
BASH
REI?! MAKO?!
NGH...
HMPH!! LITTLE MEDDLERS!!

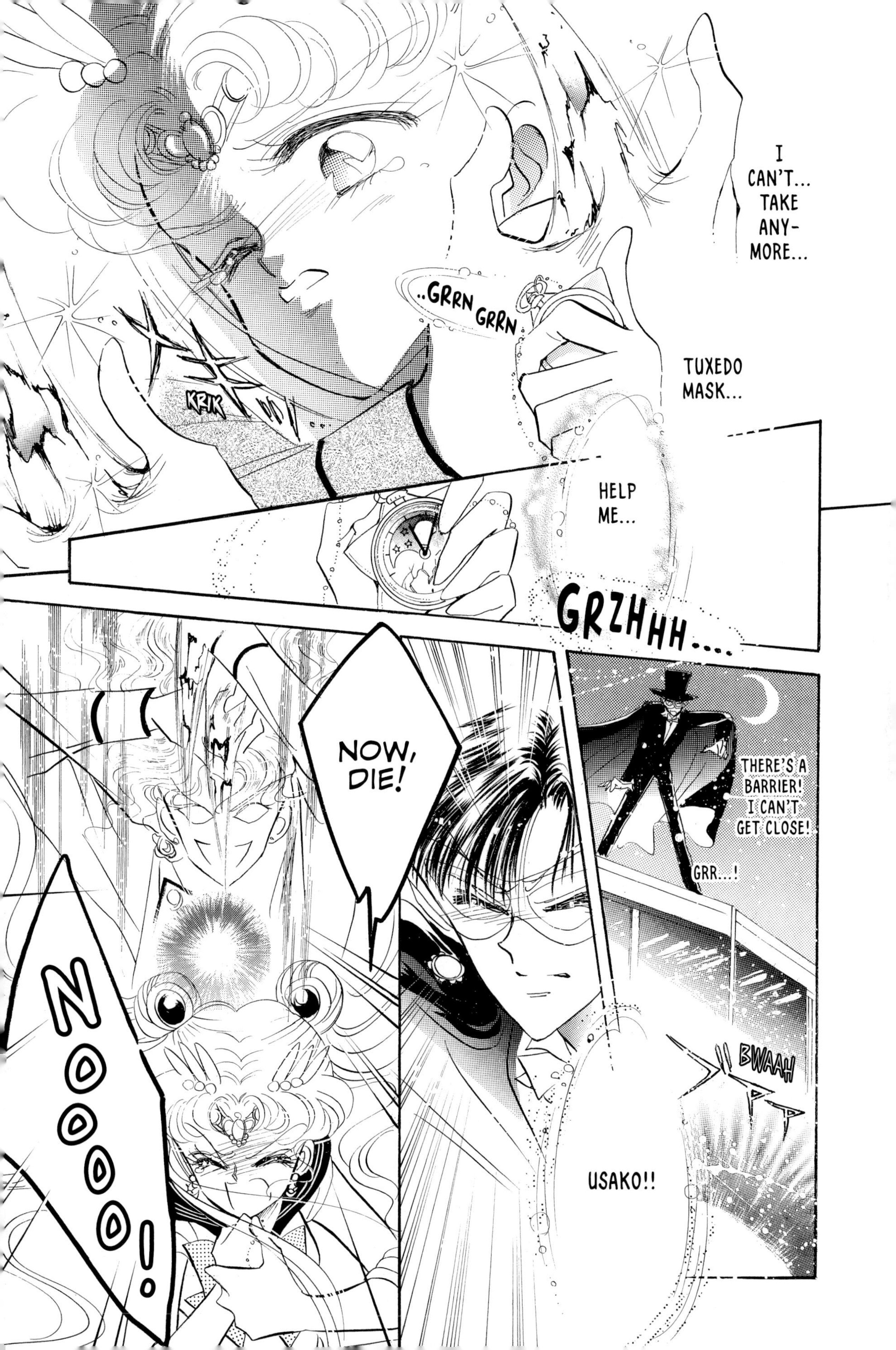
I CAN'T... TAKE ANY-MORE...
..GRRN GRRN
TUXEDO MASK...
KRIK
HELP ME...
GRZHHH....
THERE'S A BARRIER! I CAN'T GET CLOSE!
GRR...!
BWAAH
USAKO!!
NOW, DIE!
NOOOOO!

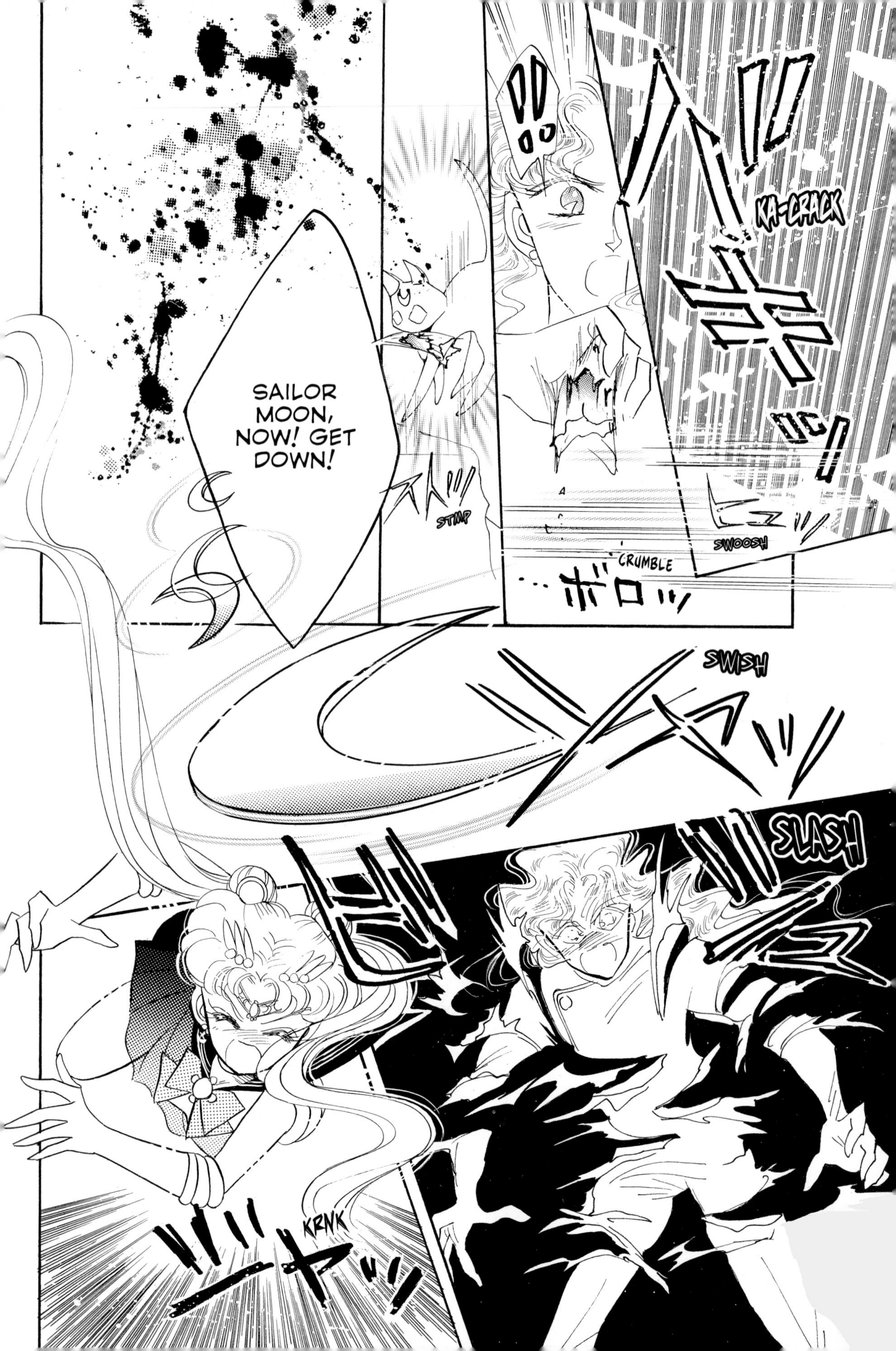
KA-CRACK
SWOOSH
CRUMBLE
STMP
SAILOR MOON, NOW! GET DOWN!
SWISH
SLASH
KRNK

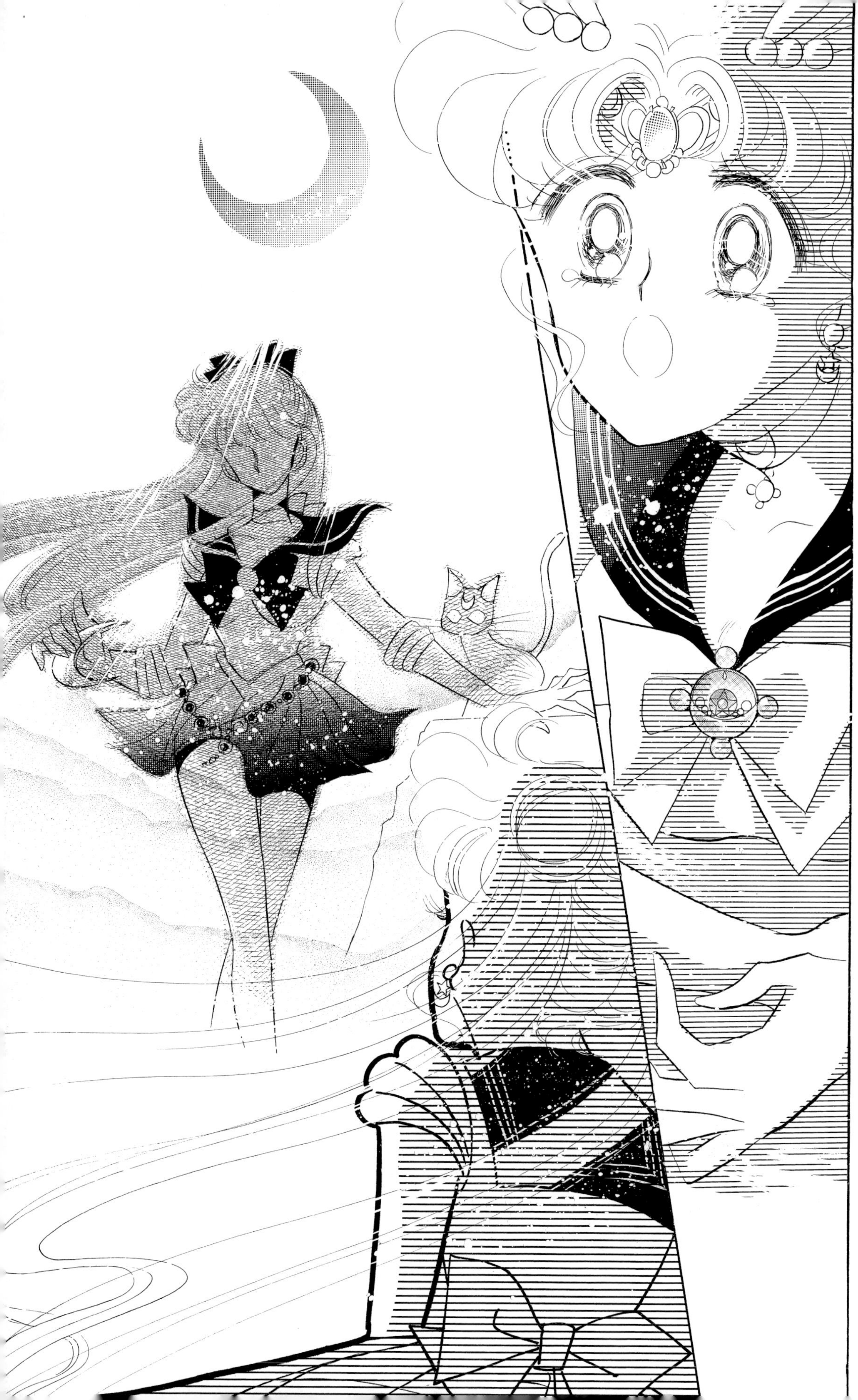

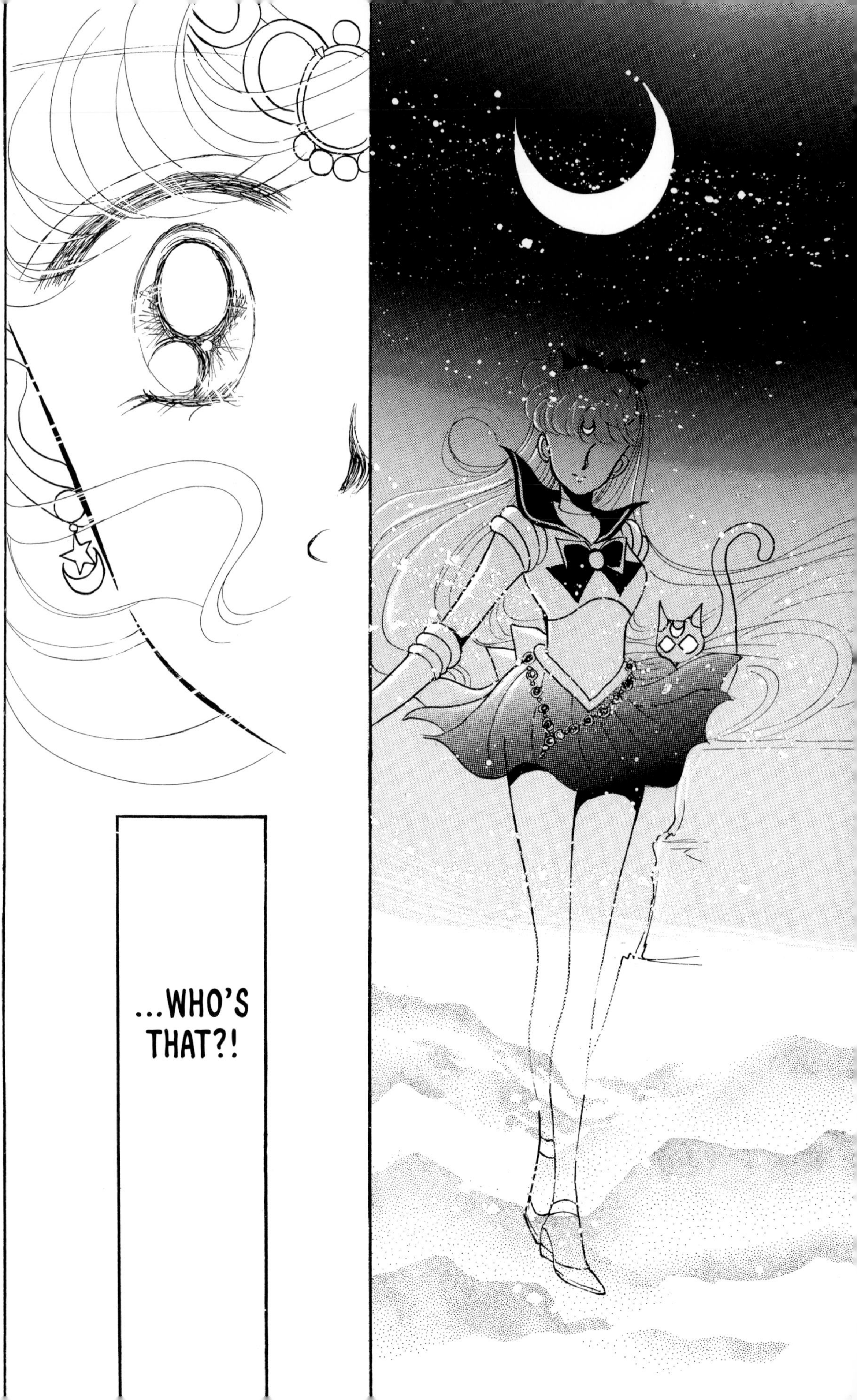
...WHO'S THAT?!

Pretty Guardian

Sailor Moon

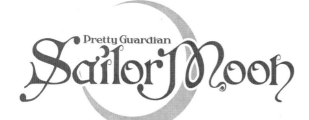

Translation Notes

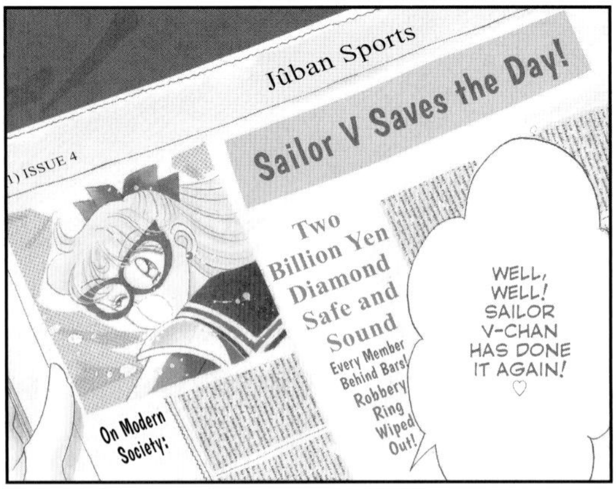

Jûban Sports
ISSUE 4
Sailor V Saves the Day!
Two Billion Yen Diamond Safe and Sound
Every Member Behind Bars! Robbery Ring Wiped Out!
On Modern Society:
WELL, WELL! SAILOR V-CHAN HAS DONE IT AGAIN! ♡

***Jûban Sports*, page 3**

Don't be fooled by the name—Usagi's mother is most likely not reading this paper for local sports news. While Japanese "sports newspapers" do cover athletic events, they also cover some news, leisure and entertainment, and, perhaps most importantly, they're a good source of celebrity gossip.

V-chan, page 3

Usagi's mother tends to add -chan to the name of every young girl she comes across. Attaching -chan to a person's name is a way to express the fact that the speaker thinks of them as a friend, as opposed to using the more distant -san. For more on honorifics, see "Call me Usagi."

Usagi Tsukino, page 7

The reader will find that the names of the main characters of this series were not chosen at random. *Usagi* means "rabbit"—hence the frequent appearance of bunnies in speech bubbles to indicate that Usagi is the one speaking. "*Tsuki no*" means "of the moon," so Usagi's full name means "rabbit of the moon," or "moon rabbit." This is a reference to the Japanese folklore tradition that the image formed on the moon's surface by its topography is that of a rabbit making *mochi* (rice cake).

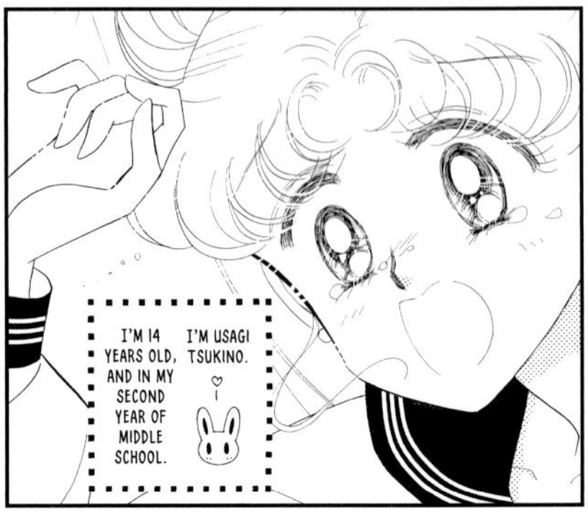

I'M USAGI TSUKINO. ♡
I'M 14 YEARS OLD, AND IN MY SECOND YEAR OF MIDDLE SCHOOL.

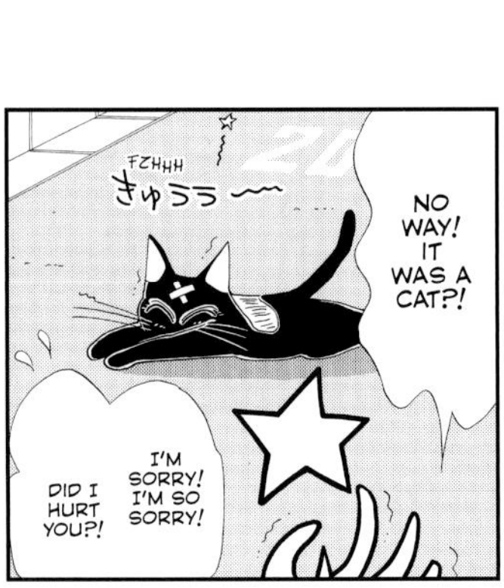

NO WAY! IT WAS A CAT?!
FZHHH
きゅうう〜
I'M SORRY! I'M SO SORRY!
DID I HURT YOU?!

Stepped on a cat, page 8

It may or may not be interesting to note that Usagi has reenacted the Japanese name of a popular piece of music to teach beginning piano students. Known in the United States as "*Der Flohwalzer*," or "The Flea Waltz," in Japan it's called "*Neko Funjatta*," or "I Stepped on a Cat." The translators recommend looking it up, as it does indeed sound like stepping on a cat (but please refrain from trying to recreate the real sound).

Haruda, page 11

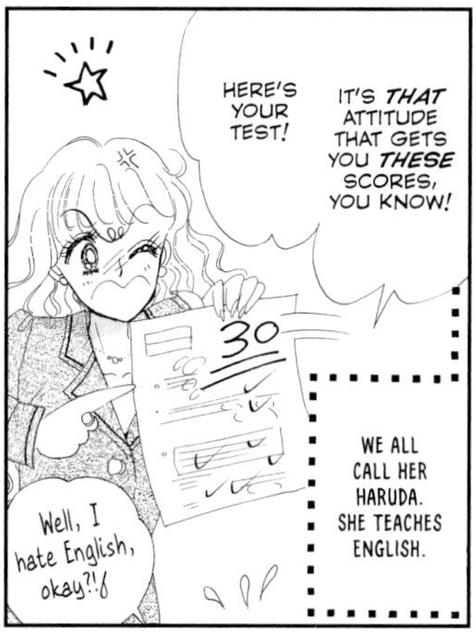
IT'S *THAT* ATTITUDE THAT GETS YOU *THESE* SCORES, YOU KNOW!
HERE'S YOUR TEST!
30
WE ALL CALL HER HARUDA. SHE TEACHES ENGLISH.
Well, I hate English, okay?!

The nickname Haruda may simply be a combination of Sakurada-sensei's given name and surname, but it may also be a play on words. First, the translators must point out that in Japan, names are listed in the order of surname first and given name second, so her full name would be said "Sakurada Haruna." "*Sakura da*" can be roughly translated as, "Look, cherry blossoms!" Cherry blossoms are a symbol of spring, so when someone looks and sees cherry blossoms, their next thought could reasonably be, "It's springtime!", which, in Japanese, is "*Haru da!*" It should also be pointed out that if the students are addressing their teacher by her given name, either they are on friendly terms with her, or they don't respect her at all. Incidentally, Sakurada-sensei first appeared in Naoko Takeuchi's earlier series, *The Cherry Project.*

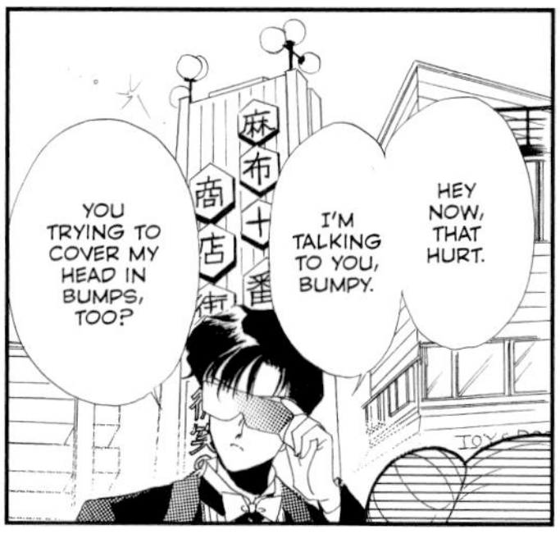
HEY NOW, THAT HURT.
I'M TALKING TO YOU, BUMPY.
YOU TRYING TO COVER MY HEAD IN BUMPS, TOO?

Azabu Jûban Shopping District, page 16

Also known as Azabu Jûban Shopping Street, this shopping district has an old Edo feel to it, and mix of new and old shops, which make it a popular spot among young people and foreign tourists. The nearby residential area is also highly sought after, due in part to its proximity to other high-end shopping and residential areas. Azabu Jûban is also where the first United States legation (home to a foreign diplomat) was established in the 19th century, and today is home to more than 20 foreign embassies.

They're called buns, page 16

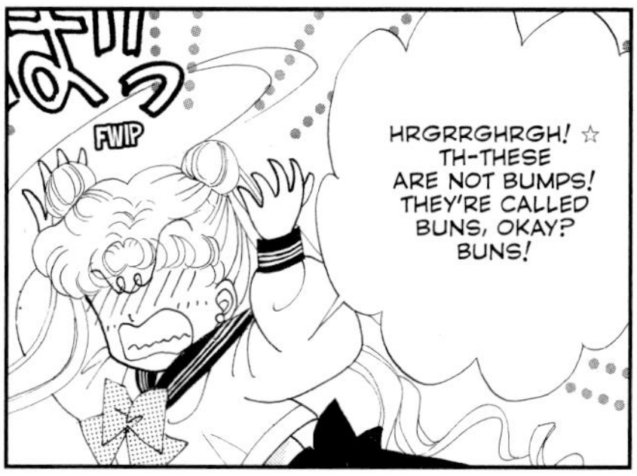
HRGRRGHRGH! ☆ TH-THESE ARE NOT BUMPS! THEY'RE CALLED BUNS, OKAY? BUNS!
FWIP

Mamoru has had several different nicknames for Usagi throughout the different incarnations of English-language *Sailor Moon.* While these translators will always have a fondness for the first English dub's "Meatball Head," names relating to buns are really more appropriate. In the original Japanese exchange, Mamoru calls her a "*tankobu* head," suggesting that she has large bumps, possibly caused by some sort of blunt impact. She informs him that the proper name for the bundles of hair on the sides of her head is not *tankobu* but *odango.* It's a bit of a play on words, because *tanko* and *dango* sound similar. An *odango* is a sweet dumpling that comes in a variety of flavors, but *odango* is also the correct Japanese name for hair buns. So not only is "bun" the correct term for her hair, but it also fits the wordplay, because it sounds like "bump." Buns and *odango* are both types of hair and types of food, so either way, Usagi has an appetizing hairstyle.

The Mystical Silver Crystal, page 17

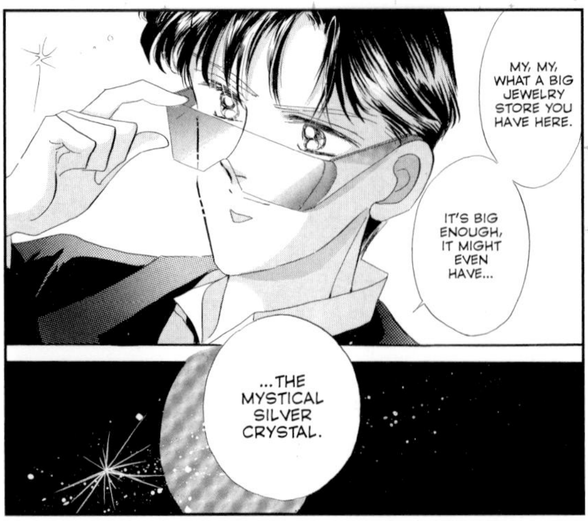
MY, MY, WHAT A BIG JEWELRY STORE YOU HAVE HERE.
IT'S BIG ENOUGH, IT MIGHT EVEN HAVE...
...THE MYSTICAL SILVER CRYSTAL.

This name of this particular magical item in Japanese is *maboroshi no ginsuishô,* and has been translated many different ways over the years, including "Legendary Silver Crystal," "Illusory Silver Crystal," and "Empyrean Silver Crystal." The one thing all translators can agree on is that it is a silver crystal. The first adjective, in Japanese, is *maboroshi no,* which can justifiably be translated many different ways. The first definition of *maboroshi* (the *no* is what makes it an adjective instead of a noun) in a Japanese language dictionary is "something that has no substance but looks like it does, or a fleeting object that disappears quickly." This definition fits the English word "illusion." However, a second definition of the Japanese word is, "something the existence of which is impossible to prove." In other words, although everyone is searching for the Silver Crystal, they have no idea what it looks like, or if it even really exists—this leads to translations such as "legendary." Longtime fans of *Sailor Moon* may remember the "Empyrean Silver Crystal," which is a more reasonable translation than it may at first appear. "Empyrean" means "of the sky or heavens," and specifically refers to the highest heaven, which is a realm of pure light and fire—very fitting of a stone as sacred as the Silver Crystal, and one that came from above the Earth.

Another favorite translation is "Phantom Silver Crystal," because of a phenomenon known as "phantom crystals," in which a quartz crystal grows over another crystal—the other crystals can be seen through the clear quartz, appearing as illusions or phantoms. Our translation uses the word "mystical," which is defined as "inspiring a sense of spiritual mystery, awe, and fascination," and "having a spiritual significance that transcends human understanding." The translators feel that this word, while not being a direct translation of *maboroshi no,* definitely applies to the Silver Crystal of the Moon Kingdom. (Furthermore, it could be argued that, in our very scientific world, because "mystical" things generally cannot be proven, the word does fit the second definition of *maboroshi.*) Whatever translation the reader prefers, the important thing is that it creates the image of something mysterious and magical.

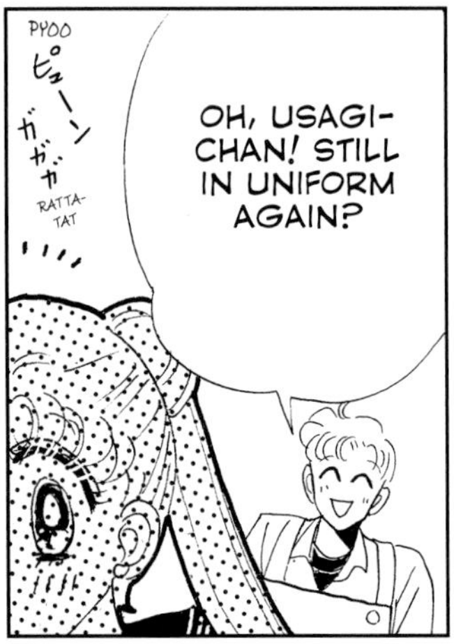
PYOO
ピュ〜
OH, USAGI-CHAN! STILL IN UNIFORM AGAIN?
ガガガ
RATTA-TAT

Still in uniform again, page 19

In Japan, most high schools and junior high schools require their students to wear uniforms. It is generally encouraged to at least go home and change clothes, and perhaps finish one's homework, before indulging in such frivolities as goofing off at the arcade.

Lupin, the gentleman thief, page 42
Usagi is speaking of Arsène Lupin, the gentleman thief and master of disguise. He first appeared in 1905 as a response to the popular detective literature of the time. Like Sherlock Holmes, he has appeared in several forms of media, including anime and manga, which is no doubt how Usagi learned of his existence. Although he doesn't have a uniform, usually wearing clothes suitable to the task at hand, he is often depicted wearing a top hat and cape, just like Tuxedo Mask.

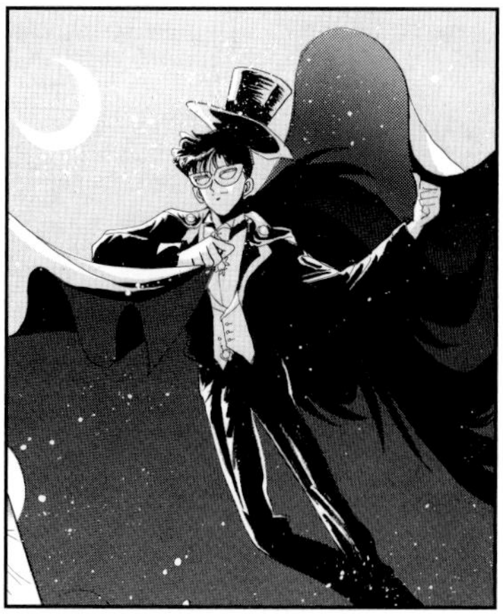

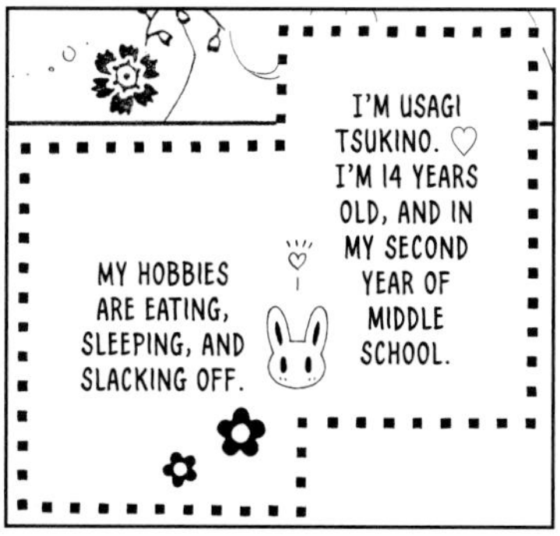
I'M USAGI TSUKINO. ♡ I'M 14 YEARS OLD, AND IN MY SECOND YEAR OF MIDDLE SCHOOL.
MY HOBBIES ARE EATING, SLEEPING, AND SLACKING OFF.

I'm Usagi Tsukino, page 51
It may seem strange that Usagi is introducing herself again, when we've all gotten to know her fairly well from the first chapter. The reason she needs to reintroduce herself is that when this story first showed up, it was published one chapter at a time in a monthly magazine. By introducing herself again, Usagi is helping readers who may have missed the previous issue for whatever reason, or who may not remember her very well after an entire month.

Princess cake, page 53
Usagi could be referring to a cake decorated to look like Cinderella or the Swedish dessert *prinsesstårta*, which has layers of cake and cream covered in marzipan. But it's not important, because in the original Japanese, she was thinking of flan. When describing Sailor Moon's mission, Luna uses the English word for princess, which is phonetically written in Japanese as *purinsesu*. Constantly hungry Usagi immediately thinks of food—in this case, *purin*, the Japanese word for flan.

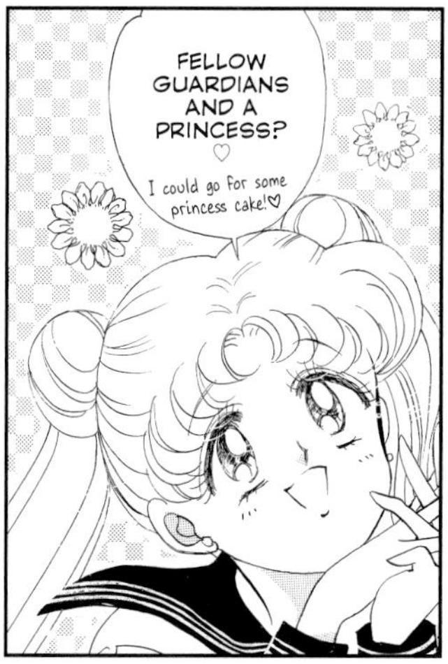
FELLOW GUARDIANS AND A PRINCESS? ♡
I could go for some princess cake!♡

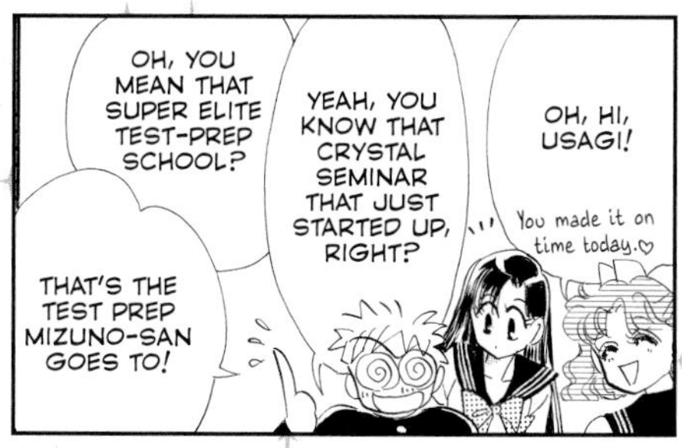
OH, HI, USAGI!
You made it on time today.♡
YEAH, YOU KNOW THAT CRYSTAL SEMINAR THAT JUST STARTED UP, RIGHT?
OH, YOU MEAN THAT SUPER ELITE TEST-PREP SCHOOL?
THAT'S THE TEST PREP MIZUNO-SAN GOES TO!

Test-prep school, page 55
In Japan, many high schools require their potential students to pass an entrance exam before they can enroll. The more elite the school, the harder the exam. To prepare for these tests, students can attend *juku*, a type of supplementary school specifically geared to help them get into the high school, and eventually college, of their choice.

I'm out of 100 yen coins, page 59
Like in America, game machines in Japan require the player to insert coins. Unlike in America, the most common coin accepted is not the quarter, but the 100 yen coin, which is worth approximately one US dollar.

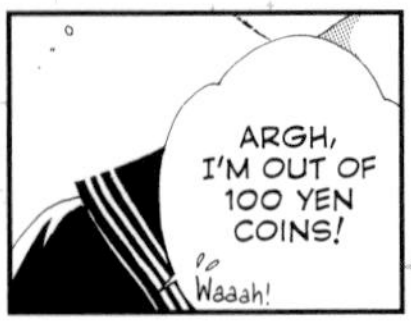
ARGH, I'M OUT OF 100 YEN COINS!
Waaah!

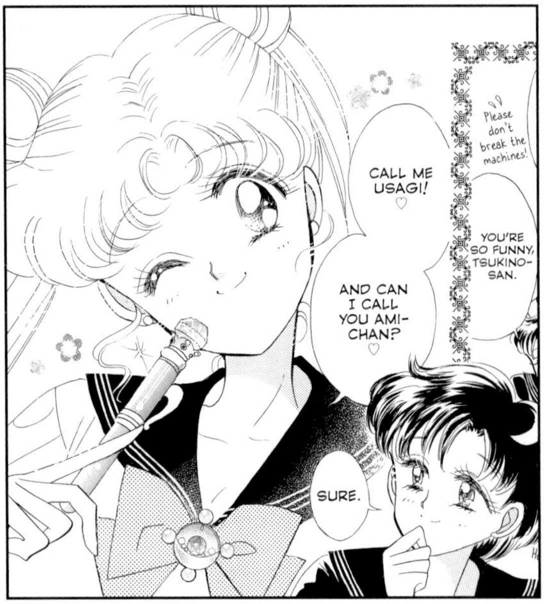
Please don't break the machines!
CALL ME USAGI! ♡
YOU'RE SO FUNNY, TSUKINO-SAN.
AND CAN I CALL YOU AMI-CHAN? ♡
SURE.

Call me Usagi, page 61
In Japan, when you're just getting to know someone, it can be very rude to address them by their given name. Sometimes it's appropriate to ask someone how they prefer to be addressed, but when that's not feasible, the safest bet in most circumstances is to call them by their surname and add the honorific -san (similar to the English "Mr." or "Miss"), as Ami did when she called Usagi "Tsukino-san." But Usagi isn't one to stand on formality, and she's happy to have her friends—even brand new ones—call her by name. However, it's still bad manners to call someone simply by name unless you're very close (and can sometimes even be a sign of enmity), so she adds -chan to Ami's name, because it is a suffix that expresses closeness and friendship. Another suffix the reader will see attached to characters' names is -kun, which is generally attached to boys' names, especially boys who are the speaker's age or younger. It is a suffix that expresses closeness and respect. The suffix -shi (seen on page 274) is somewhat more formal than -san.

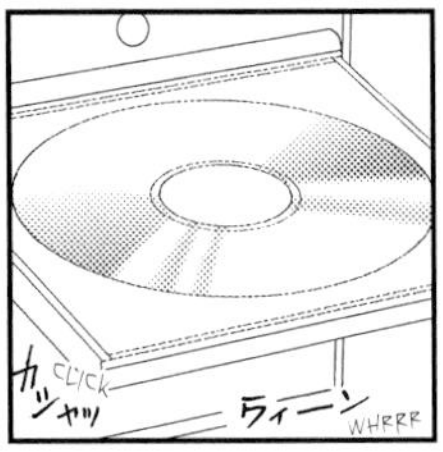
WHRRR
CLICK

Crystal Seminar discs, page 63
Before the magical days when the internet made it possible to share information instantly, if someone wanted to transfer data from one computer to another, they had to save it on what was called a "disc." You may have seen one of these old-fashioned discs in the form of a music CD or video game disc, but in the case of the Crystal Seminar, it contains a learning program.

Fauchon, page 62
Although the name may not be so well-known in the United States, Fauchon (pronounced "foe-shone") is a world-famous luxury food brand originating in France. It made a name for itself in Japan with its fruit-flavored teas in the 1960s, and opened its first retail store there in 1972.

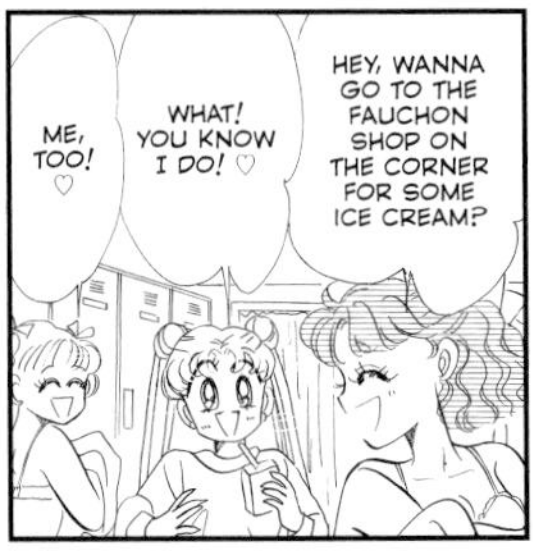
HEY, WANNA GO TO THE FAUCHON SHOP ON THE CORNER FOR SOME ICE CREAM?
WHAT! YOU KNOW I DO! ♡
ME, TOO! ♡

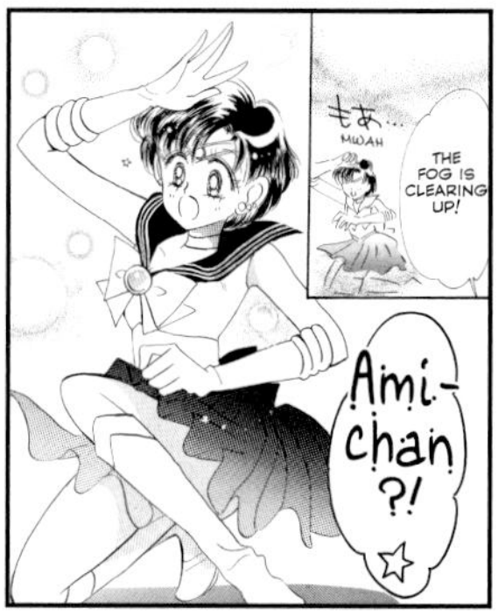
もあ…
MUAH
THE FOG IS CLEARING UP!
Ami-chan ?!

The guardian of water, page 79
Because people in East Asia didn't worship the same gods as the Romans, their astronomers came up with different names for the planets, and each of the five planets closest to the sun (excepting Earth) is associated with one of the five elements: wood, fire, earth, metal, and water. In Japanese, Mercury is *suisei,* which literally means "water star." That being the case, Sailor Mercury naturally is the guardian of water and has water powers. Fittingly, her alter-ego's surname "Mizuno" means "of water."

Hikawa Jinja, page 86
A *jinja* is a Shinto shrine, and this particular shrine's name means "fire river shrine," which is fitting because the priestess there uses fire for divination. Readers may be interested to know that this shrine is modeled after a real shrine in the real Minato Ward of Tokyo, also named Hikawa, but with different characters that mean "ice river."

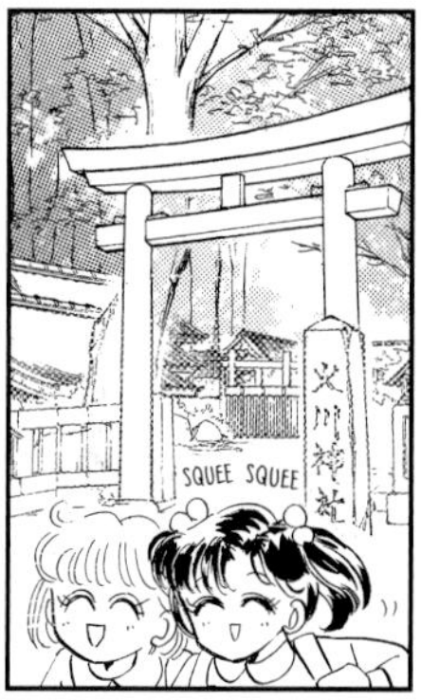
SQUEE SQUEE

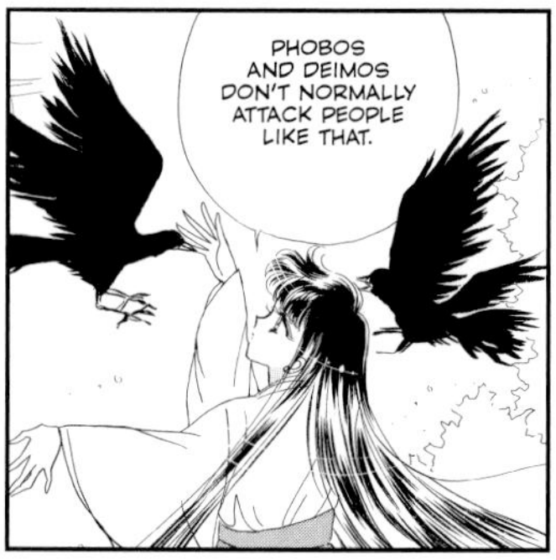
PHOBOS AND DEIMOS DON'T NORMALLY ATTACK PEOPLE LIKE THAT.

Phobos and Deimos, page 96
While Rei asserts that her pet crows are usually harmless, their names are rather intimidating. Greek for "fear" and "terror," these are also the names of the two moons of Mars, named for the sons of Ares, god of war.

Worship at a Shinto shrine, page 97
The people who have come to pray for their daughters' safe return are shown here following the procedure for worship at a Shinto shrine. This is done by bowing twice, clapping twice, then bowing again. The first bows show respect, the clapping invites the deity to you, and the last bow is to respectfully send the deity off after offering your prayer.

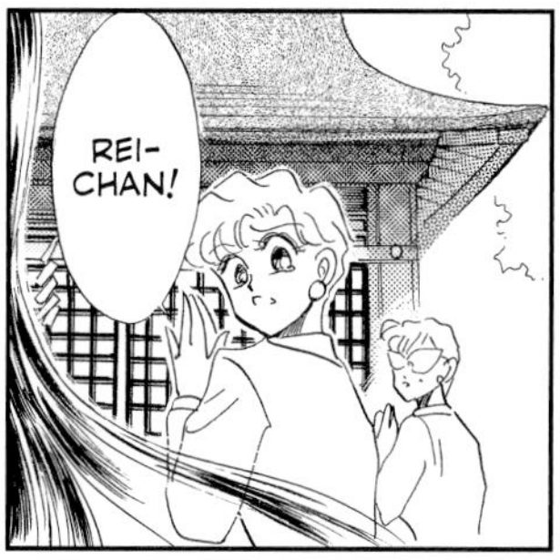
REI-CHAN!

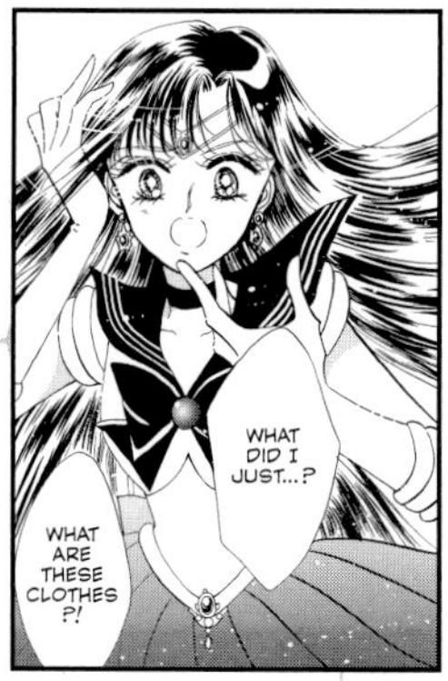
WHAT DID I JUST...?
WHAT ARE THESE CLOTHES ?!

Guardian of fire, page 122
As the red planet, it stands to reason that the planet Mars's Japanese name would be *kasei,* or "fire star." Sailor Mars's name in the Japanese name order, Hino Rei, fittingly means "spirit of fire."

Four Heavenly Kings, page 123

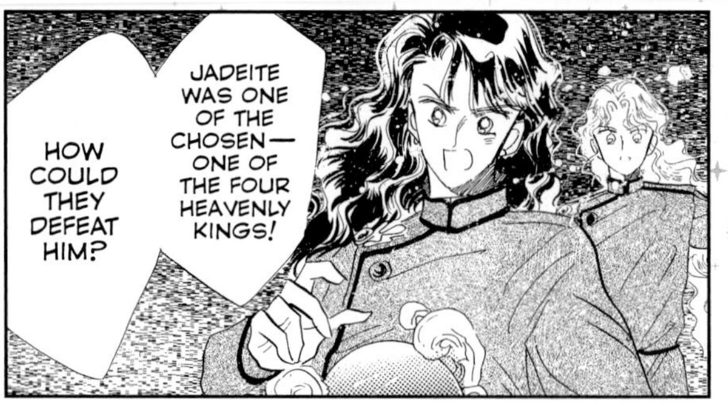
JADEITE WAS ONE OF THE CHOSEN— ONE OF THE FOUR HEAVENLY KINGS!
HOW COULD THEY DEFEAT HIM?

The reader may be wondering why the commanders of the underground Dark Kingdom would be calling themselves "heavenly" kings. The name is a direct translation of the word *Shitennô,* which is the name of a set of four Buddhist deities. The Sanskrit name of these deities simply means "four great kings," or "guardians of the world." They include Vaiśravaṇa, Virûḍhaka, Dhṛtarâṣṭra, and Virûpâkṣa, who have been charged with guarding the cardinal directions of the Earth. In other words, Jadeite and the others are four men who have been chosen to be in charge of certain regions of the map. The reader may be interested to know that, while the Four Heavenly Kings of the Dark Kingdom do have stewardships to watch over like the original Four Heavenly Kings, in modern Japan, the term *Shitennô* has come to be associated with any set of four people who are particularly well-known or powerful, especially in video games. If the reader should come across a video game with an "elite four" or "four champions," there is a good chance that set of four is also *Shitennô*.

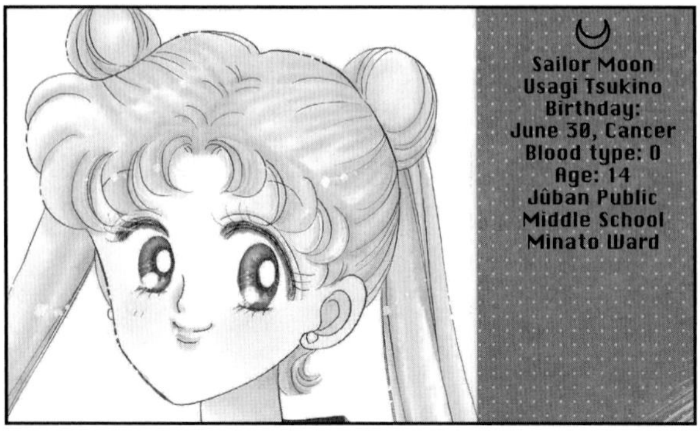
Sailor Moon
Usagi Tsukino
Birthday:
June 30, Cancer
Blood type: O
Age: 14
Jûban Public
Middle School
Minato Ward

The guardians' zodiac signs, page 125

It may seem odd to include a person's zodiac sign in their dossier, but when dealing with mystical planetary powers, it makes perfect sense. According to astrology, each zodiac sign is ruled by a celestial body. As the reader may guess, Cancer is ruled by the moon, Virgo is ruled by Mercury, and Aries is ruled by Mars.

Sendaizaka-shita, page 132

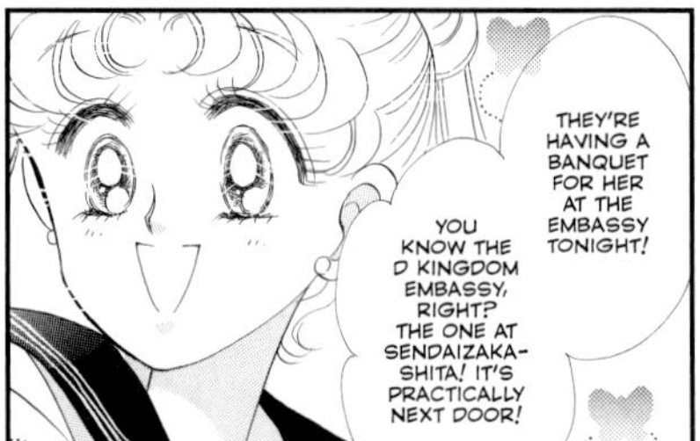
THEY'RE HAVING A BANQUET FOR HER AT THE EMBASSY TONIGHT!
YOU KNOW THE D KINGDOM EMBASSY, RIGHT? THE ONE AT SENDAIZAKA-SHITA! IT'S PRACTICALLY NEXT DOOR!

The reader will no doubt recognize Sendaizaka as the place of mysterious disappearances in the previous chapter. No need to worry about the safety of Princess D in Sendaizaka-shita, however, because not only has Sailor Moon thwarted Jadeite's evil bus plot, but the place where five slopes meet is at Sendaizaka-ue, at the top of Sendaizaka Slope (*ue* means "up" or "top"). The D Kingdom Embassy is in Sendaizaka-shita, at the bottom of the slope (*shita* means "down" or "bottom"). Of course, if D Kingdom is in any way related to the Dark Kingdom, the proximity may not be a coincidence...

June brides, page 176
June is named after the Roman goddess Juno, who happens to be the patroness of marriage. That being the case, it's easy to believe that she would smile on anyone who gets married in the month named for her.

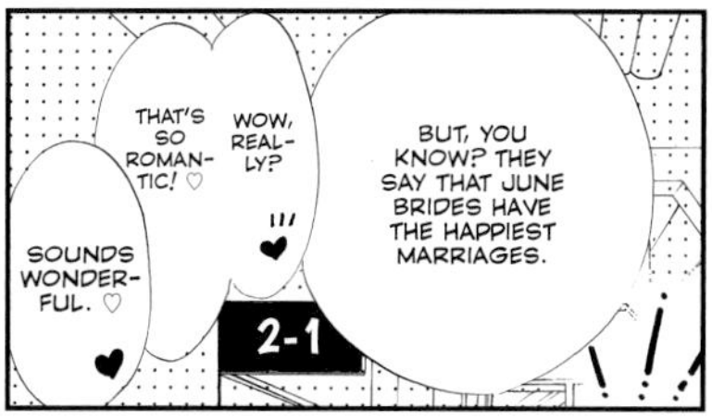
BUT, YOU KNOW? THEY SAY THAT JUNE BRIDES HAVE THE HAPPIEST MARRIAGES.
WOW, REAL-LY?
THAT'S SO ROMAN-TIC! ♡
SOUNDS WONDER-FUL. ♡
2-1

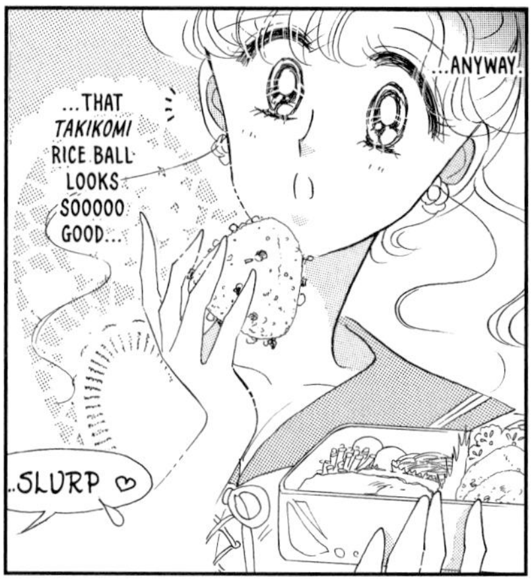
...ANYWAY
...THAT *TAKIKOMI* RICE BALL LOOKS SOOOOO GOOD...
..SLURP ♡

Takikomi rice ball, page 179
Takikomi gohan is rice (*gohan*) with ingredients cooked in (*takikomi*), as opposed to cooking the rice alone and eating it alongside other dishes. Common ingredients in this dish include dashi broth, soy sauce, vegetables, mushrooms, meat, fish, etc. Here, Makoto has packed her *takikomi gohan* into rice balls for easier portability.

Part-time priestess, page 184
Although Rei has a sixth sense that perhaps gives her an edge in spiritual professions, in modern-day Japan there are no specific qualifications required to serve as a priestess, or *miko,* at a Shinto shrine, as the part-time priestess's duties consist mainly of reception work and selling good luck charms and fortunes. Often the girls hired are attending vocational school, training to be full-time priestesses, but it would appear that Old Man Hino's only requirement is that the girls be pretty enough.

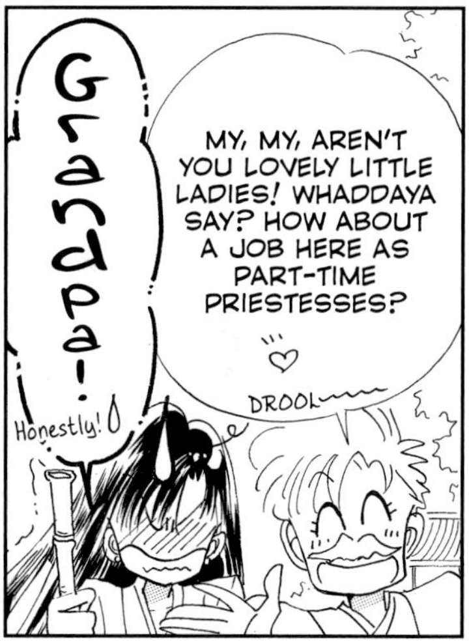
MY, MY, AREN'T YOU LOVELY LITTLE LADIES! WHADDAYA SAY? HOW ABOUT A JOB HERE AS PART-TIME PRIESTESSES?
♡
DROOL
Grandpa!
Honestly!

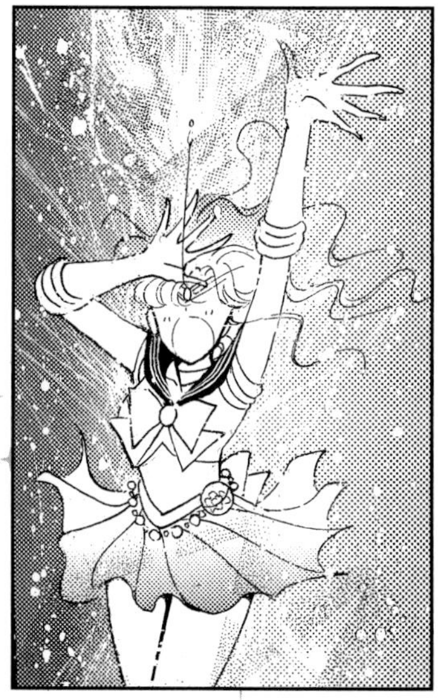

Guardian of thunder, page 200
Jupiter is the god of sky and thunder, so naturally a guardian under his protection would have thunder powers. However, the Japanese name of the planet is *mokusei,* or "wood star," which is why Sailor Jupiter also has plant-based attacks, and why her alter ego is named Kino, or "of wood." In fact, wood and thunder are related, as the eight trigrams of Daoist cosmology divide the five elements into eight, with lightning and wind being part of the wood element.

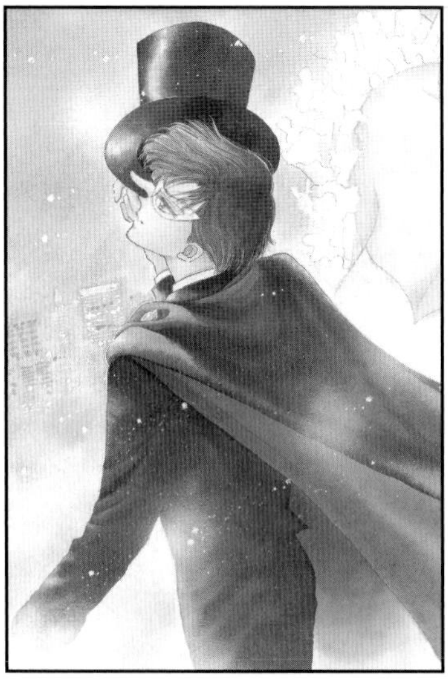

Tuxedo Kamen, page 204

Kamen is the Japanese word for "mask," and Tuxedo Kamen is the name of this well-dressed character in Japanese. The original Japanese title of this chapter is, "*Takishiido Kamen:* Tuxedo Mask," which translates to, "Tuxedo Mask: Tuxedo Mask," but mirrors the Japanese/English format of previous chapter titles (which originally left all the Sailor Guardian titles in English). Masked warriors and/or superheroes are not uncommon in greater Japanese pop culture, including the classic *Power Rangers*-esque morning children's show, *Kamen Rider.*

Moon Wand, page 207

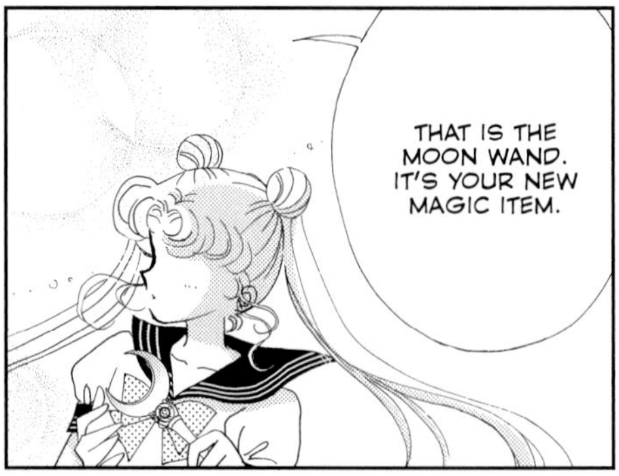
THAT IS THE MOON WAND. IT'S YOUR NEW MAGIC ITEM.

In the Japanese edition, the name of this magical item is the English "Moon Stick." "Stick" was the en-vogue word for magic wands in Japanese magical girl anime of the 1980s and '90s, and *Pretty Guardian Sailor Moon* made no exception. "Stick" is an English translation of the word *tsue,* which, in turn, is the Japanese translation of "wand." It seems likely that "stick" was the word of choice where magical girls were concerned because "stick" sounds similar to *suteki,* a Japanese adjective describing things that are "wonderful," "beautiful," "dreamy," etc. So "stick" may sound rather magical to a Japanese speaker, but in English the word is a little mundane, so the translators opted to use "wand" in this edition.

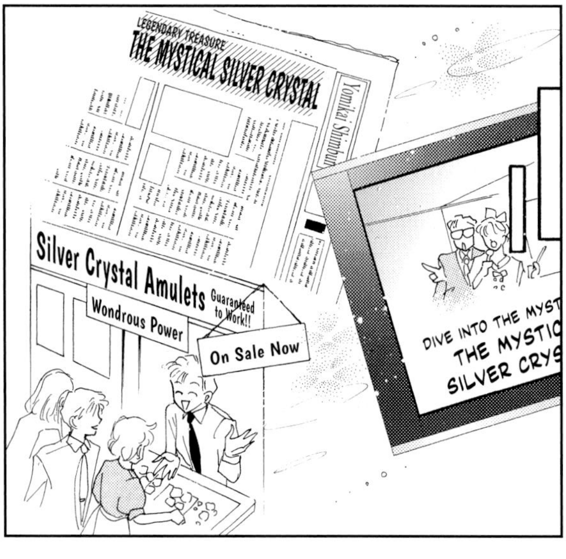
LEGENDARY TREASURE
THE MYSTICAL SILVER CRYSTAL
Yomikai Shimbun
Silver Crystal Amulets
Guaranteed to Work!!
Wondrous Power
On Sale Now

***Yomikai Shimbun*, page 223**

We've seen the local paper in Usagi's world before, and now we're seeing a national newspaper, showing just how much of a sensation Tuxedo Mask has caused. The name of this paper is a play on the famous real-world paper the *Yomiuri Shimbun. Yomiuri* means "read-sell," and comes from one of the names for the people in the Edo era who would walk the streets reading the news in a loud voice and selling fliers with the news printed on them. *Yomikai,* on the other hand, means "read-buy," perhaps in the hopes that the public will read the headlines and buy the paper, but mostly just as a parody.

Usako, page 257

Mamoru's nickname for Usagi is a combination of her real name with the suffix -ko, which is commonly found in Japanese girls' names. The reason he does this instead of calling her Usagi-chan is unclear, but there are a few possibilities. First, he likely would want a name for her that is unique to him, and so used something more original. (It may not be entirely original, though, as it is also the Japanese name for the famous Dutch rabbit character Miffy.) It's also possible that by adding the -ko he is deliberately making her name more feminine, which could be a subtle way of suggesting that he sees her as someone he would like to have a romantic relationship with, or has strong, fond feelings for.

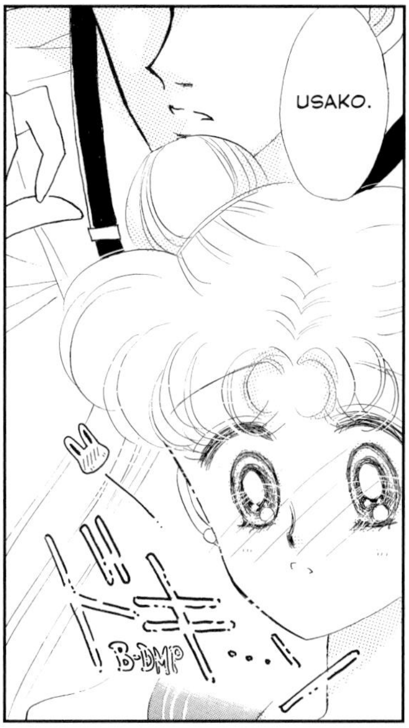
USAKO.
B-DMP

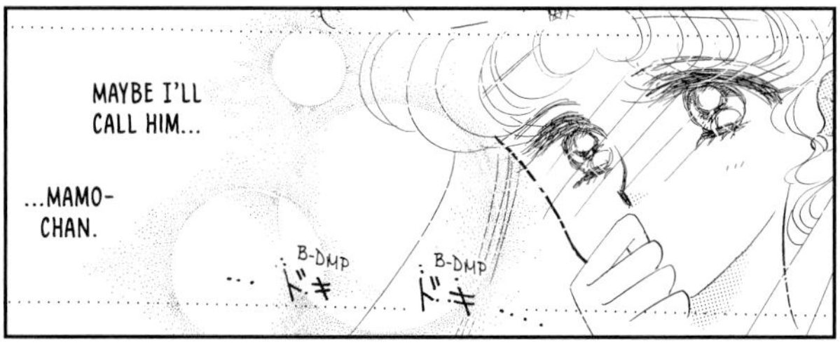
MAYBE I'LL CALL HIM...
...MAMO-CHAN.
B-DMP
ドキ
B-DMP
ドキ

Mamo-chan, page 258

Adding -chan after the first two syllables of someone's given name is an unoriginal (see: Furu-chan, Mako-chan) but effective way of showing affection for someone. But the important thing is that it gives the translators the opportunity to talk about Mamoru's name. *Mamoru* is the word that Luna constantly repeats to the sailor guardians in reference to their mission regarding the princess and the Silver Crystal; it means "to defend or protect." *Chiba* is a word that means "place" or "locality." In other words, his name means "to protect the area." (Also, since *chi* is the same *chi* used in the word for the planet Earth, it can refer to defending the earth.)

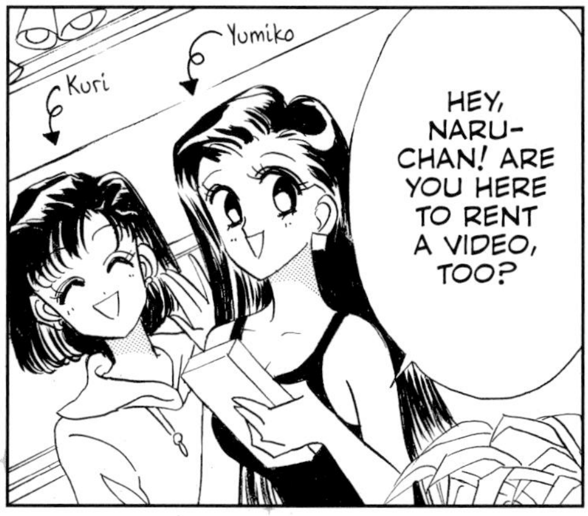
HEY, NARU-CHAN! ARE YOU HERE TO RENT A VIDEO, TOO?
Yumiko
Kuri

Rent a video, page 268

Long, long ago, before the magic of Netflix, before even DVDs, mankind recorded movies on little boxes with magnetic tape inside called "videocassettes," or "videos" for short. These videocassettes could only be viewed with an ancient machine called a VCR, and to obtain more videos, one had to set out into brick-and-mortar shops to buy them. Alternatively, if someone wanted to watch a videocassette but not necessarily own it, they could go to a rental shop, where a customer could borrow a video for a fee. Because one had to have the physical cassette in order to view the video contained thereon, if all cassettes for a certain movie were already rented out, a customer looking for that movie would be out of luck, and their only recourse would be to choose a different movie or drive across town to a different rental shop.

A Kodansha Comics Trade Paperback Original
Sailor Moon Eternal Edition volume 1 copyright © 2013 Naoko Takeuchi
English translation copyright © 2018 Naoko Takeuchi
First published in Japan in 2013 by Kodansha Ltd., Tokyo.

Published in the United States by Kodansha Comics, an imprint of Kodansha USA Publishing, LLC, New York.

Publication rights for this English edition arranged through Kodansha Ltd, Tokyo.

ISBN 978-1-63236-152-3

Printed in Canada.

www.kodanshacomics.com

9 8 7 6 5 4 3 2 1

Translation: Alethea Nibley & Athena Nibley
Lettering: Lys Blakeslee
Editing: Lauren Scanlan
Kodansha Comics edition cover design by Phil Balsman